Quantitative Business Methods Using Excel

Quantitative Business Methods Using Excel

David Whigham

OXFORD UNIVERSITY PRESS
1998

Oxford University Press, Great Clarendon Street, Oxford OX2 6DP

Oxford New York

Athens Auckland Bangkok Bogota Buenos Aires
Calcutta Cape Town Chennai Dar es Salaam
Delhi Florence Hong Kong Istanbul Karachi
Kuala Lumpur Madrid Melbourne Mexico City
Mumbai Nairobi Paris São Paolo Singapore
Taipei Tokyo Toronto Warsaw
and associated companies in
Berlin Ibadan

Oxford is a trade mark of Oxford University Press

Published in the United States
by Oxford University Press Inc., New York

British Library Cataloguing in Publication Data
Data available

Library of Congress Cataloging in Publication Data
Whigham, David, 1949–
Quantitative business methods using Excel/David Whigham.
p.   cm.
Includes bibliographical references.
1. Business mathematics—Computer programs.   2. Microsoft Excel
(Computer file)   I. Title.
HF5691.W468   1997   650'.01'51—dc21   97–38243
ISBN 0–19–877545–8 (pbk.)

10 9 8 7 6 5 4 3 2 1

Typeset by Hope Services (Abingdon) Ltd.
Printed in Great Britain
on acid-free paper by
Bookcraft Ltd.,
Midsomer Norton, Somerset

Contents

....

Preface

The purpose of this text is to provide a thematic introduction to use of the Excel 5.0 spreadsheet in the analysis of quantitative business problems. This means that it is in no way to be regarded as an extensive Excel reference manual. Rather, Excel techniques and routines are introduced and explained as and when the nature of the quantitative methods requires them. This said however, it will be found that a sufficient amount of Excel instruction is included throughout the text to take the reader to a level of expertise that is beyond that of a novice. If further expertise in the Excel techniques themselves is required, then a dedicated manual or the excellent on-line help facility should be consulted.

The text has been crafted in such a way as to provide both explanation of the overall nature of *what* is to be achieved, and instruction in *how* it is to be done with Excel. The latter hands-on directions are highlighted in bold throughout the text, and must not be omitted if the eventual recorded results are to be achieved.

In the large part, the worksheets to be used and the eventual results are displayed in the text. However, in the case of some large data files space restrictions, as well as the tedium to the reader of having to enter the data, dictated against this approach. For this reason, an accompanying disc includes a number of Excel files that can be loaded as and when instructed. In some cases these files contain no more than raw data, but in others they contain operational models that can be used to follow the arguments more closely.

Numerous exercises, with solutions, accompany each chapter, and in some cases there are suggestions for further extension of the models developed. It is suggested that these exercises are attempted as and when they are referenced in the text (rather than being attempted all at once when the chapter has been completed).

The work derives from a series of course materials prepared for various Excel based modules at Glasgow Caledonian University, and has therefore been 'live tested' by more than five hundred users. Thanks to their comments and corrections the material has been extensively edited and revised so that the author now feels confident that there are as few errors as can be possible in a text of this nature. He nevertheless welcomes any suggestions for improvement and details of any errors that have escaped correction.

I should like to thank the editorial and production staff at Oxford University Press for their efficiency in producing the book as quickly as they have. Thanks are also due to students and staff in the Department of Economics for various comments, corrections, and suggestions for improvement. As always, however, any remaining deficiencies are entirely the responsibility of the author.

David Whigham
Department of Economics
Glasgow Caledonian University
February 1998

Introduction to Excel

Contents
....

Accompanying data files to be loaded as instructed:

W1_7.XLS   W1_8.XLS   W1_9.XLS   W1_11.XLS   W1_12.XLS   W1_13.XLS   W1_14.XLS

1.1. **Terminology and navigation**

An Excel **workbook** is simply a three-dimensional stack of **worksheets** consisting of **rows** and **columns**. In any sheet the columns are identified by letters:

(A, B, C . . . Z, AA, AB, AC . . . AZ, BA, BB . . . IV)

and the rows by numbers:

(1, 2, 3, . . . 16384).

The intersection between a row and a column is known as a **cell** and therefore has a unique **cell address** or **cell reference**. Hence, the cell in the 5th row of column C has the cell address C5. Notice that the column letter *always comes first* in the cell address, followed by the row number. Thus 5C is not a valid cell reference. You therefore have what amounts to a three-dimensional electronic card index box at your disposal.

By default, the sheets of the workbook are numbered as Sheet1, Sheet2 and so on, but it is an easy matter to change this nomenclature to one that is more personal to your own work. More on this later.

Access an Excel workbook now and read on.

When Microsoft Excel is accessed for the first time a worksheet similar to the one shown in Fig. 1.1 will be observed.

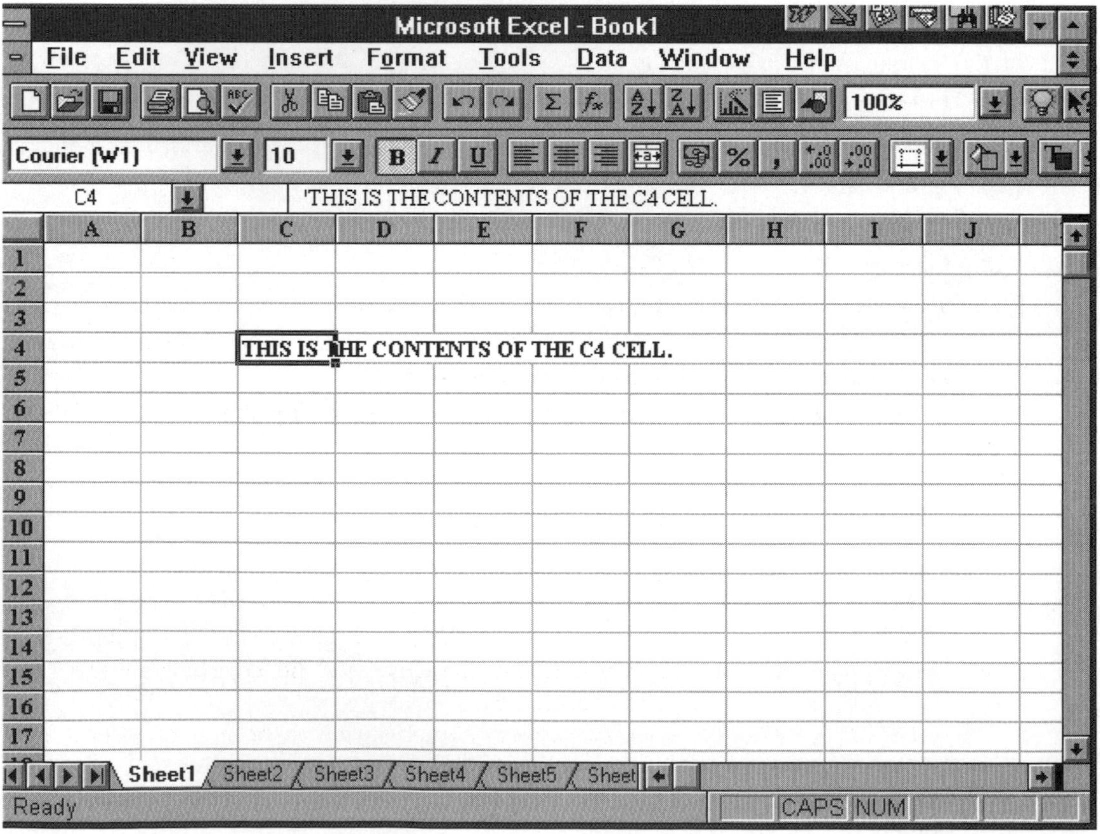

Figure 1.1

This chapter may be omitted, browsed, or read selectively by those readers who are experienced Excel users.

If this is not exactly what you see then your version of Excel may have been configured in a different way. Consult an experienced user to assist in setting up Excel in the way indicated so that you can follow the argument. Alternatively, select View from the Menu bar and experiment with the various options there until you obtain the desired effect—Formula bar and Status bar should both be ticked (click on them once if no tick shows) and under the Toolbars option the Standard and Format options should be ticked.

Navigation around the worksheet or selection of Menu or Toolbar options is usually done by placing the **Mouse pointer** over the desired option and clicking the left-hand button of the mouse once.

Try a few clicks for yourself to appreciate how it works.

Notice that when the mouse pointer is in the area of the actual worksheet it appears as a solid white cross, but when it is moved out of this area (into the Toolbar area or onto a Scroll bar for example), it turns into a solid white arrow.

At the very top of the screen is the **File name indicator**. This shows the name of file that is in use at the moment, although if a new worksheet has just been opened it will always indicate 'Book1' since Excel automatically assigns the file that name until you change it.

Immediately below the file indicator is the **Menu bar**. This contains a number of programmed facilities that will be explained in due course. Basically, they allow such things as saving, opening, printing, or creating workbooks, altering the appearance of the worksheet, and inserting or removing rows and columns, as well as providing a large number of useful tools and accessories. Click once with the left-hand button of the mouse on any of the topics to obtain further options in this category.

Try it now and then click again on the Menu bar topic to restore the original screen.

Below the Menu bar are the **Toolbars**. These duplicate many of the features of the menu bar in the form of **icons**. If their meaning is not immediately obvious, place the mouse pointer over the icon but do not click the mouse button.

Do this now.

After a few seconds a brief explanation of the icon's purpose will appear either beside the icon itself or at the bottom left hand corner of the screen. More will be said on these icons later when their features are required.

Below, and to the right of the toolbars, is the **Formula bar**. This is where the contents of any cell will be displayed. If the cell is empty the Formula bar will be blank, otherwise its contents are displayed.

Click on any cell now and enter your name. Press enter.

Your name should appear both in the cell and on the Formula bar.

Next below, are the letters identifying the columns of the worksheet and then comes the actual worksheet itself with grids indicating the cells, a solid white cross indicating the mouse pointer and a solid border indicating the active cell. The active cell's address is also shown in the bar to the left of the formula bar.

Any cell in the worksheet is made active by pointing to it with the mouse and clicking the left-hand button once. A bold or coloured border will appear around the cell, indicating that it is now the active cell. Only when a cell is active can information be entered to it, or its contents altered from the keyboard.

Practise this by making the C4 and then the E6 cell active.

To the right of, and also below, the actual worksheet area are the **Scroll bars**. These allow the screen to be moved up, down, to the right, or to the left. Simply click once on the appropriate solid arrow of the scroll bar to move one row or one column in the desired direction. If larger movements are required, place the mouse pointer on the button between the arrows of the scroll bars, depress the left-hand mouse button, and drag the button to the arrow at the opposite end of the scroll bar. This will create a movement of one full screen in any direction.

Confirm this for yourself by using the Scroll bars to move around the worksheet in a clockwise direction.

Movement around the worksheet can also be effected from the keyboard. The **cursor arrows** move the active cell up, down, right, or left by one row or column at a time. The **Page Down** and **Page Up** keys move one full screen up or down at a time, while **Tab** and **Shift Tab** move one full screen to the right or left, respectively.

Next, pressing the **Home** key makes the A1 cell active, while pressing function key five (F5) activates the Goto command. Enter the cell address of the cell that is to be made active and then click OK.

Finally, pressing the **End** key and then one of the cursor arrows will cause the active cell to move up, down, right, or left to the last occupied cell in the column or row. For example, if the active cell is currently A1, and if the cells A1 to A60 are all occupied, then End and down arrow will move to the end of this range and make the A60 cell active.

Practise using these movement keys now.

To the left of the bottom scroll bar are the **Sheet tabs.** A **tab** is simply Excel nomenclature for a 'clickable' device. When you click on any tab either an action is performed directly, or another tab or dialogue box appears requesting the user to enter information. The sheet tabs are used to select a particular sheet from the list of sheets available. For example, when a new Excel workbook is opened for the first time, Sheet1 will be the **active sheet** and this will be indicated by its having a light background. The other available sheets appear with a dark background, but they are **not active** unless you click once on them with the left-hand button of the mouse.

To the left of the sheet tabs are the **Sheet scroll bars**. These allow the user to display the names of all the sheets available in the workbook. Click on the left-hand arrow of the bar to display the first sheet in the list of those available, or on the right-hand arrow to move to the last sheet in the list. The middle two arrows move one sheet at a time in either direction throughout the list of sheets.

Check for yourself that this is the case by moving through the list of sheets.

Finally, at the very bottom of the screen is the **Status indicator bar**. Various messages will appear here and provide information upon what tasks the worksheet is performing, as well as which of several default settings has been selected.

For example, press the Caps Lock key on the keyboard and the letters CAPS will appear on the right hand side of the Status indicator bar.

Any text entered to the worksheet will now be upper case (capital letters).

Press Caps Lock again and the CAPS indicator will disappear.

Text entries will now be in lower case.

Finally, notice the icon on the Toolbar in the form of a curved left-pointing arrow. This is the **Undo** facility and can cancel the last action that you performed. Since mistakes are inevitable, and can be very time-consuming to rectify, Undo is one of the most helpful routines provided by Excel. Use it immediately you suspect that something has gone wrong in your worksheet.

Exercise 1.1 can now be attempted

1.2. Entering data

The information entered to a cell is known as **data** and can adopt four basic forms—text, number, formula or function.

A **text** entry is characterized by its first character being a letter, a space, or a punctuation mark. Text entries (often known as **labels**) are used to enter descriptive comments to the worksheet. This could be your name at the top of the sheet, or a descriptor of the worksheet's purpose, or a list of names of clients about whom you have information. The fundamental feature of a text entry is that arithmetical calculations cannot be performed on them. They are for descriptive purposes only.

To practise entering textual data, click on C1 and type your first name into this cell of your sheet and include a spelling mistake. When you have finished typing, press Enter or click on another cell.

To **edit** the contents of a cell, first make the cell active by clicking on it with the mouse. The contents of the cell will be shown in the Formula bar between the toolbar and the letters of the column identifiers. Now click once with the mouse on this Formula bar and again use the mouse to move to the section of the text that is to be altered. Then use the Backspace key or the Delete key to remove superfluous characters and type in the amendment(s) that you want to make. Press the Enter key, or click on another cell when you have finished.

Use this procedure to correct the spelling mistake that you included in your name as efficiently as possible.

Numerical data entries, on the other hand, commence with a positive or negative numerical character and contain only numerical characters thereafter. They are the raw data to which calculations can subsequently be applied and are entered directly to the sheet in the form:

23 or -19 or 167

It is important to note that text characters, spaces or punctuation marks must not be included before or after numerical characters if the contents of the cell are to be used for calculations. For example, 23 is a valid numerical entry that could be subjected to an arithmetical process (squared, cubed, etc.), but 23rd (as in 'the 23rd of June') is a text entry that cannot be manipulated mathematically. As long as Excel receives numbers, and only numbers, then the entry will be treated numerically, but once a non-numerical character such as a letter of the alphabet is introduced the whole entry becomes textual.

Practise entering numerical data in your sheet by typing 31 in C2 and 193.5 in C3.

Formula entries are what distinguish a spreadsheet from a calculator. They are *algebraic* rather than *arithmetic* concepts, and allow general rather than specific computations to be performed.

For example, suppose your annual salary is £20000 and your partner's is £25000. Your combined income is clearly £45000.

Enter your salary (as a number) into the A1 cell of your worksheet and your partner's to the A2 cell.

The task to be undertaken is to write an expression (in A3, say) that will compute the combined income.

At first sight you might be tempted to write, in A3:

A1+A2

but if you do, then you will find that it appears as text rather than as the required numerical answer of 45000.

Try it now.

The reason for this is that, as we saw above, any entry that commences with a letter will be treated by Excel as text and will not produce a numerical result.

Clearly the problem is to distinguish, for example, the 'A' of the cell reference A1 from 'A' as in the first character of a text label such as 'Asset value'. Excel allows this to be done quite simply by placing an equals sign (=) in front of any entries that require arithmetic computation on the basis of formulae using cell addresses. Thus:

=A1+A2

when entered to A3, will return 45000 if A1 and A2 contain 20000 and 25000 respectively.

Do this now and confirm that it works.

Importantly, however, if either your or your partner's annual salary should change, then all that is required is to alter the contents of A1 and/or A2 appropriately. The computed result in A3 will change automatically.

Try it for yourself on the sheet that you are using. Change the values in A1 and/or A2 and confirm that A3 computes the correct result automatically.[1]

This is what was meant when it was previously said that formulae were algebraic rather than arithmetic concepts. This is because the formula:

=A1+A2

is to be thought of as 'whatever is in A1' plus 'whatever is in A2', rather than 20000 plus 25000. This is an algebraic process rather than an arithmetic one.

It should also be noted that if numbers as well as cell addresses are to be used in formulae, then the entry must also be preceded by an equals sign. For example, an entry of 4 to a cell is a perfectly valid numerical entry if it simply represents the number 4 (a raw data item). However, if you want to add 4 to the contents of A1 then the following entry will not work:

4+A1

Try this now in any vacant cell of the sheet and notice that it appears as text.

The equals sign at the start is now essential, since the entry contains subsequent parts that are not *automatically* treated as numerical. Consequently, it must be written either as:

---

1 If the result is not correct then the chances are that the formula in A3 has not been entered correctly. There must be no spaces before the equals sign and no spaces between any of the subsequent characters.

=4+A1 or =A1+4

Type both of these entries into vacant cells of your sheet to confirm that they work.

Now observe that in this last formula there are effectively *four* distinct terms—the equals sign to tell Excel that a numerical operation is to be performed, the number 4, the plus sign, and the cell reference A1—representing the contents of the A1 cell. Clearly this implies that the contents of A1 must itself be a raw number, or the result of some other numerical calculation, otherwise no numerical answer can be obtained. Also, the plus sign is what is known as an **operator**, since it instructs Excel as to which mathematical operation is to be performed (addition in this case).

There are, however, a number of further mathematical operators that can be used in Excel formulae. The full list is:

Purpose	Operator symbol
Addition	+
Subtraction	-
Multiplication	*
Division	/
Powering	∧
Equal to	=
Greater than	>
Greater than or equal to	>=
Less than	<
Less than or equal to	<=
Not equal to	<>

These operators, in conjunction with cell references and numbers, allow very complex formulae to be written, provided that the rules governing operator use are fully appreciated. This proviso is necessary because Excel, in conjunction with all other spreadsheets, uses a strict system of **priorities** with regard to the order in which it evaluates operators in a formula. Furthermore, since expressions can become very complex, it will not always be immediately obvious whether the result obtained is in fact correct, and so it is essential that the priorities are understood and obeyed at all times.

The **priority** of an operator is quite simply an indication of which operation will be carried out first by the spreadsheet, when there is more than one mathematical operation defined by a formula.

Powering has the highest priority, and so Excel will perform any powering operation in a formula first. Then it will perform multiplication and division operations at the same level of priority, and lastly it will perform addition and subtraction operations, also at the same level of priority. For example, the expression:

=A1+A2*A3∧A4

will be evaluated by Excel in the following step-by-step way:

A3∧A4   Powering has the highest priority.
A3∧A4 is then multiplied by the contents of A2.
The product of A3∧ A4 and A2 is then added to the contents of A1.

Hence with A1 = 10, A2 = 4, A3 = 3 and A4 = 2, the formula above is equivalent to:

10+4*3∧2

which evaluates to:

$3\wedge2 = 9$
$4*9 = 36$
$10 + 36 = 46$

Now take a new sheet (click on Sheet2 on the Sheet tabs bar) and enter the above values to the A1 to A4 cells. Then, in A5 type the expression:

$=A1+A2*A3\wedge A4$

and confirm that a result of 46 is obtained.

A completely different result would have been obtained if, for example, the multiplication operation had been carried out first. Then we would obtain:

$4*3 = 12$
$12\wedge2 = 144$
$10 + 144 = 154$

Clearly the operator priority system imposes a constraint upon how formulae can be written, and from the discussion above it would appear that nothing can be done to overcome this predefined set of priorities. For example, suppose it were the case in the last illustration that we actually did want the 4 to be multiplied by the 3 before the powering by 2 took place. How could we override the default priority of powering first?

The answer is to place brackets around any terms that the user wishes to be evaluated first. Hence, while we have already seen that the expression:

$10+4*3\wedge2$

will be evaluated by Excel as 46, the expression:

$10+(4*3)\wedge2$

will be evaluated by Excel as:

$4*3 = 12$
$12\wedge2 = 144$
$10 + 144 = 154$

Confirm that this is the case by making the contents of A6 contain:

$=A1+(A2*A3)\wedge A4$

The difference between the two expressions should now be clear.

The use of brackets in the context of the last example can be further illustrated by the following two illustrations:

(a) $(10+4)*3\wedge2 = 14*3\wedge2 = 14*9 = 126$
(b) $(10+4*3)\wedge2 = (10+12)\wedge2 = 22\wedge2 = 484$

Confirm both of these results by entering the following formulae to the A7 and A8 cells:

$=(A1+A2)*A3\wedge A4$
$=(A1+A2*A3)\wedge A4$

Now compare the results obtained in A5, A6, A7, and A8 and remember that the numbers in A1 to A4 have *not changed,* yet four numerically different results have been obtained.

Notice that inside the brackets of a formula the normal default priorities again apply. For example, in the last expression the higher priority of the multiplication process ensures that the numbers inside the brackets are evaluated as:

$$4*3+10 = 12+10 = 22$$

rather than:

$$10+4*3 = 14*3 = 42$$

If this last operation was in fact what was required, then we would have to add a second set of brackets around the 10+4 term to ensure that it was evaluated first. In other words, it should be written as:

$$((10 + 4)*3)^\wedge 2 = (14*3)^\wedge 2 = 42^\wedge 2 = 1764$$

For final confirmation of this, use the A9 cell to contain:

$$= ((A1 + A2)*A3)^\wedge A4$$

and check that the correct result of 1764 is obtained.

Also notice that if there is more than one set of brackets then Excel works on an 'inside-out' basis: the innermost brackets are evaluated first, then the next innermost and so on.

Finally, to appreciate the role that brackets can play in modelling practical business problems, consider the following situation.

Individual income tax is charged at a rate of 25% on the difference between gross income and the statutory tax allowance. How can a worksheet be prepared that will compute the tax due for any entered levels of gross income and tax allowance? The solution is shown in Workbook 1.1.

To follow the argument yourself click on the Sheet1 tab and make the model up as indicated in the illustration.

Note that the entries in column C are for information only. They indicate the formula contents of the adjacent cells in column B. You do not need to make these entries. Also note that throughout the text important formulae will be shown on the formula bar along with their cell address (the one in B5 in this case).

	A	B	C	D	E	F	G	H	I
1			FORMULA IN COLUMN B						
2	Tax rate	25%	NONE						
3	Gross Income	25000	NONE						
4	Tax allowance	5000	NONE						
5	Tax due	5000	=B2*(B3-B4)						

Workbook 1.1

Notice the role played by the brackets here. If the difference between gross income and the tax allowance had not been enclosed in brackets, then the tax rate (in B2) would only have been applied to the gross income (in B3) if the formula had been written as:

=B2*B3-B4

Alternatively, the tax rate (in B2) would only have been applied to the tax allowance (in B4) if the formula had been written as:

=B3-B4*B2

Only by placing brackets around the difference between gross income and the tax allowance can the correct result be obtained. That is:

=B2*(B3-B4) or =(B3-B4)*B2

Exercise 1.2 can be attempted now.

The final form of entry to an active cell is an Excel **function**.

Excel contains a large number of pre-programmed functions that can perform sophisticated tasks as required. In Excel a function, like a formula, is always preceded by an equals sign if it is the first entry to a cell. Then the name of the function must be supplied, followed by an opening bracket. There then follows the **arguments** of the function. Some functions only have one argument, but others have several, in which case each argument is separated by a **comma**. Also, if an argument represents a **range** of cells then the required syntax is to type the address of the first cell in the range, then a colon (:), and then the address of the last cell in the required range. Finally, after all the arguments have been entered the brackets are closed.

A full list of all the functions available can be obtained from the **function wizard** (f_x icon on the toolbar) along with prompts as to the arguments that they require. For the moment, however, reconsider the formula that was written above for the combined income of the two individuals:

=A1+A2

The same result could have been obtained by using the **SUM** function. This contains only one argument—the range of cells to be summed and so we could write:

=SUM(A1:A2)

To see this, click on the Sheet1 tab to activate the sheet where the incomes of the two individuals should still be located. Now, in A4, enter:

=SUM(A1:A2)

The result will be the same as the one obtained in A3 from the expression located there, viz.

=A1+A2

Now, while typing =SUM(A1:A2) is in fact slightly less efficient than typing =A1+A2, this would not be the case if we were required to sum, say, the first 100 rows of column A. Using a formula we would have had to type:

=A1+A2+A3+ . . . and so on until . . . A99+A100

Clearly this is very tedious, especially in comparison with the functional alternative:

=SUM(A1:A100)

Appropriate Excel functions will be introduced throughout the text as and when they are required. Some are indispensable for serious quantitative analysis, but in other cases there may be no alternative to writing a formula of your own, in which case you have created what is known as a **user-defined function**.

Finally, Excel functions and user-defined functions can be used together without difficulty. For example, suppose that you wanted to find the square of the sum of the numbers contained in A1 to A100. There is no predefined Excel function that will do this, but the SUM function and the power operator can be combined to produce the required result as follows:

=SUM(A1:A100)^2

Confirm that such a procedure would work by using the A5 cell of the current sheet to contain:

=SUM(A1:A2)^2

If A1 and A2 still contain 20000 and 25000 respectively, then a value of 2025000000 should be returned to A5.

If this is not what is shown, then it is probably because the column width is too small. Excel will return the number as something like 2.03 E+09, i.e. 2.03 times 10 to the power of 9. But you can widen the column by selecting Format, Column, and then Width. The default width (8.5) will usually show, so change this to 13, say, and the result will now show in conventional form.

Exercise 1.3 can now be attempted.

1.3. **Selecting an area of the worksheet**

To follow the subsequent discussion click on the Sheet4 tab to obtain a new sheet and proceed as instructed.

Selecting an area of the worksheet in Excel is most easily done with the mouse.

Place the mouse pointer in the first cell that is to be selected, depress the left-hand button, and then drag down and/or across until the required area has been highlighted.

This area has now been **selected** and can be subjected to a variety of processes.

For example, with an area selected (A1:C9, say) click once on the B icon on the toolbar.

All entries to this area will now appear in bold lettering.

To deselect an area click on a cell outside the selected area. To remove the bold formatting that was created above, select the area once again by clicking and dragging (if you have deselected it) and then choose Edit from the Menu bar. Now select Clear and then All and the formatting will return to normal.[2] Now enter your first name, middle name and surname to the A1, A2, and A3 cells respectively and select the area A1:A3. Format this area to bold and italic by clicking click the B and then the I icon on the toolbar.

Then suppose that you wanted to move these data to the area C6 to C8.

With the area A1:A3 still selected, choose Edit from the Menu bar and then Cut.

The border around the selected area will start flashing.

Now activate the C6 cell by clicking on it, choose Edit from the Menu bar and then Paste.

It should be found that the selected area has been moved (Cut and Pasted) to the new desired area. Also notice that the bold italic formatting has also been carried over to the new area, and that any entry to the A1:A3 cells will **no longer** be bold italic.

Exercise 1.4 can be attempted now.

---

2 If you simply want to erase the contents of a range of cells while retaining any formatting (bold, currency or whatever) then select **Contents** instead of **All**. The data in the cells will be removed but the formatting will remain.

1.4. Saving, closing, and opening files

The information that you enter to an Excel workbook is contained in units known as **files**. Files can be saved, closed, and then opened again provided the correct procedures are followed.

To follow the arguments involved in these procedures more closely, begin a new session in Excel by selecting File and then Exit from the Menu bar. Click on 'No' to any Save prompts that appear, and then re-access Excel from your computer's main list of options.

The first thing to note is that when Excel is accessed for the *first* time in a *new* session a workbook with the title 'Book1' appears. This is the **File name** that Excel has *automatically* assigned to the new workbook.

Now activate the A5 cell and enter your name.

This information must now be **Saved**; to do this select **File** from the Menu bar. There are three 'Save' options on the list that now appears—**Save, Save As, and Save Workspace.** The first two of these will be used most frequently in the discussion. The distinction between Save and Save As is as follows.

Save will save the workbook with whatever name is currently displayed in the File name bar immediately above the column letters. Thus, selecting Save would save this worksheet with the file name Book1.

Save As, on the other hand, allows users to choose a name for the file that is appropriate to their filing system and usually mnemonic. Once a user-selected name has been given, however, subsequent use of the Save command will save the workbook with that given name. File names can consist of *up to* 8 characters and should not contain any blank spaces.

Consequently, select Save As from the File menu.

A screen resembling the one indicated in Fig. 1.2 will appear. This screen indicates the **default** settings for the saving procedure, which will usually be to save the workbook with the file name Book1 to the Excel directory located on the hard disk (the C drive).

Normally, however, we will want to supply our own name for the file and save it to our own disk, which is located in the A drive.

So, after ensuring that you have placed a formatted disk in drive A, click on the Drives tab in the lower middle of the screen and from the options that appear select A: by clicking.

This will ensure that the workbook is saved to your own disk.

Now click on the **File name** tab at the top left-hand side of the screen where the default file name of Book1 is currently showing.

Use the Delete key to erase the Book1 File name and then type:

Myfile1.xls

The screen should look like Fig. 1.3. If it does, click on OK.

Now, depending upon how Excel has been configured on your computer, either the file will be saved immediately to your own disk on the A drive with the name Myfile1, or a 'Summary Info' prompt will appear.

If the latter has appeared then supply as much of the information requested as you want and click OK.

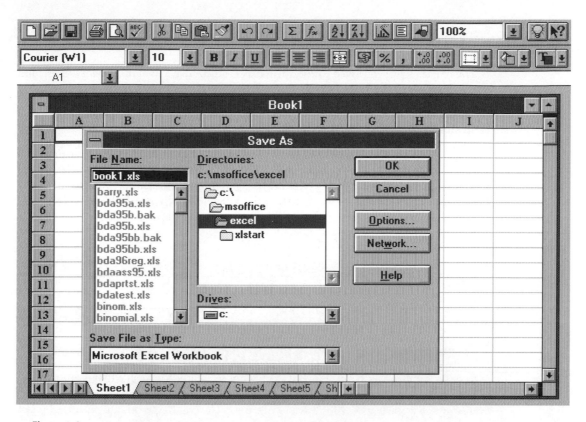

Figure 1.2

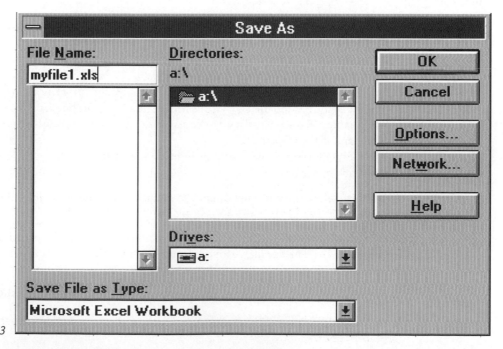

Figure 1.3

This procedure generates further information on the nature and contents of the file that can be used later on to allow easier identification of the required file from the list of all of those that are available.

The file has now been saved to your own disk on the A drive with the name Myfile1, and so the next task will be to close the file and then reopen it to ensure that the information has really been preserved.

To close a file, select File from the Menu bar and then select Close.

If you have forgotten to save any changes that you made to the file, then a prompt will automatically appear, as shown in Fig. 1.4. Usually it will be best to click on 'Yes' at this prompt if it appears, since the chances are that you have made some changes to the workbook which Excel has remembered but that you have forgotten since the last time you saved the file. However, if you are absolutely sure that this is not the case, click on 'No'. The file will now be closed and a blank screen will appear.

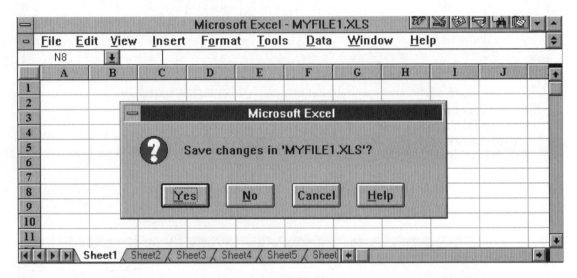

Figure 1.4 At this stage there are a number of options available. We can quit from Excel entirely by selecting File from the Menu bar and then **Exit**. We can create a new workbook by selecting File from the Menu bar and then **New**. This will create a new workbook, on-screen, with the default file name of Book2. Finally, we can open an existing workbook by selecting File from the Menu bar and then **Open**.

At the moment, assume that we want to bring the workbook that we have just saved (Myfile1) back into use.

To do this, select File and then Open. The dialogue box shown in Fig. 1.5 should now appear.

Because you selected drive A in the last save procedure, Excel is now 'logged on' to the A drive. All of the Excel files available for use from your own disk will now appear on the left-hand side of the screen.

Simply click with the mouse on the one that you want to open and then click on OK.

Myfile1 should now appear on screen as you last left it.

Now suppose that you want to work with two separate workbooks.

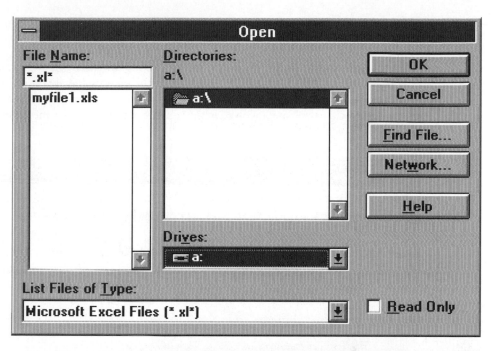

Figure 1.5

With Myfile1 still on screen, select File from the Menu bar and then New. A new workbook, by default named as Book2, will appear on screen. To move between the two workbooks click on the Window option on the Menu bar.

A number of options are now available, but the ones we require are at the bottom. Here we see a list of those Excel files that are currently open—it should show Myfile1 and Book2.

Simply click on the name of the file that you want to activate.

You now have two workbooks opened. One is called Myfile1 and the other is still called Book2 by default.

Use Window to make the Book2 workbook active and then enter your age to the A6 cell.
Now select Save As, select the A drive (if it is not already selected), and name the file as Myfile2 in the same way as before.
Now close both files by selecting File and then Close from the current screen, and then File and Close again from the screen that subsequently appears.

Both workbooks should now be closed and a blank screen displayed.

Now select File and Open. Click on the Myfile1 file name that appears in the left-hand-side list of files available for opening, depress the left-hand mouse button, and drag down to include the Myfile2 file.

Both should now be highlighted.

Select OK and both files will be opened again; you can then move between them using Window and save them again by selecting Save from the File menu.
Exercise 1.5 can be attempted now.

1.5. **Copying data**

The ability to copy text, formulae, and functions from one cell of the worksheet to another chosen range of cells is one of Excel's most powerful features. It is also quite a sophisticated process that needs careful explanation.

To appreciate the issues involved in the copying process consider the illustration shown in Workbook 1.2

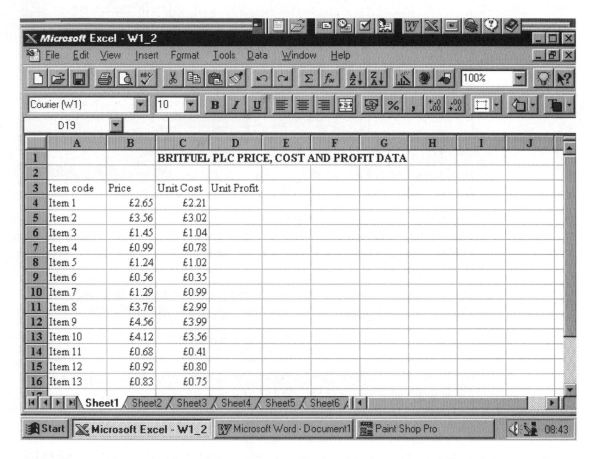

	Workbook 1.2

To create this worksheet for yourself take a blank workbook (File and then New from the Menu bar) and proceed as follows.
First enter the title of the sheet:

BRITFUEL PLC PRICE, COST AND PROFIT DATA

to the C1 cell.

Next, in the A3 to D3 cells enter the following labels to identify the data in each column:

Item Code   Price   Unit Cost   Unit Profit

Not all of the columns will be wide enough to contain these labels.

So place the mouse pointer on the vertical line to the right of the column letter at the top of the sheet. When the solid white cross of the pointer turns into a black cross with

arrows pointing left and right, depress the left-hand mouse button and drag to the right until the column width has increased sufficiently to allow all of the label's text to appear.
   Now, in A4 type the label:

   Item 1

and press Enter once.
   Now click on the A4 cell to make it active again.

Then notice that the bold or coloured border indicating that A4 is the active cell has a small 'blob' on its bottom right-hand corner. This 'blob' is known as a **handle**, and can be activated by placing the mouse pointer over it, whereupon the normal solid white cross of the pointer will become black and less solid. The handle is only active if this black cross is showing.

   Provided this is the case, depress the left-hand mouse button and then drag down column A until you reach row 16. Let go of the left-hand mouse button, and you should find that column A has been filled with the labels shown in the illustrative worksheet.

This is a very clever piece of copying, since although the source cell is a text entry (Item 1), the fact that the last term is a number means that when it is copied into the cells below Excel adds one each time to produce Item 2, Item 3, etc.[3]

   Now you must enter the raw data on price and unit cost into columns B and C.

Since there is no obvious pattern to these data, there is no quick way of doing this; just enter them as quickly as possible, but do not try to include the £ signs—these will be produced later by a special formatting procedure.

   Once these data have been entered, click on the B4 cell[4] and, while depressing the left-hand mouse button, drag down to row 16 and then three columns right into column E.

The area B4:E16 has now been selected, and we are now going to format this area to currency.

   With the B4:E16 area still highlighted, select Format from the main Menu bar and then Cells from the list of options that follows.

There then appears a list of options governing the numerical appearance of the cells in the worksheet.

   So select Currency (usually the last option on the list), and from the next option list that appears select the one showing:

   £#,##0.00;[Red] -£#,##0.00

(This is also usually the last option on the list.)

   Now click OK.

What this has done is to format all the selected cells to show a £ currency symbol with two decimal places, and this will show on screen as red if the amount is negative.

....

3   Excel also allows you to copy text entries such as Mon or Monday, or Jan or January in a 'clever' way. When either of the former two is copied the days of the week are produced, while copying either of the latter two produces the months of the year.

4   Do not activate the handle.

Column D is where we are going to compute the unit profit on Item 1 as the difference between its price and its unit cost.

Hence in D4 we should enter:

=B4-C4

Now notice that the appropriate entry in D5 for the unit profit on Item 2 would be:

=B5-C5

and by extension:

=B6-C6

in D6 for Item 3.

This logic would continue until we obtained:

=B16-C16

in D16 for Item 13.

We *could* type in each of these expressions individually, but thanks to the copying facility there is no need. *Provided there is a recognizable pattern* all we need to do is to provide *one* formula in a **source** cell and then copy this source down the sheet.

So, with the D4 cell active and containing the formula:

=B4-C4

activate the handle and, keeping the left-hand mouse button depressed, drag down from row 4 to row 16.

If this has been done properly, then the result should be the same as that shown in Workbook 1.3.

Workbook 1.3

However, before we leave this worksheet it is important to appreciate exactly what has taken place.

Activate the D4 cell and observe the formula that appears in the Formula bar just above the column letters.

It should show:

=B4-C4

This was the formula that was entered to D4.

Now click on the D5 cell and note that:

=B5-C5

shows in the Formula bar.
Keep on clicking down this column until you are satisfied that each cell contains the appropriate formula entry.

Then remember that only one formula was actually typed into the sheet. This source formula (in D4) was copied down the column, and produced, with incredible ease, exactly what was required.

The upshot of this is the observation that when Excel is instructed to copy a formula (or a function) it does so in a fully relative manner. By this, we mean that a source formula such as:

=B1+C1

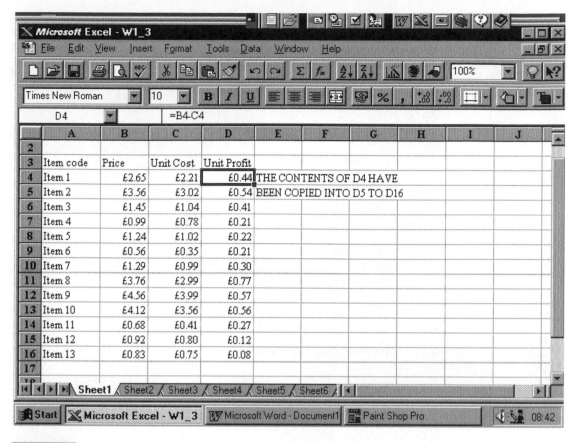

Workbook 1.3

when copied down the sheet produces:

=B2+C2   =B3+C3   =B4+C4 ... and so on.

On the other hand, when the same formula is copied across the sheet it produces:

=C1+D1   =D1+E1   =E1+F1 ... and so on.

In effect, fully relative copying means that the row numbers in a formula update by 1 as the formula is copied down the sheet and the column letters update by 1 as the formula is copied across the sheet.

Now save this file with the name:

W1_3.XLS

**since it will be used again later in the discussion.
Exercises 1.6 and 1.7 can be attempted now.**

Although fully relative copying is an exceptionally powerful tool, there can be circumstances in which it is too powerful for the requirements of our model. In other words, there may be circumstances in which we want to restrain the process. To appreciate the nature of such circumstances, consider the illustration in Workbook 1.4.

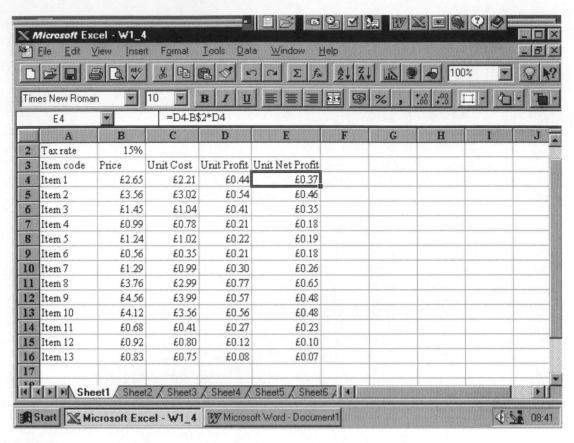

**Workbook
1.4** Here, we have taken the model constructed in Workbook 1.3 and added the information that the unit profit on each item is subject to tax at a rate of 15%.

To follow the argument open Workbook 1.3 (if it has been closed) and make the following additions.

First, in A2 enter the label:

Tax rate

and in B2 enter:

0.15 or 15%

Now, in E3 enter the label:

Unit Net Profit

This will be the profit after tax.

We now need to write a formula in E4 that will compute the unit net profit on the basis of the unit profits made by each item and the tax rate that is applied to those unit profits.

Logically, we should argue that:

Net Unit Profit = Unit Profit - Tax rate*Unit Profit

Hence, in E4 we can translate this into a formula of the form:

=D4-B2*D4

This represents the unit profit on item 1 minus the tax rate times the unit profit on item 1.

As far as Item 1 is concerned this is a completely valid formulation and would produce the correct result, but if we try to copy such a formula into the cells below, difficulties will ensue.

This is because fully relative copying means that the tax rate (in B2) will be row updated in the copying process. In other words, B2 will become B3, B4, B5, and so on, when copied down the sheet. Yet B3, B4, and B5 do not contain tax rate information. Only B2 contains this information. Consequently, we require that the B2 cell reference in the formula is always B2 and does not update in the copying process.

The two D4 references in the formula, on the other hand, must update when copied down the sheet, since they relate to each of the items that the company sells and to which the tax rate must apply.

To deal with these different requirements we must add a dollar sign ($) in front of the row number in the B2 cell address. That is, we rewrite the formula as:

=D4-B$2*D4

The dollar sign ensures that when the formula is copied down the sheet, the row number will not be updated. It will always remain as B2. The D4 references, on the other hand, without their dollar signs, will update in a fully relative manner. This will produce a formula that can be copied consistently, and that will serve our purpose.

Consequently, in E4 enter:

=D4-B$2*D4

then activate the handle and drag down to row 16.

The correct results will be obtained, and if you inspect each of the cells then you will find that the references to column D have been row updated as required but the one to B2 has remained fixed.

Save this model now as W1_4.XLS for future reference.
Exercise 1.8 can be attempted now.

Correct use of the $ symbol in copying is of such crucial importance to the efficient creation of worksheet models that it deserves further discussion. Consequently, consider the illustration shown in Workbook 1.5.

Create this now in a new workbook in line with the instructions below.

Workbook 1.5

The first step is to enter the raw data to the A1:C3 range as indicated in the illustration.
Next, in A5 enter the formula:

=A1*2

This is going to be the source cell for the copying process, and will be copied into the adjacent two columns and the adjacent two rows. In this case, however, instead of dragging the handle as before, we are going to use the Copy command from the Menu bar.

To do this, click on A5 to activate the cell. Then select Edit from the Menu bar and then click on Copy from the options that will have appeared.

The border around the active cell should change from solid to flashing, indicating that this particular cell has been selected for copying.

Now depress the left-hand mouse button and drag down two rows and then across two columns.

| Times New Roman | 10 | B | I | U | | | | | | % | , | | | | |

E3

W1_5.XLS

	A	B	C	D	E	F	G	
1	4	6	10					
2	5	2	1					
3	9	11	7					
4	SOURCE DATA							
5	8	12	20		8	12	20	
6	10	4	2		8	12	20	
7	18	22	14		8	12	20	
8	FULLY RELATIVE COPYING				SEMI-RELATIVE COPYING - ROW FIXED			
9	8	8	8		8	8	8	
10	10	10	10		8	8	8	
11	18	18	18		8	8	8	
12	SEMI-RELATIVE COPYING - COLUMN FIXED				ABSOLUTE COPYING			
13								
14								
15								
16								
17								

Sheet1 / Sheet2 / Sheet3 / Sheet4 / Sheet5 / Sh

This will select the cells A5:C7 as the range that is to be copied to.

Now press the Enter key, or select Edit and then Paste from the Menu bar.

By either method, the result of the copying process should be the same as the A5:C7 range of the illustrative worksheet.

The first thing to note is that the copying has been done in a fully relative manner, with the result that each element in the A5:C7 range is exactly double the corresponding element in the A1:C3 range. This is because the copying process that has been performed can be thought of as follows:

$$=A1*2 \text{ BECOMES } =A1*2 =B1*2 =C1*2 \text{ FULLY RELATIVE COPYING}$$
$$=A2*2 =B2*2 =C2*2$$
$$=A3*2 =B3*2 =C3*2$$

Now move to E5 and enter:

$$=A\$1*2$$

Then use the same method as above to copy this into the E5:G7 range.

In this case the dollar sign attached to the row number means that the latter will *not* update when copied down the sheet, but the column letter *will* update as copying is performed across the sheet. This has the effect of making each of the three rows in E5:G7 identical, with each element being twice the corresponding element in the A1:C1 range. The whole process can be visualized as follows:

$$=A\$1*2 \text{ BECOMES } =A\$1*2 =B\$1*2 =C\$1*2 \text{ SEMI-RELATIVE COPYING}$$
$$=A\$1*2 =B\$1*2 =C\$1*2 \text{ COLUMN RELATIVE}$$
$$=A\$1*2 =B\$1*2 =C\$1*2 \text{ ROW ABSOLUTE}$$

Next, move to A9 and enter:

=$A1*2

and copy this into A9:C11.

The results should be the same as in the illustrative worksheet, and represent the following process.

=$A1*2 BECOMES =$A1*2 =$A1*2 =$A1*2 SEMI-RELATIVE COPYING
=$A2*2 =$A2*2 =$A2*2 COLUMN ABSOLUTE
=$A3*2 =$A3*2 =$A3*2 ROW RELATIVE

Finally in E9 enter:

=$A$1*2

and copy this into E9:G11.

The appearance of dollar signs in front of both the row number and the column letter means that in the copying process the A1 cell address is absolutely fixed. Neither columns nor rows will update, since the process is equivalent to:

=$A$1*2 BECOMES =$A$1*2 =$A$1*2 =$A$1*2 ABSOLUTE COPYING
=$A$1*2 =$A$1*2 =$A$1*2
=$A$1*2 =$A$1*2 =$A$1*2

Save this model now as W1_5.XLS for future reference.

1.6. **Printing worksheets**

To follow the subsequent explanation close all files that are currently open (File, Close for as many screens as it takes, saying Yes to any Save prompts that appear). Now open a new file and enter your name and address to the A1:A5 range of the sheet.

To print some or all of the contents of a worksheet, select File from the Menu bar and then Print.

A dialogue screen resembling the one shown in Fig. 1.6 will appear.

Now decide whether you want to print the current sheet or the entire workbook (i.e. all of the sheets in the workbook) and click on the appropriate tab—Selected Sheet(s) for the former, Entire Workbook for the latter.

Normally, there will only be one sheet selected (the active sheet). However, if you want to select more than one sheet, but not the entire workbook, activate the first sheet that you want to select then depress the Shift key and while keeping it depressed click on the last sheet that is to be selected. This continuous range of sheets has now been selected, and each of them will be printed when Selected Sheets is chosen from the Print menu. To unselect a range of sheets, simply click on any sheet that has not been selected (i.e. has a dark background). (If all the currently available sheets have been selected, click on any one sheet and the rest will be unselected.)

Now note that, in order to avoid using vast amounts of superfluous paper, Excel has a Print Preview feature that allows you to see what you are likely to get from any print command that you issue.

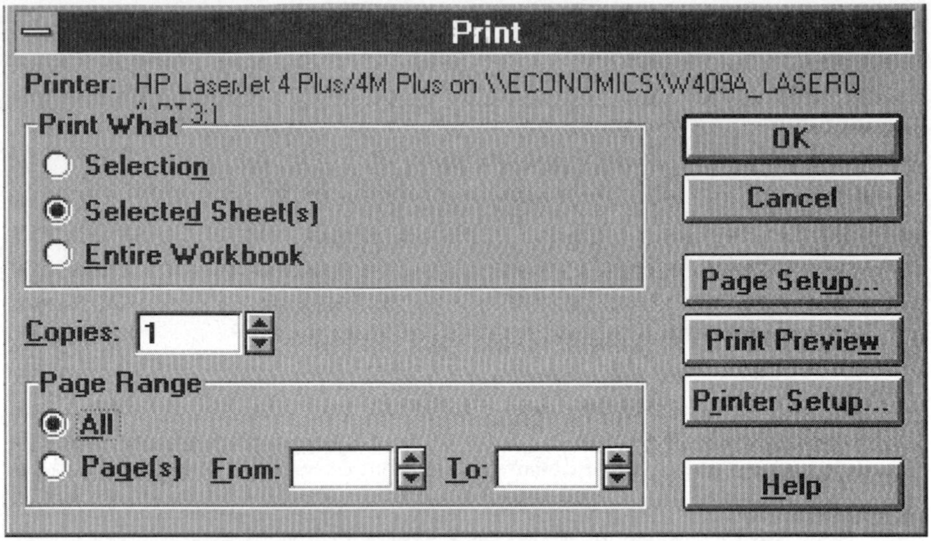

Figure 1.6

Either select File and then Print Preview from the Menu bar or click on the 'magnifying glass' icon on the Toolbar.

By either method, you will be able to see the printing selection that has been chosen.

If it appears to be incorrect, select **Close** from Print Preview and then return to the **Print** menu to reselect what you want printed.

Since in the illustration you should only have one sheet containing information, check the Print Preview, and if it looks fine select Print from the options at the top of the screen. Alternatively, close the Print Preview and then select Print and click on OK. Either way the current sheet will be printed.

If it is only a **section** (range) of the selected worksheet that you want to print, choose **Page Setup** from the dialogue screen shown in Fig. 1.6. A new dialogue screen resembling Fig. 1.7 will appear.

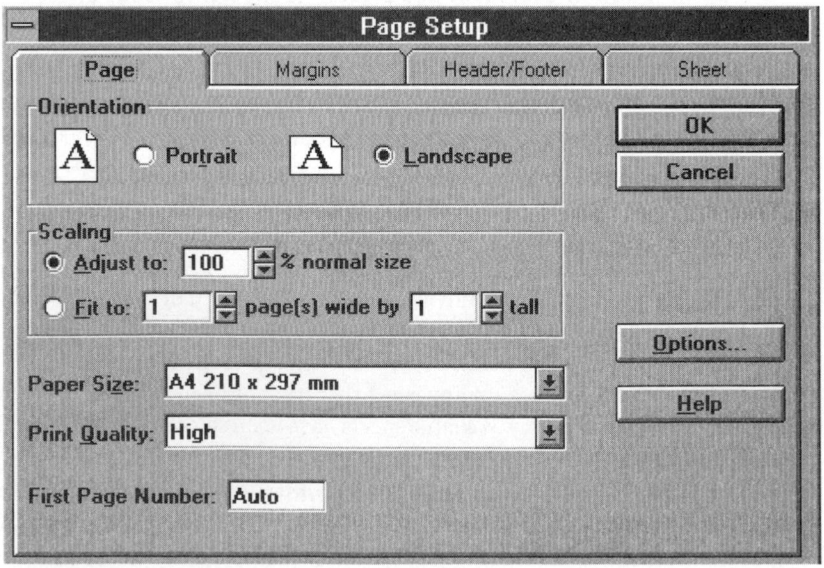

Figure 1.7

Here you can choose the orientation of the printed output—**Portrait** produces a document that is higher than it is wide, **Landscape** produces a document that is wider than it is high. (The latter can be very useful if your worksheet contains relatively few rows but lots of columns. Choosing Landscape can sometimes allow you to get the entire sheet printed on one page.)

Now click on the **Sheet** tab at the top right-hand side of the box. The dialogue screen shown in Fig. 1.8 will appear.

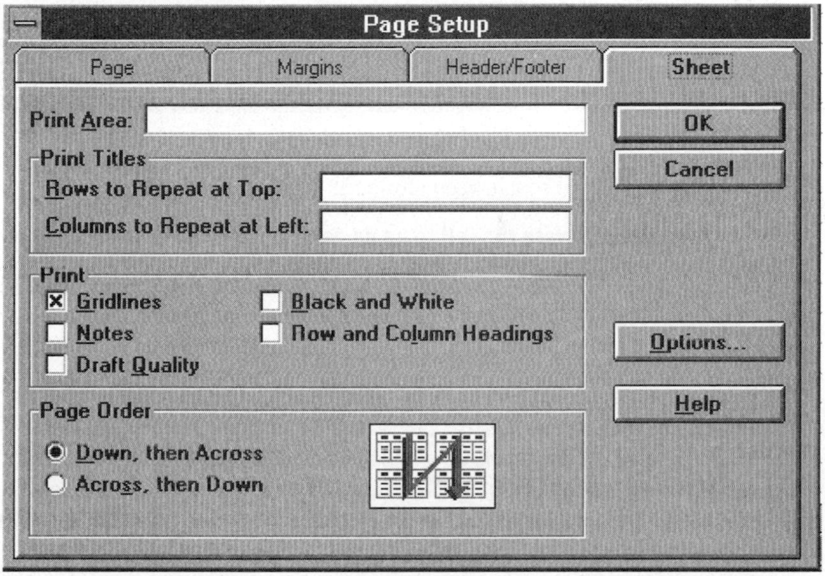

Figure 1.8

To select the range of cells to be printed click on the Print Area tab, enter the range of cells that you want printed (A1:D13, for example) and then click OK. You will be taken back to the Print dialogue box; if everything looks in order click OK.

The selected range of the document will now be printed.

Exercise 1.9 can be attempted now.

1.7. Creating and using named cells

Excel allows users to define their own names for cells, and to use these names thereafter in formulae instead of the conventional cell address (A1, B4, etc.). For example, if the B1 cell has been named as X, then the following two formulae are equivalent:

=B1+2 is the same as =X+2

Naming cells can be very useful for memory purposes. For instance, if a firm's profit for the first quarter of the year is located in the C6 cell, say, then naming this cell as Q1 is a lot easier to remember (since it has a mnemonic connotation) in subsequent formulae that need to refer to first quarter profits.

The process and effects of naming a cell are illustrated in Workbook 1.6.

Make this model up for yourself in a new workbook.

Microsoft Excel - W1_6.XLS									

Fil̲e   E̲dit   V̲iew   I̲nsert   F̲ormat   T̲ools   D̲ata   W̲indow   H̲elp

B3   =Y-X

	A	B	C	D	E	F	G	H	I	J
1	INCOME	15900								
2	EXPENDITURE	13500								
3	SURPLUS	2400	=Y-X IS THE FORMULA IN B3							
4										
5										

Sheet1 / Sheet2 / Sheet3 / Sheet4 / Sheet5 / Sheet

Workbook 1.6

Here, the B1 and B2 cells have been named as Y and X respectively.

To do this, first activate the cell to be named (click on B1 first of all), then select Insert from the Menu bar and then Name and Define.

The Name dialogue box will appear and will indicate any names that have previously been defined.

Click on the Names in Workbook tab at the top of the box and enter Y as the name, and then check that the Refers To: tab at the bottom of the box indicates Sheet1!$B$1.[5] Select OK, and the B1 cell is now known to the workbook as Y. Now click on B2 and re-peat this process for the B2 cell—naming it as X. With B1 and B2 named as Y and X re-spectively, the Surplus (Income–Expenditure) can be obtained by activating the B3 cell and entering:

$=Y-X$

This is completely equivalent to:

$=B1-B2$

when B1 and B2 have been named as Y and X respectively.

Confirm this now.
Exercise 1.10 can be attempted now.

1.8. Inserting or deleting rows or columns

Rows or columns can be inserted in the worksheet as required. Importantly however, any insertion will cause all formulae to adjust automatically to take account of the relevant in-sertions. To appreciate the importance of this point, consider Workbook 1.7.

Make this model up for yourself in a new workbook or load it from the accompanying disk (W1_7.XLS).

---

5 If it does not show this, erase what is there and then click on B1, or type in the reference as =Sheet1!$B$1.

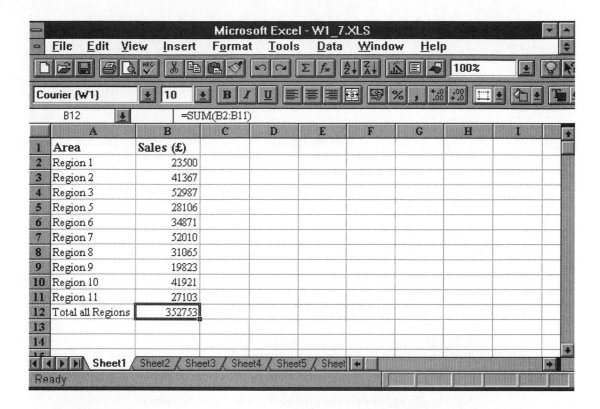

Workbook 1.7

Here, it is to be supposed that the sales information for region 4 has been inadvertently omitted. We clearly need to insert a row between row 4 and row 5 to allow the data for region 4 to be entered.

Before we do this, however, inspect the totalling formula that was entered to the B12 cell and which is indicated on the Formula bar in the illustrative worksheet. It shows:

=SUM(B2:B11)

but if we insert a new row and enter some data for that row the totalling formula should become:

=SUM(B2:B12)

Fortunately, there is no need to perform this adjustment manually, since the insertion procedure does it automatically.

To insert the required row, activate any cell in row 5 (B5 will do) and then select Insert from the Menu bar and then Rows.

The new row will be inserted.

Now click on the B13 cell, and you will find that the totalling formula has been adjusted as required. Also confirm that it operates correctly by entering a value for region 4's sales.

The column total should automatically increase by exactly the amount that you entered.

The process for inserting columns to the worksheet is identical, with the exception that **Columns** is chosen from the **Insert** menu.

Practise this now by inserting a new column between column A and column B.

Lastly, if more than one row or column needs to be inserted, activate the first cell in the insertion range and then drag down or across for as many rows or columns as are required. Then select Insert and Rows or Columns as before.

Removing rows or columns from the worksheet is done from the **Edit** option on the Menu bar. First of all, place the mouse pointer in the row or column that is to be removed, then select **Edit** and then **Delete**, and then **Entire Row** or **Entire Column**. Click OK to effect the deletion.[6]

Practise this now by removing the column that you inserted between column A and column B.
Exercise 1.11 can be attempted now.

1.9. Working with multiple sheets

As was said earlier, the sheets of a workbook are automatically named Sheet1, Sheet2, and so on, but you will often want to customize them with names *of your own* that relate to their purpose.

To follow the argument open a new workbook.
   With Sheet1 active, double click quickly with the left-hand mouse button on the Sheet1 tab. The Rename Sheet dialogue box should appear with the default name (Sheet1) highlighted in black.[7]
   Press the Delete key once to remove this name and then enter:

   1996DATA

and select OK.[8]

The new name of the sheet—1996DATA—will now appear on the sheet tabs.

Now double click rapidly on the Sheet2 tab and use the procedure explained above to rename it as 1997DATA.

Clearly, you can continue with this process until all of the sheets that you intend to use are named appropriately.

   The information contained in the various sheets of the workbook can be linked in a variety of ways. To see this proceed as follows:

Activate the 1996DATA sheet by clicking once.
   Then in A1 enter the label:

   Quarterly profits

Next, in A2:A5 enter the numbers:

   15000   21000   12500   and   8250

---

6 More care has to be exercised with deletion of rows or columns than with insertions. This is because the removal of a row or column can erase data that needs to be used by some formulae or functions elsewhere in the sheet. If this happens, one or more #REF! messages will appear and the first thing to do is click on the Undo icon on the toolbar (a curved left-pointing blue arrow). This will undo the deletion and restore the integrity of the model.

7 If this has not happened, then the time between the two clicks was too long. Try again with a sharp rapid action of the index finger on the left-hand mouse button.

8 Do not include a space between the 6 of 1996 and the D of DATA.

Now activate the A1 cell and select Edit from the Menu bar, and then Copy.

The A1 cell will flash.

What we are going to do is copy this label from the 1996DATA sheet into the 1997DATA sheet.

So click on the 1997DATA sheet tab and then click on the A1 cell of this sheet to activate it. Now press Enter, or select Edit and Paste from the Menu bar and the label will appear in the A1 cell of the 1997DATA sheet.

We now need some profit data for 1997.

So, ensuring that the 1997DATA sheet is selected and active, enter the following numbers to the A2:A5 cells:

13000   26000   15900   and   12350

What we have, therefore, is the firm's 1996 quarterly profits in the range A2:A5 of the 1996DATA sheet, and its 1997 profits in the same area of the 1997DATA sheet.

We are now going to name a new sheet as 1996-7DATA, where we will get Excel to compute the combined profits for the two years.

First, double click on Sheet3 and rename it as:

1996-7DATA

Then, in A1 enter the label:

Combined profits 1996-7

Now activate the A2 cell of the 1996-7DATA sheet.

This is where the linking of the two sheets is going to take place.

The logic is as follows. The combined annual profits for the first quarter of 1996 and 1997 are clearly the contents of A2 in the 1996DATA sheet plus the contents of A2 in the 1997DATA sheet.

Excel allows you write this logic as follows:

=1996DATA!A2+1997DATA!A2

Notice the use of the exclamation mark to separate the *sheet* reference from the *cell* reference in that sheet.

Enter this formula now to the A2 cell of the 1996-7DATA sheet.

A result of 28000 should be returned (i.e. 15000+13000).

Now activate the A2 cell of 1996-7DATA, activate the handle, and drag down to A5.

When you let go of the mouse button, the appropriate formulae for the remaining three quarters will have been entered.

Check this by inspecting each cell.

Finally, although in this illustration there were only two sheets to be combined, it is not hard to imagine circumstances where there are several sheets covering data for a large number of years. In such circumstances it is needlessly tedious to sum all the sheets *individually* as was done above—in other words to enter something like:

=1996DATA!A2+1997DATA!A2+ . . . and so on until . . . +2010DATA!A2

To overcome this tedium all we have to do is make use of the SUM function as follows:

> =SUM(1996DATA:2010DATA!A2:A2)

or, since we only have two sheets named in this way in our illustration:

> =SUM(1996DATA:1997DATA!A2:A2)

This will sum the A2 cells of all the sheets that are specified on either side of the first colon sign in the formula.

Confirm that this works by replacing the formula that you previously entered to the A2 cell of 1996–7DATA with this new version and then copying it down into A3:A5 to obtain the 2nd, 3rd, and 4th quarter totals.

1.10. **Sorting data**

One of Excel's most powerful features is the ability to perform sophisticated data sorting. To follow the argument, consider the illustration shown in Workbook 1.8.

Make this model up for yourself or load it from the accompanying disk (W1_8.XLS).

	A	B	C	D	E	F	G
1	Share Name	Share Price (£)	Dividend (£)	Capital gain %			
2	Pandora	0.95	0.19	5.60%			
3	Pan-europe	2.5	0.26	15.60%			
4	IFI	0.95	0.19	7.10%			
5	MBI	0.99	0.18	1.30%			
6	Gloxo	3.21	0.5	10.10%			
7	PR&W	2.03	0.49	2.90%			
8	AM&M	1.5	0.31	6.80%			
9	Devoors	1.5	0.31	8.90%			
10	Brutus	2.5	0.35	14.50%			
11	Cathedral Life	2.43	0.34	3.50%			
12	Spoolers	0.95	0.19	9.70%			
13	Costcut	2.5	0.35	12.40%			
14	Credit Alpha	12.21	1.65	5.20%			
15	Commercial Plus	1.67	0.21	9.10%			
16	Agricola	0.65	0.12	10.50%			
17	Regal Bank	1.56	0.4	5.80%			

Workbook 1.8 Here, we have selected financial data for a list of shares. The column headers at the top of the sheet identify what are known as **Fields**, and the individual share names are known as **Records**. Thus, each field contains information on all the records and each record has information from all the fields.

Inspection of the data indicates that there are several groups of shares with the same price. These have been indicated for you in the illustrative sheet by using bold, italics, or underline formatting.

If you are making the sheet up for yourself, there is no need to do this formatting.

It should also be clear that *of those shares with the same price* some also have the same dividend payment. However, in this illustration there are no shares with the same price and the same dividend payment and the same percentage capital gain. Next, it will be observed that the data have not been sorted into any kind of order. The task to be undertaken is to sort the data in descending order of share price and then, since some of these prices are the same, to use the dividend payment to distinguish between shares that are tied in terms of price. Once again, descending order will be used, so in the eventual sorted list two or more shares with the same price will subsequently be ranked from high to low in terms of their dividend payment.

Even then, as we have seen, there are some shares in the list that cannot be distinguished either on their price or on their dividend payment. Consequently, we will use their capital gain as the third way of separating tied ranks—once again on the basis of descending numerical value.

To initiate the sorting procedure, the first thing to do is select the entire area from A1 to D17 as the range to be sorted. This is crucial.

To understand the importance of this point remember that, although we are **not** going to use the share names as a way of sorting, if they are not included in the sort area they will become detached from their field data on price, dividend, and capital gain once we use this last information as the basis of the sorting process. Detaching one or more field values from their rightful owner in the sorting process is the commonest cause of what is euphemistically called 'computer error', and is usually enough to explain how (for example) Joe Lectric, who uses gas only to cook with, receives ICI's quarterly gas bill.

Put simply, if your worksheet contains 8 fields and 20 records, say, and even if you intend sorting those records only on the basis of one of those fields, all 8 fields and all 20 records must be included in the range selected for the sort.[9]

Consequently, with the A1:D17 range selected, choose Data and then Sort from the Menu bar.

The dialogue screen shown in Figure 1.9 should appear.

The illustrated dialogue box was created by clicking on the **Sort By** tab and selecting Share Price as the basis of the **primary** sort from the list of available fields that then appears. The **Descending** button alongside was also clicked. The **secondary** sort, to differentiate tied ranks, was defined by clicking on the first **Then By** tab and then selecting Dividend from the list and also choosing Descending. Finally, the **tertiary** sort, to differentiate between records that are tied on both the primary and the secondary sort, was defined by clicking on the second **Then By** tab and selecting Capital Gain from the list. Descending order was again selected.

Carry out these procedures now.

The results of this three-way sort are shown Workbook 1.9.

9 Sorting is a very powerful procedure and can be highly destructive if not carried out properly. The Undo feature is indispensable if a mistake is made—click on it immediately if you suspect that the sorting has destroyed the structure of your worksheet.

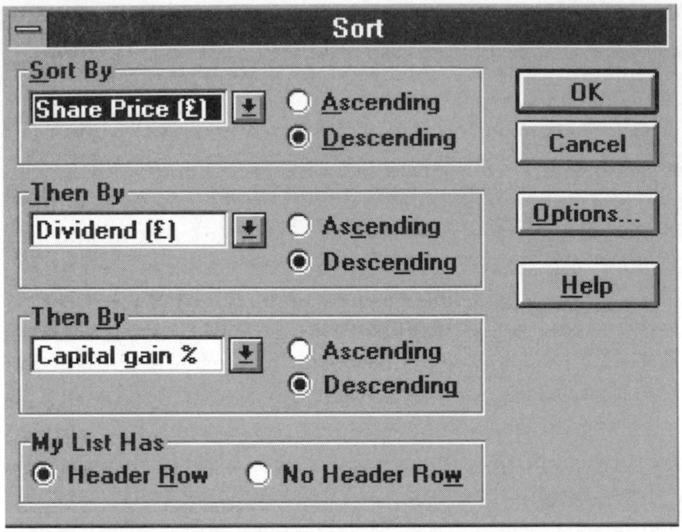

Figure 1.9

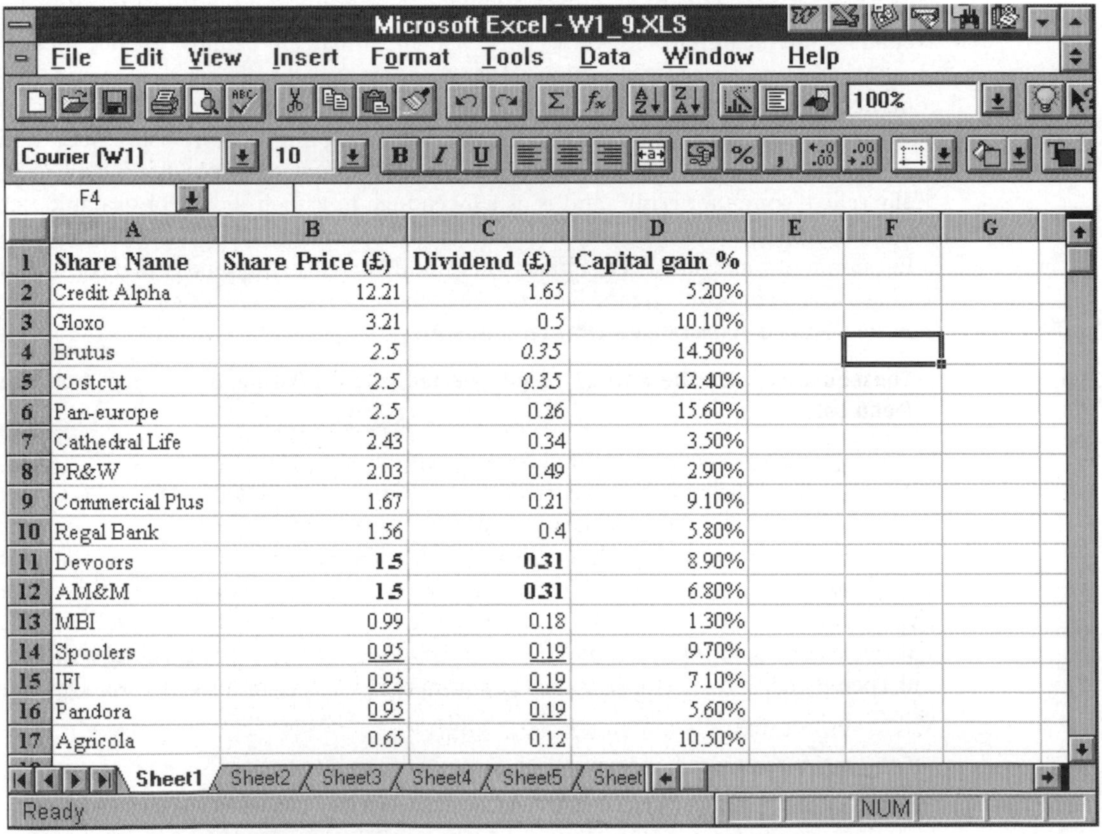

	A	B	C	D	E	F	G
1	Share Name	Share Price (£)	Dividend (£)	Capital gain %			
2	Credit Alpha	12.21	1.65	5.20%			
3	Gloxo	3.21	0.5	10.10%			
4	Brutus	2.5	0.35	14.50%			
5	Costcut	2.5	0.35	12.40%			
6	Pan-europe	2.5	0.26	15.60%			
7	Cathedral Life	2.43	0.34	3.50%			
8	PR&W	2.03	0.49	2.90%			
9	Commercial Plus	1.67	0.21	9.10%			
10	Regal Bank	1.56	0.4	5.80%			
11	Devoors	1.5	0.31	8.90%			
12	AM&M	1.5	0.31	6.80%			
13	MBI	0.99	0.18	1.30%			
14	Spoolers	0.95	0.19	9.70%			
15	IFI	0.95	0.19	7.10%			
16	Pandora	0.95	0.19	5.60%			
17	Agricola	0.65	0.12	10.50%			

Workbook 1.9

Save this sorted worksheet now as W1_9.XLS, since we will be using it again in the next section.
Exercise 1.12 can be attempted now.

1.11. **Filtering data**

....

Filtering data is the process of selecting those records from a list that meet certain requirements (**criteria**) defined by the user. It might, for instance, be all female records or all married individuals, or even all females who are also married.

The ultimate objective of filtering is to get Excel to interrogate the data list in terms of questions to which answers are required; and clearly these answers will themselves be a list of records that meet the requirements of our questions.

To follow the argument open Workbook 1.9 (W1_9.XLS) now.

You should have the sorted list of financial data for the portfolio of shares on screen.

To initiate the filtering process, the first thing to do is identify all of the **Field names** and the list of records to Excel.

Do this now by clicking on A1 and dragging down and along to D17.

The cells containing all of the information in the data base are now selected.

Next, choose Data and then Filter and then AutoFilter from the Menu bar.

When you have done this, it should be found that four arrow tabs have been inserted to the cells containing the field names (A1:D1).

To interrogate this data list, simply click on the arrow tab in the field that relates to the question that you want to ask.

For example, in the current illustration, suppose that we want to create a list of all shares with a capital gain that was more than 10%.

To do this, click on the arrow tab in the D1 cell (since this is the top of the capital gain field) and from the prompt that appears select {Custom . . .}. The dialogue box shown in Fig. 1.10 will appear.

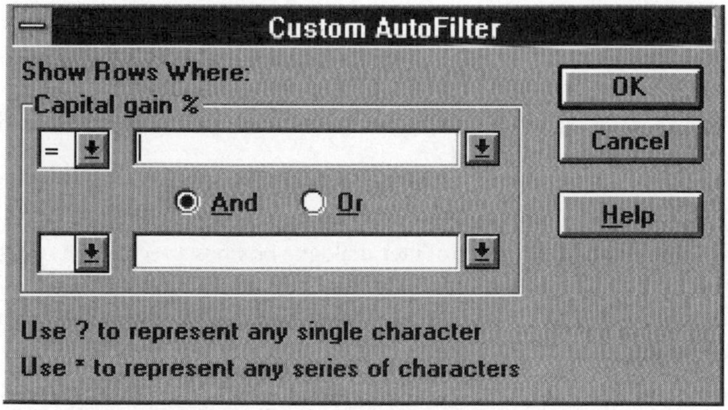

Figure 1.10

Now click on the top left-hand tab to obtain a list of arithmetic operators and from this list select 'greater than' (>).
Next, click on the adjacent box and enter the criterion—10% in this case.

The dialogue box should now resemble Fig. 1.11.

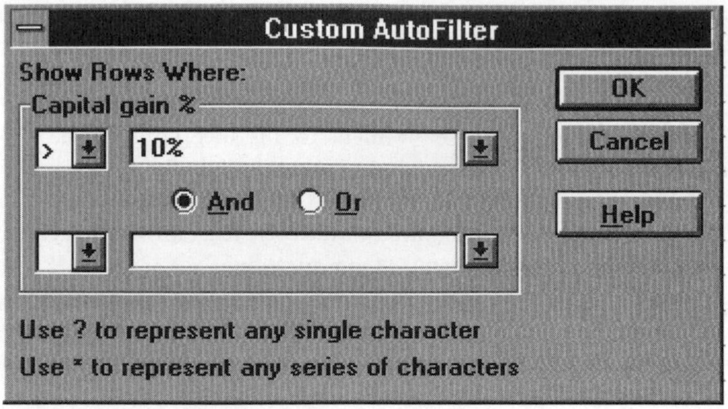

Figure 1.11

If it does, click on OK and the list will be filtered.

The effect should be the same as indicated in Workbook 1.10.

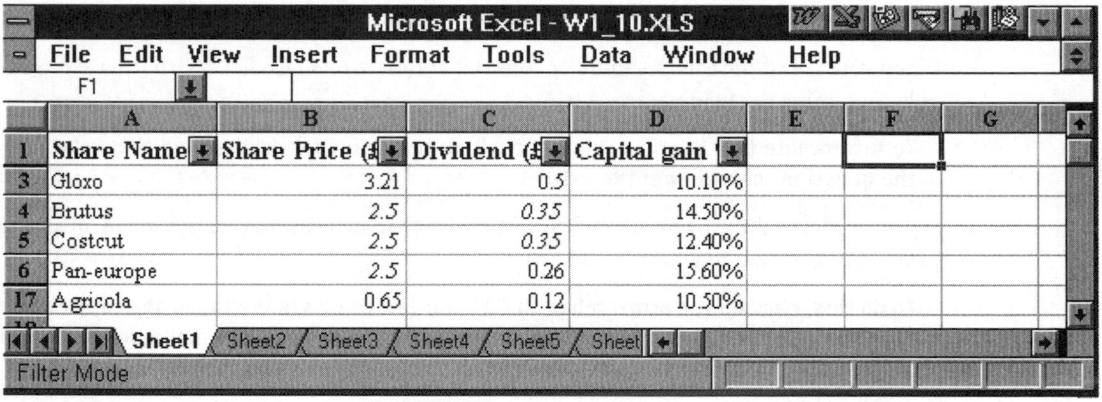

	A	B	C	D	E	F	G
1	Share Name	Share Price (£	Dividend (£	Capital gain			
3	Gloxo	3.21	0.5	10.10%			
4	Brutus	*2.5*	*0.35*	14.50%			
5	Costcut	*2.5*	*0.35*	12.40%			
6	Pan-europe	*2.5*	0.26	15.60%			
17	Agricola	0.65	0.12	10.50%			

Workbook 1.10

Notice that the arrow tab in D1 has turned from black to blue indicating that this is a **filtered** list.

To restore the original list simply click on the (blue) arrow tab and select {All} from the prompt that follows. All of the original records will be restored on screen and the arrow tab will return to its normal black colour.

Do this now.

Now notice that the Custom AutoFilter dialogue box has a second set of tabs towards the bottom of the box. These allow more complex questions to be asked.

For example, suppose we wanted a list of all shares whose capital gain was greater than 10% but did not exceed 13%.

To do this, click on the arrow tab in the Capital Gain field (D1) and then select {Custom . . .}. Then select > and enter 10% in the top two tabs. Next, make sure that And is checked in the middle of the screen and then select less than (<) and enter 13% in the bottom two tabs. Click OK and the records satisfying both of these requirements will be selected from the list.[10]

10 You should find that the list has been reduced from five to three records—Gloxo, Costcut, and Agricola.

To follow the next stage of the discussion restore all of the original records by clicking on the arrow tab in D1 and selecting All from the prompt that follows.

The previous filtering only took place on the basis of one field (Capital Gain), but it is a simple matter to interrogate the list on the basis of questions relating to more than one field.

For example, suppose that we wanted a list of all shares with more than 10% capital gain and with a dividend payment of more than £0.3.

To do this, click on the arrow tab in the capital gain field (D1) and use the same procedure as before to select all records with a capital gain of more than 10%.

Once the list has been reduced to include only these records, click on the arrow tab in the Dividend field (C1) and use the same procedure to select those records with a Dividend payment of more than £0.3.

You should find that only three records—Gloxo, Brutus, and Costcut—satisfy both of these requirements.

Now, when more than one field has been used for interrogation purposes, rather than clicking on each blue arrow tab individually and selecting All to restore the original list field by field, it is quicker to select **Data** and then **Filter** from the Menu bar and then click on **Show All**.

Do this now.

There are two further points to be noted about filtered lists.

First, when a list has been filtered, selecting Print will produce hard copy of the filtered rather than the original list. This is the easiest way of obtaining a copy of those records that satisfy the questions that you have asked.

Practise this now by printing the list of all shares with more than 8% capital gain.

Second, there will frequently be circumstances in which you require to total the values in one or more fields of a filtered list. For example, in the context of the current illustration (Workbook 1.9) we might want to obtain the total share price and the total dividend payment of those shares that had more than 10% capital gain.

At first sight it might seem simply to be a case of writing two SUM functions such as:

=SUM(B2:B17)   and   =SUM(C2:C17)

and hoping that once the list is filtered only the sum of the selected records will be produced.

However, this conventional summing procedure will only work on an unfiltered list, and will not produce the correct results when the list is filtered.

For filtered lists, Excel has a special totalling function known as SUBTOTAL.

To follow the discussion load Workbook 1.9, restore all of the original records, and read on.

Since the original list only spans 17 rows, we can use row 18 to contain our totalling formulae.

Consequently, in B18 enter:

=SUBTOTAL(9,B2:B17)

Notice that this function contains two arguments—a number (9 in this case) and the entire range of cells in the original list. The number tells Excel which of a variety of arithmetical operations is to be performed on the specified range—9 is the code for SUM—but if we had used code 1 then the list would have been averaged instead.

Now copy the SUBTOTAL formula in B18 into C18. Results of 38.1 and 6.04 should be obtained.

However, since the list has not, as yet, been filtered the two functions will at present return the totals of all the records in the Share Price and Dividend payment fields.

But now suppose that we filter the list to include only those shares that have experienced more than 10% capital gain.

Do this now by the method explained above.

It should be found that the two functions have adjusted automatically to contain the totals of the filtered list. In other words, B18 and C18 should now contain 11.36 and 1.58 respectively.

This automatic adjustment is entirely due to using the SUBTOTAL function with a first argument value of 9, rather than a simple SUM function.

Now restore all of the records and confirm that the values in B18 and C18 have returned to 38.1 and 6.04 respectively.
Exercises 1.13 and 1.14 can be attempted now.

1.12. Exercises

Exercise 1.1

(a) The intersection between a column and a row in a worksheet is known as what?

(b) What is the cell address of the 21st row of column H?

(c) An Excel workbook is a three dimensional stack of what?

(d) What is the indication that a cell is active?

(e) When can data be entered to a cell?

(f) Name three ways in which a cell can be made active.

(g) How many rows and columns are there in an Excel worksheet?

(h) Where are the contents of the active cell displayed?

(i) With the A1 cell currently active, what is the quickest way of making IV16384 become the active cell?

(j) What is the quickest way of making the BZ9999 cell active?

Exercise 1.2

Indicate how the following expressions would be evaluated by Excel

(a) =10+2^3   (b) =4*5+3^2
(c) =5+18/3^2   (d) =(9+18)/3^2
(e) =(1+18/3)^2   (f) 6/2+5*4
(g) =(3+2*6)*4   (h) =3+2*6*(3+7)
(i) =((3+2)*5)^2   (j) =((3+2)*5^2)
(k) =(3^2+1)*2^(2+1) (l) =104/2^3
(m) =4^2/2^3   (n) =4^(2/2)^3

Exercise 1.3

Identify each of the following cell entries as being one of text, number, formula, function, or a mixture of the last three.

(a) 23
(b) '96
(c) Excel
(d) 2times2
(e) A1+A2
(f) =A1*3
(g) 6*A2+A3
(h) =9*A1
(i) =SUM(H5:H55)
(j) 7*SUM(Y56:Z99)

(k) =A1*SUM(D12:D32)
(l) =9+10+A1−B1+C1−SUM(A2:C2)

Exercise 1.4

Enter some data to the A1:C6 range of a worksheet; anything will do—text and/or numbers are easiest.

(a) Format the range to underlined italics.
(b) Move the contents of A1:C6 into A8:C13.
(c) Delete the contents only of A8:C13.
(d) Remove the underlined italics formatting from A8:C13.
(e) Make A8:C13 bold formatted and then make an entry in this range to confirm that it has worked.

Exercise 1.5

Begin a new Excel session by selecting **File** and then **Exit** from the Menu bar. If Save prompts appear for workbooks that are currently open, say Yes to those that refer to files that you want to keep and/or update. Now re-access Excel from the main menu.

(a) Open a new file, enter your first name to A1, and then save the file to the A drive with the file name NEW1.

(b) Open another new file, enter your surname to A1, and save it to the A drive with the name NEW2.

(c) Satisfy yourself that you can activate either of the two files as required.

(d) Close both files.

(e) Open both files again.

(f) Replace you first name in NEW1 with that of your best friend and do the same for the NEW2 file. Save both files to the A drive with this new information.

(g) Close both files.

(h) Open both files again and confirm that the changes that you made have been saved.

(i) Make backup copies of both files on the A drive with the names New1A and NEW2A.

(j) Close both files and quit Excel.

Exercise 1.6

Use the copying facility to create the following list in column A:

Profits 1980
Profits 1981

and so on until:

Profits 2020

Exercise 1.7

Use the copying facility to produce an efficient way of creating the following series of numbers in the A1:A20 range:

4, 9, 14, 19, 24, 29, 34, 39, 44, 49, 54, 59, 64, 69, 74, 79, 84, 89, 94, 99

Exercise 1.8

Prepare the model shown in Workbook 1.11 or load it from the accompanying disk (W1_11.XLS).

Workbook 1.11

Now write formulae to complete the model in line with the requirements of the column headings.

Save the completed model as W1_11.XLS for future use.

Exercise 1.9

Print the A1:F10 range of Workbook 1.11 in Landscape form.

Exercise 1.10

The accumulated amount (A) after N years, of a principal of £P compounded at an annual interest rate of I% per annum is given by:

$$A = P*(1+I)^{\wedge}N$$

Enter the following labels to the A1:A4 range of a worksheet:

Principal   Interest Rate
Number of years Amount

Now enter the following data to the B1:B3 range:

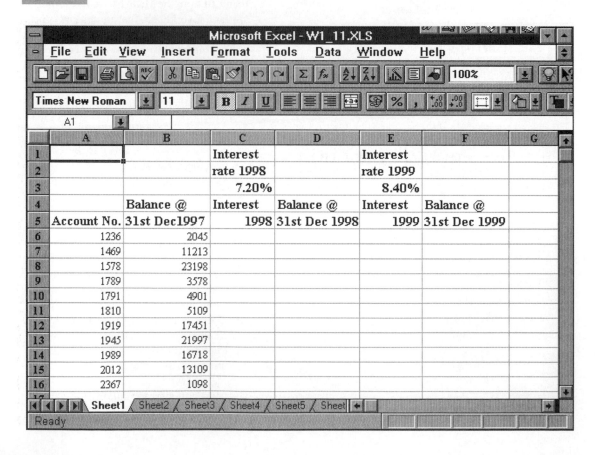

2500   8.5%   25

Name the cells B1, B2, and B3 as P, I, and N respectively, and then use these names to write a formula for the accumulated amount in B4.

Exercise 1.11

Prepare the model shown in Workbook 1.12 or load it from the accompanying disk (W1_12.XLS).

Write and copy formulae for the totals in row 11 and column G.

Now insert as many rows and columns as are required to make the product and region numbers continuous.

Check that the formulae for the totals have adjusted appropriately.

Exercise 1.12

Prepare the model shown in Workbook 1.13 or load it from the accompanying disk (W1_13.XLS).

(*a*) Sort the list of products in ascending order of sales in region 3.
(*b*) Separate any tied product ranks by performing a secondary sort in terms of sales in region 4, also in ascending order.
(*c*) Separate any product ranks that are still tied by using a descending tertiary sort on region 5.
(*d*) Sort the regions in ascending order from left to right in terms of their sales of product 5.

Exercise 1.13

Prepare the model shown in Workbook 1.14 or load it from the accompanying disk (W1_14.XLS).

Produce the following selective lists from the main data set.

(*a*) SALARY greater than £25000.
(*b*) SALARY greater than £25000 but less than £40000.
(*c*) TAKEHOME less than £10000.

Workbook 1.12

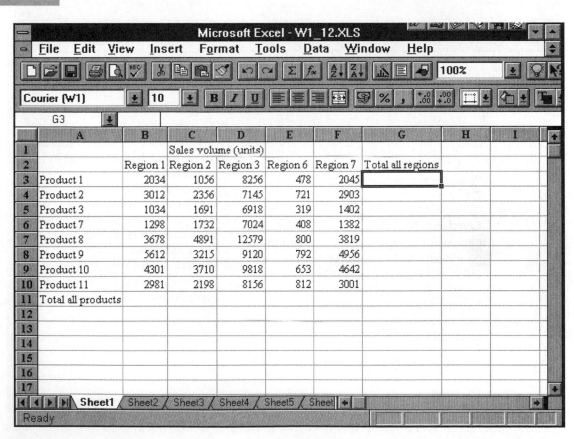

Microsoft Excel - W1_13.XLS									
File	Edit	View	Insert	Format	Tools	Data	Window	Help	

Courier (W1) · 10 · **B** *I* U

B14 · =SUM(B3:B13)

	A	B	C	D	E	F	G	H	I
1			Sales volume (units)						
2		Region 1	Region 2	Region 3	Region 4	Region 5	Total all regions		
3	Product 1	2034	1056	8256	478	2045	13869		
4	Product 2	3012	2356	7145	721	2903	16137		
5	Product 3	1034	1691	6918	319	1402	11364		
6	Product 4	692	891	6918	201	1567	10269		
7	Product 5	1932	1267	6918	201	1956	12274		
8	Product 6	1587	1935	6918	567	1835	12842		
9	Product 7	1298	1732	7024	408	1382	11844		
10	Product 8	3678	4891	12579	800	3819	25767		
11	Product 9	5612	3215	9120	792	4956	23695		
12	Product 10	4301	3710	9818	653	4642	23124		
13	Product 11	2981	2198	8156	812	3001	17148		
14	Total all products	28161	24942	89770	5952	29508	178333		
15									
16									
17									

Sheet1 / Sheet2 / Sheet3 / Sheet4 / Sheet5 / Sheet

Ready

Workbook 1.13

(d) FEMALES with TAKEHOME between £10000 and £25000 inclusive.
(e) SINGLE FEMALES with TAKEHOME between £10000 and £25000 inclusive.
(f) SINGLE MALES with TAKEHOME more than £27000.

When you have finished, save the file as W1_14.XLS.

Exercise 1.14

Using the model produced in Exercise 1.13 (Workbook 1.14), create formulae in rows 20 and 21 to compute the totals and the averages of the SALARY, TAX, SUPERANN, and TAKEHOME fields. These formulae should adjust automatically to accommodate any filtering that is done.

On the basis of these formulae, compute the following amounts.[11]

(a) The total and the average TAKEHOME of all FEMALES.
(b) The total and the average SALARY of all MARRIED MALES.
(c) The total and the average TAX of all SINGLE FEMALES.
(d) The total and the average SUPERANN of all MARRIED MALES with a SALARY in excess of £20000.
(e) The total and the average TAX of all MARRIED FEMALES with TAKEHOME between £10000 and £30000 inclusive.

---

11 Remember to restore all of the original records between each separate calculation.

```
┌─────────────────────────────────────────────────────────────────────────┐
│ ▭          Microsoft Excel - W1_14.XLS                          ▼ ▲      │
│ ▭  File  Edit  View  Insert  Format  Tools  Data  Window  Help      ♦    │
├─────────────────────────────────────────────────────────────────────────┤
│ [toolbar]   Σ ƒ×  ↓↑  100%                                               │
│ Courier (W1) ▼  10 ▼  B I U  ≡ ≡ ≡  % ,                                  │
│     A11    ▼        'REDMOND                                             │
├───┬─────────┬────────┬─────────┬─────────┬─────┬─────────┬─────────┬─────────┬───┤
│   │    A    │   B    │    C    │    D    │  E  │    F    │    G    │    H    │ I │
├───┼─────────┴────────┴─────────┴─────────┴─────┴─────────┴─────────┴─────────┴───┤
│ 1 │         MARSTAT = 1 = MARRIED, MARSTAT = 0 = SINGLE                         │
│ 2 │         SEX = F = FEMALE, SEX = M = MALE                                    │
├───┼─────────┬────────┬─────────┬─────────┬─────┬─────────┬─────────┬─────────┬───┤
│ 3 │ NAME    │ INITIAL│ SALARY  │ MARSTAT │ SEX │ TAX     │ SUPERANN│ TAKEHOME│   │
│ 4 │ ALLAN   │ L      │ 7058.27 │       1 │ M   │ 1764.57 │  705.83 │ 4587.88 │   │
│ 5 │ ALLEN   │ D      │43966.55 │       0 │ M   │14508.96 │ 4396.66 │25060.93 │   │
│ 6 │ BROWN   │ G      │53531.38 │       0 │ M   │17665.36 │ 5353.14 │30512.89 │   │
│ 7 │ BROWN   │ I      │  889.64 │       1 │ M   │  222.41 │   88.96 │  578.27 │   │
│ 8 │ BROWN   │ L      │37085.07 │       1 │ M   │ 9271.27 │ 3708.51 │24105.29 │   │
│ 9 │ COOPER  │ F      │50799.24 │       0 │ F   │16763.75 │ 3809.94 │30225.55 │   │
│10 │ DAVIES  │ R      │33501.75 │       1 │ F   │ 8375.44 │ 2512.63 │22613.68 │   │
│11 │ REDMOND │ K      │12323.86 │       0 │ F   │ 4066.87 │  924.29 │ 7332.69 │   │
│12 │ REILLY  │ G      │14764.91 │       1 │ F   │ 3691.23 │ 1107.37 │ 9966.32 │   │
│13 │ ROBERTS │ F      │35054.07 │       1 │ F   │ 8763.52 │ 2629.05 │23661.49 │   │
│14 │ SMITH   │ G      │51378.43 │       1 │ M   │12844.61 │ 5137.84 │33395.98 │   │
│15 │ SMITH   │ P      │47981.05 │       1 │ F   │11995.26 │ 3598.58 │32387.21 │   │
│16 │ SMITH   │ R      │56824.75 │       0 │ M   │18752.17 │ 5682.48 │32390.11 │   │
│17 │ STEWART │ R      │41444.09 │       1 │ F   │10361.02 │ 3108.31 │27974.76 │   │
├───┴─────────┴────────┴─────────┴─────────┴─────┴─────────┴─────────┴─────────┴───┤
│ ▶▶│ Sheet1 / Sheet2 / Sheet3 / Sheet4 / Sheet5 / Sheet  │                        │
│ Ready                                                                        │
└─────────────────────────────────────────────────────────────────────────┘
```

Workbook 1.14

1.13. Solutions to the exercises

···

Solution to Exercise 1.1

(*a*) A cell.

(*b*) H21 (not 21H).

(*c*) Worksheets.

(*d*) A bold or different coloured border.

(*e*) Only when it is active.

(*f*) Click on the cell with the mouse, or use the cursor keys, or any of Goto, Home, End, down arrow.

(*g*) 256 columns and 16384 rows.

(*h*) In the cell itself and on the Formula bar.

(*i*) End and then down arrow and then End, and right arrow.

(*j*) F5 (Goto) and then type BZ9999.

Solution to Exercise 1.2

(*a*) $10+8 = 18$.

(*b*) $20+9 = 29$.

(*c*) $5+18/9 = 5+2 = 7$.

(*d*) $27/9 = 3$.

(*e*) $(1+6)^2 = 7^2 = 49$.

(*f*) This is a text entry, but if the equals sign were there then: $3+20 = 23$.

(*g*) $(3+12)*4 = 15*4 = 60$.

(*h*) $3+2*6*10 = 3+120 = 123$.

(*i*) $(5*5)^2 = 25^2 = 625$ ('inside-out' evaluation of the brackets).

(*j*) $5*5^2 = 5*25 = 125$ ('inside-out' evaluation of the brackets).

(k) $(9+1)*2\wedge3 = 10*8 = 80$.

(l) $104/8 = 13$.

(m) $16/8 = 2$.

(n) $4\wedge1\wedge3 = 4\wedge3 = 64$.

Solution to Exercise 1.3

(a) Number.

(b) Text.

(c) Text.

(d) Text.

(e) Text.

(f) Formula and number.

(g) Text.

(h) Formula and number.

(i) Function.

(j) Text.

(k) Formula and function.

(l) Number, formula and function.

Solution to Exercise 1.4

(a) Click on A1, depress the left hand mouse button and, with it still depressed, drag down to A6 and then across to C6. Select the **B** icon and then the **U** icon from the toolbar.

(b) With A1:C6 still selected, Choose **Edit** and then **Cut**. Now click on the A8 cell and press enter or select **Edit** and then **Paste**.

(c) Select A8:C13 and then **Edit** and **Clear**. Thereafter, choose **Contents**.

(d) Select A8:C13 and then **Edit** and **Clear**. Now choose **All**.

(e) Select A8:C13 and click on the **B** icon on the toolbar.

Solution to Exercise 1.5

The command sequences are:

(a) **File**, **New**, and then enter your first name to A1. Then **File**, **Save As**, click on the drive tab and select drive A, enter NEW1 to the File Name box, and click on OK.

(b) **File**, **New**, and then enter your surname to A1. Then **File**, **Save As**, click on the drive tab and select drive A, enter NEW2 to the File Name box, and click on OK.

(c) Use Window from the Menu and select the desired file from the list.

(d) **File**, **Close** and then **File**, **Close** again.

(e) **File**, **Open**, then click on NEW1 and drag down to include NEW2. Click OK.

(f) **With NEW1 active** make the change to A1 and then select **File** and **Save** (not Save As). Then use next Window to access NEW2. Make the change and then choose **File** and **Save** again.

(g) With either file active, **File**, **Close** and then **File**, **Close** again.

(h) **File**, **Open**, then click on NEW1 and drag down to include NEW2. Click OK.

(i) **With NEW1 active**, **File**, **Save As**, and enter NEW1A to the File Name box. Use Next Window to activate NEW2 and then **File**, **Save As**, and enter NEW2A to the File Name box.

(j) **File**, **Close**, and then **File**, **Close** again. **File**, **Exit**.

Solution to Exercise 1.6

In A1, enter:

   Profits 1980

Click on A1 and then point to the handle on the bottom right-hand corner with the mouse. When the solid white cross turns to less solid black, depress the left-hand mouse button and drag down to row 41.

Solution to Exercise 1.7

In A1 enter:

   4

In A2 enter:

   =A1+5

Click on A2, activate the handle, and drag down to A20. The series:

   =A1+5; =A2+5; =A3+5 ... =A19+5

will be created in A2:A20.

Solution to Exercise 1.8

The formulae in C6, D6, E6, and F6 should be:

   in C6: =C$3*B6

   in D6: =B6+C6

   in E6: =E$3*D6

   in F6: =D6+E6

Now select C6:F6, activate the handle, and drag down this block of cells to row 16. The four source formulae will be copied.

The results should resemble those shown in Workbook 1.15.

```
┌────────────────────────────────────────────────────────────────────────┐
│ ─                    Microsoft Excel - W1_15.XLS                    ▼ ▲ │
│ ─  File  Edit  View  Insert  Format  Tools  Data  Window  Help       ▲ │
│ [toolbar icons]  Σ fx  ...  100%                              ▼  ▪    │
│ Courier (W1)  ▼ 10 ▼  B I U  ≡≡≡≡  $ % , ... ...                      │
│       C6       ▼         =C$3*$B6                                        │
├──────┬─────────┬──────────┬─────────┬──────────┬─────────┬─────────┬───┤
│      │    A    │    B     │    C    │    D     │    E    │    F    │ G │
├──────┼─────────┼──────────┼─────────┼──────────┼─────────┼─────────┼───┤
│  1   │         │          │Interest │          │Interest │         │   │
│  2   │         │          │rate 1998│          │rate 1999│         │   │
│  3   │         │          │  7.20%  │          │  8.40%  │         │   │
│  4   │         │Balance @ │Interest │Balance @ │Interest │Balance @│   │
│  5   │Account No.│31st Dec1997│  1998 │31st Dec 1998│  1999│31st Dec 1999│ │
│  6   │  1236   │   2045   │ 147.24  │ 2192.24  │ 184.15  │ 2376.39 │   │
│  7   │  1469   │  11213   │ 807.34  │12020.34  │1009.71  │13030.04 │   │
│  8   │  1578   │  23198   │1670.26  │24868.26  │2088.93  │26957.19 │   │
│  9   │  1789   │   3578   │ 257.62  │ 3835.62  │ 322.19  │ 4157.81 │   │
│ 10   │  1791   │   4901   │ 352.87  │ 5253.87  │ 441.33  │ 5695.20 │   │
│ 11   │  1810   │   5109   │ 367.85  │ 5476.85  │ 460.06  │ 5936.90 │   │
│ 12   │  1919   │  17451   │1256.47  │18707.47  │1571.43  │20278.90 │   │
│ 13   │  1945   │  21997   │1583.78  │23580.78  │1980.79  │25561.57 │   │
│ 14   │  1989   │  16718   │1203.70  │17921.70  │1505.42  │19427.12 │   │
│ 15   │  2012   │  13109   │ 943.85  │14052.85  │1180.44  │15233.29 │   │
│ 16   │  2367   │   1098   │  79.06  │ 1177.06  │  98.87  │ 1275.93 │   │
├──────┴─────────┴──────────┴─────────┴──────────┴─────────┴─────────┴───┤
│ Sheet1 / Sheet2 / Sheet3 / Sheet4 / Sheet5 / Sheet                     │
│ Ready                                                                   │
└────────────────────────────────────────────────────────────────────────┘
```

Workbook 1.15

Solution to Exercise 1.9

Select **Print** from the Menu bar and then **Page Setup**. Click on Landscape and then on the Sheet tab. Enter A1:F10 in the Print Area box and click OK. Click OK again from the Print Dialogue box and the **selected range** of the document will be printed.

Solution to Exercise 1.10

Click on B1 and then select **Insert** then **Name** and then **Define** from the Menu bar. Enter P as the name for B1.

Click on B2 and repeat the process only this time supply the name I.

Click on B3 and repeat for the name N.

Click on B4 and enter:

$$=P*(1+I)\wedge N$$

A result of 19216.91 will be returned.

Solution to Exercise 1.11

The formula in B11 should be:

$$=SUM(B3:B10)$$

and must be copied along into C11:G11.

The formula in G3 should be:

$$=SUM(B3:F3)$$

and must be copied down into G4:G10.

This procedure produces the row and column totals as well as the grand total in G11. There are three rows missing (products 4, 5, and 6), so click on A6 and drag down to A8. Select **Insert** and then **Rows** from the Menu bar. Three rows will be inserted. There are two columns missing (regions 4 and 5), so click on E1 and drag along to F1. Select **Insert** and then **Columns** and two columns will be inserted.

Click on B14 and then I3 to confirm that the range of rows to be summed has changed from B3:B10 to B3: B13 and the range of columns to be summed has changed from B3:F3 to B3:H3.

The rest of the totalling formulae have also adjusted appropriately.

Workbook 1.16

Solution to Exercise 1.12

Select the area containing the raw data and the row and column labels. In other words, click and drag over the A2:F13 range.[12]

Now choose Data and then Sort.

The primary sort is on region 3, Ascending, **Then By** region 4, also Ascending, **Then By** region 5, Descending this time. Make sure that the My List Has: Header Row is checked and then choose OK.

The results should resemble Workbook 1.16.

Sorting across columns rather than down rows is slightly trickier. First select the area containing the data—once again excluding the row and column totals and this time also excluding the row labels in column A. The selected area should therefore be B2:F13.

Then select **Data** and **Sort** from the Menu bar as before. This time, however, select **Options** and then, on the **Orientation** tab, select **Sort Left to Right** instead of the default setting of **Sort Top to Bottom**. Click OK and select the row number containing product 5 (it should be row 3 after the initial top-to-bottom sort) from the top tab on the Sort menu. Select Ascending. Then click OK again and the result shown in Workbook 1.16A should be obtained.

Solution to Exercise 1.13

Select A3:H17 as the range containing the field names and the data list and then choose **Data**, **Filter**, and **AutoFilter** from the Menu bar. The black arrow tabs will appear in the cells containing the field name.

---

12 It is neither necessary nor advisable to include the row and the column containing the totals in the area to be sorted. Since these entries are formula-based they will compute the totals automatically once the data have been sorted.

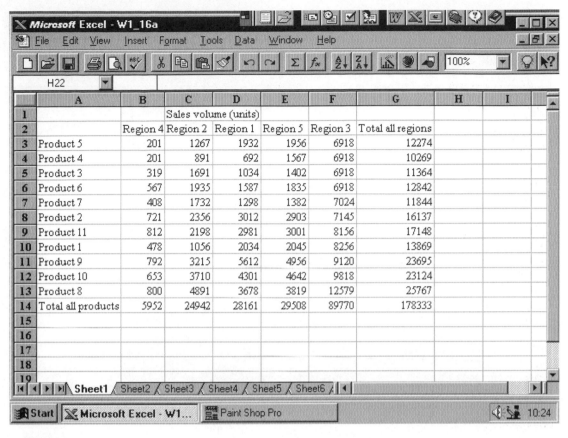

	A	B	C	D	E	F	G	H	I
1			Sales volume (units)						
2		Region 4	Region 2	Region 1	Region 5	Region 3	Total all regions		
3	Product 5	201	1267	1932	1956	6918	12274		
4	Product 4	201	891	692	1567	6918	10269		
5	Product 3	319	1691	1034	1402	6918	11364		
6	Product 6	567	1935	1587	1835	6918	12842		
7	Product 7	408	1732	1298	1382	7024	11844		
8	Product 2	721	2356	3012	2903	7145	16137		
9	Product 11	812	2198	2981	3001	8156	17148		
10	Product 1	478	1056	2034	2045	8256	13869		
11	Product 9	792	3215	5612	4956	9120	23695		
12	Product 10	653	3710	4301	4642	9818	23124		
13	Product 8	800	4891	3678	3819	12579	25767		
14	Total all products	5952	24942	28161	29508	89770	178333		
15									
16									
17									
18									
19									

Workbook 1.16A

(a) Click on the arrow tab in the SALARY field, select {Custom ...}, then select greater than (>) from the top left-hand tab and type 25000 into the adjacent box. Click OK and 10 records will be selected, beginning with Allen, D., and ending with Stewart, R. The procedures to produce the remainder of the selective lists are summarized below.

Make sure that you select Data, Filter, and Show All between each separate interrogation.

Now continue in the same way to produce the following summarized results.

(b) SALARY > 25000 < 40000
3 records selected: Brown, Davies, and Roberts

(c) TAKEHOME < 10000
4 records selected: Allan, Brown, Redmond, and Reilly

(d) TAKEHOME >= 10000 <= 25000
SEX = F
2 records selected: Davies and Roberts

(e) TAKEHOME >= 10000 <= 25000
SEX = F
MARSTAT = 0
0 records selected

(f) SEX = M
MARSTAT = 0
TAKEHOME > 27000
2 records selected: Brown and Smith

Solution to Exercise 1.14

Assuming that A3:H17 is still selected as the range of the database and that the Autofilter is still turned on, in C20 enter:

=SUBTOTAL(9,C4:C17)

and copy this into F20:H20 to give the totals.
Then, in C21 enter:

=SUBTOTAL(1,C4:C17)

and copy this into F21:H21 to give the averages.

Now perform the filters as instructed to obtain the following answers.

	TOTAL	AVERAGE			
			(c)	£20830.62	£10415.31
(a)	£154161.71	£22023.10	(d)	£8846.35	£4423.175
(b)	£96411.41	£24102.85	(e)	£27499.98	£9166.66

Principles of elementary modelling

Contents

Accompanying data files to be loaded as instructed
None

2.1. Symbols, expressions, and simple models

If the exceptional mathematical modelling power of the Excel spreadsheet is to be used to its full potential, several fundamental principles require to be understood. In the first instance, most modelling problems will be phrased in terms of a series of verbal and arithmetical statements that define the nature and structure of the problem to be solved. Usually, however, it will be necessary to rephrase these statements in symbolic rather than verbal form, and when this is carried out the result is an algebraic expression. For example, the verbal question: What is the sum of any two numbers? has its symbolic algebraic equivalent as $x + y = ?$, where x and y represent *any* two numbers.

Once the algebraic form of the problem has been obtained, the next task will be to translate it into the equivalent spreadsheet symbolic form. Thus, continuing with the example, if we choose *any* two values for x and y and enter them into cells A1 and A2 of the worksheet, then the required symbolic form can be written in A3, say, as:

=A1+A2

In this form, the statement in A3 is instructing Excel to take *whatever* value is contained in A1 and add it to *whatever* value is contained in A2. The result of this process will be returned to the A3 cell and will change automatically if any of the values in A1 and/or A2 are changed. In this sense, the spreadsheet expression in A3 is completely equivalent to the abstract algebraic form: $x + y$.

Thus, if A1 and A2 are used to contain the values of x and y respectively, then the algebraic statement: $x + y$ has its spreadsheet symbolic equivalent as: =A1+A2.

By a similar logic (and continuing to store the values of x and y in A1 and A2) the following further equivalencies can be observed.

Algebraic expression	Spreadsheet equivalent
x-y	=A1-A2
x times y	=A1*A2
x divided by y	=A1/A2
x to the power of y	=A1^A2

With these ideas in mind, we can now proceed to consider the modelling process in the context of a less abstract example.

Suppose that a firm selling kitchen units charges its customers a price of £80 per unit. However, also suppose that it offers a discount of 5% of the value of any order if payment is made in cash. Calculate the invoice to be sent to a customer who orders 50 units and pays in cash.

We can proceed by identifying the following relationships:

Order value = the number of units ordered times the price per unit = 50 times £80 = £4000

Discount offered = 5% of the order value = 5% of £4000 = 5/100 times £4000 = £200

Invoice = Order value - Discount offered = £4000 - £200 = £3800

This is clearly the answer to the specific problem that was posed, but it will be noted that a different answer would be obtained if any of the given arithmetic values were to change. Yet although this need to recompute when specific data values change will always exist, the ease and efficiency with which this recalculation is carried out will be much greater if we can specify the model in general algebraic terms rather than in specific arithmetical ones. To see this, consider the following reformulation of the problem.

Suppose that the firm selling kitchen units charges its customers a price of £P per unit. Also suppose that it offers a discount of d% of the value of any order if payment is made in cash. Calculate the invoice to be sent to a customer who orders x units and pays in cash.

Proceeding as before, we can write:

Order value = the number of units ordered times the price per unit = x times £P = £Px
Discount offered = d% of the order value = d% of £Px = d/100 times £Px = £dPx/100
Invoice = Order value - Discount offered = £Px - £dPx/100
Invoice = £Px(1 - d/100) when the £Px common term is factored out

This expression for the invoice is seen to be a completely general statement that will only adopt a specific numerical value once values are given for P, x, and d. Consequently, if we can rewrite it in its spreadsheet symbolic equivalent we will create an expression that will always produce the correct answer when we supply specific values for the price, the discount rate, and the number of units ordered.

To do this rewriting we must first choose three cells to contain the three unknowns (P, x, and d). This has been done in Workbook 2.1, where B1 contains the value of £P, B3 contains the value of x, and B2 contains the value of d.

Open a new workbook and make up this worksheet now. After entering the illustrated values for £P, d, and x to B1:B3, enter the following formula to the B4 cell:

=B1*B3*(1 - B2/100)

Then confirm that it computes the invoice accurately for any changes to the values in B1:B3.
Save this model now as W2_1.XLS.

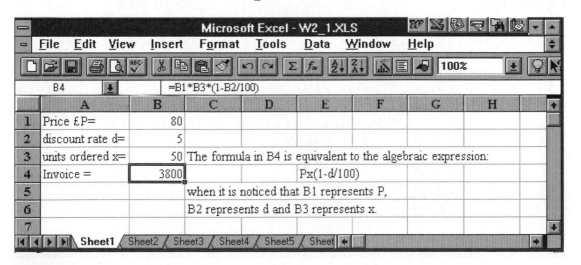

Workbook
2.1

2.2. **Creating general algebraic models**

Now, although we have satisfactorily achieved our objective of creating a general model of the problem, it might still be regarded as deficient because it can only produce the correct invoice for one chosen value of the order size. Yet there may well be circumstances in which we would want to observe the invoices that result from a *range* of different order sizes. In other words, we require to consider several values of x and their associated invoice values. (This is exactly what is meant by x being variable and the value of the invoice depending upon the value of that variable.)

To do this we can take Workbook 2.1 and modify it as indicated in Workbook 2.2, where values of x between 1 and 10 have been entered in the cells A5 to A14.

Workbook 2.2

Study this worksheet now and then make it up for yourself. Enter the labels and values shown in A1:B4. Then enter the values 1 to 10 in A5:A14. Finally, in B5 enter:

=A5*B1*(1-B2/100)

and copy this into B6:B14.

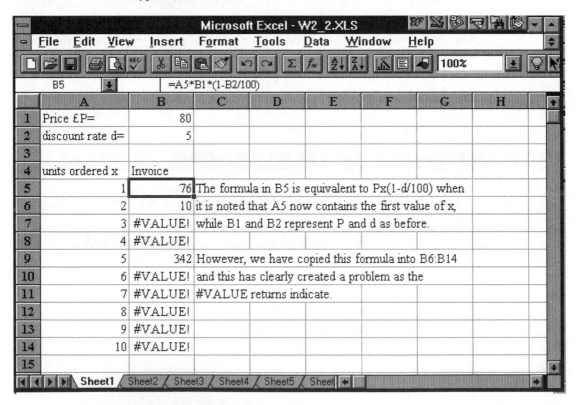

The reason for the difficulty noted in the worksheet is that as was seen in Chapter 1, Excel automatically carries out all copying of formula in a fully relative manner.[1] This means that when the entry in B5 of:

=A5*B1*(1-B2/100)

---

is copied in to B6 it becomes:

=A6*B2*(1-B3/100),

and when it is copied into B7 it becomes:

=A7*B3*(1-B4/100),

and so on, for the copies made into B8 and below.

Now, while this relative updating of the column A cell references is exactly what we require to refer to each of the 10 values of x (i.e. the column A references), it is not what we require for the B1 and B2 cell references. They must always remain as B1 and B2 and must not update in the copying process.

Consequently, both of these cell addresses will need to be 'dollar fixed' with regard to their row numbers (since we are copying down the sheet). That is, instead of writing B1 and B2 as the cell references for the price and the discount rate, we write B$1 and B$2. The row numbers of these cell references are now dollar fixed for the purposes of copying down the sheet.

This adjustment to the formula in B5 is made in Workbook 2.3, and is seen to rectify the problem perfectly since the formulae in B5 to B14 now read as:

B5:	=A5*B$1*(1-B$2/100)
B6:	=A6*B$1*(1-B$2/100)
B7:	=A7*B$1*(1-B$2/100)
	. . . etc . . .
B14:	=A14*B$1*(1-B$2/100)

Workbook 2.3	**Make this adjustment to your own model now by entering, in B5:**

=A5*B$1*(1-B$2/100)

and copying this down into B6:B14.

Now name the B1 and B2 cells as P, and d respectively and replace the formula in B5 with the equivalent formulae in terms of the *named* cells. That is:

=P*A5*(1-d/100)

and copy this down into B6:B14.

The same results should be obtained, and thus indicate another advantage of using named cells in formulae: when named, a cell is automatically treated by Excel as row and column dollar fixed ($B$1 and $B$2 in this case).

In this form the model has a high degree of generality, since if either the price charged or the discount rate offered, or both, should change, all that is required is to enter the new values in B1 and/or B2 and the new invoices will be computed automatically. It will also be noted that the generality of this approach to worksheet design derives from the fact that all operational formulae are entirely composed of cell references or named cells (as opposed to specific numbers).

This suggests a simple design rule that should always be followed: the only numbers which should appear in a formula should be those that identify the row address of the cell— 3 for B3, 6 for G6, 12 for P12, etc. Any other numbers appearing in a formula must therefore represent data elements of the problem, and should really be located in their own cells and then referred to by their cell addresses or names in any formulae that require to make use of these values. In this way formulae will never need to be edited to accommodate changing arithmetic values, and the risk of forgetting to edit a formula that needs to be altered as a result of such changes is eliminated.

	A	B	C	D	E	F	G	H
1	Price £P=	80						
2	discount rate d=	5						
3								
4	units ordered x	Invoice						
5	1	76	The dollar signs attached to B1 and B2 now					
6	2	152	ensure that they will not update when copied down the					
7	3	228	sheet.					
8	4	304	However, A5 will become A6, A7 and so on					
9	5	380	when copied, which is what is required.					
10	6	456	Alternatively, if B1 and B2 have been named as P and d					
11	7	532	respectively, then the formula in B5 can be rewritten as:					
12	8	608	=P*A5*(1-d/100)					
13	9	684	and copied down consistently.					
14	10	760						
15								

Cell reference B5: =A5*B$1*(1-B$2/100)

Workbook 2.3

In short, if a formula appears as something like:

$$=2*A1-6*B1+9*C1$$

then the cells D1, E1, and F1 (say) should be made to contain 2, -6, and 9 respectively and the formula rewritten as:

$$=D1*A1+E1*B1+F1*C1$$

Now returning to the model illustrated in Workbook 2.3, it should be noted that its flexibility can in fact be improved in relation to the *range* of x values for which the invoices are to be calculated. In the first instance these were simply entered in the normal manner (i.e. manually).

However, if the range of x values for which the invoices were to be computed needed to change (from 1 to 10 to 5 to 14, say), then at the moment manual re-entry would be the only method of doing this. With a small number of x values this is little more than a minor inconvenience, but when a large number of x values is involved it will become a major source of inefficiency.

To address this issue we can proceed as illustrated in Workbook 2.4.

Use Workbook 2.3 as a template to make the additions as suggested below.

Workbook 2.4

In C1 enter the label: Start value for x and in C2 the label: Step value for x.

Then use D1 and D2 to contain actual numerical values that we choose for these terms.

Thus, assuming that we want x to start at a value of 9 and to increase in steps of 3:

Enter 9 in D1 and 3 in D2.

With these values established we now require to 'hook up' this information with the values

	A	B	C	D	E	F	G	H
1	Price £P=	80	Start value for x	9				
2	discount rate d=	5	Step value for x	3				
3								
4	units ordered x	Invoice						
5	9	684	The formulae in A5 and A6 are:					
6	12	912	=D1					
7	15	1140	=A5+D$2					
8	18	1368						
9	21	1596						
10	24	1824						
11	27	2052						
12	30	2280						
13	33	2508						
14	36	2736						
15								

Cell B5: `=A5*B$1*(1-B$2/100)`

Microsoft Excel - W2_4.XLS

Workbook 2.4

of x that are actually to be created in A5 to A14. This will be done by two formulae and in two stages.

First, in A5 enter:

=D1

This will transfer the chosen start value for x that we have entered in D1 to the A5 cell that represents the start of the range of x values to be evaluated.

Next, in A6 write:

=A5+D$2

This will add the chosen step increase in the value of x that we have located in D2 to the start value in A5. Furthermore, the $ symbol in the D$2 term ensures that when we copy A5+D$2 from A6 into A7 to A14, the cell containing the step (D2) remains absolutely fixed, but the A5 reference becomes A6, A7, A8, . . . etc.

In other words, we get:

Cell location	Cell contents	Result
A5	=D1	9
A6	=A5+D$2	12
A7	=A6+D$2	15
A8	=A7+D$2	18
	and so on until:	
A14	=A13+D$2	36

To produce this effect, copy the contents of A6 into A7:A14.

The net effect is clearly to add the constant step amount in D2 to the *previous value of x*, and represents a highly efficient way of altering the range of x values for which the invoice is to be evaluated. (Note: the formulae in column B are the same as before.) With these formulae established, the range of x values in A5 to A14 is easily altered, simply by changing the start and/or step values contained in D1 and D2.

Practise doing this now.

Furthermore, in this illustration only 10 separate values of x have been computed, but with the formulae in A5 and A6 established it is an easy matter to copy the crucial one in A6, into as many cells below as are required. (Clearly the associated formula in column B will also have to be copied down to match any extension in the range of x values.) This will increase the number of x values to be evaluated and then, by changing the values in D1 and/or D2, the range of x values to be evaluated will also be changed.

For example, with A6 copied into A7 to A19, 15 values for x will be created. So if the start value for x is 9 (D1 contains 9), while the step value for x is 3 (D2 contains 3), then the range of x values becomes:

9, 12, 15, 18, 21, 24, 27, 30, 33, 36, 39, 42, 45, 48, and 51

Do this now in your own worksheet by copying A14:B14 into A15:B19. Then save the workbook as W2_4.XLS for future use.
Exercise 2.1 can be attempted now.

2.3. Graphing relationships in an Excel chart

With our model established in the highly flexible form shown in Workbook 2.4, we can now get Excel to produce a graph showing how the invoice to be received *varies* with the number of units ordered.

Open Workbook 2.4 now to follow the discussion and build up the model as instructed.
The first step is to click on the Chart Wizard icon on the main tools menu.
Now move to the area of the worksheet where you want the graph to be located, and click and drag the mouse to create a picture frame of appropriate size for the graph.

Once you have done this, the Chart Wizard will provide you with a series of prompts, the first of which is for the range containing the data to be graphed. To respond to this you can either click and drag over the data range (A5 to B19 in our example) or type the coordinates directly into the box in the form A5:B19. Using either method will inform Excel of the data to be plotted.

Do this now, and when you have finished click on 'Next' to obtain the subsequent prompt.

This asks for the type of graph to be constructed, and in the illustration in Workbook 2.5 we have selected a line graph.

Select this now by clicking on that box.

Clicking 'Next' again prompts for the type of line graph to be constructed, and in the illustration we have chosen a solid line graph (option 2).

Select this now.

Once again click on 'Next' to obtain a sample graph window, and pause to inspect this carefully.

This inspection is necessary because unless told otherwise Excel treats each of the specified columns of data as separate items and plots them against the number of observations, as Fig. 2.1 shows.[2]

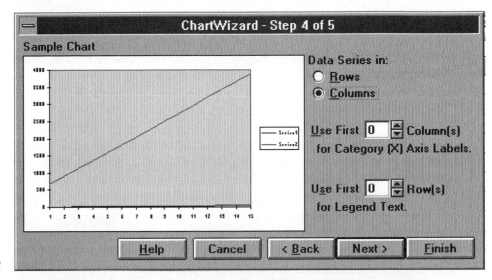

Figure 2.1

Now, while there may be occasions in which this is what is required, usually we will want to prepare graphs in which one variable is plotted against the other. In our illustration, for example, the invoice clearly depends upon the size of the order and so by convention we regard the invoice as the dependent variable, denote it by the symbol y and place it on the vertical axis.

On the other hand, the size of the order is regarded as the independent variable, is denoted by the symbol x, and placed on the horizontal axis. In mathematical terms we say that y is a function of x and denote this by:

$$y = f(x)$$

Thus we could argue that profits (y) depend upon sales (x) and write:

profits = f(sales) or $y = f(x)$

In this form, all that is being said is that profits depend upon sales in some way that is as yet unknown. However, if profits were always 16% of sales then the *general* functional form:

$$y = f(x)$$

could be replaced with the *specific* functional form:

$$y = 16x/100 \text{ or } y = 0.16x$$

With these conventions in mind, it should be clear that most of the graphs that will be used should plot each y value on the vertical axis against each x value on the horizontal axis, and this clearly means that we want the data in the first column (column A in our illustration) to be regarded as the x axis labels.

---

2 The range of x values on the horizontal axis goes from 1 to 15—i.e. the *number* of data points plotted—rather than from 9 to 51—the *range* of x values.

To do this, you must tell Excel that the first 1 column is to be used as the category x axis labels rather than the first 0 column which will usually be showing in the middle right tab of the sample chart window.

Consequently, click on the tab in the middle of 'Use First (Tab) Column(s) for the category (X) axis labels' and change the '0' to a '1'.

The sample chart will change, and should resemble the illustration in Fig. 2.2.

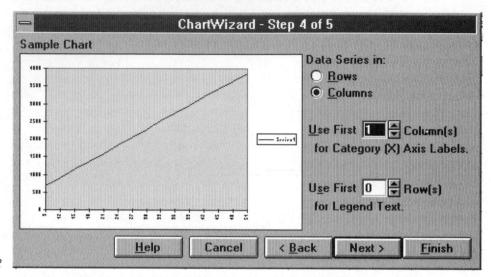

Figure 2.2

Once you have completed this procedure, click on 'Next' again to obtain the final Chart Wizard prompt which allows you to enter a title for the chart and to label the x and y axes.

Consequently, click on the graph title box and enter:

    Invoice versus order quantity

This text will now appear in the sample chart.

Then click on the X axis label box and enter:

    order quantity

Finally, click on the Y axis label box and enter:

    Invoice

If everything looks in order, select 'Finish' and the graph will be created in the worksheet, but if something does not look right, select 'Back' and alter the chosen settings appropriately before repeating the previous steps. The end result should resemble Workbook 2.5.

Workbook 2.5

Once the graph has been embedded in the worksheet, it can be resized by clicking on it once. Eight black 'handles' will appear around the frame, which can be picked up with the mouse and dragged to alter the size.

Practise resizing your chart now.

On the other hand, a double click of the mouse on the chart will create a hatched border, also with handles.

As before, these handles allow the chart to be resized. However, if the mouse pointer is placed on the hatched border itself (rather than on the handle) and the left-hand mouse

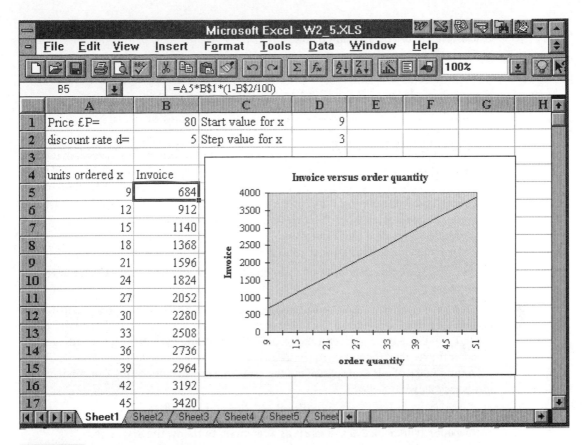

Workbook 2.5 button depressed, the border colour will change and it can be picked up with the mouse. The chart can be moved (still with its same size) to another part of the worksheet.

Practise moving the graph now.

Also, double clicking on the chart to produce the hatched border allows the components of the chart to be edited by subsequent clicking on that component (title, axis label, etc.) of the chart that is to be altered.

Practise this now by clicking on the vertical axis title and then adding a £ symbol to the end of the text that is there.[3]

Finally, it should be noted that the graph itself is 'hot' in the sense that it is sensitively linked to the data range in the worksheet that was defined in the first stage of the Chart Wizard. If these data should change, the chart will automatically redraw to reflect the new data.

To see this, try changing the price to £120 and the discount rate to 10%.

The new graph will be created instantly.

Then try altering the start value for x to 20 and the step value to 5.

Once again the graph adjusts automatically.

---

3 To remove a graph from the worksheet, simply click on it once and strike the Delete key.

Now restore the price to £80 and the discount rate to 5% and save the file as W2_5.XLS. Exercise 2.2 can be attempted now.

2.4. Expressions involving logical tests

Now recall that in the illustration we have been using it was stipulated that the discount was only to be applied if the client paid in cash. The task that we will now address is that of incorporating this stipulation into the operational worksheet model. To do this we will make use of what is known as a **logical function**. This is a pre-programmed Excel statement that can make logical decisions of the yes/no variety (higher or lower than 10, odd or even, for example). There are a number of logical functions available in Excel, but the one we will use most frequently is called the IF function.

Conceptually, and in verbal terms, it can be understood as follows:

=IF(Test of condition,Result if condition test is true,Result if condition test is false)[4]

The term outside the brackets, =IF, is known as the **function** and the three terms inside the brackets separated by commas are known as the function's **arguments**, with either one of the last two being the result returned to the cell containing the function depending upon whether the result of the test is true or false.

In the context of our example we can therefore modify this general logic (again in verbal terms) as follows:

=IF(Pay in cash, Discount offered, No discount offered)

Now open Workbook 2.5 and use it as a template to follow the discussion.

As such, the ideas involved should be fairly clear, but to put this verbal logic into action in the worksheet we require to rephrase it in numerical terms that the function can address more easily.

Consequently, in the cell A3 of Workbook 2.5 add the label:

Payment form 1= cash, 0 = other

Then, in B3 enter 1 to indicate that payment is in cash.
Next, in C3 enter the label:

Actual discount rate

Set up like this we can now use the D3 cell to house our conditional test, and build it up as follows:

=IF(B3=1, . . . i.e. if payment is in cash, THEN
B2, . . . i.e. use the discount rate contained in B2, OTHERWISE
0) . . . i.e. use a zero discount rate

Putting each of the parts together gives the D3 entry as:

=IF(B3=1,B2,0)

---

4   This is only a verbal indication of the syntax used by the IF function. It will not work as an actual operational formula until it has been translated into cell references or named cells.

Clearly this allows the D3 cell to contain *either* of two values—the discount rate fed in from B2 if payment is in cash, or zero if it is not.

Finally, we must remember to adjust the formula that is currently located in B5 since it looks to B2 for the discount rate, whereas now it should look to D3 (and discover either zero or the actual discount rate to be applied).

Consequently, edit the contents of B5 from:

=A5*B$1*(1-B$2/100) to =A5*B$1*(1-D$3/100)

and copy this into B6 to B19.

The result should resemble Workbook 2.6.

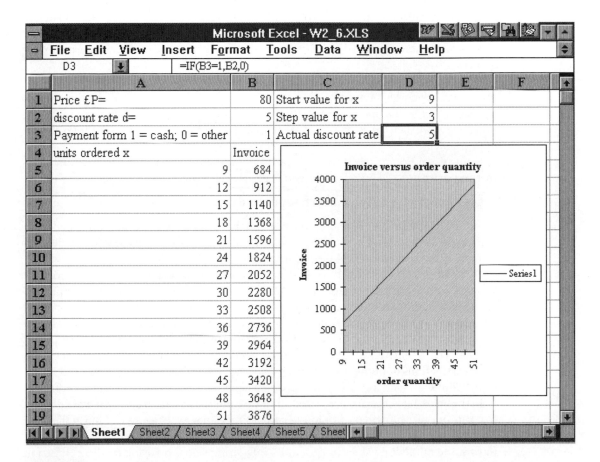

Workbook 2.6

You can now experiment with this worksheet and observe the effects upon the invoice of changes in the price charged, the discount rate offered, and whether payment is made in cash or not. For example, if the price of the kitchen units increased to £90 and the discount offered for cash increased to 7.5%, then simply change the contents of B1 and B2 to 90 and 7.5 respectively and the new invoices will be calculated and graphed automatically. These will include the discount if a value of 1 has been entered in B3, but will not include the discount if B3 has been forced to contain 0.

Experiment with this now on your own sheet, and when you have finished restore the values in B1, B2, and B3 to 80, 5, and 1 respectively.

Now save this file as W2_6.XLS for future use.
Exercise 2.3 can be attempted now.

2.5. Creating self-adjusting chart titles

At this stage it should be noted that the title of the last graph is not really producing as much information as we would like. Ideally, we would want it to indicate the price charged and the discount rate offered.

We could, of course, have typed in these values when we were creating the chart title, but the problem is that the title will then be fixed until we decide to edit it again. This will not be a real problem if both the price and the discount rate rarely or never change, but if this is not the case then the necessary editing can be inconvenient and, more importantly, easily overlooked.

Once again, the ideal outcome would be that the title of the chart displays the fixed information upon which it was based (price and discount rate in this case), and that this information in the title updates automatically in response to any changes in these values. In other words we want to create 'hot' graph titles that are sensitive to changes in the given data of the model.

Doing this is not entirely straightforward, but the eventual dividend is well worth the effort and so we proceed by using Workbook 2.6 as a template.

Load Workbook 2.6 (W2_6.XLS) now and read on.

First note that A1 and A2 contain text labels and that as far as our titles are concerned these will *always* be the same. On the other hand, B1 and B2 contain numerical values which will change as the circumstances of the problem alter.

Normally these two different types of entry cannot be combined in one cell, since they violate Excel's expectations about the nature of the input being received. For example, entering 3rd to a cell (as in the 3rd of May) will cause no problems, since the first character (3) is regarded as text and consequently the whole expression is regarded purely as text. However, if you try to enter =3rd, Excel has been told by the equals sign that a numerical expression is to be entered and the 3 treated as the number 3. Provided all subsequent entries are combinations of numbers, operators (+, -, *, /, ^) or functions, the entry will be accepted, but the 'r' and the 'd' in this expression are none of these and so are unacceptable.

In the light of this, the problem faced is how to combine these two different types of entry to create one text entry that will allow the numerical values to behave as text but at the same time adjust as the numbers on which they are based are changed. The secret to doing this is to turn the numerical values in B1 and B2 into string values by using the Excel function known as FIXED. This function takes two arguments and has the following general syntax:

=FIXED(Cell Reference, Number of Decimal Places)

Consequently, in E1 type:

=FIXED(B1,2)

80.00 should be returned to E1, but crucially this is now a text entry. Yet it is a text entry that will change if the contents of B1 change.

Check this now by changing the value in B1 and observing the effect upon the contents of E1. Then restore the value in B1 to 80.

Now do the same in E2 for the B2 cell.

That is, in E2 type:

=FIXED(B2,2)

5.00 should be returned, but once again this is a text entry which changes in accordance with changes in the contents of B2.

Check this again for yourself, and when you have finished restore the value in B2 to 5.

Now we come to the last stage of creating the required label. The trick is to *join up* the contents of A1 with those of E1 and the contents of A2 with those of E2, and then join up these two joinings to create one long string of text. This would produce something like:

Price £P= 80.00 discount rate d = 5.00

but would become something like:

Price £P= 90.00 discount rate d = 4.00

if the price were increased to £90 and the discount rate offered were reduced to 4%.

The joining-up process is known as **concatenation**, and uses the & symbol to join together the required cell references.

In other words an entry in C4, say, such as:

=A1&E1

will join the contents of A1 and E1 (provided they are both text entries) to produce, in our illustration:

Price £P= 80.00

(since A1 contains 'Price £P =' and E1 contains the string form of the number 80).

Consequently, extending this logic, in C4 type:

=A1&E1&A2&E2

This creates a text label in the C4 cell that will change as the values in B1 and/or B2 change and forms the basis of our 'hot' graph title.

Check this now by changing the values in B1 and B2 and observing the effect upon C4. Then restore the original values of 80 and 5.

However, before we incorporate this expression into our chart, remember that what appears in C4 will be identical to the text that has been typed in A1 and A2 and the string values entered to E1 and E2. At the moment its appearance is typographically unsatisfactory.

If you want to enhance the appearance of the eventual graph title then you must edit A1 and/or A2 (to add spaces for example), whereupon C4 will adjust automatically. Furthermore (as will usually be the case), if a space is required between the '80.00' and the 'd' of discount you can insert it with the term &" " &—i.e. ampersand, double quotes, space bar, double quotes, ampersand.

This means that the entry in C4 should be changed to:

=A1&E1&" "&A2&E2

in order to incorporate the required space.

Finally, we really require that the % symbol appears at the end of our title, so we can use any vacant cell (F1, say), enter the % symbol there, and add &F1 to the end of the formula in C4.

Now make the formula in C4 look like:

=A1&E1&" "&A2&E2&F1

and notice that it will display as something like:

Price £P = 80.00 discount rate d = 5.00%

Now we are ready to incorporate the 'hot' label in the C4 cell into our chart.

So double click on the chart to edit it.

A coloured hatched border will appear.

Then click on the existing title.

Now, and this is crucial:

click on the Formula bar at the top of the worksheet (just above the letters indicating the columns), and type:

=Sheet1!$C$4

(This is the sheet and cell reference of the cell containing the concatenated label.)

Press Enter

and what you see at this stage should resemble Workbook 2.7.

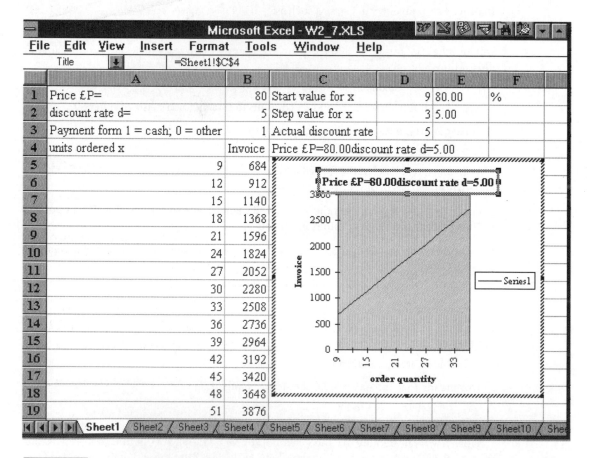

Workbook 2.7   Now click on any cell and click again to exit entirely from graph edit mode, and notice that the new title of the chart will change automatically to reflect the contents of C4, which in turn is determined by the values entered in B1 and B2.

This is a 'hot' graph title which is sensitively linked to the C4 cell.[5]

Save this worksheet now as W2_7.XLS.
Exercise 2.4 can be attempted now.

2.6. Linear functions in business

As another illustration of the process of modelling business and economic relationships on a spreadsheet, we can discuss the following example. Consider the types of cost that typically are incurred by a business enterprise in carrying out its line of activity. On the one hand, there are costs such as rent on premises, local taxes, and insurance premiums, that do not vary regardless of the level of activity. These costs must be borne if the enterprise is to remain operational, and *cannot be avoided* except by closing down. They are frequently referred to as overheads or fixed costs and are characterized by their invariance with regard to the scale of operations.

On the other hand, there are also categories of cost that depend upon the level of operational activity and that (usually) increase with that level. Wage, delivery, raw material, and energy costs typically come into this category, and are regarded as variable costs in the sense that they vary with the level of activity. Clearly they must be viewed in a different way from fixed costs in the modelling process.

We can make this distinction more formal if we argue as follows:

Total Costs (TC) = Fixed Costs (FC) + Variable Costs (VC)

Now consider an enterprise that has an activity level that is denoted by x. The units in which x is measured could be units of output per day, number of clients seen per day, or any other of a large range of measures of activity. The point is that x represents the variable, and it is this value of x that will determine the variable costs, since these are the only ones that change with the level of activity.

With this idea in mind we can now reason as follows:

TC = FC + VC times x

This is a mathematical statement of the composition of total costs between their two constituent parts. However, letting y, a, and b represent Total Costs, Fixed Costs, and Variable Costs respectively, we can rewrite the last expression as:

$y = a + bx$

This is known as a linear equation, since when y is plotted against x the resulting graph shows a straight line starting at the value of 'a' on the vertical axis and rising upwards by 'b' units on the vertical scale for every 1 unit along the horizontal scale. Thus:

$y = a + bx$

is the general mathematical form of any of the countless number of straight lines that could be drawn.

However, to define a *specific* straight line requires that numerical values be assigned to the 'a' and 'b' terms. Thus:

---

5 For some strange reason Excel will not allow you to use a cell reference as the title when you are creating the graph for the *first* time. Consequently, if you want to create 'hot' titles you should enter any set of characters as the title when creating the chart at first. Then use the edit facility as outlined in the discussion to include the cell reference containing your 'hot' title on the Formula bar.

$$y = 10 + 2x$$

defines a straight line that starts at a value of 10 on the vertical axis, and which rises by 2 units on the y axis for every 1 unit increase in the value on the horizontal axis. We can see this in Workbook 2.8, which uses the principles outlined in the previous worksheets to create a model that can calculate and graph any linear function for various values of x if the values for 'a' and 'b' are supplied.

Open a new workbook and make up the model in line with the subsequent instructions.

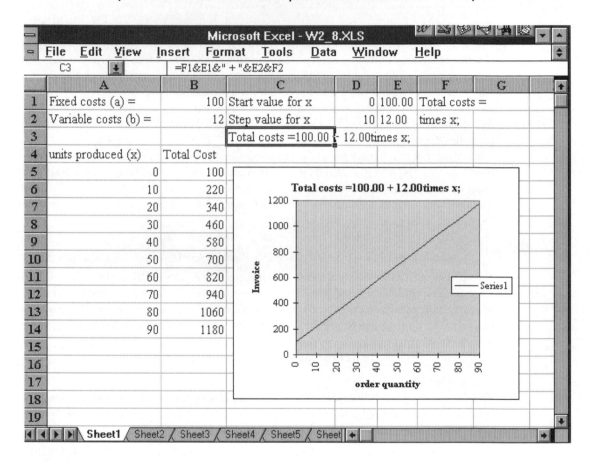

| **Workbook 2.8** | This worksheet has been constructed using the same principles as previous ones, with the exception that the formula in B5 reflects the new nature of the problem. |

Hence, if x represents the number of units produced, total costs (y) are given generally by:

$$y = a + bx$$

and if the B1 and B2 cells contain 'a' and 'b' respectively, then with the first value of x located in A5:

$$y = a + bx$$

has:

=B$1+B$2*A5

as its spreadsheet equivalent in B5.

Enter this now to the B5 cell.
Then copy this formula into the B6 to B14 cells—again noticing the use of the dollar symbols to allow consistent copying.

The chart was prepared as before with a data range defined as A5:B14

Create this chart now in the indicated area, and for the moment enter your name to the chart title box.

Now notice that the C3 cell contains a concatenated label. The formula to do this is shown on the Formula bar in Workbook 2.8, and the cell entries referred to in this formula are given below.

Enter these now.
In E1: =FIXED(B1,2)   In E2: =FIXED(B2,2)
In F1: Total costs   In F2: times x;

Now, to create the 'hot' title double click on the chart to edit it and then click on the title box.

With the title available for editing,

click on the Formula bar and enter the cell reference:
=Sheet1!$C$3

Now make some changes to the contents of B1 and B2 and observe the effects upon the graph and the 'hot' title.
When you have finished, restore the values in B1 and B2 to 100 and 12 respectively and save this workbook as W2_8.XLS.
Exercise 2.5 can be attempted now.

However, although costs are an important aspect of all business activity, it should be noted that they constitute only *one* side of the concept of profit. The other side is revenue—defined as the number of units sold times the price at which they were sold. If this price is constant, and denoted by p, then revenue, represented by R is defined as:

$$R = px$$

where x once again represents the level of (selling) activity.

Open Workbook 2.8 (W2_8.XLS) to continue with the discussion.

We can modify Workbook 2.8 to calculate the revenue received from each of the levels of activity (x values). This has been done in column C of Workbook 2.9.

| Workbook 2.9 |

To reproduce this sheet make the following additions.
In A3 and C4 add the labels:
Product price
Revenue

Now enter the product price of 17 to B3.
In C5 enter the formula:
=B$3*A5

This is equivalent to:

$$R = px$$

when it is noted that B3 contains the value of p and the x values commence in A5.

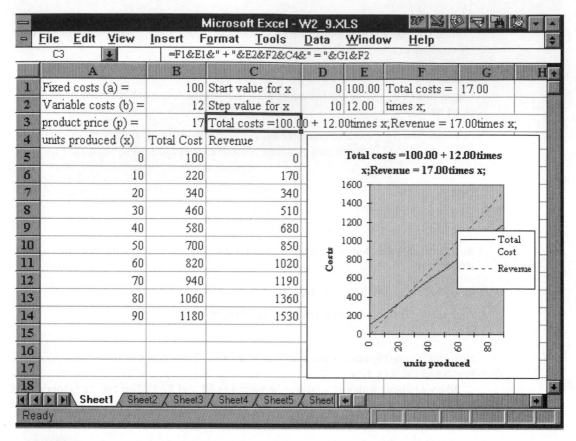

<table>
<tr><th>Workbook
2.9</th><td>**Now copy the contents of C5 into C6:C14.**</td></tr>
</table>

To allow the graph title to display the revenue information we must turn the product price data into a string value.

So in G1 enter:

=FIXED(B3,2)

Now we must alter the string formula in C3 to include the revenue details.

Do this by *adding* the following terms to the existing formula in C3:

&C4&" = "&G1&F2

C3 should now be the same as the formula indicated on the Formula bar in Workbook 2.9.

Next, since we now have **two** sets of data (Costs and Revenue) that are both to be plotted against x, we need to redefine the data range to include the extra column of data.

To do this, click on the original chart once and then on the Chart Wizard icon. Now click and drag to select the A4:C14 area.

By including the revenue data in column C in this range and also including the column headers in B4 and C4, the results shown in the chart in Workbook 2.9 are obtained.

Now select Next to obtain the sample chart.

Notice that since we now have two data series plotted against x, the legends—Total Cost and Revenue—are now vital as a way of identifying which line is which.

To define Series 1 as the label in B4 and Series 2 as the label in C4, from the sample chart screen click on the tab in

> Use first (Tab) Rows for Legend text

to supply a value of 1.

The sample chart should now change to show the data series legends (Total Cost and Revenue).

Finally, notice that to distinguish between the cost and revenue data series Excel assigns a different colour to each line. This is fine on a colour screen, and fine too if a colour printer is being used, but in monochrome the two lines will be indistinguishable. Consequently, it will usually be necessary to assign a different style to one or more of the lines (dotted or dashed, for example).

To do this, double click on the chart to enter edit mode. Then click on the line whose style you want to alter.

In the illustration we have chosen the revenue series.

A series of black squares representing the data points will appear.

Now double click on any one of these squares.

The **Format Data Series** dialogue box will appear.

Next, click on the Line Style tab and select the dashed style and then click OK. When you have finished, click on any cell to leave edit mode and click again if necessary to return to data entry mode.

The style of the line will change both on the actual chart and in the series legend box and the chart should now resemble the one in Workbook 2.9.

Save this file now as W2_9.XLS.

Now it should be noted that inspection of the chart in Workbook 2.9 suggests that Costs and Revenues are equal at an output level of 20 units. This is known as the break-even level of output, since at output levels lower than 20 units costs exceed revenues and a loss is being made, while at output levels in excess of 20 units revenues exceed costs and a profit is being made. Only when output equals 20 units are costs and revenues the same, with the result that profits are zero.

These ideas allow us to define profit in terms of revenue and cost as:

> Profit = Revenue - Total Costs

or, symbolically and in the context of our current example:

$$\text{Profit} = px - (a + bx) = px - a - bx$$

Now, we have already seen from the chart that the break-even level of output is 20 units. However, we *could* obtain the same result by reasoning mathematically as follows:

The break-even level of output requires that profit be zero. Hence:

$$\text{Profit} = px - a - bx = 0$$

Collecting together any terms in x and transferring the 'a' term to the other side of the equality sign with an opposite algebraic sign gives:

$$px - bx = a$$

which can be rewritten after factoring as:

$$x(p - b) = a$$

whereupon:

$$x = a/(p - b)$$

This expression will compute the break-even value of x when the values of a, b, and p are supplied.

Notice that in verbal terms this expression amounts to saying that the break-even level of output is obtained by dividing the level of fixed costs by the difference between the price charged for a unit of the product and the variable cost of producing that unit.

With these notions established, we can now create a worksheet to facilitate the computations as indicated in Workbook 2.10.

Make up this new sheet now by entering the labels shown in A1:A4 and the values shown in B1:B3.

Then name the B1, B2, and B3, cells as a, b, and p respectively.

		Microsoft Excel - W2_10.XLS						
File	Edit	View	Insert	Format	Tools	Data	Window	Help
B4		=a/(p-b)						
	A	B	C	D	E	F	G	H
1	fixed costs (a)	100						
2	variable costs (b)	12						
3	product price (p)	17						
4	break even level of output	20						

Sheet1 / Sheet2 / Sheet3 / Sheet4 / Sheet5 / Sheet

Workbook 2.10

Now, in B4 enter the formula:

=a/(p-b)

and observe how this automatically calculates the break-even level of output for any values entered to B1:B3.[6]

Save this file as W2_10.XLS.
Exercises 2.6 and 2.7 can be attempted now.

Now suppose that, for the foreseeable future at least, the cost terms (a and b) can be taken as given but that the price received for the product frequently varies within a range of £3 either side of £15.50: that is, the price varies between £12.50 and £18.50. While the formula in B4 will still calculate the break-even level of output correctly for any *given* value of p, we might like to observe how the break-even level varies with changes in the price. Workbook 2.11 has been constructed with this task in mind.

Use Workbook 2.10 as a template to follow the discussion.

Workbook 2.11

First, establish the specified range of values for the product price in column A. Then compute the break-even level of output alongside in column B by entering, in B7:

=a/(A7-b)

and copying this into B8:B19. Add the labels shown in A6, B5, and B6.

....

6 Note that this will only work if you have named the B1 to B3 cells as instructed.

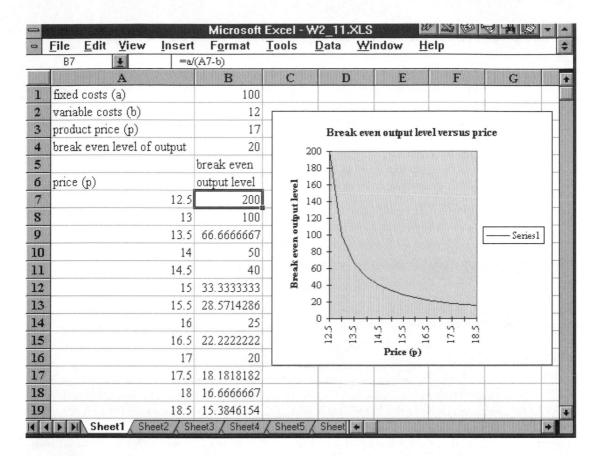

Now create the chart as outlined in the previous discussion and save the model as W2_11.XLS.

As is clear from the chart in Workbook 2.11, as the price received increases, the break-even level of output decreases, but the relationship is not linear. This is because the denominator in the expression for the break-even level of output (p - b) clearly increases as p increases with b remaining constant. Thus, the constant numerator (a) is being divided by an increasing denominator, which must inevitably lead to a declining quotient (i.e. the ratio between the numerator and the denominator).

Also notice that if the price were £12 then (p - b) would evaluate to zero and any value divided by zero becomes undefined. (Excel would return the message #DIV/0!, indicating that such an action is mathematically undefined.)

However, there is more than a purely mathematical implication of this situation. If the unit variable cost and the price are the same, then clearly each unit of the product is being sold at its variable cost of production (i.e. with zero profit). If there were no fixed costs involved then this would imply break-even at any level of output. But with positive fixed costs and with the absence of any profit contribution from sales of the product, there will never be enough surplus from these sales to cover the fixed costs.

Therefore, break-even can never be achieved. Either the fixed costs must disappear or the difference between price and unit variable cost must become positive if a break-even level of production is to exist.

Exercise 2.8 can be attempted now.

2.7. **Linear functions involving logical tests**

Now consider a simple income tax system in which a fixed allowance of £4000 is awarded against gross income. In other words, no tax is paid on the first £4000 of gross income. Thereafter, all income is taxable, but at two different rates.

To be exact, suppose that the first £16000 of taxable income is taxed at a rate of 20%, and any taxable income above £16000 is taxed at a higher rate of 25%. (Note: it is only the amount of taxable income above £16000 that is taxed at the higher rate.) Calculate the tax due and hence the net income of an individual who earns a gross income of £30000.

For this *arithmetic* problem we can proceed as follows.

Taxable income (TI) = £30000 - £4000 = £26000

The first £16000 of this £26000 is taxed at 20%, giving:

$$\text{Tax due}_1 = 20/100(\pounds16000) = 0.2(\pounds16000) = \pounds3200$$

The remaining £10000 (£26000 - £16000) of taxable income is taxed at 25% giving:

$$\text{Tax due}_2 = 25/100(\pounds10000) = 0.25(\pounds10000) = \pounds2500$$

Consequently, the total tax bill = Tax due$_1$ + Tax due$_2$ = £3200 + £2500 = £5700
Net income is therefore

£30000 - £5700 = £24300

Now consider the following more general formulation of the problem.

An income tax system contains a fixed allowance of £A which is awarded against gross income. Thereafter, all income is taxable, but at two different rates. The first £M of taxable income is taxed at a rate of t_1%, and any taxable income above £M is taxed at a higher rate of t_2%.

Calculate the tax due and hence the net income of an individual who earns a gross income of £G.

We can proceed in the same way as with the arithmetic example, only using symbols instead of numbers. Hence:

Taxable income (TI) = G - A

However, although this appears to be a reasonable enough statement, the difficulties that can arise when moving from the specific to the general are immediately encountered. This is because the possibility exists that G could be less than A, in which case TI would be negative. Mathematically this would imply a negative amount of tax due (i.e. a rebate to the taxpayer), yet few tax systems allow for this eventuality.

In general practice, if an individual's gross income is less than their fixed allowance then their taxable income is regarded as zero rather than some negative amount. Consequently, with a view to modelling the problem on a spreadsheet, we require some form of *test* to be applied to the expression for taxable income that will prevent negative values being returned for low gross incomes. In other words, we need something for TI like:

=IF(G-A<0,0,G-A)

This will test the difference between G and A and return 0 if that difference is less than 0, but return the actual (positive or zero) difference otherwise.

Turning to the tax due on *positive* taxable incomes, we again note that this will *depend* upon the magnitude of that taxable income.

To be exact, if TI is less than or equal to £M, then the tax due is simply given by:

Tax due = t_1TI   (i.e. the lower tax rate times the taxable income)

However, if TI exceeds M then the tax due is composed of two parts:

$$t_1 M + t_2(TI - M)$$

That is, the lower tax rate times the threshold value of taxable income for the higher tax rate to apply (M), plus the higher tax rate times the difference between taxable income and the threshold.

Translating these ideas into an IF statement gives:

$$=IF(G-A<=M,t_1*(G-A),t_1*M+t_2*(G-A-M))$$

or, in terms of TI:

$$=IF(TI<=M,t_1*TI,t_1*M+t_2*(TI-M))$$

Now consider Workbook 2.12, where the verbal logic above has been translated into spreadsheet form and then applied.

Open a new workbook and proceed as instructed.

	A	B	C	D	E	F	G
1		TAX CALCULATOR					
2			FORMULAE IN COLUMN B				
3	Fixed allowance (A) =	4000	NONE				
4	Lower tax rate (t1) =	0.2	NONE				
5	Higher tax rate (t2) =	0.25	NONE				
6	Threshold for higher tax rate (M) =	16000	NONE				
7							
8	Gross Income (G)	30000	NONE				
9	Taxable income (TI)	26000	=IF(G-A<0,0,G-A)				
10	Tax due (TD)	5700	=IF(TI<=M,tl*TI,tl*M+th*(TI-M))				
11	Net income (NI)	24300	=G-B10				

Workbook 2.12

First, enter the indicated labels in A3:A11 and then the values to B3:B8. Leave B9:B11 empty for the moment.

Note that the two tax rates have been entered in their decimal form (i.e. 20% = 20/100 = 0.2). If these tax rates were to change then they must be entered in this form, otherwise the calculations will be in error by a factor of 100.

In other words, in this model a tax rate of 18% must be entered as 0.18 or 18% and not as 18.

Now name the following cells:[7]

B3 as A   B4 as tl   B5 as th   B6 as M   B8 as G   B9 as TI

The IF statements in B9 and B10 correspond exactly to those outlined in the discussion above when the cells have been named as suggested.

[7] t_1 and t_2 are not allowed by Excel as valid names, so we use tl (for lower) and th (for higher) as the names of the cells containing the two tax rates.

Consequently, in B9 enter:

=IF(G-A<0,0,G-A)

Then in B10 enter:

=IF(TI<=M,tl*TI,tl*M+th*(TI-M))

Finally, to compute net income use B11 to contain:

=G-B10

The tax calculator is therefore completely general, and will accurately compute the tax due and the net income for any value of gross income that is entered to B8. Furthermore, it can clearly accommodate changes in the tax regime and/or gross income simply by making the relevant changes to any or all of the B3 to B8 cells. For example, use the model to compute the tax due for an individual who earns a gross income of £45000 if the fixed allowance has been increased to £6000, the lower tax increased to 23%, the higher tax rate increased to 35%, and the threshold for the higher tax rate increased to £19000.

If the model has been prepared correctly, then figures of £11370 and £33630 should be obtained for the tax due and the net income respectively.

Save the model as W2_12.XLS.

Now consider how to obtain a chart of tax due versus gross income for a range of gross income values.

Open a new workbook to follow the argument.

The first step will be to create our flexible scale adjuster for the variable to be placed on the horizontal axis (gross income). The procedure is the same as before—define start and step values for gross income and then link these to the range that is to contain these values with a formula that adds the defined step on to each previous value. This has been done in Workbook 2.13 for a tax system in which A = £5000, t_1 = 0.25, t_2 = 0.5, and M = £19000.

Workbook 2.13

Enter these new labels and values now as indicated in the A1:E5 range of Workbook 2.13.
Then in A6, enter:

=E1

and in A7 enter:

=A6+E$2

and copy this into A8 to A19.
Finally, name the B1:B4 cells as A, tl, th, and M respectively.

The rest of the worksheet has been constructed as follows:

In B6 the taxable income is computed and then forced to become zero if the result turns out to be negative.

To do this use B6 to contain:

=IF(A6-A<0,0,A6-A)

and then copy this into the B7 to B19 cells.
Then, in C6 write:

=IF(B6<M,tl*B6,tl*M+th*(B6-M))

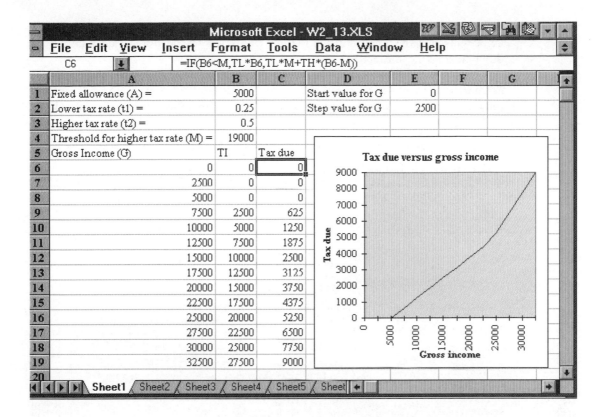

Workbook 2.13 This tests whether the taxable income figure in B6 is lower than the threshold for the upper rate of tax. If it is, then the tax due is simply the lower rate of tax times the taxable income. However, as with the model in Workbook 2.12, if taxable income exceeds the threshold then the higher rate of tax is applied to the amount by which taxable income exceeds the threshold and added to the (fixed) amount of the lower tax rate times the threshold.

Now copy the contents of C6 into C7 :C19.
To produce the illustrated graph, define the data range as:

    A6:A19,C6:C19

(i.e. missing out the column B data).

Once again, use the first column as the values for the data to be plotted on the horizontal axis.

As can be seen from the chart in Workbook 2.13, the tax due goes through three distinct phases. First, as long as gross income is lower than the fixed allowance there is no tax due. This is shown by the line coinciding with the horizontal axis. Second, once taxable income becomes positive, but still lower than the threshold, the tax due rises by £25 for every extra £100 of taxable income. This continues until the threshold for the higher rate of tax is reached, whereupon the tax due is the constant 25% of £19000 (£4750) plus £50 for every extra £100 of taxable income.

These three phases are clearly indicated on the chart, and illustrate the power of the worksheet in giving a clear visual impression of what is by no means a trivial problem.

Save this model now as W2_13.XLS.

Finally, it might well be asked: What proportion of various different amounts of gross income is taken by the tax authorities? In other words, what is the *average* rate of tax paid at different gross income levels?

To answer this, we simply have to note that the average rate of tax will be the total tax due as a percentage of gross income. Workbook 2.13 contains all the data required to perform these calculations, and then to graph the results when modified as shown in Workbook 2.14.

Use Workbook 2.13 as a template to produce the results indicated in Workbook 2.14.

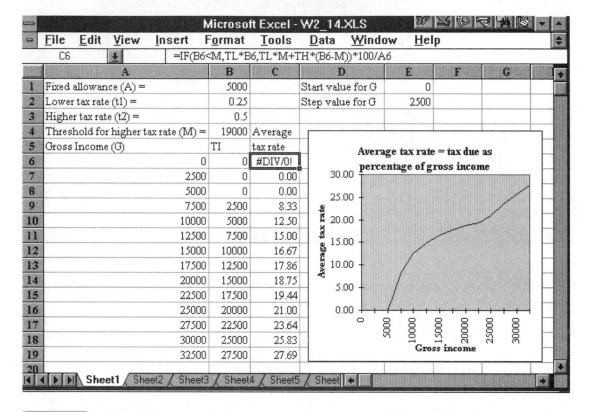

| Workbook 2.14 | Workbook 2.14 was easily obtained from Workbook 2.13 by altering the formula in C6 in line with the recent discussion above and as indicated on the formula bar at the top of the sheet. |

That is, the previous contents of C6 were multiplied by 100 and the result divided by A6.

This is clearly the worksheet formulation of the total tax due as a percentage of gross income.

Make this adjustment now, and then copy this new version of the formula in C6 into C7:C19.

Lastly, change the label for the data in column C to:

average tax rate

and edit the title and vertical axis labels in the chart to reflect the changed nature of the problem.

Clearly the average tax rate, although always rising with gross income, goes through a series of 'phases' that are determined by the levels of taxable income at which each of the three tax rates (0%, 25%, and 50%) come into play. These correspond to the 3 phases of the chart in Workbook 2.13, although the movement between the phases is no longer linear.

However, what is not clear from the chart in Workbook 2.14 is whether the average tax rate *continues* to rise indefinitely as the level of gross income increases. Logically, we should expect that it *would not*, since in this tax regime even multi-billionaires will never pay tax at any rate in excess of 50%. True, the vast majority of such individuals' gross income will be taxed at 50%, but they will still be entitled to the fixed allowance of £5000 and will still only pay tax at the lower rate of 25% on the first £19000 of their taxable income.

Consequently, as gross income gets larger and larger we should expect that the *average* rate of tax gets closer and closer to 50%—but never quite gets there (49.99% for example).

Confirm this in Workbook 2.14 by altering the start and step values for G to £30000 and £50000 respectively.

The graph of the average tax rate will now be seen to have lost its phases, since only individuals who pay tax at the higher rate are included in the gross income range. At the same time however, the graph will display a smooth and steady approach towards the limit of 50% as the level of gross income increases.

In general, then, if an income tax system consists of a fixed allowance and several increasing tax rates, the average rate of tax will increase steadily with increases in gross income, but will reach a definite limit that is determined by the highest rate of tax in the system.

The various tax rates that apply at different levels of taxable income are known as marginal tax rates, since they represent the tax rate to be applied to each extra (marginal) unit of income above each of the defined income thresholds. Therefore, it will always be the case that the *average* rate of tax approaches the highest marginal rate of tax as the limiting case when gross incomes become very large.

Save this model now as W2_14.XLS.
Exercises 2.9 and 2.10 can be attempted now.

2.8. Linear functions involving numerous logical tests

The previous discussion has indicated how the logical IF function can be used to address problems in which there are two or three possible outcomes depending upon the circumstances (for example, no tax paid, all tax paid at the lower rate, tax paid at both the lower and the higher rates). However, the question arises of how to deal with situations in which there are considerably more than two or three possible outcomes. In theory, the necessary series of IF statements could be composed and entered to the worksheet, but in practice the effort and complexity of doing this means that a more efficient mechanism should be sought.

To discover this mechanism, consider the following reformulation of the 'discount rate' problem. To be exact, imagine that the firm selling kitchen units offers a range of discount rates depending upon the size of the order quantity:

For orders of fewer than 10 units no discount is offered.

For orders of at least 10 units but fewer than 25 units a 4% discount is offered.
For orders of at least 25 units but fewer than 45 units a 6% discount is offered.
For orders of at least 45 units but fewer than 75 units a 7% discount is offered.
For orders of at least 75 units but fewer than 100 units a 7.5% discount is offered.
For orders of 100 units or more a 9% discount is offered.

Clearly in this scenario there are six different discount rates that can be applied, depending upon the order size, and the task is to get Excel to select the correct one and then apply it to the order quantity so that the correct invoice can be calculated. Notice, however, that unlike the previous income tax example these discount rates are not assumed to be applied marginally. In other words, each appropriate discount rate is applied to *all* units in the order.

The mechanism for dealing with this situation is indicated in Workbook 2.15.

Open a new workbook and proceed as instructed.

	Microsoft Excel - W2_15.XLS							
File **Edit** **View** **Insert** **Format** **Tools** **Data** **Window** **Help**								
B2		=VLOOKUP(B3,D3:E8,2)						
	A	**B**	**C**	**D**	**E**	**F**	**G**	**H**
1	price (£P)	80		VERTICAL LOOKUP TABLE				
2	discount rate applied (d%)	0.07		order size (x)	discount rates			
3	order quantity (x)	70		0	0			
4	discount obtained (£)	392		10	0.04			
5	Invoice (£)	5208		25	0.06			
6				45	0.07			
7				75	0.075			
8				100	0.09			
9								
	Sheet1 Sheet2 Sheet3 Sheet4 Sheet5 Sheet							

Workbook 2.15

First enter the indicated labels to A1:A5, and D1:E2.
Then enter the illustrated values to B1 and B3.
Leave B2, B4, and B5 blank for the moment.
Next enter the 6 different-order threshold values and their associated discount rates into a table located in the range D3:E8.

Notice that the labels in the rows directly above are for information only—the range of values eventually to be addressed are in D3 to E8. Also notice that the discount rates have been entered as decimals, i.e. 4% = 4/100 = 0.04.

This has been called a vertical lookup table—vertical because the values have been entered in columns rather than rows, and lookup because we are going to get Excel to look up in this table any value of x that we care to enter and return the discount rate that lies immediately to the right of that x value.

The function that will do this is called =VLOOKUP and takes three arguments (separated, as usual, by commas).[8]

The first argument is *what* is to be looked up in the table . This can be an actual value (2, 6, etc.) or an actual label (A, X, etc.), or, more usually, a cell reference containing either of these. In our illustration we require to find the discount rate associated with any *order quan-*

---

8 There is also an equivalent horizontal lookup function (=HLOOKUP) if the data has been entered in rows rather than columns.

tity, so it is the latter that we use as the first argument. Furthermore, since the order quantity has been housed in the B3 cell we can use this cell reference as the first argument.

Thus, building the function up step by step, we have:

> =VLOOKUP(B3 . . .

The next argument is the location of the table where the looking up is to be done. In our illustration we have previously noted that this range is D3:E8. However, notice that although we only have 2 columns in our illustrated table there is nothing to stop us having more if necessary—the third argument of the VLOOKUP function will tell us which column of the table contains the data that is to be returned.

Continuing with building up the function, we now have:

> =VLOOKUP(B3,D3:E8, . . .

Finally, the third required argument is known as the **column offset** and defines which of the columns in the table is the one to be associated with the looked up value. The offset starts at 1 (i.e. the first column of the table) and increases in steps of 1 for every subsequent column of data. Notice, however, that since in our illustration we have defined the lookup table to be the range D3:E8, this means that there are only two columns in use as far as the illustration is concerned. Hence the column offset for our illustration *can only* be 1 or 2. However, with three columns defined in a table (D to F, for example) the legal offset values become 1, 2, or 3.

Consequently, since in this example it is the discount rate associated with the requested order size that we want to be returned to whatever cell contains our VLOOKUP function, the required offset in this case is 2.

The completed function is therefore:

> =VLOOKUP(B3,D3:E8,2)

Enter this now to the B2 cell.

Once this has been done, the lookup capability is completely operational.

Notice that this particular lookup function can be read to mean the following.

Look up the value contained in the B3 cell in the first column of the table contained in D3:D8 and return the associated value contained in the second column of that table.

Now enter any order quantity in B3 and confirm that B2 will contain the associated discount rate.

Once again, notice that *any* order quantity can be entered to B3, not just one of the 6 contained in the first column of the lookup table.

The worksheet is completed in a similar way to our previous illustration by writing formulae to compute the monetary value of the discount and the net invoice.

Hence, in B4 enter:

> =B1*B3*B2

and in B5 write:

> =B1*B3-B4

Now confirm that the correct invoice is computed for any entered value of the order, and then save this model as W2_15.XLS.

Two final points should be noted about the VLOOKUP function.

First, the values in the first column of any lookup table (containing *what* is to be looked up) *must* be arranged in *ascending* numerical order if they are values, or in *ascending* alphabetical order if they are text.

Second, although in the example only 6 values have been entered in the first column on the lookup table, Excel regards the values to be looked up as continuous within this range. In other words, the first value (0) is effectively regarded as 0 to 9.99999 inclusive, and the second value (10) as 10 to 24.99999 inclusive.

This continues for the rest of the values in the first column of the lookup table and explains why any value—not just those six contained in the first column of the lookup table—can be entered to the B3 cell.

2.9. Combining conditional statements with lookup functions

....

Now suppose that the discounts used in the illustration were in fact *only* for cash payments, and that for non-cash payments the equivalent discounts were:

0%, 1.5%, 2.5%, 3.5%, 4%, and 4.5%.

The task to be undertaken now is to modify the worksheet to take account of this added distinction.

This has been done in Workbook 2.16

Use Workbook 2.15 as a template to produce Workbook 2.16.

		Microsoft Excel - W2_16.XLS		
File	**Edit**	**View**	**Insert**	**Format** **Tools** **Data** **Window** **Help**

B2 =VLOOKUP(B3,D3:F8,B7)

	A	B	C	D	E	F
1	price (£P)	80		VERTICAL LOOKUP TABLE		
2	discount rate applied (d%)	0.07		order size (x)	discount rates (cash)	discount rates (other)
3	order quantity (x)	70		0	0	0
4	discount obtained (£)	392		10	0.04	0.015
5	Invoice (£)	5208		25	0.06	0.025
6	payment form: 1= cash; 0 = other	1		45	0.07	0.035
7	Column offset for lookup table	2		75	0.075	0.04
8				100	0.09	0.045
9						

Sheet1 / Sheet2 / Sheet3 / Sheet4 / Sheet5 / Sheet

Workbook 2.16

First, add the labels shown in A6:A7.

Second, enter the non-cash discount rates in column F alongside those that apply for cash.

Notice that the first implication of this is that the lookup table will have to be *redefined* as D3:F8 to accommodate this extra column of information.

Next, as in previous versions of this problem we have used a cell (B6 in this case) to contain a code that tells whether (1) or not (0) payment is in cash.

So enter 1 to B6.

Now notice that the heart of the problem created by the introduction of another set of discount rates lies in getting the VLOOKUP function to apply the proper column offset in the lookup table. This is because, if payment is in cash, the column offset in the VLOOKUP function should be 2, whereas if it is not in cash the offset value should be 3.

Consequently, we require a cell that will contain a value of 2 if payment is in cash (i.e. B6 = 1) or a value of 3 if payment is not in cash (i.e. B6 = 0).

Do this in the B7 cell with the following IF statement:

=IF(B6=1,2,3)

Clearly B7 will now always contain the correct lookup offset, and so the final step is to include B7 *in cell address form* as the third argument of the VLOOKUP function.

That is, change the formula in B2 to:

=VLOOKUP(B3,D3:F8,B7)

Note carefully how the inclusion of B7 in the formula means that the lookup function can be forced to refer to either the second or the third column of the lookup table depending upon the value that B7 adopts, which in turn depends upon whether or not payment is in cash (i.e. whether B6 contains 1 or 0).

After making these alterations, confirm that the correct invoice is obtained for any order amount and any payment form (i.e. cash or other).
Now save this model as W2_16.XLS.
Exercise 2.11 can now be attempted.

Finally, by using the same methods as in previous illustrations we can extend Workbook 2.16 to provide a chart that will indicate how the invoice varies with the order size—for both cash and non-cash payment forms.

Open a new workbook and make up Workbook 2.17 as explained in the text below the illustration.

<table><tr><td>Workbook
2.17</td><td>**First, fill all of the indicated cells with the illustrated labels and data values except for those in B5:C16. These will be created by formulae.**</td></tr></table>

Now we can use the lookup function as a replacement for the cell that contained the discount rate in previous illustrations.

In other words with P, x, and d representing the price, order quantity, and discount rate (as a decimal) respectively, the entry in B5 should represent:

$$Px - Pxd = px(1- d)$$

Therefore in B5 enter:

=B$1*A5*(1-VLOOKUP(A5,D$3:F$8,2))

Notice that the address of the lookup table (D3:F8) has had its row numbers dollar fixed. This is essential to prevent the address of the table updating erroneously when the formula in B5 is copied into B6 to B16.[9] Also observe that, since this column is for payment in cash, the column offset in the lookup function can be fixed at 2.

Now, in C5, make the equivalent entry:

=B$1*A5*(1-VLOOKUP(A5,D$3:F$8,3))

---

9 You could get round this need to dollar fix by naming the lookup table. That is, select D3:F8 and then choose Insert, Name, and Define from the Menu bar. Then supply a name such as TABLEA and refer to this named range thereafter in any lookup functions that are written.

	Microsoft Excel - W2_17.XLS							
File **Edit** **View** **Insert** **Format** **Tools** **Data** **Window** **Help**								
B5		=B$1*A5*(1-VLOOKUP(A5,D$3:F$8,2))						
	A	**B**	**C**	**D**	**E**	**F**	**G**	**H**	**I**
1	Price (£P) =	80		order size (x)	discount rate applicable (d)				
2					cash	non cash			
3		Cash	Non cash	0	0	0			
4	Order size (x)	invoice	invoice	10	0.04	0.015			
5	0	0	0	25	0.06	0.025			
6	9	720	720	45	0.07	0.035			
7	10	768	788	75	0.075	0.04			
8	24	1843.2	1891.2	100	0.09	0.045			
9	25	1880	1950						
10	44	3308.8	3432						
11	45	3348	3474						
12	74	5505.6	5712.8						
13	75	5550	5760						
14	99	7326	7603.2						
15	100	7280	7640						
16	110	8008	8404						
17									

Sheet1 / Sheet2 / Sheet3 / Sheet4 / Sheet5 / Sheet

Notice that the only change from the entry in B5 is that that the column offset has become 3 instead of 2.

Workbook 2.17

Now copy B5:C5 into B6:C16.
Next, plot these three data series (A3:C16) with appropriate titles and legends AND WITH THE FIRST *TWO* ROWS USED FOR THE LEGEND TEXT, to obtain the chart shown in Fig. 2.3.

As can clearly be seen, the data create a 'step-like' graph that shows both the cash and the

Figure 2.3 non-cash invoices rising in steps until the maximum discount of 9% for cash or 4.5% for

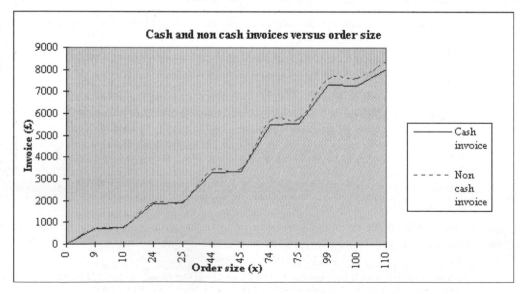

non-cash is reached. Thereafter, the graph for both payment forms would rise steadily and without any steps.

Now save this worksheet with its embedded chart as W2_17.XLS.

Finally, the invoice *per unit ordered* could also be calculated and plotted simply by reforming the B5 and C5 entries.

Use Workbook 2.17 (W2_17.XLS) as a template and then make the following alterations.
    Rewrite the formula in B5 as:

=B$1*A5*(1-VLOOKUP(A5,D$3:F$8,2))/A5

Or, after cancelling the A5 term from top and bottom as:

=B$1*(1-VLOOKUP(A5,D$3:F$8,2))

Then rewrite the formula in C5 as:

=B$1*A5*(1-VLOOKUP(A5,D$3:F$8,3))/A5

or, again after cancellation:

=B$1*(1-VLOOKUP(A5,D$3:F$8,3))

Finally, copy B5 and C5 into B6 to C16.[10]

When this is done (using the second versions of the formulae) the results shown in Workbook 2.18 should be obtained.

	Microsoft Excel - W2_18.XLS						
File	**Edit**	**View**	**Insert**	**Format**	**Tools**	**Data**	**Window**	**Help**
B5		=B$1*(1-VLOOKUP(A5,D$3:F$8,2))					

	A	B	C	D	E	F	G
1	Price (£P) =	80		order size (x)	discount rate applicable (d)		
2					cash	non cash	
3		Cash invoice	Non-cash invoice	0	0	0	
4	Order size (x)	per unit ordered	per unit ordered	10	0.04	0.015	
5	0	80	80	25	0.06	0.025	
6	9	80	80	45	0.07	0.035	
7	10	76.8	78.8	75	0.075	0.04	
8	24	76.8	78.8	100	0.09	0.045	
9	25	75.2	78				
10	44	75.2	78				
11	45	74.4	77.2				
12	74	74.4	77.2				
13	75	74	76.8				
14	99	74	76.8				
15	100	72.8	76.4				
16	110	72.8	76.4				

Sheet1 / Sheet2 / Sheet3 / Sheet4 / Sheet5 / Sheet

Workbook 2.18 Notice that since we are using Workbook 2.17 as a template the graph will have adjusted automatically to reflect the new nature of the data, but the title, the axis labels, and the legends for the data series still refer to the previous illustration.

10 If you use the first versions of these formulae, then B5 and C5 will show #DIV/0, since this is exactly what is being done in row 5. You can fix this by making the first value for order size = 0.001 rather than zero.

Use the editing facility to make the necessary changes so that your graph resembles the one shown in Fig. 2.4, and then save the new version as W2_18.XLS.

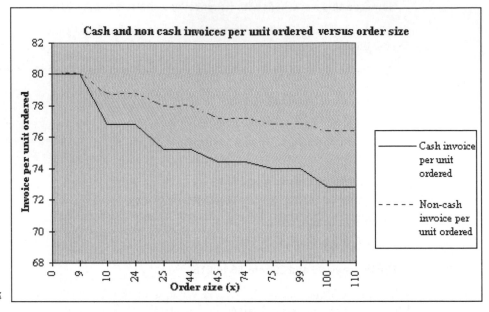

Figure 2.4

Once again, as in the previous income tax example, these invoices per unit of order size reach a limit that is determined by the highest discount rate that the firm offers. To be exact, *once an order size of 100 units has been achieved* then the invoice per unit is simply the price less 9% of the price if payment is in cash, or the price less 4.5% of the price if the payment form is non-cash.

This is the same as (100% - 9%) = 91% of the price for cash payments or (100% - 4.5%) = 95.5% of the price for non-cash payments.

2.10. Exercises

Exercise 2.1

A firm's profits (y) are known to be r% of the value of its capital assets (x). Set up a worksheet that will calculate the value of the firm's profits for any value of r and for each of 50 specified values of x.

These 50 values of x should be able to include any required numerical range simply by changing the values contained in two chosen cells that are used to house the start and step values for the range of x values.

When you have finished, save the file as W2_19.XLS for future use.

Exercise 2.2

Using the data created in Exercise 2.1, prepare a suitably labelled and titled graph indicating how the firm's profits vary with the value of its capital assets.

Exercise 2.3

The fire insurance premium on factories is £10 per square metre (m²) of floor space if that space is 500m² or less, but £15 per m² for all larger areas.

(i) Prepare a worksheet that can calculate the total insurance due when the floor space of the factory is entered.

(ii) Prepare a suitably labelled and titled graph showing how the total insurance due varies with the floor space of the factory for any range of floor spaces that are entered.

(Use the principles established in Exercises 2.1 and 2.2 and then save the file as W2_20.XLS.)

Exercise 2.4

Prepare a 'hot' graph title for the graph created in Exercise 2.3. This should allow the title to change appropriately if there are changes in either or both of the actual premiums, or the floor area determining when the premium increases. In other words, in the graph title, the premiums themselves and the floor area at which the premium increases should be linked sensitively to the data cells in the worksheet.

Exercise 2.5

In foreign currency transactions a bank charges customers a fixed amount of £15 per transaction, plus a commission of 1% of the value of the transaction for deals of £5000 or less. For larger deals the fixed charge is still £15, but the commission rate reduces to 0.75% of the value of the entire transaction.

Prepare a worksheet that will compute, and a graph that will display, the transaction costs associated with foreign currency purchases by clients between values of £1000 and £20000 in steps of £1000.

The worksheet should allow easy alteration of any of the fixed data elements and also of the range of transaction values to be computed.

Exercise 2.6

In order to fund a trip to France, a businesswoman needs to convert sterling (£) into French Francs (FF). She can do this in either of two ways:

Purchase Travellers' Cheques at an exchange rate of £1 =FF7.15 and pay a commission of 1.5% of the value of the transaction. Purchase French currency at an exchange rate of £1 = FF7.1 and pay a fixed commission of £10 regardless of the value of the transaction.

(i) Prepare a worksheet containing a chart that will indicate, for each of the methods, how the cost of obtaining various amounts of FF *differs* with the number of FF required.

The worksheet should be completely flexible and thereby allow easy alteration of the specifications of the problem.

(ii) Use the chart created in part i) to determine the number of FF for which the two methods are equally expensive (i.e. the break-even quantity of FF).

When you have finished the exercise, save the file as W2_22.XLS.

Exercise 2.7

Suppose, in Exercise 2.6, that the commission paid on travellers' cheques also includes an insurance element that guarantees replacement in the event of loss or theft. The currency commission does not include such an element, and has to be purchased separately at a cost of 0.1% of the value of the transaction (excluding the commission).

Modify the worksheet created in Exercise 2.6 above (W2_22.XLS) to take account of this added information, and prepare a chart that will indicate the new break-even quantity of FF if the businesswoman regards insurance cover as essential.

Exercise 2.8

Prepare a new worksheet containing a formula that will compute the break-even quantity of FF for the problem defined in Exercise 2.7 (i.e. including insurance arrangements).

The model should be completely flexible, and perform the calculations correctly regardless of whether insurance cover is regarded as essential.

Exercise 2.9

A builder can obtain concrete from any of four suppliers.

Supplier W charges £12 per ton for the concrete and a fixed delivery charge of £50 regardless of the quantity ordered.
Supplier X charges £14 per ton including delivery.
Supplier Y charges £11.5 per ton for the concrete and a fixed delivery charge of £100. However, for orders in excess of 40 tons delivery is free from supplier Y.
Supplier Z charges £11 per ton for the concrete, £2 per ton delivery charge and a fixed delivery charge of £20.

(i) Prepare a worksheet and a graph that will indicate, for a range of order amounts, the total cost of concrete ordered from each of the four suppliers.

(ii) Prepare a worksheet and a graph that will indicate, for a range of order amounts, the cost per unit of concrete ordered from each of the four suppliers.

Exercise 2.10

The cost of electricity to domestic users is composed of a standing charge of £10 per quarter, a charge of £0.14 per metered unit for the first 2000 units consumed, and a charge of £0.11 per metered unit for all units in excess of 2000 units that are used.

Prepare a worksheet that can calculate and graph the quarterly cost per metered unit for a range of usage levels. What is the limiting value of the cost per metered unit as the number of units used becomes very large?

Exercise 2.11

A firm sells 6 different products (A, B, C, D, E, and F), each of which is available in 4 different sizes (S, M, L, XL). Table 2.1 indicates the prices charged (in £s) for the products (see Table 2.1).

Table 2.1

TYPE	SIZE			
	S	M	L	XL
A	15	17	18	19.50
B	21	26	29	32
C	43	52	67	78
D	3	5	8	9
E	29	34	38	49
F	63	69	73	81

Prepare a worksheet that will compute the invoice to be sent to a customer when any product type, any size, and any order quantity are entered to three cells of the sheet.

2.11. Solutions to the exercises

Solution to Exercise 2.1

A section of the solution worksheet along with explanation of the formulae used is shown in Workbook 2.19.

Solution to Exercise 2.2

Using Workbook 2.19 define the data range as B7:C56 and use the first column for the x axis labels. Then add a title and text for the x and y axes to produce the chart shown in Fig. 2.5.

Solution to Exercise 2.3

(i) The solution is shown in Workbook 2.20A.

(ii) The data for the graph are calculated as shown in Workbook 2.20B, and the graph constructed in Figure 2.6 from a data range of B14:C27. Fixed titles were added as indicated.

Solution to Exercise 2.4

The formulae used to create the 'hot' title are shown in Workbook 2.20C, and the fixed title of the chart in Workbook 2.20B was edited to contain the cell reference:

=SHEET1!A38

Solution to Exercise 2.5

Workbook 2.21 illustrates the formulae used for the calculations, and the graph can be obtained by defining the data range as B9:C28.

Solution to Exercise 2.6

(i) Name the following cells as indicated.

B3 as: TE	(i.e. travellers' exchange rate)
D3 as: CE	(i.e. currency exchange rate)
B4 as: TPC	(i.e. travellers' proportional commission)
D4 as: CPC	(i.e. currency proportional commission)
B5 as: TFC	(i.e. travellers' fixed commission)
D5 as: CFC	(i.e. currency fixed commission)

We can now argue that the sterling cost of travellers' cheques (ST) is given by the number of FF required, divided by the travellers' cheque exchange rate, plus the proportional commission times the sterling value of the purchased FF, plus any fixed commission.

Workbook 2.19

	Microsoft Excel - W2_19.XLS					
File	**Edit** **View**	**Insert**	**Format** **Tools**	**Data**	**Window**	**Help**
B1		0.15				
	A	B	C	D	E	
1	Value of r (%)	15%				
2	Start value for x	100				
3	Step value for x	1000				
4						
5	FORMULAE IN			FORMULAE IN		
6	IN COLUMN B	Capital asset value (x)	Profits (y)	COLUMN C		
7	=B2	100	15	=B$1*B7		
8	=B$3+B7	1100	165	=B$1*B8		
9	=B$3+B8	2100	315	=B$1*B9		
10	=B$3+B9	3100	465	=B$1*B10		
11	AND SO ON	4100	615	AND SO ON		
12	AFTER COPYING	5100	765	AFTER COPYING		
13	B8 INTO B9:B56	6100	915	C7 INTO C8:C56		
14		7100	1065			

Sheet1 / Sheet2 / Sheet3 / Sheet4 / Sheet5 / Sheet

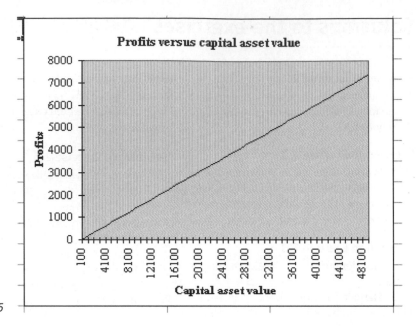

Figure 2.5

Now, with the first value for FF required located in A10, symbolically, and in terms of the named cells, this gives:

$$ST = A10/TE + TPC*A10/TE + TFC$$

By a similar logic the sterling cost of Currency (SC) is given by:

$$SC = A10/CE + CPC*A10/CE + CFC$$

Workbook 2.20A

Workbook 2.22. performs these calculations in the B13 and C13 cells, which, after copying, produces the costs of the two methods for the indicated range of FF required.

Finally, the cost differential between the two methods is computed in column D, and Fig. 2.7 is generated by defining the data range as A9:A29,D9:D29.

(ii) The chart clearly indicates that break-even is obtained at approximately FF9000.

	Microsoft Excel - W2_20A.XLS						
File	**Edit**	**View**	**Insert**	**Format**	**Tools**	**Data**	**Window**	**Help**

B7   =IF(B6<=B3,B2*B6,B4*B6)

	A	B	C	D	E	F
1			FORMULA IN COLUMN B			
2	Insurance premium 1	10	NONE			
3	Maximum floor space for insurance premium 1	500	NONE			
4	Insurance premium 2	15	NONE			
5						
6	Floor space (square metres)	700	NONE			
7	Insurance premium due	10500	=IF(B6<=B3,B2*B6,B4*B6)			
8						
9						
10						
11						

Sheet1 / Sheet2 / Sheet3 / Sheet4 / **Sheet5** / Sheet

	Microsoft Excel - W2_20B.XLS			
File Edit View Insert Format Tools Data Window Help				
C14		=IF(B14<=B$3,B$2*B14,B$4*B14)		

	A	B	C	D
9	Start value for floor space	0		
10	Step value for floor space	100		
11				
12		Floor	Premium	
13	FORMULA IN COLUMN B	Space	Due	FORMULA IN COLUMN C
14	=B9	0	0	=IF(B14<=B$3,B$2*B14,B$4*B14)
15	=B14+B$10	100	1000	=IF(B15<=B$3,B$2*B15,B$4*B15)
16	=B15+B$10	200	2000	=IF(B16<=B$3,B$2*B16,B$4*B16)
17	=B16+B$10	300	3000	=IF(B17<=B$3,B$2*B17,B$4*B17)
18	AND SO ON AFTER COPYING	400	4000	AND SO ON AFTER COPYING
19	DOWN TO ROW 27	500	5000	DOWN TO ROW 27
20		600	9000	
21		700	10500	
22		800	12000	
23		900	13500	

Sheet1 / Sheet2 / Sheet3 / Sheet4 / Sheet5 / Sheet

Ready

**Workbook
2.20B**

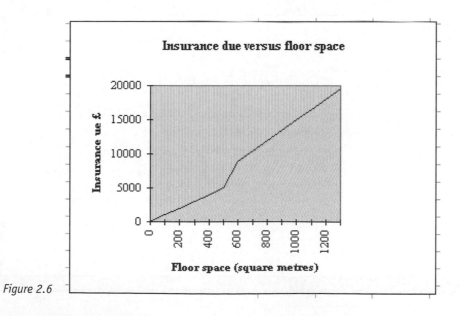

Figure 2.6

Microsoft Excel - W2_20C.XLS

| File | Edit | View | Insert | Format | Tools | Data | Window | Help |

A38   =A31&A32&A33&A34&A35&A36&A37

	A	B	C	D	E	F
30		FORMULA IN COLUMN A				
31	Insurance = £	NONE				
32	10.00	=FIXED(B1,2)				
33	per square metre for floor areas <=	NONE				
34	500	=FIXED(B2,0)				
35	square metres; £	NONE				
36	15.00	=FIXED(B3,2)				
37	per square metre otherwise.	NONE				
38	Insurance = £10.00 per square metre for floor areas <= 500 square metres; £15.00 per square metre otherwise.					
39						
40	THE FORMULA IN A38 IS:					
41	=A31&A32&A33&A34&A35&A36&A37	AND THIS CELL REFERENCE WAS USED FOR THE				
42		GRAPH TITLE BY ENTERING:				
43		=Sheet1!A38				
44						

Sheet1 / Sheet2 / Sheet3 / Sheet4 / Sheet5 / Sheet

Workbook 2.20C

Workbook 2.21

Microsoft Excel - W2_21.XLS

| File | Edit | View | Insert | Format | Tools | Data | Window | Help |

C9   =IF(B9<=B$4,B$2*B9,B$3*B9)+B$1

	A	B	C	D	E	F	G
1	Fixed commission charge	15					
2	Commission rate 1	1.00%					
3	Commission rate 2	0.75%					
4	Minimum Purchase for commission rate 2	5000					
5	Start value for transaction amount	1000					
6	Step value for transaction amount	1000					
7	FORMULA IN COLUMN B	Transaction	Transaction	FORMULA IN COLUMN C			
8		Amount	Cost				
9	=B5	1000	25	=IF(B9<=B$4,B$2*B9,B$3*B9)+B$1			
10	=B9+B$6	2000	35	=IF(B10<=B$4,B$2*B10,B$3*B10)+B$1			
11	=B10+B$6	3000	45	=IF(B11<=B$4,B$2*B11,B$3*B11)+B$1			
12	=B11+B$6	4000	55	=IF(B12<=B$4,B$2*B12,B$3*B12)+B$1			
13	AND SO ON AFTER COPYING	5000	65	AND SO ON AFTER COPYING			
14	DOWN TO ROW 28.	6000	60	DOWN TO ROW 28.			
15		7000	67.5				
16		8000	75				
17		9000	82.5				
18		10000	90				

Sheet1 / Sheet2 / Sheet3 / Sheet4 / Sheet5 / Sheet

	A	B	C	D	E	F	G
		Microsoft Excel - W2_22.XLS					
			=A10/CE+CPC*A10/CE+CFC				
1		Travellers'		Foreign			
2		Cheques		Currency			
3	Exchange rate	7.15		7.1			
4	Commission per £	1.50%		0			
5	Fixed commission	0		10			
6	Start value for FF	8500					
7	Step value for FF	100					
8		Travellers'	Foreign	Cost			
9	FF needed	Cheques cost	Currency cost	difference	FORMULAE USED:		
10	8500	1206.64	1207.183099	0.54	IN B10:		
11	8600	1220.84	1221.267606	0.43	=A10/TE+TPC*A10/TE+TFC		
12	8700	1235.03	1235.352113	0.32	COPIED DOWN TO ROW 29		
13	8800	1249.23	1249.43662	0.21	IN C10:		
14	8900	1263.43	1263.521127	0.09	=A10/CE+CPC*A10/CE+CFC		
15	9000	1277.62	1277.605634	-0.02	COPIED DOWN TO ROW 29		
16	9100	1291.82	1291.690141	-0.13	IN D10:		
17	9200	1306.01	1305.774648	-0.24	=B10-C10		
18	9300	1320.21	1319.859155	-0.35	COPIED DOWN TO ROW 29		
19	9400	1334.41	1333.943662	0.46			

Sheet1 / Sheet2 / Sheet3 / Sheet4 / Sheet5 / Sheet

**Workbook
2.22**

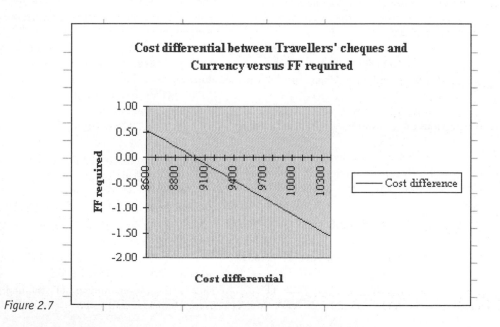

Figure 2.7

	A	B	C	D	E
		Travellers'		Foreign	
2		Cheques		Currency	
3	Exchange rate	7.15		7.1	
4	Commission per £	1.50%		0	
5	Fixed commission	0		10	
6	Insurance cost per £			0.10%	
7	Start value for FF	8500			
8	Step value for FF	100			
9		Travellers'	Foreign	Cost	
10	FF needed	Cheques cost	Currency cost	difference	FORMULAE USED:
11	8500	1206.64	1208.380282	1.74	IN B11:
12	8600	1220.84	1222.478873	1.64	=A11/TE+TPC*A11/TE+TFC
13	8700	1235.03	1236.577465	1.54	COPIED DOWN TO ROW 30
14	8800	1249.23	1250.676056	1.45	IN C11:
15	8900	1263.43	1264.774648	1.35	=A11/CE+CPC*A11/CE+CFC+IC*A11/CE
16	9000	1277.62	1278.873239	1.25	COPIED DOWN TO ROW 30
17	9100	1291.82	1292.971831	1.15	IN D11:
18	9200	1306.01	1307.070423	1.06	=B11-C11
19	9300	1320.21	1321.169014	0.96	COPIED DOWN TO ROW 30

Workbook 2.23

Solution to Exercise 2.7

We have modified Workbook 2.22 by inserting a row at row 6 to contain the insurance premium in the D6 cell of Workbook 2.23.

The D6 cell was then named as IC, and the formulae in C11 adjusted as indicated to include this premium and then copied down to row 30.

Finally, the same principles as in the previous exercise were used to create the chart shown in Fig. 2.8.

As Fig. 2.8 indicates, the two methods are now equally expensive when approximately FF10,300 are purchased.

Solution to Exercise 2.8

Using the same named cells as before, recall that the sterling costs for each of the methods (ST and SC) were given by:

$$ST = TFF/TE + TPC*TFF/TE + TFC$$

and:

$$SC = CFF/CE + CPC*CFF/CE + CFC+IC*CFF/CE$$

where TFF and CFF are the number of FF required in travellers' cheques and currency respectively.

The break-even number of FF occurs when these two costs are the same (ST = SC) for either method of purchase (FF = TFF = CFF).

Putting these two ideas together gives the break-even requirement as:

$$FF/TE + TPC*FF/TE + TFC = FF/CE + CPC*FF/CE + CFC+IC*FF/CE$$

This can be rearranged with *only* terms in FF on the left-hand side as:

$$FF/TE + TPC*FF/TE-FF/CE- CPC*FF/CE -IC*FF/CE = CFC-TFC$$

Now factor out the terms in FF on the left-hand side to obtain:

$$FF*(1/TE + TPC/TE-1/CE -CPC/CE- IC/CE) = CFC-TFC$$

Thus the break-even number of FF is found from:

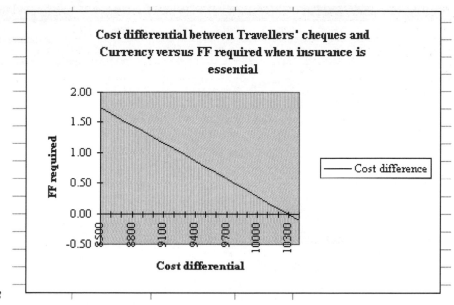

Figure 2.8

FF = (CFC-TFC)/(1/TE + TPC/TE-1/CE-CPC/CE-IC/CE)

This is the formula that has been entered to the B7 cell of Workbook 2.24, and will compute the break-even number of FF for the two methods available.

If insurance is not regarded as essential, then simply set the contents of the D6 cell equal to *zero* and the new break-even number of FF will be computed. The results are shown in Workbook 2.24.

You can now use this model to confirm that the exact break-even amounts of FF are 8984.95 if insurance is not regarded as essential or 10286.73 if the insurance is regarded as essential.

Solution to Exercise 2.9

(i) A section of the calculations required to produce the total cost are shown in Workbook 2.25, and these data are then graphed in Fig. 2.9 from the data range: A8:E24 (i.e. including the column headers to provide the data series legends).

(ii) Workbook 2.25 is easily modified to compute the unit as opposed to the total cost of concrete from each of the suppliers. All that needs to be done is divide the previous expressions for total cost by the number of tons ordered.

After cancelling any common terms from the top and the bottom, this produces the formulae shown in Workbook 2.26. Thus:

B9 becomes: =(B$2*A9+B$5)/A9 = B$2+B$5/A9
C9 becomes: =(C$2*A9)/A9 = C$2
D9 becomes: =IF(A9>D$4,D$2*A9/A9, (D$2*A9+D$5)/A9)

which is equivalent to:

=IF(A9>D$4,D$2,D$2+D$5/A9)
E9 becomes: =((E$2+E$3)*A9+E$5) /A9 = (E$2+E$3)+E$5/A9

When the data produced by these calculations are graphed, the chart shown in Fig. 2.10 is obtained.

The data range is the same as in Exercise 2.9, but the titles and column headers have been changed to reflect the changed nature of the calculations.

Solution to Exercise 2.10

The B1:B4 cells were named as S, ch, cl, and TQ respectively.

The calculations and formulae used are shown in Workbook 2.27 and then graphed in Fig. 2.11, where a data range of A9:A37,C9:C37 has been used.

Clearly, as the number of metered units increases the cost per unit approaches a limit of £0.11.

Microsoft Excel - W2_24.XLS

| | File | Edit | View | Insert | Format | Tools | Data | Window | Help | |

| | 100% | | |

B7 =(CFC-TFC)/(1/TE+TPC/TE-1/CE-CPC/CE-IC/CE)

	A	B	C	D	E
1		Travellers'		Foreign	
2		Cheques		Currency	
3	Exchange rate	7.15		7.1	
4	Commission per £	1.50%		0	
5	Fixed commission	0		10	
6	Insurance cost			0.10%	
7	Break even FF	10286.72746			
8					

Sheet1 / Sheet2 / Sheet3 / Sheet4 / Sheet5 / Sheet

Ready

Workbook 2.24

Workbook 2.25

Microsoft Excel - W2_25.XLS

| | File | Edit | View | Insert | Format | Tools | Data | Window | Help | |

D9 =IF(A9>D$4,D$2*A9,D$2*A9+D$5)

	A	B	C	D	E	F	G	H	I
1	Supplier	W	X	Y	Z				
2	Cost per ton	12	14	11.5	11				
3	Delivery charge per ton	0	0	0	2				
4	Threshold for free delivery	0	0	40	0				
5	Fixed delivery charge	50	0	100	20				
6	Start value for order amount	6							
7	Step value for order amount	3							
8	Amount ordered	Cost W	Cost X	Cost Y	Cost Z	FORMULAE:			
9		6	122	84	169	98	B9: =B$2*A9+B$5		
10		9	158	126	203.5	137	COPIED DOWN TO ROW 24		
11		12	194	168	238	176			
12		15	230	210	272.5	215	C9: =C$2*A9		
13		18	266	252	307	254	COPIED DOWN TO ROW 24		
14		21	302	294	341.5	293			
15		24	338	336	376	332	D9: =IF(A9>D$4,D$2*A9,D$2*A9+D$5)		
16		27	374	378	410.5	371	COPIED DOWN TO ROW 24		
17		30	410	420	445	410			
18		33	446	462	479.5	449	E9: =(E$2+E$3)*A9+E$5		
19		36	482	504	514	488	COPIED DOWN TO ROW 24		
20		39	518	546	548.5	527			

Sheet1 / Sheet2 / Sheet3 / Sheet4 / Sheet5 / Sheet

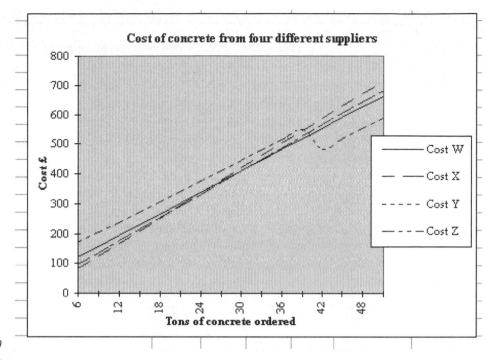

Figure 2.9

Workbook 2.26

	A	B	C	D	E	F	G	H
1	Supplier	W	X	Y	Z			
2	Cost per ton	12	14	11.5	11			
3	Delivery charge per ton	0	0	0	2			
4	Threshold for free delivery	0	0	40	0			
5	Fixed delivery charge	50	0	100	20			
6	Start value for order amount	6						
7	Step value for order amount	3						
8	Amount ordered	Cost W	Cost X	Cost Y	Cost Z	FORMULAE:		
9	6	20.33333	14	28.16667	16.33333	B9: =B$2+B$5/A9		
10	9	17.55556	14	22.61111	15.22222	COPIED DOWN TO ROW 24		
11	12	16.16667	14	19.83333	14.66667			
12	15	15.33333	14	18.16667	14.33333	C9: =C$2		
13	18	14.77778	14	17.05556	14.11111	COPIED DOWN TO ROW 24		
14	21	14.38095	14	16.2619	13.95238			
15	24	14.08333	14	15.66667	13.83333	D9: =IF(A9>D$4,D$2,D$2+D$5/A9)		
16	27	13.85185	14	15.2037	13.74074	COPIED DOWN TO ROW 24		
17	30	13.66667	14	14.83333	13.66667			
18	33	13.51515	14	14.5303	13.60606	E9: =(E$2+E$3)+E$5/A9		
19	36	13.38889	14	14.27778	13.55556	COPIED DOWN TO ROW 24		
20	39	13.28205	14	14.0641	13.51282			

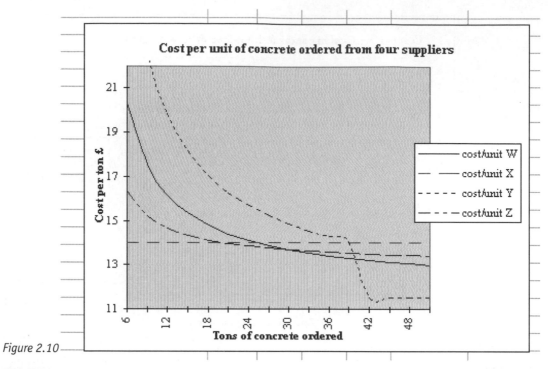

Figure 2.10

Workbook
2.27

	A	B	C	D	E	F	G	H
		B9		=IF(A9<=TQ,S+ch*A9,S+TQ*ch+cl*(A9-TQ))				
1	Standing charge	10						
2	Charge per metered unit 1	0.14						
3	Charge per metered unit 2	0.11						
4	Minimum consumption for charge 2	2000						
5	Start value for usage	10						
6	Step value for usage	200						
7			Cost per					
8	Usage (metered units)	Total cost	metered unit	FORMULAE:				
9	10	11.4	1.14	IN B9:				
10	210	39.4	0.187619048	=IF(A9<=TQ,S+ch*A9,S+ch*TQ+cl*(A9-TQ))				
11	410	67.4	0.164390244	COPIED DOWN TO ROW 37				
12	610	95.4	0.156393443					
13	810	123.4	0.152345679	IN C9: =B9/A9				
14	1010	151.4	0.14990099	COPIED DOWN TO ROW 37				
15	1210	179.4	0.148264463					
16	1410	207.4	0.147092199					
17	1610	235.4	0.14621118					

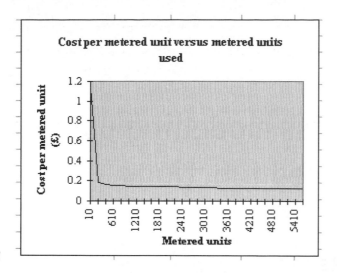

Figure 2.11

Solution to Exercise 2.11

The solution is shown in Workbook 2.28. The main lookup table has been located in B9: F14. However, notice how we have created a second lookup table in B16:C19 containing the sizes of the items (in ascending alphabetical order) in the first column and the appropriate column offsets in the main table in the second column.

The formula in B5 then uses this second table to look up the appropriate offset for the main table, and this allows the contents of B5 to be used as the **offset argument** in the lookup formula that has been located in B6.

Workbook 2.28

	A	B	C	D	E	F	G	H	I	J
1			FORMULA IN COLUMN B							
2	Product type	A	NONE							
3	Product size	XL	NONE							
4	Number of units	20	NONE							
5	Column offset	5	=VLOOKUP(B3,B16:C19,2)							
6	Value of order	390	=B4*VLOOKUP(B2,B9:F14,B5)							
7		Size	S	M	L	XL				
8		Product								
9		A	15	17	18	19.5				
10		B	21	26	29	32				
11		C	43	52	67	78				
12		D	3	5	8	9				
13		E	29	34	38	49				
14		F	63	69	73	81				
15		LOOKUP TABLE FOR COLUMN OFFSET VALUE								
16		L	4							
17		M	3							
18		S	2							
19		XL	5							
20										

Microsoft Excel - W2_28.XLS

File Edit View Insert Format Tools Data Window Help

B6 = =B4*VLOOKUP(B2,B9:F14,B5)

Sheet1 / Sheet2 / Sheet3 / Sheet4 / Sheet5 / Sheet

Business modelling using more advanced functions

Contents

Accompanying data files to be loaded as instructed.

None.

3.1. Introduction

In the previous chapter it was shown how Excel could be used to model linear functions in the context of business and economic applications. Unfortunately, however, not all real-life applications can be modelled within a linear framework. To appreciate this, recall that any linear function either rises, falls, or stays constant over its entire range. It cannot, for example, rise and then fall, fall and then rise, or rise, stay constant, and then fall. Linear functions are therefore said to be **monotonic** in the sense that if they start to increase or decrease they will continue to do so monotonously.

Nevertheless, it is clear that there are a variety of business and economic variables that do not always behave in such a monotonic manner. For example, profits, revenues, or unit costs are all capable of changing direction over any given range of sales or output values. For this reason we must define and consider a number of additional mathematical functions that will provide the extra flexibility needed to allow non-linear behaviour to be modelled satisfactorily.

The first of these functions to be considered is known as a **quadratic function**.

3.2. Quadratic functions

A quadratic function is fundamentally distinguished from a linear function by the introduction of a term containing x^2, and can be written in the following form:

$$y = f(x) = ax^2 + bx + c$$

where a, b, and c are constant terms known as **coefficients** or **parameters**.

In its most general form, a quadratic function often represents a U- or inverted U-shaped curve, but the specific shape of the curve is ultimately determined by the values of the coefficients *a*, *b*, and *c*.

Workbook 3.1

To see how these influence the shape that a quadratic curve adopts, prepare Workbook 3.1.
    First, enter the labels and values shown in A1:D3.
    Next, create a flexible range of x values in C4:C22 by using C4 and C5 to contain the formulae:
        =D1   and   =C4+D$2

Then copy C5 into C6:C22.
    Leave D4:D22 blank for the moment—a formula will be written and copied to create these entries.

With the first value for x located in C4, it then follows that the entry in D4 should be:
        =B$1*C4^2+B$2*C4+B$3

This is equivalent to $ax^2 + bx + c$ when it is remembered that B1 contains *a*, B2 contains *b*, B3 contains *c*, and the first value for x is located in C4.

Enter this formula now to D4 and then copy it into D5:D22.

Now you can use this worksheet to investigate the respective properties of the various types of quadratic function, since these are entirely determined by the values adopted by *a*, *b*, and *c*.

	A	B	C	D	E	F	G	H
1	Coefficient of x² (a)	-1	Start value for x	0				
2	Coefficient of x (b)	50	Step value for x	5				
3	Constant (c)	400	x	y				
4			0	400				
5			5	625				
6			10	800				
7			15	925				
8			20	1000				
9			25	1025				
10			30	1000				
11			35	925				
12			40	800				
13			45	625				
14			50	400				
15			55	125				
16			60	-200				
17			65	-575				
18			70	-1000				
19			75	-1475				

Sheet1 / Sheet2 / Sheet3 / Sheet4 / Sheet5 / Sheet6

Workbook 3.1

To aid this investigation, create a chart frame and then define the data range as C4:D22, select an XY scatter graph, and use the first column as the X axis data.

The resulting graph should resemble Fig. 3.1

In respect of the shape that any quadratic graph adopts, three key aspects should be appreciated.

1. The value adopted by c determines where the graph of the function intersects the

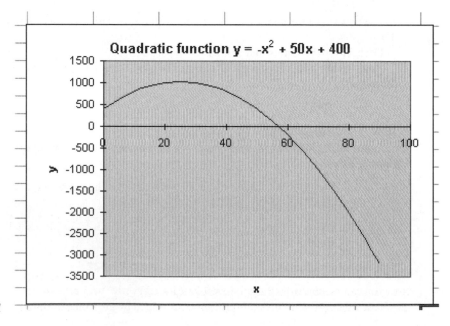

Figure 3.1

vertical axis (since when x = 0, y = f(x) = a(0²) + b(0) + c = c). The value of *c* therefore influences the general position, but not the overall shape, of the graph.

> **To see this, increase the value of *c* from 400 to 450. The general shape of the graph will not change, but for each value of x the value of y will be 50 units more than previously. Confirm this now.**

2. If the value adopted by *a* is negative, then the graph of the function will rise and then fall, while if *a* is positive then the opposite is the case. (If *a* = 0 then the graph becomes linear of course, since this is equivalent to y = bx + c.)

> **To see the effect of a being positive as opposed to negative, restore the value for *c* in B3 to 400 and then change the value in B1 from -1 to 2.**

The graph obtained should now resemble Fig. 3.2.

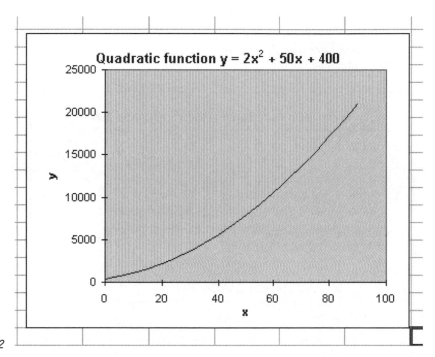

Figure 3.2

3. Whether the graph of any quadratic function intersects the horizontal axis is determined by the algebraic sign of what is known as the **discriminant** of the function. This is defined for:

$$y = ax^2 + bx + c$$

by the following expression:

$$\text{discriminant} = b^2 - 4ac$$

To understand its importance, use the A4 and B4 cells of Workbook 3.1 to contain the following label and formula:

Discriminant   =B2^2-4*B1*B3

Now, if the discriminant is negative, then you will find that there is no intersection between the graph of the function and the horizontal axis.

On the other hand, if the discriminant is greater than 0 then the x axis will be intersected twice, while if it is exactly equal to 0, then the graph of the function will just touch the x axis at one value of x.

Now generate each of these possibilities for yourself by entering the following values for a, b, and c.

1. $a = 0.1, b = 0.1, c = 100$ Discriminant $= 0.1^2 - 4(0.1)(100) = 0.01-40 = -39.99$

The graph of this function ($y = 0.1x^2 + 0.1x + 100$) does not intersect the x axis for any real value of x.

2. $a = 1, b = -100, c = 2100$ Discriminant $= -100^2 - 4(1)(2100) = 10000 - 8400 = 1600$

The graph of this function ($y = x^2 - 100x + 2100$) intersects the x axis twice—at $x = 30$ and $x = 70$.

3. $a = 1, b = -80, c = 1600$ Discriminant $= -80^2 - 4(1)(1600) = 6400 - 6400 = 0$

The graph of this function ($y = x^2 - 80x + 1600$) just touches the x axis at $x = 40$.

These results are confirmed by the graphs shown in Figs. 3.3, 3.4, and 3.5 that should have been obtained.

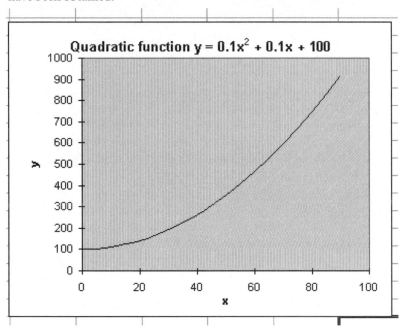

Figure 3.3

Save the file now.

Now, the last two circumstances (discriminant ≥ 0) will often be of interest, since it should be clear that, if the x axis is intersected at all, this implies that the value of the function is 0, and that the intersection value(s) of x represent the **solution value(s)** of the following **quadratic equation:**

$$y = f(x) = ax^2 + bx + c = 0$$

For example, if you alter the step value for x to 0.75, and enter values of a = 1, b = -13, and c = 36, then you should find that the graph of the function intersects the x axis at values of x = 4 and x = 9.

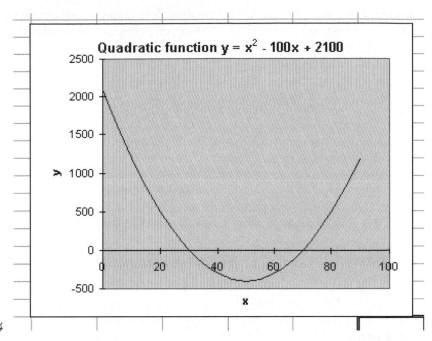

Figure 3.4

Do this now.

These two values ($x_1 = 4$ and $x_2 = 9$) are known as the **characteristic roots** of this quadratic equation, and can be thought of as the values of x which solve the equation formed by setting the functional expression equal to 0.

Hence, in the example under consideration, the selected values for *a*, *b*, and *c* imply that:

$$y = x^2 - 13x + 36$$

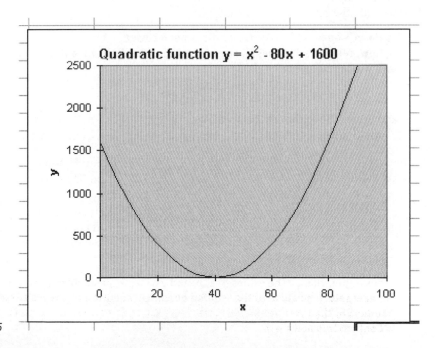

Figure 3.5

Consequently, since the characteristic roots of this equation have been shown to be $x_1 = 4$ and $x_2 = 9$, this means that y will adopt a value of 0 when x is either 4 or 9.

This is easily confirmed as follows.

$$\text{when } x = 4: \quad y = 4^2 - 13(4) + 36 = 0$$
$$\text{when } x = 9: \quad y = 9^2 - 13(9) + 36 = 0$$

Thus $x_1 = 4$ and $x_2 = 9$ are the solution values to the quadratic equation given by:

$$y = x^2 - 13x + 36 = 0$$

In this example, the values chosen for a, b, and c ensured that the graph of the function provided a clear indication of the values of x at which the horizontal axis was intersected. However, the solution values for x will not always be so easily observed from the graph, and for this reason we require an algebraic method of obtaining the exact values of the characteristic roots of any given quadratic function.

This is done by the application of what is known as the **quadratic formula**. This states that the characteristic roots (x_1 and x_2) of the equation:

$$y = ax^2 + bx + c = 0$$

are given by:

$$x_1, x_2 = [-b \pm (b^2 - 4ac)^{0.5}]/2a$$

Accordingly, if we apply this formula to our last illustration (a = 1, b = -1,3 and c = 36) then we obtain:

$$x_1, x_2 = [-(-13) \pm ((13^2 - 4(1)(36))^{0.5}]/(2)(1)$$
$$x_1, x_2 = [13 \pm (169 - 144)^{0.5}]/2$$
$$x_1, x_2 = [13 \pm (25)^{0.5}]/2$$
$$x_1 = (13+5)/2 = 9$$
$$x_2 = (13-5)/2 = 4$$

This confirms the previous result obtained from the graph.

Sometimes the calculations involved in evaluating the quadratic formula can be tedious, so we will now get Excel to do them for us.

To do this open Workbook 3.1, if it has been closed.

Now, remembering that B4 already contains the discriminant, use A5 and A6 to contain the labels:

$$x_1 \quad \text{and} \quad x_2$$

and B5 and B6 to contain the formulae:

$$= (-B2+B4^0.5)/(2*B1) \quad \text{and} \quad = (-B2-B4^0.5)/(2*B1)$$

These two expressions are equivalent to $[-b + (b^2 - 4ac)^{0.5}]/2a$ and $[-b - (b^2 - 4ac)^{0.5}]/2a$ when it is remembered that the values of a and b are held in B1 and B2 respectively, and that the computed value of the discriminant is contained in B4.

Provided you are still using values of a = 1, b = -13, and c = 36, then B5 and B6 will contain the solution values that were obtained earlier ($x_1 = 9$ and $x_2 = 4$).

More importantly however, these formula will adjust automatically to any set of new coefficients that you enter.

For example, change the values of a, b, and c to 1, -12, and 20 and you should find that the new solution values to the implied quadratic equation of $y = x^2 -12x + 20$ are $x_1 = 10$ and $x_2 = 2$.

Confirm this now.

Finally, change the values of a, b, and c to 2, 1, and 3 and you should find that because the discriminant is negative, its square root cannot be computed by Excel and so error messages (#NUM!) are returned for the two characteristic roots.

Notice what this means. It does *not* imply that the quadratic equation ($y = 2x^2 + x + 3$) is illegal, or that it cannot be graphed (the graph should be on screen). It simply means that the graph of this quadratic function does not intersect the horizontal axis for any real value of x, and consequently that there are no real values for x_1 and x_2 that produce a zero value for the equation. In other words, $y = 2x^2 + x + 3 = 0$ cannot be solved for real values of x.

Now save this file as W3_1A.XLS.

As an application of quadratic functions in business, consider the following illustration. In Chapter 2 it was shown that if the price (p) at which a firm sells its product is constant, then the total revenue (R) obtained by selling x units is given by:

$$R = px$$

This is a linear equation emanating from the origin ($R = 0$ when $x = 0$) and rising monotonically as x increases.

However, now suppose that in order to sell more of the product, the price had to be reduced. In other words, suppose that the price charged was an indirect **function** of the number of units sold.

In these circumstances the total revenue obtained is no longer a simple linear function of the number of units sold. Rather, it depends upon the number of units sold (as before), but also upon how the number of units sold have affected the price that is received.

So, suppose that the relation between p and x is given by:

$$p = b - ax$$

(i.e. a linear demand relation in which p decreases as x increases).

It now follows that with the definition of total revenue still being generally given by the price received times the quantity sold, the exact expression for total revenue becomes:

$$R = px = (b - ax)x = bx - ax^2 = -ax^2 + bx$$

This is clearly a quadratic function of the standard form (but with $c = 0$).

Now suppose that $b = 200$ and $a = 5$, implying a revenue function of the form:

$$R = -5x^2 + 200x$$

To see the behaviour of this revenue function, open Workbook 3.1A (W3_1A.XLS) and change the labels in C3 and D3 to:

x (sales)   and   y (revenue)

Save this file immediately as W3_2.XLS.
Then enter the coefficient values (-5, 200, and 0) to the B1, B2, and B3 cells and change the step value for the scale from 5 to 2.5.

The graph obtained should resemble Fig. 3.6, and the solution values for x_1 and x_2 should be returned as 0 and 40, implying that zero revenue is obtained when either 0 units or 40 units are sold. In between these two polar values the revenue function first rises, then flattens out (at its maximum value), and then declines.

Next suppose that, in order to produce the product, a factory had to be leased at a fixed cost of £750 per time period, and that the labour and raw material costs were £25 per unit of the product produced.

Clearly, total cost (C) will be given by the following linear function of x:

$$C = 750 + 25x$$

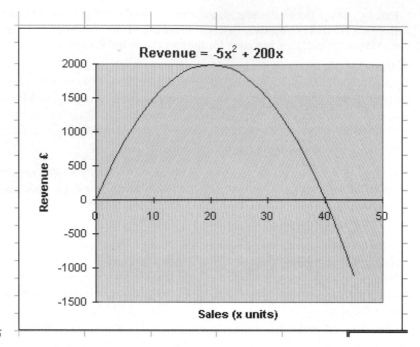

Figure 3.6

To incorporate this extra information into the model in Workbook 3.2 make the following additions.

First, in A8 and A9 enter the labels:

Fixed cost   and   Unit cost

Then enter values of 750 and 25 to B8 and B9.

Next, in E3 and E4 enter the label and the formula:

Total cost   and   =B$8+B$9*C4

and copy E4 into E5:E22.

Finally, double click on the chart to allow editing, select the Chart Wizard and then redefine the data range as C4:E22 to include the new cost information.

Now save the file as W3_2.XLS.

The results should resemble Fig. 3.7 and clearly indicate that the break-even levels of sales are around 5 and 30 units.

Notice that, unlike the case discussed in Chapter 2, where both the revenue and the cost functions were linear, there are now two levels of sales at which break-even occurs.[1] These have been indicated approximately in Fig. 3.7, but can be calculated accurately as follows.

We have:

$$R = -5x^2 + 200x \quad C = 750 + 25x$$

Hence:

$$\text{Profit} = -5x^2 + 200x - 750 - 25x = -5x^2 + 175x - 750$$

For break-even we require that profit is 0.

---

1 This is simply because any two straight lines cannot intersect more than once, whereas a line and a curve can intersect twice.

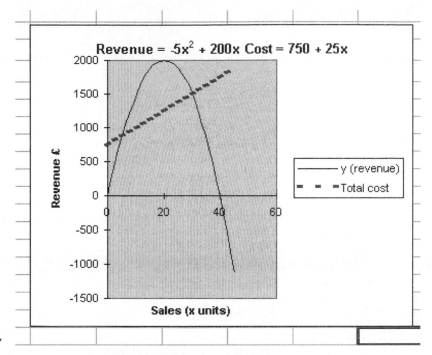

Figure 3.7

Therefore, we require the solution values of:

$$\text{Profit} = -5x^2 + 175x - 750 = 0$$

To find these values, open Workbook 3.1A and use B1, B2, and B3 to contain -5, 175, and -750 respectively.

The values for x_1 and x_2 returned to B5 and B6 should be 5 and 30.

Finally, it should be noted that the parameters of either the revenue function or the cost function, or both, can be such that break-even is not feasible.

To demonstrate this, open Workbook 3.2 (W3_2.XLS) and then increase the fixed element of total cost in B8 from 750 to 2000.

As the graph will indicate, the cost function no longer intersects the revenue function and so break-even is impossible.

Furthermore, it may also be the case that the parameters of the cost and revenue function are such that there is only one break-even level of sales. This will happen in the illustrative example if the (linear) cost function just touches the (quadratic) revenue function at one single value of x.

To demonstrate this make B8 and B9 contain 750 and 75 respectively (implying C = 750 + 75x).

Now it should be found that there is only one break-even value of x—namely, x = 10 with revenue and cost both equal to 1500.

Exercises 3.1 and 3.2 can be attempted now.

3.3. **Cubic functions**

A cubic function can be obtained from a quadratic function simply by adding a term in x^3. Thus:

$$y = ax^3 + bx^2 + cx + d$$

is the general form of any cubic.

We have already seen that a linear function (highest power of x = 1) cannot change direction, and that a quadratic function (highest power of x = 2) can only change direction once. From this we should expect that a cubic function having a highest power of x = 3 can change direction twice. This is indeed the case.

Workbook 3.3

To investigate the properties of any cubic function, open Workbook 3.1 (W3_1.XLS) and, using it as template, make the additions and changes shown in the A1:B4 range of Workbook 3.3.

	A	B	C	D	E	F	G
1	Coefficient of x^3 (a)	0.02	Start value for x	0			
2	Coefficient of x^2 (b)	-0.8	Step value for x	2			
3	Coefficient of x (c)	12	x	y			
4	Constant (d)	1000	0	1000			
5			2	1020.96			
6			4	1036.48			
7			6	1047.52			
8			8	1055.04			
9			10	1060			
10			12	1063.36			
11			14	1066.08			
12			16	1069.12			
13			18	1073.44			
14			20	1080			
15			22	1089.76			
16			24	1103.68			
17			26	1122.72			
18			28	1147.84			
19			30	1180			

Sheet1 / Sheet2 / Sheet3 / Sheet4 / Sheet5 / Sheet

Then change the formula in D4 to:

=B$1*C4^3+B$2*C4^2+B$3*C4+B$4

If you use the values for *a*, *b*, *c*, and *d* indicated in the worksheet (a = 0.02, b = -0.8, c = 12, and d = 1000) then Fig. 3.8 should be obtained.[2]

Save this file now as W3_3.XLS.

The class of curve shown in Fig. 3.8 is frequently used in economics to represent the behaviour of total costs (y) in terms of output (x).

---

2 Your own graph may not appear exactly as shown, but you can achieve the illustrated effect if you double click on the graph to allow editing and then double click on any value on the vertical scale. Now select Scale from the menu that appears and set the minimum value to 900.

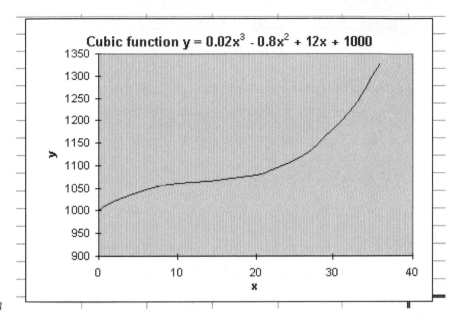

Figure 3.8

Thus, when output equals 0 the fixed costs are given by d.

As x increases, so too do total costs, but in such a manner that the rate of increase at first declines. This means that the slope of the curve tends to flatten out (implying that total costs at this stage are not increasing significantly as output expands).

Eventually, however, further increases in output cause total costs to start rising again, and this time they do so at an increasing rate. The total cost curve therefore becomes steeper and steeper.

Given this typical behaviour of the total cost function, there are implications for the behaviour of average costs.

To appreciate these implications, make the following additions to Workbook 3.3. First use E3 to contain the label:

    Average costs

Now, since average costs are defined as total costs per unit of output, it follows that the entry in E4 should be the total cost (D4) divided by the number of units produced (C4).

Consequently in E4 enter:

    =D4/C4

and copy this into E5:E22.

Now observe that the entry in E4 is #DIV/0!

This means that to obtain a satisfactory graph of average costs versus output we should ignore the entries in C4 and E4.

Consequently, draw a new frame and define the data range as C5:C22,E5:E22.
    Now increase the value of the step in which x increases from 2 to 5, and after adding labels the effect should resemble Fig. 3.9.

This is the typical U-shaped average cost curve that elementary economic theory predicts.

Exercise 3.3 can be attempted now.

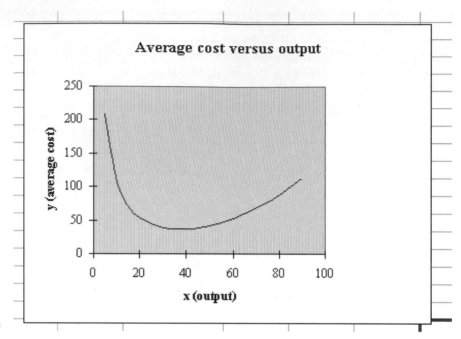

Figure 3.9

3.4. **Asymptotic functions**

An asymptote is simply the mathematical name used to describe a curve that gets closer and closer to one or more straight lines without ever actually touching any of them. Frequently these straight lines will be the horizontal and/or vertical axes.

Asymptotic functions are frequently created when some average quantity is being modelled, since this will often involve dividing the function representing the total by x, and will create difficulties if any constant term contained in the function has to be divided by an x value of 0. They are also created when an x value used as a divisor becomes infinitely large. This can be seen quite clearly in the following example.

The quarterly bill for domestic gas is made up of two components, a standing charge of £15 per quarter and a variable charge of £0.4 per unit consumed. This means that the total bill (y) will clearly be given in terms of units consumed (x) by the following linear function:

$$y = 15 + 0.4x$$

From this, it follows that the cost per unit consumed (c) will be given by:

$$c = (15 + 0.4x)/x = 15/x + 0.4$$

Inspection of this expression indicates that when 0 units are consumed the cost per unit is infinite (since $15/0 = \infty$), but that as the number of units consumed increases, the term $15/x$ gets smaller and smaller. This means that c will get closer and closer to a value of £0.4, but will never quite get there.

Therefore, the expression: $c = 15/x + 0.4$ is asymptotic to the horizontal line with a value on the vertical axis of 0.4.

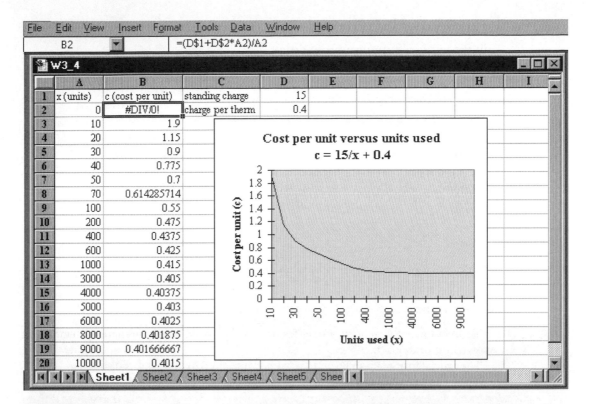

File Edit View Insert Format Tools Data Window Help

B2 =(D$1+D$2*A2)/A2

W3_4

	A	B	C	D	E	F	G	H	I
1	x (units)	c (cost per unit)	standing charge	15					
2	0	#DIV/0!	charge per therm	0.4					
3	10	1.9							
4	20	1.15							
5	30	0.9							
6	40	0.775							
7	50	0.7							
8	70	0.614285714							
9	100	0.55							
10	200	0.475							
11	400	0.4375							
12	600	0.425							
13	1000	0.415							
14	3000	0.405							
15	4000	0.40375							
16	5000	0.403							
17	6000	0.4025							
18	8000	0.401875							
19	9000	0.401666667							
20	10000	0.4015							

Sheet1 / Sheet2 / Sheet3 / Sheet4 / Sheet5 / Shee

Cost per unit versus units used

$c = 15/x + 0.4$

Workbook 3.4

To see this, open a new workbook and make the entries indicated in Workbook 3.4.

The values and labels in A1:A20 were entered directly, as were the labels and values in B1 and C1:D2.

The formula in B2 is:

=(D$1+D$2*A2)/A2

and this was copied into B3:B20.

Notice the error message that is returned to B2 when Excel tries to divide by zero.

The range for the graph was A3:B20 (to exclude the #DIV/0! entry in B2), and a line graph was selected.

When you have made all the entries save the file as W3_4.XLS.

Clearly, the value of c is approaching a value of £0.4 as the value of x increases, and is therefore asymptotic to a value of c = 0.4 on the x axis. In other words, as x tends to infinity, c tends towards £0.4 per unit used.[3]

Exercise 3.4 can be attempted now.

---

3 The cost per unit is also asymptotic to the vertical axis, since as the number of units used gets closer and closer to zero, the cost per unit approaches infinity.

3.5. **Exponential functions**

The linear, quadratic, and cubic functions that have previously been explained are all members of a general class of function known as **polynomials**.

The general form of such a function is given by:

$$y = a_0 + a_1x + a_2x^2 + a_3x^3 + \ldots a_nx^n$$

With a view to subsequent discussion, the important point to note is that the variable (x) is the **base** to which the various constant powers (or exponents) are applied.

An exponential function, on the other hand, reverses this process and uses the variable as the **exponent** to be applied to a constant base. For example:

$$y = x^2 \text{ is a polynomial function}$$

whereas:

$$y = 2^x \text{ is an exponential function.}$$

The general form of an exponential function is given by:

$$y = ab^{cx}$$

where *a*, *b*, and *c* are the parameters of the function.

Workbook 3.5

To investigate the general properties of this class of function, prepare the worksheet shown in Workbook 3.5.

The crucial formula is in B5 and was copied into B6:B20.

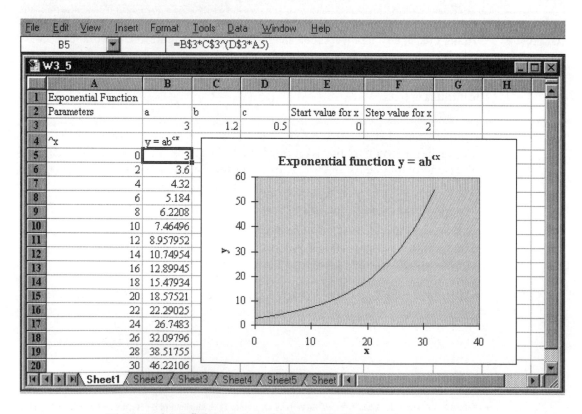

When you have finished, save the file as W3_5.XLS.

This model can now be used to confirm the following general properties of the exponential class of function.

As a general rule it is the **sign** of c and the **magnitude** of b that exercise the greatest influence on the overall appearance of the graph of the function.

To understand the influence exerted by the values of b and c, three things should be appreciated.

1. For positive values of a and c, the value of ab^{cx} will increase as x increases if b is greater than 1, and decrease if b is less than one.

Confirm this now in Workbook 3.5 by changing the value of b from 1.2 to 0.8.

The graph should change from rising when b was greater than 1 to falling when b is less than 1.

2. For negative values of c the value of ab^{cx} will decrease as x increases if b is greater than 1 and increase if b is less than 1.

Confirm this now by changing the value of c from 0.5 to -1.

With b = 0.8 and a still positive the graph will increase, but will fall if b is increased back to its original value of 1.2.

3. The value of a determines the value at which the curve cuts the vertical axis. This is because when x = 0, y = ab^0 = a.

The value of a also influences how steeply the curve rises or falls. If the curve is rising it will do so more rapidly the greater is the value of a (for given values of b and c). Similarly, if the curve is falling, it will do so more rapidly the larger is the value of a (again for given values of b and c).

Exponential functions with b < 0 can be useful in a number of modelling circumstances because they approach the x axis in a way that often represents a much more realistic description of many types of business variable. Asset value as a function of time, sales, or market share as a function of price are just a few examples of this. These variables rarely decline in a simple linear manner that could eventually lead to negative values for y. Rather, they usually get closer and closer to the horizontal axis without ever quite reaching it. Such behaviour has been noted in the section on asymptotic functions, but the simple functions used there behave in a way that does not allow the modelling process as much control over the way in which the function approaches the x axis as does the exponential class of function. For example, suppose that the value of a firm's assets (y) are believed to depend upon the passage of time (x) as follows:

$$y = 2500(1.25^{-0.9x})$$

This means that, in terms of y = ab^{cx}, a = 2500, b = 1.25, and c = -0.9.

Enter these values now to the appropriate cells of Workbook 3.5.

As the graph that should now appear on screen indicates, the value of the firm's assets approach a value of 0 as time increases. However, the behaviour is asymptotic, and implies that a zero asset value will never actually be reached.

It is now time to mention a special type of exponential function that has a widespread currency in business and economics.

We have seen that the base of any exponential function is denoted by b, but there is a special case in which the value of b is taken as 2.7182. This number is known as e, and possesses a number of remarkable properties that are of particular use in modelling. Clearly, this means that if:

$$b = e = 2.7182$$

then the expression for the exponential class of function becomes:

$$y = ae^{cx}$$

Since this is no more than a special case, the previous comments that have been made about the general behaviour of this class of function remain valid.

A full appreciation of the special additional properties possessed by exponential functions with a base of e must wait until later in the text, so at the moment it will simply be necessary to obtain a graph of the function.

To do this, open Workbook 3.5 if it has been closed and make the following entry to the C3 cell.

$$=EXP(1)$$

This is the Excel version of the number e and should return a value of 2.7182.

Now change the value for c in D3 from negative to positive (after altering the scale necessary if) and confirm that $y = ae^{cx}$ is simply a special case of an exponential function with $b > 1$.

In other words, with c being positive, the function rises monotonically for positive values of x, while with c being negative it declines monotonically and asymptotically to the x axis for positive values of x.

Confirm this now in your own worksheet.

Finally, we should note that although the Excel function $=EXP(1)$ is equivalent to e^1, different powers of e are easily calculated.

For example: $=EXP(0.6)$ is equivalent to $e^{0.6}$; $=EXP(-0.1)$ is equivalent to $e^{-0.1} = 1/e^{0.1}$; and $=EXP(A1)$ is equivalent to e^{A1}.

This last expression means that if, for example, the A1 cell contains the product of c and x (i.e. cx), then $= EXP(A1)$ is equivalent to e^{cx}.

Exercise 3.5 can be attempted now.

3.6. Logarithmic functions

To appreciate the behaviour of the class of functions known as logarithmic functions, it is first of all necessary to understand the concept of a logarithm. This is defined in terms of a variable (x) and a base (b) as follows.

The logarithm of x to the base b is the power to which b must be raised in order to equal x. We write this in general terms as: $\log_b x$, i.e. the logarithm of x to the base b.

From this definition we can derive the following illustrations.

$$\log_2 16 = 4 \qquad \text{since } 2^4 = 16$$
$$\log_{10} 100 = 2 \qquad \text{since } 10^2 = 100$$
$$\log_{10} 1000 = 3 \qquad \text{since } 10^3 = 3$$
$$\log_b 1 = 0 \qquad \text{since } b^0 = 1$$

Note that this last result is completely general—the logarithm of 1 to any base is always zero, since any base to the power of zero is always 1.

Now notice that in each of the illustrations the 'convenience' of the x values and the bases was such that the logarithms were easily calculated by simple arithmetic.

However, what would be the value of $\log_{10}500$? To answer this question we can argue as follows:

We know that $\log_{10}100 = 2$ and that $\log_{10}1000 = 3$.
Hence we should expect that $\log_{10}500$ lies between 2 and 3. But where exactly?

**Workbook
3.6**

To find out, open a new workbook and make the entries shown in Workbook 3.6.

	A	B	C	D	E	F	G	H	I
1	Number (x)	500							
2	Base (b)	10							
3	Guess for logarithm	2.5							
4	b$^{\text{guess for logarithm}}$	316.2278	The formula in B4 is =B2^B3						
5									

File Edit View Insert Format Tools Data Window Help
H2
W3_6
Sheet1 Sheet2 Sheet3 Sheet4 Sheet5 Shee

With this workbook established, keep changing the guess for the logarithm of 500 to the base 10 (in B3) until the value in B4 becomes equal to the required value of 500.

Eventually, this trial-and-error approach should produce a value of 2.69897 as the logarithm of 500 to the base 10.

Confirm this now.

However, although this method works it is needlessly tedious, since all we have to do is use the Excel function called =LOG(number).

To see how this works, add the following label and formula to the A5 and B5 cells of the workbook.

$\quad$ $\log_{10}x$ $\quad$ and $\quad$ =LOG(B1)

The value previously obtained of 2.69897 should be returned to B5.

Now confirm our previous observation that the logarithm of 1 is zero by changing the value in B1 to 1.

A value of 0 will be returned to B5.

**Furthermore, if you now enter a value of 0 to B1 then you will find that Excel returns an error message (#NUM!), since there is no mechanism whereby raising a positive base to any given power can produce a result which is 0 or negative.
Confirm this now.**

For this reason the logarithm of 0, and of all negative numbers, is undefined.

This does not mean, however, that a logarithm itself cannot adopt a negative value (it is the logarithm of a negative number that is undefined). In fact, since the logarithm of 1 is always 0, it should be suspected that the logarithm of any number lying between 0 and 1 will be negative. This is indeed the case.

Confirm this now by entering a value of 0.6 to B1, whereupon a value of -0.2218 will be returned to B5.

What this means is that the required power to which 10 must be raised in order to equal 0.6 is negative, and that as a result a reciprocal has been formed. In other words:

$\log_{10} 0.6 = -0.2218$ because:
$10^{-0.2218} = 1/10^{0.2218} = 0.6$

Or, as another example:

$\log_{10} 0.1 = -1$ because:
$10^{-1} = 1/10 = 0.1$

Now prepare the following workbook to see some of the further implications of logarithmic expressions.

	A	B	C	D	E	F	G	H	I
1	Value of x	5							
2	Log x	0.69897							
3	Value of y	20							
4	Log y	1.30103							
5	Log x + Log y	2							
6	$10^{(\log x + \log y)}$	100							

W3_7

Sheet1 / Sheet2 / Sheet3 / Sheet4 / Sheet5 / Shee

Workbook 3.7

The entries in B2 and B4 are :

=LOG(B1)   and   LOG(B3)

while the entries in B5 and B6 are:

=B2+B4   and   =10^B5

Now enter a value of 5 in B1 and a value of 20 in B3.

You will find that the result in B5 is 2, and that B6 contains 100. But what is the significance of these results?

We know that the product of 5 and 20 is 100, and that the logarithm of 100 to the base 10 is 2. We also know that $10^2 = 100$, and that $\log_{10} 5 + \log_{10} 20 = 2$.

This should suggest that adding the logarithms of any two numbers is performing a process that is equivalent to multiplying the two numbers together. It should also suggest that when the resulting sum of the two logarithms is used as the index to which 10 is raised, then the product of the two numbers is obtained.

In other words, if x and y are any two positive numbers then:

$xy = 10^{(\log_{10} x + \log_{10} y)}$

The reason for this is easy to understand, since all the process of taking logarithms does is express each number in index form as a power of 10.

For example, suppose you want to multiply 100 by 1000. The answer is clearly 100000. But, using indices we can express (100)(1000) as:

$(10^2)(10^3)$ which is equal to:
$10^{(2+3)} = 10^5 = 100000$

Furthermore, as has already been seen, the logarithms to the base 10 of 100 and 1000 are 2 and 3 respectively, and so their sum is 5. Consequently:

$10^{(\log_{10} 100 + \log_{10} 1000)} = 10^{(2+3)} = 10^5 = 100000$

This discussion can be summarized by one of the first rules of logarithmic operations:

If $z = xy$ where x and y are both > 0

Then:

$\log z = \log x + \log y$

It will be noticed that we have not defined a base for these logarithms in this case. This is because it is a general statement that is true regardless of the base employed.

By a similar logic we would also argue that if:

$z = x/y$ where x and y are both > 0

then, since this could be rewritten as:

$z = x(y^{-1})$ it follows that:
$\log z = \log x - \log y$

Now suppose that two numbers of the same magnitude are to be multiplied together. In other words, we require:

$z = (x)(x)$ where $x > 0$

By our basic rule of logarithms we can write:

$\log z = \log x + \log x = 2(\log x)$

In other words, the logarithm of the square of any number is twice the logarithm of that number.

Now this should give us an idea for a more general rule, since, following the previous logic, we would expect that:

$\log (x^3) = 3(\log x)$ and that:
$\log (x^5) = 5(\log x)$ and that:
$\log (x^n) = n(\log x)$

This last line means that if, for example, we have an equation such as:

$y = x^n$ then:
$\log_b y = n(\log_b x)$ and:
$\log_b x = (\log_b y)/n$ whereby:
$x = b^{\left[(\log_b y)/n\right]}$

For example, if:

$y = x^{3.5}$ then by the rules of indices:
$x = y^{1/3.5} = y^{0.2857142}$
So, if $y = 45$ then $x = 45^{0.2857142} = 2.96719$

Alternatively, taking logarithms to the base 10:

$x = 10^{\,\log_{10} 45/3.5}$
$x = 10^{1.6532125/3.5} = 10^{0.4723464} = 2.96719$

Once again, it is easy to see that logarithmic operations are no more than a modification of the rules of indices.

This being the case, it may then be asked why time has been spent on what is apparently no more than an alternative to the rules of indices. The answer is that there are circumstances which arise from certain types of equation which require that logarithms are used in order to provide a solution. Knowledge of index operations alone will not be enough in these cases.

These types of equation derive from the exponential class of function and must be solved as follows. Suppose we have:

$$y = ab^{cx}$$

and are required to solve for x.

Using the most recently explained rule of logarithms, we can rewrite this expression as follows.[4]

$$\log y = \log a + cx \log b$$

Then, transferring terms, we have

$$cx = (\log y - \log a)/\log b$$

whereupon:

$$x = (\log y - \log a)/c \log b$$

For example, suppose a region's population (y) grows over time (x) in such a way that the value of y is always given by:

$$y = 1000000(1.2^{0.1x})$$

Now imagine that we are required to calculate the length of time before the region's population first reaches 2000000.

We clearly require to find the value of x such that:

$2000000 = 1000000(1.2^{0.1x})$ or dividing both sides by 1 million, x such that:
$2 = 1.2^{0.1x}$

Therefore:

$\log 2 = 0.1x \log 1.2$
$0.1x = \log 2/\log 1.2$
$x = 10 \log 2/\log 1.2 = 10(0.30103)/0.0791812 = 3.0103/0.0791812 = 38.02$ time periods

Clearly the use of logarithms is the only analytical method of solving for the exponent in the exponential class of functions.

Finally, it should be noted that up until now only logarithms to the base 10 have been considered. However, there is another base that is frequently encountered when working with logarithms. This is the base e = 2.7182, usually written as ln x, and calculates what is known as the natural logarithm of x (as opposed to the common logarithm, when a base of 10 is used).

Excel supports logarithms to both bases of e and 10. The latter has already been encountered as =LOG(number), and the syntax of the former is =LN(number).

Thus, for example, if A1 is made to contain 60, then =LOG(A1) will return a value of 1.7781, while =LN(A1) will return a value of 4.0943.

Confirm this now in any vacant cell of a blank workbook.
Exercise 3.6 can be attempted now.

---

4   If this does not make sense, imagine that c and x are 2 and 3 respectively, so that cx = 6.
    Then $y = ab^6$.
    Now let $b^6 = m$, so that the expression for y becomes y = am.
    Then log y = log a + log m.
    But we know that $m = b^6$.
    So $\log m = \log(b^6) = 6 \log b$. Therefore log y = log a + 6 log b = log a + cx log b.

3.7. **Logistic functions**

A logistic function is a function in which the value of y increases steadily with increases in the value of x, but does so in such a way that as the value of x becomes large, the increase in the value of y eventually becomes very close to zero. In other words, as the value of x becomes very large the value of y approaches some constant limiting value.

Logistic functions are useful for modelling processes that are subject to **saturation**. For example, as advertising expenditure rises, sales volume will usually rise quite rapidly at first. However, as more and more is spent on advertising, the effect of each extra pound of expenditure often becomes less and less until the effect upon sales volume becomes negligible. This is the saturation effect.[5]

One of the most commonly encountered forms of logistic function is given by:

$$y = a(1 - e^{-cx})$$

where *a* and *c* are the parameters of the expression and e = 2.71828.

Workbook 3.8

To investigate the behaviour of this function more closely, open a new workbook and make up the model indicated in Workbook 3.8.

The crucial formula in B4 is shown on the Formula bar and was copied into B5:B19.

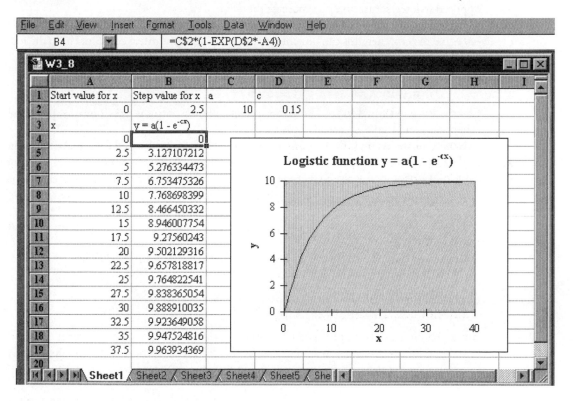

---

5 Another example is to be found in terms of the Principle of Diminishing Returns, where the eventual effect of applying more and more amounts of some resource to a fixed amount of another resource eventually means that there is no appreciable increase in the output obtained.

With the values for a and c indicated in the workbook, it is clear that the value of y commences at 0 when x = 0 and then rises towards a limiting value of 10.

Workbook 3.8 can now be used to confirm the following general features of this type of logistic function.

1. The value of y when x = 0 is given by 0.

This is because when x = 0; $y = a(1 - e^{-0}) = a(1 - 1) = a(0) = 0$.

2. The constant limiting value that y approaches is always given by the value of a.

This is because when $x = \infty$; $y = a(1 - e^{-\infty}) = a(1 - 0) = a$.

Both of these features are easily seen from the graph in Workbook 3.8.

3. The speed with which the value of y approaches the constant limit is determined by the value of c.

With the illustrated value of $c = 0.15$, the saturation process clearly only really begins to take effect once x exceeds a value of about 20.

However, now change the value of c from 0.15 to 0.9 and it will be found that saturation sets in much earlier (for x values roughly in excess of 5).

This clearly means that, for any given value of c, the way to make the model exhibit early, as opposed to later, saturation is to increase the value of c.

Finally, it should be noted that if the model to be created is to start at a value of y that is *not* equal to zero, then this can be achieved by including an additive constant (b) in the following manner.

$$y = a(1 - e^{-cx}) + b$$
$$\text{Then, when } x = 0, y = a(1 - 1) + b = b$$

Clearly, if b is set equal to zero then this model collapses into the previous one, but in all other cases y will have a value of b when x = 0.

Notice, however, that the introduction of the term in b has also had the effect of altering the limiting value of the function. That is, the function will now asymptotically approach a value of $a + b$ rather than a value of a as before.

Exercise 3.7 can be attempted now.

3.8. **Algebraic series**

Any algebraic series is simply a collection of numerical terms in which each term is related to the previous one by a known relationship. It is the fact that there is such a known relationship which distinguishes a series from any other haphazard collection of numerical terms.

The exact nature of the relationship between each term and the previous one can adopt a variety of forms, but as long as a pattern can be identified, then order is brought to the terms and more general investigation can be carried out.

Spreadsheets are an ideal vehicle for creating algebraic series, since once the pattern has been established the copying facility can easily generate the series for as many terms as are required.

3.8.1. Arithmetic series

One of the simplest series identifiable is known as an arithmetic series (or progression), and is characterized by the fact that each term differs from the previous term by a constant amount.

An arithmetic series has already been encountered when creating the flexible scales used for graphing functions, since these took a starting value and then added a constant step amount to each x value in order to obtain the next value of x. This is exactly what is meant by an arithmetic series.

However, when dealing with more complex series there are a few points of definition that have to be established in order to further understanding. Viewed in terms of their pattern the numbers:

$$4, 7, 10, 13$$

are the first 4 terms of an arithmetic series in which the first term (start value) is 4, and in which the common difference (step value) is 3.

This common difference can be positive or negative, and is often denoted by the symbol d. Furthermore, the first term in the series is usually denoted by a, the number of terms in the series by n, and the nth term in the series by u_n.

In this notation u_n is a subscripted variable, with the subscript defining any particular term in the series. So, for example, u_1 is the first term of the series (a), u_4 is the fourth term, and u_n is the nth term.

Using this notation means that any arithmetic series can be generally represented by the following statement:

$$u_n = u_{n-1} + d \text{ or: } u_n - u_{n-1} = d$$

With these ideas established, we can put them into practice in a worksheet.

Workbook 3.9   **Open a new workbook and make the entries indicated in Workbook 3.9 and explained below.**

The term numbers (n) were created by entering a value of 1 to the A4 cell, and then using the A5 cell to contain:

$$=A4+1$$

This was then copied down into A6:A19.

The first term (a) and the common difference (d) were located in C1 and C2 respectively and the following formulae in B4 and B5:

$$=C1 \quad \text{and} \quad =B4+C\$2$$

The entry in B5 was then copied down into B6:B19.

Clearly this has produced the first 16 terms of the series, but if more are required all that needs to be done is copy A19:B19 further down the sheet.

However, although the workbook has generated the first 16 terms of the series effortlessly, there could be circumstances in which we only require to know the value of one term—the 13th, say. Using the worksheet approach, the only way to obtain the value of this term is to evaluate the previous 12 terms, so that the 13th term can be obtained by adding the common difference to the 12th. With only a few terms this is hardly a problem, but with a large number of terms it can use up a lot of worksheet space.

Clearly, it would be preferable if we could obtain some algebraic expression that will identify the value of any one specified term in the series without having to evaluate all the previous ones.

To derive this expression we can argue as follows:

| | L1 | ▼ | | Term number | | | | | | | | |

W3_9

	A	B	C	D	E	F	G	H	I
1		First term in series (a)	5						
2		Common difference (d)	3						
3	Term number (n)	Term value (u$_n$)							
4	1	5							
5	2	8							
6	3	11							
7	4	14							
8	5	17							
9	6	20							
10	7	23							
11	8	26							
12	9	29							
13	10	32							
14	11	35							
15	12	38							
16	13	41							
17	14	44							
18	15	47							
19	16	50							
20									

Sheet1 / Sheet2 / Sheet3 / Sheet4 / Sheet5 / She

Workbook 3.9

Term number	1	2	3	4	5…	12…	n
Term value	a	a + d	a + 2d	a + 3d	a + 4d…	a + 11d…	a + (n - 1)d

This clearly means that:

$$u_n = a + (n-1)d$$

We can incorporate this result into Workbook 3.9 as follows.

In D1 enter the label:

Term number

and in E1 enter the numerical value of the required term number (say 6). Then in F1 enter the label:

is

and in G1 the formula:

=C1+(E1-1)*C2

Assuming that the first term and common difference are still 5 and 3 respectively, the D1:G1 cells should show:

Term number   6   is   20

Now consider the following example.

A firm's workforce currently consists of 10 employees, but 4 new employees are added each year. Calculate the size of the workforce after 16 years.

The answer is clearly the 16th term in an arithmetic series with a = 10 and d = 4. Thus:

$$u_{16} = 10 + 15(4) = 70$$

Confirm this now in Workbook 3.9 by making the appropriate entries to the C1, C2, and E1 cells.

Now suppose we were required to find the total number of employees who were employed over the entire 16-year period.

The answer is clearly:

$$10 + 14 + 18 + \ldots + 70$$

To get the worksheet to compute this total, make the following additions.
In C3 add the label:

Sum of terms

and in C4 enter the formula:

=SUM(B$4:B4)

and copy this into C5:C16 to create a running total of the numbers in column B.

As is clear from the entry in C19, a total of 640 employees have been employed over the entire period.

This figure is known as the sum of the first 16 terms in the arithmetic series.

Once again however, although the worksheet has supplied the answer, it can often be better to derive and include a formula that will sum the first n terms in the series, without having to evaluate the sum of all of the previous terms.

Defining the sum of the first n terms in an arithmetic series as S_n, it can be shown, after some algebra, that:

$$S_n = n/2[2a + (n - 1)d]$$

Hence, with n = 16, a = 10, and d = 4, we have:

$$S_n = 16/2[(2)(10) + (16 - 1)(4)] = 8[20 + 15(4)] = 8(80) = 640$$

which is the result that was obtained earlier.

For ease of calculation, we should now incorporate this formula into the most recent version of Workbook 3.9 as follows.

In D2 enter the label:

Sum of first

and in E2 enter the numerical value of the required term number (16 in this case).
Then in F2 enter the label:

terms is

and in G2 the formula:

=E2/2*(2*C1+(E2-1)*C2)

With a = 10 and d = 4, the D1:G1 cells should show:

Sum of first   16   terms is   640

Exercise 3.8 can be attempted now.

3.8.2. Geometric series

The next important series is known as a **geometric series** and is characterized by a constant **common ratio** (or factor) as opposed to a common difference in arithmetic series. This means that each term in a geometric series is a constant multiple of the previous term. For example, the series:

10, 20, 40, 80, 160 . . .

is characterized by the fact that each term is exactly twice the previous term, while the series:

100, 50, 25, 12.5 . . .

has each term being exactly half the previous term.

Therefore, they can be thought of as geometric series in which the first terms are respectively 10 and 100, and in which the common factors are 2 and 0.5 respectively. More generally, if we denote this common factor by m, then we can define any geometric series by the following statement:

$u_n = m \, u_{n-1}$ or: $u_n / u_{n-1} = m$

You should be able to see that if m is greater than 1 the terms in the series are increasing in magnitude, but if m is less than 1 the terms are decreasing in magnitude, while if m is equal to 1 the terms are all identical and equal to the first term.

A geometric series can be an extremely useful modelling device if, for example, we were required to force some base value (a) to increase at a rate of (say) 10% per period. Under these circumstances, the behaviour of the base value could be represented by a geometric series in which the common factor was 1.1. That is:

Term number	1	2	3	4	etc.
Term value	a	a(1.1)	a(1.1)(1.1)	a(1.1)(1.1)(1.1)	etc.
Term value	a	a(1.1)	a(1.1²)	a(1.1³)	etc.

Inspection of the pattern should now suggest that any term (u^n) in this geometric series can be calculated from:

$u_n = a(1.1^{n-1})$

Alternatively, if the base value were required to decrease at a rate of 10% per time period then we could use a geometric series in which the common factor was 0.9 (i.e. 1- 0.1).That is:

Term number	1	2	3	4	etc.
Term value	a	a(0.9)	a(0.9)(0.9)	a(0.9)(0.9)(0.9)	etc.
Term value	a	a(0.9)	a(0.9²)	a(0.9³)	etc.

Inspection of this pattern should now suggest that any term (u_n) in this geometric series can be calculated from:

$u_n = a(0.9^{n-1})$

Furthermore, if a common factor of m is applied to a base value of a, the then nth term in the series will be given by:

$u_n = a(m^{n-1})$

In general, if some base value (a) is required to grow at a rate of g% per period (or decline at g% per period), then the behaviour of the variable can be modelled by a geometric series in which the common factor (m) is (1+g/100) for positive growth, or (1-g/100) for negative growth (decline).

The behaviour of any geometric series can be investigated by using Workbook 3.9 as a template and making the following alterations.

Load Workbook 3.9 (W3_9.XLS) now.

First, change the label in B2 from common difference to common factor and change the values in C1 and C2 to 100 and 1.1 respectively.

Next, since any term in the series is now defined as the previous term times the common factor, change the formula in B5 from:

=B4+C$2   to   =B4*C$2

and then copy B5 into B6:B19.

Column B now contains each of the first 16 terms in this geometric series, while column C, without any adjustment, contains the sum of the terms.

However, you will notice that the values computed in G1 and G2 no longer match the terms and sums in columns B and C. This is because the formulae in G1 and G2 will have to be altered to reflect the logic of a geometric as opposed to an arithmetic series.

The first alteration is easily done, since we have already seen that:

$$u_n = a(m^{n-1})$$

Hence with *a* contained in C1, *m* contained in C2, and *n* contained in E1 we can write the expression for u_n in terms of cell references as:

=C1*(C2^(E1-1))

Enter this expression now to the G1 cell.

You should find that with a = 100, m = 1.1, and n = 8, the nth term is returned to G1 as 194.8717 and now tallies with the value in B11.

Now, however, deriving a formula for the sum of the first n terms in a geometric series is a bit more complex that in an arithmetic series. The reason for this is that the expression derived for the sum of the first n terms in a geometric series is different depending upon whether the common factor is greater than or less than one. To be exact:

When m > 1:
$$S_n = a(m^n - 1)/(m - 1)$$
But, when m < 1:
$$S_n = a(1 - m^n)/(1 - m)$$

This means that the formula to be applied in G2 must be made conditional upon whether the value of m in C2 is greater than or less than 1.

Consequently we should write an =IF statement such as the following.

=IF(C2>1,C1*(C2^E2-1)/(C2-1),C1*(1-C2^E2)/(1-C2))

Do this now, and then confirm that the sum of the first 13 terms is 2452.271, and that this now tallies with the value in the C16 cell.[6]
If it does, save this file now as W3_10.XLS.

Now use this model to consider the following example.

A manager's annual salary was £10000 for the year 1990 and was increased by 20% per annum in each of the subsequent 5 years. Find both the salary earned in 1995 and the total salary earned over the entire period (i.e. after the inclusion of the 1995 salary).

....

6 It may have been noticed that we have not stated the formula for the sum of the first n terms in a geometric series in which m is exactly equal to 1. In this case the formula in G2 will always return an error message, since either version of the formula will be forced to divide by a denominator that is 0. However, if m = 1 then each term is the same as the first term, and so the sum of the first n terms is simply (na).

To do this, we note that total income earned in the years 1990–5 inclusive is given by the sum of the first 6 terms of the geometric series with:

a = 10000, and m = 1.2

Consequently, using Workbook 3.10, we should enter values of 10000 to C1, 1.2 to C2, and 6 to E1 and E2.

Do this now.

You should find that the annual earnings in 1995 are £24883.2 and the earnings over the entire period are £99299.2.

Exercise 3.9 can be attempted now.

3.9. Exercises

Exercise 3.1

A firm sells its product in a market where the demand is given by:

$$p = 1000 - 2x$$

where p represents the price charged, and x represents the annual quantity demanded of the product, expressed in appropriate units.

The firm also receives income from the lease of a property which produces an annual income of £1 million.

The firm's total costs of production (c) are known to be given by:

$$c = x^2 + 500x + 750000$$

Use Workbook 3.1A to calculate the output levels that make the firm break even.

Exercise 3.2

A local authority has just taken delivery of a new bridge at a total cost of £10 million.

(i) Assuming that there are no maintenance costs, what price (p) should be charged per crossing if the local authority requires to recover 5% of the total cost in the first year, and if the annual number of crossings (x) depends upon the price as follows:

$$x = 1 - 0.01p$$

(where x is measured in millions)?

(ii) If, in addition to the fixed cost of £10 million, there were maintenance costs of £0.03 per crossing, what price would now have to be charged if 5% of the fixed cost and all of the annual maintenance costs had to be recovered in the first year?

Exercise 3.3

A firm's quarterly profits (£y) are known to have varied over time (x) in a manner that is given by:

$$y = x^3 - 15x^2 + 63x + 10000$$

(i) Prepare a graph indicating the behaviour of profits with regard to x over the range x = 0 to x = 10.8.

The threshold for a corporate tax rate on profits of 15% to apply is £10050.

(ii) Prepare a graph indicating the behaviour of the firm's tax liability over the period.

Exercise 3.4

A firm's capital equipment has a value of 0.5 million just now, and depreciates in such a way that its eventual scrap value is never less than £0.05 million.

Derive an asymptotic function that will describe the behaviour of the value (v) of the firm's assets over time (x months).

Graph this derived function for x values between 0 and 180 in steps of 10.

Exercise 3.5

A firm's accountant has estimated that the value (v) of any asset that the company purchases depreciates over time (t) in accordance with:

$$v = ae^{-0.2t}$$

where a is the initial purchase value of the asset (i.e. v = a when t = 0).

For tax purposes however, the government employs a depreciation function that is given by:

$$v = a/(1 + 0.5t)$$

(i) For values of t between 0 and 20 in steps of 0.5, prepare a suitably labelled and titled graph comparing the firm's evaluation of the value of an asset that was purchased for £10000 with that of the government.

(ii) Estimate from the graph, as accurately as you can, the value of t for which the firm's and the government's evaluations of the asset's value are the same.

Exercise 3.6

Consider the function:

$$y = 20x^4$$

(i) Prepare a workbook model that can graph y versus x for x values between 1 and 100 in steps of 5.

Now rewrite $y = 10x^4$ in its logarithmic form and then graph $\log_{10} y$ versus $\log_{10} x$, again for x values between 1 and 100 in steps of 5.

(ii) What has been the most obvious effect of using the logarithmic form of the function?

Exercise 3.7

A firm's market share (y%) when advertising expenditure (£x million) is zero is 2%. No matter how much it spends on advertising, its market share can never exceed 100%. When advertising expenditure is £30 million, the market share is 95%

Use Workbook 3.8 to model this situation by choosing appropriate values for a, b, and c.

Exercise 3.8

An occupation's salary scale starts at £9000 and rises in equal annual increments of £500 to a maximum of £15000

(i) How many 'points' are there in the salary scale?

(ii) How much would an individual be earning if they were on salary point 8?

(iii) What would be the total earnings for the period of an individual who progressed from point 1 to the maximum point and then remained at the maximum for 11 years?

Exercise 3.9

A firm's sales of its product was 100000 units in 1986 and increased by a constant 10% per annum in the years 1987–92 inclusive.

The price at which the product was sold was £15 in 1986 and was increased by a constant 7% per annum over the period 1987–92.

(i) Find the firm's sales in 1992.

(ii) Find the price of the product in 1992.

(iii) Find the firm's revenue from sales in 1992.

(iv) Find the total revenue earned over the period 1986–92 inclusive.

3.10. Solutions to the exercises

Solution to Exercise 3.1

The firm's revenue (r) and cost (c) functions will be given by:

$$r = (1000 - 2x)x + 1000000$$
and
$$c = x^2 + 500x + 750000$$

Hence profit = revenue minus cost is given by:

$$\text{Profit} = 1000x - 2x^2 + 1000000 - x^2 - 500x - 750000$$

Collecting terms and rearranging gives:

$$\text{Profit} = -3x^2 + 500x + 250000$$

If we enter these coefficient values (-3, 500, and 250000) to the B1, B2, and B3 cells of Workbook 3.1A, then the solution values for x_1 and x_2 will be calculated in B5 and B6 as:

$$-217.12 \text{ and } 383.79$$

Consequently, since a negative output (-217.12) makes no economic sense we can ignore this solution value and conclude that there is only one relevant break-even level of sales—at x = 383.79.

Solution to Exercise 3.2

(i) The cost in millions (c) of the bridge is given by:

$$c = £10$$

and, since 5% must be recovered in the first year, an income of £0.5 million must be generated.

The income (r) will depend upon the price charged (p) and the number of crossings (x) which take place at that price. So:

$$r = (1 - 0.01p)p = p - 0.01p^2$$

Consequently, since we require r = 0.5, this implies that:

$$-0.01p^2 + p - 0.5 = 0$$

Now enter values for a, b, and c of -0.01, 1, and -0.5 to the B1, B2, and B3 cells of Workbook 3.1A. The solution values $-p_1$ and p_2 will be computed in B5 and B6 as £0.50 and £99.50 (when expressed to 2 decimal places).

This implies that the local authority has a choice of prices to charge, since in either case the required £0.5 million will be raised. (Check this for yourself by evaluating the expression for revenue when each of the prices is charged.)

(ii) The introduction of maintenance costs at £0.03 per crossing means that the generated income must now recover:

$$c = 500000 + 0.03x$$

Therefore:

$$(1000000 - 10000p)p = 500000 + 0.03x$$

But since we know that:

$$x = 1000000 - 10000p$$

we can rewrite the previous expression entirely in terms of p as:

$$1000000p - 10000p^2 = 500000 + 0.03(1000000 - 10000p)$$

Implying that:

$$1000000p - 10000p^2 = 500000 + 30000 - 30p$$

Collection of terms and rearrangement then produces:

$$-10000p^2 + 1000030p - 530000 = 0$$

When you enter these coefficient values to the appropriate cells of Workbook 3.1A, the solution values for p are obtained as £0.53 and £99.47.

Notice the implication of this result, since it would appear to be the case that when the maintenance cost are included the lower price should be increased (from £0.5 to £0.53), and that the higher price should be decreased (from £99.50 to £99.47). This has a logical interpretation when it is remembered that the introduction of maintenance costs depending upon the number of crossings will have a greater effect when the price is low and the number of crossings is high than when the price is high and the number of crossings is low.

Solution to Exercise 3.3

(i) Load Workbook 3.3 (W3_3.XLS) and change the values in B1:B4 to 1, -15, 63, and 10000 respectively.

Then change the step value for the scale from 2 to 0.6.

The graph produced should show profits rising until x is roughly 3, then falling until x reaches roughly 7 and then rising again thereafter.

(ii) Use the E1 and E2 cells of Workbook 3.3 to contain the tax threshold (10050) and the tax rate (0.15). Then add the label :

Tax due

to the E3 cell.

Next, in E4 write:

=IF(D4<=E$1,0,E$2*D4)

and copy this into D5:D22.

This formula will calculate the tax due for each of the time period values depending upon whether or not profits exceeded the threshold.

The graph of tax due versus time should resemble Fig. 3.10 when the data range is defined as C4:C22, E4:E22, and an XY scatter graph type 2 selected.

Solution to Exercise 3.4

We require the function to do two things:

Adopt a value of 0.5 when x = 0, i.e. = f(x) such that f(0) = 0.5

And:

Asymptotically approach a value of 0.05, i.e. v = f(x) such that f(∞) = 0.05

The simplest form for v would be:

$$v = f(x) = 0.5/x$$

But this has a value of ∞ when x = 0 (not 0.5 as required), and asymptotically approaches a value of 0 when x becomes infinitely large (not 0.05 as required).

However, if we write:

$$v = f(x) = 0.45/(x + 1) + 0.05$$

then both of these objections are answered.

This is because when x = 0, v = 0.45/(0 + 1) + 0.05 = 0.5
while when x = ∞ v = 0.45/∞ + 0.05 = 0 + 0.05 = 0.05

You can appreciate the general shape of the function that has been created if you open a blank workbook and make the entries indicated in Workbook 3.11.

Then graph the A2:B20 range as an XY scatter graph to obtain the diagram shown in the illustrated worksheet.

Solution to Exercise 3.5

(i) The solution is shown in Workbook 3.12 and Fig. 3.11.

The formulae in B5 and C5 are:

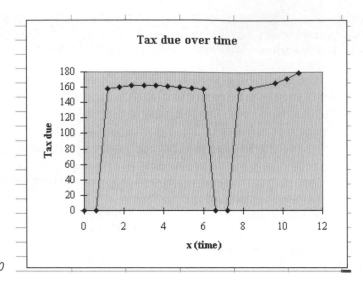

Figure 3.10

=D$1*EXP(-0.2*A5)   and
=D$1/(1+0.5*A5)

and these were copied into B6:C45.

These are equivalent to:

**Workbook
3.11**

$$v = ae^{-0.2t} \quad \text{and} \quad v = a/(1+0.5t)$$

when it is remembered that the D1 cell has

been used to contain the value of *a*, and A5:A45 contain the values for the time variable.

(ii) An approximate value for t such that the firm's and the government's estimates of the asset's value are equal would be somewhere between 7.9 and 8.3.

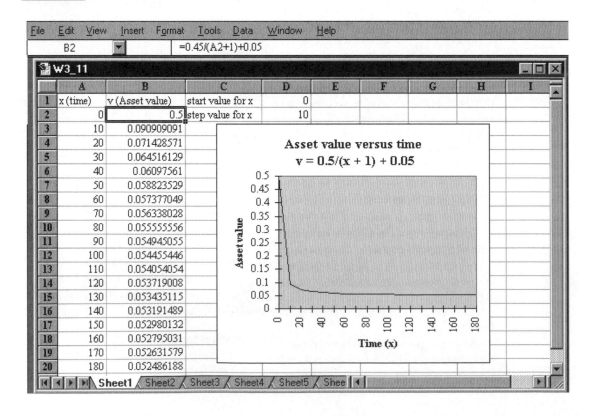

```
w3_12                                                           _ □ ×
        A              B              C            D      E      F      G      H
1   Start value for t              0  Initial purchase value (a)  10000
2   Step value for t            0.5
3                      Firm's estimate  Government's
4   Time (t)           of value       estimate of value
5              0      10000          10000
6            0.5      9048.37418     8000
7              1      8187.307531    6666.666667
8            1.5      7408.182207    5714.285714
9              2      6703.20046     5000
10           2.5      6065.306597    4444.444444
11             3      5488.116361    4000
12           3.5      4965.853038    3636.363636
13             4      4493.289641    3333.333333
14           4.5      4065.696597    3076.923077
15             5      3678.794412    2857.142857
16           5.5      3328.710837    2666.666667
17             6      3011.942119    2500
18           6.5      2725.31793     2352.941176
19             7      2465.969639    2222.222222
20           7.5      2231.301601    2105.263158
```

Sheet1 / Sheet2 / Sheet3 / Sheet4 / Sheet5 / She

Workbook 3.12

However, you can improve the accuracy of this estimate if you change the chart type to a line graph, increase the start value for t to 7.5, and reduce the step value for t to 0.02. This will focus more closely on the intersection between the two curves, and will produce a much more accurate estimate of the value for t at which the two curves intersect (8.1 seems quite accurate).

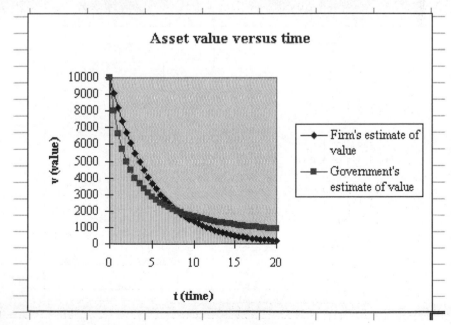

Figure 3.11

Solution to Exercise 3.6

(i) The equation:

$$y = 20x^4$$

is rewritten in logarithmic form as:

$$\log_{10} y = \log_{10} 20 + 4 \log_{10} x$$

Workbook 3.13 shows the relevant calculations, and the graphs of y versus x and log10 y versus log 10 x, respectively.

The formula in B5 is:

=20*A5^4

and this was copied down into B6:B25.

The formula in C5 and D5 are:

=LOG(A5)   and
=LOG(20)+4*LOG(A5)

(ii) When the C5:D25 range is graphed as an XY scatter chart, the clear effect has been to turn the curved relationship between y and x into a linear relationship between log10 y and log10 x.

This is because $\log_{10} y = \log_{10} 20 + 4 \log_{10} x$ is of the standard linear form: $y = a + bx$ when y is regarded as $\log_{10} y$ and x is regarded as log10 x.

Workbook 3.13

Solution to Exercise 3.7
Open Workbook 3.8.

This workbook evaluates the expression:

$$y = a(1-e^{-cx})$$

which has y = 0 when x = 0

However, it is an easy matter to modify it to accommodate the more general form:

$$y = a(1-e^{-cx}) + b$$

which has y = b when x = 0.

To do this, use E1 to contain the label: *b* and then enter a value of 2 to the E2 cell. The formula in B4 must now be amended from:

=C$2*(1-EXP(D$2*-A4))   to
=C$2*(1-EXP(D$2*-A4))+E$2

Now copy B4 into B5:B19 and save the file as W3_8A.XLS.

Clearly, if b is set equal to zero then there is no difference between these last two expressions and the logistic curve will start at the origin. In all other cases however, the curve will start at a value on the horizontal axis that is given by b.

This is what is required by the question, since the market share when there is no advertising expenditure is to be 2%.

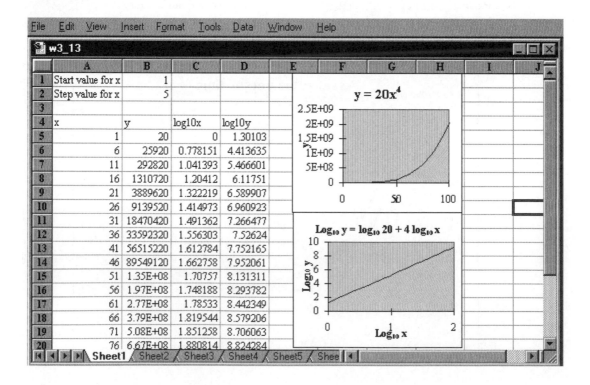

With a value of 2 entered to E2, we now require to decide upon the value of a. To do this note that when $x = \infty$, $y = a + b$. Hence, since we know that b = 2, and that when $x = \infty$, y should equal 100%, it follows that the value of a must be given by:

$$a = y - b = 100 - 2 = 98$$

Enter this value (98) now to the C2 cell, and notice that we have satisfactorily achieved 2 out of 3 of the question's requirements— market share equalling 2% when x = 0, and market share never exceeding 100% no matter how large x becomes.

The final requirement is to ensure that a market share of 95% is achieved when x = 30.

This will involve finding an appropriate value for *c*. The way to do this is to note that when x = 30:

$$y = 98(1 - e^{-30c}) + 2$$

With y required to be 95 this means that:

$$95 = 98(1 - e^{-30c}) + 2$$

Hence:

$$93 = 98(1 - e^{-30c})$$

And:

$$93/98 = 1 - e^{-30c}$$

Whereby

$$e^{-30c} = 1 - 93/98 = 0.0510204$$

Now taking natural logarithms (ln) of both sides we obtain:

$$-30c \ln e = \ln 0.0510204$$

But since $\ln e = 1$ by definition:

$$c = \ln 0.0510204 / -30 = 0.0991843$$

Enter this value now to the D2 cell and you will find that the market share is almost exactly 95% when x = 30.

Solution to Exercise 3.8

(i) This problem can be modelled by an arithmetic series in which a = £9000, d = £500 and n is initially unknown.

Now, since the nth term of an arithmetic series is given by:

$$u_n = a + (n-1)d$$

we can write:

$$u_n = 9000 + (n-1)(500)$$

and then note that this must equal 15000 (the maximum point).

Therefore:

$$9000 + (n-1)(500) = 15000$$

Implying that:

$$500 (n-1) = 15{,}000 - 9{,}000 = 6000$$

And that:

$$(n-1) = 6000/500 = 12$$

Consequently:

$$n = 13$$

The salary scale therefore has 13 'points'.

Now load Workbook 3.9 (W3_9.XLS).

(ii) Enter values n = 8, a = 9000, and d = 500 to the appropriate cells of the worksheet. An answer of £12500 should be returned to the G1 cell.

(iii) The progression from point 1 to point 13 on the salary scale produces 13 annual salaries of:

$$9000, 9500 \ldots 15000$$

The sum of these 13 terms can be obtained from Workbook 3.9 by entering a value of 13 for n to the E2 cell, whereupon the value returned to the G2 cell will be £156000.

However, since this individual stays at the maximum for 11 years there are a further 10 maximum salaries of £15000 to be added on. The total accumulated income is therefore:

$$£156000 + 10(£15000) = £306000$$

Solution to Exercise 3.9

Open Workbook 3.10 and then use it as follows.

(i) The firm's sales can be represented by a geometric series in which a = 100000 and m = 1.1.

The period 1986–92 inclusive represents 7 years, so n = 7.

Enter these values to the appropriate cells of Workbook 3.10 to obtain the sales achieved in 1992 as 177156.1.

(ii) The behaviour of the product's price is modelled by a geometric series with a = £15, m = 1.07, and n = 7.

Enter these values now to obtain the price in 1992 as £22.51.

(iii) Revenue in 1992 is therefore $(177156.1)(22.51) = £3987953$.

(iv) This is a more difficult question to answer, since it requires that we find the sum of 7 annual revenue terms.

In other words, letting $R_1, R_2 \ldots R_7$ denote

the revenue earned in each of the years 1986, 1987 ... 1992, we require:

$$R_1 + R_2 + \ldots + R_7$$

Now, since the revenue in each year will be that year's price times that year's sales, we can let:

$$S_1 \ldots S_7 \text{ and } P_1 \ldots P_7$$

represent sales and price respectively, in the years 1986–92.

This allows us to rewrite the revenue expression above as:

$$R_1 + R_2 + \ldots + R_7 = S_1 P_1 + S_2 P_2 + \ldots + S_7 P_7$$

We could of course evaluate each of these terms individually and then sum to obtain the required result, but the issue that will be posed here is whether our knowledge of geometric progressions can be used to simplify this task.

The answer is that it can, but that we must be careful how we do it. The problem can be solved as follows:

> Sales are in geometric progression with $m = 1.1$, $a = 100000$, and $n = 7$
>
> Price is in geometric progression with $m = 1.07$, $a = 15$, and $n = 7$

Therefore: Revenue = (Sales)(Price) is in geometric progression with:

> $a = (15)(100000) = 1.5$ million
>
> $m = (1.1)(1.07) = 1.177$ and:
>
> $n = 7$

Enter these values now to the C1, C2, G1, and G2 of the worksheet, and you should find that the revenue earned in 1992 is returned to G1 as £3987953 (confirming the result that we obtained in part (iii)), and that the total revenue earned over the entire period is £18044184.

Equation solving and optimization using the Excel Solver

Contents

Accompanying data files to be loaded as instructed

W4_10.XLS   W4_11.XLS   W4_12.XLS   W4_15.XLS

4.1. **Introduction**

The process of modelling business relationships frequently creates situations which call for methods of solving equations. This chapter discusses the elementary algebraic principles of equation solving and then shows how to use the Excel Solver to solve equations that are not so amenable to such direct solution methods. Once these principles have been explained, the Solver will be used to consider optimization procedures.

4.2. **Principles of solving equations**

An equation is simply a symbolic statement of the equality between two mathematical relationships—the left-hand side (LHS) and the right-hand side (RHS). Thus:

LHS = RHS

is an equation that has been written in its *explicit* form (i.e. with the equals sign located between the LHS and the RHS).

However, equations can also be written in what is known as their *implicit* form as:

LHS - RHS = 0

In either form the information that is being conveyed is the same, but as regards using the Excel Solver the implicit form will often be more useful.

In most practical cases both the LHS and the RHS will be composed of a number of *terms*—which can either be *known* or *unknown*. The known terms will either be numbers (2, 6, 11 etc.) or symbols representing known numbers ($\pi = 22/7$, e = 2.71828 etc.). The unknown terms will be shown as symbols, but these can be either of two types—*parameters* or *variables*.

Parameters represent the constant information of the model in the sense that although over time they can change, they are regarded as being constant for the time span with which the model is concerned and apply generally rather than individually.

For example, in an income tax model the current rate of taxation would be regarded as a parameter since although the tax authorities could decide to change its value, it would still be the same for all people who pay income tax. This is not true for the incomes themselves, since individuals can clearly earn different amounts, meaning that income should be regarded as a variable in the model.

In short, if an income tax system is composed of a single tax rate (t—a parameter) then the tax due (y) will depend upon the income earned (x—a variable) and the tax rate to be applied, in the following way:

y = tx

Here, tax due—y, is regarded as the *dependent* variable, since it depends upon the *independent* variable representing income and defined as x, as well as the parameter t. If the tax rate were to change then so too would the amount of tax due, but it would do so in a way that was the same for all levels of income.

To make these ideas more clear in the context of equation solving, consider two countries (A and B) who employ different corporate tax regimes.

Country A charges all firms a fixed tax charge of £a plus a tax rate of t_a% of firms' reported profits.

Country B has a similar regime but the respective parameters are £b and t_b%.

It should be clear that the tax due in each of the countries (TD_a and TD_b) can be written as:

$$TD_a = a + t_a x$$
$$TD_b = b + t_b y$$

where x and y are independent variables representing the reported profits of firms in countries A and B respectively.

Now suppose that we are required to find the level of reported profits earned by a firm that makes the tax due the same in country A as in country B. Clearly we require:

$$TD_a = TD_b$$

which is equivalent to:

$$a + t_a x = b + t_b y$$

Furthermore, since we are seeking a level of profits that is to be the same in each country we can deduce that x must equal y for this to be the case. Consequently, introduce a new variable (z) that is defined to be equal to *both* x and y and then rewrite the last equation as:

$$a + t_a z = b + t_b z$$

Now transfer the term that contains z to the LHS and the term that does not contain z to the RHS after changing its algebraic sign. This gives:

$$t_a z - t_b z = b - a$$

which is equivalent to:

$$z(t_a - t_b) = (b - a)$$

whereupon:

$$z = (b - a)/(t_a - t_b)$$

The terms on the RHS of this last expression represent the solution to the equation that was defined above and will give the value of reported profits ($z = x = y$) that produces the same amount of tax due, regardless of the country in which the firm is located.

Of course, to obtain a definite numerical solution requires that values are assigned to a, b, t_a and t_b.

For example, suppose that:

$$a = £5000, b = £7000, t_a = 0.25, t_b = 0.20$$

Then:

$$z = (£7000 - £5000)/(0.25 - 0.2) = £2000/0.05 = £40,000$$

This means that if a firm in either country earns reported profits of £40,000 then they will pay exactly the same amount of tax, since:

$$TD_a = £5000 + 0.25(£40000) = £15,000$$

and:

$$TD_b = £7000 + 0.2(£40000) = £15,000$$

However, suppose that the tax regimes of the two countries were now defined by:

$$a = £5000, b = £7000, t_a = 0.20, t_b = 0.20$$

We now have:

$$z = (£7000 - £5000)/(0.2 - 0.2) = £2000/0 = \text{infinity}$$

The reason for this is quite simple—with the rate of tax being the same in both countries the lines representing the amount of tax due have the same slope (0.2) and are therefore parallel. They will never intersect and so there is no finite solution to the equation. That is, there is no level of profits that will yield the same tax. Because country B has a higher fixed tax charge than country A (£7000 > £5000), firms in B with the same reported profits as those in A will always pay more tax and so there is no possibility that they could pay the *same* amount.

Another difficulty with the model can be seen if we consider tax regimes in which:

$$a = £5000, b = £7000, t_a = 0.20, t_b = 0.25$$

Substitution into the solution expression now gives:

$$z = (£7000 - £5000)/(0.2 - 0.25) = £2000/-0.05 = -£40000$$

In this case a solution can only be obtained when *losses* of £40,000 are made, and whether this is a realistic solution depends upon whether the tax regimes in the two countries reimburse losses as well taking a share of profits.

With these principles established we can now transfer the logic to an Excel worksheet as indicated in Workbook 4.1.

Make up this workbook now in line with the illustration and the instructions.

	A	B	C	D	E	F
	W4_1					
1			FORMULAE IN COLUMN B			
2	Country A fixed tax charge (a)	5000				
3	Country A tax rate t_a	25%				
4	Profits of firm in country A (x)	60000				
5	Tax due by firm in country A (TD_a)	20000	=B2+B3*B4			
6	Country B fixed tax charge (b)	7000				
7	Country B tax rate t_b	20%				
8	Profits of firm in country B (y)	60000				
9	Tax due by firm in country B (TD_b)	19000	=B6+B7*B8			
10						
11	Tax due in country A = tax due in country B when profits =	40000	=(B6-B2)/(B3-B7)			
12						

Sheet1 / Sheet2 / Sheet3 / Sheet4 / Sheet5 / Shee

Workbook 4.1 Most of the entries in the sheet should be self explanatory when it is remembered that B2, B3, and B4 represent a, t_a, and x respectively, while B6, B7, and B8 represent b, t_b, and y. Thus the formula in B11 is exactly equivalent to:

$$z = (b - a)/(t_a - t_b)$$

and reproduces the result that was obtained earlier.

4.3. **Iterative solution methods**

In the two-country tax model discussed in section 4.2 above, the simple nature of the relationships meant that an analytical solution for z was easily obtained. However, more complex models nearly always produce equations that are more difficult to solve. In some cases they can still be solved analytically by advanced mathematical methods, but in others there may be no alternative to using what are known as *iterative* methods.

Put simply, an iterative solution is one that is based upon trial and error methods—a value for the variable is substituted into the equation (tried), the difference between the LHS and the RHS is noted and treated as error, and then another value for the variable is tried and the error associated with this value noted. This process continues until a value for the variable is found that produces an error of zero (LHS = RHS).

Clearly, even with relatively simple equations such a process can become extremely time consuming, although if the model is correctly set up on a worksheet then the procedure becomes more efficient.

Workbook 4.2 indicates how this can be done for the two-country tax model that has already been 'solved'.

Make up this model now.

	A	B	C	D	E
			FORMULAE IN COLUMN B		
1					
2	Country A fixed tax charge (a)	5000			
3	Country A tax rate t_a	25%			
4	Country B fixed tax charge (b)	7000			
5	Country B tax rate t_b	20%			
6	Profits of firms in either country A or B (z)	50000			
7	LHS = Tax due by firm in country A (TD_a)	17500	=B2+B3*B6		
8	RHS = Tax due by firm in country B (TD_b)	17000	=B4+B5*B6		
9	LHS - RHS = Tax difference between firms in A and firms in B	500.00	=B7-B8		
10					
11					

Sheet1 / Sheet2 / Sheet3 / Sheet4 / Sheet5 / She

Workbook 4.2

The worksheet is structured as follows. First, the parameters of the model are entered at the top of the sheet (B2:B5). Second, the variable whose value is going to be changed in the trial process, is entered in its own cell (B6 in this case). This is the variable in this model and so it is the value in this cell that is going to be changed, by trial and error, until our target of the same amount of tax being paid in each country is achieved.

Next, and this is the crucial step, the LHS and the RHS of the equation are entered as formulae in B7 and B8 that refer to the cell addresses of the parameters and the variable. Thus, B7 gives the tax due by a firm in country A that earns whatever amount of profits have been entered to B6. Equivalently, B7 gives the tax due by a firm in country B that also earns whatever value for profits have been entered in B6.

Finally, the difference between the LHS and the RHS is computed from the formula entered to B9 representing the error associated with the trial value of the variable (z = x = y). Hence, with a trial value for z of 50000 the tax due for firms in A and B are 17500, and 17000 respectively. The difference between the amounts of tax due is therefore 500—given the trial value of 50000.

Set up like this, it should be clear that solving the equation simply requires that the value entered to B6 is changed until the value of the error in B9 reaches its target value of zero. From our previous analytical solution this will occur when you let the value in B6 become 40000.

Confirm this now in your own worksheet and then save the file as W4_2.XLS.

4.4. **Using the Excel Solver**

The trial and error procedure explained above is simple but inefficient.

However, now that we know what we are trying to achieve, and how we are trying to do it, we can get the Excel Solver to do it for us. Before doing so however, we must translate the logic of our trial and error process into Excel parlance.

What we are trying to do is known as the **target**, and the cell of the worksheet containing that target is called the **target cell**. The value that the target cell must achieve (a difference of zero between the LHS and the RHS) is known as the **target value**. How we are trying to achieve our target is by changing the value in B6, and so this is known as the **changing cell**. Thus we have:

> Target cell = B9
> Target cell value = 0
> Changing cell = B6

Now, load Workbook 4.2 and make the value in B6 equal to 50000. Next select Tools and then Solver.[1]

The dialogue box shown in Fig. 4.1 will appear.

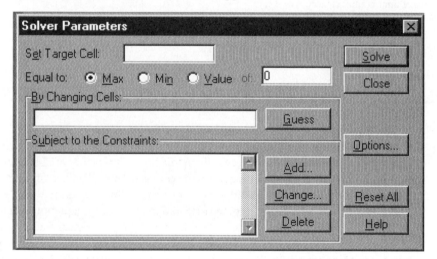

Figure 4.1

Now, in line with the most recent discussion make this dialogue box resemble Fig. 4.2.

When you have done this click on Solve and the dialogue box shown in Fig. 4.3 will appear.

Here, you have the option to keep the original value for the changing cell, or force Excel to replace the original value with the solution value that it has found. Usually the latter will be what is required and this is the default, so choose OK, whereupon Excel will insert a value of 40000 to the B6 cell. This is clearly the solution value that we obtained earlier.[2]

As a final point in this section it should be noted that the Solver is not fully 'hot'. By this we mean that if the parameters of the problem should change the Solver routine will have to

---

1 If Solver does not appear on the Tools menu it may not have been added in. Select Tools and then Add-Ins and then choose Solver from the list that appears. The Solver should now be installed.

2 If you do not want the solution values to be entered to the worksheet click on the lower button and the original values for the changing cells will be restored.

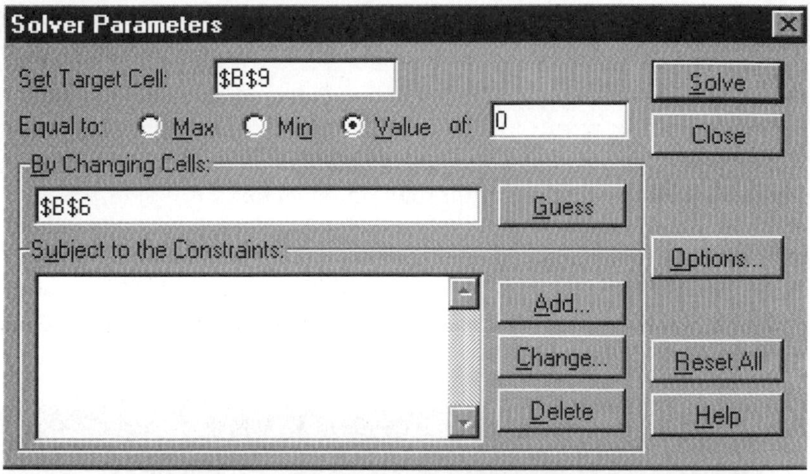

Figure 4.2

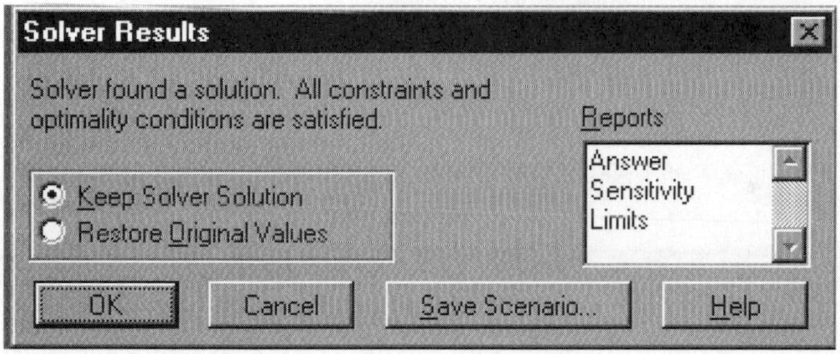

Figure 4.3

be run again to get the new solution. However, unless the structure of the problem has changed, the original Solver settings can be **accepted** and so it is only a matter of clicking again on Solve.

For example, suppose that the tax rate in country A was reduced to 20%.

Using the most recent version of Workbook 4.2, change the value in B3 to 20%.

Clearly the previous solution value (40000) is no longer correct.

Now run the Solver with the given settings.

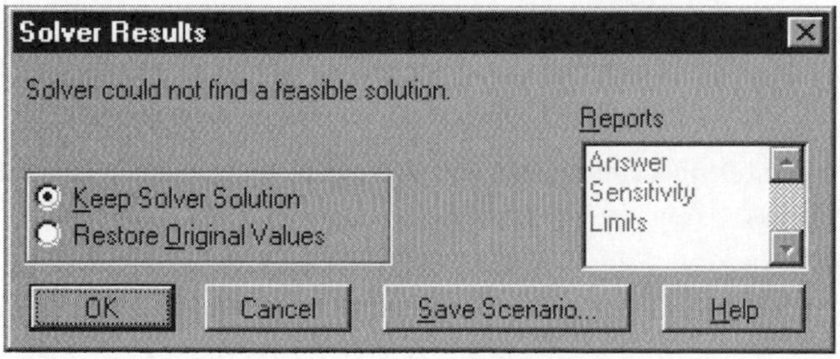

Figure 4.4

You should now find that the Solver produces the message shown in Fig. 4.4.

The reason for this is quite simple and was noted earlier in the discussion. That is, the lines representing the tax due in each of the countries are parallel and therefore do not intersect, and so there is no solution possible.

Exercise 4.1 and 4.2 can be attempted now.

4.5. **Solving more complex equations using the Excel Solver**

Chapter 3 showed how to solve quadratic equations using the quadratic formula. For example, it was shown there that the solution values to:

$$y = x^2 - 13x + 36 = 0$$

were $x_1 = 4$ and $x_2 = 9$.

To get the Solver to find these solutions, open a new workbook and make the entries indicated in Workbook 4.3.

	A	B	C	D	E	F	G	H	I
	W4_3								
1			FORMULA IN COLUMN B						
2	Value of x	5							
3	Coefficient of x^2 (a)	1							
4	Coefficient of x (b)	-13							
5	Constant (c)	36							
6	$y = ax^2 + bx + c =$	-4	= B3*B2^2+B4*B2+B5						
7									
8									

Sheet1 / Sheet2 / Sheet3 / Sheet4 / Sheet5 / She

Workbook 4.3

Now notice that in terms of this problem the target cell is B6 and the target cell value is 0. Also, the cell that is to be changed in order to achieve this target is B2 (i.e. the value of x).

Enter these settings now to the Solver and you should find that a solution value of 4 is returned to the B2 cell.

However, although this solution is correct, it is clearly incomplete—since the other solution value of x = 9 has not been located.

This is because the Solver can only find one solution value at a time, and the one that it finds will be the value that is closest to the starting value that was used for the changing cell. In this illustration the value for x was initially set at x = 5 (without any good reason). However, since 5 is closer to 4 than it is to 9, the Solver found the nearest solution value. Consequently, to obtain the other solution value it will be necessary to alter the initial value used in B2.

Do this now by entering a value of 15 to the B2 cell, and then run the Solver again with the same settings.

It will be found that Excel now settles down at the higher solution value of x = 9.

Up until now, the Solver has been used to solve equations for which analytical solution methods exist (the quadratic formula in the last example). However, it should be appreciated that the true power of the Solver is experienced when analytical solution methods either do not exist or involve extremely complex mathematics.

For example, reconsider Exercise 3.5. There, it was required to find the value of t for which the value of an asset was the same under two different evaluation schemes i.e.

$$v = 10000e^{-0.2t} \text{ for the firm, and } v = 10000/(1 + 0.5t) \text{ for the government}$$

The worked solution used a graph of the two evaluation functions to determine approximately where they intersected. This was the only method available at that stage, since solution of the two equations is not easy.

However, we can now use the Solver to obtain a more accurate estimate of the required value of t.

To do this, make up the model indicated in Workbook 4.4.

W4_4							
	A	B	C	D	E	F	G
1			FORMULAE IN COLUMN B				
2	Time (t)	5					
3	Initial value of the asset	10000					
4	Firm's estimate of the asset's value	3678.794	=B3*EXP(-0.2*B2)				
5	Government's estimate of the asset's value	2857.143	=B3/(1+0.5*B2)				
6	Firm's estimate - government's estimate	821.6516	=B4-B5				
7							
8							

Sheet1 / Sheet2 / Sheet3 / Sheet4 / Sheet5 / She

Workbook 4.4

Set up like this, it should be clear that the task is to find the value of t that makes the values in the B4 and B5 cells identical. However, in this formulation we have calculated the difference between the two evaluations in the B6 cell, and so the Solver problem can be defined as:

Target cell = B6
Target cell value = 0
Changing cell = B2

Now use these settings in the Solver and you should find that a solution value of t = 8.093943 is obtained.

This is very close to the solution value of 8.1 that was obtained by inspection of the graph in Chapter 3.

Exercises 4.3 and 4.4 can be attempted now.

4.6. Using the Solver in optimization procedures

Optimization is the process of making some function representing the **objective**, or **target**, as large or as small as possible by changing the value adopted by the independent variable or variables. Thus we may want to find the value of sales that makes revenue as large as possible or the value of output that makes unit costs as small as possible.

Whatever the objective, the procedure will always be to model the problem in a worksheet in terms that the Solver can understand. If this can be done, then either the Max or the Min button in the Solver dialogue box can then be chosen (instead of the value of: button that has been selected up until now).

To see how this works reconsider the revenue function that was produced in Figure 3.6. This was defined by:

$$Revenue = -5x^2 + 200x$$

and as the graph indicated, reached a maximum value when sales (x) were approximately 20 units.

To obtain the exact value at which revenue is maximized, make up the model indicated in Workbook 4.5.

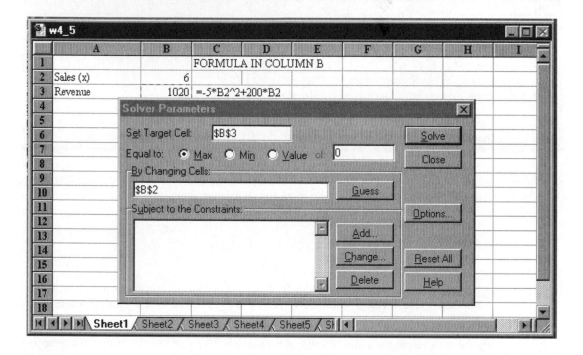

Workbook 4.5 With the Solver settings indicated (notice that the Max button has been checked instead of the Value one) it will be found that the greatest revenue obtainable is £2000 and that this is achieved when sales are equal to 20 units.

Confirm this now.

Now reconsider the cubic total cost function that was investigated in Chapter 3. That was:

$$Total\ cost = 0.02x^3 - 0.8x^2 + 12x + 1000$$

Then recall the discussion on the nature of the average cost function that such a total cost function implies—namely that:

$$Average\ cost = Total\ cost/output = (0.02x^3 - 0.8x^2 + 12x + 1000)/x$$

Therefore:

$$Average\ cost = 0.02x^2 - 0.8x + 12 + 1000/x$$

Suppose now that we are required to find the output level that minimizes the average (or unit) cost of production. This is not easy to do without a lot of mathematical skill.

To do this with the Solver, make up the model indicated in Workbook 4.6.

	A	B	C	D	E	F	G	H	I	
1			FORMULA IN COLUMN B							
2	Output (x)	4								
3	Total cost	1036.48	=0.02*B2^3-0.8*B2^2+12*B2+1000							
4	Average cost	259.12	=B3/B2							
5										
6										

Sheet1 / Sheet2 / Sheet3 / Sheet4 / Sheet5 / She

Workbook 4.6

Now access the Solver, define the target cell as B4 and select the Min option. The changing cell should be defined as B2.

Now click on Solve and it should be found that Excel determines the value of output that minimizes average cost to be 37.64298 units, and that the minimum average cost attainable is £36.79087.

Exercise 4.5 can be attempted now.

Up until now, the discussion has only considered problems that could be represented by one dependent variable as a function of one independent variable. However, it should be clear that realistic modelling will often require that the dependent variable is related to one or more independent variables. Thus, sales usually depend upon the product price and the level of advertising and the level of household incomes. Or, investment depends upon the level of retained profits and the cost of borrowing funds.

In either of these cases the model will have at least two independent variables, and this inevitably introduces a degree of complexity that was not present in the previous simple models.

However, the Excel Solver finds no difficulty in dealing with this added complexity, provided the model has been properly set up in a worksheet. To see this consider the following example.

A firm sells its product in each of two distinct markets—A and B. In market A the quantity demanded (Q_A) is given in terms of the price charged in that market (P_A) by:

$$Q_A = 2000 - 0.5P_A^2$$

The equivalent demand function for market B is:

$$Q_B = 2500 - 0.75P_B^2$$

There are no fixed costs, and variable production costs are constant and equal to £4 per unit. If the firm wishes to maximize its profit from sales in both markets, what prices should it charge?

To answer this optimization problem we can argue that the revenues obtained from each of the markets $(R_A$ and $R_B)$ are given by:

$$R_A = P_A(2000 - 0.5P_A^2)$$
$$R_B = P_B(2500 - 0.75P_B^2)$$

Thus the combined revenue (R) is given by:

$$R = R_A + R_B$$

The total costs of production (C) will be given by:

$$C = 4Q_A + 4Q_B = 4(Q_A + Q_B)$$

Thus the total profit from sales in both markets (Z) will be:

$$Z = R - C = R_A + R_B - 4(Q_A + Q_B)$$

$$Z = P_A(2000 - 0.5P_A^2) + P_B(2500 - 0.75P_B^2) - 4(Q_A + Q_B)$$

This expression contains terms in both prices and quantities. However, since we are required to find the prices that should be charged in order to make the greatest profit we must rewrite the RHS entirely in terms of price variables. This is easily done as:

$$Z = P_A(2000 - 0.5P_A^2) + P_B(2500 - 0.75P_B^2) - 4(2000 - 0.5P_A^2 + 2500 - 0.75P_B^2)$$

Notice that the first term on the RHS of this expression is simply R_A as a function of P_A, the second term is R_B as a function of P_B, and the last term is C as a function of P_A and P_B.

Now open a new workbook and make the entries indicated in Workbook 4.7.

	A	B	C	D	E	F	G	H	I
1			FORMULA IN COLUMN B						
2	Price charged in A (P_A)	3							
3	Price charged in B (P_B)	6							
4	Revenue from A (R_A)	5986.5	=B2*(2000-0.5*B2^2)						
5	Revenue from B (R_B)	14838	=B3*(2500-0.75*B3^2)						
6	Total costs (C)	17874	=4*(2000-0.5*B2^2+2500-0.75*B3^2)						
7	Total Profits (Z)	2950.5	=B4+B5-B6						
8									
9									

Workbook 4.7

Set up like this, it should be clear that the model computes the overall profit obtained as a result of whatever values for P_A and P_B are entered to the B2 and B3 cells.

Given this, it would seem logical to regard the changing cells in the Solver as B2 and B3, and the target cell to be maximized as B7.

Consequently, open up the Solver and make these entries now—target cell = B7, target cell value = Max, changing cell(s) = B2:B3.
Now click on Solve and observe the results.

Excel has found the optimal solution to be to charge a price of 37.87 in market A and a price of 34.69 in market B. This will ensure that the profits obtained from sales in both markets are as large as possible (92478.72 to be exact).

There is one final thing to note about this model. Although the total revenue obtained depends upon two independent variables (P_A and P_B) these two variables do not interact. In other words R_A depends only on P_A and R_B depends only on P_B.

This might be felt to be unsatisfactory if, as will usually be the case, consumers can make their purchases in either market—usually the one with the lower price. This means that unless the two markets can be completely separated there will be a tendency for prices to equalize. We can deal with this objection if we respecify the model in such a way that the demand functions in each market depend not only on the price charged in that market, but also on the price charged in the other market.

For example, suppose that the two demand functions were defined as:

$$Q_A = 2000 - 0.5P_A^2 + 0.1P_B \text{ and:}$$
$$Q_B = 2500 + 0.15P_A - 0.75P_B^2$$

The structure of this model clearly implies for each market, as the price charged in that market increases, the quantity demanded declines (as in the previous formulation), but also that as the price charged in the other market rises the quantity demanded in this market also rises.

With these demand relations established the derivation of the new revenue and cost functions is the same as before. Thus:

$$R_A = P_A(2000 - 0.5P_A^2 + 0.1P_B)$$
$$R_B = P_B(2500 + 0.15P_A - 0.75P_B^2)$$
$$C = C_A + C_B = 4(Q_A = Q_B) = 4(2000 - 0.5P_A^2 + 0.1P_B + 2500 + 0.15P_A - 0.75P_B^2)$$

Now open Workbook 4.7 and use it as a template to make the alterations indicated in Workbook 4.8.

	A	B	C	D	E	F	G	H	I
1			FORMULA IN COLUMN B						
2	Price charged in A (P_A)	20							
3	Price charged in B (P_B)	40							
4	Revenue from A (R_A)	36080	=B2*(2000-0.5*B2^2+0.1*B3)						
5	Revenue from B (R_B)	52120	=B3*(2500+0.15*B2-0.75*B3^2)						
6	Total costs (C)	12428	=4*(2000-0.5*B2^2+0.1*B3+2500+0.15*B2-0.75*B3^2)						
7	Total Profits (Z)	75772	=B4+B5-B6						
8									
9									

Sheet1 / Sheet2 / Sheet3 / Sheet4 / Sheet5 / She

Workbook 4.8

When you have finished save the file as W4_8.XLS.

As you can see the only major alteration is the reformulation of the formulae in B4, B5, and B6 to take account of the added variable.

Now take the Solver settings as specified, since the structure of the problem has not altered, and then activate the Solver.

It should be found that the new prices that maximize the total profit are $P_A = 37.95$ and $P_B = 34.75$, with a maximum profit of 92771.

Exercise 4.6 can be attempted now.

4.7. Linear optimization subject to linear constraints (linear programming)

Optimization is usually viewed in terms of the eternal business problem of choosing the best way to achieve a given objective in the face of limitations upon the resources available to be used, and in the light of a number of different ways in which these resources can be employed.

In this section however, the word 'linear' is crucial to the argument, since in the context of linear programming this means that a linear function of two or more variables is to be used as a mathematical representation of the objectives to be achieved by the business activity being undertaken. Accordingly, this function is always referred to as the **objective**

function and will usually be a mathematical representation of variables such as output, revenue, cost or profit.

However, since we have already said that the objective function will always be linear, it follows that there will be no finite maximum or minimum value that it can adopt, unless we introduce some modification to the analysis which constrains the function to values which are less than plus or minus infinity.

To see this point, suppose we ask the question: what is the greatest sum of 2 positive numbers?

Clearly there is no sensible answer to be obtained unless we introduce some added information such as 'the sum of the first number and twice the second number must never exceed 20'. This added restriction means that the maximum value that the first number can adopt is 20 (when the second number is 0), while the maximum value that the second number can adopt is 10 (when the first number is 0). In between these two extremes there is a large number of combinations of values that the two numbers can adopt, but which all satisfy the requirement that the sum of the first and twice the second never exceeds 20.

However, although a combination such as 4 for the first number and 8 for the second number does not violate the restriction, it should be clear that the resulting sum (12) is not as large as it could be. Intuition would suggest that we should let the first number be as large as possible (20) and let the second number be as small as possible (0), and then we will obtain the greatest sum (20) without disobeying the restriction, (since $20 + 2(0) = 20$ does not exceed 20, whereas $0 + 2(20) = 40$ does).

What this simple illustration shows is that the process of optimizing linear functions cannot take place unless there is at least one constraint upon the values which the variables of the function can adopt.

In the context of business analysis you can see another version of this idea more clearly if you try to answer the question: what is the minimum cost of production?

On the face of it this would appear to be a reasonable question, until it is remembered that production costs will be 0 when nothing is produced. Consequently, the answer to this question will always be: zero.

On the other hand, if the question were rephrased as: What is the minimum cost of producing 500 units of output?, then the requirement that 500 units be produced has turned this into a meaningful question. The introduction of a constraint has brought substance and definition to the problem.

Bearing this in mind means that in the context of linear programming the constraints will also be linear functions of some or all of the same variables as are included in the objective function, and will always represent the physical and/or financial restrictions imposed upon the optimization process.

In summary, we can state that linear programming is fundamentally concerned with optimizing a linear objective function (representing the target to be achieved) subject to the restrictions imposed by a set of linear constraints (representing the limited availability of the resources needed to achieve the specified target).

Viewed in this manner, many of the fundamental allocation problems of elementary business economics can be written in terms of a linear program, provided of course, that the objective function and the relevant constraints can reasonably be modelled by linear relationships.

In respect of this modelling process, it should be stressed at the outset that one of the fundamental difficulties encountered in the formulation of linear programming exercises stems from the failure to distinguish between **variables** and **variable names**.

For example, in an exercise that refers to the production of nuts and bolts, statements such as:

'let x = nuts' and 'let y = bolts'

are frequently made. Such statements, when carefully inspected, are seen to be almost meaningless since the feature of nuts and bolts that is supposed to be measured by the x and y variables is not defined. Hence x could be the weight of nuts, the diameter, the steel content or any other of a number of characteristics that nuts possess. As a result, the statement 'let x = nuts' is so vague as to be effectively useless in helping us to model the problem. This is because x should be a numeric variable—capable of adopting specific numerical values, whereas 'nuts' is a variable name which is quantitatively unspecified in terms of the feature of nuts that is to be measured.

In the light of this discussion we must recognize that the choice of what to let the variables represent must be conditioned by the objective of the linear program, since x, y (and any other variables) will always be the unknowns of the problem. Hence if nuts and bolts are produced and sold, and if the objective of the program is to make the greatest profit from this process, then the variables should be defined as the production levels of nuts and bolts and the linear program should be employed to find those values of the variables which, when sold, produce the greatest revenue or profit.

That is:

Let x = the number of nuts produced per time period
Let y = the number of bolts produced per time period

We could then use these carefully defined variables to write the Linear Program that will find those values of x and y which will maximize profit.

As a more concrete example, consider a firm which uses three inputs (labour, capital, and steel) to produce two outputs (steel girders and steel casings). The labour input will usually be specified in terms of man hours while the capital input (following the economic definition of capital) will be defined in terms of machine time. The input of steel will, of course, be specified in physical units as kilos or tonnes per time period.

Suppose, in addition, that the technical relationship between inputs and outputs (frequently called the production function) is known to the firm, and is specified in terms of the minimum necessary amounts of each of the three inputs required for the production of a unit of the respective outputs. Hence we might know, for example, that each girder requires 2 units of labour time, 1 unit of machine time, and 5 units of steel, while each casing requires 2 units of labour time, 5 units of machine time, and 2 units of steel.

In addition, the overall availability of the three inputs must also be known, and for the immediate future at least, must be regarded as fixed. (This last assumption stems from the fact that the need to allocate resources between competing ends is only pressing if such resources are limited in availability).

For the purposes of this illustration we will take these overall availabilities to be the following:

Labour : 24 man hours per day
Capital : 44 machine hours per day
Steel : 60 tonnes per day

These technical requirements form the basis of the constraints of the linear program, since the combined usage of each input in the production of girders and/or casings cannot exceed the availability of that input. Hence, if it was decided to produce 10 girders and 20 casings then the total labour usage would be 10 times 2 = 20 man hours (for girders) plus 20 times

2 = 40 man hours (for casings) giving an overall usage of 60 man hours which exceeds the available amount by 36 hours. The constraint upon labour availability is therefore **violated** and such an output combination (10 girders and 20 casings) is said to be **non-feasible** (i.e. unattainable given the constraint upon labour availability).

It should be recognized however, that the purpose of any linear program is to determine the production levels of girders and/or casings rather than assume them to be 10 and 20 or any other combination. Towards this end we require to formulate the constraints in terms of unknown variables that represent the respective outputs of girders and casings. To do this, we will denote the daily production of girders by x and the daily production of casings by y. It should now be clear that we can write the following linear expression as a representation of the total labour usage resulting from producing x girders and y casings per day.

$$2x + 2y = \text{Total Labour usage per day}$$

(Remember that each girder uses 2 units of labour and each casing also uses 2 units of labour. Consequently, x girders will use 2x units of labour and y casings will use 2y units of labour).

The expression above has to be related in some way to the total daily labour hours available, and we do this by noting that the total daily labour usage cannot exceed (i.e. must be less than or equal to) the total daily labour availability. We therefore have a general expression for our first constraint as:

$$2x + 2y \leq 24$$

Notice that this expression is a linear **inequality** rather than an equality since it allows for the possibility that all the available labour hours will not be used, in which case the constraint is said to be **non-binding**. Alternatively, when the values of x and y are such that the inequality becomes an equality then the constraint is said to be **binding**.

The constraints which refer to the usage of machine time and steel can be developed by a similar logic. Hence, if x girders and y casings are produced each day they will require:

$$1x + 5y \text{ hours of machine time per day, and}$$
$$6x + 2y \text{ tonnes of steel per day}$$

As before, these requirements must be related to the total machine time and steel which the firm has available, and when this is done we obtain the complete set of constraints governing this allocation problem to be:

$$2x + 2y \leq 24 \quad \text{Labour time constraint}$$
$$1x + 5y \leq 44 \quad \text{Machine time constraint}$$
$$6x + 2y \leq 60 \quad \text{Steel constraint}$$
$$x \geq 0$$
$$y \geq 0$$

You will notice that we have added two further constraints (x and y both ≥ 0). The reason for this is that we must preclude negative (but not zero) valued output levels from our model. From now on these restrictions will be presumed to be present without actually being presented in future programs.

Having derived mathematical expressions for the constraints of this problem, we must now perform a similar exercise for the objective function. As with the constraints, this must always be expressed in terms of the unknown variables x and y, and will reflect the behavioural motivation of the firm.

In the simplest case, an objective of maximizing the combined daily output of girders and casings would be written as:

Maximize: $1x + 1y = Q$

where Q represents the combined daily output objective function of girders and casings. Although simple, such an objective function is perfectly reasonable if, for example, the two products were completely complementary in the sense that they had to be sold together (such as nuts and bolts). In this case, there is effectively only **one** product (nuts and bolts) and the objective function would have to address itself to the question of how many nuts and bolts should be produced per day.

But in most cases the firm will attach a higher priority to one product than to the other, since the products will usually not be sold at the same price and will not be completely complementary. This complication means that the objective function will usually be denominated in monetary as opposed to physical units with the respective selling prices of the products being used to 'weight' their outputs, and the resulting expression having a monetary dimension defined as Total Revenue (R).

So, for example, if the firm were able to sell girders at £15 each and casings at £16 each then its total daily revenue would be given by:

$15x + 16y = R$

Our complete Linear Program therefore becomes:

Maximize $15x + 16y = R$
Subject to $2x + 2y \leq 24$
and: $\quad x + 5y \leq 44$
$\quad 6x + 2y \leq 60$

The next task is to derive a method of solving for the optimal values of x and y (i.e. those unique values that satisfy the desired objective of maximizing total daily revenue subject to the relevant constraints). In this respect it is important to recognize the crucial function performed by the constraints in obtaining a determinate finite solution, since on its own the expression:

$15x + 16y = R$

has no finite maximum value and no finite optimal values for x and y. Only when the constraints are introduced is a 'boundary' created within which a finite solution can be obtained.

To use the Excel Solver to solve this linear program, set up the workbook indicated in Workbook 4.9.

Workbook 4.9

First of all , enter the labels shown in A1, A2, and A4. Then enter values of 4 and 6 to the B1 and B2 cells.

These are our initial (trial) values for x and y.

Next, in B4 enter the formula:

$=15*B1+16*B2$

This computes the revenue obtained from 4 units of x and 6 units of y. However, if you change the value of x from 4 to 9 the revenue will be recomputed automatically.

Do this now and then change the value of x back to 4.

Consequently, B4 is eventually going to be our target cell and the value in this cell is to be maximized. Furthermore, this is to be achieved by changing the values in B1 and B2.

Now introduce the constraints to the model as indicated in the A6:C9 range.

	A	B	C	D	E	F	G	H	I
1	Variable 1 (x)	4							
2	Variable 2 (y)	6							
3									
4	Revenue	156							
5									
6		LHS	RHS						
7	Constraint 1	20	24						
8	Constraint 2	34	44						
9	Constraint 3	36	60						
10									

Sheet1 / Sheet2 / Sheet3 / Sheet4 / Sheet5 / She

Workbook 4.9   The entries in B7:B9 are the left-hand sides of the constraints expressed in terms of the cell references B1 (for x) and B2 (for y).

Hence the formulae in B7:B9 are:

=2*B1+2*B2   and   =B1+5*B2   and   =6*B1+2*B2

Make these entries now.

These LHS values represent the usage of the three resources stemming from producing the amounts of the two products (x and y) that have been entered to B1 and B2.

Finally, add the right-hand sides of each constraint to the C7:C9 range and change x from 4 to 9.

Set up like this the model can automatically compute the revenue and resource usage implications of any chosen combination of x and y values. For example, with the values in the worksheet (x = 9 and y = 6), it is clear that a revenue of £231 would be obtained.

However, as is also clear from the A7:C9 range, the constraint upon the usage of the first resource (labour time) is violated (usage when x = 9 and y = 6 = 30, available = 24). Constraint number 3 (steel usage) is also violated (66 > 60). Consequently, producing 9 girders and 6 casings is not a **feasible** option.

Now reduce the value of y from 6 to 2.

It will now be found that no constraints are violated and that this option is feasible. The revenue produced is £167.

Clearly you *could* keep on changing the values for x and y until eventually you were satisfied that the revenue could not be improved without violating at least one of the constraints. However, there is no need to do this since the Solver will do it for you.

Consequently, open up the Solver and specify the target cell to be B4, that this target cell should be a Max(imum), and that the changing cells are B1:B2.

So far this procedure is the same as the Solver routines that have previously been carried out. However, in this case we must also inform the Solver that the maximization process that has been defined is to be carried out in the context of the constraints that have been identified.

To do this click on the Add tab below and to the right of the 'Subject to the Constraints' label.

The new dialogue screen shown in Fig. 4.5 will appear.

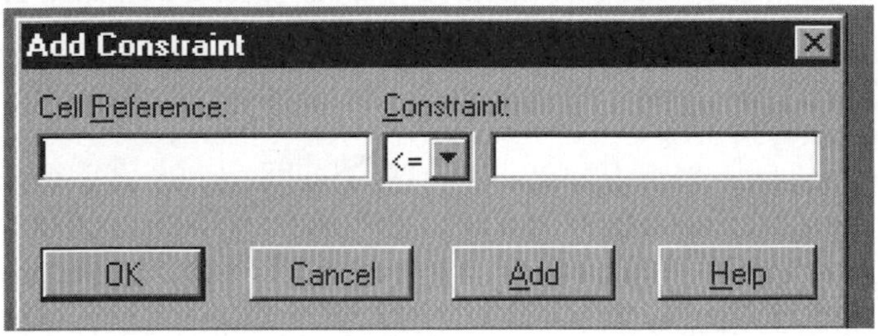

Figure 4.5

Now enter the left-hand sides of each constraint all at once by clicking and dragging on B7:B9. Then click on the middle tab shown in Figure 4.5 and make it indicate <= if it does not already do so.

Finally click on the right-hand box and then click and drag from C7:C9. This will enter the right-hand side values of the constraints.

Now notice that if this procedure has included all of the constraints of the problem then OK should be clicked. The first Solver dialogue box will reappear and after checking that everything looks in order Solve should be clicked.

If however, more constraints (of a different nature) are to be entered then instead of clicking OK, select Add.

This is what we want in this case since we have not as yet included the non-negativity requirements ($x, y \geq 0$), and these must be included.

Consequently, select Add and then click and drag over the B1:B2 range containing the two variables of the model. Then click in the centre tab and select >= from the list.

Finally, click on the right-hand box and enter a value of 0.

All relevant constraints have now been entered so select OK to return to the main Solver menu.

It should now resemble Fig. 4.6.

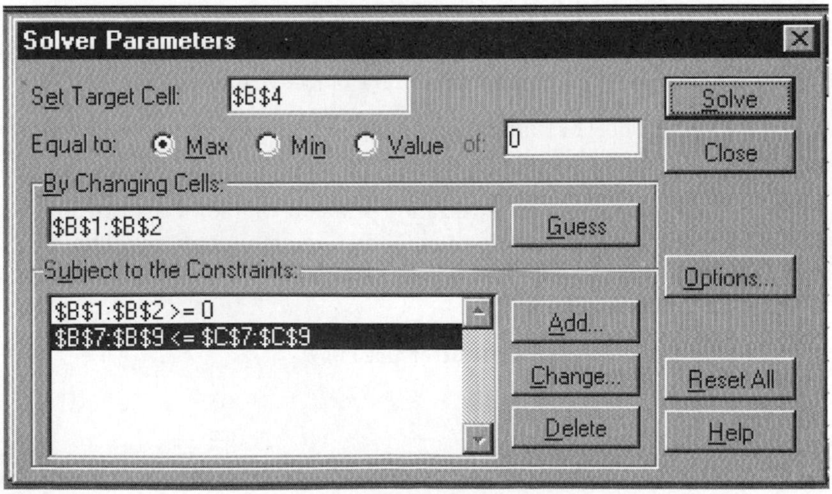

Figure 4.6

If it does, click on Solve whereupon it should be found that the solution values for x and y are returned as 4 and 8 respectively, and produce a maximum total revenue of £188.

If this is what shows at the last dialogue box, select OK to have these values placed in the worksheet (Keep Solver solutions).

Then notice that only two of the constraints are binding—labour time and machine time. The third constraint upon steel usage is not binding since in the optimal solution (x = 4, y = 8), only 40 units are used of the total of 60 that are available.

The amount of any resource that is unused in the optimal solution is known as slack, and so for this program we have the slack associated with the third resource being 60 - 40 = 20.

Exercise 4.7 can be attempted now.

4.8. A general linear programming Solver model

The model developed in the previous section was **specific** in the sense that it could only address linear programs containing two variables and three constraints. Also, if any of the coefficients in either the constraints or the objective function should change then some of the formulae would need to be edited to reflect the parameters of the new program. This can not only be inconvenient, but allows scope for errors and omissions. Both of these limitations have been overcome in the general model prepared in Workbook 4.10.

Load Workbook 4.10 (W4_10.XLS) now.

Workbook 4.10

This worksheet can accommodate linear programs containing up to 6 variables and 6 constraints, but if there are less than this, all that needs to be done is to set the coefficient values for the non existent variables and/or constraints to zero.

This has been done in the workbook that was loaded and clearly represents a linear program with 3 variables and three constraints. That is:

$$\text{Maximize Revenue} = 3600x_1 + 2100x_2 + 2400x_3$$
$$\text{Subject to} \quad 0.3x_1 + 0.4x_2 + 0.2x_3 \leq 60$$
$$0.2x_1 + 0.3x_2 + 0.1x_3 \leq 80$$
$$0.4x_1 + 0.2x_2 + 0.3x_3 \leq 70$$

The Solver settings have also been made and produce the solution shown ($x_1 = 160$, $x_2 = 30$ and $x_3 = 0$), with a maximum value for the objective function of 639000.

Confirm this now by running the Solver.

Furthermore, these Solver settings will only need alteration if either the program changes from a maximization to a minimization problem, or if some or all of the constraints change from less than or equal to, to greater than or equal to, or just equal to.

After studying the structure of the workbook including the Solver settings, use it to answer Exercises 4.8 and 4.9.[3]

Exercises 4.8 and 4.9 can be attempted now.

---

3 Make sure that you only make data entries to the highlighted areas, otherwise you will destroy formulae. If you should do this, close the file immediately without saving and then open it again.

4.9. Sensitivity analysis

Up until now, although linear programs have been solved, there has been no attempt to investigate the way in which the optimal solution responds to changes in the parameters of the model. Such investigation is called **sensitivity analysis**, and involves asking a series of 'what if?' questions that are designed to indicate how the optimal solution changes if, for example, more or less of specific resources are available, or if the production process requires more or less of specific resources.

Sensitivity analysis can also investigate the effects of changes in the contribution to the value of the objective function of any of the variables.

To see how to conduct sensitivity analysis in the context of the Excel Solver, load Workbook 4.10.

This should contain the linear program that was considered in the last section. If it has been changed, restore the values to those that were present in the first version of Workbook 4.10:

$$\text{Maximize Revenue} = 3600x_1 + 2100x_2 + 2400x_3$$
$$\text{Subject to} \quad 0.3x_1 + 0.4x_2 + 0.2x_3 \leq 60$$
$$0.2x_1 + 0.3x_2 + 0.1x_3 \leq 80$$
$$0.4x_1 + 0.2x_2 + 0.3x_3 \leq 70$$

To conduct sensitivity analysis efficiently, the first thing to do is make a **perfect clone** of the linear programming model in a new sheet.

To do this, select Edit and then Move or Copy sheet. Then click on the Create a copy tab and then position the new sheet before the Sheet2 label displayed in the central area of the dialogue box.
Now click OK and the new sheet will be inserted after Sheet1 and before Sheet2 at the chosen location with the default name Sheet1(2).
To rename it, double click on the sheet tab and enter the new name as something like Sheet1 Clone.

Notice that because the actual **sheet** was copied, rather than just its contents, the Solver settings from the original sheet have been copied as well.

If the process outlined above has not produced the required effect, load a prepared version of the file now from the accompanying disk (W4_11.XLS).

We are now going to think of the Sheet1 model as the 'before' situation and the Sheet1 Clone model as the 'after' situation (i.e. after one or more of the parameters have been changed). Consequently, suppose that the availability (70) of the resource associated with the third constraint increased to 71.

Click on the Sheet1 Clone tab and change the entry in D16 from 70 to 71.
Now run the Solver with the established settings and it will be found that the optimal solution has changed from $x_1 = 160$, $x_2 = 30$, $x_3 = 0$ to $x_1 = 164$, $x_2 = 27$, $x_3 = 0$.

It will also be noted that the maximum value of the objective function has increased from 639000 to 647100.

This clearly means that if an extra unit of this resource could be obtained, then the value of the objective function (Revenue) would increase by £8100. Consequently, we can deduce that the firm would be willing to pay up to £8100 for that extra unit, since the net contribution to profit would be positive for all amounts paid that are less than £8100, (and zero for a value of £8100).

This figure (£8100) is known as the **shadow price** of the resource, and is defined as the maximum amount that the firm would pay for an extra unit of the resource with that shadow price.

Now restore the value in the D16 cell of Sheet1 Clone to 70, but increase the value in B16 from 60 to 61.

This represents a unit increase in the availability of the resource associated with the first constraint.

Now run the Solver again and it will be found that the optimal solution has changed from $x_1 = 160$, $x_2 = 30$, $x_3 = 0$ to $x_1 = 158$, $x_2 = 34$, $x_3 = 0$.

It will also be found that the maximum value of the objective function has changed from 639000 to 640200.

This represents an increase of £1200, and so we conclude that the shadow price of the resource associated with the first constraint is £1200.

Finally, restore the value in B16 to its original value of 60 and increase the value in C16 from 80 to 81.

This represents an extra unit of the resource associated with the second constraint becoming available.

However, before running the Solver to investigate the effects of this extra availability, notice that in the 'before' situation optimal solution, only 41 units of the 80 units available were used. Consequently, the slack on this resource is 39 units.

Given this, we should expect that an extra unit being available would have no effect upon the optimal solution or the maximum revenue (since there were 39 units unused anyway).

Confirm this now by running the Solver on the 'after' situation and noting that there is no change apart from there being an extra unit of this resource being unused (i.e. the slack on the second constraint has increased from 39 to 40).

Also notice that the implication of a resource not being fully used is that its shadow price is zero. This is intuitively obvious when it is remembered that there is no economic sense in paying any positive amount for an extra unit of a resource that is not being fully used. Consequently, positive shadow prices indicate scarce resources and zero shadow prices indicate non scarce resources.

Save this file now as W4_11.XLS.

In summary, and for ease of reference in subsequent discussion we can show the optimal solution for this problem in Table 4.1.

It should also be noted that this 'before and after' approach can also be used to investigate the effects of changes in the actual coefficient values of the program (as opposed to the RHS values of the constraints).

For example, suppose that the contribution made to the objective function by the third variable increased from 2400 to 2600. It is an easy matter to change the value in the D4 cell of Sheet1 Clone to 2600, and discover that this has no effect upon the optimal solution. It is still optimal to have the third variable zero valued. The value of the objective function is also unchanged.

Confirm this now.

Table 4.1

	NO.	OPTIMAL VALUE		
Variable	1	160		
Variable	2	30		
Variable	3	0		
Variable	Revenue	639000		

	NO.	OPTIMAL VALUE	SLACK	RESOURCE SHADOW PRICE
Constraint	1	60	0	1200
Constraint	2	41	39	0
Constraint	3	70	0	8100

However, if the third variable's contribution to the objective function should increase to 2700 then it will be found that the optimal solution changes quite radically. To be exact it is now the first variable that should be zero valued while the optimal values for the second and third variables become 50 and 200 respectively. Also, the value of the objective function has increased from 639000 to 645000.

Confirm this now.
Exercise 4.10 can be attempted now.

The method of conducting sensitivity analysis explained above, although simple and effective, is deficient in one respect—it does not automatically supply the shadow prices of the resources or provide information on the limits within which the values of the variables that produce the optimal solution will remain unchanged. We have to compute these for ourselves by trial and error.

Ideally therefore, we would like to be given such information automatically, and to obtain this we must ask Excel for a **Sensitivity Report**.

This is easily done at the last Solver dialogue screen.

Consequently, make sure that the most recent version of Workbook 4.11 is on screen and that Sheet1 is active.

Now run the Solver routine as before, but at the last dialogue screen instead of clicking OK straight away, click on the Answer Report tab in the window on the right-hand side of the screen. Now keep the shift key depressed and click on the last item on this list. All three should now be highlighted. If they are, click on OK and Excel will automatically create three new sheets in your workbook—the Answer Report, the Sensitivity Report, and the Limits Report.

Each of these reports supply information on how the optimal solution would change if there were small changes in the parameters of the program.

For example, click on the Answer Report sheet and you should find that the information that was summarized in Table 4.1 is produced in a very similar format (although the shadow prices do not appear in this report).

Now click on the Sensitivity Report sheet, ignore the top section, but observe that the shadow prices that were computed from the 'before and after' approach are reproduced exactly in the column under the Lagrange Multiplier heading.

Finally, click on the Limits Report to obtain a summary of the values that the

objective function would adopt if each of the variables in turn adopted a zero value when the others were at their optimal value.

For example, with the illustrative values currently being used the first line of the Limits report shows that if the value of x_1 was set to zero with x_2 and x_3 being at their optimal values of 30 and 0 respectively, the value of the objective function would be 63000. Similarly, line 2 of the report shows that if x_2 was set equal to zero, with x_1 and x_3 being at their optimal values of 160 and 0 respectively, then the value of the objective function is 576000.

Finally, since the optimal value of x_3 is in fact zero, line 3 shows that the optimal solution would be unchanged at 639000 if x_3 were set to zero.

Exercises 4.11 and 4.12 can be attempted now.

4.10. Solving simultaneous equations

Modelling various types of business and economic relationships frequently generates what are known as **systems** of linear equations.

When this happens, resolution of the model will usually require that unique solution values are obtained for all of the variables that the model contains. To do this requires that each of the equations in the model is considered **collectively** rather than individually so that the simultaneous solution can be obtained.

The implication of this is that if a system of equations contains m variables, then to obtain unique solution values for all of them requires that the system contains an equal number of independent equations.

For example, suppose that 2 firms (A and B) each purchase two types of concrete (I and II) from the same supplier. Also suppose that the supplier charges the same price to each firm for each type of concrete.

Now suppose that firm A purchases 100 tons of type I and 400 tons of type II and receives an invoice for £2400. Firm B on the other hand, purchases 300 tons of type I and 200 tons of type II and receives an invoice for £2200.

The task is to determine the prices charged by the supplier for the two types of concrete. To do this we can proceed as follows. Let x = the price of type I concrete and y = the price of type II concrete.

Then for firm A we have:

$$100x + 400y = 2400$$

and for firm B:

$$300x + 200y = 2200$$

To solve these two equations simultaneously, we must take the information supplied by one of them and include it in the other.

Thus the first equation can be rewritten as:

$$100x = 2400 - 400y \text{ implying } x = 24 - 4y \text{ after dividing throughout by 100.}$$

This means the second equation can be rewritten entirely in terms of y as:

$$300(24 - 4y) + 200y = 2200 = 300(24) - 300(4y) + 200y = 2200$$

Therefore:

$$7200 - 1200y + 200y = 2200$$
$$5000 = 1000y$$
$$y = 5$$

This value for y can now be substituted into either of the original equations to give the value of x.

Hence:

$$100x + 400(5) = 2400$$

Implying that:

$$100x = 400$$
$$\text{Hence, } x = 4$$

Thus x = 4 and y = 5 are the simultaneous solution values for the system of equations that were defined.

When the number of variables is small, the analytical solution method that has just been used is satisfactory. However, as the number of variables increases, so too must the number of equations, and then the models can be tedious to solve.

The Solver can help here however, since the method of solving systems of linear equations is very similar to the method of solving linear programs that has already been explained.

To see this, load Workbook 4.12 (W4_12.XLS).

This is simply Workbook 4.10 with a few modifications.

First the labels were changed to reflect the fact that we are now dealing with equations rather than constraints. Then the system was considered in terms of LHS and RHS **equalities** (rather than inequalities).

Now, since there is no objective function *as such* that is to be maximized or minimized, we must adjust the solver settings to take account of this.

The method is to regard the first equation as the objective by using the LHS of the equation as the target cell and the RHS as the target value. As before, the cells that must change in order to achieve this target are the variable values in B2:G2.

In addition however, we must regard the left-hand and right-hand sides of the remaining equations as the constraints of the model. But in this case they will all be in the form of strict equalities.

The general effect of this structure is to create a model in which the LHS of the first equation is to be equated with its target RHS. Since however, this can be done in a variety of ways, the model is made definite by the introduction of the requirements that the left-hand sides and the right-hand sides of the remaining equations must also be equal. In this way unique solution values for each of the variables will be obtained.

This means that the Solver settings should resemble Fig. 4.7.

When these modifications have been made the Solver model is now capable of solving systems of equations containing up to six variables and six equations.

For the moment however, we will use the model to solve the two equations in two unknowns that were solved above.

Therefore, make the appropriate entries to the B7:C8 and the B16:C16 ranges of Workbook 4.12, if they are not already there in the loaded file, and ensure that all other highlighted cells are zero valued or blank.

Now run the Solver, and the results obtained earlier by the analytical method should be confirmed (x = 4, y = 5).

Exercise 4.13 can be attempted now.

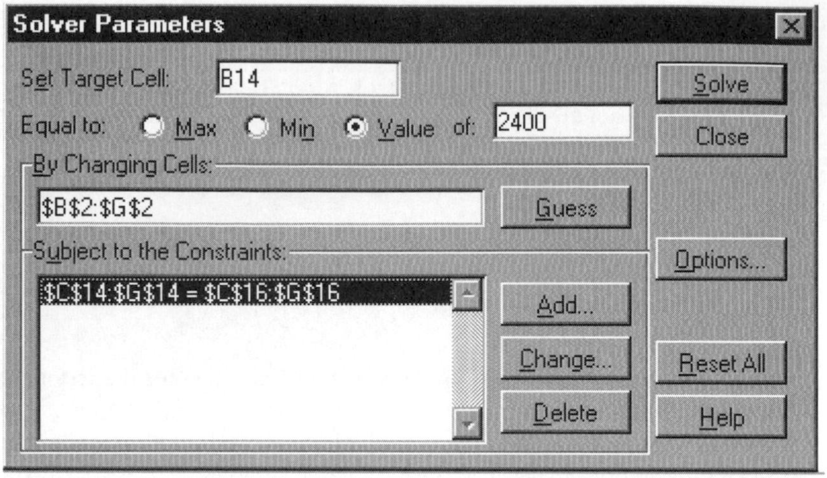

Figure 4.7

4.11. **Non-linear optimization subject to constraints**

In the context of optimization, the discussion up until now has considered non linear optimization without constraints (Section 4.6) and linear optimization subject to linear constraints (Section 4.7).

It is now time to turn our attention to the logical next step—non-linear optimization subject to linear or non-linear constraints.

Optimization problems of this type crop up frequently in business and economics and would normally require methods based upon differential calculus. However, with an understanding of the Solver, they can be modelled and solved without a knowledge of such techniques. To see how, consider a firm that uses three inputs (labour time, machine time, and a raw material) to produce a finished product.

Also suppose that the relationship between the amount of the inputs used (x, y, and z respectively) and the output produced (q) is given by:

$$q = x^{0.3}y^{0.2}z^{0.4}$$

Finally, imagine that the unit costs of each of the inputs are £2, £5, and £3 respectively. This means that the total cost of production (c) is given in terms of the amounts of the inputs used by:

$$c = 2x + 5y + 3z$$

Now consider a situation in which the department producing the product is allocated a budget of £2000. This budget must be spent in its entirety but cannot be exceeded.

The scenario faced by the department can therefore be summarized verbally in terms of an objective of producing the greatest output possible given the size of the allocated budget. This translates into the following mathematical program:

$$\text{Maximize } q = x^{0.3}y^{0.2}z^{0.4}$$

File	Edit	View	Insert	Format	Tools	Data	Window	Help

B6 ▼ =B1^D1*B2^D2*B3^D3

	A	B	C	D	E	F	G	H	I
1	Labour time	200	coefficient	0.3					
2	Machine time	50	coefficient	0.2					
3	Raw materials	100	coefficient	0.4					
4									
5									
6	Output	67.62433							
7									
8	Unit labour time cost	2							
9	Unit machine time cost	5							
10	Unit raw material cost	3							
11									
12	Total cost	950							
13	Budget	2000							
14									

Sheet1 / Sheet1 (2) / Sheet2 / Sheet3 / Sheet4 /

Subject to $c = 2x + 5y + 3z = 2000$

The procedure for setting up this program for the Solver is shown in Workbook 4.13.

Workbook 4.13 The formula in B6 is shown on the Formula bar and the one in B12 is:

$$= B1 * B8 + B2 * B9 + B3 * B10$$

Make up this worksheet now and then run the Solver with the target cell of output in B6 being required to adopt a maximum value by changing the B1:B3 cells, subject to the constraint that that the total cost in B12 must be equal to the budget available in B13.

The solution values for each of the variables should be calculated as 333.33, 88.88, and 296.29 respectively for labour time, machine time, and raw material usage. Also, the greatest output that can be obtained from this budget is 136.56.

The model outlined above can also be formulated in slightly different terms by removing the fixed budget and assuming that the department is required to fulfil a **given** order of (for example) 500 units, and do so at the **lowest** cost possible.

This means that the program becomes:

Minimize $c = 2x + 5y + 3z$
Subject to $q = x^{0.3}y^{0.2}z^{0.4} = 500$

This program can be solved in Workbook 4.13 if the Solver settings are adjusted appropriately.

To do this, first copy the A1: D13 range into Sheet2.

Then add the Solver settings that will minimize the target cell (Total cost in B12), by changing the values in B1:B3. This is to be done subject to the constraint that the output produced in B6 is equal to 500 units.

Now run the Solver for this problem to produce solution values of labour time = 1409.795, machine time = 375.9354, and raw material usage = 1253.145. Also, the minimum cost of producing the required 500 units is 8458.702.

Now re-save the file as W4_13.XLS.

Both of these programs view the optimization process from different perspectives.

In the first case, the given budget must be used as effectively as possible in order to make the greatest possible output. In the second case, the given output specified in the order must be produced at the minimum possible cost.

In both cases however, the ultimate objective is to find the usage levels of the three inputs that satisfy these different objectives.

Exercises 4.14 and 4.15 can be attempted now.

4.12. Exercises

Exercise 4.1

A firm's annual fixed costs of operation are £2 million, with unit costs of production being £4.

The product produced sells at a constant price of £8.

Use the Excel Solver to determine the annual break-even level of production if all the output produced can be sold at the price of £8.

Exercise 4.2

The demand for an industry's product (d) is given in terms of the price charged (p) by:

$$d = 2100 - 0.1p$$

The amount supplied (s) by the industry is given in terms of p by:

$$s = 2p$$

Use the Excel Solver to determine the price at which the supply and the demand are equal.

Exercise 4.3

Reconsider part (ii) of Exercise 3.2.

Use the Excel Solver to confirm the solution values for p of £0.53 and £99.47 that were obtained in the worked solution to that problem.

Exercise 4.4

A firm's market share (y%) in terms of advertising expenditure (£x million) is given by:

$$y = 100(1 - e^{-mx})$$

Use the Excel solver to determine the value of m that will ensure that the market share is 50% when x = £10 million.

Exercise 4.5

The annual quantity demanded of a firm's product (q) is given in terms of the price charged (p) by:

$$q = 3000 - 0.2p^2$$

The total costs of production (c) are given in terms of output by:

$$c = 1000 + q^2$$

Use the Excel Solver to determine the price that should be charged if the firm is required to make the greatest profit.

Exercise 4.6

A firm's sales volume (y) is given in terms of its level of advertising expenditure (£x thousand) by:

$$y = 200(1 - e^{-0.4x})$$

The product sells at a constant price of £10.

Use the Excel Solver to determine the level of advertising expenditure that should be carried out if the firm wishes to maximize the net revenue from sales (i.e. total revenue minus advertising expenditure).

Exercise 4.7

Consider the worked example from Section 4.7:

Maximize $15x + 16y =$ Revenue

Subject to $2x + 2y \leq 24$
(labour time constraint)

and: $x + 5y \leq 44$
(machine time constraint)

$6x + 2y \leq 60$
(steel constraint)

Now imagine that units of labour time, machine time, and steel had to be purchased at prices of £2, £1.50, and £1 respectively, and that the firm's objective was to maximize profit. Reformulate the linear program to take account of this new information and then use the model developed in Workbook 4.9 (W4_9.XLS) to solve for the values of x and y that produce the greatest profit.

Exercise 4.8

A building company has acquired 250000 square metres land, for which it paid £2000000 and on which it plans to build three types of dwelling: terraced, semi-detached, and detached.

Each terraced block consists of 4 individual units which each require 180 square metres of land and which will be sold for £40000 per unit.

Each semi-detached block consists of 2 individual units which each require 250 square metres of land and which will be sold for £50000 per unit.

Each detached block consists of one individual unit which requires 400 square metres of land and which will be sold for £62000 per unit.

The construction costs for the three types of unit are £34000, £42000, and £52000 for terraced, semi-detached, and detached units respectively.

A total of 25000 square metres will have to be earmarked for access and recreational facilities.

The Planning Authorities will not allow the total number of blocks on the site to exceed 300, nor the number of terraced blocks to exceed 150, while the mortgage situation is such that the builder feels that the number of detached blocks should not exceed 50.

Formulate and solve the linear program which will maximize the building company's profit.

Exercise 4.9

An oil fired power station burns three grades of oil: grades A, B, and C.

The efficiency with which electricity can be produced from the burning of these oils depends upon the presence of three ingredients (X, Y, and Z) which are known to be present in each ton of the three grades as shown in Table 4.2.

Table 4.2	TONS OF INGREDIENT PER TON OF OIL		
	X	Y	Z
Grade A	0.2	0.4	0.3
Grade B	0.1	0.3	0.2
Grade C	0.3	0.2	0.4

Maximum efficiency in the burning process requires the presence of at least 200 tons of ingredient X, at least 175 tons of ingredient Y, and at least 300 tons of ingredient Z, in 1 hour of continuous electricity production.

The power station purchases the oil at prices of £60, £80, and £70 per ton for grades A, B, and C respectively, and is required to operate for 12 hours per day.

(i) Formulate the linear program which will minimize the total daily cost of electricity production.

(ii) Obtain the optimal utilization rates of the three grades of oil.

Exercise 4.10

Reconsider Exercise 4.9.

By using a before and after approach, answer the following questions.

(i) If a new burning process became available which meant that the minimum necessary amount of ingredient X was reduced to 150 tons per hour, what changes would this induce in the optimal solution obtained in the previous solution?

(ii) If a new grade of oil were to become available at the same price as grade A, but which contained 0.2, 0.41, and 0.31 tons of ingredients X, Y, and Z respectively, should the new grade of oil be used in preference to grade A?

Exercise 4.11

Reconsider Exercise 4.8.

Generate an appropriate Excel report to answer the following questions. Obtain a measure of the cost to the firm of the Planning Authorities' restrictions that:

(i) the total number of blocks must not exceed 300

(ii) the number of terraced blocks must not exceed 150

(iii) If it were later discovered that 15,000 square metres of the land was unsuitable for building purposes what difference would this imply for the optimal solution?

(iv) What difference would be implied for the optimal solution if the firm had received a 10% discount on the price it paid for the land?

Exercise 4.12

A publishing company sells its major textbook at home, in the USA, and in Australasia. The production costs per textbook are £8 regardless of the book's market destination, but transport costs per textbook are £0.5, £1.00, and £1.50 for books distributed to the home, US, and Australasian markets respectively. The selling prices for the textbook are £10, £12, and £14 in the respective markets (home, US, and Australasian), while demand conditions are such that at these prices, annual sales in each of the markets cannot exceed 12000, 4000, and 8000 respectively.

(i) The publisher has just completed a production run of 20000 copies, and requires you to write and solve a linear program that will determine the sales volumes that should be allocated to each of the three markets if profits are to be maximized.

(ii) On completion of this task you discover that as a result of import controls introduced by the US government the maximum volume of sales in that market has been reduced by 5%. Indicate the effect upon the optimal solution of such a change.

(iii) How would the company's profits have been affected if it had been the Australasian market in which the maximum sales volume had been reduced by 5%?

(iv) On the basis of your analysis can you recommend an increase in the production run?

(v) You are also asked to consider the following suggestion for an alteration in the company's pricing policy viz.

> Selling price per unit = 1.15 (unit production costs) + (unit transport costs),

and are told that for every 1% reduction (increase) in selling price, maximum sales in each of the markets will increase (decrease) by 0.25% of their previous value.

Re-write and solve the linear program to take account of this proposal.

Exercise 4.13

A firm produced 4 products in annual quantities that were given by x_1, x_2, x_3, and x_4. All units of output produced were sold. The products are sold at prices of £4, £6, £2, and £8 respectively, and the annual revenue was £8800.

The unit production costs of the products were £2, £5, £1, and £3 respectively, and the total annual cost of production was £4700. The unit advertising costs for each product were £0.2, £0.4, £0.3, and £0.1 respectively, and the total annual advertising costs were

£530. The unit distribution costs for each of the products were £0.4, £0.2, £0.1, and £0.3 respectively, and the annual distribution costs were £370.

Calculate the output and sales that must have occurred to have produced the revenue and cost amounts given.

Exercise 4.14

Reconsider the illustration from Section 4.11:

> Minimize $c = 2x + 5y + 3z$
> Subject to $q = x^{0.3}y^{0.2}z^{0.4} = 500$

Now suppose that the product being produced sells for a constant price of £15.

By reformulating the model in terms of total revenue and total cost determine the usage levels of the three inputs that will produce the greatest revenue subject to the constraint that profits must be at least 10% of total costs.

Exercise 4.15

Consider a firm that owns two distinct production plants (X and Y), each with its own separate cost functions (Cx and Cy) that are given in terms of the output produced (Qx and Qy) by:

> $Cx = 0.6Q^3 - 27Q^2 + 450Q + 15000$
> $Cy = Q^3 - 36Q^2 + 500Q + 20000$

Now suppose that the firm must meet a demand of 40 units for the product.

(i) Determine the output that should be produced from each of the plants if the demand is to be met at the minimum cost of production.

Suppose that the demand for the product depends upon the price charged (p) as follows: demand = 5000 - 2p

(ii) Determine the price that should be charged, and the output that should be produced from each of the plants if profits are to be maximized.

4.13. **Solutions to the exercises**

Solution to Exercise 4.1

Open up a new workbook and then use the A1:A4 range of a workbook to contain the labels:

Output   Total cost
Total revenue   Profit

Enter any value to B1 as the output produced. Then use B2:B4 to contain the formulae:

$$= 2000000 + 4*B1 \qquad = 8*B1$$
$$= B3 - B2$$

Now set up the Solver so that:

Target cell = B4
Target cell value = 0
(Break-even implies zero profit)
Changing cell = B1

Now click on Solve to obtain the break-even level of output of 500000 units.

Solution to Exercise 4.2

Open up a new workbook and then use the A1:A4 range of a workbook to contain the labels:

Price   Demand   Supply
Surplus (+)/Shortage(-)

Enter any value to B1 as the price charged. Then use B2:B4 to contain the formulae:

=2100-0.1*B1   =2*B1   =B3-B2

Now set up the Solver so that:

Target cell = B4
Target cell value = 0
(Neither surplus nor shortage when demand equals supply)
Changing cell = B1

Now click on Solve to obtain the 'equilibrium' price of £1000.

Solution to Exercise 4.3

Workbook 4.14

The solution method is shown in Workbook 4.14.

Make this workbook up as indicated and then run the Solver with the settings shown. Because the entered trial value for price (60) is closer to 100 than it is to 0, the higher break-even price of £99.49 will be returned.

However, if the trial price is decreased to 30, which is closer to 0 than to 100, then the other break-even price of £0.532 will be found.

Solution to Exercise 4.4

Open up a new workbook and then use A1:A3 to contain the labels:

Advertising expenditure   Value of m
Market share

Then use B1:B3 to contain the following values and formula

10   0.1   =100*(1-EXP(-B2*B1))

The value in B2 is the trial value for m, so this is the changing cell.

The target cell is B3 and the target value is 50.

Make these settings and then click on Solve to obtain a value of m = 0.0693. This ensures a market share of 50% when £10 million is spent on advertising.

Solution to Exercise 4.5

Open up a new workbook and then use A1:A5 to contain the labels:

Price   Quantity demanded
Total revenue   Total cost   Profit

	W4_14							
	A	**B**	**C**	**D**	**E**	**F**	**G**	
1	Total cost (£millions)	10						
2	% of total cost to be recovered in 1st year	5%						
3								
4	Price charged per crossing (£)	60	Changing cell is B4					
5	Number of crossings (millions)	0.4	= 1-0.01*B4					
6	Revenue generated (£millions)	24	=B4*B5					
7								
8	Maintenance costs per crossing (£)	0.03						
9	Annual maintenance costs (£millions)	0.012	=B8*B5					
10								
11	Required annual revenue (£millions)	0.512	=B2*B1+B9					
12								
13	Revenue generated - required revenue	23.49	=B6-B11	Target cell is B13				
14				Target cell value is 0				

Sheet1 / Sheet2 / Sheet3 / Sheet4 / Sheet5 / She

Enter any positive value to B1 as the price charged, and then use B2:B5 to contain the following formulae:

> In B2: =3000-0.2*B1^2
> (the quantity demanded)
> In B3: =B2*B1
> (revenue = quantity demanded times price)
> In B4: =1000+B2^2
> (cost = 1000 plus the square of quantity demanded)
> In B5: =B3-B4
> (profit—revenue minus cost)

The target cell is B5 (profit) and the target cell value is to be maximized.

The changing cell is the one containing the price (B1).

Make these settings and then click on Solve to obtain a value of £121.24 as the price that should be charged in order to make the greatest profit.

Solution to Exercise 4.6

Open up a new workbook and then use A1:A5 to contain the labels:

> Advertising expenditure
> Sales volume   Price
> Gross revenue   Net revenue

Enter a trial value of 100 to B1.

Now use B2:B5 to contain the formulae:

> In B2: =200*(1-EXP(-0.4*B1))
> (sales volume)
> In B3: =10
> (price)
> In B4: =B3*B2
> (gross revenue = price times sales volume)
> In B5: =B4-B1
> (net revenue = gross revenue minus advertising expenditure)

The target cell is net revenue in B5 and the target cell value is to be maximized.

The changing cell is the one containing the level of advertising expenditure (B1)

Make these settings and then click on Solve to obtain a value of 16.71 thousand for the amount of advertising expenditure that is most cost effective with regards to sales revenue.

Solution to Exercise 4.7

Each girder requires 2 units of labour time, 1 unit of machine time, and 6 units of steel. Therefore the cost of producing one girder is $2(2) + 1(1.50) + 6(1) = £11.50$, and the cost of producing x girders is £11.50x.

For casings, a similar logic reveals that each casing requires 2 units of labour time, 5 units of machine time, and 2 units of steel.

Therefore the cost of producing one casing is $2(2) + 5(1.50) + 2(1) = £13.50$, and the cost of producing y casings is £13.50y.

Consequently, the total cost (C) of producing x girders and y casings is:

> $C = 11.50x + 13.50y$

With revenue being given by:

> $R = 15x + 16y$

it follows that profit (Z) is defined by:

> $Z = (15 - 11.50)x + (16 - 12.50)y = 3.50x + 2.50y$

We therefore need to maximize profit subject to the same constraints upon resource availability as before.

To obtain the solution, load Workbook 4.9 (W4_9.XLS).

Now enter the new profit expression to the B4 cell as the modified objective function. That is, change the contents of B4 from:

> =15*B1+16*B2   to:
> =3.5*B1+2.5*B2

The Solver settings do not require adjustment, so click on Solve to obtain the optimal solution of x = 9, y = 3 as the output levels of girders and casings that produce the greatest profit.

Notice that these are not the same as the values that produce the greatest revenue (x = 4, y = 8).

You can also see a more flexible model that can solve linear programs of this type (2 variables, 3 constraints) if you load Workbook 4.15 (W4_15.XLS).

By making appropriate entries to the yellow highlighted cells (and only those cells) use this model now to solve the problem that has just been completed.

Then imagine that the prices of each of the three inputs were zero. Make these changes to the worksheet and then re-solve the model. The revenue-maximizing solution of x = 4,

$y = 8$ will be returned (since with zero costs maximizing revenue is the same as maximizing profit).

Solution to Exercise 4.8

Let T = the number of terraced blocks constructed.

Let S = the number of semi-detached blocks constructed.

Let D = the number of detached blocks constructed.

The objective function of maximizing profit (P) can then be identified as:

Maximize: $4(40000-34000)T + 2(50000-42000)S + 1(62000-52000)D = P = 24000T + 16000S + 10000D$

Subject to: $4(180)T + 2(250)S + 1(400)D \leq 225000 = 720T + 500S + 400D$

$T + S + D \leq 300$

$T \leq 150$

$D \leq 50$

Now load Workbook 4.10 (W4_10.XLS) and make the following entries (with zeros everywhere else in the highlighted areas).

	B	C	D	E
ROW 4	24000	16000	10000	
ROW 7	720	500	400	
ROW 8	1	1	1	
ROW 9	1	0	0	
ROW 10	0	0	1	
ROW 16	225000	300	150	50

Now run the Solver to find that the optimal solution is to build 150 terraced blocks and 150 semi-detached blocks. This will leave 42000 square metres of land unused, and so the restriction on the number of detached blocks does not operate as an effective constraint at all.

When the £2.5 million that was paid for the land is subtracted this leaves a net profit of £4.5 million.

Solution to Exercise 4.9

(i) The objective function is easily identified as:

Minimize: $60a + 80b + 70c = Cost$

Where:

a = the number of tons of grade A coal burned per day

b = the number of tons of grade B coal burned per day

c = the number of tons of grade C coal burned per day

These tonnages must supply at least 200, 175, and 300 tons of ingredients X, Y, and Z in one hour of continuous electricity production. Therefore the requirement that the power station must operate for 12 hours per day means that at least $12(200) = 2400$ tons of X must be supplied, at least $12(175) = 2100$ tons of Y must be supplied, and at least $12(300) = 3600$ tons of Z must be supplied.

The ingredients are present in the various grades of oil as indicated, so that burning c tons of grade C oil, for example, will supply 0.3c tons of ingredient X and 0.2c tons of ingredient Y, and so on. We therefore have the following 3 constraints:

$0.2a + 0.1b + 0.3c \geq 2400$

i.e. (Ingredient X supply) $\geq$ (Ingredient X requirement).

$0.4a + 0.3b + 0.2c \geq 2100$

i.e. (Ingredient Y supply) $\geq$ (Ingredient Y requirement).

$0.3a + 0.2b + 0.4c \geq 3600$

i.e. (Ingredient Z supply) $\geq$ (Ingredient Z requirement).

(ii) Now load Workbook 4.10 (W4_10.XLS) and make the following entries (with zeros everywhere else in the highlighted areas).

	B	C	D
ROW 4	60	80	70
ROW 7	0.2	0.1	0.3
ROW 8	0.4	0.3	0.2
ROW 9	0.3	0.2	0.4
ROW 16	2400	2100	3600

The Solver settings will have to be changed to reflect the fact that this is a minimization problem. So, alter the setting from Max to Min for the target cell value, and change all the constraints from $\leq$ to $\geq$.

Now run the Solver to find the optimal solution to be to burn 1200 tons of grade A oil and 8100 tons of grade C oil. Grade B oil should not be used, the minimum necessary amount of ingredient X is exceeded by 270 units, and the minimum cost is £639000.

Save this file as W4_10A to have a separate

model that can address minimization problems.

Solution to Exercise 4.10

(i) Load Workbook 4.10A (W4_10A.XLS), and then make a copy of Sheet1.

Now reduce the value in B16 from 2400 to 1800 (i.e. 12*150) and run the Solver again. It should be found that the optimal allocation is unchanged as a result of this reduced ingredient X requirement.

This is only to be expected, since the supply of ingredient X is already excess to requirements, and so the introduction of the new process will simply mean that the excess supply will increase from 270 tons to 870 tons (since the minimum requirement is now 1800 tons per 12 hour shift as opposed to 2400 previously).

(ii) Since the new grade of oil contains the same amount of ingredient X and more of both ingredients Y and Z than grade A oil, it follows that burning the same tonnage of the new grade will supply more of ingredients Y and Z than would grade A oil. Furthermore, since the constraints upon ingredients Y and Z are binding in the optimal solution, (and since ingredient X is over-supplied) it also follows that the required supply of all ingredients could be provided by burning less of the new grade of oil. Since this new grade is available at the same price as grade A oil, it also follows that the total cost would be reduced.

This can be confirmed by using the 'after' sheet to contain the program with the new constraints:

$$0.2a + 0.1b + 0.3c \geq 2400$$
$$0.41 + 0.3b + 0.2c \geq 2100$$
$$0.31a + 0.2b + 0.4c \geq 3600$$

That is, change the value in B16 back to 2400 and then change B8 and B9 to 0.41 and 0.31 respectively.

The new solution will be to burn 1176.47 tons of the new grade of oil (instead of 1200 tons of grade A oil), 8088.24 tons of grade C oil, at a minimum total cost of £636764.71.

Solution to Exercise 4.11

Load Workbook 4.10, and if necessary make the coefficient entries as indicated in the solution to Exercise 4.8.

Now run the Solver and select the Sensitivity report.

(i) Line 2 of the bottom half of the report indicates that the shadow price associated with the constraint on the total number of buildings is 16000. This indicates that the opportunity cost to the company of this particular restriction is £16000. That is, profit would increase by £16000 if the restriction on the total number of blocks was relaxed by 1.

(ii) Line 3 of the report indicates that the shadow cost of the restriction upon the number of terraced blocks is 8000. Thus, profit would increase by £8000 if the restriction on the total number of blocks was relaxed by 1.

(iii) The zero shadow price associated with the land constraint indicates that it is not a scarce resource; and since there are 42000 square metres of land left over in the optimal solution, all that will happen is that this surplus will be reduced by 15000 (to 27000 square metres).

(iv) The fact that the price paid for the land is a 'sunk' cost means that it exercises no influence over the best way of using the land that was acquired. In other words, any discount will not affect the optimal number of dwellings of each type that should be constructed. All that will happen is that the maximum profit will be increased by the amount of the discount received, with this maximum being achieved in the *same way* as without the discount.

Solution to Exercise 4.12

(i) Let h = sales to the home market.
Let u = sales to the US market.
Let a = sales to the Australasian market.
Then:

Profit per book sold in the home market = £10 - £8 - £0.5 = £1.50
Profit per book sold in the US market = £12 - £8 - £1 = £3.00
Profit per book sold in the Australasian market = £14 - £8 - £1.50 = £4.50

We therefore require to:

Maximize: $1.5h + 3u + 4.5a = $ Profit

This profit function is subject to the following constraints:

$h + u + a \leq 20000$

That is, total sales to all 3 markets cannot exceed the production run of 20000 copies.

$h \leq 12000$

$u \leq 4000$

$a \leq 8000$

That is, the demand restrictions mean that sales to *each* of the markets are confined as above.

Now load Workbook 4.10 (W4_10.XLS) and make the following entries (with zeros everywhere else in the highlighted areas).

	B	C	D	E
ROW 4	1.5	3	4.5	
ROW 7	1	1	1	
ROW 8	1	0	0	
ROW 9	0	1	0	
ROW 10	0	0	1	
ROW 16	20000	12000	4000	8000

Now run the Solver to obtain the optimal solution of selling 8000 copies in the home market, 4000 copies in the US market, and 8000 copies in the Australasian market. This produces a maximum profit of 60000.

(ii) Since the maximum volume of sales in the US market has fallen by 5%, u must now be less than or equal to 3800.

Make a copy of the sheet and then reduce the value in the D16 cell from 4000 to 3800. Then run the Solver with the same settings.

As should be seen, 200 copies have been diverted from the US market to the home market, and as a result the profit has fallen by £300.

(iii) Run the Solver on the Clone sheet after having restored the maximum sales in the US market to 4000 and reducing the maximum sales in the Australasian market to 7600. This will show that 400 copies (5% of 8000) would have to be diverted from the Australasian market to the home market, and that the profit would fall by £600.

(iv) Generate a Sensitivity report on the first sheet. Since there is demand unsatisfied in the home market, this is indicated by the shadow price of 1.5 in line 1 of the report. Therefore an increase in production would be justified, provided that the cost per copy did not increase by more than £1.50.

(v) Under this new pricing policy the prices in the 3 markets would become:

Home market price 1.15(£8) + £0.5 = £9.70

US market price 1.15(£8) + 1.00 = £10.20

Australasian market price 1.15(£8) + 1.50 = £10.70

The price in the home market has fallen by (£10 - £9.7)/10 = 3%, and so maximum sales in that market will increase by 3(0.25)% of 12000 = 90 (i.e. to 12090).

By a similar logic it should be found that sales in the US market will increase by 15(0.25)% of 4000 =150 (i.e. to 4150), and that sales in the Australasian market will increase by 23.57(0.25)% of 8000 = 471 (i.e. to 8471).

The profit per copy is now £1.20 in all three markets, so the new program becomes:

Maximize: $1.2h + 1.2u + 1.2a = $ Profit

Subject to: $h + u + a \leq 20000$

$h \leq 12090$

$u \leq 4150$

$a \leq 8471$

When these new coefficients are entered to the second (copied) sheet of the worksheet and the Solver run, it should be found that the result of this new pricing strategy has been to alter the allocation to each of the markets. The way in which it is done, however, is entirely arbitrary. This is because, with copies sold in each market being equally profitable, it makes no difference where the copies are sold, as long of course as none of the maximum sales constraints is violated. This means that the Solver will find whatever values are closest to the trial values, provided these trial values are feasible.

With any allocation however, the effect of the new pricing policy is to reduce the profit by £36000 (from £60000 to £24000).

Now create the Sensitivity report for the new model in the *copied* sheet. It should indicate that, since sales are now equally profitable in each of the markets, the shadow costs of the demand restrictions have all become 0.

The only real constraint is the size of the production run (shadow cost = 1.2), and this indicates that if production could be increased it would be profitable to do so, but that it would not matter from the point of view of profit alone, in which market this extra production was sold.

Solution to Exercise 4.13

The following system of linear equations models the problem.

$$4x_1 + 6x_2 + 2x_3 + 8x_4 = 8800$$
(revenue)
$$2x_1 + 5x_2 + x_3 + 3x_4 = 4700$$
(production cost)
$$0.2x_1 + 0.4x_2 + 0.3x_3 + 0.1x_4 = 530$$
(advertising cost)
$$0.4x_1 + 0.2x_2 + 0.1x_3 + 0.3x_4 = 370$$
(distribution cost)

Now load Workbook 4.12 (W4_12.XLS) and make the following entries.

	B	C	D	E
ROW 7	4	6	2	8
ROW 8	2	5	1	3
ROW 9	0.2	0.4	0.3	0.1
ROW 10	0.4	0.2	0.1	0.3
ROW 16	8800	4700	530	370

Now change the target cell value to 8800 and Solve to obtain the solution values of:

$$x_1 = 100, x_2 = 400, x_3 = 1000, \text{ and } x_4 = 500$$

Solution to Exercise 4.14

The structure and formulae of the solution model is shown in Workbook 4_16. The target cell is B15 (revenue) and the target cell value is to be maximized.

The changing cells are the usage levels of the three inputs contained in B1:B3, and these must also be constrained to be greater than or equal to zero.

The final constraint is that the profit made must be at least 10% of the total costs incurred. Thus B16 (profit) must be $\geq 0.1*B12$

When these settings are made to the Solver, the optimal solution shown in the illustration should be obtained.

Solution to Exercise 4.15

(i) The structure and formulae of the solution model is shown in Workbook 4_17.

The formulae in B8 and C8 are:
$$=B2*B7^3+B3*B7^2+B4*B7+B5$$
and
$$=C2*C7^3+C3*C7^2+C4*C7+C5$$
While B9 and B10 contain:
$$=B7+C7 \qquad \text{and} \qquad =B8+C8$$
The Solver settings are as follows.

The target cell is B10 (total cost), and the target cell value is to be minimized.

The changing cells are the outputs from each of the factories (B7:C7) and these must be constrained to be greater than or equal to zero.

Workbook 4.16

	A	B	C	D	E	F	G	H	I
1	Labour time	163.2301	coefficient	0.3					
2	Machine time	43.52804	coefficient	0.2					
3	Raw materials	145.0936	coefficient	0.4					
4									
5									
6	Output	71.8213	=B1^D1*B2^D2*B3^D3						
7									
8	Unit labour time cost	2							
9	Unit machine time cost	5							
10	Unit raw material cost	3							
11									
12	Total cost	979.3814	=B8*B1+B9*B2+B10*B3						
13									
14	Price	15							
15	Revenue	1077.32	=B14*B6						
16	Profit	97.93814	=B15-B12						
17									

W4_16

Sensitivity Report 1 / **Sheet1** / Sheet1 (2) / Sheet2

	A	B	C	D	E	F	G	H	I
1	Cost coefficients	Plant X	Plant Y						
2	Coefficient of x^3	0.6	1						
3	Coefficient of x^2	-27	-36						
4	Coefficient of x	450	500						
5	Fixed cost	15000	20000						
6									
7	Output	22.71261	17.28739						
8	Cost	18322.34	23051.36						
9	Total output	40							
10	Total cost	41373.69							
11	Demand	40							
12									

Sheet1 / Sheet2 / Sheet3 / Sheet4 / Sheet5 / Sh

Workbook 4.17

The final constraint is that the combined output from the two factories must at least equal the demand for the product. Thus:

B9 must be ≥ B11

After making these settings run the Solver to obtain the optimal solutions shown in the illustrative workbook.

(ii) The introduction of a price function means that the demand for the product can no longer be taken as given, but rather will be determined by the price that the firm decides to charge. Given this, the next task will be to determine the optimal output from each of

Workbook 4.17A

the plants that meets the demand that has been created.

This is to be done within the overall global objective of maximizing profit.

The structure and formulae of the solution model is shown in Workbook 4_17A.

The additional formulae are as follows. In B11 the demand relationship is entered as:

=5000-2*B6

Then the revenue and profit were calculated in B12 and B13 from:

=B11*B6   and   =B12-B10

	A	B	C	D	E	F	G	H	I
1	Cost coefficients	Plant X	Plant Y						
2	Coefficient of x^3	0.6	1						
3	Coefficient of x^2	-27	-36						
4	Coefficient of x	450	500						
5	Fixed cost	15000	20000						
6	Price	2454.414							
7	Output	51.23863	39.93339						
8	Cost	47884.7	46239.18						
9	Total output	91.17202							
10	Total cost	94123.88							
11	Demand	91.17196							
12	Revenue	223773.7							
13	Profit	129649.9							
14									

Sheet1 \ **Sheet2** / Sheet3 / Sheet4 / Sheet5 / Sh

The target cell for this variant of the model is now profit (in B13), and the target cell value is to be maximized.

As before, the changing cells are the output levels of the two plants in B7:C7, and once again these must be constrained to be greater than or equal to zero. In addition however, the price (in B6) is also to be regarded as a changing cell. This means the changing cells box should contain the following entry:

B7:C7, B6

and B6 should also be constrained to be greater than or equal to zero.

Finally, the output produced (in B9) must satisfy the demand that has been created by the pricing strategy (in B11). Thus, the final constraint is that:

B9 must be $\geq$ B11

Make these settings and then click on Solve to obtain the optimal solution shown in the illustrative worksheet.

Financial mathematics

Contents
....

Accompanying files to be loaded as instructed:

None

5.1. **Introduction**

This chapter considers the effect that the passage of time, and the consequent payment of interest, exercises upon the value of any given sum of money after different lengths of time. The simplest starting-point is the notion that if any sum of money, called the principal, bears interest at a rate of r% per annum, then after one year has passed this principal has earned interest that is equal to the principal times (r/100). When this interest is added to the principal then the value of the account has become: principal plus (principal times r/100).

For example, a principal of £200 that was deposited at an interest rate of 10% per annum would bear an annual interest payment of:

$$£200(10/100) = £20$$

Furthermore, the value of the deposit when the annual interest has been included is easily seen to have increased from £200 to £200 + the annual interest payment, i.e. £200 + £20 = £220.

In general then, we can state:

amount after 1 year = principal + (principal)(r/100)

Now, although we have referred to the interest rate as a percentage rate per annum, it will usually be more convenient to convert it to a decimal expression, denoted as i. This means that an interest rate of 15% per annum, for example, can be re-expressed as 15/100 = 0.15.

In general, of course, we could say that an interest rate of r% per annum could be written in decimal form (i) as:

$$i = r\%/100$$

This means that the expression above for the amount after 1 year can now be rewritten as:

amount after 1 year = principal + (principal)(i)

Furthermore, since the right-hand side of the last expression above can have the principal factored out of it, we can rewrite it as:

amount after 1 year = (principal)(1 + i)

Obviously it becomes extremely tedious to write out lengthy expressions like the ones above, and so we should use the following generally recognized symbols as abbreviations:

t   = the number of years for which the principal is deposited.
i   = the interest rate expressed as a decimal.
P = the principal.
A_t = a subscripted variable representing the amount after t years have passed.

Taking these last two definitions together, it should be clear that we can also write:

$$P = A_0$$

That is, the principal is by definition the same as the amount after 0 years have passed. Furthermore, using these symbols more extensively, we can state that the amount after one year (A_1) is given by:

$$A_1 = P(1 + i) = A_0(1 + i)$$

For example, to find the amount after 1 year of a principal of £1500, if interest is paid at a rate of 6% per annum, we would evaluate:

$$A_1 = 1500(1 + 0.06) = 1500(1.06) = £1590$$

It should now be noted that the procedure illustrated above is perfectly adequate if only one year's interest is to be calculated; but it is easy to envisage circumstances in which we are required to find the value of a deposit after 2, 3, or more years have passed. In this case we must identify from the outset whether the annual interest rate is being applied on a simple or on a compound basis, since the calculation methods are significantly different in each case.

5.2. Simple interest

If interest is calculated on a simple basis, what this means is that at the end of each year for which the principal was deposited a constant interest payment of £iP is paid. This means that the annual interest received is the same regardless of the length of time for which the principal has been deposited.

It is easy to see that simple interest can be represented in terms of an arithmetic progression in which the first term is the principal, and the common difference is iP. We therefore have:

$$A_0 = P$$
$$A_1 = P + iP$$
$$A_2 = P + iP + iP = P + 2iP$$
$$A_3 = P + iP + iP + iP = P + 3iP$$

Following this sequence through, it should be clear that the amount after t years, denoted by A_t, will be given by:

$$A_t = P + iP + iP + \ldots + iP = P + tiP.$$

and that this can then be rewritten as:

$$A_t = P(1 + ti)$$

For example, to find the amount after 5 years of a deposit of £2500, if the annual simple interest rate for the period is 13% per annum we should evaluate:

$$2500[1 + 5(0.13)] = 2500(1 + 0.65) = 2500(1.65) = £4125$$

It should now be noticed that in the explanation to date we have made use of what is known as a recursive relationship. That is, each term in the series is related to the previous term in a constant, known fashion. Hence, for example, A_t is always equal to A_{t-1} plus the interest accruing during the year.

Identifying any recursive relationships that exist in a problem can often aid understanding and modelling, but on their own they are relatively weak computational aids. This is because before any chosen term can be evaluated, all previous terms must have been calculated.

Nevertheless, as we saw above, inspection of the recursive relationship often displays an expression that can be applied to any particular term to be evaluated. This was the obviously the case in our simple example, since we were easily able to derive, from the recursive relationship, an expression for A_t:

$$A_t = P(1 + ti)$$

These ideas are easily translated into an Excel workbook, as indicated in Workbook 5.1.

Make this up now.

	A	B	C	D	E	F	G	H	I
1	Principal (P)	2500							
2	Interest rate (i)	13%							
3	Number of years (t)	5							
4	Amount after t years (A_t)	4125							
5									

Sheet1 / Sheet2 / Sheet3 / Sheet4 / Sheet5 / She

Workbook 5.1

The entries in B1:B3 will be the given data of any simple interest problem, and the terminal amount after the specified number of years is calculated in B4 from:

=B1*(1+B3*B2)

For example, with P = 2500, i = 13%, and t = 5, use this worksheet to confirm the result obtained above for the terminal amount after 5 years (£4125).

In the previous example it was required to find the amount after a specified number of years (i.e. A_t), but this need not always be the problem posed. Nevertheless, simple algebraic transposition of the expression for A_t will always be sufficient to determine the value of any specified argument in the equation. To see this, suppose that it was required to find the annual simple interest rate which, if applied to the whole period, caused a principal of £2000 to amount to £3260 after 7 years.

To answer this we can start from

$$A_t = P(1 + ti)$$

and then write:

$$A_t/P = 1 + ti$$

whereby:

$$ti = A_t/P - 1$$

and:

$$i = (A_t/P - 1)/t$$

Therefore:

$$i = (3260/2000 - 1)/7 = (1.63 - 1)/7 = 0.09$$

The required interest rate is 9% per annum.

As another illustration, suppose we were required to find the number of years that it will take for a principal of £4000 to amount to £6400 if the annual simple interest rate for the period is 12%. To answer this we can again start from:

$$A_t = P(1 + ti)$$

and then write:

$$A_t/P = 1 + ti$$

whereby:

$$ti = A_t/P - 1$$

and:

$$t = (A_t/P - 1)/i$$

Therefore:

$$t = (6400/4000 - 1)/0.12 = (1.6 - 1)/0.12 = 5$$

We therefore can conclude that it will take 5 years for a deposit of £4000 to amount to £6400 if the annual simple interest rate is 12% for the entire period.

Finally, it may be the case that we are required to find the principal that would need to be deposited just now in order to amount to a given sum after t years when the interest rate is i per annum. Once again we can start from:

$$A_t = P(1 + ti)$$

whereby:

$$P = A_t/(1 + ti)$$

For example, if a principal of £P amounts to £6000 after 5 years when the annual simple interest rate is 10%, then the principal that must have been deposited is calculated from:

$$P = 6000/(1 + 5(0.1)) = 6000/1.5 = £4000$$

Each of these transformations of the basic formula can be incorporated into Excel worksheets as shown in Workbooks 5.2, 5.3, and 5.4.

Make these up now.

	A	B	C	D	E	F	G	H	
1	Principal (P)	2000							
2	Number of years (t)	7							
3	Amount after t years (A$_t$)	3260							
4	Required interest rate (i)	0.09							
5									

W5_2 — Sheet1 / Sheet2 / Sheet3 / Sheet4 / Sheet5 / She

Workbook 5.2 The given data of the problem should be entered to the B1:B3 range. Then the required interest rate is computed in B4 from:

=(B3/B1-1)/B2

	A	B	C	D	E	F	G	H	
1	Principal (P)	4000							
2	Interest rate (i)	12%							
3	Amount after t years (A$_t$)	6400							
4	Required number of years (t)	5							
5									

W5_3 — Sheet1 / Sheet2 / Sheet3 / Sheet4 / Sheet5 / She

Workbook 5.3 The given data of the problem should be entered to the B1:B3 range. Then the required number of years is computed in B4 from:

=(B3/B1-1)/B2

Workbook 5.4 The given data of the problem should be entered to the B1:B3 range. Then the required principal is computed in B4 from:

=B2/(1+B3*B1)

Exercise 5.1 can be attempted now.

	A	B	C	D	E	F	G	H
1	Interest rate (i)	12%						
2	Amount after t years (A$_t$)	7000.00						
3	Number of years (t)	6						
4	Required Principal (P)	4069.767						
5								

W5_4

Sheet1 / Sheet2 / Sheet3 / Sheet4 / Sheet5 / She

Workbook 5.4

5.3. Compound interest

The important point to have noted in the previous discussion was that because simple interest was being paid, the principal did not increase in magnitude as each subsequent year's interest was paid. However, this is contrary to our normal expectation that if a principal of £500 were deposited at a simple interest rate of 10% per annum, then after one year had passed the interest payment due would be £50, and that this payment should then be added to the account. The value of the account upon which the next year's interest is calculated would then become £550.

This would once again attract interest at an annual rate of 10%, and would mean that the second year's interest payment would be £55 (as opposed to £50 under simple interest). When this payment is added to the account, the value of the account at the start of the next period becomes £605, and the interest due at the end of the third year becomes £60.5. This steady increase in the size of the interest payment that results from the previous period's interest payment being added to the account and being left on deposit to gain further interest is the crucial feature of compound as opposed to simple interest.

Furthermore, since compound interest is by far the more prevalent practice amongst financial institutions, it is crucial that its logic is fully understood.

This logic can be more generally appreciated as follows. For the first year the situation is identical to simple interest. Hence:

$$A_1 = P + iP = P(1 + i)$$

After two years, however, it should be apparent that the amount accumulated is equal to the amount after 1 year plus i times that amount. That is:

$$A_2 = A_1 + iA_1$$

However, since we already know that $A_1 = P(1 + i)$, we can rewrite this last expression as:

$$A_2 = P(1 + i) + iP(1 + i)$$

Which, upon factoring the term in $P(1 + i)$, becomes:

$$A_2 = P(1 + i)(1 + i) = P(1 + i)^2$$

By a similar logic, we could find the amount after 3 years to be:

$$A_3 = A_2 + iA_2$$

Then, once again using our knowledge that $A_2 = P(1 + i)^2$, we can rewrite this as:

$$A_3 = P(1 + i)^2 + iP(1 + i)^2$$

This, upon factoring the term in $P(1 + i)^2$, then produces:

$$A_3 = P(1+i)^2(1+i) = P(1+i)^3$$

Careful inspection of the relationships that have been built up here should provide an obvious expression for the amount after t years. That is:

$$A_t = P(1+i)^t$$

To confirm this expression, consider the process of finding the compounded amount, after 3 years, of an initial deposit of £1000 if interest is compounded at a rate of 8% per annum for the period.

We therefore have:

$$P = A_0 = 1000$$
$$i = 8/100 = 0.08$$
$$t = 3$$

Therefore:

$$A_1 = £1000 + £1000(0.08) = £1080$$
$$A_2 = £1080 + £1080(0.08) = £1166.4$$
$$A_3 = £1166.4 + £1164.4(0.08) = £1259.71$$

However, this result could have been obtained more easily from the expression that was derived above:

$$A_t = P(1+i)^t$$

which, upon substituting the given values, produces:

$$A_3 = 1000(1+0.08)^3 = 1000(1.25971) = £1259.71$$

These ideas can be translated into an Excel worksheet, as indicated in Workbook 5.5.

Make this up now.

	A	B	C	D	E	F	G	H	I
1	Principal (P)	1000							
2	Interest rate (i)	5%							
3	Number of years (t)	6							
4									
5	Amount (A_t)	1340.10							
6									

Workbook 5.5 The given values for P, i, and t are entered to the B1:B3 range, and then the compounded amount calculated in B5 from the formula:

=B1*(1+B2)^B3

Exercise 5.2 can be attempted now.

As was the case in the discussion on simple interest, the basic compound interest formula derived above can be transformed to allow solution for any of the arguments that it contains. For example, suppose it were required to find the annual compound rate that is being received on a principal of £2000 that amounted to £3500 after 5 years.

We can proceed as follows.

$$A_t = P(1+i)^t$$

Therefore:

$$A_t/P = (1+i)^t$$

Now take the tth root of both sides to obtain:

$$\sqrt[t]{A_t/P} = (1+i)$$

whereby:

$$i = \sqrt[t]{A_t/P} - 1$$

To aid eventual transfer to Excel this should now be written in index form as:

$$i = (A_t/P)^{1/t} - 1$$

Thus with P, A_t, and t being given as £2000, £3500, and 5 respectively, we have:

$$i = (3500/2000)^{1/5} - 1 = 1.750^{0.2} - 1 = 1.118427 - 1 = 0.118427 = 11.8427\%$$

The annual compound rate for the period must have been 11.8427% if a principal of £2000 amounted to £3500 after 5 years.

To assist computation, these relationships can be translated into an Excel worksheet, as indicated in Workbook 5.6

Make this up now.

	A	B	C	D	E	F	G	H	I
1	Principal (P)	2000							
2	Amount (A$_t$)	3500							
3	Number of years (t)	5							
4									
5	Interest rate received	0.118427							
6									

Workbook 5.6 The entries in B1:B3 are the given values of P, A_t, and t, and the interest rate being received is calculated in B5 from the formula:

=(B2/B1)^(1/B3)-1

This is clearly the spreadsheet equivalent of the expression that was derived above, and confirms the result that was calculated manually from that expression.

Exercise 5.3 can be attempted now.

Now suppose that it were required to find the number of years that it will take for a principal of £1000 to amount to £2000 if the annual compound rate of interest is 15%. As before, we start with the basic compound interest formula:

$$A_t = P(1+i)^t$$

Therefore:

$$A_t/P = (1+i)^t$$

Now take logarithms of both sides to obtain:

$$\log(A_t/P) = t\log(1+i)$$

Therefore:

$$t = \log(A_t/P)/\log(1+i)$$

With the values given, this means that:

$$t = \log(2000/1000)/\log(1.15) = \log 2/\log 1.15 = 4.959 \text{ years}$$

It will therefore take almost 5 years for the principal of £1000 to double in value if the annual compound rate of interest is 15%.

Once again, the calculations can be simplified by entering them to an Excel worksheet. This is done in Workbook 5.7.

Make this up now.

	A	B	C	D	E	F	G	H
1	Principal (P)	1000						
2	Amount (A$_t$)	2000						
3	Interest rate	15%						
4								
5	Required number of years	4.959484						
6								

Sheet1 / Sheet2 / Sheet3 / Sheet4 / Sheet5 / She

Workbook 5.7

The given data of the problem—P, A$_t$, and i are entered to the B1:B3 range, and then the required number of years calculated in B5 from the formula:

=LOG(B2/B1)/LOG(1+B3)

The result obtained earlier (4.959 years) will be obtained.

Exercise 5.4 can be attempted now.

Finally, it is an easy matter to perform the last logical transformation of the basic compounding equation to obtain the principal that must be deposited just now in order to receive a specified amount after t years when the annual compound interest rate is i. This is done simply by rewriting:

$$A_t = P(1+i)^t$$

as:

$$P = A_t/P(1+i)^t$$

Hence, for example if an amount of £5000 is received after 6 years when the annual compound rate of interest is 8%, then the principal that must have been deposited in order to secure this terminal amount is calculated as:

$$P = 5000/(1.08)^6 = 5000/1.586874 = £3150.85$$

A worksheet that can perform calculations of this type is shown in Workbook 5.8.

Make this up now.

Workbook 5.8

The formula in B5 is:

=B1/(1+B2)^B3

When this is evaluated by Excel, the result obtained above (£3150.85) will be returned to the B5 cell.

Exercise 5.5 can be attempted now.

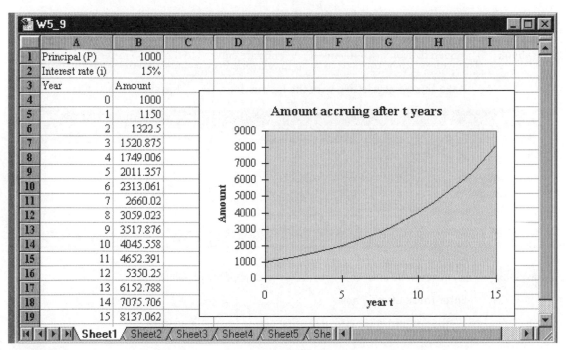

	A	B	C	D	E	F	G	H	
1	Amount (A_t)	5000							
2	Interest rate	8%							
3	Number of years	6							
4									
5	Required principal	3150.848							
6									

W5_8 — Sheet1 / Sheet2 / Sheet3 / Sheet4 / Sheet5 / She

Workbook 5.8

It should now be pointed out that, in the previous discussion, when the principal and the interest rate were given, the derived compounding formula calculated the amount accruing after a selected number of years (t). However, it will be instructive to investigate how the amount accruing varies with the passage of time. To do this we must evaluate A_t for each of a specified number of years.

An Excel worksheet that can do this efficiently is shown in Workbook 5.9.

Make this up now in line with the explanation.

W5_9

	A	B	C	D	E	F	G	H	I	
1	Principal (P)	1000								
2	Interest rate (i)	15%								
3	Year	Amount								
4	0	1000								
5	1	1150								
6	2	1322.5								
7	3	1520.875								
8	4	1749.006								
9	5	2011.357								
10	6	2313.061								
11	7	2660.02								
12	8	3059.023								
13	9	3517.876								
14	10	4045.558								
15	11	4652.391								
16	12	5350.25								
17	13	6152.788								
18	14	7075.706								
19	15	8137.062								

Sheet1 / Sheet2 / Sheet3 / Sheet4 / Sheet5 / She

Chart title: **Amount accruing after t years**, y-axis: Amount, x-axis: year t

Workbook 5.9

First of all enter the values and labels indicated in the A1:B3 range.

 Then name the B1 and B2 cells as P and i respectively (use Insert, Name, Define with the cursor located firstly in B1 and then in B2).

 Next, enter the year values 0 to 15 in the A4:A19 range.

 Finally, in B4 enter the formula:

$$=P*(1+i)\wedge A4$$

This will return a value that is identical to the principal in year zero.

Now copy B4 into B5:B19.

This will compute the amount accruing in each of the years 1 to 15. The results shown in the illustrative worksheet should now be obtained.

Now, chart the A4:B19 range as an XY Scatter graph to obtain the diagram shown in Workbook 5.9.

As is clear from this graph the amount accruing rises steadily as the number of years increases, and does so at an increasing rate.

In all of the previous examples it will have been noticed that the interest rate was constant over the entire period under consideration. However, it is easy to envisage circumstances in which the rate changes from time to time.

To deal with this additional complication, the problem can be approached as follows. Let i_1, i_2, i_3, etc. be the interest rates received respectively for periods of t_1, t_2, t_3, etc. years. It then follows that the amount after t_1 years (A_{t_1}) is given by:

$$A_{t_1} = P(1+i_1)^{t_1}$$

This amount can then be regarded as the principal to which the next period's interest rate (i_2) will apply for the whole of the next period (t_2). Consequently the amount after $t_1 + t_2$ years will be given by:

$$A_{t_1 + t_2} = P(1+i_1)^{t_1}(1+i_2)^{t_2}$$

By a similar logic, the amount after $t_1 + t_2 + t_3$ years will be given by:

$$A_{t_1 + t_2 + t_3} = P(1+i_1)^{t_1}(1+i_2)^{t_2}(1+i_3)^{t_3}$$

These ideas can be transferred to an Excel worksheet, as indicated in Workbook 5.10.

Make this up now in line with the instructions.

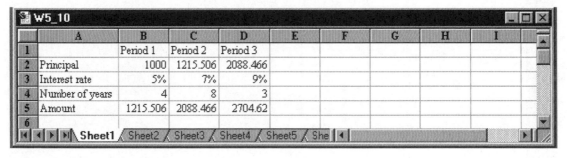

	A	B	C	D	E	F	G	H	I
1		Period 1	Period 2	Period 3					
2	Principal	1000	1215.506	2088.466					
3	Interest rate	5%	7%	9%					
4	Number of years	4	8	3					
5	Amount	1215.506	2088.466	2704.62					
6									

Sheet1 / Sheet2 / Sheet3 / Sheet4 / Sheet5 / She

Workbook 5.10

The entries in B2 and B3:D4 are the given data of the problem.

Enter these directly now.

In B5 the amount at the end of the first period is calculated from:

=B2*(1+B3)^B4

Enter this formula now.

Since this relationship will also be true for each of the subsequent periods it can be copied along the row.

So copy B5 into C5:D5.

Then, the amount at the end of the first period must be transferred to the C2 cell to become the principal at the start of the second period.

So make an entry in C2 of:

=B5

and then copy it into D2.

The model is now complete, and can easily be extended to include further periods by copying the key formulae in D2 and D5 along the sheet.

Exercise 5.6 can be attempted now.

5.4. **Fractional years**

In the previous discussion the number of years for which the principal was deposited was always a whole number. But consideration should be given to situations in which a deposit is made for 2.5 or 3.6 years, or some other non-whole number of years. In this respect it would be reasonable to expect that the basic compounding formula ($A_t = P(1 + i)^t$) would still apply, with the obvious difference being that t no longer adopts an integer value.

In fact this is not the case, since virtually all financial institutions evaluate interest payments on what is known as a daily basis. What this means is that interest is compounded for the integer number of years for which the principal has been deposited, and any extra non-integer number of years is then treated on a pro rata basis in relation to the annual interest rate.

For example, suppose £1000 were deposited at an annual compound interest rate of 7% for 2 years and 100 days. The amount after 2 years is easily calculated to be:

$$A_2 = 1000(1.07)^2 = £1144.9$$

This amount then attracts that proportion of the interest rate that corresponds to the proportion of 365 days for which the funds have been deposited. Consequently, since the interest rate is 7%, and the funds have been on deposit for 100/365 of a year; the additional interest payment due is therefore given by:

$$1144.9(100/365)(0.07) = £21.96$$

When this interest payment is added to the previous value of the account then we obtain:

$$£1144.9 + £21.96 = £1166.85$$

The same result could, of course, have been obtained from the following expression:

$$A_{2,100} = [1000(1.07)^2][1+(100/365)(0.07)] = £1166.85$$

Where $A_{2,100}$ represents the amount after 2 years and 100 days.

In general, then, if funds are deposited for t years and d days, at an annual compound rate of i per annum, then the accumulated amount at the end of this period ($A_{t,d}$) is given by:

$$A_{t,d} = [P(1 + i)^t][1+(d/365)(i)]$$

Notice that if the £1000 were deposited for 2 years and 365 days (i.e. 3 years) then the formula above remains correct, since:

$$A_{t,d} = 1000[(1.07)^2][1+(365/365)(0.07)]$$
$$A_{t,d} = (1144.9)(1.07) = 1225.04$$

which is identical to:

$$A_3 = 1000(1.07)^3$$

To perform this type of calculation on Excel, consider Workbook 5.11.

	A	B	C	D	E	F	G	H
1	Principal	1000						
2	Interest rate	7%						
3	Number of years	2.273973						
4	Integer number of years	2						
5	Remaider number of years	0.273973						
6	Compounded value	1144.90						
7	Partial year value	21.96						
8	Terminal value	1166.86						
9								

Sheet1 / Sheet2 / Sheet3 / Sheet4 / Sheet5 / She

**Workbook
5.11**

**Make this up now in line with the instructions.
Enter the given data for the problem to B1:B3.**

Notice that 2 years and 100 days is the same as 2.273973 years.

Now calculate the integer number of years in B4 from the formula:
=INT(B3)

This function returns the pre-decimal point portion of any number.

Next, calculate the remainder number of years in B5 from the formula:
=MOD(B3,1)

This function calculates the remainder of the first argument divided by the second argument. Thus in our illustration B3 = 2.273973, so B3/1 also equals 2.273973. The remainder of this is clearly 0.273973 and this is the value that =MOD(B3,1) will return.

Next, use B6 to calculate the value of the principal after the whole number of years contained in B4 from:
=B1*(1+B2)^B4

A value of £1144.9 will be returned.

Then calculate the interest for the partial year in B7 from:
=B6*B2*B5

A value of £21.95 will be returned.

Finally calculate the terminal value of the principal in B8 from:
=B6+B7

The answer obtained previously (£1166.85) will be returned.

Exercise 5.7 can be attempted now.

5.5. Variations in the compounding period

All of the discussion to date has assumed that interest is compounded on an annual basis (i.e. once a year). However many financial organizations offer savings schemes on which interest is compounded on a half-yearly, quarterly, or even daily basis. Such variations in what is known as the compounding period exercise a considerable effect upon the eventual value of any given principal, even when the annual interest rate and the length of time of the investment are the same.

To see this effect, consider a principal of £500 that is deposited for 2 years at an interest rate of 12% per annum. If interest is compounded annually, it is an easy matter to calculate the amount after 2 years to be:

$$A_2 = 500(1.12)^2 = £627.2$$

Suppose now, however, that interest was compounded semi-annually (i.e. twice per year). What this means is that after 6 months half a year's interest is actually credited to the account, and therefore increases the account's value accordingly. This larger value then forms the base upon which the next 6 months' interest is calculated, and so on.

Now since the annual interest rate is 12%, this clearly implies that the appropriate rate for the half year will be 12%/2 = 6%. Furthermore, since the funds are deposited for 2 years this means that the problem can be viewed in terms of 4 half-year periods in each of which the appropriate interest rate is 6%.

Bearing these points in mind means that the amount after 2 years can be calculated from:

$$A_2 = 500(1.06)^4 = £631.24$$

The fact that this new amount is £4.04 greater than under annual compounding is entirely due to the greater number of compounding periods (since all other factors are the same).

Continuing this line of reasoning, it should be clear that if interest were compounded quarterly, then the amount after 2 years could be derived from viewing the problem in terms of 8 periods of 3 months, in each of which the effective interest rate was 12%/4 = 3%. Therefore:

$$A_2 = 500(1.03)^8 = £633.38$$

Once again, the effect of increasing the number of compounding periods in the year (from 2 to 4) is seen to increase the amount after 2 years from £631.24 to £633.38.

Now suppose that interest is compounded on a monthly basis. Clearly, the amount after 2 years can be calculated from evaluating the following expression:

$$A_2 = 500(1.01)^{24} = £634.86.$$

(since there are 24 periods in which the interest rate for each period is 12%/12 = 1%).

It should now be possible to generalize this result to deal with any number of compounding periods that are contained in a year. To do this, it is simply necessary to recognize that if interest is compounded m times per annum, then any period of t years contains m times t = mt compounding periods. Furthermore, if the annual interest rate is represented, as usual, by i, then the relevant interest rate for each of these periods must be given by i/m.

This means that the amount after t years will be given by:

$$A_t = P(1 + i/m)^{mt}$$

For example, if interest were compounded weekly, then there would be 52 compounding periods in one year, and therefore m = 52. Consequently:

$$A_t = P(1 + i/52)^{52t}$$

In order to keep our symbols consistent, however, we really should recognize the effect exercised by variations in the compounding period by including it in the symbol for the amount. Consequently, we should define:

$A_{t,m}$ to be the amount after t years when interest is compounded m times per annum.

Of course, if interest is compounded on an annual basis, then m = 1 and the expression above becomes:

$$A_{t,1} = P(1 + i)^t$$

which reproduces the basic compound interest formula.

In all other cases, however, the amount after t years will be given by:

$$A_{t,m} = P(1 + i/m)^{mt}$$

For example, to find the value after 1 year of £3000 deposited in an account that bears interest at a rate of 10% per annum, compounded quarterly, the following expression should be evaluated.

$$A_{1,4} = 3000(1 + 0.1/4)^4 = 3000(1.025)^4 = £3311.44$$

Or, to find the value after 4 years of £5000 deposited in an account that bears interest at a rate of 9% per annum, compounded semi-annually, the following expression should be evaluated:

$$A_{4,2} = 5000(1 + 0.09/2)^8 = 5000(1.045)^8 = £7110.5$$

A more efficient way of investigating the effects of variations in the compounding period can be seen in Workbook 5.12.

Make this up now in line with the instructions.

	A	B	C	D	E	F	G
1	Principal	6000					
2	Annual interest rate	8%					
3	Number of years	7					
4	Number of compounding periods per annum	1					
5	Total number of compounding periods	7					
6	Interest rate per compounding period	0.08					
7	Terminal value	10282.95					
8							

Workbook 5.12

Enter the given data of the problem directly to the B1:B4 cells.

Then, in B5 calculate the total number of compounding periods in the term of the investment from:

=B3*B4

Next, in B6 calculate the interest rate for each compounding period from:

=B2/B4

Finally, calculate the terminal amount in B7 from:

=B1*(1+B6)^B5

This is analogous to the algebraic expression derived earlier for $A_{t,m}$ when it is noticed that B6 has been forced to contain i/m and B5 to contain mt.

From this worksheet it should be clear that the terminal value of a principal of £6000 that is deposited for 7 years at an annual interest rate of 8%, compounded annually, is £10282.95. It is also an easy matter to use this worksheet to confirm that if interest were compounded quarterly the terminal value would be £10446.15.

Now use Workbook 5.12 to confirm the two results obtained earlier (£3311.4 and £7110.5).

It is now time to point out that an important result emerges if we choose certain values for P, i, m, and t in the expression for $A_{t,m}$. To see this, consider the following example.

Find the value after 1 year of £1 deposited in an account that bears interest at a rate of 100% per annum, compounded annually.

To find this value, use Workbook 5.12 with values of 1 in each of the B1:B4 cells.

A result of 2 will be returned to B7, since $A_{t,m} = P(1 + i/m)^{mt}$ will be evaluated as:

$$A_{1,1} = 1(1 + 1/1)^1 = 2$$

Now suppose that interest is compounded semi-annually. This means that the entry in B4 should become 2.

Make this entry now.

The result in B7 will become 2.25.

Now suppose that we let the number of compounding periods in the year go through a steadily increasing sequence, and that we calculate the associated value of $A_{t,m}$ for each of these values of m. Worksheet 5.13 performs the necessary calculations.

Make this up now.

	A	B	C	D	E	F	G	H
1	Principal	1						
2	Annual interest rate	1						
3	Number of years	1						
4								
5		Annual number						
6		of compounding	Terminal					
7		periods (m)	amount					
8		1	2.0000					
9		2	2.2500					
10		4	2.4414					
11		12	2.6130					
12		52	2.6926					
13		365	2.7146					
14		8760	2.7181					
15		525600	2.7183					
16		31536000	2.7183					
17								

W5_13 — Sheet1 / Sheet2 / Sheet3 / Sheet4 / Sheet5 / She

Workbook 5.13

Enter the given values for P, i, and t (all = 1) to the B1:B3 range.
   Next, in B8:B16 enter the indicated values for the number of compounding periods in the year.

These represent the process of annual, semi-annual, quarterly, monthly, etc. compounding, right down to B16, where interest is regarded as being compounded every second.

Now use C8 to contain the formula:

$$=B\$1*(1+B\$2/B8)\wedge(B\$3*B8)$$

and copy this into C9:C16.

This formula is equivalent to the expression for $A_{t,m}$ when it is noticed that B1, B2, and B3 contain the values for P, i, and t , while B8:B16 contain the varying values for m.

Clearly, what happens is that the value of $A_{t,m}$ at first increases quite dramatically but, as the number of compounding periods increases, $A_{t,m}$ starts to increase less rapidly. This suggests that the value of $A_{t,m}$ is approaching some limit as the value of m increases, and this limit can be shown to be e = 2.7183. This limit is reached when the number of compounding periods in the year (i.e. the value of m) becomes infinitely large, and consequently, when the time between compounding periods becomes infinitesimally small.

In symbols it is said that the limit as m tends to infinity of $1(1+1/m)^m = e = 2.7183$.

5.6. **Continuous compounding**

As has previously been said, when m becomes infinitely large the time between compounding periods becomes infinitesimally small, and can effectively be regarded as zero. When this happens we refer to such a situation as continuous compounding, since instead of there being a countable period of time between compounding periods there is so little time that the process can be regarded as continuous. It is almost as if the interest for a millisecond is added to the principal in the instant of its passing, and hence forms an infinitesimally larger base upon which the interest for the next millisecond is calculated.

The sceptical reader will no doubt argue that few financial institutions would ever offer terms as beneficial to the lender as continuous compounding implies, and on this there is no dispute. However, many natural phenomena do not recognize the accounting habits of banks and building societies, and insist upon growing in a fashion that is most appropriately modelled by continuous compounding and the use of e.

To see how this can be done, we should now relax some of the restrictive values that were imposed upon P, i, and t in the illustration in the previous section (i.e. P = i = t = 1).

First of all, we should allow the value of the interest rate to be i as usual, instead of 100%. When this is done the expression for $A_{t,m}$ can be written as:

$$A_{1,m} = 1(1 + i/m)^m$$

Now we have already seen that if i = 1 then the limit of this expression as m tends to infinity is 2.7183 = e.

So the question arises of what happens when i adopts some value other than 1. In particular, does this expression also reach a definite limit, and if so, what is it? The answer to the first question is 'yes', although the algebra to prove it is beyond the scope of this text. Nevertheless, it can be taken on trust that the limit of:

$$A_{1,m} = 1(1 + i/m)^m$$

as m tends to infinity is given by:

$$A_{1,m} = 1(1 + i/m)^m = e^i$$

This can be confirmed by an appropriate modification of the model in Workbook 5.13.

To do this, enter a value of 0.1 (for example) in B2, whereupon it will be found that a value of 1.1052 will be returned to the C16 cell.

This is indistinguishable from $e^{0.1}$ as is easily confirmed by entering the following formula to any vacant cell of the worksheet:

$=EXP(0.1)$

Now suppose that the principal of £1 is deposited for more than one year and continuously compounded at an annual rate of i. The expression for $A_{t,m}$ becomes:

$A_{t,m} = 1(1 + i/m)^{mt}$

Now if we rewrite this as:

$A_{t,m} = [1(1 + i/m)^m]^t$

it can be seen that, since the limit of the expression inside the square brackets has already been stated to be e^i, we can write:

$A_{t,m} = (e^i)^t = e^{it}$

In other words, the limit of $1(1 + i/m)^{mt}$ as m tends to infinity is given by e^{it}.

Keeping the same figures as were used in the last example: $(i = 0.10, P = 1)$, this result can be confirmed by making the following modifications to Workbook 5.13.

In B3 enter a value of 5 (i.e. 5 years), and in any vacant cell enter:

$=EXP(B2*B3)$

It will now be found that with hourly compounding the results returned to C14 onwards will be the same as that obtained from the exponential function (1.6487). This, of course, is because:

$1(1+i/m)^{mt} = 1(1 + 0.1/8760)^{(5)(8760)} = 1.6487$

and:

$e^{(5)(0.16)} = e^{0.8} = 1.6487$

Finally, if a principal of £P is deposited then we have:

$A_{t,m} = P(1+i/m)^{mt}$

It is left as an exercise to confirm that the limit of this expression as m tends to infinity is given by:

$A_{t,m} = Pe^{it}$

Exercise 5.8 can be attempted now.

5.7. The equivalent annual rate

The discussion in the previous section has produced the important implication that the effective rate of interest being paid on deposited funds depends not only upon the quoted nominal rate but also upon the frequency with which interest is compounded (i.e. the value of m). In other words, with any nominal annual rate of interest, a given principal will amount to more if that interest is compounded monthly than if it is compounded annually. Clearly, this implies that the effective rate on the monthly compounded funds exceeds that on the annually compounded funds.

This idea gives rise to the concept of the equivalent annual rate (EAR) that allows any nominal annual rate (NAR) to be expressed in terms that take account of the frequency with which interest is compounded. To do this, note that if interest is compounded m times per annum at the quoted NAR, then the amount after t years is given by:

$$A_{t,m} = P(1 + NAR/m)^{mt}$$

However, in the simplest case of annual compounding the fact that m = 1 means that this expression reduces to:

$$A_{t,1} = P(1 + NAR)^t$$

This implies that only under annual compounding will the nominal and the equivalent rates be the same, and this knowledge allows us to rewrite the last expression as:

$$A_{t,1} = P[1 + EAR]^t$$

If we now equate the right-hand sides of the first and third of these last expressions, we obtain:

$$P(1 + EAR)^t = P(1 + NAR/m)^{mt}$$

Eliminating P from both sides and then raising both sides to the power of 1/t produces:

$$(1 + EAR) = (1 + NAR/m)^m$$

Therefore:

$$EAR = (1 + NAR/m)^m - 1$$

For example, if a savings scheme offers quarterly compounding at a nominal annual rate of 12%, then the last expression above would become (with NAR = 0.12 and m = 4):

$$EAR = (1 + 0.12/4)^4 - 1 = 1.03^4 - 1 = 0.1255$$

The effect of quarterly compounding has been to make the nominal annual rate of 12% become equivalent to an annually compounded rate of 12.55%. Furthermore, if the compounding process is continuous, then it should be clear that the expression for the EAR becomes:

$$EAR = (e^{NAR}) - 1$$

which, if NAR = 0.15, for example, implies that the annual equivalent rate of a nominal rate of 15% compounded continuously is given by:

$$e^{0.15} - 1 = 0.1618 \text{ i.e. } 16.18\%$$

This is clearly the highest value, for any given nominal rate, that the equivalent annual rate can adopt.

The result of this discussion is the conclusion that the EAR increases steadily with any increases in the number of compounding periods in the year, and approaches a limit of e^{NAR} as m approaches infinity. These results are summarized in Table 5.1

Table 5.1

ANNUAL NO. OF COMPOUNDING PERIODS (M)	EAR
1	NAR
2	$(1 + NAR/2)^2 - 1$
4	$(1 + NAR/4)^4 - 1$
12	$(1 + NAR/12)^{12} - 1$
...	...
m	$(1 + NAR/m)^m - 1$
...	...
∞	$e^{NAR} - 1$

Furthermore, it is an easy matter to translate these expressions into Excel terms to create a worksheet that can perform the necessary calculations. This is shown in Workbook 5.14.

Make this up now in line with the explanation.

	A	B	C	D	E	F
1	Nominal annual rate	10%				
2	Number of compounding periods per annum	4				
3	Equivalent annual rate	0.103812891				
4						

W5_14 — Sheet1 / Sheet2 / Sheet3 / Sheet4 / Sheet5 / She

Workbook 5.14

Enter the given labels and values as indicated A1:B2 as shown.
Next, in A3 enter the label:

Equivalent annual rate

and in B3 the formula:

=(1+B1/B2)^B2-1

Now use this workbook to confirm the result obtained above—that a nominal annual rate of 12% is equivalent to a rate of 12.55% if interest is compounded quarterly. Exercises 5.9 and 5.10 can be attempted now.

5.8. Growth rate calculations

It has already been suggested that, although financial institutions do not offer continuously compounded interest rates, there are a number of naturally occurring processes in which the growth in the variable's value is of a continuous or almost continuous nature. Population growth, the rate of inflation, Gross National Product, and the appreciation or depreciation of company assets are all examples of such continuous growth processes. In each of these cases the most important feature is that, although analysts may measure the value of the variable at one point in time and then measure it again at some later date, the variable is in fact changing continuously throughout the duration of the measurement period. In other words, it does not remain constant for 99.99% of the measurement period and then suddenly change its value at the time of the second measurement.

What this means is that the arbitrary choice of the length of the measurement period will influence how the growth in the value of the variable is perceived and calculated. Of course, continuous monitoring of the variable's value is the only way to remove this problem completely, yet this would be a time-consuming and expensive practice. Nevertheless, knowledge of the process of continuous compounding and its relationship with the exponential function allows us to calculate the appropriate growth rate as if it had been subject to continuous monitoring.

To see this, consider the following example. An accountant estimates the value of a company's assets to be £1.64 million on 1 January 1997, and to be £2.14 million 2 years later. The task is to calculate the implied rate of growth of the company's assets over the period. To deal with this problem, it must be decided whether the growth process is to be regarded as simple or compound, and, if it is compound, the assumed number of compounding periods per annum must be determined.

Each of these alternatives can be considered as follows.

5.8.1. Simple growth

In this case the value of i can be calculated from transposition of the formula for simple interest. That is:

$$A_t = P(1 + ti)$$

implies that:

$$i = [A_t/P - 1]/t$$

Therefore:

$$i = [(2.14/1.64) - 1]/2 = 0.1524.$$

The simple growth rate is 15.24% per annum.

5.8.2. Annual compound growth

In this case, the most recent version of the compound interest formula should be used and then transposed to produce an expression for i as follows:

$$A_t = P(1 + i/m)^{mt}$$
$$A_t/P = (1 + i/m)^{mt}$$
$$(A_t/P)^{1/mt} = (1 + i/m)$$
$$(A_t/P)^{1/mt} - 1 = i/m$$
$$m[(A_t/P)^{1/mt} - 1] = i$$

Now since for annual compounding we have m = 1, and can write:

$$1[(2.14/1.64)^{1/2} - 1] = i$$

implying that i = 0.1423, and the annually compounded growth rate is 14.23% per annum.

5.8.3. Quarterly compound growth

In this case we have m = 4, and so:

$$4[(2.14/1.64)^{1/8} - 1] = i = 0.13453$$

The quarterly compounded growth rate is 13.53% per annum.

5.8.4. Monthly compound growth

For this case, we have m = 12, and so:

$$12[(2.14/1.64)^{1/24} - 1] = i = 0.1337$$

The monthly compounded growth rate is 13.37% per annum.

5.8.5. Continuous compound growth

In this case, we must make use of the expression for continuous compound growth as follows:

$$A_t = Pe^{it}$$

Therefore

$$A_t/P = e^{it}$$
$$\ln(A_t/P) = it \ln e$$

But ln e = 1 by definition, so

$$[\ln(A_t/P)]/t = i$$

For the figures of the example this produces:

$$i = [\ln (2.14/1.64)]/2$$
$$i = 0.1330$$

The continuous compound growth rate is 13.3% per annum.

As is clearly illustrated from these calculations, the calculated growth rate is highly sensitive to the number of compounding periods used. Nevertheless, as might be expected by now, the growth rate approaches a lower limit that is provided by the continuous compound rate as the number of compounding periods in the year approaches infinity.

Exercise 5.11 can be attempted now.

5.9. Annuities

So far we have only considered the process of calculating the future or terminal value of a single principal that has been placed on deposit for some specified number of years. However, many popular savings schemes allow for a number of equal principals to be deposited at periodic (usually annual) intervals.

Such schemes are known as annuities, and to calculate their terminal value immediately after the last principal has been deposited, requires that account is taken of all the deposits, and all the interest payments that each of these deposits attracts. The method of doing this can be illustrated as follows.

Suppose that, starting today, 4 annual deposits of £2000 are made to an account that bears interest at an annual rate of 11% per annum, compounded annually over the entire period during which the deposits are made.

The task is to calculate the terminal or future value of the account immediately after the 4th deposit has been made. To do this we can argue as follows.

The first deposit will attract interest at the prevailing rate for 3 years, and consequently will have a terminal value given by:

$$A_3 = 2000(1.11)^3 = £2735.26$$

Similarly, the second deposit will attract interest for a period of 2 years, and will therefore have a terminal value of:

$$A_2 = 2000(1.11)^2 = £2464.20$$

The third deposit will only bear interest for 1 year, and therefore has a terminal value of

$$A_1 = 2000(1.11)^1 = £2200.00$$

Finally, since it is required to calculate the value of the account immediately after the 4th deposit has been made, this 4th deposit must be included in the calculations without any interest added to it. Hence:

$$A_0 = 2000(1.11)^0 = £2000.00$$

Clearly the total future value (FV) of the account can be obtained by adding each of these individual terminal values together, to produce:

$$FV = £2735.26 + £2464.20 + £2200 + £2000 = £9419.46$$

Viewed in this methodical way, the calculation of the terminal value of an annuity is easily understood. However, such an approach is needlessly laborious, since Excel has a dedicated function that can perform such calculations. The function is called future value (=FV), and has the following general syntax:

FV(Interest rate,Number of periods,Periodic equal payment,*Present value,Type*)

where those arguments in *italics* are optional, i.e. need not necessarily be included. Their exact meaning is explained below.

Interest rate is the interest rate per period. It will be the annual rate if interest is compounded annually, but will be the equivalent annual rate $(1+ i/m)^m - 1$ if interest is compounded m times per annum, and if payments to the annuity are on an annual basis.

If interest is compounded with the same annual frequency as deposits are made to the annuity then the appropriate value for this argument is the periodic rate i/m.

Number of periods is the total number of periods in which payments are made to the annuity. If payments are made on an annual basis, then the number of periods is the number of years of the annuity (its term) plus one. (Remember that an annuity with a term of 3 years consists of 4 equal payments if the first payment is made just now.)

If payments are made more frequently than annually, and if interest is compounded with the same frequency (m times per annum, say), then the number of periods is the term of the annuity plus 1 times the frequency of payments in the year. For example, an annuity with a term of 3 years has 4 annual payments, 8 semi-annual payments, 16 quarterly payments, 48 monthly payments, etc.

Consequently, an annuity with a term of t years and with m payments per annum will consist of a total of (t + 1)m periods, in each of which the interest rate is i/m if the annual interest rate is i.

Periodic equal payment is the payment made to the annuity in each period. It cannot change over the life of the annuity.

Present value is an optional argument that is not relevant to the discussion at the moment. It is assumed to be 0 if it is omitted.

Type is another optional argument that indicates when the future value of the annuity is to be calculated. If omitted, its value is assumed to be 0 and means that the future value is to be calculated immediately after the last payment has been made. On the other hand, if *Type* is set to 1 then the last payment is assumed to remain on deposit for one more period and so will attract an extra period's interest.

For example, to replicate the result that was obtained for the future value of the annuity illustrated earlier (£9419.46), take a blank worksheet and make the following entry to any vacant cell.

=FV(11%,4,-2000,0,0)

A result of £9419.46 will be returned, and since the *Type* argument has been set to 0, indicates that this future value is based on the value of the annuity immediately after the last payment has been made.

However, suppose that this future value (£9419.46) had been left on deposit for a further year at the going interest rate of 11%. Clearly it will then amount to 9419.46(1.11) = £10455.60. This would be the value returned by the FV function if its last argument had been set to 1.

Confirm this now.
Exercise 5.12 can be attempted now.

Now consider the following situation. An annuity with a term of 15 years has annual payments of £1500. The interest rate for the period is 10% per annum compounded quarterly. Calculate the future value of the annuity immediately after the last payment has been made.

To answer this, we note that there are 16 annual payments of £1500, and that the value of the account is to be calculated immediately after the last deposit is made. Also, since interest is compounded on a quarterly basis but payments are made annually, we require to calculate the equivalent annual rate implied by the quarterly compounding. This is easily done from:

$$EAR = (1 + i/m)^m - 1 = (1 + 0.1/4)^4 - 1 = 0.10381 = 10.381\%$$

Consequently, the interest rate to be used as the first argument of the FV function should be 10.381%. Taken together, these observations mean that the completed FV function should be:

=FV(10.381%,16,-1500,0,0)

Enter this now to a vacant cell of a worksheet to obtain an answer of £55722.11.

Notice that if the annual interest rate of 10% had in fact only been compounded annually, then the future value of the annuity would decline to £53924.59.

Confirm this now by changing the first argument value from 10.381% to 10%.
Exercise 5.13 can be attempted now.

Now consider an annuity with a term of 13 years to which quarterly payments of £500 are made. The interest rate attracted is 8% per annum compounded quarterly.

To calculate the future value of this annuity immediately after the last deposit has been made, we can note that the frequency of the payments to the annuity (quarterly) also matches the frequency with which interest is compounded. Consequently, the annuity can be thought of as 14(4) = 56 quarterly payments of £500 that attract a quarterly interest rate of 8%/4 = 2% in each quarter.

The future value of this annuity is therefore calculated from:

=FV(2%,56,-500,0,0)

Enter this formula to a vacant cell of a worksheet to obtain a result of £50779.13 as the future value of this scheme.
Exercise 5.14 can be attempted now.

As a final point in this section, the role of the optional present value argument should be explained.

Reconsider the simple annuity that was illustrated at the start of the section: 4 equal annual payments of £2000 to an account that provided interest of 11% per annum compounded annually. Now recall that the future value of this annuity, immediately after the last payment was made, was £9419.46. However, suppose that the account to which these annuity payments were made contained an initial amount of £1000. The future value of the account (as opposed to the annuity itself) will clearly be greater as a result of this initial amount.

To be exact, after the last deposit of £2000 has been made, the account will be worth £9419.46 plus the initial deposit of £1000, plus the interest received on the initial deposit over a period of 3 years. That is, the future value will be:

$$£9419.46 + £1000(1.11)^3 = £9419.46 + 1367.63 = £10787.09$$

This is the value that the Excel future value function should return when a value of -1000 is used as the optional present value argument.

In fact, however, on many versions of Excel there is a 'bug' in the function that has the effect of returning a result that is only consistent with the initial value of the account having attracted interest for one more year than it actually did.

To see this, use any vacant cell of a worksheet to contain:

$$=FV(11\%,4,-2000,-1000,0)$$

A result of £10937.53 will be returned. Clearly, this exceeds the previously calculated future value of £10787.09 by an amount of £150.44.

This is exactly the amount of interest that would be paid on a sum of £1000 invested for 3 years at 11% per annum (£1367.63) plus the annual interest for another year on that amount $0.11(1367.63) = £150.44$.

This means that, as constituted, the Excel FV function must be modified downwards if the future value of the account is to be computed satisfactorily when the account to which the annuity payments are made contains an initial sum, and when the value of the account is to be calculated immediately after the last deposit has been made. In other words, we must write:

$$=FV(11\%,4,-2000,-1000,0)-1000*0.11*(1.11)^{\wedge}3$$

Now confirm that this amended version of the function returns the correct result (£10787.09).

It should be noticed, however, that this 'bug' does not exist in the FV formula when the last argument (*Type*) is set to a value of 1. To see this, suppose that the account with an initial deposit of £1000, and with 4 annual payments of £2000, all receiving interest at an annually compounded rate of 11% per annum, was allowed to gather one more year's interest. The future value would then become:

$£9419.46 + £1000(1.11)^3 = £9419.46 + 1367.63 = £10787.09$ after 3 years, plus one year's interest on £10787.09.

This clearly gives:

$£10787.09(1.11) = £11973.67$

Now, remembering that the last argument of the FV function should be 1 rather than 0 (since we require the future value one year after the last deposit was made), take a vacant cell of the worksheet and enter:

$$=FV(11\%,4,-2000,-1000,1)$$

A result of £11973.67 will be obtained, thereby indicating that the Excel future value function performs correctly when its last argument value is 1, but not when it is 0.

Exercise 5.15 can be attempted now.

Now recall that it was shown earlier that an annuity with a term of 3 years and with 4 annual payments of £2000 had a future value of £9419.46 when the interest rate was 11% per annum compounded annually.

However, suppose that we now asked the following question. How many annual payments of £2000 must be made to an account in order to ensure a terminal value of £9419.46, if the interest rate for the period is 11% per annum compounded annually? Clearly the answer is 4.

But the issue to be addressed now is whether an equivalent answer could be obtained to variations on this type of problem. In other words, we are required to calculate the total number of equal periodic payments that must be made to an annuity if a future value of FV is to be obtained, immediately after the last payment is made, and if the interest rate for the period is i per annum.

The solution to this type of problem is provided by the Excel function called NPER (short for 'number of periods'). It has the following general syntax.

$$=NPER(\text{Interest rate},\text{Equal periodic payment},\text{Present value},\textit{Future value},\textit{Type})$$

where those arguments in italics are optional, and need not necessarily be included. Their exact meaning is explained below.

Interest rate is the interest rate per period. It will be the annual rate if interest is compounded annually, but the equivalent annual rate $(1+ i/m)^m - 1$ if interest is compounded m times per annum, and payments to the annuity are on an annual basis.

Equal periodic payment is the amount that is paid in to the annuity in each period of the term of the annuity.

Present value is the value just now of the account into which the periodic payments are made. If the account is established with a balance of zero, then the value of this argument is 0.

Future value is an optional argument representing the future amount that is to be secured by the annuity.

Type is another optional argument that indicates when the future value of the annuity is to be calculated. If omitted it is assumed to be 0, and means that the future value is to be calculated immediately after the last payment has been made. On the other hand, if *Type* is set to 1 then the last payment is assumed to remain on deposit for one more period, and so will attract an extra period's interest.

Consequently, to obtain the result that was obtained above by simple inspection (4 periods) we should enter:

=NPER(11%,-2000,0,9419.46,0)

Do this now and confirm that a result of 4 is obtained.

Now reconsider the solution to Exercise 5.15.

This showed that 9 equal annual payments of £1000 to an account containing £5000 to start with, would produce a future value of £25382.94, one year after the last deposit was made, if interest were paid at an annual equivalent rate of 9.2025%. Consequently, we should expect that the NPER function would evaluate to 9 if the arguments were set to values of 9.2025%, -1000, -5000, 25382.94, and 1 respectively.

Confirm this now by using any vacant cell of a worksheet to contain:

=NPER(9.2025%,-1000,-5000,25382.94,1)

A value of 9 should be returned.

Exercise 5.16 can be attempted now.

5.10. **Sinking funds**

A sinking fund is the name given to the process of setting up a series of equal periodic payments that are designed to secure some specified future value when the number of payments and the interest rate that they attract are given.

For example, suppose that the basic annuity example from the previous section was rephrased in the following way. An annuity with a term of 3 years is required to supply a future value of £9419.46 when the interest rate that it attracts is 11% per annum compounded annually. What is the required size of the 4 equal annual payments to the annuity if the specified future value is to be achieved? Once again, the answer is easily obtained by inspection and prior knowledge to be £2000. To replicate this result on Excel, however, use must be made of the PMT function. This has the following general syntax:

=PMT(Interest rate,Number of periods,Present value,*Future value,Type*)

The exact meaning of each of these arguments is the same as with the FV and the NPER functions.

Consequently, use any vacant cell of a worksheet to contain:

=PMT(11%,4,0,9419.46,0)

A value of -£2000 will be returned, thereby confirming what is already known—that 4 equal annual payments of £2000 are required to secure a future value of £9419.36 in 3 years' time if the interest rate furnished by the annuity is 11% per annum compounded annually. Now consider the solution to Exercise 5.15 again. There it was shown that 9 equal annual payments of £1000 to an account containing £5000 to start with, would produce a future value of £25382.94, one year after the last deposit was made, if interest were paid at an annual equivalent rate of 9.2025%.

So, suppose that the necessary annual payments required to achieve this target future amount were unknown. They can easily be calculated from the PMT function if the following argument values are used.

=PMT(9.2025%,9,-5000,25382.94,1)

**Now confirm that this function will return the required value of £1000.
Exercise 5.17 can be attempted now.**

5.11. Debt repayments

The Excel PMT function can also be used to calculate the periodic repayments that will have to be made in order to repay any debt that is incurred just now. For example, suppose that a loan of £D is secured at an annually compounded interest rate of i%. This debt is to be repaid in 3 equal annual instalments of £X, with the first repayment being made immediately.

If the debt is administered on a reducing balance basis, the task is to calculate the size of the 3 equal annual repayments required to pay off the debt. Since the first repayment is to be made immediately, this means that the size of the debt on which interest is charged is given by:

$(D - X)$

This outstanding debt then attracts interest charges, so that at the end of the first year the outstanding debt becomes:

$(D - X)(1 + i)$

When the second payment of £X is made, this outstanding debt reduces to:

$[(D - X)(1 + i) - X]$

which then attracts interest charges in such a way that at the end of the second year the outstanding debt is:

$[(D - X)(1 + i) - X](1 + i)$

When the 3rd and final repayment of £X is made, then the debt must be cleared (i.e. outstanding debt = 0). We can therefore derive the following equation for this example:

$[(D - X)(1 + i) - X](1 + i) - X = 0$

Collecting terms and simplifying gives:

$$(D - X)(1 + i)^2 - X(1 + i) - X = 0$$

Therefore:

$$D(1 + i)^2 - X(1 + i)^2 - X(1 + i) - X = 0$$

and:

$$D(1 + i)^2 - X[(1 + i)^2 + (1 + i) + 1] = 0$$

Consequently:

$$X = D(1 + i)^2/[(1 + i)^2 + (1 + i) + 1]$$

For example, if a debt of £10000 is incurred just now at an annual interest rate of 10%, and is to be repaid in 3 equal annual instalments, with the first instalment being paid just now, then the size of each instalment is given by:

$$X = 10000(1.1)^2/[1.21 + 1.1 + 1] = 12100/3.31 = £3655.59$$

The debt will then be cleared after 2 years.

However, many reducing-balance debts allow the debtor to have a one period delay before the first payment has to be made. This being the case, then for the last example (with one year's delay) we have:

Initial Debt = D
Debt after 1 year = $D(1 + i)$
Debt after 1st repayment = $D(1 + i) - X$
Debt after 2 years = $[D(1 + i) - X](1 + i) = [D(1 + i)^2 - X(1 + i)]$
Debt after 2nd repayment = $[D(1 + i)^2 - X(1 + i) - X]$
Debt after 3 years = $[D(1 + i)^2 - X(1 + i) - X](1 + i) = [D(1 + i)^3 - X(1 + i)^2 - X(1 + i)]$
Debt after 3rd repayment = $[D(1 + i)^3 - X(1 + i)^2 - X(1 + i) - X]$

Setting this last term equal to 0, collecting terms and solving for X as before produces:

$$X = [D(1 + i)^3/[(1 + i)^2 + (1 + i) + 1]$$

For example, with the same figures as before, the 3 equal annual instalments are given by:

$$10000(1.1)^3/(1.21 + 1.1 + 1) = 13310/3.31 = £4021.15$$

Three equal annual instalments of £4021.15 will be required to pay off this debt after 3 years when the first repayment is made in one year's time. Notice how this contrasts with the lower figure obtained earlier of £3655.59 if the first repayment is to be made immediately.

To replicate these results with the PMT function we can write:

=PMT(10%,3,10000,0,1)

Enter this now to a vacant cell of a worksheet and confirm that by setting the last argument value to 1, this forces the function to regard the repayments as being immediate.

Also notice that the optional Future value argument has been set to zero. This is because the repayments must exactly clear the debt, with neither surplus nor deficit.

Now confirm that if the first repayment is delayed by one year, then the result obtained earlier (£4021.15 as opposed to £3655.59) can be obtained from:

=PMT(10%,3,10000,0,0)

In other words, by setting the *Type* argument value to 0 the function has been forced to regard the repayments as commencing in one period's time.

Also notice that both functions will return negative values, since these are the repayments necessary to pay off the initial positive loan.

Exercise 5.18 can be attempted now.

5.12. Exercises

Exercise 5.1

(i) Calculate the amount after 20 years, of a principal of £2000 if simple interest is paid at an annual rate of 8.25%.

(ii) Calculate the length of time required for a principal of £3000 to amount to £5400 if simple interest is paid at a rate of 8% per annum.

(iii) Calculate the principal that must have been deposited, if an amount of £6000 is received after 15 years and simple interest paid at a rate of 10% per annum.

(iv) Calculate the simple interest rate being received if a principal of £4000 amounts to £8000 after 10 years.

Exercise 5.2

A principal of £3000 is deposited for 20 years at a compound interest rate of 7.75% per annum. Calculate the compounded amount after 20 years.

Exercise 5.3

Find the annual compound rate of interest being received on a principal of £10000 that amounts to £20000 after 7 years.

Exercise 5.4

Calculate the length of time for which £3500 must be deposited if it is to amount to £10000 when the annual compound rate of interest is 5.5%.

Exercise 5.5

Calculate the size of the principal that must be deposited just now if a terminal sum of £20000 is to be obtained after 10 years when the annual compound rate of interest for the period is 9.9%.

Exercise 5.6

A principal of £6000 is deposited just now. The annual interest rate for the coming year is 8%. This interest rate increases at a compound rate of 5% per annum for all subsequent years.

Modify the model created in Workbook 5.10 (W5_10.XLS) to allow calculation of the value of the account after 10 years have passed.

Exercise 5.7

Find the amount accruing to a principal of £5000 that is deposited at an annual interest rate of 8% per annum, for a period of 5.7824 years.

Exercise 5.8

Use Workbook 5.13 to compare the terminal value of a principal of £2500 that is compounded by the second at an annual rate of 11.5% for a period of 7 years, with the amount that would accrue if interest were only compounded once per annum. Also demonstrate that continuous compounding is indistinguishable from compounding by the second, when calculated to two decimal places.

Exercise 5.9

Find the equivalent annual rate being supplied by an account that bears interest at a nominal annual rate of 25% compounded daily.

Exercise 5.10

Calculate the required number of compounding periods in a year if a nominal annual rate of 10% is to have an equivalent annual rate of 10.5%.

Exercise 5.11

Calculate the continuous compound annual rate of inflation if the index of retail prices was 134.67 on the 1st of January 1995, and had risen to 204.78 by the 1st of January 2000.

Exercise 5.12

Calculate the future value, immediately after the last deposit has been made, of an annuity with a term of 12 years, consisting of annual payments of £5000, if the interest rate is 9% per annum compounded annually.

Exercise 5.13
Calculate the future value, immediately after the last deposit is made, of an annuity with a term of 19 years, in which annual payments of £10000 attract interest at an annual rate of 18% compounded monthly.

Exercise 5.14
Calculate the future value of an annuity with a term of 25 years, immediately after the last deposit has been made, if the monthly payments are £50, and if the rate of interest is 18% per annum compounded monthly.

Exercise 5.15
An account containing £5000 is to be the recipient of an annuity with a term of 8 years, and a periodic payment of £1000. The interest rate for the period is 9% per annum compounded semi-annually.

   Calculate the future value of the account one year after the last deposit has been made.

Exercise 5.16
Calculate the number of equal annual payments of £6000 that are required to supply a future value of £306528.05 immediately after the last payment is made, if the account is empty to start with, and gathers interest at a quarterly compounded rate of 15% per annum.

Exercise 5.17
An annuity scheme attracts interest at a monthly compounded rate of 10% per annum. It is intended to make 20 equal annual payments to this fund, with the objective of securing a future amount of £300000. The fund contains an amount of £10000 when the first payment is made.

   (i) Calculate the required size of the 20 equal annual payments if:

   (a) the future sum is to be available immediately after the last payment is made.
   (b) the future sum is to be available one year after the last deposit is made.

   (ii) Repeat both of these calculations if the account were empty when the first annuity payment is made.

   (iii) Suppose that the value of the account when the first payment is made is £50000. Calculate the size of the 20 equal annual payments that are required to supply the future value of £300000 immediately after the last deposit is made.

Exercise 5.18
Calculate the size of the 15 equal annual payments required to pay off a debt of £7000 incurred at an interest rate of 17% per annum if the first repayment is to be made:

   (a) one year from now.
   (b) immediately.

5.13. Solutions to the exercises

Solution to Exercise 5.1
   (i) Enter values of 2000, 8.25%, and 20 to the B1, B2, and B3 cells of Workbook 5.1. (W5_1.XLS). The amount after 20 years will be returned to B4 as £5300 when formatted to 2 decimal places.

   (ii) Enter values of 3000, 8%, and 5400 to the B1, B2, and B3 cells of Workbook 5.3 (W5_3.XLS). The required number of years will be returned to B4 as 10.00 years when formatted to 2 decimal places.

   (iii) Enter values of 10%, 6000, and 15 to the B1, B2, and B3 cells of Workbook 5.4 (W5_4.XLS). The principal that must have been deposited will be returned to B4 as £2400 when formatted to 2 decimal places.

   (iv) Enter values of 4000, 10, and 8000 to the B1, B2, and B3 cells of Workbook 5.2 (W5_2.XLS). The required simple interest rate will be returned to B4 as 0.1 (10%) when formatted to 2 decimal places.

Solution to Exercise 5.2

Enter values of 3000, 7.75%, and 20 to the B1, B2, and B3 cells of Workbook 5.5 (W5_5.XLS). The compounded amount will be returned to B5 as £13349.56 when formatted to two decimal places.

Solution to Exercise 5.3

Use the B1:B3 cells of Workbook 5.6 (W5_6.XLS) to contain 10000, 20000, and 7 respectively. The compound rate of return being received is calculated in B5 as 0.10409, i.e. 10.409%.

Solution to Exercise 5.4

Enter values of 3500, 10000, and 5.5% to the B1:B3 cells of Workbook 5.7 (W5_7.XLS). The required number of years will be computed in B5 as 19.6 when formatted to two decimal places.

Solution to Exercise 5.5

Enter values of 20000, 9.9%, and 10 to the B1:B3 cells of Workbook 5.8 (W5_8.XLS). The required principal will be calculated in B5 as £7781.31.

Solution to Exercise 5.6

Enter the principal of £6000 to the B2 cell, and then copy D1 into E1:K1 to give 10 periods. Make the number of years for each period equal to 1 by entering 1 to B4 and copying this into C4:K4.

Copy D2 and D5 into E2:K2 and E5:K5.

Next, enter 8% to the B3 cell and 1.05*B3 to the C3 cell. This calculates the increase in the interest rate in the second period.

Finally, copy C3 into D3:K3 to obtain the interest rate in each of the subsequent years.

This completes the model, and the terminal value of the account should be returned to K5 as £15638.07.

Solution to Exercise 5.7

Use Workbook 5.11 (W5_11.XLS) to contain the following values.

> In B1: 5000   In B2: 8%   In B3: 5.7824

The worksheet will evaluate the terminal amount to be £7806.48.

Solution to Exercise 5.8

Enter values of 2500, 11.5%, and 7 to B1:B3.

The terminal amount when interest is compounded by the second case is returned to C16 as £5591.74, as opposed to the value in C8 of £5356.29 representing annual compounding.

For continuous compounding, the terminal amount can be obtained by using any vacant cell of the worksheet to contain:

> =B1*EXP(B2*B3)

A value of £5591.74 will be returned when formatted to two decimal places.

Solution to Exercise 5.9

Enter values of 25% and 365 to the B1 and B2 cells of Workbook 5.14.

The EAR will be calculated in B3 as 0.2839 = 28.39%.

Solution to Exercise 5.10

There is no easy way to solve this problem manually, since we require to find m such that:

$$0.105 = (1 + 0.1/m)^m$$

and this is not amenable to simple manipulative solution methods. However, if you load Workbook 5.14 (W5_14.XLS) then the Excel Solver can be used.

First, enter the given NAR of 0.1 to the B1 cell. The target cell is B3 and the target cell value is to be 0.105. The changing cell is B2 and this must be constrained to be greater than zero.

When these entries and Solver settings are made to the worksheet, a result for m = 32 is obtained. Interest must therefore be compounded 32 times per annum if the nominal annual rate of 10% is to have an equivalent annual rate of 10.5%.

Solution to Exercise 5.11

We have

$$P = 134.67, t = 5, A_5 = 204.78$$

Therefore

$$i = [\ln (204.78/134.67)]/5 =$$
$$\ln (1.5206)/5 = 0.4191/5$$
$$i = 0.0838.$$

The continuously compounded inflation rate for the period was therefore 8.38% per annum.

Solution to Exercise 5.12

The periodic interest rate is the annual rate in this case, i.e. 9%. The number of periods is the term plus 1 = 12 + 1 = 13.

The equal periodic payment is -5000. The present value argument is entered as 0 or omitted. The future value is to be found immediately after the last deposit has been made, so the *Type* argument value is 0.

Consequently, we should enter:

=FV(9%,13,-5000,0,0)

and obtain a value of £114766.92.

Solution to Exercise 5.13

The equivalent annual rate must be calculated before the Excel FV function can be used, since payments are annual but interest is compounded monthly. Therefore we require:

$$EAR = (1 + i/m)^m - 1 = (1 + 0.18/12)^{12} - 1 = 0.1956 = 19.56\%$$

This can then be used in the FV function as follows:

=FV(19.56%,20,-10000,0,0)

A value of £1770040.18 will be obtained.

Solution to Exercise 5.14

The periodic rate is 18%/12 = 1.5% per month, and this matches the periodic payments of £50 per month. There are 26(12) = 312 periods in the term of the annuity, in each of which the payment is £50. Consequently, the structure of the required future value function is:

=FV(1.5%,312,-50,0,0)

A result of £343630.28 for the future value will be returned.

Solution to Exercise 5.15

First calculate the equivalent annual rate from:

$$EAR = (1 + 0.09/2)^2 - 1 = 0.092025 = 9.2025\%$$

Then remember that the *Type* argument should be set to 1, since the future value is to be calculated one year after the last deposit is made. This also means that the FV function performs properly, unlike the case when the *Type* argument value is 0.

The future value can therefore be obtained from:

=FV(9.2025%,9,-1000,-5000,1)

This should return a value of £25382.94.

Solution to Exercise 5.16

First, the equivalent annual rate must be calculated from:

$$=(1 + 0.15/4)^4 - 1 = 0.15865 = 15.865\%$$

The answer is then given by the NPER function with the following argument values:

=NPER(15.865%,-6000,0, 306528.05,0)

This should return a value of 15 for the required number of annual payments to be made over a timespan of 14 years.

Solution to Exercise 5.17

First calculate the equivalent annual rate from:

$$EAR = (1 + 0.1/12)^{12} - 1 = 0.1047 = 10.47\%$$

(ia) The answer is obtained from:

=PMT(10.47%,20,-10000,300000,0)

The 20 required annual payments are £3752.46 and this will secure the required annual amount after 19 years (20 payments).

(ib) All that is needed is to change the last argument value from 0 to 1. Hence:

=PMT(10.47%,20,-10000,300000,1)

The 20 required annual payments are £3396.81 and this will secure the required annual amount after 20 years.

(iia) Change the present value argument from -10000 to 0, and then enter:

=PMT(10,47%,20,0,300000,0)

The 20 required annual payments are £4964.96 and this will secure the required annual amount after 19 years.

(iib) Use a present value argument of 0 and a *Type* argument of 1. Then enter:

=PMT(10.47%,20,0,300000,1)

The 20 required annual payments are £4494.39, and this will secure the required annual amount after 20 years.

(iii) Change the present value argument to -50000 and set the *Type* argument to 0. That is:

=PMT(10.47%,20,-50000,300000,0)

Now notice that Excel returns a positive amount (£1097.54) for this function. This is because the initial account value of £50000 on its own will amount to more than £300000 after 19 years' compound interest. (The

£50000 will be worth £331673.2, to be exact.) Consequently, there is no need to make any annual payments to the account in order to secure the target sum. In fact, the value returned by the PMT function (£1097.54) in this case indicates the annual amount that the account can pay out and still have a future value of £300000.

Solution to Exercise 5.18

The answers are obtained from:

    a) =PMT(17%,15,7000,0,0)

A value of £1314.75 should be returned.

    b) =PMT(17%,15,7000,0,1)

A value of £1123.72 should be returned.

Discounting techniques

Contents

Accompanying files to be loaded as instructed:

W6_3.XLS   W6_4.XLS   W6_5A.XLS   W6_6.XLS   W6_11A.XLS   W6_13.XLS

6.1. **Present value (PV)**
....

The ideas of compounding explained in the previous chapter have an important extension in an area known as **discounting**. To understand the issues involved ask the following question: 'When is a pound not a pound?'

One answer would be: 'When it is received at some future date rather than at the present.' What this means is that £1 (or any other amount) that is to be received 10 years from now is worth less than £1 that is to be received 5 years from now; which is worth less than £1 which is to be received 1 year from now. Only if the funds are received just now is their present worth the same as their nominal worth.

This idea can be stated more formally as follows. Any two or more nominally equal monetary sums must be regarded as unequal in current magnitude unless they are received at exactly the same time. Furthermore, the current magnitude of these monetary sums is only equal to their nominal magnitude if the funds are received just now.

This explicit introduction of the time dimension to the calculation of the present worth of funds that are to be received at some future date means that any future sum must have its nominal value modified downwards in order to take account of the reduction in present value caused by the time lapse that exists before the funds are received.

This reduction stems entirely from the fact that the recipient of the funds must wait for a finite period of time before the money is available to be spent or reinvested, and the reduction in current value compared to nominal value therefore represents the lost interest cost to the individual of having to wait for the funds to be received.

The procedure of modifying nominal values into current values is known as discounting, and there are two things that must be understood about it. First, the word discount is not used in the popular sense of the word to mean a reduction in the price paid for an article expressed as a percentage of the higher price. 'Discounting' as used here *does* mean a systematic reduction in the nominal value of monetary sums, but, as will be seen, it is not done in a simple percentage manner.

Secondly, the cost of having to wait mentioned above has nothing to do with the existence of a positive inflation rate. It is true that if inflation exists, then the penalty of having to wait becomes higher; but this penalty exists whether there is inflation or not, and is to be understood in terms of the interest payments that have to be given up as a result of having to wait for the funds to be received.

As in the case of some of our previous analyses, a simple transposition of a basic equation is sufficient to illustrate the basic idea. This is because it will be remembered that the basic compounding formula developed in Chapter 5 stated that:

$$A_t = P(1+i)^t$$

Now, if a principal of £P amounts to £A_t after t years when the interest rate is given by i, it follows that if a sum of £A_t is to be received after t years, then this is equivalent to a principal just now of:

$$P = A_t / (1+i)^t$$

When this transposition is made, the term P is usually referred to as the **present value** (PV) of the future amount A_t and the i term is known as the **discount rate** (i.e. the interest rate used for discounting purposes). We therefore have:

$$PV = A_t / (1 + i)^t$$

For example, to find the present value of an amount of £1000 that is to be received in 10 years' time when the interest rate for the period is 10% per annum, we must evaluate:

$$PV = 1000/(1 + 0.1)^{10} = 1000/1.1^{10} = £385.54$$

The implication of this calculation is that an individual would be indifferent between the choice of £1000 to be received in 10 years' time, and £385.54 to be received just now. This is because the present sum of £385.54 could be placed on deposit for 10 years at the 10% compound interest rate and would eventually amount to:

$$385.54(1.1)^{10} = £1000.$$

As has already been said, the further into the future a given sum is to be received, then the less is its present value for any given discount rate.

**This can be confirmed by preparing a worksheet similar to Workbook 6.1.
Do this now.**

W6_1

	A	B	C	D	E	F	G	H	I
1	Start value for t	0							
2	Step value for t	2							
3	Future amount	1000							
4	Discount rate %	0%	5%	10%	15%	20%	25%		
5	t (periods)	PV	PV	PV	PV	PV	PV		
6	0	1000	1000.00	1000.00	1000.00	1000.00	1000.00		
7	2	1000	907.03	826.45	756.14	694.44	640.00		
8	4	1000	822.70	683.01	571.75	482.25	409.60		
9	6	1000	746.22	564.47	432.33	334.90	262.14		
10	8	1000	676.84	466.51	326.90	232.57	167.77		
11	10	1000	613.91	385.54	247.18	161.51	107.37		
12	12	1000	556.84	318.63	186.91	112.16	68.72		
13	14	1000	505.07	263.33	141.33	77.89	43.98		
14	16	1000	458.11	217.63	106.86	54.09	28.15		
15	18	1000	415.52	179.86	80.81	37.56	18.01		
16	20	1000	376.89	148.64	61.10	26.08	11.53		
17	22	1000	341.85	122.85	46.20	18.11	7.38		
18	24	1000	310.07	101.53	34.93	12.58	4.72		

Sheet1 / Sheet2 / Sheet3 / Sheet4 / Sheet5 / She

Workbook 6.1

The crucial formula is contained in B6:

=$B$3/((1+B$4)^$A6))

Now copy this formula down the sheet to show how the present values change as the number of periods increase, and then copy the whole block in B6:B18 along the sheet to show how the present values change as the discount rate increases.

The results shown in Workbook 6.1 should be obtained.

Furthermore, when the A4:G18 range is graphed as an XY scatter graph using the first 2 rows for the legend text, Fig. 6.1 is produced.

Prepare this graph now, and when you have finished save the file as W6_1.XLS.

Clearly, as the time before the funds are received increases, the present value of any given amount decreases, and this decrease in present value is greater, the greater the discount rate.

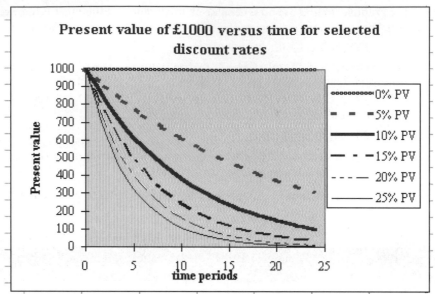

Figure 6.1

Fig. 6.1 also shows that there is one special case when present and future values are the same—when the discount rate is zero. This should be intuitively obvious, since if no interest is paid on deposited funds then there is no penalty involved in having to wait for the funds to be received.

Exercise 6.1 can be attempted now.

6.2. **Discounting multiple amounts**

The ideas involved in the basic notion of discounting can of course be extended to situations in which there is more than one future payment. In this respect, consider the following example.

Imagine a situation in which a sum of £1000 was to be received just now, and after 1 year, and after 2 years, and after 3 years. Also assume that the interest rate is 14% per annum compounded annually. What is the present value of this stream of income receipts?

To answer this question, notice that the £1000 that is received just now simply has a present value of £1000 (i.e. its nominal worth), while the receipt of £1000 that is to be received in one year's time has a present value of £1000/(1.14) = £877.19.

By a similar logic the final two receipts will have present values of £1000/$(1.14)^2$ =£769.47 (for the receipt after 2 years) and £1000/$(1.14)^3$ = £674.97 (for the receipt after 3 years).

Consequently, the combined present value of all 4 income receipts (i.e. the present value of the entire income stream) must be given by:

£1000 + £877.19 + £769.47 + £674.97 = £3321.63.

What this means is that, with an annual interest rate of 14%, a lump sum payment just now of £3321.63 is equivalent to an income stream of 4 annual receipts of £1000, with the first receipt being received immediately and the remaining equal receipts of £1000 being received after 1, 2, and 3 years respectively.

In other words, £3321.63 is the present value of the stream of 4 equal annual receipts of £1000 when the first receipt is received just now.

Exercise 6.2 can be attempted now.

Now, a moment's consideration should reveal that there are numerous savings and pension schemes available which use exactly this notion. For example, suppose that, in exchange for a specified (but as yet unknown) lump sum payment just now, a savings scheme guaranteed to provide 5 payments of £5000 after 1 year, 2 years, 3 years, 4 years, and 5 years. What must be the size of this lump sum payment if the interest rate over the period is 12.5%?

Clearly the answer to this question can be obtained by finding the present value of the guaranteed income stream, since no rational saver would agree to pay more than this present value as the initial lump sum payment required to secure the specified income stream. Similarly, no rational borrower would be willing to accept less than the present value of the income stream as the initial payment.

In either case, the size of the initial payment would differ from the present value of the income stream that the initial payment was designed to secure. This initial lump sum payment must therefore be equal to the present value of the secured income stream, which is given by:

$$5000/1.125 + 5000/1.125^2 + 5000/1.125^3 + 5000/1.125^4 + 5000/1.125^5 = £17802.84$$

From what we have done, it should be clear that we can derive a general expression for the present value of any given income stream of £R per annum, receivable at the end of each of t years, when the interest rate is i (=r/100)% per annum.

Assuming that the first income receipt is received a year from now, this would be:

$$PV = R/(1 + i) + R/(1 + i)^2 + \ldots + R/(1 + i)^t$$

Of course, it is possible that the first receipt in an income stream is actually received just now, in which case the last expression becomes:

$$PV = R/(1 + i)^0 + R/(1 + i)^1 + R/(1 + i)^2 \ldots + R/(1 + i)^t$$

where, of course, $R/(1 + i)^0 = R$.

Clearly, if several years are involved these calculations, although arithmetically simple, can become extremely tedious. This is where Excel can help with its dedicated present value function, the general syntax of which is:

=PV(Interest rate,Number of periods,Equal periodic amount,*Future value,Year start or end*)

where, as usual, optional arguments have been italicized.

Consequently, to reproduce the answer obtained in the last illustration (£17802.84) we can identify the following arguments of the Excel PV function.

Interest rate = 12.5%
Number of periods = 5
Equal periodic amounts = 5000
Future value = 0—since it is an optional argument that is not relevant to the current discussion.
Year start or year end = 0.

This is a simple **switch** argument—enter 0 or omit the argument if the payments or receipts occur at the end of the period, or enter 1 if they occur at the start of the period. In the worked illustration the first receipt of £5000 was to be received after one year, i.e. at the end of the period, and so a value of 0 should be used in this case.

Taken together these figures mean that the PV function should be specified as:

=PV(12.5%,5,5000,0,0)

Enter this now to any vacant cell of a workbook, and confirm that the present value of this stream of income is £17802.84.

Also notice that Excel in fact returns the present value as a negative amount. This is because the constant amounts were positive—representing receipts as opposed to outgoings (in which case they should be entered as negative amounts). This means that the calculated present value represents the negative amount that would have to be laid out just now in order to secure the specified future stream of positive receipts.

Now suppose that the scheme illustrated promised an immediate return of £5000, followed by a further 4 returns of £5000 after 1, 2, 3, and 4 years. The effect of this alteration to the problem is to bring the whole stream of payments forward by one year. Consequently the present value would be given by:

$$PV = 5000/1.125^0 + 5000/1.125^1 + 5000/1.125^2 + 5000/1.125^3 + 5000/1.125^4 = £20028.20$$

To reproduce this result in Excel, all that needs to be done is alter the last argument of the previous PV function from 0 to 1.

Do this now, and confirm that the correct answer (£20028.20) is obtained. Exercise 6.3 can be attempted now.

Before leaving the Excel PV function, the role of the optional 4th argument (future value) should be explained.

Consider a savings scheme that, in exchange for a lump sum payment just now of £3000, promises to pay 4 equal annual amounts of £600 after 1, 2, 3, and 4 years. Additionally however, a terminal bonus of £1000 is paid along with the last payment of £600. If the interest rate for the period is 9% per annum compounded annually, calculate the present value of the scheme.

This problem differs from the previous illustrations in the sense that the payments (including the terminal bonus) are not all equal, and so the PV function is not immediately applicable. However, if we regard the problem in terms of the present value of the following income stream, then a solution can be obtained:

$$PV = 600/1.09 + 600/1.09^2 + 600/1.09^3 + 600/1.09^4 + 1000/1.09^4 = £2652.26$$

Clearly this is simply the present value of the 4 equal receipts of £600 plus the present value of the 'one-off' payment of £1000 received after 4 years.

In terms of the PV function this one-off payment is regarded as the **future value** argument.

Consequently, make the following entry to a blank cell of a worksheet.

=PV(9%,4,600,1000,0)

The answer obtained above (£2652.26) should be returned, and represents the amount of the lump sum payment that has to be laid out just now in order to secure the given stream of equal annual amounts, plus the one-off terminal bonus.

The result of this discussion is that the optional future value argument in the PV function is to be used if the stream of constant amounts also contains one (and only one) additional and perhaps different amount that accrues with the last constant amount.

Furthermore, since, in the illustration, a lump sum of £3000 was required to be laid out just now in order to secure a future stream of income with a present value of £2652.26, it can be deduced that the savings scheme offered is less attractive than simply placing the £3000 on deposit at the prevailing interest rate of 9%. This is because the savings scheme is equivalent to giving away £3000 just now in exchange for a return of £2652.26 received just now. In other words a net present giveaway of £347.74.

Finally, the future value argument can also be used to allow calculation of the present value of a single future amount simply by setting the equal periodic amount to zero and using the single future amount as the future value argument.

For example, in section 6.1 of this chapter the present value of a single payment of £1000 to be received in 10 years' time when the discount rate was 10% per annum was calculated as £385.54 (i.e. $1000/1.1^{10}$).

Confirm that this result could also be obtained from:

=PV(10%,10,0,1000,0)

Exercise 6.4 can be attempted now.

6.3. Variations in the discounting period

It will have been noticed that the foregoing discussion has only considered situations in which interest is discounted on an annual basis. Yet, as was the case with compounding, account should be taken of situations in which interest is discounted more frequently than once per year.

For example, consider an amount of £2000 that is to be received 5 years from now. If the current interest rate is 7% compounded annually, then the present value of this amount is easily obtained from:

$$PV = 2000/(1.07^5) = £1425.97$$

or, in Excel from:

=PV(7%,5,0,2000,0)

Now suppose that the interest rate of 7% per annum was compounded half-yearly. Then, in the same way as any sum deposited just now would be worth more after a given number of years than under annual compounding, any sum received in the same given number of years will be worth less than if annual discounting prevailed. To be exact:

$$PV = 2000/(1 + 0.07/2)^{5(2)} = 2000/(1.035^{10}) = £1417.83$$

The figure above results from the fact that there are now 10 discounting periods in each of which the interest rate is 3.5%.

By a similar logic, if interest were compounded quarterly, monthly, weekly, or daily; then the present values would be given by:

Quarterly:
$$PV = 2000/(1 + 0.07/4)^{5(4)} = 2000(1.00875^{20}) = £1413.65$$
Monthly:
$$PV = 2000/(1 + 0.07/12)^{5(12)} = 2000(1.00583^{60}) = £1410.81$$
Weekly:
$$PV = 2000/(1 + 0.07/52)^{5(52)} = 2000(1.00135^{260}) = £1409.70$$
Daily:
$$PV = 2000/(1 + 0.07/365)^{5(365)} = 2000(1.00019^{1825}) = £1409.42$$

Inspection of the pattern in these results should now suggest that if some future amount (A) is to be received in t years' time when the interest rate is i = r/100% per annum, compounded m times per annum, the present value will be given by:

$$PV = A/(1 + i/m)^{mt} = A(1 + i/m)^{-mt}$$

That is, the present value is to be viewed in terms of m times t periods in each of which the interest rate is i/m.

It should now be clear how the PV function can be adapted to take account of variations in the compounding period. Hence the semi-annual, quarterly, monthly, weekly, and daily discounted amounts produced above would be obtained from the following versions of the Excel present value function.

Confirm these results now in your own worksheet.

Semi-annual =PV(7%/2,5*2,0,2000,0)
Quarterly   =PV(7%/4,5*4,0,2000,0)
Monthly   =PV(7%/12,5*12,0,2000,0)
Weekly   =PV(7%/52,5*52,0,2000,0)
Daily   =PV(7%/365,5*365,0,2000,0)

Furthermore, it is an easy matter to write a more general version of the present value function that will never need editing for any variations in the compounding period. This is shown in Workbook 6.2.

Make this up now.

The entries in B1:B4 are the given data of the problem and are therefore entered directly. The value in B5 is obtained from:

=B3*B4

i.e. the number of years of the investment times the number of compounding periods in the year.

The value in B6 is the discount rate per compounding period and is obtained from:

=B2/B4

Finally, the present value is calculated in B8 from:

=PV(B6,B5,0,B1,0)

Workbook 6.2

	A	B	C	D	E	F	G
	w6_2						
1	Single future amount	2000					
2	Annual discount rate	7%					
3	Number of years	5					
4	Number of compounding periods per annum	12					
5	Total number of compounding periods	60					
6	Interest rate per compounding period	0.00583333					
7							
8	Present value	-£1,410.810					
9							
10							

Sheet1 / Sheet2 / Sheet3 / Sheet4 / Sheet5 / She

Now use this model to confirm the results that were obtained above by making successive alterations to the value in B4.

As was the case with compounding, the effect of increasing the frequency with which interest is discounted, is at first quite dramatic but eventually exercises an almost negligible additional effect. Clearly the expression for the present value is approaching some limit as the frequency of discounting increases.

Now it should be remembered that as compounding became effectively continuous (i.e. as the number of compounding periods (m) tended to infinity), the expression:

$$A_t = P(1+i/m)^{mt} \text{ tended towards } Pe^{it}$$

By a similar logic we would therefore expect that the equivalent discounting expression:

$$PV_t = A/(1+i/m)^{mt}$$

would tend towards A/e^{it}. This is indeed correct, and is the discounting equivalent of continuous compounding. That is, if an interest rate of i is discounted m times per annum, then the present value of an amount of £A to be received t years from now is given by:

$$PV_t = A/(1+i/m)^{mt}$$

which tends towards A/e^{it} as m tends to infinity.

Using the figures from our last illustration, this means that with continuous discounting we would obtain:

$$PV = 2000/e^{0.07(5)} = 2000/e^{0.35} = £1409.376.$$

This figure is, of course, almost identical to the one obtained on the basis of daily discounting (£1409.42)

Confirm this now in Workbook 6.2 by imagining that the annual interest rate was discounted by the second. There are therefore 365(24)(60)(60) = 31536000 periods of 1 second in a year. So enter this value to the B4 cell and the present value will be computed as 1409.376 (when formatted to 3 decimal places).

Clearly the difference between continuous discounting and discounting every second can only be observed if more than 3 decimal places are used.

Exercise 6.5 can be attempted now.

Now, in just the same way as continuous compounding was used to model growth processes that did not fall into discrete accounting patterns (population growth etc.) continuous discounting should be used to calculate the present value of such processes. For example, suppose that a forestry commission has planted an area of young trees that is expected to have a value of £10 million in 15 years' time. If the value of useable wood is believed to grow at a continuous exponential rate of 4% per annum, calculate the present value of the tree plantation.

To answer this, note that since growth is taken to be at an exponential rate of 4% per annum we have:

$$PV = 10/e^{0.04(15)} = 10/e^{0.6} = £5.48 \text{ million}$$

As a final point in this section, it should now be shown how the Excel present value function can be used in situations where there are a series of equal periodic payments or receipts, but where these periods are not necessarily of one year.

For example, suppose that, in order to buy a car, an individual agrees to a loan with the following scheme of repayments: 24 monthly repayments of £200, with the first repayment being made in 1 month's time. If the annual interest rate is 12% compounded monthly, calculate the size of the sum borrowed.

To answer this question we note that the monthly interest rate is 12%/12 = 1%, and that over the term of the debt there are a total of 24 monthly periods. Consequently we require:

=PV(1%,24,-200,0,0)

Now confirm that this evaluates to £4248.68, as the sum that was borrowed.

A generic worksheet model that can solve problems of this type is contained on the accompanying disk in the file called W6_3.XLS.

Load this now and study its structure.
Exercise 6.6 can be attempted now.

6.4. Net present value (NPV)

The techniques illustrated above have important applications in any attempt to evaluate the relative merits of financial projects that yield differing returns at different points in time. Consider a firm that is trying to decide whether to purchase a new machine with an initial cost of £10000. Suppose also that this machine is expected to provide revenue of £6000 at the end of both its 1st and 2nd year of use. Thereafter, the machine is scrapped without any scrap value. If the market interest rate is 12% per annum, compounded annually, does this machine represent a viable investment?

It should be clear that the stream of income furnished by the machine must be brought back to the present so that it can be compared with the current cost of £10000. Consequently, we must evaluate:

$$PV = 6000/(1.12) + 6000/(1.12^2) = £10140.30$$

This figure, representing the value just now of the future stream of income from the machine, must be compared with the cost of £10,000 that must be laid out just now in order to produce the income stream. Consequently, we can form the difference between the present value of the income stream and the initial cost, to obtain a figure that is known as the **net present value** (NPV):

$$NPV = PV - C$$

where C represents the initial cost of the machine.

In our example the NPV is £140.30 (£10140.30-£10000) and since this figure is positive we would recommend that that the machine be purchased in preference to the alternative available—with that alternative being to place the funds on deposit at the going market rate of interest of 12%. This means that the implication of a positive (negative) NPV is that the project being appraised provides an implied rate of return that is greater (less) than the currently available market rate of return.

To see this, imagine that the funds had been placed on deposit for two years at the prevailing rate of 12% per annum (compounded annually). The amount accruing after 2 years is easily calculated as:

$$10000(1.12)^2 = £12544.00$$

Now this raises an apparent difficulty in the light of our declared preference for the project, since simple arithmetic suggests that the machine will provide a terminal sum of £6000 + £6000 = £12000, i.e. less than the £12544 that could be obtained from the bank.

Yet this is to forget that the first return of £6000 from the machine occurs after 1 year and is therefore available to be placed on deposit at the going market rate (which is assumed to be 12%). When this is done, the terminal value of the returns from the machine are calculated to be:

£6000(1.12) + £6000 = £12720.00

This figure exceeds the terminal value that would have been obtained from the bank by £176.00, thereby confirming our conclusion that purchasing the machine is a superior financial project to the alternative use of the funds.

A problem arises, however, when we attempt to measure this superiority. This is because we have two apparently conflicting measures. On the one hand, on the basis of the net present value calculation, the machine appears to be £140.30 superior to a 12% rate of return. On the other hand, however, when viewed at the end of the period this superiority has also been calculated to be £176.00. In fact, there is no conflict here, since it should be clear that a terminal superiority of £176.00 is identical to a current superiority of £140.30 if the current market rate of interest is 12%. This is because the present value of £176.00, discounted at 12% for 2 years is £140.30.

The net result of this discussion is twofold. First, the net present value technique assumes that the incoming funds are placed on deposit at the going market rate immediately they become available. Second, the net present value figure gives the current net superiority of the project being appraised, in comparison with the rate of return available from the alternative uses of the funds. This last rate of return is the figure to be used as the discount rate in the net present value calculations, and will usually be taken as the current market rate of interest.

Excel can carry out net present value calculations with its NPV function, the general syntax of which is:

=NPV(Discount rate, Range of amounts from year 1 onwards) + Initial cost

For example, to reproduce the result from the last example, make the following entries to a blank worksheet.

In A1:A5 enter the labels:

| Initial cost | First return | Second return | Discount rate | Net present value |

Then in B1:B4 enter the values:

| -10000 | 6000 | 6000 | 12% |

Finally in B5 calculate the NPV from the formulae:

=NPV(B4,B2:B3)+B1

The previously obtained result of £140.30 should be returned.

Notice how Excel has been forced to obtain the present value of the year 1 and year 2 receipts and then add on the (negative) initial cost at its nominal value.

This means that correct usage of the NPV function requires that the stream of returns from year one onwards are entered in the range specified in the second argument. The first element in this range should always be the receipt to be received one year from now, and the last element in the range should always be the last receipt. All cost items should be entered as negative terms, but initial (i.e. immediately incurred) costs (as opposed to recurring costs) should not be entered in the second argument of the function. Rather, they are added on at their nominal worth outside the NPV function.

Also notice that the crucial distinction between the PV function and the NPV function is that the former can only calculate the present value of a stream of equal amounts and a single terminal amount (future value). The NPV function on the other hand, does not require that the amounts are all equal.

As might be imagined, the net present value figure obtained for any problem is highly dependent upon the discount rate that is used. This can be seen more clearly in Workbook 6.4, where the NPV for the last example has been calculated for a variety of discount rates.

Load this Workbook (W6_4.XLS) now from the accompanying disk and study the formulae in D2:D14.

When the results are graphed, Fig. 6.2 is obtained.

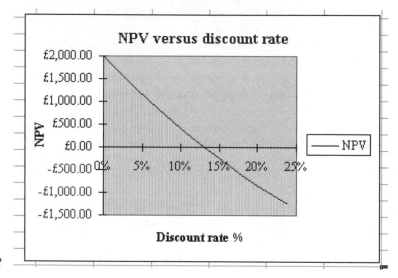

Figure 6.2

As should be clear, the NPV declines steadily as the discount rate increases, and becomes negative for rates in excess of about 13%. This is an important point, since it indicates the threshold value of the discount rate that will make viable projects non-viable. In this sense, as will be seen in the next section, the value of the discount rate that makes the value of NPV = 0 can be interpreted as a measure of the rate of return being supplied by the project.

The full power of the NPV function in saving calculation time can be appreciated in the following example. A power station is to be constructed just now at an initial capital cost of £100 million. Its expected useful lifetime is 16 years, and during this time is expected to produce an average of one million megawatt hours (MWH) per annum. The operational costs of the power station are estimated to be £10 million per annum in its first year of operation, and these are expected to increase at an average rate of 6% over the power station's operational life.

The electricity produced is sold at a price of £25 per MWH in its first year of operation, but this price will be raised at an annual rate of 4% per annum.

Assuming that all costs and revenues (apart from the initial capital cost) accrue at the end of each operational year and that the company employs a discount rate of 15%, calculate the net present value of the project and comment on its financial viability.

The cash flows are indicated in Workbook 6.5.

Make up this model now in line with the explanation below.

	A	B	C	D	E	F	G	H	I	J
1	Year	Costs	Revenue	Net income	NPV					
2	0	-100		-100	£0.84					
3	1	-10	25	15						
4	2	-10.6	26	15.4						
5	3	-11.236	27.04	15.804						
6	4	-11.9102	28.1216	16.21144						
7	5	-12.6248	29.24646	16.6216944						
8	6	-13.3823	30.41632	17.03406678						
9	7	-14.1852	31.63298	17.44778434						
10	8	-15.0363	32.89829	17.86199189						
11	9	-15.9385	34.21423	18.27574551						
12	10	-16.8948	35.5828	18.68800572						
13	11	-17.9085	37.00611	19.09763016						
14	12	-18.983	38.48635	19.50336582						
15	13	-20.122	40.02581	19.90384075						
16	14	-21.3293	41.62684	20.29755508						
17	15	-22.609	43.29191	20.68287163						
18	16	-23.9656	45.02359	21.05800571						
19										

Sheet1 / Sheet2 / Sheet3 / Sheet4 / Sheet5 / She

Workbook 6.5

Three formulae have been used to generate the cost, revenue, and net income entries:

In B4:   =B3*(1.06) which is then copied into the cells B5:B18.

In C4:   =C3*(1.04) which is then copied into the range C4:C18.

In D2:   =C2+B2 which is then copied to the range D4:D18.

Finally, the NPV is calculated from the formula in E2 as:

=NPV(15%,D3:D18)+D2

Since the NPV is positive (£0.84 million), this means that the power station is supplying a rate of return in excess of the 15% discount rate that was applied to the project. Assuming that 15% is the best alternative rate of return that can be achieved, then building and operating the power station is the superior use of the funds.

Exercises 6.7 and 6.8 can be attempted now.

Up until now the NPV technique has only been used to compare the benefits of carrying out a single project with the alternative of placing the funds on deposit at the going market rate of interest (the discount rate). However, it will often be the case that the NPV approach will be of value in allowing rational choices to be made between two or more alternative projects. For example, suppose that in the last illustration there had been an alternative type of power station available with its own different initial and recurring costs. (The output and revenue stream can be assumed to be the same.)

These new cost data have been added to Workbook 6.5A, along with some labels to identify the power stations as A and B.

Now load this workbook (W6_5A.XLS) from the accompanying disk.

The NPV for power station B has been calculated in H3 from the formula:

=NPV(15%,F4:F19)+F3

As can be seen, the NPV for power station B is greater than that for station A and so, if only one of the power stations is to be built it should be station B—because of its greater NPV. However, although B is superior to A at the 15% discount rate that was employed, it does not necessarily follow that B will always be superior to A at all discount rates.

To see whether this is the case, we should evaluate the NPV values of both projects over a range of different discount rates. This has been done in the J1:L22 range of Workbook 6.5A for discount rates between 0% and 20% in steps of 1%. Furthermore, when these data are graphed, Fig. 6.3 is produced.

As is clear from this diagram, the NPV values of the two stations cross over at a discount rate of about 14%. For discount rates less than this station A is superior to station B, while for discount rates in excess of 14% station B is superior to station A.

This said, however, it is also clear that the superiority of station B at discount rates in excess of 14% is only a viable superiority for discount rates that are less than roughly 16%. In other words, both projects have negative NPVs for discount rates in excess of about 16% and so neither is really viable in comparison with placing the funds on deposit at a going rate of about 16%.[1]

To find the exact value of the cross over discount rate we can use the Excel Solver in Workbook 6_5A as follows.

First, use H5 to contain a trial value for the discount rate (13% say).
   Then use H6 to calculate the NPV of station A at the discount rate contained in H5 by entering:

=NPV(H5,E4:E19)+E3

With the trial value of 13% a value of £12.65 will be returned as the NPV for power station A.

Next, compute the NPV for station B in H7 by entering:

=NPV(H5,F4:F19)+F3

With the trial value of 13% for the discount rate, the NPV for station B will be evaluated as £10.25.

Now use H8 to compute the difference between the NPV values for stations A and B from:

=H6-H7

In terms of using the Solver, this cell (H8) is going to be our target cell, and its target value will be zero (implying that the NPV values for stations A and B are the same). The changing cell will be the trial value of the discount rate that has been located in H5.

Now enter these settings to the Solver and then click on Solve.

A result of 14.02% will be returned to the H5 cell (when formatted to 2 decimal places) and indicates the exact value of the crossover discount rate (i.e. the discount rate that equates the NPV figures for the two power stations).

It is also an easy matter to use the Solver to calculate the values of the discount rate that make the NPV figures for each of the power stations equal to zero.

---

1 Trial and error with the value of the discount rate used will show that station A only has a positive NPV at discount rates of 15% or less, while station B only has a positive NPV at discount rates of 16% or less. Thus B is both viable and superior to A only for discount rates between 15% and 16%. Similarly A is both viable and superior to B only for discount rates that are less than 15%.

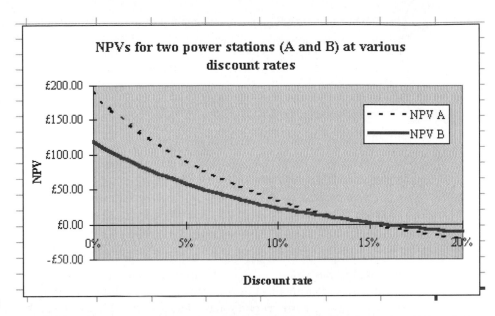

Figure 6.3

To do this for station A, change the target cell in the Solver from H8 to H6 and then click on Solve.

A result of 15.16% will be returned, indicating that the NPV of station A is zero when a discount rate of 15.16% is employed.

To obtain the equivalent figure for station B, change the target cell from H6 to H7 and then click on Solve.

A value of 15.91% will be returned, indicating that the NPV of station B is zero when a discount rate of 15.91% is employed.

This idea of the discount rate that makes the NPV of an investment project exactly equal to zero is an important one, since it gives rise to a crucial concept in investment appraisal known as the **internal rate of return**.

Exercise 6.9 can be attempted now.

6.5. **The internal rate of return (IRR)**

If we now reconsider the machine example of the previous section, then it will be remembered that it was shown that with a discount rate of 12% the NPV of the project was £140.32. Now this must surely mean that the implied rate of return on this project was somewhat in excess of 12%, otherwise the net present value would be zero.

Nevertheless, somewhat in excess of 12% is not a sufficiently exact statement, so the question arises of how to obtain an exact figure for the implied rate of return provided by the project. The answer to this question is supplied by a concept known as the internal rate of return (IRR), and is defined as that rate of return (i), which, if used as the discount rate, would make the NPV of the project exactly equal to 0. In other words:

IRR = i such that: PV - C = 0

If we apply this idea to the machine illustration then we are required to find:

i such that: $6000/(1 + i) + 6000/(1+i)^2 - 10000 = 0$

This should be recognized as a quadratic equation, which, if we let $x = (1 + i)$, can be rewritten and solved as follows:

$6000/x + 6000/x^2 - 10000 = 0$

Now multiply all terms by x^2 to produce:

$6000x + 6000 - 10000x^2 = 0$

Then divide through by 1000 and rearrange to obtain:

$-10x^2 + 6x + 6 = 0$

Finally, solve by the quadratic formula to obtain:

$x = 1.1306$ or $x = -0.5306$

Now since we have already defined $x = (1 + i)$ this means that $i = 0.1306$ or -1.5306, and when we ignore the meaningless negative root we have:

$IRR = i = 0.1306$ (i.e. 13.06%)

This confirms our earlier statement that the IRR would be somewhat in excess of 12%.

You can also confirm that this is indeed the IRR by substituting a value of $i = 0.1306$ into the NPV expression, whereupon you will find that the NPV does in fact become zero. This will only be the case for the data in our example if $i = 0.1306$. That is:

$6000/(1.1306) + 6000/(1.1306^2) - 10000 = 0.$

As a further illustration of this concept consider the following example. Find the internal rate of return of the following cost and income stream:

> an initial expenditure of £12000, followed by revenue of £8000 after 1 year and revenue of £6000 after 2 years

To do this we require i such that:

$PV - C = NPV = 8000/(1+i) + 6000/(1+i)^2 - 12000 = 0$

Using the same method as before, this can be reduced to the following quadratic equation:

$-12x^2 + 8x + 6 = 0$

which has the following positive solution:

$x = 1.11506$, implying that $i = 0.11506 = 11.506\%$

There are, however, a number of potential difficulties with the IRR technique when more difficult problems are considered. In particular, where the costs and/or revenues are spread over more than 2 years, then solving for i involves finding the solution to high-order polynomials. Fortunately, Excel has a dedicated internal rate of return function called IRR which, provided we recognize its limitations, can eliminate these computational difficulties. The structure of the IRR function is:

=IRR(Range of outgoings and receipts, Guess)

This means that on the basis of a (preferably realistic) guess of the IRR, the Excel IRR function will calculate the internal rate of return of the range of costs and revenues entered as the first argument. This range should be constructed so that initial costs precede 1st-year costs and revenues, which in turn should precede 2nd-year costs and revenues, etc. Once again, costs should be entered as negative items and revenues as positive items. The results of the last illustration can now be confirmed.

To do this, take a blank worksheet and make the following entries.
In A1:A4 enter the labels:

| Initial cost | First-year revenue | Second-year revenue | Internal rate of return |

Then, in B1:B3 enter the values:

-12000   8000   6000

Finally, in B4 enter the formula:

=IRR(B1:B3,0.1)

It will be found that the previously obtained result (11.506%) for the IRR is returned to B4.

Now use the IRR function to find the internal rate of return of the stream of costs and revenues associated with the two power stations example from the last section.
To do this, load Workbook 6.5A and use G4 and H4 to contain the labels:

IRR station A   and   IRR station B

Then use G5 and H5 to contain the formulae:

=IRR(E3:E19,0.1)   and   =IRR(F3:F19,0.1)

Results of 15.16% and 15.91% will be obtained, thereby confirming our previous conclusion made at the end of that illustration.

As was hinted at earlier, however, there are limitations upon the validity of the IRR under certain patterns of cash flow. In particular, an unambiguous result will only be obtained from any Excel IRR calculation if the signs of the net cash flows correspond to one of the following patterns.

(*a*) -+++ i.e. costs just now, revenues later
(*b*) --++++ i.e. costs just now and after 1 period, revenues thereafter
(*c*) -++++++ - i.e. costs just now and at the end of the project, revenues in between

If the actual pattern of net cash flows does not correspond to one of these forms, then the IRR as calculated can often be ambiguous and even misleading.

Furthermore, in complex problems spanning several years the IRR as calculated by Excel is sensitive to the initial guess. For this reason it is always advisable to try several guesses to see if the calculated IRR changes.

Exercises 6.10, 6.11, and 6.12 can be attempted now.

6.6. The annual percentage rate (APR)

The notion of the annual percentage rate (APR) as frequently quoted in credit terms stems from the idea that if the stream of repayments needed to repay a given debt are not on the same time basis as quoted in the nominal rate of interest, then the effective rate of interest will differ from this nominal rate.

As will be seen, the APR is very closely related to the IRR concept, but before we make this association explicit consider the following illustration. A lender quotes a flat rate of 10% per annum, and requires that a debt of £5000 is to be repaid in 2 equal annual instalments, with the 1st repayment being made one year from now.

The fact that it is a flat rate that has been quoted has two important implications. First, it means that the repayments are not treated on a reducing balance basis. Secondly, it means that interest is calculated on a simple rather than a compound basis. This means that the total interest on the debt is calculated to be:

$$0.1(5000) = £500 \text{ for each of the two years for which the debt is outstanding}$$

This gives a total interest requirement of £1000 and a total debt to be repaid of £6000. From this it is easy to see that two annual instalments of £3000 are needed to repay the debt plus interest.

Now, if the 1st repayment is to be made in one year's time, and if the 2nd is to be made in 2 year's time, then we can calculate the annual compound percentage rate of interest that will make the present value of this stream of repayments exactly equal to the sum that was borrowed. In other words, we can solve for i in the following expression:

$$3000/(1+i) + 3000/(1+i)^2 = 5000 \text{ implying } 3000/(1+i)^2 + 3000/(1+i) - 5000 = 0$$

Now the similarity with the IRR concept should be clear, since this last expression can be solved for i by using the Excel IRR function. The formula is:

$$= \text{IRR(A1:A3,0.1)} \qquad \text{when A1} = -5000, \text{A2} = \text{A3} = 3000$$

Do this now in any cell of a blank worksheet, and confirm that a value of 13.06% is obtained.

This figure is called the annual percentage rate (APR), and in the context of the illustration indicates that the quoted flat rate of 10% is in fact equivalent to an effective compound rate that is slightly in excess of 13%.

Two points are worth noting about the APR.

(a) Like the IRR, it is frequently difficult to calculate, and subject to the same reservations when complex loan arrangements are considered.

(b) If the repayments on the debt are made on an annual reducing balance basis, then the APR and the nominal rate are the same. To see this, suppose that a debt of £5,000 is to be repaid in 2 equal annual instalments on a reducing balance basis. If the nominal interest rate is 10% compounded annually, then the Excel PMT function will calculate the required repayments to be:

$$=\text{PMT(0.1,2,5000)} = -£2880.95$$

Confirm this now.

In other words, 2 equal annual payments of £2880.95 are needed to pay off the £5000 debt after 2 years—with the first repayment being made 1 year from now.

Now since these repayments have been said to be on a reducing balance basis, and since it is assumed that the 1st payment will be made after 1 year, the APR on this debt can be found from calculating the value of i such that:

$$2880.95/(1 + i) + 2880.95/(1+i)^2 - 5000 = 0$$

Now confirm in the current worksheet that the IRR for this expression is 10%.

This shows that equal annual repayments on an annual reducing balance basis at a nominal annual interest rate of i, represent the only situation in which the calculated APR is the same as the quoted nominal rate.

Of course, very few debts are actually repaid on an annual basis, as anyone who has a mortgage or a bank loan will appreciate. In these cases monthly repayments tend to be the norm, and this means that any quoted annual rate (even if repayments are on a reducing balance basis) will not represent the APR unless the repayments are also annual. This can be seen in the following two examples.

Suppose that the following credit terms are offered by a kitchen unit manufacturer for one of its range of kitchen units.

Special credit offer 3% interest	(APR = 5.65%)
Unit list price	£3637.82
List price less 25% deposit	£2728.37
First year's interest (3% flat)	£81.85
Second year's interest (3% flat)	£81.85
Total debt plus interest	£2892.07
Number of monthly instalments	24
Monthly repayments (2892.07/24)	£120.50

The question that needs to be addressed is how a flat rate of 3% becomes equivalent to an APR of 5.65%, and the answer derives from finding the value of i such that:

$$2728.37 = 120.5/(1+i) + 120.5/(1+i)^2 + \ldots + 120.5(1+i)^{24}$$

To solve this on Excel, open a new workbook and use A1 to contain the total debt (2728.37) and then A2:A25 to contain the 24 monthly repayments (-120.5).
   Now use A26 to contain:

=IRR(A1:A25,0.1)

A result of 0.4713% will be obtained when formatted to 4 decimal places. However, since the repayments are monthly this last figure is the monthly rate, and so to obtain the APR it must be multiplied by 12 to obtain 5.65% per annum.

As another example, suppose that a £30000 mortgage is taken out over 25 years at a guaranteed nominal rate of 13% per annum. The repayments on this debt are made monthly, but the debt is serviced on an annual reducing balance basis. The task is to calculate the size of the monthly repayments and the APR on this debt.

To do this, open a new workbook and in B1 enter:

=PMT(0.13,25,30000)

This will evaluate to -£4092.77, and implies that 25 equal annual repayments of this amount are required to repay the mortgage. Consequently, the monthly repayments are:

- 4092.77/12 = -£341.06.

The APR on this debt is i such that

$$30000 = 341.06/(1+i) + 341.06(1+i)^2 + \ldots + 341.06(1+i)^{300}$$

Accordingly, enter the sum borrowed in A1 and the 300 repayments of £341.06 as negative items in A2:A301. Then in B2 enter:

=IRR(A1:A301,0.01)

A value of 1.0933% will be returned and so the APR on this debt is therefore 12(1.0933%) = 13.1198% per annum, and exceeds the nominal rate (13%) for no other reason than the fact that the repayments are made on a monthly basis while the outstanding balance of the debt is only reduced annually.

Exercise 6.13 can be attempted now.

6.7. **Financial security appraisal**

There is one crucial difference between compounding and discounting that has not yet been considered. This derives from the notion that while the terminal value of an annuity of n payments can be obtained from the sum to n terms of the appropriate geometric progression, the fact that the common factor $m = (1 + i)$ of this series is greater than one means that the sum to infinity does not exist. In other words, the series does not reach a definite limit.

In discounting, on the other hand, the common factor is given by $m = 1/(1 + i)$ which, being less than 1, means that a sum to infinity can be obtained. This is done by noting that:

$$S_n = a(1 - m^n)/(1 - m)$$

and that, since m is less than 1, this means that as n becomes very large, m^n will become very small. Thus the expression $(1 - m^n)$ will tend to 1 and so $S_n = a(1 - m^n)/(1 - m)$ will tend to $a/(1 - m)$.

This is the sum to infinity (S_∞) of the series.

Consider, for example, an annuity of £100 per annum received in perpetuity (i.e. forever) with the first annual receipt being received just now. If the interest rate is represented by i and is compounded annually then this has a present value that is given by :

$$PV = 100 + 100/(1 + i) + 100/(1 + i)^2 + \ldots + 100/(1 + i)^n$$

Now as n tends to infinity this expression has a sum to infinity (S_∞) that is given by :

$$PV = S_\infty = a/(1-m) \text{ where m is the common factor.}$$

Furthermore, since we know that $m = 1/(1 + i)$ this means that:

$$PV = S_\infty = 100/[1-1/(1+i)]$$

which, after some algebra, reduces to:

$$PV = S_\infty = 100(1 + i)/i$$

Hence if $i = 0.1$ we have:

$$PV = 100(1.1)/0.1 = £1100$$

This may seem at first sight both perplexing and irrelevant, since perpetual annuities might be thought to be uncommon securities and would surely be expected to have a present value that is considerably more than indicated above. However, this is a mistaken view on two counts.

First, many government bonds (such as consols) are undated securities that promise to pay a fixed interest coupon in perpetuity, and can properly be regarded as perpetual annuities. Second, the fact that some of the income elements are received so far in the future means that when these are discounted (i.e. divided) by $(1 + i)$ raised to a very large power they become insignificant. For this reason, most of the numerical worth of the PV figure is obtained from the terms in the earlier years, with subsequent terms becoming increasingly insignificant.

This can be appreciated by considering a fixed interest security that is purchased for £100 and promises to bear 8% per annum in perpetuity. This means that there is an infinite stream of payments of $(0.08)(10) = £8$ and if we use a discount rate of 8% per annum to bring this stream back to the present we obtain:

$$PV = 8 + 8/1.08 + 8/1.08^2 + \ldots + 8/1.08^n$$

Then, as n tends to ∞ the value of PV tends to S_∞ and we have:

$$S_\infty = (8)(1.08)/0.08 = £108.$$

It is however, slightly unrealistic to assume that the purchased security provides its first £8 interest coupon immediately it is purchased, and so we should modify the stream accordingly.

Assuming that the first interest coupon is received 1 year after the purchase of the bond, the stream of interest payments becomes:

$$8/1.08 + 8/1.08^2 + \ldots + 8/1.08^n$$

which is an infinite geometric progression in which the first term is 8/1.08 and the common factor is 1/1.08.

The sum to infinity is therefore given by:

$$S_\infty = (8/1.08)(1-1/1.08) = 8/0.08 = £100.$$

In general, then, if an undated security promises to bear a fixed interest coupon of £R per annum in perpetuity, and if the first coupon is to be received 1 year from now, the present value of that perpetual stream of income is given by:

$$PV = R/i$$

where i is the current market discount rate.

Now if the purchase price of the security is denoted by £M and if the fixed interest rate on the bond is i per annum, it follows that $R = iM$ and so the present value becomes:

$$PV = R/i = iM/i = M$$

This is an important result, since it implies that when a new undated bond is issued the purchase price (M) must be the same as the infinite sum of the discounted values of its fixed interest coupons.

Suppose, however, that after this security is issued (bearing what will then be the current market rate of interest), this market rate falls. What will happen to the price that could be obtained for the security if it were offered for sale?

In answering this it should be clear that, if new bonds bear less than old bonds, then the old ones are relatively more attractive, and consequently one would expect their market price to rise above their nominal price (i.e. the price at which they were issued). This is indeed the case as the following illustration will indicate.

Nominal purchase price   £100
Fixed interest rate   0.1
Fixed interest coupon   £10
Present value of coupons 10/0.1 = £100

Now assume that the market rate falls to 8%. New bonds with a nominal purchase price of £100 now bear a coupon of £8. That is:

Nominal purchase price   £100
Fixed interest rate   0.08
Fixed interest coupon   £8
Present value of coupons 8/0.08 = £100

However, if we apply the new (lower) interest rate as the discount rate for the appraisal of the old bond (with the £10 coupon) then we obtain:

$$10/0.08 = £125.00$$

This figure represents the maximum price that could be received for the old bond with the £10 coupon. This is because if £125 is paid for a bond with a £10 coupon this will produce an annual stream of income that represents the same annual percentage return ($10/125 =$ 8%) as that from a bond with an £8 coupon for which £100 was paid.

If the interest rate subsequently rises to 12%, for example, then the 10% bond has a PV of $10/0.12 = £85$, while the 8% bonds have a PV of $8/0.12 = £67.50$. These are the maximum prices at which each of these securities can be sold.

There is a final point to be drawn from this analysis which can be seen by considering the following illustration. Suppose that the current market rate of interest is 8%. Then all bonds previously issued at rates that were less than 8% have a market value that is less than their nominal price. Any investor who is forced to sell one of these bonds will therefore take a capital loss. Conversely, any securities issued at the current rate of interest, or previously issued at rates in excess of this current rate, have a market value that is at least equal to their nominal price, and could therefore be sold without capital loss and often with capital gain.

This principle explains why all financial newspapers find it necessary to quote the going market prices for a wide range of undated securities.

Exercises 6.14 and 6.15 can be attempted now.

6.8. Exercises

Exercise 6.1
Use Workbook 6.1 to indicate how the present value of £500 varies over a period of 12 years at discount rates of 1%, 2%, 4%, 8%, 16%, and 32% respectively.

Exercise 6.2
Use Workbook 6.1 to calculate the present value of £2000 to be received at the end of each of the next 5 years if the discount rate is 11% per annum.

Exercise 6.3
Reconsider Exercise 6.2. Write an Excel function that will provide the same answer as was obtained in that exercise.

Exercise 6.4
Find the present value of 25 equal annual receipts of £50, if the first receipt is to be received just now, if the interest rate for the period is 8% compounded annually, and if a terminal bonus of £2000 is to be received with the last receipt of £50.

Exercise 6.5
Find the present value of an amount of £3500 to be received in 10 years' time if the interest rate is 16% per annum compounded: (*a*) quarterly; (*b*) monthly; (*c*) daily; (*d*) continuously.

Exercise 6.6
What size of loan would require 12 equal quarterly payments of £300, with the first payment being made in one quarter's time, if the quoted annual interest rate were 16% per annum compounded quarterly?

Exercise 6.7
A firm is considering the purchase of a new computer that is expected to produce annual net savings in labour costs of £8000 in each of the 6 years of its operational life. The computer has an initial cost of £30000, and annual maintenance costs of £1000. All savings and maintenance costs accrue at the end of each relevant year. The company has access to funds at the current market interest rate of 14% per annum, compounded annually, and wishes to decide whether the purchase of the computer is a worthwhile investment.

(i) By calculating the NPV of the proposed expenditure decide whether the computer should be purchased.

(ii) If the market rate of interest fell to 8.5% per annum would the decision reached in (i) above be altered?

(iii) In an attempt to finalize the sale, the computer salesperson offers the firm a 'trade-in' after 6 years, the terms of which guarantee a £7500 reduction in the price of a replacement computer. Would such an offer alter the decision reached in (i) above (i.e. at the 14% interest rate)?

Exercise 6.8
A firm wishes to acquire a new photocopier, but has to decide whether it should purchase the item outright or lease one from a leasing company. It intends to keep the photocopier for 3 years and employs a 12% discount rate in all of its investment projects. The relevant expenditures for the alternative acquisition schemes are given below.

A. Purchase of photocopier
    Purchase Price = £5000
    Service contract for maintenance, service, repair etc. (payable at the start of years 1 and 2) = £200
    Resale value of the photocopier after 3 years = £3500

B. Leasing scheme
    Annual Lease (payable at the start of each year for a minimum of 3 payments) = £1000
    Maintenance costs and resale value = 0

(i) Which of the two schemes should the firm choose?

(ii) Suppose that because of the cash flow situation the £5000 for the purchase of the photocopier would have to be borrowed from the bank at an interest rate of 12%, and repaid in equal annual instalments at the end of each of the 3 years. What difference does this make to the choice of schemes?

(iii) If the borrowing rate demanded by the bank is increased to 18% and the repayment method is as in (ii), what difference does this make to the choice of schemes?

Exercise 6.9

Reconsider Exercise 6.8. Prepare a worksheet that can graphically compare the net present values of the purchase and the leasing scheme for discount rates between 0% and 15% in steps of 1%. What conclusions can be drawn?

Exercise 6.10

Reconsider Exercise 6.7. Calculate the IRR of the proposed purchase of the computer, both with and without the 'trade-in'. Should the computer be purchased if the current market rate of interest is 7% per annum?

Exercise 6.11

A whisky manufacturer has just completed a production run of 10000 barrels of whisky at a unit production cost of £400 per barrel. The whisky must be matured for 5 years before it can be sold, and this will impose storage costs of £10 at the end of each of the next 5 years. Bottling and labelling a mature barrel of whisky will cost £4 per barrel. The current selling price of a barrel of this whisky is £500, but this is expected to increase, on average, by 10% per annum in each of the next 5 years.

Calculate the internal rate of return of this investment, and decide whether it is worthwhile if the current market rate of interest is 11% per annum.

Exercise 6.12

A forestry commission has just planted an area of land with 100000 saplings at a cost of £11 per tree, £1 of which was planting costs (the remainder being purchase cost). The trees will be ready for cutting after 10 years at the earliest, and during the maturing period grow at an annual compound rate such that the value of usable wood increases each year by 20% of the initial purchase cost of each tree.

During the maturing period the annual cost of tending the plantation is expected to be equal to 1.5% of the value of the plantation at the start of that year, payable at the start of the second and all subsequent years. (The first year's tending costs are included in the planting cost at the start of the first year.)

Calculate the IRR of this investment if the forestry commission decides that all of the trees are to be felled as soon as they mature, and if the cost of this felling is 5% of the value of trees felled.

Exercise 6.13

A shipping company has just taken delivery of an £8 million cargo vessel. The payment terms imposed by the shipyard are that 25% of the amount due must be paid immediately, but that the outstanding balance can be repaid in 5 equal annual instalments. The shipyard will, however, charge an annual flat rate interest charge of 10% of the incurred debt for each year that there is any debt outstanding.

(i) If the first instalment is to be made one year from now, calculate the size of the 5 equal payments that will have to be made by the shipping company, and the APR on this loan arrangement.

(ii) Funds are also available from the shipping company's bankers at a rate of 10.5% per annum compounded annually. This would mean that the outstanding debt to the builders could be borrowed from the bank and cleared off immediately. Which of the two loan arrangements should the shipping company use in terms of offering the lowest APR?

(iii) In addition however, suppose that the shipyard offered the shipping company a deal whereby (after the initial 25% payment) no interest was charged and no further payments were due until 2 years after the ship was delivered, would this make any difference to the decision reached in (ii) above?

Exercise 6.14

An individual's current stock of assets consists of the following portfolio.

800 undated bonds, each with a nominal value of £1 and an annual

interest coupon of £0.09 in perpetuity
2000 undated bonds, each with a
nominal value of £1 and an annual
interest coupon of £0.10 in perpetuity
3000 undated bonds, each with a
nominal value of £1 and an annual
interest coupon of £0.07 in perpetuity

In order to raise funds all of these securities
have to be sold now.

If the current rate of interest being offered
on undated bonds is 8.5%, how much will be
raised by the sale of the portfolio?

Exercise 6.1

A pension fund is set up just now with an
initial value of £P million. The funds will be
invested at an annual compound rate of r%
over the next 20 years. Repayments from the
fund are £X million per annum, commence
after one year, and are increased by a constant
annual amount of £M each year.

(i) Set up a worksheet that can calculate the
net value of the pension fund after 20 years
when any given values are entered for P, r, X,
and M. Make sure that the worksheet is
flexible enough to allow easy alteration of the
parameter values. In other words locate P, r,
X, and M in their own cells and then refer to
these cell addresses in all formulae that are
written.

Suppose that the operators of the fund
require that the net value of the fund after 20
years is the same as its initial value, and also
suppose that this was £10 million.

(ii) Given values for r and M of 12% and
£0.1 million respectively, calculate the size of
the first repayment (£X million) that will
achieve this objective.

(iii) Given values for r and X of 12% and
£0.9 million respectively, calculate the
maximum allowable annual increase in the
amount of the repayment that is allowed if the
initial value of the fund is to be retained after
20 years.

(iv) Given values for X and M of £1 million
and £0.1 million respectively, calculate the
annual compound rate of growth of the fund
that must be achieved if the initial value of the
fund is to be retained after 20 years.

(v) Given values for X, M, and r of £1
million, £0.1 million, and 12% respectively,
calculate the initial size of the fund that would
be required to make these repayments and at
the same time retain its initial value after 20
years.

6.9. Solutions to the exercises

Solution to Exercise 6.1
Load Workbook 6.1 and change the entry in
B3 to 500. Then alter the step value for t from
2 to 1. Finally, enter values of 1%, 2%, 4%,
8%, 16%, and 32% to the B4:G4 cells.

The results will be calculated and graphed
automatically (although you will have to
change the value in the graph title from £1000
to £500 manually).

Solution to Exercise 6.2
Load Workbook 6.1 and change the entry in
B3 to 2000 and make sure that the step value
for t is 1. Then enter 11% to the B4 cell.
The present values of a single amount of £2000
after 1, 2, 3, 4, and 5 years are contained in
B7:B11 respectively. Consequently the present
value of the stream of 5 future payments of
£2000 is given by:
=SUM(B7:B11) = £7391.79

Solution to Exercise 6.3
The appropriate PV function is:
=PV(11%,5,2000,0,0)
and this evaluates to £7391.79.

Remember that the last argument value
should be set to 0 since the first payment is to
be received one year from now.

Solution to Exercise 6.4
The appropriate PV function is:
=PV(8%,25,50,2000,1) = £868.47

That is, the terminal bonus is included as the 4th argument, and since the first payment is received just now the last argument is set to a value of 1.

Solution to Exercise 6.5

All that needs to be done is make the appropriate entries in Workbook 6.2 and the correct results will be obtained:

(a) B1 = -3500, B2 = 16%, B3 = 10, B4 = 4 giving PV = £729.01
(b) B1 = -3500, B2 = 16%, B3 = 10, B4 = 12 giving PV = £714.15
(c) B1 = -3500, B2 = 16%, B3 = 10, B4 = 365 giving PV = £706.88
(d) Use any cell to contain:
     =3500/(EXP(0.16*10))

This gives an answer of £706.64

Solution to Exercise 6.6

The size of the loan is calculated from:
    =PV(16%/4,4*3,-300,0,0) = £2815.52

Notice how the repayments on the loan are regarded as comprising 12 quarterly instalments, each of which are discounted at a rate of 16%/4 = 4% per quarter.

Alternatively, the same result can be obtained by making the following entries to Workbook 6.3:

B1 = 0, B2 = -300, B3 = 16%, B4 = 3, and B5 = 4

Finally, this result can be confirmed from the PMT function as follows:
    =PMT(4%,12,2815.52,0,0)

A result of -£300 will be obtained, and indicates that 12 quarterly repayments of £300 are required to pay off a debt of £2815.52 that is incurred just now at an annual interest rate of 16% compounded quarterly.

Solution to Exercise 6.7

(i) The relevant costs and returns are illustrated in Workbook 6.6.

The entry in E3 is: =SUM(B3:D3), and this was copied into E4:E9.

The entry in B12 is: =NPV(B11,E4:E9)+E3.

Being negative, the NPV figure of -2779.33 indicates that the project is not viable at the discount rate employed.

(ii) Change the discount rate in B11 to 8.5% and it will be found that the NPV has risen to £1875.11. The project has become viable as a result of the reduction in the implied cost of credit.

(iii) The £7500 trade-in means that an extra income item after 6 years is to be received. Add this to the existing entry in B6 (so that it becomes 15,500), and then notice that even with a 14% discount rate the effect of the trade-in has been to make the NPV on the project positive (£637.58 to be exact). The project is now viable at a 14% discount rate, but only because of the trade-in.

Workbook 6.6

	A	B	C	D	E	F	G	H	I
1		Labour cost	Maintenance	Purchase					
2	Year	Savings	Costs	Cost	Net revenue				
3	0	0	0	-30000	-30000				
4	1	8000	-1000	0	7000				
5	2	8000	-1000	0	7000				
6	3	8000	-1000	0	7000				
7	4	8000	-1000	0	7000				
8	5	8000	-1000	0	7000				
9	6	8000	-1000	0	7000				
10									
11	Discount rate	14.00%							
12	Net Present value	-£2,779.33							
13									
14									

Sheet1 / Sheet2 / Sheet3 / Sheet4 / Sheet5 / She

W6_7

	A	B	C	D	E	F	G	H	I
1		Purchase	Purchase	Purchase	Purchase	Lease			
2		Resale	Service	Purchase	Net	Annual			
3	Year	Value	Contract	Price	Revenue	Lease			
4	0	0		-5000	-5000	-1000			
5	1	0	-200	0	-200	-1000			
6	2	0	-200	0	-200	-1000			
7	3	3500	0	0	3500	0			
8									
9									
10	Discount rate	12%							
11	Purchase NPV	-£2,846.78							
12	Lease NPV	-£2,690.05							
13									

Sheet1 / Sheet2 / Sheet3 / Sheet4 / Sheet5 / She

Workbook 6.7

Solution to Exercise 6.8

Worksheet 6.7 tabulates the relevant costs and revenues for both the purchase and the leasing scheme. The relevant formulae are:

In E4: =SUM(B4:D4) copied into E5:E7.

In B11: =NPV(B10,E5:E7)+E4

In B12: =NPV(B10,F5:F7)+F4

As can be seen:

(i) The leasing scheme has a less negative NPV and is therefore to be preferred.

(ii) The 3 equal annual payments to repay the loan of £5000 can be obtained from:

=PMT(12%,3,5000) = -£2081.74

Workbook 6.8

These can then be included as cash flow items as shown in Workbook 6.8.

Clearly the situation is unchanged as a result of the new arrangements. This should have been expected, since if the firm applies a discount rate of 12% to the project, then this is effectively charging itself an interest rate of 12% for the use of the funds. Since this charge is the same as that made by the bank, there will be no change in the NPV of the project.

(iii) It would be possible to go through arithmetic if necessary, but really there is no need, since we can reason as follows. The increased bank lending rate means that the annual repayments on the loan will be higher,

W6_8

	A	B	C	D	E	F	G	H	I
1		Purchase	Purchase	Purchase	Purchase	Lease			
2		Resale	Service	Purchase	Net	Annual			
3	Year	Value	Contract	Price	Revenue	Lease			
4	0	0			0	-1000			
5	1	0	-200	-2081.74	-2281.74	-1000			
6	2	0	-200	-2081.74	-2281.74	-1000			
7	3	3500	0	-2081.74	1418.26	0			
8									
9									
10	Discount rate	12%							
11	Purchase NPV	-£2,846.77							
12	Lease NPV	-£2,690.05							
13									
14									

Sheet1 / Sheet2 / Sheet3 / Sheet4 / Sheet5 / She

	A	B	C	D	E	F	G	H	I
		Purchase	Purchase	Purchase	Purchase	Lease	Discount	Purchase	Lease
1									
2		Resale	Service	Purchase	Net	Annual	Rate	NPV	NPV
3	Year	Value	Contract	Price	Revenue	Lease	0%	-£1,900.00	-£3,000.00
4	0	0		-5000	-5000	-1000	1%	-£1,997.01	-£2,970.40
5	1	0	-200		-200	-1000	2%	-£2,090.18	-£2,941.56
6	2	0	-200		-200	-1000	3%	-£2,179.70	-£2,913.47
7	3	3500	0		3500	0	4%	-£2,265.73	-£2,886.09
8							5%	-£2,348.45	-£2,859.41
9							6%	-£2,428.01	-£2,833.39
10	Discount rate	12%					7%	-£2,504.56	-£2,808.02
11	Purchase NPV	-£2,846.78					8%	-£2,578.24	-£2,783.26
12	Lease NPV	-£2,690.05					9%	-£2,649.18	-£2,759.11
13							10%	-£2,717.51	-£2,735.54
14							11%	-£2,783.33	-£2,712.52
15							12%	-£2,846.78	-£2,690.05
16							13%	-£2,907.94	-£2,668.10
17							14%	-£2,966.93	-£2,646.66
18							15%	-£3,023.83	-£2,625.71

Sheet1 / Sheet2 / Sheet3 / Sheet4 / Sheet5 / She

Workbook 6.9

which with a 12% discount rate means that the NPV of the loan scheme will become more negative. Now since the leasing scheme was preferable before the NPV of the purchase scheme became more negative, it follows that it must be even more preferable now. Consequently, there will be no change in the choice of schemes.

Solution to Exercise 6.9

The solution is shown in Workbook 6.9.

The crucial formulae are located in H3 and I3, and are:

=NPV(G3,E$5:E$7)+E$4 and
=NPV(G3,F$5:F$7)+F$4

These were then copied into H4:I18.

When the G1:I18 range is graphed as an XY Scatter graph, using the 1st column as the

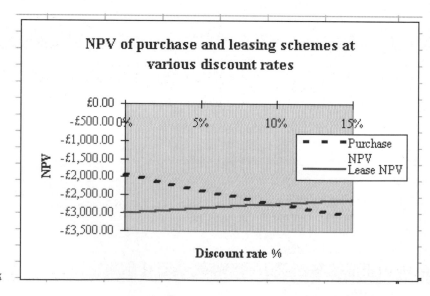

Figure 6.4

horizontal axis and the first 2 rows for the legend, then Fig. 6.4 is obtained.

This clearly shows that the purchase scheme is superior to the leasing scheme (less negative NPV) for discount rates that are lower than about 10.5%. Thereafter the leasing scheme is superior.

Solution to Exercise 6.10

Load Workbook 6.6. Use B13 to contain the formula:

$$=IRR(E3:E9,0.1)$$

When this is formatted to two decimal places a value of 10.55% will be returned. To calculate the IRR when the trade-in is included, change the value in B9 to 15500, and the IRR will increase to 14.7%.

With a current market rate of interest of 14%, the fact that the IRR with the trade-in exceeds this figure means that the project is superior to the alternative of placing the funds on deposit. Notice that this confirms the conclusion that was obtained on the basis of NPV analysis.

Solution to Exercise 6.11

The selling price (P) of a barrel of whisky in 5 years' time will be:

$$P = 500(1.1)^5 = £805.25$$

The storage, production, and bottling costs per barrel, and the eventual income, give rise to the stream of costs and receipts indicated in Workbook 6.10.

The IRR per barrel is calculated in B10 from the formula:

$$=IRR(F3:F8,0.1)$$

and returns a value of 12.98% when formatted to 2 decimal places. The fact that this exceeds the cost of borrowing funds (11%) suggests that the project should be carried out.

Solution to Exercise 6.12

The Value (V) of an average tree on maturity will be given by:

$$V = 10(1.2)^{10} = £61.92.$$

The associated costs and revenues give rise to the stream of amounts shown in Workbook 6.11. The important formulae are:

In B4: = B3*1.2: this computes the value of the average tree in each of the years, and was copied into B5:B13.

In C13: =B13: this translates the value of the average tree into gross revenue once felling takes place.

In F4: =1.5%*-B4: this computes the tending cost as 1.5% of the value of the average tree and was copied into F5:F13.

In G13: =5%*-B13: this calculates the felling cost of the average tree as 5% of its final value.

In H3: =SUM(C3:G3): this calculates the net revenue as the gross revenue less all costs, and was copied into H4:H13.

Finally the IRR of the stream costs and revenue is calculated in B15 from:

$$=IRR(H3:H13,0.1)$$

Workbook 6.10

	A	B	C	D	E	F	G	H	I	J
		Storage	Production	Bottling	Gross	Net				
1		Costs	Cost	Cost	Income	Income				
2	Year									
3	0		-400	0	0	-400				
4	1	-10	0	0	0	-10				
5	2	-10	0	0	0	-10				
6	3	-10	0	0	0	-10				
7	4	-10	0	0	0	-10				
8	5	-10	0	-4	805.25	791.25				
9										
10	IRR	12.98%								
11										

W6_10 — Sheet1 / Sheet2 / Sheet3 / Sheet4 / Sheet5 / She

	A	B	C	D	E	F	G	H	I	J
1		Value of	Gross	Purchase	Planting	Tending	Felling	Net		
2	Year	Average tree	Revenue	Cost	Cost	Cost	Cost	Revenue		
3	0	10.00	0.00	-10	-1	0	0	-11.00		
4	1	12.00	0.00	0	0	-0.18	0	-0.18		
5	2	14.40	0.00	0	0	-0.22	0	-0.22		
6	3	17.28	0.00	0	0	-0.26	0	-0.26		
7	4	20.74	0.00	0	0	-0.31	0	-0.31		
8	5	24.88	0.00	0	0	-0.37	0	-0.37		
9	6	29.86	0.00	0	0	-0.45	0	-0.45		
10	7	35.83	0.00	0	0	-0.54	0	-0.54		
11	8	43.00	0.00	0	0	-0.64	0	-0.64		
12	9	51.60	0.00	0	0	-0.77	0	-0.77		
13	10	61.92	61.92	0	0	-0.93	-3.10	57.89		
14										
15	IRR	16.50%								
16										

Workbook 6.11

and returns a value of 16.5% when formatted to 2 decimal places. Consequently, the forest is a worthwhile investment as long as the market rate of interest is less than 16.5%.

A more general model for this problem is contained on the accompanying disk as Workbook 6.11A (W6_11A.XLS). Load this now and then use it answer the following supplementary question. With the data as given in the original question, calculate the minimum required rate of growth of the trees if the project is to yield an internal rate of return of 20%.

The answer can be obtained from the Solver with a target cell of B19 (the IRR) and a target cell value of 20%. The changing cell is B1 (the growth rate of the trees). When these settings are made and the Solver run, a solution value of 23.6% will be returned (when formatted to 2 decimal places).

Solution to Exercise 6.13

(i) The solution is shown in Workbook 6.12, where the size of the 5 equal annual repayments is calculated from:

$$(6 + 5(0.1)6)/5 = 9/5 = £1.8 \text{ million}$$

The formula in B6 is therefore:

$$= - (B3+B5*B4*B3)/B5$$

The APR of the builder's first scheme is calculated in B18 from:

$$=IRR(B9:B14,0.1)$$

and returns a value of 15.24%.

(ii) This is clearly greater than the annual rate of 10.5% charged by the bank and so the bank loan is to be preferred.

(iii) The effect of the moratorium on the repayments to the builders is displayed in column C of the worksheet, and the APR of this scheme calculated in C18 from:

$$=IRR(C9:C16,0.1)$$

Clearly the effect of the moratorium has been to reduce the APR on the debt to the builders to 10.97%, but this is still not quite enough to make it preferable to the bank loan. However, it is an easy matter to confirm that if an extra year's moratorium were offered then the APR would fall by enough to alter the decision as to which scheme should be chosen. The calculations for this have been entered into column D of the worksheet, and the new APR (8.59%) calculated in D18 from:

$$=IRR(D9:D16,0.1)$$

Clearly the builder's scheme with the 3-year moratorium now has a lower APR than the bank loan.

Solution to Exercise 6.14

The current market price of an undated bond with an annual interest coupon of £0.09 is found by dividing the coupon value by the current rate of interest being offered on equivalent bonds. Thus bonds with an annual coupon of £0.09 will sell for £0.09/£0.085 = £1.06, and since 800 of them are owned, their sale would realize £847.06.

By a similar logic, the remaining bonds will sell at prices of 0.1/0.085 = £1.18 and £0.07/£0.085 = £0.82 respectively, and so will realize £2352.94 and £2470.59. Consequently, sale of the entire portfolio will realise a total of £5670.69.

Solution to Exercise 6.15

(i) There are no dedicated Excel functions that can answer this question directly. Consequently, a model will have to be developed from first principles. A section of a template model ready for completion is shown in Workbook 6.13. Either make up the model as indicated, or load it from the accompanying disk (W6_13.XLS) and complete it as follows.

The given values for P, r, X, and M are entered to the A2:D2 range. The initial size of the fund (P) in A2 is fed into the B4 cell from the formula located there:

=A2

Next, since the repayments from the fund are

zero in the first year enter a value of zero to the C4 cell.

Then, in D4 compute the net value of the fund from:

=B4-C4

This formula will apply to all subsequent entries in that column so copy it into the D5:D24 range.

Now observe that it is this net value of the fund that grows at the annual compound rate located in B2. Consequently, in B5 enter:

=D4*(1+B$2)

This computes the new gross value of the fund at the end of the year when the net value has grown at the given rate located in B2. This is also a general relationship for all subsequent periods so copy B5 into the B6:B24 range.

The first disbursement from the fund is the value that has been located in C2, so feed this into the C5 cell by using it to contain:

=C2

Next, note that the increase in the size of the disbursement is the initial disbursement plus the increment that has been located in D2. Consequently, the entry in C6 should be:

=C5+D$2

This is also a general relationship for all

Workbook 6.12

	A	B	C	D	E	F	G	H
1	Cost of ship	8	Bank loan	Equivalent annual rate (EAR)		10.50%		
2	Deposit	25%						
3	Balance	6.00						
4	Flat rate	0.10						
5	Number of repayments	5.00						
6	Size of repayments	-1.80						
7		Scheme 1	Scheme 2	Scheme 3				
8	Year	Repayments	Repayments	Repayments				
9	0	6.00	6	6				
10	1	-1.80	0	0				
11	2	-1.80	-1.80	0				
12	3	-1.80	-1.80	-1.80				
13	4	-1.80	-1.80	-1.80				
14	5	-1.80	-1.80	-1.80				
15	6		-1.80	-1.80				
16	7			-1.80				
17		APR	APR	APR				
18		15.24%	10.97%	8.59%				

Sheet1 / Sheet2 / Sheet3 / Sheet4 / Sheet5 / She

	A	B	C	D	E	F	G	H
1	P	r	X	M	Change in net value			
2	10	13%	0.5	0.09				
3	Time period	Gross value of fund	Repayments	Net value of fund				
4	0	value of P		0 ?				
5	1	??	value of X	?				
6	2	??	???	?				
7	3	??	???	?				
8	4	??	???	?				
9	5	??	???	?				
10	6	??	???	?				
11	7	??	???	?				
12	8	??	???	?				
13	9	??	???	?				
14	10	??	???	?				
15	11	??	???	?				
16	12	??	???	?				
17	13	??	???	?				

Workbook 6.13

subsequent years, and so when C6 is copied into C7:C24 the model is complete.

With the parameters being used (P = 10, r = 13%, X = 0.5, and M = 0.09) it should be found that the terminal value of the fund is £32.563 million.

(ii) Enter the given values of P = 10, r = 12%, and M = 0.1 to the A2, B2, and D2 cells. Then in E2 enter the formula:

=D24-A2

This computes the change in the value of the fund over the period.

Now note that to answer the question we require that the change in the value of the fund be zero. Consequently, in Solver terms E2 is the target cell and the target cell value is 0. This target is to be achieved by changing the value of the first disbursement (X) contained in C2. Consequently C2 is the changing cell, and it must be constrained to be greater than or equal to zero.

When these settings are entered to the Solver and the routine activated, it will be found that a value of £0.597979 million is returned as the only initial disbursement that will satisfy the requirements.

(iii) Enter the given values of P = 10, r = 12%, and X = 0.9 to A2, B2, and C2 respectively. The target cell and its value are the same as before, but the changing cell is now D2 (i.e. the annual amount by which the disbursement from the fund increases). When these alterations to the Solver settings are made, it will be found that the increment that satisfies the requirement is £0.0498 million.

(iv) This question is solved in the same way as the previous two, with the exception that the changing cell is now the growth rate of the fund (B2). With the given values for P, X, and M of 10, 1, and 0.1 respectively, it will be found that the fund must grow at an annual compound rate of 15.3% if the conditions are to be met.

(v) In this case the changing cell is the initial size of the fund (A2) and the B2:D2 cells must be made to contain values of 12%, 1, and 0.1 respectively. The Solver should find that the fund must be set up with an amount of £13.35 million if the disbursal commitments and requirements are to be met.

Matrix algebra

Contents

Accompanying data files to be loaded as instructed:

None

7.1. **Introduction**

We are all familiar with the idea of using a table to present numerical data items in summary form. Furthermore, we all recognize that provided these data items are of a conventional mathematical form, then each individual item can be subject to normal arithmetical or algebraic operations. However, the question arises of whether the items that constitute the table can be manipulated collectively (i.e. as a unit as opposed to individually). To answer this question we must refer to the concept of a **matrix.**

In its simplest form a matrix is merely a table (or rectangular array) of data elements, in which each element is uniquely identified by means of two numerical subscripts (denoted generally by i and j). The first subscript (i) always refers to the row of the matrix in which the element is located, while the second subscript (j) identifies the column location of the element.

Clearly, this notation is very similar to that which has been used when referring to any cell in an Excel worksheet, with the exception that instead of using a letter to identify a column, another number is used. (There is also another slight difference: Excel employs the convention: 'column letter, row number' to identify a cell address, while matrix algebra reverses this convention and uses 'row number, column number'.) Apart from these two points an Excel worksheet can effectively be thought of as an exceptionally large matrix.

Conventionally, upper-case letters are used to symbolize the whole matrix (i.e. the collection of elements), and lower-case subscript letters to symbolize individual elements. This means that we can define a_{ij} as the element in the ith row of the jth column of the matrix A.

In this notation, the values adopted by i and j define what is known as the **dimension** of the matrix and is said to be i times j (read as i by j). For example, a matrix with 5 rows and 3 columns would be said to be of dimension 5 by 3 and would contain 15 elements.

To see the operation of matrices in practice consider the following illustration. In the first 6 months of a given year a firm produces 3 different products at 3 different factories. The task is to form a matrix that represents the outputs (measured in thousands) of the 3 products from each of the factories.

The structure of the required matrix is shown below.

	Product		
	1	2	3
1	Output from		
Factory 2	factory location i		
3	of product type j		

This means that the required matrix (A) can be thought of as

$$A = \begin{bmatrix} a_{11} & a_{12} & a_{13} \\ a_{21} & a_{22} & a_{23} \\ a_{31} & a_{32} & a_{33} \end{bmatrix} \text{ and is clearly 3 by 3}$$

Now, if we know the actual output values that were produced then we could rewrite this matrix as (for example):

$$A = \begin{bmatrix} 100 & 50 & 90 \\ 65 & 34 & 72 \\ 80 & 43 & 96 \end{bmatrix}$$

As should be clear, the matrix **A** contains 9 ordered elements that each identify the output of product i from factory j. Hence $a_{23} = 72$ represents the output from the 2nd factory of the 3rd product, while $a_{31} = 80$ represents the output from the 3rd factory of the 1st product.

Now notice that since the definition of a matrix simply specifies a rectangular array of elements, there is no need for the values of m and n to be equal. But if they are, then this produces what is known as a **square matrix**. As will be seen later, square matrices possess particular properties that are of considerable value in mathematical modelling; but at the moment it is sufficient to note that there is no necessity for a matrix to be square.

In fact, there are two other dimensions which are of considerable use in the modelling process, and neither of them is square. These are defined by either i or j being equal to 1, in which case, if i = 1 a **row vector** is obtained, while if j = 1 a **column vector** results. Conventionally, vectors are represented by lower-case letters while matrices are represented by upper-case letters, and both are written in bold.

Finally, if both i and j are equal to 1 then this defines a **scalar number**, and illustrates the point that all conventional numbers can be regarded as special cases of i by j matrices in which i = j = 1.

These points can be seen more clearly as follows:

$$\mathbf{a} = [\, a_{11} \, a_{12} \ldots a_{1j} \,]$$

is a row vector of dimension 1 by j.

$$\mathbf{a} = \begin{bmatrix} a_{11} \\ a_{21} \\ \ldots \\ \ldots \\ a_{i1} \end{bmatrix}$$

is a column vector of dimension i by 1.

$$\mathbf{a} = [\, a_{11} \,]$$

is a scalar number of dimension 1 by 1.

7.2. Special types of matrix

Just like normal algebra, matrix algebra operations follow a number of formal rules. Before proceeding to these, however, it will be useful to identify a few special matrix types and clarify their function.

7.2.1. The identity matrix

The identity matrix (**I**) is a square matrix of any dimension that acts as the matrix algebra equivalent of the scalar number 1 in conventional algebra. It is characterized by being composed entirely of ones and zeros.

$$[1] = \begin{bmatrix} 1 & 0 \\ 0 & 1 \end{bmatrix} = \begin{bmatrix} 1 & 0 & 0 \\ 0 & 1 & 0 \\ 0 & 0 & 1 \end{bmatrix}$$

are all identity matrices of different dimension.

As should be clear, the terms that comprise what is called the **principal diagonal** of the matrix (top left to bottom right) are always equal to 1, while zeros appear elsewhere. It will also be noted that the identity matrix can be of **any** dimension as long as it is square. This means that an appropriate identity matrix can always be found for certain specific algebraic operations. This is important since, as will be seen later, any square matrix remains unchanged after being multiplied by an identity matrix of appropriate dimension, thereby confirming the earlier statement about **I** performing the matrix algebra equivalent of 1 in scalar algebra.

7.2.2. The null matrix

This matrix (**O**) is the equivalent of 0 in scalar algebra, and is characterized by being comprised entirely of zero elements. It can be of any dimension (i.e. not necessarily square) and has the feature that when multiplied by any matrix of appropriate dimension it reproduces the null matrix (i.e. itself) as the product. Thus:

$$[0] \quad [0 \ \ 0 \ \ 0] \quad \begin{bmatrix} 0 \\ 0 \end{bmatrix} \begin{bmatrix} 0 & 0 \\ 0 & 0 \end{bmatrix} \quad \begin{bmatrix} 0 & 0 \\ 0 & 0 \\ 0 & 0 \end{bmatrix}$$

are all null matrices of different dimensions.

It also has the feature that if the null matrix is added to, or subtracted from any other matrix of appropriate dimension, then the latter remains unchanged in value.

Now it may have been noticed that the preceding discussion has placed much emphasis on the phrase 'of appropriate dimension'. This is because the algebraic operations of addition, subtraction, multiplication, and division are only defined in matrix algebra under certain circumstances. This means that we can only perform collective arithmetic operations on sets of matrices if certain conditions are met.

These conditions relate largely to the dimensions of the matrices that are to be the subjects of the proposed operations, and for this reason we must always be clear as to when certain processes can be carried out and when they cannot.

7.2.3. The matrix transpose

Transposition of a matrix is the process of exchanging each row with each column of the matrix to obtain a new matrix. Thus, row 1 of the original matrix becomes column 1 of the new matrix, row 2 becomes column 2, and so on.

The transpose of any matrix is indicated by adding the superscript 'T' to the matrix letter. Thus A^T denotes the transpose of the matrix **A**. For example:

$$\text{If } A = \begin{bmatrix} 100 & 50 & 90 \\ 65 & 34 & 72 \\ 80 & 43 & 96 \end{bmatrix} \text{ then } A^T = \begin{bmatrix} 100 & 65 & 80 \\ 50 & 34 & 43 \\ 90 & 72 & 96 \end{bmatrix}$$

Transposition of matrices can often be very useful when particular types of matrix algebra operation require to be carried out. More will be said on this later.

7.3. **Matrix addition and subtraction**

As we have just said, compared to conventional algebra it will be found that there are a number of additional conditions that govern whether particular arithmetic operations can be performed on any two or more matrices.

As regards addition and subtraction of matrices, this can only be done if the matrices to be added or subtracted are of the same dimension. This being the case, then the sum or difference is obtained by adding or subtracting the terms in the same relative location. For example:

If $A = [a_{11} \ a_{12}]$ and $B = [b_{11} \ b_{12}]$
Then $A \pm B = [(a_{11} \pm b_{11}) \ (a_{12} \pm b_{12})]$

It is now an easy matter to confirm our previous statement with regard to the null matrix. To do this, suppose that A is given by:

$$A = \begin{bmatrix} 1 & 6 \\ 5 & 3 \end{bmatrix}$$

The associated null matrix of appropriate dimension is:

$$O = \begin{bmatrix} 0 & 0 \\ 0 & 0 \end{bmatrix}$$

Then:

$$A + O = \begin{bmatrix} 1 & 6 \\ 5 & 3 \end{bmatrix} + \begin{bmatrix} 0 & 0 \\ 0 & 0 \end{bmatrix} = \begin{bmatrix} 1 & 6 \\ 5 & 3 \end{bmatrix} = A$$

From this it should also be clear that:

$$A - O = A$$

Furthermore, it should also be noted that any two or more matrices are regarded as equal to one another if and only if they are of the same dimension and all their elements are equal and identically located. For example:

$$\text{if } A = \begin{bmatrix} 1 & 2 \\ 3 & 4 \end{bmatrix} \text{ and } B = \begin{bmatrix} 1 & 2 \\ 4 & 3 \end{bmatrix} \text{ and } C = \begin{bmatrix} 1 & 2 \\ 4 & 3 \end{bmatrix}$$

then A equals B but neither A nor B equals C (because the elements in row 2 of C, although numerically the same as those in row 2 of A and B, are in different locations). It is also the case that if $A = B$ then $A + B = 2A = 2B$. This can be seen this in the following illustration.

$$\text{if } A = \begin{bmatrix} 1 & 2 \\ 3 & 4 \end{bmatrix} \text{ and } B = \begin{bmatrix} 1 & 2 \\ 3 & 4 \end{bmatrix}$$

$$\text{Then } A + B = \begin{bmatrix} 2 & 4 \\ 6 & 8 \end{bmatrix} = 2 \begin{bmatrix} 1 & 2 \\ 3 & 4 \end{bmatrix} = 2A = 2B$$

This last result stems from the fact that any matrix multiplied by a scalar number produces a new matrix in which every element is multiplied by that scalar. (Notice that this is a very special case of matrix multiplication. Normally it is not as simple as this.)

Now consider the following illustration. Suppose, in the factory example, that in addition to the outputs for the first 6 months (the matrix **A**), the outputs of the 3 products from the 3 factories in the second 6 months of the year were given by the matrix **B**, where:

$$\mathbf{B} = \begin{bmatrix} 67 & 39 & 50 \\ 45 & 23 & 90 \\ 82 & 56 & 40 \end{bmatrix}$$

The task is to form a matrix that will give the total annual output of all 3 products from all 3 factories.

To do this we can represent the required matrix by **P** and define it as the sum of **A** and **B**. This gives:

$$\mathbf{P} = \mathbf{A} + \mathbf{B} = \begin{bmatrix} 100 & 50 & 90 \\ 65 & 34 & 72 \\ 80 & 43 & 96 \end{bmatrix} + \begin{bmatrix} 67 & 39 & 50 \\ 44 & 23 & 90 \\ 82 & 56 & 40 \end{bmatrix} = \begin{bmatrix} 167 & 89 & 140 \\ 109 & 57 & 162 \\ 162 & 99 & 136 \end{bmatrix}$$

Now suppose, in addition, that the firm had annual sales that were given by the matrix **S**, where:

$$\mathbf{S} = \begin{bmatrix} 150 & 80 & 125 \\ 99 & 50 & 162 \\ 143 & 89 & 121 \end{bmatrix}$$

We can now form a matrix **E** that will represent the firm's annual excess production of each of the products at each of the factories. This is done as follows.

$$\mathbf{E} = \mathbf{A} + \mathbf{B} - \mathbf{S} = \mathbf{P} - \mathbf{S}$$

Therefore:

$$\mathbf{E} = \begin{bmatrix} 167 & 89 & 140 \\ 109 & 57 & 162 \\ 162 & 99 & 136 \end{bmatrix} - \begin{bmatrix} 150 & 80 & 125 \\ 99 & 50 & 162 \\ 143 & 89 & 121 \end{bmatrix} = \begin{bmatrix} 17 & 9 & 15 \\ 10 & 7 & 0 \\ 19 & 10 & 15 \end{bmatrix}$$

Exercise 7.1 can be attempted now.

7.4. Matrix multiplication

Unless (as we saw earlier) one of the matrices is in fact a **scalar**, matrix multiplication is only possible when the matrices that are to form the product are what is known as conformable. This will be the case if and only if the number of columns in the first matrix of the product is equal to the number of rows in the second matrix of the product.

A little reflection will confirm that this requirement means that the order in which a particular multiplication is to be carried out is of considerable importance, since if **A** is a 3 by 2 matrix and **B** is a 2 by 4 matrix then the product **AB** is conformable ($2 = 2$), but the product **BA** is not ($4 \neq 3$).

The implications of conformability are considerable, and create a number of possibilities as regards any matrix product. These can be understood as follows.

1. Neither of the products **AB** nor **BA** exist (both are non conformable). For example, if **A** has dimension 3 by 2 and **B** has dimension 4 by 5, then neither product exists ($2 \neq 4$ for

AB and $5 \neq 3$ for **BA**).

    2. **AB** exists but **BA** does not. For example, if **A** has dimension 3 by 2 and **B** has dimension 2 by 4, then **AB** can be formed ($2 = 2$) but **BA** cannot ($4 \neq 3$).

    3. **BA** exists but **AB** does not. For example, if **A** has dimension 2 by 4 and **B** has dimension 3 by 2, then **BA** can be formed ($2 = 2$) but **AB** cannot ($4 \neq 3$).

    4. Both **AB** and **BA** exist[1] but will not be equal except in very special circumstances.

To appreciate the significance of these statements we need further understanding of how a matrix product is created from two or more conformable matrices. Consequently, look at the two matrices below.

$$A = \begin{bmatrix} 3 & 1 \\ 5 & 2 \end{bmatrix} \quad B = \begin{bmatrix} 4 & 6 \\ 3 & 5 \end{bmatrix}$$

It should immediately be noticed that since both of the matrices are square the conformabilty requirements are met for both the product **AB** and the product **BA**.

Now, to obtain the product **AB** we must multiply each element in the first row of **A** by each corresponding element in the first column of **B**, and then take the sum of these individual products. This produces the first element (row 1 column 1) of the product matrix. The process can be thought of as 'diving' the first row of A into the first column of B. Thus when row 1 of A 'dives' beside column 1 of B, we get:

    3   4
    1   3

Now multiply each of the row terms together and take the sum of all products to give:

    $(3)(4) + (1)(3) = 12 + 3 = 15$

This is the first element of the product matrix.

We then multiply each element in the first row of **A** by each corresponding element in the second column of **B** and then take the sum of these individual products. This produces the next element (row 1 column 2) of the product matrix.

To obtain the remaining elements in the product we repeat the last procedure, but this time using the second row of **A** with initially the first, and then the second column of **B**.

These operations produce the following product for our illustrative matrices.

$$AB = \begin{bmatrix} 3 & 1 \\ 5 & 2 \end{bmatrix}\begin{bmatrix} 4 & 6 \\ 3 & 5 \end{bmatrix} = \begin{bmatrix} (3)(4)+(1)(3) & (3)(6)+(1)(5) \\ (5)(4)+(2)(3) & (5)(6)+(2)(5) \end{bmatrix}$$

Therefore:

$$AB = \begin{bmatrix} 15 & 23 \\ 26 & 40 \end{bmatrix}$$

It should be clear from this last illustration that the processes involved in matrix multiplication necessarily mean that a matrix of dimension n by m multiplied by a matrix of dimension m by p will produce a new matrix of dimension n x p. In effect what happens is that the dimension of the product is determined by the row dimension of the 1st matrix in the product and the column dimension of the 2nd matrix in the product. In other words, **M** which is 5 by 3, times **N** which is 3 by 8, produces **MN** which is 5 by 8.

Now that it is known how to perform matrix multiplication we can confirm our earlier statement that even if both products exist they will not usually be identical. To do this, all we have to do is form the product **BA** from the two earlier matrices. This produces:

---

1 Clearly **AB** and **BA** can only both exist if **A** and **B** are both square and of the same dimension.

$$BA = \begin{bmatrix} 4 & 6 \\ 3 & 5 \end{bmatrix} \begin{bmatrix} 3 & 1 \\ 5 & 2 \end{bmatrix} = \begin{bmatrix} (4)(3)+(6)(5) & (4)(1)+(6)(2) \\ (3)(3)+(5)(5) & (3)(1)+(5)(2) \end{bmatrix}$$

Therefore:

$$BA = \begin{bmatrix} 42 & 16 \\ 34 & 13 \end{bmatrix}$$

Clearly the product $AB = \begin{bmatrix} 15 & 23 \\ 26 & 40 \end{bmatrix}$ is different from the product $BA = \begin{bmatrix} 42 & 16 \\ 34 & 13 \end{bmatrix}$.

The results of this discussion clearly suggest that unlike scalar algebra, where it is always true that ab = ba, in matrix algebra there is a difference between pre-multiplication of **B** by **A** (**AB**) and post-multiplication of **B** by **A** (**BA**). It also means that care must always be taken to ensure that the appropriate product is being evaluated, since even if both products exist they will rarely have the same meaning.

Although the process of matrix multiplication is arithmetically simple, it can become tedious when large matrices are involved. This is where Excel can help. For example, to calculate the matrix product **BA** that was obtained above we can proceed as follows.

First, enter the elements of the B matrix to the A1:B2 range, and those of the A matrix to the D1:E2 range of a blank worksheet.

The Excel function that performs matrix multiplication is called MMULT and has the following general syntax.

=MMULT(Matrix 1,Matrix 2,Matrix 3, . . . Matrix n)

where the Matrix 1 . . . Matrix n arguments are the cell range addresses or named ranges of the matrices that are to be multiplied together (A1:B2 and D1:E2 in our example).

However, the MMULT function is not entered to the worksheet in the same way as other standard Excel functions. There is a special procedure that must always be observed.

The first thing to do is calculate the dimension of the product that is to be formed, and then use the mouse to select an area of the worksheet that corresponds to that dimension. For example, if a matrix of dimension 4 by 3 is to be post multiplied by a matrix of dimension 3 by 5, then, as we have already seen, the resulting product will have dimension 4 by 5. Consequently, an area of the worksheet consisting of 4 rows and 5 columns will have to be selected to contain the computed product.

In the current example the matrices to be multiplied are both of dimension 2 by 2, and so the product will also be of dimension 2 by 2.

Therefore, use the mouse to select the area G1:H2.

This area should now be highlighted.

Now, and this is crucial, with the G1:H2 area still selected, type:

=MMULT(A1:B2,D1:E2)

When this has been typed, do not press Enter yet!

As we have said, matrix functions have to be entered in a special way.

So, press the Shift and the Control keys together, and while keeping them depressed, press Enter.

This is the standard way of entering matrix functions to Excel, and if it has been done properly, it will return all of the elements of the matrix product to the selected cells.

Confirm this now.

The previously derived product **BA** should be returned to the G1:H2 range as:

$$BA = \begin{bmatrix} 42 & 16 \\ 34 & 13 \end{bmatrix}$$

Then confirm our previous statement about BA and AB not necessarily being equal by calculating AB in the J1:K2 range.

The previous results should be obtained and should resemble Workbook 7.1

	A	B	C	D	E	F	G	H	I	J	K	L	M	N	O	P
1	4	6		3	1		42	16		15	23					
2	3	5		5	2		34	13		26	40					
3	Matrix B			Matrix A			Matrix BA			Matrix AB						
4																
5																

Sheet1 / Sheet2 / Sheet3 / Sheet4 / Sheet5 / She

Workbook 7.1

It should now be noted that these matrix products are 'hot' like any other Excel functions.

To see this, change the b_{11} element from 4 to 2, and the a_{11} element from 3 to 2.

The new products **BA** and **AB** will be recomputed automatically by Excel and should become:

$$BA = \begin{bmatrix} 34 & 14 \\ 31 & 13 \end{bmatrix} \quad \text{and} \quad AB = \begin{bmatrix} 7 & 17 \\ 16 & 40 \end{bmatrix}$$

It is now appropriate to confirm our earlier statement that multiplication of any square matrix by an identity matrix of the same dimension leaves the original matrix unchanged.

To do this, open a new workbook and in A1:C3 enter the following matrix.

$$A = \begin{bmatrix} 6 & 1 & 4 \\ 3 & 9 & 8 \\ 11 & 2 & 1 \end{bmatrix}$$

Then, in E1:G3 enter a 3 by 3 identity matrix. That is:

$$I = \begin{bmatrix} 1 & 0 & 0 \\ 0 & 1 & 0 \\ 0 & 0 & 1 \end{bmatrix}$$

Next, in I1:K3 calculate the product of A and I by selecting this area and then typing:
=MMULT(A1:C3,E1:G3)

Now enter this as a matrix with the Shift, Control, Enter routine.

The result will be **A** when formatted to zero decimal places.

You should also now confirm that I times A is also A.
Do this by selecting I4:K6 with the mouse and typing:

=MMULT(E1:G3,A1:C3)

Enter this as a matrix in the usual way and the result will again equal A.

In summary, the identity matrix is unique in the sense that **AI** always equals **IA**.
Now, referring back to the most recent version of the factory example, suppose that, in addition to the matrix **P** representing the 3 factories' annual production of the 3 products, we also had information on the usage levels of 3 fuel inputs (C, E, and G), per unit of each of the 3 products. Letting this latter matrix be represented by **U**, the task is to form a matrix product that will represent the total usage of each of the 3 fuel inputs at each of the 3 factories as a result of producing all 3 products.

Clearly we require some data for the **U** matrix, so take it as:

$$\mathbf{U} = \begin{bmatrix} 3 & 6 & 2 \\ 1 & 5 & 7 \\ 4 & 2 & 3 \end{bmatrix}$$

where the rows represent products 1 to 3 and the columns represent inputs C, E, and G. In other words, the u_{23} element represents each unit of product 2's usage of input G.

$$\text{Also recall that } \mathbf{P} = \begin{bmatrix} 167 & 89 & 140 \\ 109 & 57 & 162 \\ 162 & 99 & 136 \end{bmatrix}$$

These are the outputs of each of the products (j = 1, 2, 3) at each of the factories (i = 1, 2, 3)

Now enter the elements of P matrix to the A1:C3 range of a blank worksheet and the elements of U to the E1:G3 range.

At this stage, care will have to be exercised in deciding which particular product is to be formed in order to achieve the required objective. This is because both **PU** and **UP** can be formed—but will have completely different meanings. To see this, consider the product **UP** first of all.

The first element will be formed as:

3(167) + 6(109) + 2(162)

Inspection of each of these terms reveals that they represent:

(Usage of C by product 1) times (Output of product 1 at factory 1)   plus:
(Usage of E by product 1) times (Output of product 1 at factory 2)   plus:
(Usage of G by product 1) times (Output of product 1 at factory 3)

Clearly, the sum formed involves adding the physical usage levels of the three different fuel inputs and this makes little sense. (What, for example, is the sum of 10 tonnes of coal, 6 MWh of electricity, and 4 m^3 of gas? The mathematical answer is 20, but the fact that different units are being summed means that this figure contains very little useful information.)

On the other hand, if we form the product **PU** then the first element will be given by:

167(3) + 89(1) + 140(4)

Inspection of each of these terms reveals that they represent:

(Output of product 1 at factory 1) times (Usage of C by product 1)   plus:
(Output of product 2 at factory 1) times (Usage of C by product 2)   plus:
(Output of product 3 at factory 1) times (Usage of C by product 3)

Summing these terms clearly gives the factory 1 usage of input C in the production of all 3 products.

Clearly this figure makes much more sense, as do the rest of the elements in the product matrix. **PU** can therefore be thought of as:

Factory i usage of fuel input j in the production of all 3 products

Thus the 2nd element in the 3rd row of **PU** is factory 3's total usage of input E in the production of all 3 products. Consequently, **PU** as opposed to **UP** is the required product.

Form this product now in the I1:K3 range of the worksheet, by selecting this range and then typing:

=MMULT(A1:C3,E1:G3)

Then, with the Shift and Control keys simultaneously depressed, press Enter.

The required product will be calculated in I1:K3 and should be:

$$\mathbf{PU} = \begin{bmatrix} 1150 & 1727 & 1377 \\ 1032 & 1263 & 1103 \\ 1129 & 1739 & 1425 \end{bmatrix}$$

Thus, for example, 1150 units of input C are used at factory 1, 1103 units of input G are used at factory 2, and 1739 units of input E are used at factory 3.

Now save this file as W7_2.XLS for future use.
Exercise 7.2 can be attempted now.

As another illustration of the methods that can be used to ensure that any matrix product is appropriate to the stated objective, consider the following example.

A firm sells each of its three products (X, Y, and Z) in each of three distinct markets (A, B, and C). The prices (in £s) that it charges for each product (i = 1, 2, 3), in each market, (j = 1, 2, 3) are given in the matrix **P** where:

$$\mathbf{P} = \begin{bmatrix} 8 & 7 & 6 \\ 15 & 18 & 16 \\ 25 & 29 & 27 \end{bmatrix}$$

The total sales (in 000s of units) of the products to each of the markets are given in the matrix **S**, where:

$$\mathbf{S} = \begin{bmatrix} 2.1 & 3.4 & 7.1 \\ 8.2 & 5.5 & 6.0 \\ 3.9 & 7.6 & 4.2 \end{bmatrix}$$

The task is to form a matrix product that will give the total revenue generated in each market from the sales of all products.

Now open a new workbook and enter the elements of P to the A1:C3 range and the elements of S to the E1:G3 range.

Now we must be careful, since both **P** and **S** are conformable, and if the product is simply formed randomly, then it will never be certain that the result is the required one. Bearing this in mind, we can form the product **PS** and observe that the first element will be calculated as:

$$(8)(2.1) + (7)(8.2) + (6)(3.9)$$

Clearly, this gives the price of X in A times the sales of X in A, plus the price of X in B times the sales of Y in A, plus the price of X in C times the sales of Z in A. Equally clearly, some of the terms are 'mixed' in the sense that the prices and sales refer to different products, and so we conclude that **PS** is not an appropriate product.

If we form **SP**, on the other hand, then the first element is calculated as:

$$(2.1)(8) + (3.4)(15) + (7.1)(25)$$

This represents the sales of X in A times the price of X in A, plus the sales of X in B times the price of Y in A, plus the sales of X in C times the price of Z in A. Once again the terms are 'mixed', and so this product is also inappropriate.

However, if we form the transpose of S (i.e. S^T) then progress can be made.

To do this, select the range containing S (E1:G3) and then select Edit and then Copy from the Menu bar.

Now click on the A5 cell. This will be the first cell in the range where the transpose is to be located.

Now select Edit and then Paste Special and check the Transpose box.

Select OK and the transpose of S will be located in A5:C7.

If we now form the product $S^T P$, the first element will be calculated as:

$$2.1(8) + 8.2(15) + 3.9(25)$$

This represents the sales of X in A times the price of X in A, plus the sales of Y in A times the price of Y in A, plus the sales of Z in A times the price of Z in A—that is, the revenue from sales of all products in market A. This is clearly the product that the question calls for, since it represents the total revenue from the sales of each of the products in market A.

Now force Excel to form this product ($S^T P$) in the E5:G7 range.

The results should resemble Workbook 7.3.

	A	B	C	D	E	F	G	H	I	J	K	L	M	N
1	8	7	6		2.1	3.4	7.1							
2	15	18	16		8.2	5.5	6							
3	25	29	27		3.9	7.6	4.2							
4	Matrix P				Matrix S									
5	2.1	8.2	3.9		237.3	275.4	249.1							
6	3.4	5.5	7.6		299.7	343.2	313.6							
7	7.1	6	4.2		251.8	279.5	252							
8	Matrix S^T				Matrix $S^T P$									
9														

Workbook 7.3

Also notice that the product **PS^T** also exists and will have as its first element:

$$8(2.1) + 7(3.4) + 6(7.1)$$

This represents the price of X in A times the sales of X in A, plus the price of X in B times the sales of X in B, plus the price of X in C times the sales of X in C. Consequently, this product represents the revenue obtained in all markets from the sales of product X.

Finally, notice that the matrices $S^T P$ and PS^T only provide actually observed amounts for those elements on the principal diagonal (top left to bottom right). The elements 'off' the principal diagonal are hypothetical, since they indicate, for example, what revenue would have been if sales in market A had taken place at market B's prices.

In short, the elements on the principal diagonal of S^TP are:

Revenue from the sale of all products in market A
Revenue from the sale of all products in market B
Revenue from the sale of all products in market C

On the other hand, the elements on the principal diagonal of PS^T are:

Revenue from the sale of product X in all markets
Revenue from the sale of product Y in all markets
Revenue from the sale of product Z in all markets

Exercise 7.3 can be attempted now.

7.5. Matrix inversion

It may have been noticed that we have studiously avoided the process of matrix division in the discussion so far. This is because matrix division is far from straightforward and requires to be handled with extreme care. Basically, the principle is the same as in scalar algebra, but the process is considerably different.

For example, suppose that we had the following scalar algebra equation:

$$ax = b$$

If we multiply both sides of the equation by the inverse of a ($1/a = a^{-1}$), we obtain:

$$a^{-1}ax = a^{-1}b$$

implying that:

$$x = a^{-1}b \text{ (since } a(1/a) = aa^{-1} = 1)$$

Clearly, the process of multiplying any expression by an inverted term is equivalent to dividing that expression by the term. Equally clearly, the product $aa^{-1} = 1$, and so we might try to apply this idea to matrices. For example, consider the following matrix:

$$A = \begin{bmatrix} 3 & 1 \\ 5 & 2 \end{bmatrix}$$

What we are looking for is a second matrix (A^{-1} which is read as A inverse) such that if we multiply A by this matrix then we obtain the identity matrix (I). In other words, we require:

$$A^{-1} \text{ such that } A^{-1}A = I$$

If this can be done then we can proceed to perform the matrix equivalent of division. However, it is not quite as simple as this.

First, finding the inverse of a matrix is arithmetically complex, although Excel can help. Secondly, the inverse of a matrix only exists for square matrices, and so there may be certain division operations on matrices that are not square which cannot be carried out. Thirdly, even if the matrix to be inverted is square, this is no guarantee that an inverse exists. In particular, if one or more columns or rows is a constant multiple of any other column or row then the inverse cannot be calculated.

However, provided these restrictions are observed we can use Excel to find the inverse of the matrix A as follows.

First of all place the following matrix:

$$A = \begin{bmatrix} 3 & 1 \\ 5 & 2 \end{bmatrix}$$

in the A1:B2 range.

Now, remembering that the inverse of A must necessarily be of the same dimension as A, select the D1:E2 range with the mouse.

Now, with D1:E2 still selected, type:

=MINVERSE(A1:B2)

Then press Shift and Control simultaneously and press Enter.

The inverse of A, if it exists, will be returned to D1:E2, and should be:

$$A^{-1} = \begin{bmatrix} 2 & -1 \\ -5 & 3 \end{bmatrix}$$

To confirm that this is indeed the inverse of A, select A5:B6 and then enter:

=MMULT(A1:B2,D1:E2)

Then enter this as a matrix in the usual way.

This forms the matrix product:

AA⁻¹

and when formatted to zero decimal places will return:

$$I = \begin{bmatrix} 1 & 0 \\ 0 & 1 \end{bmatrix}$$

Now select the D5:E6 range and use it to confirm that A⁻¹A is also equal to I.

The results should resemble Workbook 7.4.

	A	B	C	D	E	F	G	H	I	J
1	3	1		2	-1					
2	5	2		-5	3					
3	Matrix A			Inverse of A = A⁻¹						
4										
5	1	0		1	0					
6	0	1		0	1					
7	AA⁻¹			A⁻¹A						
8										

Sheet1 / Sheet2 / Sheet3 / Sheet4 / Sheet5 / She

Workbook 7.4

This clearly means that the order of multiplication is not important when the inverse matrix is the other part of the product, since it should be clear that $AA^{-1} = A^{-1}A = I$.

Now, finding the inverse of a matrix is an extremely useful process, as will soon be seen.

7.6. Using matrix algebra to solve sets of linear equations

The primary purpose of inverting a matrix is to allow computers to solve sets of simultaneous linear equations. For example, in order to solve the following set of equations:

$$2x + 5y + 3z = 28$$
$$x - y + z = 5$$
$$3x + 2y - z = 9$$

we can proceed as follows.

Rewrite the equations in matrix form as:

$$\mathbf{As} = \mathbf{b}$$

where **A** is the 3 by 3 matrix of variable coefficients, **s** is the 3 by 1 column vector of unknown solution values for x , y, and z, and **b** is the 3 by 1 column vector of right-hand side constant terms. That is:

$$\mathbf{As} = \mathbf{b} \Rightarrow \begin{bmatrix} 2 & 5 & 3 \\ 1 & -1 & 1 \\ 3 & 2 & -1 \end{bmatrix} \begin{bmatrix} x \\ y \\ z \end{bmatrix} = \begin{bmatrix} 28 \\ 5 \\ 9 \end{bmatrix}$$

Now, if we pre-multiply both sides by $\mathbf{A}^{-1}$ we obtain:

$$\mathbf{A}^{-1}\mathbf{As} = \mathbf{A}^{-1}\mathbf{b}$$

Then, since $\mathbf{A}^{-1}\mathbf{A} = \mathbf{I}$, we have:

$$\mathbf{Is} = \mathbf{A}^{-1}\mathbf{b}$$

Therefore:

$$\mathbf{s} = \mathbf{A}^{-1}\mathbf{b} \text{ (since } \mathbf{Is} = \mathbf{s})$$

Now take a blank workbook and proceed as follows.

First, enter the A matrix to the A1:C3 range, and the b column vector to the E1:E3 range.

Next, select the A6:C8 range and enter:

=MINVERSE(A1:C3)

and enter this as a matrix.

Then select the E6:E8 range to contain the product of $\mathbf{A}^{-1}$ and b by entering the matrix expression:

=MMULT(A6:C8,E1:E3)

This creates the solution vector s where:

$$\mathbf{s} = \mathbf{A}^{-1}\mathbf{b} = \begin{bmatrix} 3 \\ 2 \\ 4 \end{bmatrix}$$

Finally, to confirm that these values (2, 3, and 4) are in fact the solution values for x, y, and z, use G6:G8 to contain the matrix product As.

That is, select G6:G8 and then enter the matrix expression:

=MMULT(A1:C3,E6:E8)

The original vector **b** containing the right-hand side values will be reproduced, thereby indicating that **As = b**.

The result of these procedures should resemble Workbook 7.5.

	A	B	C	D	E	F	G	H	I	J
1	2	5	3		28					
2	1	-1	1		5					
3	3	2	-1		9					
4	Matrix A				Vector b					
5										
6	-0.0303	0.333333	0.242424		3		28			
7	0.121212	-0.33333	0.030303		2		5			
8	0.151515	0.333333	-0.21212		4		9			
9	Matrix A⁻¹				s = A⁻¹b		As			
10										

Sheet1 / Sheet2 / Sheet3 / Sheet4 / Sheet5 / She

Workbook 7.5   **Now use this workbook to confirm our previous statement, that if any row or column is a constant multiple of any other, then the system of equations cannot be solved. To do this make the entries in C1:C3 become 4, 2, and 6 respectively.**

Each of the values in column 3 of **A** is now exactly twice the value of those contained in column 1. The inverse of **A** no longer exists, as the #NUM entries in A6:C8 indicate, and so there is no solution vector for this set of equations.

Exercises 7.4 and 7.5 can be attempted now.

7.7. Input–output analysis

Input–output analysis, like linear programming, is one of the prime examples of a mathematical technique that which has been developed for the specific purpose of modelling the relationships that constitute business and economic systems. The essential idea of the input–output technique is a recognition of the fact that many products not only represent finished, marketable output but are also used as inputs in the production of other finished products and in the production of that product itself.

The simplest example of such relationships would be in a basic agricultural system that produces only wheat and cattle. Under such circumstances, the production of wheat must satisfy the following:

    1. Final consumer demand for wheat (to make flour)
    2. Food requirements of the cattle
    3. Seed requirements for the next year's harvest

The effect of these requirements is that wheat is not only a final product (flour) but also an input in the production of cattle, and an input in the production of itself (seed).

By a similar logic, the production of cattle must satisfy the following:

    1. Final consumer demand for meat and milk
    2. The fertilizer requirements of wheat production

3. The requirements to breed more cattle

Once again, cattle are not only a final product but also an input in the production of wheat and an input in the production of themselves.

Viewed in this way, the task of input–output analysis is to find those production levels of both cattle and wheat that meet all requirements from all sources.

As a more concrete illustration consider the following example. A simple economic system produces only 3 products: coal, electricity, and steel. Each product is used as an input in the production not only of itself but also of the other 2 products as well, in such a way that:

Each unit of coal requires 0.2 units of coal itself, 0.15 units of electricity, and 0.12 units of steel
Each unit of electricity requires 0.2 units of coal, 0.16 units of electricity itself, and 0.15 units of steel
Each unit of steel requires 0.3 units of coal, 0.40 units of electricity, and 0.22 units of steel itself

The final consumer demands for the three products are 100 units of coal, 250 units of electricity, and 200 units of steel. The task is to calculate the required output levels of all three products if all demands are to be met exactly. To achieve this task:

Let c = the required output of coal.
Let e = the required output of electricity.
Let s = the required output of steel.

Clearly, the value of c must be such that it meets its own input requirements, the requirements of the other two products, and the requirements of final consumption. Now its own requirements depend upon its own production (c), while the requirements of the other two products depend upon their respective outputs (e and s). Consequently, the value of c must be such that:

$$c = 0.2c + 0.2e + 0.3s + 100$$

The logic of this expression is:

Output of coal = coal needed by coal + coal needed by electricity + coal needed by steel + final demand for coal

This is equivalent to:

Output of coal = 0.2 units per unit of coal + 0.2 units per units of electricity + 0.3 units per unit of steel + 100 units of final demand

Therefore:

$$c = 0.2c + 0.2e + 0.3s + 100$$

By a similar logic we can also write:

$$e = 0.15c + 0.16e + 0.4s + 250$$
$$s = 0.12c + 0.15e + 0.22s + 200$$

Now, if we let **x** be a 3 by 1 column vector of unknowns (c, e, and s), then in matrix terms the 3 equations above can be written as:

$$\mathbf{x} = \mathbf{Ax} + \mathbf{b}$$

where

$$\mathbf{x} = \begin{bmatrix} c \\ e \\ s \end{bmatrix} \quad \mathbf{A} = \begin{bmatrix} 0.2 & 0.2 & 0.3 \\ 0.15 & 0.16 & 0.4 \\ 0.12 & 0.15 & 0.22 \end{bmatrix} \quad \text{and} \quad \mathbf{b} = \begin{bmatrix} 100 \\ 250 \\ 200 \end{bmatrix}$$

Therefore:

$$x - Ax = b$$

And, taking care to ensure conformability:

$$(I - A)x = b$$

(Notice that $x(I - A)$ is non conformable.)

Now pre-multiply both sides by the inverse of $(I - A)^{-1}$ to obtain

$$[(I - A)^{-1}](I - A)x = [(I - A)^{-1}]b$$

Therefore:

$$x = [(I - A)^{-1}]b$$

since:

$$[(I - A)^{-1}](I - A) = I$$

To solve this matrix equation on Excel, the first thing to do is enter the matrix of technical coefficients (A) in A1:C3, and the final demand vector (b) in I1:I3.

Do this now.

Now enter a 3 by 3 identity matrix to A5:C7.

We are now going to calculate the (I - A) matrix in the E1:G3 range.

So select E1:G3 with the mouse and type:

=A5:C7-A1:C3

This must now be entered as a matrix with Shift, Control, and Enter.

The matrix (I - A) will be computed in E1:G3 as:

$$(I - A) = \begin{bmatrix} 0.8 & -0.2 & -0.3 \\ -0.15 & 0.84 & -0.4 \\ -0.12 & -0.15 & 0.78 \end{bmatrix}$$

Confirm this now.

The procedure from now on is the same as was used in the last section to solve sets of linear equations.

Consequently, calculate the inverse of (I - A) in E5:G7 from:

=MINVERSE(E1:G3)

Then form the product of $(I - A)^{-1}$ and b in the I5:I7 range from:

=MMULT(E5:G7,I1:I3)

This will create the solution vector for the required outputs of the 3 products that meet all demands in the system.

The completed worksheet should resemble Workbook 7.6. Clearly the outputs of c, e, and s must be 433.735, 582.269, and 435.113 respectively.

Workbook 7.6

At this stage it is appropriate to point out that the matrix containing the technical coefficients (A) in the above example was carefully chosen to avoid a potential difficulty that can arise. To see this, it must be remembered that negative outputs are not acceptable solutions to the equation system, and so the structure of A must be such that these are avoided. But under what circumstances will A only produce positive solutions?

First of all, it should be clear that no product can use more than 100% of its own output

	A	B	C	D	E	F	G	H	I	J
1	0.2	0.2	0.3		0.8	-0.2	-0.3		100	
2	0.15	0.16	0.4		-0.15	0.84	-0.4		250	
3	0.12	0.15	0.22		-0.12	-0.15	0.78		200	
4	Matrix A				Matrix (I - A)				Vector b	
5	1	0	0		1.465396	0.494867	0.817392		433.7346	
6	0	1	0		0.406234	1.44767	0.898639		582.2685	
7	0	0	1		0.303567	0.354531	1.580619		435.1134	
8	Matrix I				Matrix (I - A)$^{-1}$				x = (I - A)$^{-1}$b	
9										

Sheet1 / Sheet2 / Sheet3 / Sheet4 / Sheet5 / She

Workbook 7.6

as an input. This means that all of the elements on the principal diagonal of A must be less than or equal to 1 (but ≥ 0).

Now use Workbook 7.6 to confirm that this is the case, by successively letting the a_{11}, a_{22}, and a_{33} values become 1.

In each case, the only solution values for c, e, and s that can be obtained will involve at least one negative value.

There are some other restrictions on the values that the sum of the a_{ij} coefficients in any row or column can adopt, but detailed examination of these exceeds the scope of this text. However, a graphic example of some of the effects can be seen if the following entries are made to the A1:A3 cells of Workbook 7.6.

First change A1 from its previous value to 0.6.

The sum of the a_{ij} coefficients in row 1 now exceed 1, but the solution values are consistent and positive.

Now increase the value in A2 from its previous value to 0.7 (with A1 still containing 0.6).

Now the sum of the a_{ij} coefficients in both rows 1 and 2 exceed 1. Once again however, the output solution values are positive.

Finally, increase the value in A3 from its previous value to 0.8 (with A1 and A2 still containing 0.6 and 0.7 respectively).

It will now be found that the only output solution values that can be found are negative. From this we conclude that if an input–output system contains n equations, then only n-1 of them can have row coefficient values that sum to more than unity. Otherwise negative solution values will be generated.

Finally, if the coefficient values in all of the rows sum to exactly 1, then no solution at all is obtainable.

To see this, make the A1, A2, and A3 values become 0.5, 0.44, and 0.63 respectively.

The $(I–A)^{-1}$ matrix will return #NUM! values throughout, indicating that there is no feasible solution to this problem.

Exercise 7.6 can be attempted now.

7.8. Exercises

....

Exercise 7.1

The matrix **X** represents the sales of 3 products (j = 1, 2, 3) in each of two markets (i = 1, 2) in the first 4 months of 1999.

The matrix **Y** contains the same information for the next 4 months, and the matrix **Z** gives the same information for the last 4 months of that year. Where:

$$X = \begin{bmatrix} 10 & 4 & 11 \\ 12 & 2 & 8 \end{bmatrix} \quad Y = \begin{bmatrix} 15 & 6 & 3 \\ 4 & 1 & 21 \end{bmatrix}$$

$$Z = \begin{bmatrix} 3 & 7 & 20 \\ 8 & 3 & 7 \end{bmatrix}$$

Form a new matrix **T** that will give the total sales of each product in each of the markets for the whole year.

Exercise 7.2

Use the matrix **PU** from section 7.4, and Worksheet 7.2, to form a matrix product that represents the firm's total fuel costs at each of the factories, if it is known that the unit costs of C, E, and G are £5, £4, and £6 respectively.

Exercise 7.3

A transport company owns 4 lorries, which in a particular week travel distances of 2000, 1800, 1890, and 2080 miles. The respective fuel consumption rates (in litres per mile) for each of the lorries are 0.3, 0.25, 0.4, and 0.35.

(i) Form a matrix product that will give the firm's total weekly fuel consumption.

(ii) Form another matrix product that will give the firm's weekly fuel consumption by each of the lorries.

(iii) Form another matrix product that will give the fuel consumption of each of the lorries and the fuel consumption that would result if each of the lorries also travelled each of the other lorries' distances at each of the other the other lorries' fuel consumption rates.

Exercise 7.4

A firm uses 3 inputs (L, K, and R) to produce 3 products (U, V, and W).

Each unit of product U requires 2 units of L, 4 units of K, and 3 units of R

Each unit of product V requires 5 units of L, 2.5 units of K, and 6 units of R

Each unit of product W requires 1 unit of L, 5.5 units K, and 3.5 units of R.

Over a particular period the firm used a total of 1000 units of L, 2500 units of K, and 2000 units of R.

(i) Calculate the output levels of the 3 products over this period.

(ii) In the next period the firm's usage of the 3 inputs was 1100, 2400, and 2100 of L, K, and R respectively. Calculate the new output levels of the 3 products.

Exercise 7.5

The process of making a particular dietary supplement involves combining 3 compounds (X, Y, and Z) into a 100-gram capsule.

The supplement must contain exactly 22% of vitamin A and 24% of vitamin B, while the vitamin contents of the compounds to be combined are as follows.

Each gram of compound X contains 0.2 grams of Vitamin A and 0.3 grams of Vitamin B

Each gram of compound Y contains 0.3 grams of Vitamin A and 0.12 grams of Vitamin B.

Each gram of compound Z contains 0.1 grams of Vitamin A and 0.4 grams of Vitamin B.

Form a matrix equation that will allow solution for the required amounts of each compound that should be used in the blend.

Exercise 7.6

A simple economic system involves the production of 2 products (X and Y). The conditions of production are such that each unit of X requires 0.2 units of X and 0.6 units of Y, while each unit of Y requires 0.4 units of X and 0.3 units of Y. The final demand for the two products is 32 units and 64 units for X and Y respectively.

(i) Calculate the outputs of the two products necessary to satisfy all the demands of the system.

(ii) As a result of a change in the conditions of production, it is now the case that each unit of X requires 0.3 units of X and 0.4 units of Y, while each unit of Y requires 0.8 units of X and 0.7 units of Y.

Calculate the new outputs of the two products.

7.9. Solutions to the exercises

Solution to Exercise 7.1

The matrices **X**, **Y**, and **Z** are all of the same dimension (2 by 3) and so can be added together to form **T** as follows.

$$T = X + Y + Z = \begin{bmatrix} 10 & 4 & 11 \\ 12 & 2 & 8 \end{bmatrix} +$$
$$\begin{bmatrix} 15 & 6 & 3 \\ 4 & 1 & 21 \end{bmatrix} + \begin{bmatrix} 3 & 7 & 20 \\ 8 & 3 & 7 \end{bmatrix} =$$
$$\begin{bmatrix} 28 & 17 & 34 \\ 24 & 6 & 36 \end{bmatrix}$$

To get Excel to perform this calculation proceed as follows.

Enter the **X**, **Y**, and **Z** matrices to the ranges A1:C2, A4:C5 and A6:C7 of a blank workbook. Now select the A8:C9 range with the mouse so that it is highlighted. Then enter =A1:C2+A4:C5+A6:C7 and press Shift, Control, and Enter.

The matrix **T** that was manually computed above will be returned to the A8:C9 range.

Solution to Exercise 7.2

Since **PU** has dimension 3 by 3, the unit costs of the inputs should be formed into a vector (**m**) that is consistent with the rules of conformability. However, this can be done in either of two ways.

Thus if **m** is made to be 1 by 3 then **mPU** is conformable but **PUm** is not. Alternatively, if **m** is made to be 3 by 1 then **mPU** is not conformable but **PUm** is. Furthermore, which of these 2 possible products should be formed depends upon the objective and the nature of the **PU** matrix.

Thus if **m** is made to be 1 by 3 then the 1st element of **mPU** will be given by:

$$5(1150) + 4(1032) + 6(1129)$$

Now, since the numbers 5, 4, and 6 refer to the units costs of C, E, and G respectively, whereas the terms from the 1st column of **PU** all refer to input C, it should be clear that this product, although conformable, is inappropriate.

So, having eliminated **mPU** as a possible product, we should consider making **m** a 3 by 1 column vector, and then form the product **PUm**. The first element of this product will be evaluated as:

$$1150(5) + 1727(4) + 1377(6)$$

In this case, the terms 1150, 1727, and 1377 refer to the usage levels at factory 1 of C, E, and G, while the terms 5, 4, and 6 are the unit costs of C, E, and G.

Consequently, this product will give the fuel costs sustained at each factory in the production of all 3 products.

Therefore, load Workbook 7.2 and enter **m** as a column vector $\begin{bmatrix} 5 \\ 4 \\ 6 \end{bmatrix}$ in M1:M3.

Then, remembering that **PUm** will have dimension 3 by 1, select O1:O3 to contain this product. The matrix formula should be:

=MMULT(I1:K3,M1:M3)

and when entered by the now familiar method should produce:

$$PUm = \begin{bmatrix} 20920 \\ 16830 \\ 21151 \end{bmatrix}$$

These are the fuel costs at each of the factories as a result of producing all 3 products.

Solution to Exercise 7.3

(i) Let the distances be contained in a row vector (**d**) and the litres per mile in a column vector (**g**).

Take a blank worksheet and enter the elements of **d** to A1:D1, and the elements of **g** to F1:F4. The product **dg** will be a scalar (1 by 1), so click on H1 and type:

=MMULT(A1:D1,F1:F4)

Now enter this as a matrix to obtain a value of 2534 for **dg**. This is the total fuel consumption by all 4 lorries over all 4 routes.

(ii) To answer this question, use the A6:D9 range to contain the matrix **D**, where:

$$\mathbf{D} = \begin{bmatrix} 2000 & 0 & 0 & 0 \\ 0 & 1800 & 0 & 0 \\ 0 & 0 & 1890 & 0 \\ 0 & 0 & 0 & 2080 \end{bmatrix}$$

Notice how the 'active' elements have been placed on the principal diagonal, with zeros placed everywhere else. This allows post-multiplication of **D** by **g** to produce a 4 by 1 column vector containing the fuel usage levels for each of the lorries.

Locate this product in F6:F9 from the formula:

=MMULT(A6:G9,F1:F4)

entered as a matrix. The result will be:

$$\mathbf{Dg} = \begin{bmatrix} 600 \\ 450 \\ 756 \\ 728 \end{bmatrix}$$

(iii) In this case, we should form the product **gd**. So, remembering that **gd** will be 4 by 4 select the area A12:D15 to contain this product. Then with A12:D15 selected enter:

=MMULT(F1:F4,A1:D1)

The following matrix (**M** = **gd**) will be returned to A12:D15.

$$\mathbf{M} = \mathbf{gd} \begin{bmatrix} 600 & 540 & 567 & 624 \\ 500 & 450 & 472.5 & 520 \\ 800 & 720 & 756 & 832 \\ 700 & 630 & 661.5 & 728 \end{bmatrix}$$

This has produced a 4 by 4 matrix in which the first element is the actual fuel usage of lorry 1. However the second element in the first row will contain the fuel usage that lorry 2's distance would have used if it had travelled its distance at lorry 1's fuel consumption rate. In other words, the elements 'off' the principal diagonal give hypothetical usage rates that can

be used to answer questions such as 'what if lorry j travelled its distance at lorry i's fuel consumption rate?'.

Questions such as these can often provide useful management information, since it should be clear that if the firm wanted to reduce its total fuel usage, then a reallocation of the lorry distances could do this. To be exact, lorry 2 should take over lorry 4's route, lorry 4 should take over lorry 3's route, and lorry 3 should take over lorry 2's route. Now the lorries with the best fuel consumption rates are travelling the longest distances and the vector **g** could be rewritten as:

$$\mathbf{g} = \begin{bmatrix} 0.30 \\ 0.4 \\ 0.35 \\ 0.25 \end{bmatrix}$$

Now change the values in F1:F4 in line with this reallocation of lorries to routes, and observe that the total fuel usage for all vehicles given by **dg** has declined from 2534 to 2501.5.

Solution to Exercise 7.4

(i) If we let u, v, and w represent the (unknown) output levels of the 3 products, then the total usage of input L will be given by:

2u + 5v + w = usage of L

Similarly, the usage levels of K and R would be given by:

4u + 2.5v + 5.5w = usage of K

and:

3u + 6v + 3.5w = usage of R

In matrix terms this can be written as:

$$\mathbf{As} = \mathbf{b} \Rightarrow \begin{bmatrix} 2 & 5 & 1 \\ 4 & 2.5 & 5.5 \\ 3 & 6 & 3.5 \end{bmatrix} \begin{bmatrix} u \\ v \\ w \end{bmatrix} = \begin{bmatrix} 1000 \\ 2500 \\ 2000 \end{bmatrix}$$

Pre-multiplication of both sides of this equation by $\mathbf{A}^{-1}$ gives:

$$\mathbf{A}^{-1}\mathbf{As} = \mathbf{A}^{-1}\mathbf{b} \Rightarrow \mathbf{Is} = \mathbf{A}^{-1}\mathbf{b} \Rightarrow \mathbf{s} = \mathbf{A}^{-1}\mathbf{b}$$

Now load Workbook 7.5 (W7_5.XLS) and change the elements of **A** and **b** appropriately. The solution vector (**s**) will contain the values

153.85, 76.92, and 307.69 for the output levels of products U, V, and W respectively.

(ii) All that needs to be done is change the values in the **b** vector to reflect the new usage levels of the 3 inputs. The results will be returned automatically to the **s** vector and should give: u = 91.02, v = 120.51, w = 315.38.

Solution to Exercise 7.5

Letting x, y, and z represent the amounts of the 3 compounds to be combined in the blend we have:

x + y + z = 100   (the capsule must contain 100g of the blend)
0.2x + 0.3y + 0.1z = 0.22(100) = 22 (the supply of Vitamin A from each of the compounds must equal 22% of 100g).
0.3x + 0.12y + 0.4z = 0.24(100) = 24 (the supply of Vitamin B from each of the compounds must equal 24% of 100g).

This system of equations can be written in matrix terms as:

$$\mathbf{As} = \mathbf{b} \Rightarrow \begin{bmatrix} 1 & 1 & 1 \\ 0.2 & 0.3 & 0.1 \\ 0.3 & 0.12 & 0.4 \end{bmatrix} \begin{bmatrix} x \\ y \\ z \end{bmatrix} = \begin{bmatrix} 100 \\ 22 \\ 24 \end{bmatrix}$$

Now load Workbook 7.5 (W7_5.XLS) and change the elements in the **A** matrix and the **b** vector to reflect these values.

The solution will be returned to the **s** vector and should indicate that 20g of compound X should be blended with 50g of compound Y and 30g of compound Z.

Solution to Exercise 7.6

(i) The input–output equations are:
x = 0.2x + 0.4y + 32
y = 0.6x + 0.3y + 64

Now load Workbook 7.6 (W7_6.XLS).

Enter values of 0.2 and 0.4 to A1 and B1, and values of 0.6 and 0.3 to A2 and B2, and erase all other elements in the **A** matrix. Then enter 32 and 64 to I1 and I2 and erase I3. The solution will be returned to the x vector, and indicates that 150 units of X and 220 units of Y should be produced.

(ii) Enter values of 0.3 and 0.8 to A1 and B1, and values of 0.4 and 0.7 to A2 and B2. Because the sum of the elements of **A** are greater than 1 for both rows of the matrix, it will be found that there is no positive solution.

Introductory statistical analysis

Contents
....

Accompanying data files to be loaded as instructed:

W8_1.XLS   W8_5.XLS   W8_7.XLS   W8_17.XLS   W8_19.XLS

8.1. **Preliminaries**

Whether you realize it or not, at some time or another you will almost certainly have performed some kind of elementary statistical analysis. This is because, at base, statistics is concerned with the process of making sense from, and bringing order to, collections of data observations. Your monthly bank statement, your end of term assessment marks, or your quarterly telephone bill, are all examples of data observations that can be collected together (over several months, terms or quarters) to form what is known as a **data set**, thereby creating the basic unit of statistical analysis.

Given this basic unit, the purpose of elementary statistical analysis can be summarized in terms of five fundamental objective:

1. Data collection.
2. Data collation.
3. Visual portrayal of the data's properties.
4. Summary measures of the data's characteristics.
5. Drawing conclusions on the basis of the foregoing analysis.

Taking each of these objectives in turn, we must consider a number of issues.

8.1.1. Data collection

In many cases, the nature of the problem to be investigated will be such that there is little relevant information available. In this case the investigator will have to use interview and/or questionnaire techniques to extract the raw data from a group or groups of identified respondents.

In other cases however, it may be possible to use (and amend if necessary) data that has already been collected and made accessible in one or more of the numerous statistical data banks now available. These often exist in electronic form and can simply be downloaded in raw form into an Excel workbook.

8.1.2. Data collation

Once collected (from whatever source) the data will then have to be brought together and presented in some manageable form. This is known as **collation**, and will frequently involve summarizing and/or tabulating the information so that it can be interpreted and analysed more efficiently.

8.1.3. Visual portrayal of the data

After collation, it will often be desirable to produce a pictorial display of the data's features. As you have already seen Excel supports a number of graphic techniques, and the primary task in this regard will always be to choose the most appropriate chart so that a clear visual impression of the data's properties is produced. This will obviously be conditioned by the nature of the data itself, and by the purposes to which it is to be put.

8.1.4. Summary characterizations

Particularly in the case of large data sets, it will usually be necessary to obtain one or more summary statistics that measure certain characteristics of the data set.

As far as elementary statistical analysis is concerned there are two basic features that require to be measured:

(*a*) Measurement of the data's central or 'average' value.
(*b*) Measurement of the extent to which the data is dispersed around its central value.

As we will see, there are in fact a number of measures of central tendency, and as a consequence, a number of measures of dispersion, each related to the particular measure of centralization that has been employed.

8.1.5. Drawing conclusions

Once the previous four objectives have been achieved, the data can then be used as part of the decision-making process. This will always involve the task of drawing conclusions on the basis of the information that has been provided by the data, and in some cases can be a straightforward matter.

In many cases however, the old adage that there are 'lies, damned lies, and statistics' will be particularly apposite, and will mean that conclusive interpretation of the data will have to be subject to a number of reservations.

8.2. Collating the data

8.2.1. Frequency distributions

One of the most effective ways of collating data is to create what is known as a frequency distribution. To see how this works, consider the data contained in Workbook 8.1.

Load the file called W8_1.XLS from the accompanying disk now.

The data in column A are the number of occupants observed to be in each of 100 cars that arrived at a motorway service station over a period of 30 minutes on a particular day. Clearly the data are in 'raw' form, and as such are not easy to interpret until it is noticed that the number of occupants observed was always between 1 and 5 inclusive.

To collate this data without using Excel would require that a manual count of the number of cars containing 1 person was made, then a manual count of the number of cars containing 2 persons, and so on for the number of cars with 3, 4, and 5 persons.[1] If you can be bothered to do this manual count, then you will find that in this data set there were:

> 22 cars with 1 occupant, 32 cars with 2 occupants, 27 cars with 3 occupants, 12 cars with 4 occupants and 7 cars with 5 occupants

Now, if we regard the number of occupants as a statistical variable (since in this case its value can vary between 1 and 5 inclusive), and denote it by the symbol x, then each value of x can be associated with the number of times that it was observed—its frequency (denoted by f). Thus, a value of $x = 2$ has an associated frequency of 32 in the illustrative data set.

Finally, if we consider each value of x that *could* be observed and attach alongside the associated frequency of that value of x, then we obtain what is known as the **frequency distribution** of the x variable. For the illustrative data this would be written as:

Variable (x)	1	2	3	4	5
Frequency (f)	22	32	27	12	7

---

1 You are quite likely to have done something like this at some time or other with the 'five-bar gate' tallying device.

This is the frequency distribution of the statistical variable x, and simply indicates the number of times that a particular value of x was observed.

However, if you actually went through the manual counts for this data set you should appreciate that it is a extremely tedious process—even with only 100 observations. With 10000 or 20000 observations it would become a Herculean task. This is where Excel can help.

Make sure that you have Workbook 8.1 on-screen and proceed as follows.
First, in B1 reproduce the header contained in A1 (number of occupants). Then, in B2:B6 enter the 5 distinct values that the variable can adopt (i.e. 1, 2, 3, 4, and 5).

In Excel parlance this will be known as the 'bin', and simply provides information to the program as to which values of the variable it is to use in calculating the frequencies of the raw data. For example, if you only supplied a bin range of 2, 4, and 5 then Excel would compute the combined frequencies of 1 and 2, 3 and 4, and then 5 alone. However, with the bin established in this case as 1, 2, 3, 4, and 5, all that remains is to access Tools from the Menu bar and then Data Analysis.

Do this now.[2]
From the list of options that appears select Histogram.

The dialogue box shown in Fig. 8.1 should now appear.

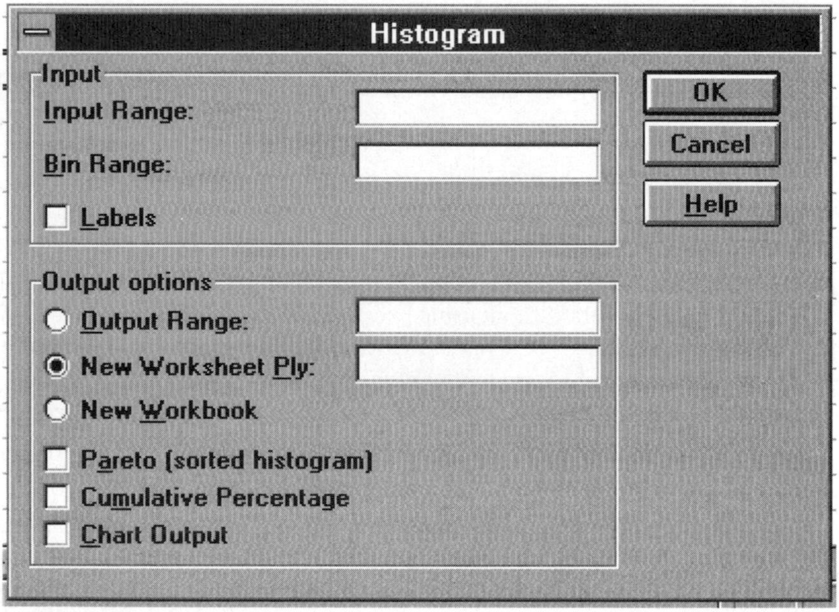

Figure 8.1

Excel must now be apprised of the range containing the raw data, as well as the range containing the bin values to be used, so that it can perform the classification.

Consequently, click on the Input Range box and then click on the A1 cell and drag down to A101. Alternatively enter the range directly to the box as A1:A101.

---

2 If you cannot find Data Analysis on the list of Tools options then this routine may not have been 'added in'. To do this, click on Tools and then Add-Ins. From the list that appears, select Analysis ToolPak by checking the box. This Add-In will now be available.

This will define the range containing the data observations.

Next, click on the Bin Range box and then click on B1 and drag down to B6.

This will define B1:B6 as the range of x values to be used in the classification.

Next, since we have included the column headers in both the Input and Bin ranges, click on the Labels tab so that a cross appears.

This tells Excel to expect labels as well as numerical values in the data range. Only the latter can be used in the classification process, and so with this tab checked Excel will ignore any text entries used as labels.

Finally, click on the Output Range tab and then on the adjacent box and enter C1.

This tells Excel where to put frequency distribution that it is about to compute. (If you do not specify an output range, Excel will create a new sheet and place the results there.) The worksheet and Histogram dialogue box should now resemble Workbook 8.1.

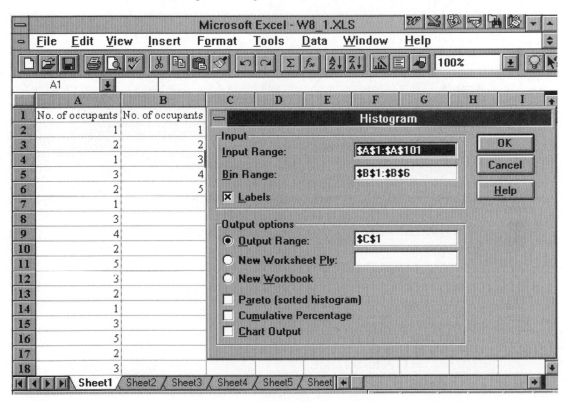

Workbook 8.1	**If it does, click on OK.**

After a few seconds the frequency distribution will be computed, and your worksheet should resemble Workbook 8.2.

Workbook 8.2	Notice that these are exactly the results that were obtained from the manual procedure explained above.

Now save this file as W8_2.XLS.

```
 ─                    Microsoft Excel - W8_2.XLS            𝑤 ▨ ▧ ▨ ▥ ▨  ▼ ▲
 ─    File   Edit   View   Insert   Format   Tools   Data   Window   Help        ▲
                                                                                 ▼
   □ ⌷ 🖫  🖨 🔍 ✓  ✂ 🗋 📋 ✎  ↻ ↺  Σ ƒ×  ↕ ↕  ▦ ▤ ◢  100%           ▼  ♡ ▶
      F10          ▼
            A              B          C        D        E      F      G      H      I   ▲
 1  No. of occupants  No. of occupants   Bin    Frequency                                 ▼
 2              1              1           1        22
 3              2              2           2        32
 4              1              3           3        27
 5              3              4           4        12
 6              2              5           5         7
 7              1                       More        0
 8              3
 │◀ ◀ ▶ ▶│ \ Sheet1 / Sheet2 / Sheet3 / Sheet4 / Sheet5 / Sheet │ ◀ │        ▶│
 Ready
```

Workbook 8.2

Also notice that Excel has added an extra category—'*More*'—to the bin. In this case the associated frequency is zero, but in other cases it will indicate the number of observations that cannot be classified in terms of the bin that was defined. For example, had there in fact been 4 cars with 6 occupants, with the bin still being defined as 1 to 5 inclusive, then the frequency associated with *More* would have been 4 (with one or more of the other frequencies being reduced by a total of 4).

The frequencies that this Excel routine produces are known as **absolute** frequencies in the sense that they indicate the actual number of occurrences of x values of 1, 2, 3, 4, or 5. However, it will sometimes be useful to convert these absolute frequencies into what are known as **relative** frequencies. Quite simply, a relative frequency is simply each absolute frequency expressed as a proportion or percentage of the total number of frequencies.

The Excel Data Analysis routine does not compute relative frequencies automatically, but it is an easy matter to write formulae in the worksheet that perform this task. To see how, use the most recent version of Workbook 8.2 as a template and read on.

The first thing to do is compute the total number of frequencies in the data set.

Do this now in the D8 cell by entering the formula:

=SUM(D2:D7)

For the illustration, a value of 100 should be returned.

Now name D8 as FT (for frequency total).
Next, in E1 enter the label:

Frequency %

and then, in E2 the formula:

=D2/FT

Now copy the contents of E2 into E3:E7.

The results show each of the frequencies as a proportion of the total number of frequencies, and at the moment these are expressed in **decimal** form.

To make them display as percentages, select the E3:E7 area with the mouse and then Format from the Menu bar. Then choose Cells and then Percentage and use two decimal places.

The results should resemble Workbook 8.3.

	Microsoft Excel - W8_3.XLS						
File **Edit** **View** **Insert** **Format** **Tools** **Data** **Window** **Help**							

FT =SUM(D2:D7)

	A	B	C	D	E	F	G	H
1	No. of occupants	No. of occupants	Bin	Frequency	Frequency %			
2	1	1	1	22	22.00%			
3	2	2	2	32	32.00%			
4	1	3	3	27	27.00%			
5	3	4	4	12	12.00%			
6	2	5	5	7	7.00%			
7	1		More	0	0.00%			
8	3			100				
9	4							

Sheet1 / Sheet2 / Sheet3 / Sheet4 / Sheet5 / Sheet

Ready

Workbook 8.3

Now save this file as W8_3.XLS.
Exercise 8.1 can now be attempted

8.2.2. Cumulative frequency distributions

Absolute and relative frequencies tell us about the number and proportion of times each particular value of x occurs. However, suppose we were concerned with the frequency of occurrence of more than one particular value of x.

Simple inspection of the data suggests that a total of 54 (= 22 + 32) cars had 1 or 2 occupants. Similarly, a total of 81 (= 22 + 32 + 27) cars had 1 or 2 or 3 occupants. Continuing with this logic reveals that 93 cars had 1 or 2 or 3 or 4 occupants, and 100 had 1 or 2 or 3 or 4 or 5 occupants.

Another way of phrasing this argument is to work in terms of 'x occupants or fewer'. Thus, 22 cars had 1 occupant or fewer, 54 cars had 2 occupants or fewer, 81 cars had 3 occupants or fewer, 93 cars had 4 occupants or fewer and 100 cars had 5 occupants or fewer.

When the variable is regarded as 'x or fewer' as opposed to 'exactly equal to x', then what is known as a **cumulative frequency distribution** is produced. Furthermore, these absolute cumulative frequencies could also be translated into percentage terms to obtain a relative cumulative frequency distribution. Both of these are produced below from the data obtained in the discussion above.[3]

Exactly x occupants	1	2	3	4	5
Absolute frequency	22	32	27	12	7
x occupants or less	1	2	3	4	5
Cumulative frequency	22	54	81	93	100
Cumulative frequency %	22	54	81	93	100

However, now that we understand how cumulative frequencies are derived, we can get Excel to calculate them for us.

---

3 Because there were exactly 100 cars observed, the absolute and the relative frequencies are the same in this case. However, with any number of frequencies other than 100 this will not be the case.

Use Workbook 8.3 as a template to follow the discussion.

The first thing to do is run the Histogram routine again and define the Input, Bin, and Output ranges as in the previous illustration.[4]

Now click on the Cumulative Percentage tab in the bottom half of the dialogue box, and while you are there also click on the Chart output tab. Then click OK.

Excel knows that, since you have not changed the Output range, some of the previous information contained there will be overwritten, and warns you of this fact.

In this case this is all right, so click OK.[5]

The calculations will now be performed, and the sheet should resemble Workbook 8.4. As you can see from the worksheet, the cumulative percentage frequencies have been calculated in addition to the individual absolute frequencies, and the former are identical to the ones that were calculated manually. Furthermore, checking the Chart Output tab has caused Excel to graph both sets of frequencies automatically.[6]

Workbook 8.4

	A	B	C	D	E	F	G	H
1	No. of occupants	No. of occupants	Bin	Frequency	Cumulative %			
2	1	1	1	22	22.00%			
3	2	2	2	32	54.00%			
4	1	3	3	27	81.00%			
5	3	4	4	12	93.00%			
6	2	5	5	7	100.00%			
7	1		More	0	100.00%			
8	3			100				
9	4							
10	2							
11	5							
12	3							
13	2							
14	1							
15	3							
16	5							
17	2							
18	3							
19	2							
20	4							

4 Unless you have made any changes to the specification of the histogram, then these settings will have been retained by Excel and you can just accept them. Otherwise specify the settings again as A1:A101, B1:B6, and C1 respectively for the Input, Bin, and Output ranges.

5 In other circumstances you may want to retain the original frequency distribution, in which case specify a new Output range.

6 The histogram graph will not be produced in exactly the same location nor with exactly the same dimensions as indicated in Workbook 8.4. However, it is an easy matter to move the chart and then resize it to obtain the illustrated effect.

Notice that the heights of the columns represent absolute individual frequencies as measured on the left-hand scale, whereas the line graph represents the cumulative percentage frequencies as measured on the right-hand scale.

It should now be an easy matter to answer questions such as:

(i)   How many cars contained exactly 3 occupants? (Answer = 27)
(ii) What proportion of cars contained 4 occupants or less? (Answer = 93%)
(iii) What is the most frequently observed number of car occupants? (Answer = 2 with a frequency of 32 observations)
(iv) What proportion of cars contained 3 occupants or more? (Answer = 100% minus the 54% with 2 occupants or less = 46%)

Now save this file as W8_4.XLS.
Exercise 8.2 can be attempted now.

8.2.3. Discrete and continuous data sets

It should now be pointed out that in this illustration the data (number of occupants) is to be regarded as **discrete**. That is, only whole numbers can be observed.

Not all data are discrete however; sometimes they are **continuous** (i.e. capable of being measured to a large number of decimal places). When this is the case, we must modify the approach that is used in the creation of frequency distributions.

To understand the issues involved, load the file called W8_5.XLS from the accompanying disk.

Here, we have created a second data set in column B from the 100 car observations, by assuming that each of the occupants was asked to reveal their age (correct to 2 decimal places). With 100 cars containing 250 occupants this means that we have 250 observations on age, and unlike the number of occupants this new variable must be regarded as continuous.

The difficulties that continuous as opposed to discrete data sets create for the collation process can be appreciated by noting that the ages range from close to zero to over 80, and that they are measured to 2 decimal places. This means that to include every possible age that *could* be observed, our bin would have to start at 0.01 and increase in steps of 0.01 until a value of 99.99 (say) was reached. This would give almost 10000 values for the bin and so, with only 250 actual observations, approximately 97.5% of these bin values would have a zero frequency. Far from summarizing the data set, such a procedure for defining the bin would actually increase the amount of information that would have to be considered.

The answer to this difficulty is to think of the bin in terms of a series of class intervals rather than in terms of individual values. Thus, we could define the bin in terms of 9 intervals of 10 years and then classify the data into each of these intervals.

Consequently, in C1 enter the label:

  Age

and then enter:

  10, 20, 30, 40, 50, 60, 70, 80, and 90

to the C2:C10 range.

This will be the bin for the new problem.

Before performing the classification, however, notice how Excel treats these intervals.

The first bin value (10) will include all occupants whose age is less than or equal to 10. The second bin value (20) will include all occupants who are older than 10 but less than or equal to 20. This logic then continues for the remainder of the defined intervals.

> Now access Tools from the Menu bar and then Data Analysis and Histogram.
> Define the Input, Bin, and Output ranges as B1:B251, C1:C10, and D1 respectively.
> Then click on the Cumulative Percentage and the Chart Output tabs and click OK.

The results should resemble Workbook 8.5A.

Workbook 8.5A

It is now an easy matter to answer questions such as:

(i) What proportion of occupants are 40 years old or less? (Answer = 50.00%)
(ii) What proportion of occupants are over 60 years old? (Answer = 100% minus the 74.8% who are 60 years old or less = 25.2%)
(iii) What proportion of occupants are over 20 but not over 60? (Answer = the 74.8% who are 60 or less minus the 21.2% who are 20 or less = 53.6%)

> Now save this file as W8_5A.XLS.
> Exercise 8.3 can be attempted now.

8.2.4. Principles of selecting class intervals

In the two previous illustrations the user selected the bin values to be employed, and in both cases the nature of the data was such that the choice of values or intervals was fairly straightforward. However, particularly when large data sets are involved the process of choosing appropriate class intervals is not always so easy.

The problem derives from the inevitable trade-off between the process of summarizing data and the information loss that results from summary procedures. By this we mean that the smaller each class interval is the more there are of them, and so the frequencies associated with each interval will tend to be lower than otherwise. There will therefore be relatively few frequencies in each class compared to a situation in which there were fewer intervals of larger width.

Now remember that any individual frequency simply tells us the number of observations that were observed in a particular interval, and tells us nothing about the actual values of the individual observations apart from the fact that they lie in that interval. Consequently, the wider a class interval is the greater is the scope for variation in the individual values and the greater the potential loss of information

To see this, consider an examination in which the mark can lie between 0% and 100% inclusive. Also assume that the marks are all rounded to the nearest whole number and that the pass mark is 50% or more.

Now suppose that a given number of students sat the examination and that the assessor chose a class interval of 100 percentage marks for classifying the marks. Clearly, such an interval only allows the conclusion that 100% of examinees obtained between 0% and 100%—a classic example of a statistical statement of the obvious.

Now suppose that 2 intervals, each comprising 50 percentage marks, were used (i.e. 0% to 49% inclusive and 50% to 100% inclusive). Although not ideal, these intervals are significantly better, since they would allow a conclusion such as x% of the examinees obtained 49% or less (and therefore failed) while the remainder passed by obtaining 50% or more.

Moving from 1 class interval to 2 has clearly improved our ability to draw conclusions from the data. At the same time, however, with such a wide interval we are unable to draw any conclusions about whether those who failed did so narrowly or abysmally, or whether those who passed did so marginally or with great ease.

To draw conclusion such as these requires that more intervals are employed—implying that each interval becomes narrower.[7] Consequently, the assessor might decide to use intervals of 10 percentage marks (9%, 19%, 29%, 39%, etc.).

Once again this will allow more detailed conclusions to be drawn, but the cost is that the data is less compact than with only 2 intervals.

So far, the process of increasing the number of class intervals has increased the amount of information that the summarized data set can offer. Indeed, this will always be the case. However, suppose the assessor now decides to use intervals of 1 percentage mark (0%, 1%, 2%, etc.). You should be able to see that such a classification system simply reproduces the raw data set. There will be absolutely no loss of information, but at the same time there is very little summarizing taking place.

The upshot of this discussion is that there are no hard and fast rules for choosing the ideal number of class intervals, or their ideal width. As a rough rule of thumb, however, there should rarely be fewer than 6 and rarely more than 16 class intervals. Within these limits the trade-off between information loss (too few intervals) and summarization (too many intervals) is usually at acceptable levels.

Also notice that in both of the illustrations, and in the most recent discussion, it has been implied that the intervals are of equal width. Thus, given the range of the data, if the number of intervals is chosen then their width is determined, or if the width is chosen then the

---

7 Assuming, as we are at the moment, that each interval has the same width.

number of intervals is determined. However, it is not hard to envisage data sets that might call for unequal class intervals.

For example, suppose that 80% of the values in a data set lie between 0 and 10 inclusive, but that the remaining 20% are spread out over a range of 11 to 5000. Clearly, we require a different set of class intervals for the 80% of observations in the narrow range from those to be applied to the 20% of observations in the wide range. Unequal class intervals are needed, and so we might try something like:

2, 4, 6, 8, 10, 1000, 2000, 3000, 4000, and 5000

Once again, however, whether this produces satisfactory results will depend entirely on how the individual data observations are distributed within the proposed classification system. Trial and error until a 'reasonable' shape to the frequency distribution is obtained may well be the only answer.

Given the potential difficulties involved in choosing appropriate class intervals, it is useful to know that Excel can choose them for us, although its methods are by no means perfect and it will never produce unequal class intervals.

To force Excel to make up its own class intervals, simply erase the Bin Range box in the Histogram dialogue screen.

To see this, reload Workbook 8.5A (W8_5A.XLS).
Keep the same Input range as before (B1:B251), but erase the contents of the Bin Range box (if there is anything there).
Finally, to prevent overwriting specify the Output range as D24 and *deselect* the Chart Output tab.

Workbook 8.6

The results should resemble Workbook 8.6

	A	B	C	D	E	F	G	H	I
23		23.41							
24		35.89		Bin	Frequency	Cumulative %			
25		43.81		0.13	1	.40%			
26	3	30.99		5.707333	15	6.40%			
27		69.21		11.28467	13	11.60%			
28		76.81		16.862	12	16.40%			
29	2	15.11		22.43933	25	26.40%			
30		46.81		28.01667	15	32.40%			
31	1	60.23		33.594	25	42.40%			
32	3	28.75		39.17133	15	48.40%			
33		40.70		44.74867	23	57.60%			
34		13.87		50.326	22	66.40%			
35	5	0.13		55.90333	9	70.00%			
36		36.14		61.48067	15	76.00%			
37		17.76		67.058	21	84.40%			
38		43.87		72.63533	18	91.60%			
39		0.52		78.21267	13	96.80%			
40	2	33.86		More	8	100.00%			
41		50.12							

Microsoft Excel - W8_6.XLS

File   Edit   View   Insert   Format   Tools   Data   Window   Help

Sheet1 / Sheet2 / Sheet3 / Sheet4 / Sheet5 / Sheet

Workbook 8.6

Whether this is an improvement on the set of intervals that we previously specified for this illustration (10, 20, 30, . . . 90) is difficult to say. There are 15 equal intervals of approximately 5.57 years and a 'catch-all' of more than 78.21267 years. But the numbers themselves are a bit 'messy', especially computed as they are, to 5 or 6 decimal places. However, you can rectify this last problem by formatting.

Select the D26:D40 range and then Format and Cells from the Menu bar. Then select Number and choose 0 (decimal places).

The bin values will now become whole numbers, although the frequencies will still be computed on the basis of the six decimal place bin values, and this can create confusion. For example, the first bin value as computed by Excel originally was 0.13004 years and there was 1 car occupant who was less than or equal to 0.13004 years old. This clearly must still be true after formatting the bin values to whole numbers, yet the 0.13004 becomes 0 and so it appears as if there is 1 occupant whose age is less than or equal to zero.

To remove this confusion, reformat the D26:D40 range to 2 decimal places (the 0.00 option).

The bin values are now specified to the same number of decimal places as the raw data, and this is probably the best we can do *when we let Excel choose the values for the bin*. Notice however, that if you run the Histogram routine again, with the same specifications, then the 2 decimal place formatting that we have just established will *not* be retained. Excel will revert to the 5 or 6 decimal place format.

Exercise 8.4 can be attempted now.

8.2.5. Creating histograms with unequal class intervals

We have previously mentioned the possibility of using unequal class intervals in the creation of frequency distributions. In some cases it will just be desirable but in other cases it will be essential. However, using unequal class intervals creates a difficulty for the construction of histogram charts that must be addressed.

To consider the issues, load Workbook 8.7

Workbook 8.7

Here, Excel has been used to create the illustrated frequency distribution and the histogram chart of the marks obtained by 125 students in an examination. It is to be noted that the class intervals employed are, in the first instance, the same (10 percentage marks wide).

Now when the class intervals are equal like this, plotting the actual frequencies as the heights of the columns will ensure that the area of the rectangles are proportional to the frequencies. *This is what is always required by a correctly constructed histogram.* However, with unequal class intervals this proportionality between the areas of the rectangles and the frequencies is destroyed, and some adjustment will have to be made.

For example, if a data set is classified into 3 intervals of 10, 20, and 30 units, and if the associated frequencies are 8, 12, and 15, then since the 2nd interval is twice the width of the 1st, the plotted height of the column in the histogram should only be 6 (= 12/2) as opposed to 12. Similarly, since the 3rd interval is 3 times as wide as the first, the plotted height of the column for this interval should only be 5 (=15/3) as opposed to 15. In this way the required proportionality between areas and frequencies is re-established.

To see whether Excel will perform these adjustments for us, take the current workbook (W8_7.XLS) and set up a new bin range in B13:B16 of:

29, 79, and 100

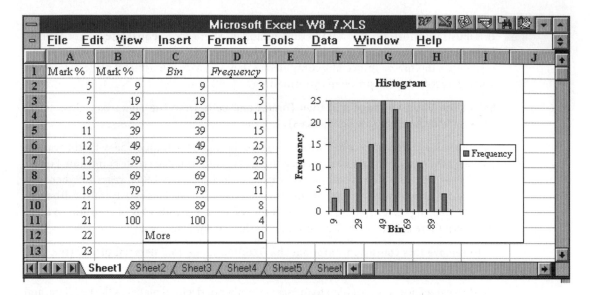

Then use the methods previously explained to classify the data into these intervals and output the frequency distribution and the histogram to the C13 range.

Workbook 8.8

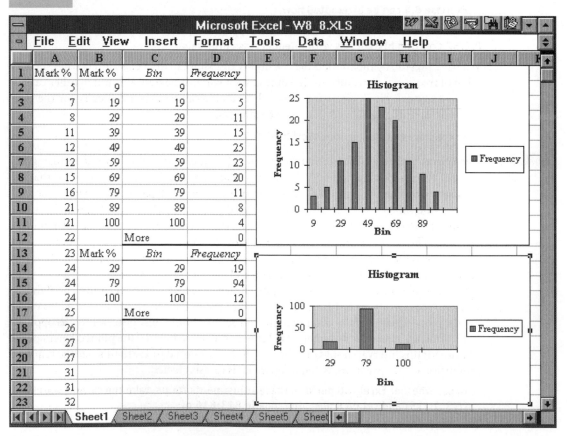

Workbook 8.8

The results should resemble Workbook 8.8, and clearly indicate that it is the actual frequencies that have been plotted as the heights of the columns rather than the adjusted frequencies. Also, the widths of the columns are all the same. Consequently, to produce a 'proper' histogram chart when unequal class intervals are being used, we will need to abandon the programmed Histogram routine, write formulae to adjust the frequencies, and create a customized chart for ourselves.

To do this, open a new workbook and in consultation with the explanation below make the entries indicated in Workbook 8.9.

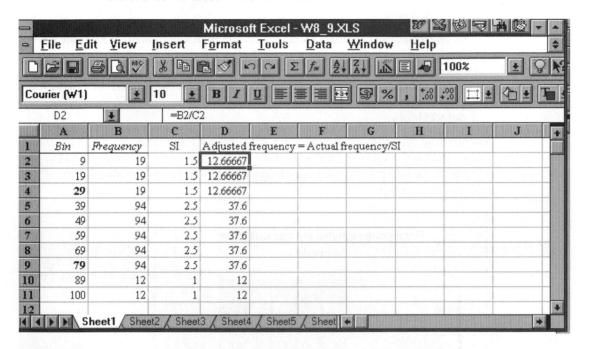

Workbook 8.9

Column A contains the intervals 9, 19, 29, etc., but since we want to accommodate the unequal class intervals identified in bold, the frequencies in column B are replicated for each of the sub-intervals. That is, the interval 0 to 29 is regarded as being composed of 3 intervals of 0 to 9, 9 to 19 and 19, to 29, each with a frequency of 19 (i.e. the frequency of the larger interval). A similar logic is then applied to the other two intervals.

Make these entries now.

Then notice that the widths of the unequal class intervals are 30, 50, and 20 percentage marks respectively. The smallest of these is 20, and so we will call this the **standard interval**.

Now, by simple proportion it follows that the 1st interval is $30/20 = 1.5$ standard intervals and that the 2nd interval is $50/20 = 2.5$ standard intervals.

Now enter these standard intervals to the C1:C11 area of the worksheet as indicated. Next, compute the first adjusted frequency in D2 from the formula:

$=B2/C2$

This divides the first actual observed frequency by its standard interval value, and will always proportionately reduce the height to be plotted unless the interval itself happens to be of standard width. In this case, since the first interval (30) is 1.5 times the standard interval (20), dividing the first interval's frequency by 1.5 will restore the proportionality requirement.

A similar logic prevails for the remaining 2 intervals, so the formula in D2 can be copied down consistently

Accordingly, copy D2 into D3:D11.

The calculations are now complete, and all that remains is to choose an appropriate way of charting them so that a 'proper' histogram is created.

To do this, click on the Chart Wizard icon, draw a frame of appropriate size, and then define the data range as:

A2:A11,D2:D11

Now select Next and choose a Column chart and then option number 8 for the type of Column chart. Click on Next again to obtain the sample chart and use the first column as the Category (X) Axis Labels.

Finally, click on Next and supply appropriate titles for the graph itself and the X and Y axes.

Select Finish.

The resulting chart should resemble Fig. 8.2. This is an adjusted histogram with the adjustment reducing the heights of the columns to compensate for the unequal interval widths. The areas of those rectangles with equal heights will now be proportional to the frequencies in those class intervals.

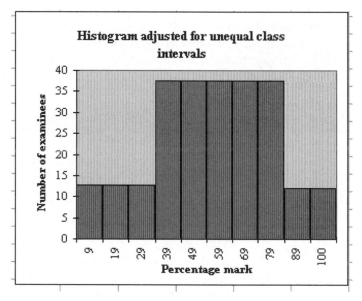

Figure 8.2

8.2.6. Further uses of cumulative distributions

Previous discussion has shown how much useful information can be produced by cumulative frequencies. But the accumulation process can also be usefully applied to the values of the variable itself.

To appreciate the issues involved, consider Workbook 8.10.

Workbook 8.10

Make up this workbook now.

Here, we have a frequency distribution of income after tax, with the values in column A once again representing the class intervals employed in the collation

```
┌─────────────────────────────────────────────────────────────────────────────┐
│ ─                    Microsoft Excel - W8_10.XLS        🖉 📊 📖 🔽 📇 📗 ▼ ▲ │
│ ─   File   Edit   View   Insert   Format   Tools   Data   Window   Help    ▲ │
│        A          B          C      D      E      F      G      H      I   J ▲│
│  1              Number of                                                     │
│  2  Income     Individuals                                                    │
│  3  after tax (£)  (000's)                                                    │
│  4        2500      1407.00                                                   │
│  5        5000      6293.00                                                   │
│  6        7500      6672.00                                                   │
│  7       10000      4400.20                                                   │
│  8       20000      2493.00                                                   │
│  9       40000       297.00                                                   │
│ 10       60000        33.70                                                   │
│ 11      370000         4.10                                                   │
│ 12                                                                          ▼ │
│ ◄◄ ◄ ► ►│  Sheet1 / Sheet2 / Sheet3 / Sheet4 / Sheet5 / Sheet │◄│          ►│
└─────────────────────────────────────────────────────────────────────────────┘
```

Workbook 8.10

process.[8] As before, we will compute the cumulative percentage frequencies to give us an indication of what percentage of the total population at least earn a particular level of income. However, in this example we are also going to accumulate the actual income figures (as opposed to their frequencies). This immediately creates a minor problem, since it is clear that the income data are the upper values in each of the class intervals. They are not, therefore, truly representative of the majority of values in each of the intervals.

We can deal with this difficulty by taking the midpoints of each class interval and using these midpoint values as an indicative value and then accumulating these.

Workbook 8.11

To follow the discussion, use Workbook 8.10 as a template and make the amendments and additions indicated in Workbook 8.11 and explained below.

```
┌─────────────────────────────────────────────────────────────────────────────┐
│ ─                    Microsoft Excel - W8_11.XLS        🖉 📊 📖 🔽 📇 📗 ▼ ▲ │
│ ─   File   Edit   View   Insert   Format   Tools   Data   Window   Help    ▲ │
│      D4         ↓           =B4*C4                                            │
│        A         B         C         D          E         F         G         H         I  ▲│
│  1  Income  Number of  Income   Income of            Cumulative Cumul-    Cumul    Equal     │
│  2  after   Individuals Mid-    groups    Cumulative Income    -ative Freq- -ative Inc- shares │
│  3  tax (£)  (000's)   points (£) (£000's)  Frequency  (£000's)  -ency %   -ome %    curve    │
│  4    2500   1407.00    1250     1758750    1407.00   1758750.00   6.51%    1.14%    6.51%     │
│  5    5000   6293.00    3750    23598750    7700.00  25357500.00  35.65%   16.42%   35.65%     │
│  6    7500   6672.00    6250    41700000   14372.00  67057500.00  66.54%   43.42%   66.54%     │
│  7   10000   4400.20    8750    38501750   18772.20 105559250.00  86.91%   68.35%   86.91%     │
│  8   20000   2493.00   15000    37395000   21265.20 142954250.00  98.45%   92.57%   98.45%     │
│  9   40000    297.00   30000     8910000   21562.20 151864250.00  99.83%   98.34%   99.83%     │
│ 10   60000     33.70   50000     1685000   21595.90 153549250.00  99.98%   99.43%   99.98%     │
│ 11  370000      4.10  215000      881500   21600.00 154430750.00 100.00%  100.00%  100.00%     │
│ 12          21600.00          154430750.00                                                    │
│ ◄◄ ◄ ► ►│  Sheet1 / Sheet2 / Sheet3 / Sheet4 / Sheet5 / Sheet │◄│          ►│
└─────────────────────────────────────────────────────────────────────────────┘
```

8 You can think of this frequency distribution as the result obtained by using Excel to classify a raw data set of 21.6 million individual income observations into intervals of £2500 or less, over £2500 but £5000 or less, . . . etc.

Column C contains the midpoint values of the income variable and have simply been entered by hand.

Enter these values now.

Next, we must compute an estimate of the income of all the members in each income group on the basis of the midpoint income values. Thus, the first income group has 1407.00 thousand members each with a midpoint income value of £1250. The estimated income of this group is therefore 1407.00 thousand times £1250 = £1758750 thousand. Similar calculations apply for the remainder of the groups.

Consequently in D4 enter:

=B4*C4

and then copy this formula into D5:D11.

In columns E and F the cumulative absolute frequencies and incomes have been computed from 'clever' formulae.

Therefore, in E4 and F4 enter:

=SUM(B$4:B4) and =SUM(D$4:D4)

and copy both E4 and F4 into E5:F11.

Inspection of these formulae should reveal how the accumulation process has been effected. The dollar sign attached to the first argument of the SUM function ensures that it will always retain the address of the first cell specified. However, the absence of the dollar sign in the second argument means that, when *copied*, this address will update, giving:

=SUM(E$4:E4); =SUM(E$4:E5); =SUM(E$4:E6) . . . =SUM(E$4:E11)

Clearly, each value in the range is being added to the sum of the previous values in the range to create a 'running total'—and this is exactly what is meant by a cumulative process.

The formulae explained above create absolute cumulative frequencies. However, for our purposes we really require percentage values. Columns G and H perform these calculations, as explained below.

First, compute the total number of frequencies and the total midpoint income of all the groups in B12 and D12 from the formulae:

=SUM(B4:B11) and = SUM(D4:D11)

Then name these cells as TF (for total frequency) and TI (for total income) respectively.
Next, in G4 and H4 enter:

=E4/TF and =F4/TI

and copy these formulae down into G5:H11.

Columns G and H now contain the cumulative frequencies expressed as a proportion of the total number of frequencies and the total income after tax income.

To convert these proportions into percentages, select the G4:H11 area and then choose Format from the Menu bar, then Cells and then Percentages. Choose 2 decimal places (0.00) and the required formatting will be done.
Finally, in I4 enter:

=G4

and copy this into I5:I11

This will create an 'equal shares' curve, since the values in column I will always be identical to those in column G.[9] The results obtained by this process should now resemble Workbook 8.11.

With all the necessary calculations performed, we are now going to produce a graph showing how the cumulative percentage frequencies vary with the actual cumulative percentage incomes. This is known as a **Lorenz** curve, and simply indicates what percentage of the total income earned after tax is received by what percentage of the total earning population.

Clearly, an equal distribution of income would have 10% of the total income being earned by 10% of the population, 20% of the total income being earned by 20% of the population, and so on, in a one-to-one manner.

Now you should appreciate the purpose of the entries in column I, since when charted these will clearly indicate 6.51% of the population earning 6.51% of the total income, 35.65% of the population earning 35.65% of the total income, and so on. Plotting these values against each other will give the equal shares curve, against which the actual shares can be compared. Any deviation from this simple one-to-one relationship indicates inequalities in the distribution of income, and the Lorenz curve makes this clear by curving as opposed to adopting the straight-line form that the equal-shares curve would produce.

Create the Lorenz curve now by defining the data range in the Chart Wizard as:

G1:I11

choosing an XY{Scatter} graph, Option 2, and using the first column for the horizontal axis values and the first 3 rows for the Legends Text. Then add the graph and axes titles indicated in Fig. 8.3.[10]

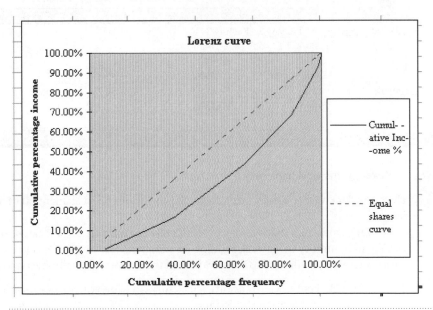

Figure 8.3

---

9 The equal shares curve indicates 10% of the total income being earned by 10% of the total population, 20% by 20%, 30% by 30%, and so on.

10 You must choose a scatter type of graph rather than a line graph to achieve the illustrated effect. A scatter graph uses a scale of equal intervals on the horizontal axis, whereas line graphs use the actual values of the data in the column that has been used for the Category (X) Axis Labels. (Thanks to John Houston.)

The end results should resemble Fig. 8.3.

If they do, save this file now as W8_11.XLS.

Clearly this particular Lorenz curve is displaying significant inequality in the distribution of income, with at one stage 86.91% of the population earning only 68.46% of the total income, (and, by implication, the remaining 31.56% of total income being earned by only 13.09% of the population).

Finally, note that the area between the Equal shares curve and the Cumulative percentage income curve is known as the area of inequality, and indicates the extent to which the actual distribution of incomes deviates from an equal distribution.

Exercise 8.5 can be attempted now.

8.3. Pictorial representation of data sets

We have already noted that Excel supports a number of charting options. To see how these can be used most effectively, consider Workbook 8.12.

	A	B	C	D	E	F	G	H	I
1	Daily cost element	Factory 1	Factory 2	Factory 3					
2	Labour	£1,200	£1,450	£1,140					
3	Raw materials	£930	£780	£1,020					
4	Fuel	£340	£250	£400					
5	Interest payments	£90	£75	£85					
6	Other	£110	£100	£120					
7									

Workbook 8.12

Make up this workbook now.

Here, the data refer to a daily breakdown of 5 constituent cost elements at each of 3 factories.

However, although this is not an exceptionally complex data set, it can be displayed pictorially in a number of ways, depending on which particular feature is to be emphasized. Consequently, we will need to decide which of the following possibilities is to be graphed:

1. Each cost element's occurrence at each factory (in which case the factory number will be used as the variable on the horizontal axis).
2. Each factory's burden of each cost element (in which case the cost elements will be used as the variable on the horizontal axis).
3. Each factory's share of all cost elements.
4. Each cost element's share of costs at all factories.

Taking each of these options in turn, we can proceed as follows:

8.3.1. Option 1
Use the Chart Wizard to draw a frame and then define the data range as:
A1:D6

Select Next and then choose a Column chart, and then Next again and pick Option 1 for the type of Column chart.
Select Next and the sample chart screen will appear.

Now we have to exercise care in order to make sure that the graph meets our requirements. This is because the data set is a 6 by 4 rectangle of values and labels and can clearly be regarded either as 6 rows with 4 items each or as 4 columns with 6 items each. How the graph will eventually appear depends entirely on which of these views is adopted, and Excel can be instructed to take either.

To view the data in row terms, click the top right-hand tab on the sample chart screen (Data Series In:) and select Rows.

This will force Excel to collect together the 5 cost elements (rows) for each factory.

Now ensure that Excel uses the first (1) row(s) for the Category (X) Axis Labels, and the first (1) column(s) for the Legend Text.

The X axis labels will therefore be factory 1, factory 2, and factory 3 and the 5 cost observations for each factory will be used as the chart legend.

Finally, select Next and supply some titles and then choose Finish.

The graph should resemble Fig. 8.4.

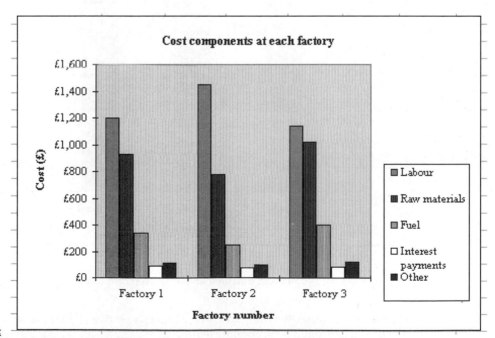

Figure 8.4

The chart shown in Figure 8.4 is a simple Column chart with the height of each column representing the amounts of the cost elements. However, it is an easy matter to change the type of Column chart into either a component, or a percentage component chart.

To do this, double click on the chart in Workbook 8.12 to go into edit mode and then select Format from the Menu bar and then Chart Type.

The current type of chart (Column) will be highlighted, but other types (Area, Pie, etc.) are available by clicking. Furthermore, you can also change the type of Column chart by selecting Options.

Keep the Column type of chart highlighted and click on Options.

Three possibilities will be presented. The 1st is simply the current chart, but the 2nd and 3rd are component and percentage component charts.

Click on the second option and a preview will appear.

As you can see, this component chart contains only 1 column for each factory, so the height of each column represents total costs (i.e. the sum of all cost elements) for each factory. Within this total cost, each of the cost elements is displayed as an absolute amount and shaded for identification purposes.

If you want to replace the original chart by this new one, click OK and the change will be effected.

Do this now, and the result should resemble Fig. 8.5.

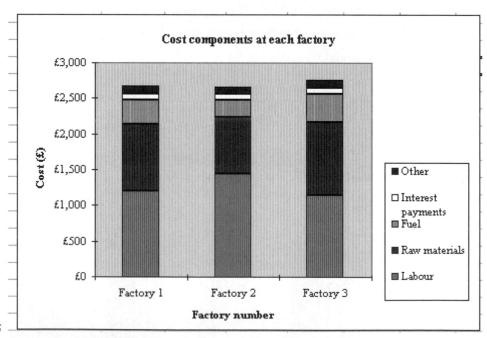

Figure 8.5

Now repeat the process outlined above to alter the chart type and this time select the third option.

The preview indicates that the heights of the columns are now all the same and that the vertical scale has changed from absolute figures (£) to percentages. This is a percentage component column chart, with each cost element for each factory being shown as a percentage of the total costs incurred by that factory.

With this last option highlighted, click OK and the graph in the workbook will change.

The effect should resemble Fig. 8.6.

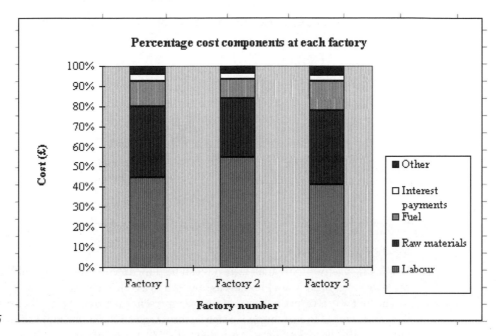

Figure 8.6

Now experiment with the different types of graph, other than Column, that are available and when you have finished restore the original chart (Column, Option 1).

8.3.2. Option 2

To display each cost element for all factories, we need to force Excel to view the data in columns rather than in rows as in the previous discussion.

To do this, click on the Chart Wizard, draw a new frame, and provide the same information as before (A1:D6 for the data range, Column graph, Option 1), but when the sample chart screen appears make sure that the tab for the Data Series is checked to *columns*.

Then use the first column for the Category (X) Axis Labels, and the first row for the Legend Text.

Finally, supply titles and Finish.

Something resembling Fig. 8.7 should be produced.

As is clear from the chart, factory 2 has got the highest labour costs while factory 3 has got the highest raw material and fuel costs. Once again, the type of Column chart could be changed by editing and then choosing Format and Chart Type as previously explained.

Practise this now by changing the chart first of all to a component column chart and then to a percentage component column chart.

When you have finished, restore the original simple column chart.

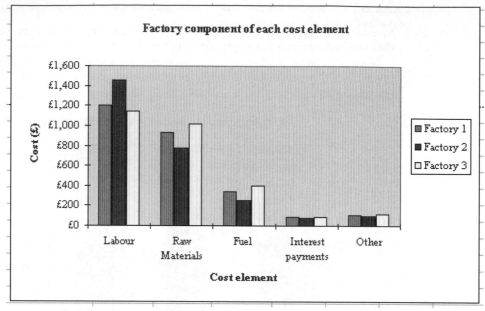

Figure 8.7

8.3.3. Options 3 and 4

Displaying all cost items at all factories can be done in either of 2 ways, although in both cases we are going to use a **Pie chart** as opposed to a Column chart.

The first way is to let the 'slices' of the pie represent each factory, in which case we obtain the percentage of all costs borne by each factory (Option 3). For example, the total costs sustained by all 3 factories can be computed to be £8090, and of these £2670 are borne by factory 1. Thus £2670/£8090 = 33% of all costs are attributable to factory 1. This would be the factory 1 'slice' in the Pie chart.

On the other hand, the slices of the pie could be used to represent each of the cost elements for all 3 factories (Option 4). Thus total labour costs for all three factories are easily computed as £3790, and with the total costs sustained in all cost categories and for all factories still being £8090, the labour cost slice of the pie would be calculated as £3790/£8090 = 46.84%.

Clearly we require the row and column totals to perform these calculations.

So, in the B7 cell of Workbook 8.12 enter the formula:

> =SUM(B2:B6)

and copy this into C7:D7.

This will produce the column totals (i.e. the total of all cost categories at each factory).

Then in E2 enter:

> =SUM(B2:D2)

and copy this into E3:E6.

The values in E2:E6 are the row totals (i.e. the total for all factories in each cost category). With these computations completed, we can now prepare our pie charts.

To make the slices of the pie represent factories, the data series must be defined as:

> B1:D1,B7:D7

i.e. the factory labels and the total costs at each factory.

Now click on Chart Wizard, define the data range as B1:D1,B7:D7, and select Pie and then Option 7 for the type of pie chart.
When the sample chart screen appears, make sure that the data series tab is checked to *rows* and then use the first row for the Pie Slice Labels and the first 0 columns for the Chart title.
Select Next and supply the title as indicated in Fig. 8.8.

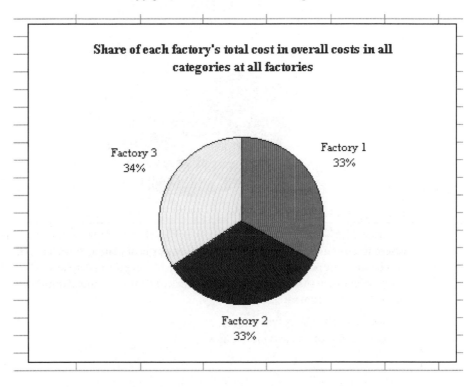

Figure 8.8

Clearly, factory 3 has the highest share of overall costs sustained by all factories.
To make the slices of the pie represent cost elements the data range must be transposed.

To do this, create another frame and repeat the procedure above, except defining the data range to be A2:A6,E2:E6.

That is, the cost element labels and the total costs in each category at all factories.

Then at the sample chart screen make sure that the data series is checked to columns and that the first column is used for the pie slices and the first row for the chart title. Then add the new title indicated in Fig. 8.9.

Notice one final thing about pie charts. Like percentage component column charts, they are relative graphs. That is, they convey no information about the absolute magnitude of the data, only about the shares in the grand total. For example, if each of the cost elements for each of the factories was multiplied by 10, then the pie charts in Figs. 8.8 and 8.9 would retain the same shape. Yet a tenfold increase in all costs is likely to create significant difficulties for the factories concerned, and pie charts will not give any indication of this. On the other hand, they will show whether a particular cost category or a particular factory is taking up a more than proportionate share of all the costs that have to be endured. In short,

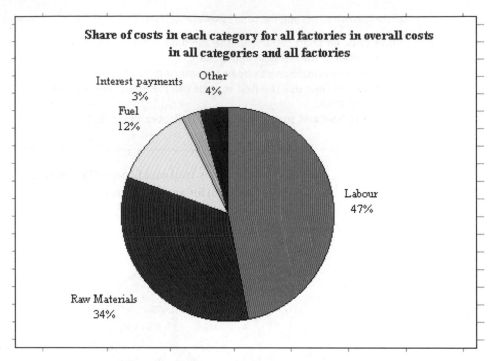

Figure 8.9

where relative as opposed to absolute behaviour is of primary concern, then pie charts or percentage component column charts are the best pictorial displays. When, however, it is the absolute magnitude of the data that needs to be shown, then simple or component column charts perform satisfactorily.

Now save this file as W8_12.XLS.
Exercise 8.6 can be attempted now.

8.4. Measures of central tendency

Because there will usually be several values of the observed variable, it will frequently be instructive to calculate some single value that measures the central or 'average' value of the data set. This measure of central tendency may well be the same as one of the observed data elements, but there is no necessity that this be the case, since the averaging process is capable of calculating a central value that is not the same as any one of the observed data items. Furthermore, even in the case of discrete data sets, there is no requirement that the central value is also integer valued. This means that the central value could be one which is actually incapable of being observed (2.5 car occupants, for example).

Bearing these ideas in mind, we can proceed by explaining the 5 most commonly used measures of central tendency that statistics employs.

8.4.1. The arithmetic mean

The **arithmetic mean** is the name that statistics uses for what we more commonly refer to as the 'average'. To see how it can be calculated, consider the following example.

The following data are the daily number of clients placed by an employment agency over a period of 11 working days.

x (number of clients placed) 15, 28, 21, 13, 19, 23, 21, 16, 21, 17, 26

Calculate the arithmetic mean of the data set.

For any data set, the arithmetic mean is calculated by obtaining the total arithmetic worth of all the observations and then dividing this total by the number of observations. For our data this would produce:

$(15 + 28 + 21 + 13 + 19 + 23 + 21 + 16 + 21 + 17 + 26)/11 = 220/11 = 20$ client placements per day.

This means that 'on average' 20 clients were placed each day, and although this happens to be a whole number, you can see that there was no actual occasion over the 11-day period when 20 clients were actually placed. It should also be clear that there is no necessity for the arithmetic mean to be a whole number even when it is computed from a discrete data set such as the one being currently used. For example, with one fewer clients being placed on any particular day the mean would become:

$219/11 = 19.9090$

More generally, we can use the following notational conventions to define the arithmetic mean for any unclassified data set.

Let n = the total number of observations in the data set.
Let x_i = the ith observation in the data set where i can be any integer value in the range 1 to n (we say: $i = 1 \ldots n$).
Let Σx_i represent the sum of the n observations, i.e. $(x_1 + x_2 + \ldots + x_n)$.
Let $\bar{x}$ represent the arithmetic mean of the data set.

Then:

$\bar{x} = \Sigma x_i / n$

If you now apply this formula to the data in the illustration, you will find that:

$\Sigma x_i = 220$, and $n = 11$

Therefore:

$\bar{x} = 220/11 = 20.00$

Excel can also perform these calculations with its AVERAGE function, which has the following general syntax:

=AVERAGE(DATA RANGE)

To see this in operation, open a new workbook and enter a heading (Clients placed) in A1 and the 11 data observations in the range A2:A12. Then in B1 enter the formula:

=AVERAGE(A2:A12)

This will calculate the arithmetic mean of the data set and should equal 20 if the data has been correctly entered.

Notice that this formula for the arithmetic mean will change automatically if the value of any of the data observations changes.

Confirm this now by reducing the value of any one of the observations by 1. Then restore the original value.

8.4.2. The mode

The second measure of central tendency is known as the **mode**, and is quite simply defined as that value of the variable that occurs most often. For our illustrative data set simple inspection of the data shows there is only one value of x which occurs more than once (21), and so we conclude that this is the modal value of the data set.

To calculate the mode (as opposed to observe it from inspection) we can use the Excel function called =MODE. This has the general syntax:

=MODE(DATA RANGE)

Confirm that the calculated mode for the illustrative data set is 21 by using B2 to contain:

=MODE(A2:A12)

Also notice that there may be no unique value for the mode if more than one value of x occurs with equal frequency. In this case the distribution could be bi-modal, tri-modal, or even multi-modal.

8.4.3. The median

For simple data sets you can think of the **median** as representing the 'middle' value of the variable when these values have been placed in order of magnitude. This is because the exact definition of the median is:

that value of x, above and below which, 50% of the observations lie

Now, since the data in our example contains 11 observations, all we have to do is order the observations and then select the value of x associated with the 6th (i.e. middle) observation. This would produce:

x (number of clients placed)	13, 15, 16, 17, 19, 21, 21, 21, 23, 26, 28
observation number	1 2 3 4 5 6 7 8 9 10 11

The median is clearly seen to be 21 and in this case is equal to the mode.

As with the previous 2 measures of central tendency, Excel can calculate the median from its function:

=MEDIAN(DATA RANGE)

Therefore, use the B3 cell of the current workbook to contain:

=MEDIAN(A2:A12)

and confirm that a result of 21 is obtained.

Workbook 8.13

The results obtained so far should resemble Workbook 8.13.

You should now note that calculation of the median was straightforward in this last case because of the fact that there was an odd number of observations, and the 'middle' one was clearly the 6th. If, however, there was an even number of observations then the middle 2 observations must be selected and then averaged (i.e. added together and then divided by 2) to produce an estimate of the median value.

Confirm this now by removing the last observation (26) from the data set (click on A12 and press the Delete key).

Both the mean and the median values in B1 and B3 will change automatically (to 19.4 and 20 respectively) but the mode in B2 is unaffected.

Now select Undo and the deleted observation will be restored.

	A	B	C	D	E	F	G	
1	Clients placed (x)	20	Arithmetic mean					
2	15	21	Mode					
3	28	21	Median					
4	21							
5	13							
6	19							
7	23							
8	21							
9	16							
10	21							
11	17							
12	26							

Microsoft Excel - W8_13.XLS

File Edit View Insert Format Tools Data Window Help

Workbook 8.13

Now save this file as W8_13.XLS.

8.4.4. Comparison between the mean, the median, and the mode

At this stage it is fair to ask which of these 3 measures of central tendency is the 'best'. The answer is that 'best' is not really the correct word, since we are more concerned with appropriateness. This means that the alternative measures should be viewed as being complementary rather than competitive, with the most appropriate being dependent upon the nature of the data to be investigated. To see this, consider the following example.

The following data refer to the daily output of a particular component produced by each of 5 machines in a factory's production system:

x (daily output) 490, 510, 495, 490, 1000

Calculate the most appropriate measure of central tendency which will allow you to advise the management on its proposed policy of scrapping the whole system if the output per machine is less than 550 units per day, or if more than 50% of the machines have a daily output of less than 500 units.

Enter the data to a new workbook and compute the arithmetic mean, the median, and the mode as previously explained.

The arithmetic mean output is 597 units per day, so on the 1st criterion the system should not be scrapped (597 > 550), but since the median daily output is 495 units, on the 2nd criterion it should be. (It should be clear, in fact, that 60% of the machines will have an output which is less than 500 units per day.) You would have to ask the management to give you more information on which of the 2 criteria is to be given more weight, since the single extreme observation of 1000 is exercising a disproportionate effect on the value of the arithmetic mean.

Finally, the mode is 490 units and indicates that an output that is fewer than 500 units occurs most frequently.

In conclusion, it is generally true that the arithmetic mean is much more sensitive to extreme observations than either the median or the mode, but that neither the median nor the mode give any indication of the arithmetic extent to which the other observations in the data set differ from the central value.

Exercise 8.7 can be attempted now.

8.4.5. The geometric mean

The **geometric mean** is a measure of central tendency that takes account of the fact that for certain types of data the arithmetic mean is not the most appropriate measure of central tendency. To see what is meant by this, consider the following example.

An individual's salary was £10000 in 1990, but was increased by 10% in 1991, by 15% in 1992, by 25% in 1993, and by 30% in 1994. What is the 'average' rate of growth of the individual's salary for these five years?

First instincts are usually to calculate the arithmetic mean of 10%, 15%, 25%, and 30%, and obtain:

$$(10\% + 15\% + 25\% + 30\%)/4 = 20\%$$

However, if this is in fact an appropriate measure of central tendency, then it should, when applied for 4 years to the £10000 initial salary, produce the same figure for 1994 as was actually earned. To see whether this is indeed the case, we can argue as follows.

After four years the individual's actual salary would be computed as:

£10000 + £10000(0.1) = £10000(1 + 0.1) = £10000(1.1) = £11000 after 1 year
£11000 + £11000(0.15) = £11000(1 + 0.15) = £11000(1.15) = £12650 after 2 years
£12650 + £12650(0.25) = £12650(1 + 0.25) = £12650(1.25) = £15812.5 after 3 years.
£15812.5 + £15812.5(0.3) = £15812.5(1 + 0.3) = £15812.5(1.3) = £20556.25 after 4 years

If we now apply the computed arithmetic mean growth rate of 20% to the initial £10000 for four years, then the predicted eventual salary is:

£10000 + £10000(0.2) = £10000(1 + 0.2) = £10000(1.2) = £12000 after 1 year
£12000 + £12000(0.2) = £12000(1 + 0.2) = £12000(1.2) = £14400 after 2 years
£14400 + £14400(0.2) = £14400(1 + 0.2) = £14400(1.2) = £17280 after 3 years
£17280 + £17280(0.2) = £17280(1 + 0.2) = £17280(1.2) = £20736 after 4 years

Clearly the predicted eventual salary (£20736) exceeds the actual salary (£20556.25) by £179.75, and so using the arithmetic mean as the measure of the 'average' growth rate has produced a degree of error. The answer to this difficulty is to compute the geometric as opposed to the arithmetic mean. The former is defined for n observations as the nth root of the product of all the observations.

Furthermore, since in this illustration it is the growth factors (1 + the growth rates) that concern us, we should compute the nth root of these growth factors rather than the nth root of the growth rates. For the illustration this would give:

$$[(1 + 0.1)(1 + 0.15)(1 + 0.25)(1 + 0.3)]^{(1/4)} = [(1.1)(1.15)(1.25)(1.3)]^{(1/4)} = 1.19739$$

This is the mean growth factor, so the mean growth rate is:

$$1.19739\text{-}1 = 0.19739 \text{ or } 19.739\%$$

If we now apply this mean growth rate to the initial salary for 4 years we obtain:

£10000(1.19739) = £11973.90 after 1 year
£11973.90(1.19739) = £14337.45 after 2 years
£14337.45(1.19739) = £17167.53 after 3 years
£17167.53(1.19739) = £20556.25 after 4 years

Clearly this now produces the actual salary that was earned, and so we conclude that the mean rate of salary growth should be taken as the geometric mean of 19.739%, rather than the arithmetic mean of 20%.

Now it can be pointed out that Excel possesses a function to calculate the geometric mean. It is called =GEOMEAN and has the general syntax:

=GEOMEAN(DATA RANGE)

To confirm the results obtained above, take a new workbook and enter the growth *factors* (1.1, 1.15, 1.25, and 1.3) to the A1:A4 cells.
Then in B1 enter:

=GEOMEAN(A1:A4)

As with the manual calculation, a result of 1.19739 should be obtained, implying a mean growth rate of $0.19739 = 19.739\%$.

The upshot of this discussion is that where the data represent a variable that is measured as a percentage rate of growth, then the geometric as opposed to the arithmetic mean is the most appropriate measure of central tendency.

8.4.6. The harmonic mean

The **harmonic mean** is another statistic which can be used in circumstances where the nature of the data is such that the simple arithmetic mean does not produce a satisfactory measure of central tendency. To see some of the issues involved, consider the following example.

A van driver has to make 3 deliveries to 3 different shops on a particular day, with a schedule that is outlined in Table 8.1. We are required to calculate the 'average' speed of the driver over all 4 journeys.

Table 8.1

JOURNEY	DISTANCE (MILES)	SPEED (M.P.H.)
Depot to Shop 1	30	25
Shop 1 to Shop 2	30	30
Shop 2 to Shop 3	30	20
Shop 3 to Depot	30	40

Once again, the temptation might be to calculate the arithmetic mean of the 4 speeds and obtain a value of:

$(25 + 30 + 20 + 40)/4 = 115/4 = 29.25$ m.p.h.

However, this method would only give an accurate estimate of the average speed if the speeds of each journey were all the same. Clearly this is not the case, and so we should approach the problem from first principles as follows.

The 1st journey will take the driver $30/25 = 1.2$ hours, the 2nd journey will take $30/30 = 1$ hour, the 3rd journey will take $30/20 = 1.5$ hours, and the 4th journey will take $30/40 = 0.75$ hours. Consequently, the total driving time is 4.45 hours, and in that time a total distance of 120 miles has been travelled. The average speed for all 4 journeys is therefore given by:

$120/4.45 = 26.96629$ m.p.h.

Having solved the problem from first principles, it can now be noted that the 'average' speed for this problem is in fact measured by what is known as the harmonic mean of the 4 speeds. This is defined as the number of observations divided by the sum of the reciprocals of the x values (speeds).

For the illustrative data this would produce:

$$4/(1/25 + 1/30 + 1/20 + 1/40) = 4/0.14833 = 26.96629 \text{ m.p.h.}$$

Excel can do these calculations for you with its HARMEAN function, which has the general syntax:

=HARMEAN(DATA RANGE)

To see this, open a new workbook and enter the 4 speeds to the A1:A4 range. Then in B1 enter:

=HARMEAN(A1:A4)

A result of 26.96629 should be obtained.

The conclusion of this discussion is that, as a general rule, the harmonic mean is frequently the most appropriate measure of central tendency for data sets in which the variable is measured in terms of units of one variable *per* unit of another (miles per hour, miles per gallon, metres per second etc.).

8.5. **Measures of dispersion**

Data sets are like individuals or objects—they can be described in terms of a number of characteristics. The previous section has explained one of these characteristics—central tendency—but since the eventual purpose of descriptive statistics is to allow the investigator to observe the differences between one or more data sets, a single characteristic will rarely be sufficient. This would be like trying to distinguish between two individuals simply in terms of their height rather than in terms of their height *and* weight *and* hair colour and so on. Clearly a full description of any object usually requires that more than one characteristic is defined.

In descriptive statistics the most frequently used second characteristic is known as **dispersion**, and attempts to measure the extent to which the observations are spread out. One of the simplest measures of dispersion is the range, quite simply defined as the maximum observed value of the variable minus the minimum observed value. In Excel the range is easily computed by combining the MAX and the MIN functions as follows:

=MAX(DATA RANGE)-MIN(DATA RANGE) = RANGE

However, although easy to calculate, the range suffers from the major deficiency that it only considers the two extreme observations in the data set, whereas ideally we would like to measure dispersion in terms of all of the observations. Furthermore, the range is what is known as an absolute measure of dispersion, since its value is not related to any other characteristic of the data set. Ideally, we would like to create a dispersion measure that was relative in the sense that it is related to one of the central-tendency characteristics. To deal with these deficiencies, we should think in terms of measuring the difference (or deviation) of each individual x value from its central (arithmetic mean) value, and then using the sum of these deviations as our measure of dispersion. That is, we define the deviation (d_i) of each individual x value (x_i) from its arithmetic mean value ($\bar{x}$) as:

$$d_i = (x_i - \bar{x}) \ (i = 1 \ldots n).$$

And the sum of these deviations as:

$$\Sigma d_i = \Sigma(x_i - \bar{x}) \ (i = 1 \ldots n).$$

You can see how this can be done in Workbook 8.14, where the data in column A are the outputs from a particular factory over a period of 7 days.

	Microsoft Excel - W8_14.XLS						
File	Edit	View	Insert	Format	Tools	Data	Window	Help

Courier (W1) ▾ 10 ▾ **B** *I* U

A13 ▾ =VARP(A2:A8)

	A	B	C	D	E	F	G
1	Daily output (x)	d_i	d_i^2				
2	45	-0.714285714	0.510204082				
3	56	10.28571429	105.7959184				
4	23	-22.71428571	515.9387755				
5	48	2.285714286	5.224489796				
6	50	4.285714286	18.36734694				
7	46	0.285714286	0.081632653				
8	52	6.285714286	39.51020408				
9	Arithmetic mean	Sum of deviations	Sum of squared deviations				
10	45.71428571	0.00	685.4286				
11							
12	variance		variance				
13	97.91836735		97.91836735				
14							
15							
16	standard deviation		standard deviation				
17	9.895371006		9.895371006				

Sheet1 / Sheet2 / Sheet3 / Sheet4 / Sheet5 / Sheet

Workbook 8.14

Make up this new workbook for yourself as indicated.
First, enter the labels and raw data to the A1:A9 range and then compute the arithmetic mean of the data set in A10 from:

=AVERAGE(A2:A8)

Now name this cell as MEAN.

Next, in column B we need to subtract the mean from each value of x to produce the 7 individual deviation values.

Therefore, in B2 enter the formula:

=A2-MEAN

and then copy this into B3:B8.
Finally, in B10 calculate the sum of these deviations from the formula:

=SUM(B2:B8)

As you can see, this sum turns out to be zero[11] for this data set, and therein lies the fundamental problem with this approach. By this we mean that it is not coincidence that the sum

---

11 Depending upon the width of the column and the decimal place formatting, Excel may show the result in summarized scientific notation. To remedy this, either widen the column or format the entry to 2 or 3 decimal places to obtain a 'true' value of 0.

of deviations is zero. This will always be the case for all data sets, since the process of subtracting the arithmetic mean from each observation inevitably produces positive and negative deviations which collectively sum to zero. In short, this means it is always the case that:

$$\Sigma d_i = 0 \ (i = 1 \dots n)$$

This creates a serious problem for our attempts to devise a satisfactory measure of dispersion, since the clear implication is that as measured by the summed deviations from the arithmetic mean, all data sets will have the same index of dispersion, and that this index will always be zero. As a method of distinguishing between different degrees of dispersion in various data sets, such an index is obviously useless.

However, the principle involved in our definition of dispersion in terms of deviations from the mean remains sound, and if we could only devise some way of preventing the positive and negative deviations from cancelling one another out, then the method could be retained. This is easily done by squaring each deviation (to eliminate the negative deviations) and then calculating the associated sum of squared deviations. This means that we calculate:

$$d_i^2 = (x^i - \bar{x})^2$$

and then sum each of these squared deviations to obtain:

$$\Sigma d_i^2 = \Sigma (x_i - \bar{x})^2$$

Do these calculations now in the C2 cell of the current workbook from the formula:

=B2^2

and then copy this into C3:C8.
   Next calculate the sum of these squared deviations in C10 from:

=SUM(C2:C8)

As you can see, this returns a value of 685.4285, and so:

$$\Sigma d_i^2 = 685.4286$$

This is the sum of squared deviations.

This statistic is (nearly) our best measure of dispersion in relation to the arithmetic mean, but it must be remembered that it is inevitably sensitive to the total number of observations. This would mean that a widely dispersed data set with only a few observations could have a lower value for the sum of squared deviations than a concentrated data set in which there was a large number of observations. In other words, more observations mean more deviations, and this implies that there will always be a higher value for the sum of squared deviations than for a similarly dispersed data set containing fewer observations.

To deal with this fact we must standardize the index of dispersion (as measured by the sum of squared deviations) by dividing it by the total number of observations (n). This produces the following statistic which is known as the **variance** of x:

$$\text{Variance of } x = \Sigma (d_i)^2 / n$$

Calculate this now in the C13 cell of your own workbook from the formula:

=C10/7

Finally, to compensate for having squared the deviations earlier, we can take the square root of the variance to produce a statistic known as the **standard deviation**.

$$\text{Standard deviation of } x = [\Sigma (d_i)^2 / n]^{0.5}$$

Now calculate this statistic in the C17 cell of your own workbook from the formulae:

$=C13^0.5$

As you can see, values of 97.91 and 9.895 are returned to C13 and C17 respectively.

Now that you have learnt the logic on which the variance and the standard deviation are founded, you can get Excel to save you some time by using its dedicated variance and standard deviation functions. These have the following general syntax: [12]

    =VARP(DATA RANGE)
    =STDEVP(DATA RANGE)

For our illustration the data range is A2:A8, so enter the appropriate functions in the A13 and A17 cells.

You should find that the same results are returned as were calculated in C13 and C17 from first principles. When you have finished save the file as W8_14.XLS.

Exercise 8.8 can now be attempted.

The variance and the standard deviation are by far the most frequently used measures of dispersion, and are to be interpreted as meaning that the higher the arithmetical value is of either of these statistics then the greater the degree of dispersion displayed by the data set from which they were calculated—provided that both data sets are measured in the same or comparable units.

This can be seen by inspecting Workbook 8.15, where the percentage examination marks for 2 groups of students have been entered in columns A and C.

Make up Workbook 8.15 now, leaving A17:A19 and C17:C19 blank for the moment.

Workbook 8.15	**Using the methods explained above, use Excel functions to calculate the arithmetic mean, the variance, and the standard deviation marks for both sets of students in the A17:A19 and C17:C19 ranges.**

The formulae in A17:A19 should be:

    =AVERAGE(A2:A16)
    =VARP(A2:A16)
    =STDEVP(A2:A16)

Then copy these formulae into C17:C19.

The results of the calculations are shown in the illustrative workbook and clearly indicate that, although both sets of students have the same arithmetic mean mark (55), the dispersion of these marks is much greater for group A than for group B. This is only to be expected when it is noted that all of the students in group B obtained the same mark. The mean is therefore identical to the value of each of the observations, and there is therefore no deviation from the mean by any of these individual marks. Consequently, as measured by the variance and the standard deviation, the degree of dispersion in this data set is zero.

However, a slight problem arises with the general conclusion that a higher standard deviation or variance means a greater degree of dispersion when this dispersion is to be compared between 2 data sets that are measured in different units. To understand this point more clearly, consider the 2 data sets shown in Workbook 8.16, which refer to the weekly take home pay of 7 British and 7 French employees, measured in £s and FF respectively.

---

12 Excel also has two related functions—STDEV and VAR—which are used when the data is the result of a sampling procedure. In the context of the current discussion, however, it is assumed that the data represents a population, and so STDEVP and VARP are the appropriate functions.

	Microsoft Excel - W8_15.XLS						
File	Edit	View	Insert	Format	Tools	Data	Window	Help

	A	B	C	D	E	F	G
1	Group A % marks		Group B % marks				
2	65		55				
3	7		55				
4	31		55				
5	87		55				
6	25		55				
7	36		55				
8	78		55				
9	65		55				
10	53		55				
11	67		55				
12	42		55				
13	49		55				
14	59		55				
15	61		55				
16	100	Group A	55	Group B			
17	55	Arithmetic mean	55	Arithmetic mean			
18	554.9333333	Variance	0	Variance			
19	23.55702302	Standard deviation	0	Standard deviation			
20							

Sheet1 / Sheet2 / Sheet3 / Sheet4 / Sheet5 / Sheet

Workbook 8.15

Workbook 8.16

Make up the first four columns of this workbook now.

First, enter the two data sets into columns A and C of the worksheet and then calculate the arithmetic means, variances, and standard deviations of both data sets in rows 9 to 11 as indicated.

Finally, add the labels in rows 8 to 11 of columns B and D.

As you can see, both the arithmetic mean and the standard deviation take-home pay for the French employees is considerably higher than for their British counterparts, but we should immediately suspect such a simple conclusion on the grounds that the units in which the variables are measured are also different. To be exact, since at the moment one pound sterling is approximately equivalent to 7.5 French francs, we really should adjust one or other of the data sets to take account of this fact.

Do this now in column E of the workbook by entering to E2 the formula:

$$=C2/7.5$$

and copying it into E3:E8.

This will convert the FF data into approximate sterling values.

Now copy the formulae in C9:C11 into E9:E11.

The mean, variance, and standard deviation for the adjusted series will now be computed in E9:E11.

As you can see, the large absolute differences in central tendency and dispersion that

	A	B	C	D	E
1	UK take home pay (£)		French take home pay (FF)		FF/7.5
2	140.23		1500.56		200.0746667
3	156.5		1410.76		188.1013333
4	123.21		1300		173.3333333
5	99.99		1000.78		133.4373333
6	178.87		1850.56		246.7413333
7	147.67		1450.8		193.44
8	161.25	UK	1670.9	France	222.7866667
9	143.96	Arithmetic mean	1454.908571	Arithmetic mean	193.98781
10	580.9291714	Variance	62495.9721	Variance	1111.0395
11	24.10247231	Standard deviation	249.9919441	Standard deviation	33.3322592
12			16.74247868		17.18265663
13					
14					
15					

Workbook 8.16

were previously observed have been reduced considerably, although it is still true that in France there is a higher mean take-home pay and a greater dispersion of this take-home pay than in the UK.

However, in this case, we were able to use our knowledge of the exchange rate to convert one of the data sets to the same or similar units as the other. But what should we do if such a conversion factor is not readily available? The answer is that we can form a statistic known as the coefficient of variation (CV), which is defined for each data set as:

$$CV = 100(\text{standard deviation/arithmetic mean}) \%$$

This statistic provides a relative measure of dispersion in the sense that the overall dispersion in the data set (as measured by the standard deviation) is related to the arithmetic mean value, thereby compensating for any overestimation that may have occurred as a result of differences in measurement units. If any difference in dispersion as calculated by the standard deviation is entirely due to different measurement units, then the coefficient of variation will return an equal value for both data sets.

Now calculate the coefficients of variation for the two data sets in A12 and C12 of the current workbook from the two formulae:

=100*A11/A9 and =100*C11/C9

As you can see, without making recourse to given information on the exchange rates between the two currencies, the relative dispersion in the two data sets, as now measured, is no more than 1.1%. That is:

$$CV_{UK} = 16.74\% \text{ and } CV_{France} = 17.18\%$$

Exercise 8.9 can be attempted now.

8.6. **Statistical analysis of selected data subsets**

The previous discussion has shown how to compute the mean, variance, and standard deviation for all of the observations in a given data set. However, it will often be the case that we require measures of central tendency and dispersion that apply only to certain selected observations from the data set. This means that we are only concerned with what is known as a data subset.

For example, in a data set of the marks obtained by all of the students who sat a particular examination we may want to know the mean and standard deviation mark of only the female examinees, or of only those examinees who were over 25 years of age.

Computations such as these require that we re-deploy the **data filtering** process that was explained in section 1.11, and then use some of the SUBTOTAL functions that were also explained in that section.

Workbook 8.17

To see how this selective data analysis can be achieved, load Worksheet 8.17 now.
Now select the A3:H17 area with the mouse and then select Data, Filter and then Autofilter.

The data set can now be filtered as required to produce selected subsets.

Next, recall that to compute summary statistics in a filtered list requires that we use an appropriate SUBTOTAL function. These functions produce different summary statistics depending upon the numerical value adopted by their first argument. (The second argument is simply the range of each of the fields for which calculations are to be performed—C3:C17, D3:D17, . . . H3:H17 in this case.)

The full list of first argument numbers used in SUBTOTAL functions is:

1 = AVERAGE (i.e. the arithmetic mean)
2 = COUNT (i.e. the number of items in the list that are numbers)
3 = COUNTA (i.e. the number of items in the list that are numbers or text or messages)[13]
4 = MAX (i.e. the maximum value in the list)
5 = MIN (i.e. the minimum value in the list)
6 = PRODUCT (i.e. the product of all the values in the list)
7 = STDEV (i.e. the standard deviation of a sample data set)
8 = STDEVP (i.e. the standard deviation of a population data set)
9 = SUM (i.e. the sum of the values in the list)
10 = VAR (i.e. the variance of a sample data set)
11= VARP (i.e. the variance of a population data set)

In the context of our current knowledge of statistics the relevant function arguments are 1, 2, 4, 5, 8, and 11.

Consequently, to obtain these summary statistics for each of the fields, first of all enter the labels and numbers to the column A and B ranges as shown in Workbook 8.17A.

---

[13] Neither COUNT nor COUNTA includes cells that are blank in the counting process.

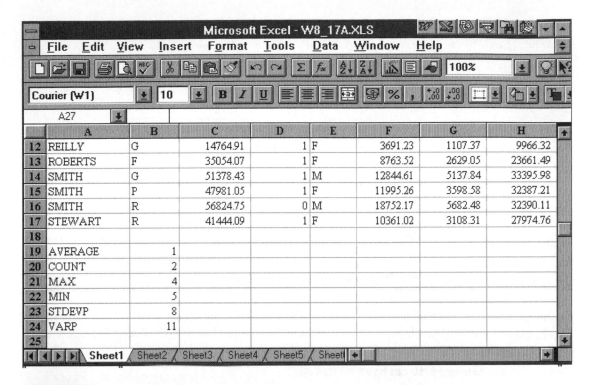

	A	B	C	D	E	F	G	H
12	REILLY	G	14764.91	1	F	3691.23	1107.37	9966.32
13	ROBERTS	F	35054.07	1	F	8763.52	2629.05	23661.49
14	SMITH	G	51378.43	1	M	12844.61	5137.84	33395.98
15	SMITH	P	47981.05	1	F	11995.26	3598.58	32387.21
16	SMITH	R	56824.75	0	M	18752.17	5682.48	32390.11
17	STEWART	R	41444.09	1	F	10361.02	3108.31	27974.76
18								
19	AVERAGE	1						
20	COUNT	2						
21	MAX	4						
22	MIN	5						
23	STDEVP	8						
24	VARP	11						
25								

Workbook 8.17A

Next, in C19 enter the formula:

=SUBTOTAL($B19,C$4:C$17)

and copy it down into C20:C24.

This uses the column B entries as the first argument of the SUBTOTAL functions, while the dollar signs ensure consistent copying both down and across the sheet. Clearly this process will produce the specified summary statistics for the SALARY field.

To obtain equivalent statistics for the remaining fields, copy the C19:C24 block into D19:H24. And then, for identification purposes, copy C3:H3 (the field labels) into C25:H25.

Workbook 8.17B

The results should resemble the section shown in Workbook 8.17B. Notice that the values produced in columns D and E are of little use, since the data in column E is merely a numerical code to identify marital status, while those in column E are text entries to identify gender. The summary statistics for these fields therefore have no statistical meaning, although the field data themselves can be used for filtering purposes.

Now notice that at the moment the summary statistics refer to the entire data list (i.e. all the observations in each of the fields). This is because the list has not been filtered yet. So, suppose now that we require to compute the mean salary and the mean tax due for the female subset.

To do this, click on the SEX field filter tab and select F from the list.

The summary statistics in rows 19 to 14 will adjust automatically, and if the model has been prepared correctly it is an easy matter to observe that for this subset the mean salary is £33695.57 and the mean tax is £9145.30.

Finally, to obtain the summary statistics for all married females, say, with the SEX field

			Microsoft Excel - W8_17B.XLS					
File	**Edit**	**View**	**Insert**	**Format**	**Tools**	**Data**	**Window**	**Help**
	A	**B**	**C**	**D**	**E**	**F**	**G**	**H**
14	SMITH	G	51,378.43	1	M	12844.61	5137.84	33395.98
15	SMITH	P	47,981.05	1	F	11995.26	3598.58	32387.21
16	SMITH	R	56,824.75	0	M	18752.17	5682.48	32390.11
17	STEWART	R	41,444.09	1	F	10361.02	3108.31	27974.76
18								
19	AVERAGE	1	34,757.36	0.64	#DIV/0!	9931.89	3054.54	21770.93
20	COUNT	2	14.00	14.00	0.00	14.00	14.00	14.00
21	MAX	4	56,824.75	1.00	0.00	18752.17	5682.48	33395.98
22	MIN	5	889.64	0.00	0.00	222.41	88.96	578.27
23	STDEVP	8	17,931.87	0.48	#DIV/0!	5711.52	1747.31	10888.26
24	VARP	11	321,551,998.40	0.23	#DIV/0!	32621484.50	3053102.76	118554269.55
25			**SALARY**	**MARSTAT**	**SEX**	**TAX**	**SUPERANN**	**TAKEHOME**
26								
27								

Sheet1 / Sheet2 / Sheet3 / Sheet4 / Sheet5 / Sheet

Workbook 8.17B still selecting females, click on the MARSTAT field filter tab and select 1 (for married). The mean salary and the mean tax paid should be returned as £34549.17 and £8637.29 respectively.

Exercise 8.10 can be attempted now.

8.7. **Exercises**

....

Exercise 8.1

Using the data from Workbook 8.1 (W8_1.XLS), use Excel to classify the cars according to the numbers that respectively have:

> only 1 occupant; 2 or 3 occupants; 4 or 5 occupants

Exercise 8.2

(i) Using the data from Workbook 8.1 (W8_1.XLS), use Excel to produce an absolute and a cumulative percentage frequency distribution of the number of cars that respectively have:

> only 1 occupant; 2, 3 or 4 occupants; 5 occupants

(ii) Chart the absolute and cumulative percentage frequencies in a histogram.

(iii) What proportion of cars have 4 or less occupants?

(iv) What proportion of cars have more than 1 occupant?

Exercise 8.3

(i) Using the data from Workbook 8.5

(W8_5.XLS), classify the occupants of the cars according to whether their age is:

> 15 or less; over 15 but 20 or less; over 20 but 40 or less; over 40 but 60 or less; over 60

(ii) What proportion of occupants are 40 or less?

(iii) What proportion of occupants are over 20?

(iv) What proportion of occupants are over 15 but not over 60?

Exercise 8.4

Load Workbook 8.1 (W8_1.XLS) and let Excel choose the bin values with which to classify the number of car occupants. Then create the frequency distribution and state whether you are satisfied with the results.

Exercise 8.5

Suppose that the income distribution shown in Workbook 8.10 was for country A, and that the equivalent frequencies for a second country (B) are as indicated in Workbook 8.18. Use Workbook 8.11 as a template to add

Workbook 8.18

	A	B	C	D	E	F	G	H	I	J
1		Number of								
2	Income	Individuals								
3	after tax (£)	in B (000's)								
4	2500	4.10								
5	5000	33.70								
6	7500	297.00								
7	10000	1407.00								
8	20000	6293.00								
9	40000	6672.00								
10	60000	4400.20								
11	370000	2493.00								

Microsoft Excel - W8_18.XLS
File   Edit   View   Insert   Format   Tools   Data   Window   Help
C14
Sheet1 / Sheet2 / Sheet3 / Sheet4 / Sheet5 / Sheet

Table 8.2

	STREPO	ROSEWAITE	PO-OC	CESTO	SAVE-KWIK
England	71.4	34.2	41.6	102.5	59.8
N. Ireland	7.4	0.2	2.1	4.8	3.1
Scotland	3.9	0.2	12.3	1.2	4.6
Wales	8.6	2.3	3.5	0.9	5.8

the second set of frequencies and then perform the necessary calculations to create the Lorenz curve for country B.

What conclusions about differences in the equality of the distributions of income can be drawn from the Lorenz curves for the two countries?

Exercise 8.6

The data in Table 8.2 are the annual sales in £m by 5 supermarket chains in the 4 regions of the UK. Enter the data to a new workbook and then prepare charts to answer the following questions.

(i) In which region does Cesto sell the highest proportion of its total sales?
(ii) Which supermarket has got the highest share of the Scottish market?
(iii) Which region has the lowest share of the UK market?
(iv) Which supermarket has got the highest share of the entire UK market?

Exercise 8.7

Load the data contained in Workbook 8.5 (W8_5.XLS). Now use Excel statistical functions to calculate the mean, median, and mode of both the number of car occupants and the age of those occupants.

When you have finished, save this file as W8_24.XLS.

Exercise 8.8

Load the data contained in Workbook 8.24 (W8_24.XLS). Now use Excel statistical functions to calculate the variance and the standard deviation of both the number of car occupants and the age of those occupants. What conclusions can be drawn from these statistics?

When you have finished, save this file as W8_25.XLS.

Exercise 8.9

Load the data contained in Workbook 8.25 (W8_25.XLS). By computing the coefficient of variation for both the number of occupants and the age of those occupants, determine which of the 2 data sets has the greatest degree of relative dispersion.

When you have finished, save this file as W8_26.XLS.

Exercise 8.10

Make up Workbook 8.19 or load it from the accompanying disk (W8_19.XLS).

(*a*) Use the Excel Data Filtering device in conjunction with appropriate SUBTOTAL functions to complete Table 8.3.

(*b*) Use the worksheet prepared in part (*a*) to determine:

(i) The subject in which females performed best.
(ii) The subject in which males performed best.
(iii) The subject in which females performed worst.
(iv) The subject in which males performed worst.
(v) The subject with the least dispersion of marks for students aged under 18.
(vi) The subject with the greatest dispersion of marks for students aged over 20.

(*c*) Use the worksheet prepared in part (*a*) to complete Table 8.4 and then make some comments about the relative performance of the different groups of students in the different subjects.

When you have finished, save this file as W8_27.XLS.

Table 8.3	MARK OBTAINED IN ECONOMICS	COUNT	ARITHMETIC MEAN	STANDARD DEVIATION	MAXIMUM	MINIMUM
	Females					
	Males					
	Aged under 18					
	Aged over 30					
	Males with over 40% in Maths					
	Females with under 40% in Law					
	Females aged under 20					
	Males aged under 20					
	Over 40% in both Law and Maths					

Table 8.4		FEMALES AGED UNDER 20	MALES AGED UNDER 20	FEMALES AGED 18 OR OVER	MALES AGED 18 OR OVER
	LAW mean				
	LAW std. devn.				
	MATHS mean				
	MATHS std. devn.				
	ACCOUNTS mean				
	ACCOUNTS std. devn.				
	INFOTECH mean				
	INFOTECH std. devn.				
	ECONOMICS mean				
	ECONOMICS std. devn.				
	STATS mean				
	STATS std. devn.				

8.8. Solutions to the exercises

Solution to Exercise 8.1

Keep the Input Range as A1:A101 but redefine the bin values in B2:B4 as 1, 3, and 5. Make sure the Labels tab is checked.

Output the results to C1 and do not check any of the tabs below the Output Range tab. Something resembling Workbook 8.20 should be obtained.

Solution to Exercise 8.2

(i) Keep the Input Range as A1:A101 but redefine the bin values in B2:B4 as 1, 4, and 5.

Make sure the Labels tab is checked. Output the results to C1 and check the Cumulative Percentage tab.

(ii) Check the Chart Output tab and repeat the previous Histogram routine. The results should resemble Workbook 8.21.

(iii) 93%

(iv) 100% - 22% = 78%.

Solution to Exercise 8.3

(i) Keep the Input Range as B1:B253 but redefine the bin values in C2:C5 as 15, 20, 40,

```
┌────────────────────────────────────────────────────────────────────────────────┐
│ ─          Microsoft Excel - W8_19.XLS          🗗 🗔 🗔 🗔 🗔 🗔  ▼ ▲         │
│ ─  File   Edit   View   Insert   Format   Tools   Data   Window   Help      ▲   │
│ ┌──┬──┬──┬──┬──┬──┬──┬──┬──┬──┬──┬──┬──┬──┬──┬──┬──┬──┐                          │
│ │  │  │  │  │  │  │  │ Σ │ ƒ │  │  │  │  │  │ 100% │ ▼ │                          │
│                                                                                  │
│     A         B       C    D    E       F         G          H          I          J          │
│  1 Surname  Initial  Age  Sex  Law%   Maths %  Accounts %  Infotech %  Economics %  Stats %  │
│  2 Aitken    R       17   F     45      78        56          92          8          72       │
│  3 Arnold    S       18   F     67      56        58          91          23         51       │
│  4 Brown     H       18   M     56      82        54          85          57         80       │
│  5 Carter    F       24   F     21      56        39          87          89         58       │
│  6 Dodds     E       37   M     48      12        38          79          76         19       │
│  7 Draper    O       45   F     83      51        45          78          12         54       │
│  8 Fraser    H       17   F     24      58        47          69          24         59       │
│  9 French    D       18   M     36      72        48          92          13         75       │
│ 10 Hastie    E       19   M     79      90        38          95          87         93       │
│ 11 Jones     R       17   F     67      21        53          83          88         26       │
│ 12 Masters   P       21   M     56      25        57          85          43         21       │
│ 13 Naylor    D       24   F     54      67        54          86          35         69       │
│ 14 Roberts   L       43   F     24      69        38          88          37         70       │
│ 15 Smith     P       51   M     79      61        45          76          34         64       │
│ 16 Taylor    K       19   F     82      56        47          78          78         59       │
│ 17 Turner    W       17   M     45      45        48          73          60         48       │
│ 18 Walters   J       19   M     40      49        51          74          21         47       │
│ 19 West      D       18   F     38      79        38          69          35         80       │
│ 20 Wright    M       21   F     59      80        39          92          56         79       │
│ 21                                                                               │
│ ◄ ◄ ► ►◄ Sheet1 / Sheet2 / Sheet3 / Sheet4 / Sheet5 / Sheet ◄                  │
└────────────────────────────────────────────────────────────────────────────────┘
```

Workbook 8.19

,and 60. Output the results to D1 and check the Cumulative Percentage tab. The results are shown in Workbook 8.22.

(ii) 50% are 40 or less.

(iii) 21.2% are 20 or less. So 100% - 21.2 % = 78.8% are over 20.

(iv) 74.8% are 60 or less (i.e. not over 60),

Workbook 8.20

and 13.6% are 15 or less. Therefore, 74.8% - 13.6% = 61.2% are over 15 but not over 60.

Solution to Exercise 8.4

When Excel is allowed to choose the bin values for itself it does so as indicated in Workbook 8.23. As you can see, the bin values are not whole numbers, and so are rather unsatisfactory in the context of this data set where the number of occupants is clearly a discrete variable.

```
┌────────────────────────────────────────────────────────────────────────────────┐
│ ─          Microsoft Excel - W8_20.XLS          🗗 🗔 🗔 🗔 🗔 🗔  ▼ ▲         │
│ ─  File   Edit   View   Insert   Format   Tools   Data   Window   Help      ▲   │
│ ┌──┬──┬──┬──┬──┬──┬──┬──┬──┬──┬──┬──┬──┬──┬──┬──┬──┬──┐                          │
│ │  │  │  │  │  │  │  │ Σ │ ƒ │  │  │  │  │  │ 100% │ ▼ │                          │
│     D8      ▼                                                                     │
│        A                B              C        D        E    F    G    H        │
│  1 No. of occupants  No. of occupants  Bin   Frequency                           │
│  2        1                1            1        22                               │
│  3        2                3            3        59                               │
│  4        1                5            5        19                               │
│  5        3             More                     0                                │
│  6 ◄ ◄ ► ►◄ Sheet1 / Sheet2 / Sheet3 / Sheet4 / Sheet5 / Sheet ◄               │
└────────────────────────────────────────────────────────────────────────────────┘
```

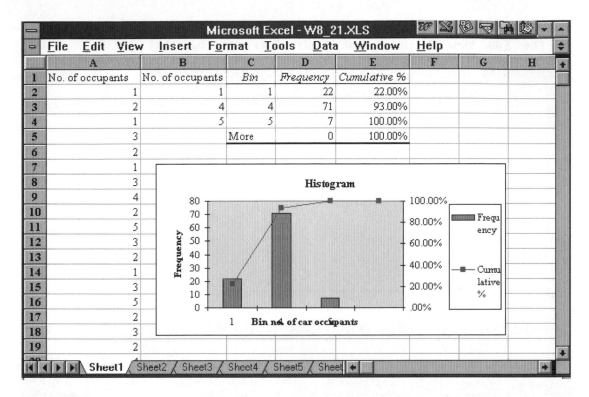

Workbook
8.21

Solution to Exercise 8.5

Load Worksheet 8.11 and then immediately Save As W8_18.XLS. Now replace the data in C4:C14 with the new data for country B given in Workbook 8.18 above. The new calculations will be performed automatically for this new data.

The chart will now change automatically to produce the Lorenz curve for the country B data, and should resemble Fig. 8.10.

As you can see by comparing Fig. 8.3 with Fig. 8.10, in country A approximately

87% of the population earn roughly 68% of the total income. Whereas in country B the equivalent approximate figures are 88% and 58%.

Solution to Exercise 8.6

Enter the data to the A1:F5 range of a workbook. Click on the Chart Wizard icon and then draw a frame. Define the data range as A1:F5 and then click Next to proceed through the Chart Wizard prompts.

(i) Since this question asks for the share of

Workbook
8.22

	A	B	C	D	E	F	G	H	I
	No. of occupants	Age	Age	Bin	Frequency	Cumulative %			
1	1	24.07	15	15	34	13.60%			
2	2	49.42	20	20	19	21.20%			
3		34.78	40	40	72	50.00%			
4	1	62.13	60	60	62	74.80%			
5	3	29.69		More	63	100.00%			
6		49.91							

	A	B	C	D	E	F	G	H
1	No. of occupants	*Bin*	*Frequency*	*Cumulative %*				
2	1	1	22	22.00%				
3	2	1.4	0	22.00%				
4	1	1.8	0	22.00%				
5	3	2.2	32	54.00%				
6	2	2.6	0	54.00%				
7	1	3	27	81.00%				
8	3	3.4	0	81.00%				
9	4	3.8	0	81.00%				
10	2	4.2	12	93.00%				
11	5	4.6	0	93.00%				
12	3	More	7	100.00%				
13	2							
14	1							

Workbook 8.23

total sales, we will use a percentage component Column chart (Column type, Option 5). Also, since we require the supermarkets to be on the horizontal axis, tell Excel to view the data in rows and use the 1st row for the X axis labels and the 1st column for the legend text. After adding titles the chart should resemble Fig. 8.11. From this figure it is

clear that, proportionately, Cesto sells most of its produce in England.

(ii) Double click on the current chart and then click on the Chart Wizard icon. Accept the defined data range by clicking on Next, and then from the screen that appears tell Excel to view the data series as being in columns. Edit the titles to produce Fig. 8.12.

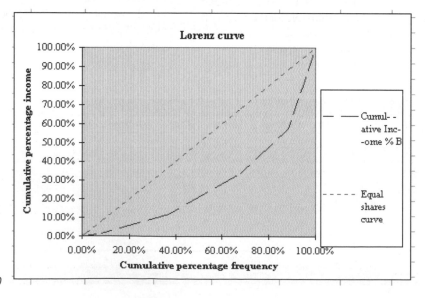

Figure 8.10

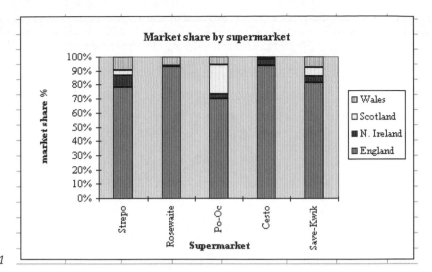

Figure 8.11

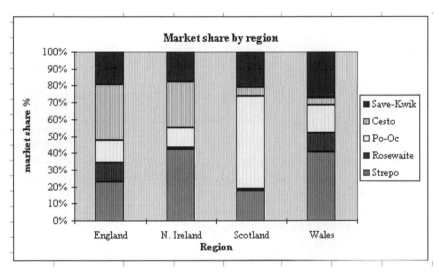

Figure 8.12

From this chart it is clear that in the Scottish market, Po-Oc has the biggest share.

(iii) Total the sales of each region in column G from the formulae in G2:

=SUM(B2:F2)

and copy this into G3:G5.

Use the Chart Wizard to draw a frame and define the data range as:

A2:A5,G2:G5

Select Pie for the type of chart and then Option 7. Fig. 8.13 will be produced. From this pie chart it is clear that Northern Ireland has the smallest share of all supermarket sales.

(iv) Total the sales of each supermarket in row 6 from the formulae in B6:

=SUM(B2:B5)

and copy this into C6:F6. Use the Chart Wizard to draw a frame and define the data range as:

B1:F1,B6:F6

Select Pie for the type of chart and then Option 7. Fig. 8.14 will be produced. Clearly the highest share of the UK market is attributable to Cesto.

Solution to Exercise 8.7

The results are shown in Workbook 8.24. As you can see, the returned value for the modal age is 0.78. However, this would not be the case if the data were measured to the nearest

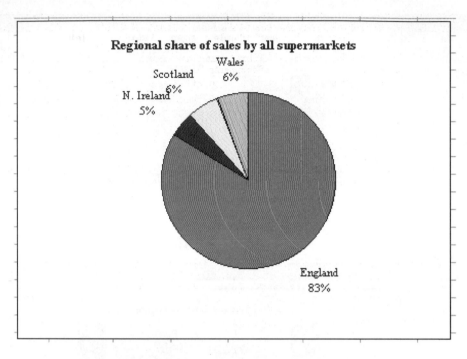

Figure 8.13

year. To see this, use the H2 cell of the worksheet to contain:

=ROUND(B2,0)

i.e. round the contents of B2 to 0 decimal places. Then copy H2 into H3:H252.

Now use I1 to contain:

=MODE(H2:H251)

and confirm that for this data set the most frequently observed age, when measured to the nearest year, is 30.

Solution to Exercise 8.8

The results are shown in Workbook 8.25. As measured by the variance and the standard deviation, it is clear that the dispersion in the Age variable is considerably greater than for the Number of occupants variable.

This is only to be expected, since there is clearly much more variation that can take place in the age of the occupants than in the number of occupants. (We would however,

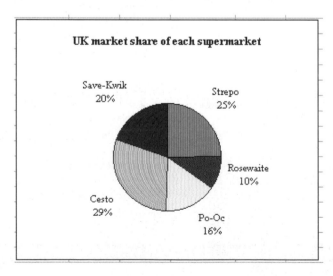

Figure 8.14

Microsoft Excel - W8_24.XLS

File Edit View Insert Format Tools Data Window Help

	A	B	C	D	E	F	G
1	No. of occupants	Age		No. of occupants	FORMULA	Age	FORMULA
2	1	24.07	**Mean**	2.50	=AVERAGE(A2:A251)	40.38	=AVERAGE(B2:B251)
3	2	49.42	**Median**	2.00	=MEDIAN(A2:A251)	40.25	=MEDIAN(B2:B251)
4		34.78	**Mode**	2.00	=MODE(A2:A251)	0.78	=MODE(B2:B251)
5	1	62.13					
6	3	29.69					
7		49.91					

Sheet1 / Sheet2 / Sheet3 / Sheet4 / Sheet5 / Sheet

Workbook 8.24

Microsoft Excel - W8_25.XLS

File Edit View Insert Format Tools Data Window Help

	A	B	C	D	E	F	G
1	No. of occupants	Age		No. of occupants	FORMULA	Age	FORMULA
2	1	24.07	**Mean**	2.50	=AVERAGE(A2:A251)	40.38	=AVERAGE(B2:B251)
3	2	49.42	**Median**	2.00	=MEDIAN(A2:A251)	40.25	=MEDIAN(B2:B251)
4		34.78	**Mode**	2.00	=MODE(A2:A251)	0.78	=MODE(B2:B251)
5	1	62.13	**Variance**	1.35	=VARP(A2:A251)	506.13	=VARP(B2:B251)
6	3	29.69	**St. Devn.**	1.16	=STDEVP(A2:A251)	22.50	=STDEVP(B2:B251)
7		49.91					
8		61.99					

Sheet1 / Sheet2 / Sheet3 / Sheet4 / Sheet5 / Sheet

Workbook 8.25

expect the measured difference in dispersion to be reduced if, for example, it had been coaches rather than cars that formed the basis of the study.)

Workbook 8.26

Solution to Exercise 8.9

The solution is shown in Workbook 8.26. As the coefficients of variation indicate, even when allowance is made for the fact that age and number of occupants are measured in different units, the relative dispersion of the ages is almost 21% greater than that for the number of occupants.

Microsoft Excel - W8_26.XLS

File Edit View Insert Format Tools Data Window Help

	B	C	D	E	F	G	H	I
1	Age		No. of occupants	FORMULA	Age	FORMULA		
2	24.07	**Mean**	2.50	=AVERAGE(A2:A251)	40.38	=AVERAGE(B2:B251)		
3	49.42	**Median**	2.00	=MEDIAN(A2:A251)	40.25	=MEDIAN(B2:B251)		
4	34.78	**Mode**	2.00	=MODE(A2:A251)	0.78	=MODE(B2:B251)		
5	62.13	**Variance**	1.35	=VARP(A2:A251)	506.13	=VARP(B2:B251)		
6	29.69	**St. Devn.**	1.16	=STDEVP(A2:A251)	22.50	=STDEVP(B2:B251)		
7	49.91	**CV**	46.47580015	=100*D6/D2	55.72	=100*F6/F2		

Sheet1 / Sheet2 / Sheet3 / Sheet4 / Sheet5 / Sheet

Table 8.5

MARK OBTAINED IN ECONOMICS	COUNT	ARITHMETIC MEAN	STANDARD DEVIATION	MAXIMUM	MINIMUM
Females	11	44.09	28.01	89	8
Males	8	48.88	24.24	87	13
Aged under 18	4	45	31.16	88	8
Aged over 30	4	39.75	23.05	76	12
Males with over 40% in Maths	6	45.33	25.34	87	13
Females with under 40% in Law	4	46.25	25.17	89	24
Females aged under 20	6	42.67	29.72	88	8
Males aged under 20	5	47.6	27.2	87	13
Over 40% in both Law and Maths	10	45	25.51	87	8

Solution to Exercise 8.10

Define the data list as A1:J20 and then switch the Autofilter on. Enter the numbers 1, 2, 4, 5, 8, and 11 to the A22:A27 range and then the labels AVERAGE, COUNT, MAX, MIN, STDEVP, and VARP to the B22:B27 range.

Then, in E22 enter the formula:

=SUBTOTAL($A22,E$2:E$20)

and copy this into E23:J27.

The worksheet now contains the summary statistics for the unfiltered list.

(*a*) To fill in the table, click on the appropriate field filter tab, select the required filter and note the results. These are shown in Table 8.5.

(*b*) Once again use appropriate filters to produce the summary statistics for the selected list of observations and then choose the subject that meets the requirements of the question.

(i)   Infotech (mean = 83)
(ii)   Infotech (mean = 82.38)
(iii) Economics (mean = 44.09)
(iv)   Accounts (mean = 47.28)
(v)   Accounts (standard deviation = 3.67)
(vi)   Economics (standard deviation = 23.28)

(*c*) The completed table is shown in Table 8.6. The calculated statistics would suggest the following general conclusions.

Table 8.6

	FEMALES AGED UNDER 20	MALES AGED UNDER 20	FEMALES AGED 18 OR OVER	MALES AGED 18 OR OVER
LAW mean	53.83	51.2	53.5	56.29
LAW std. devn.	19.83	15.43	22.53	15.93
MATHS mean	58	67.6	64.25	55.86
MATHS std. devn.	19.23	17.81	10.46	26.88
ACCOUNTS mean	49.83	47.8	44.75	47.29
ACCOUNTS std. devn.	9.3	5.38	7.28	6.88
INFOTECH mean	80.33	83.8	83.63	83.71
INFOTECH std. devn.	9.3	9.02	7.4	7.32
ECONOMICS mean	42.67	47.6	45.63	47.29
ECONOMICS std. devn.	29.72	27.2	24.95	25.52
STATS mean	57.83	68.6	65	57
STATS std. devn.	17.1	18.21	10.39	26.38

(i) Males under 20 seem to be considerably better at MATHS than their female counterparts. The opposite is true for the 18 or over age group. (Notice that 18- and 19-year-olds will be included in both of these groups.)

(ii) The ACCOUNTS marks, although not producing the highest mean score for any of the groups, are clearly the least dispersed, meaning that very few students did exceptionally well or exceptionally badly.

(iii) The ECONOMICS marks have a similar mean to those for ACCOUNTS, but unlike the latter, the dispersion was very large for all of the student groups. There were therefore a number of students with extremes of good and poor performance.

(iv) The patterns observed for the MATHS marks are repeated for the STATS marks (perhaps not surprisingly, since both are quantitative subjects and skills in one can be transferred easily to the other).

(v) The INFOTECH marks are clearly the highest, with a very low degree of dispersion across all of the student groups. In fact, the marks are so high with so little dispersion in comparison to those for the other subjects that one would want to question either the standard of the examination or the rigour of the marking, or both.

Further descriptive statistical methods

Contents

Accompanying data files to be loaded as instructed:

W8_5.XLS   W9_1.XLS   W9_18.XLS   W9_19A.XLS   W9_21.XLS   W9_22.XLS   W9_23.XLS

9.1. Calculating the mean, variance, and standard deviation from frequency distributions

The previous chapter has indicated the techniques and statistical measures used in the description of simple data sets. However, sometimes the nature of the data require the use of additional descriptive measures and/or the development of further methods of computing the standard statistical measures.

As an illustration of the latter, consider Workbook 9.1. Here, the data from Workbook 8.5 has been reproduced with a few amendments.

	A	B	C	D	E	F	G	H
	Microsoft Excel - W9_1.XLS							
	File **Edit** **View** **Insert** **Format** **Tools** **Data** **Window** **Help**							
	A	B	C	D	E	F	G	H
1	Mean	Mean	Occupants	*Bin*	*Frequency*			
2	2.50	40.38	1	1	22			
3	Variance	Variance	2	2	32			
4	1.35	506.13	3	3	27			
5	Standard deviation	Standard deviation	4	4	12			
6	1.16	22.50	5	5	7			
7	No. of occupants	Age		More	0			
8	1	24.07						
9	2	49.42						
10		34.78						
11	1	62.13	Age	*Bin*	*Frequency*			
12	3	29.69	10	10	26			
13		49.91	20	20	27			
14		61.99	30	30	40			
15	2	18.45	40	40	32			
16		23.21	50	50	39			
17	1	69.30	60	60	23			
18	3	77.46	70	70	32			
19		22.33	80	80	29			
20		76.55	90	90	2			
21	4	61.25	More		0			
22		81.64						
23		17.68						

Sheet1 / Sheet2 / Sheet3 / Sheet4 / Sheet5 / Sheet

Workbook 9.1

Load Workbook 9.1 (W9_1.XLS) now.

First, the mean, variance, and standard deviation of both the number of occupants and their ages have been placed at the top of the sheet under appropriate labels. These are for comparison purposes later in the discussion. Second, the Histogram routine was used to prepare absolute frequency distributions of both variables (number of occupants and age) as indicated. Now imagine that after these frequency distributions have been created, both raw data sets were destroyed and hence, along with them, the ability to compute the means, variances, and standard deviations.

The question that arises is whether, in the absence of the raw data, the frequency distributions provide sufficient information to allow us to calculate the means, variances, and standard deviations. The answer is a qualified 'yes', the qualification being that when frequency distributions are used, the computed values for the mean, variance, and standard deviation will only be estimates of their true values. This is because the collation of the data into frequency distributions will usually (but not always) involve some loss of raw data.

For example, with the data on the number of occupants, the fact that every possible value for this data set was included in the bin means that, by working backwards, the frequency distribution can be used to recreate the raw data set perfectly. In this case therefore, the estimate of the mean, variance, and standard deviation will be identical with the statistics obtained from the raw data.

This is not the case, however, for the age data. Here, class intervals of 10 years were used and so the frequencies for each class interval do not tell us enough about the actual values that were observed, apart from the fact that they were located in those intervals. It would, for example be impossible to replicate the raw data set perfectly, if only the frequency distribution data were available.

Clearly, in this case, any calculation to be performed must assume that the actual values were evenly distributed throughout each class interval, and if this were indeed the case then the estimated values for the mean, variance, and standard deviation would be fairly accurate. However, to the extent that the actual values are not evenly distributed within each class interval, error will occur, and the calculated estimates will differ from the true values.

This means that when we are only presented with frequency distribution data, calculation of the mean, variance, and standard deviation becomes slightly more difficult, since there are no dedicated Excel statistical functions that can be employed.

Nevertheless, Excel will still be of value in writing the formulae that have to be used. Considering the data on the number of occupants first, we can start by calculating the arithmetic mean as follows.

The total number of occupants in the 100 cars is:

$$(1 + 1 + \ldots + 1) + (2 + 2 + \ldots + 2) + (3 + 3 + \ldots + 3) + (4 + 4 + \ldots + 4) +$$
(22 terms)   (32 terms)   (27 terms)   (12 terms)
$$(5 + 5 + \ldots + 5)$$
   (7 terms)

Thus the total arithmetic worth of these observations can be obtained by multiplying each different x value (number of occupants) by its corresponding frequency (number of times which that occupancy value occurred) and then summing these products:

$$\Sigma f_i x_i = f_1 x_1 + f_2 x_2 + f_3 x_3 + f_4 x_4 + f_5 x_5 = 22(1) + 32(2) + 27(3) + 12(4) + 7(5) = 250$$

This is the total arithmetic worth of all the observed x values i.e. the total number of occupants.

Furthermore, since the total number of cars = Σf_i = 100, it follows that the arithmetic mean for this frequency distribution will be given by:

$$\bar{x} = \Sigma f_i x_i / \Sigma f_i = 250/100 = 2.5 \text{ occupants per car.}$$

We can now use columns E and F of the current worksheet to perform these calculations.

First, in E8 calculate the total number of frequencies (cars) from the formula:

=SUM(E2:E6)

Then, in F1 enter the label:

fx

and in F2 the formula:

$=D2*E2$

and copy this into F3:F6.

This will compute the arithmetic worth of each of the 5 different observed x values.

Next, compute the total arithmetic worth in F8 from:

$=SUM(F2:F6)$

Finally, compute the arithmetic mean number of occupants in F9 from:

$=F8/E8$

and add the label:

Mean $=$

to the E9 cell.

As we predicted, because this frequency distribution could recreate the raw data exactly the estimated mean and the true mean are identical (2.5 occupants in both cases).

To compute the variance and the standard deviation directly from the frequency distribution we require to employ the same principles.

Clearly, since there are 100 observations there will be 100 deviations and 100 squared deviations from the mean that has just been computed in the F9 cell. Thus the deviations from the mean for each distinct value of x are:

$(x_i - \bar{x}) = (1 - 2.5)$	$(2 - 2.5)$	$(3 - 2.5)$	$(4 - 2.5)$	$(5 - 2.5)$
$(x_i - \bar{x}) = -1.5$	-0.5	0.5	1.5	2.5

The squared deviations are therefore:

$(x_i - \bar{x})^2 = (1 - 2.5)^2$	$(2 - 2.5)^2$	$(3 - 2.5)^2$	$(4 - 2.5)^2$	$(5 - 2.5)^2$
$(x_i - \bar{x})^2 = (-1.5)^2$	$(-0.5)^2$	$(0.5)^2$	$(1.5)^2$	$(2.5)^2$
$(x_i - \bar{x})^2 = 2.25$	0.25	0.25	2.25	6.25

Once again, however, the arithmetic worth of each of these squared deviations must be computed on the basis of the number of times that the particular squared deviation occurred. Thus, there are a total of 22 observations of x = 1 and therefore a total of 22 squared deviations of 2.25.

Their arithmetic worth is therefore:

$22(2.25)$

A similar logic applies for the rest of the individual squared deviations, and so the total sum of squared deviations (SSD) is:

$$SSD = 22(2.25) + 32(0.25) + 27(0.25) + 12(2.25) + 7(6.25) = 135$$

Given that the figures inside brackets are the individual squared deviations and the figures attached to them are the frequencies associated with those squared deviations, it therefore follows that:

$$SSD = f_1(x_1 - \bar{x})^2 + f_2(x_2 - \bar{x})^2 + \ldots + f_5(x_5 - \bar{x})^2 = \Sigma f_i(x_i - \bar{x})^2$$

Lastly, to standardize for the number of observations, we obtain the variance by dividing the SSD by the total number of observations. As with the calculations for the mean, the number of observations is given by the sum of the frequencies (Σf_i), and so the variance is given by:

$$\text{Variance} = \Sigma f_i(x_i - \bar{x})^2 / \Sigma f_i$$

and the standard deviation by:

Standard deviation = $\text{Variance}^{0.5}$

To put these ideas into practice in the worksheet, we need to use a new column (H).

First, in H1 enter the label:[1]

$f(x - \text{mean})^2$

Next, in H2 enter the formula:

=E2*(D2-F$9)^2

This is the first squared deviation times its frequency, with the dollar sign attached to the F9 reference ensuring that it will always be the F9 cell (the mean) that is subtracted when copying is done.

Now copy H2 into H3:H6
Next, in H8 enter:

=SUM(H2:H6)

This computes the SSD.

Finally, to compute the variance number of occupants use H9 to contain:

=H8/E8

i.e. the SSD divided by the sum of the frequencies.

Then take the square root of the variance to obtain the standard deviation by using H10 to contain:

=H9^0.5

The worksheet should now resemble Workbook 9.2.

Microsoft Excel - W9_2.XLS

	A	B	C	D	E	F	G	H
1	Mean	Mean	Occupants	Bin	Frequency	fx		f(x - mean)²
2	2.50	40.38	1	1	22	22		49.5
3	Variance	Variance	2	2	32	64		8
4	1.35	506.13	3	3	27	81		6.75
5	Standard deviation	Standard deviation	4	4	12	48		27
6	1.16	22.50	5	5	7	35		43.75
7	No. of occupants	Age		More	0			
8	1	24.07			100	250		135
9	2	49.42		Mean =		2.5	variance	1.35
10		34.78					std dev.	1.161895004

Sheet1 / Sheet2 / Sheet3 / Sheet4 / Sheet5 / Sheet

Workbook 9.2

As predicted earlier, these estimates of the variance and standard deviation are identical to the true values obtained from the raw data. This is entirely due to the fact that the data were whole numbers and that the values used in the frequency distribution were able to recreate the raw original data set perfectly.

When we address the age data, the fact that the frequency distribution used class intervals creates a problem that has already been encountered—namely, which of the interval

---

1 To obtain the power symbol, enter the text as f(x - mean)2, then, on the Formula bar, click and drag on the 2, select Format, Cells, and then Superscript.

values of x to use. Once again, the remedy is to use the midpoint values of the intervals as representative of the x values.

Consequently, and still using Workbook 9.2, in F11 enter the label:

X_m

and then fill F12:F20 with the values:

5	15	25	35	45	55	65	75	85

These are the midpoint values of each of the class intervals.

Thereafter, the procedure is the same as with the data on the number of occupants explained above. Therefore:

use G11 to contain the label:

fX_m

and G12 to contain the formula:

=E12*F12

Then copy G12 into G13:G20.
   In E22 sum the frequencies from:

=SUM(E12:E20)

and compute ΣfX_m in G22 from:

=SUM(G12:G20)

Finally, calculate the mean in F23 from:

=G22/E22

To compute the variance age of the occupants in H11, add the label:

$f(X_m - mean)^2$

and in H12 the formula:

=E12*(F12-F$23)^2

Then copy this into H13:H20.
   Next, in H22 calculate the SSD from:

=SUM(H12:H20)

and the variance in H23 from:

=H22/E22

The standard deviation can then be computed in H24 from:

=H23^0.5

When these calculations have been completed and appropriate labels added, the results should resemble the section of Workbook 9.3 shown.

Workbook 9.3

Save this model now as W9_3.XLS.

As you can see, the values for the mean, variance, and standard deviation age of occupants calculated from the frequency distribution are not exactly the same as those obtained from the original raw data. The errors are not huge, but they none the less exist, and represent the difference between the actual values of the mean and the standard deviation and the estimated values.

	Microsoft Excel - W9_3.XLS						

File Edit View Insert Format Tools Data Window Help

H23   =H22/E22

	A	B	C	D	E	F	G	H
				Bin	Frequency	X_m	fX_m	$f(X_m - mean)^2$
11	1	62.13 Age						
12	3	29.69	10	10	26	5	130	32582.16
13		49.91	20	20	27	15	405	17419.32
14		61.99	30	30	40	25	1000	9486.40
15	2	18.45	40	40	32	35	1120	933.12
16		23.21	50	50	39	45	1755	825.24
17	1	69.30	60	60	23	55	1265	4902.68
18	3	77.46	70	70	32	65	2080	19365.12
19		22.35	80	80	29	75	2175	34717.64
20		76.55	90	90	2	85	170	3978.32
21	4	61.25		More	0			
22		81.64			250		10100	124210
23		17.68			mean =	40.4	variance	496.84
24		71.85					std dev.	22.28990803
25	2	40.58						
26		14.47						

Sheet1 / Sheet2 / Sheet3 / Sheet4 / Sheet5 / Sheet

Workbook 9.3

The extent of such errors will depend upon two things. First of all is the class intervals used to create the frequency distribution, and therefore the values of the midpoints. The fewer the number of intervals (i.e. the wider the class interval), the greater the likelihood of the errors being large.

Second is the extent to which the raw data are evenly distributed within each of the class intervals. If this distribution is completely even, the midpoint values will be fairly representative and the estimation error will tend to be small. On the other hand, if many of the actual observations are concentrated at the top or at the bottom of the intervals, the midpoint values will underestimate or overestimate the actual worth of the values in the interval, and the scope for estimation error increases.

Exercise 9.1 can be attempted now.

9.2. Alternative measures of dispersion

The variance and the standard deviation measure dispersion in relation to the mean. However, in Chapter 8 we saw that for certain data sets the mean is not always the most appropriate measure of central tendency. In such circumstances the question therefore arises of how to measure dispersion in a way that is not related to the mean.

One answer is to split the data into what are known as **quartiles**. These are denoted by Q_1, Q_2, Q_3, and Q_4 and are respectively defined as:

the value of the variable (x) below which 25%, 50%, 75%, and 100% of the observations lie

Thus, Q_2 is simply the median since we already have this defined as the value of x above and below which 50% of the observations lie. Also Q_4 will simply be the maximum value in the data set, since 100% of the observation must be less than or equal to this value.

Q_1 and Q_3 are known respectively as the lower and upper quartiles, since 25% of the observations will lie below a value of $x = Q_1$ (75% will therefore lie above this value), while 25% of the observations will lie above a value of $x = Q_3$ (with 75% therefore lying below this value).

Consequently, it also follows that 50% of the observations will lie between the lower and the upper quartiles. This range between the upper and lower quartiles is known as the **interquartile range**, and is simply defined as:

Interquartile range $= Q_3 - Q_1$

The interquartile range is clearly a crude measure of dispersion, since it can be related to the overall range (the maximum value of x minus the minimum value of x) to give an indication of the extent to which the middle 50% of observations span a range of x values that is large or small in relation to the overall range of values that x adopts.

For example, consider 2 data sets (A and B) with the following ranges and interquartile ranges.

	Data set A	Data set B
Range	£500	£500
Interquartile range	£400	£250

Clearly, the middle 50% of observations in data set A cover a range of x values that is much larger in relation to the overall range (£400:£500) than is the case in data set B (£250:£500). Thus although both data sets span the same overall range, data set A is much more dispersed within this overall range than data set B.

We can get Excel to calculate the quartiles for any data set from its =QUARTILE function, the general syntax of which is:

=QUARTILE(Data range,Required quartile)

Workbook 8.5

To see how this works, load Workbook 8.5.

Here we have the data on car occupancy and the age of those occupants, and the task is to calculate the quartiles for both data sets.

First, use C1:E1 to contain the labels:

Quartile   Occupants   Age

and then fill C2:C5 with the numbers 1, 2, 3, and 4.

These are the 4 values that the second argument of the =QUARTILE function can adopt.
Next, in D2 enter:

=QUARTILE(A$2:A$251,$C2)

and copy this into D3:D5.
Next, copy D2:D5 into E2:E5 to obtain the quartiles for the age data set.

Finally, to confirm our previous suggestion that the second quartile is simply the median we should calculate the latter.

So, in C6 enter the label:

Median

and in D6 the formula:

=MEDIAN(A2:A251)

Then copy D6 into E6 to obtain the median for the age data.

The results should resemble Workbook 9.4.

Workbook 9.4

Save this file now as W9_4.XLS.

Now it is an easy matter to calculate the interquartile ranges for each data set. Thus:

for the number of occupants: $Q_3 - Q_1 = 3 - 2 = 1$ occupant
for the ages of the occupants: $Q_3 - Q_1 = 60.12 - 21.99 = 38.13$ years

The interquartile range should always be employed to indicate dispersion when the median has been adopted as the most appropriate measure of central tendency. However, although simple to compute, it is generally less satisfactory as a measure of dispersion than the variance. This is because it takes into account the spread of only 2 values of the variable (the upper and lower quartile values) and therefore gives no indication of the rest of the dispersion within the distribution.

On the other hand, if a data set contains one or two extreme observations, then the fact that the mean is much more sensitive to these extreme values than is the median suggests that the interquartile range may be a more appropriate measure of dispersion than the variance or the standard deviation.

Finally, it will often be useful to classify the data into percentiles rather than quartiles. This is easily done with Excel's =PERCENTILE function, which has the following general syntax.

=PERCENTILE(Data range, Required percentile)

For example, if the **deciles** are required, then use 10%, 20%, . . . 100% as the second arguments of the functions.

Do this now in the current workbook by making the following entries.
   In C7:E7 enter the labels:

Percentile   Occupants   Age

and in C8:C17 enter the percentile values either as decimals (0.1, 0.2 etc.) or as actual percentages (10%, 20% etc.).
   Next, in D8 enter the formula:

=PERCENTILE(A$2:A$251,$C8)

and copy this into D9:D17.
Then copy D8:D17 into E8:E17.

The results should resemble Workbook 9.5.

	A	B	C	D	E	F	G	H	I
	No. of occupants	Age	Quartile	Occupants	Age				
1									
2	1	24.07	1	2	21.9875				
3	2	49.42	2	2	40.25				
4		34.78	3	3	60.1175				
5	1	62.13	4	5	83.79				
6	3	29.69	Median	2	40.25				
7		49.91	Percentile	Occupants	Age				
8		61.99	0.10	1	9.368				
9	2	18.45	0.20	1	19.05				
10		23.21	0.30	2	25				
11	1	69.30	0.40	2	32.002				
12	3	77.46	0.50	2	40.25				
13		22.35	0.60	3	46.366				
14		76.55	0.70	3	55.558				
15	4	61.25	0.80	3	64.654				
16		81.64	0.90	4	71.232				
17		17.68	1.00	5	83.79				
18		71.85							
19	2	40.58							
20		14.47							

Microsoft Excel - W9_5.XLS

File Edit View Insert Format Tools Data Window Help

E8 — =PERCENTILE(B$2:B$251,$C8)

Sheet1 / Sheet2 / Sheet3 / Sheet4 / Sheet5 / Sheet

Workbook 9.5

Now save this model as W9_5.XLS.

As with the quartile analysis, various interpercentile ranges can be computed. Thus, for example, the middle 80% of observations lie between $P_{90\%}$ and $P_{10\%}$ and span a range of x values given by:

$$P_{90\%} - P_{10\%} = 71.232 - 9.368 = 61.864$$

Exercise 9.2 can be attempted now.

9.3. Further descriptive measures of data sets

As was suggested in Chapter 8, data sets are like individuals and can be described in terms of a number of characteristics. So far in the discussion we have only considered 2 descriptive characteristics—central tendency and dispersion. But 2 more characteristics require measurement before we possess the ability to distinguish accurately between data sets.

The first of these characteristics is known as **skewness**, and can be thought of as the extent to which a graph of the frequency distribution is off-centre or asymmetric. The second characteristic is the extent to which the graph of the frequency distribution is very pointed with wide tails or humped with short tails. This peakedness characteristic is known as **kurtosis.**

9.3.1. Skewness

Skewness characterizes the degree of asymmetry of a distribution around its mean value. Positive skewness indicates a distribution with an asymmetric tail extending towards more positive values. Negative skewness indicates a distribution with an asymmetric tail extending towards more negative values.

Excel calculates skewness from the function:

=SKEW(Data range)

Notice that if there are fewer than three data values, or the sample standard deviation is zero, =SKEW returns the #DIV/0! error value.[2]

For example, to calculate the skewness of the data on the number of occupants we proceed as follows.

Workbook 8.5

Load Workbook 8.5 (W8_5.XLS).

> **Then in D1 enter the label:**
>
> skewness
>
> **and in D2 and E2 the labels:**
>
> Occupants   Age
>
> **In D3 enter the formula:**
>
> =SKEW(A2:A252)

A figure of 0.4854 should be returned indicating positive skewness, i.e. off-centre to the left.

> **Now copy D3 into E3.**

This will give the skewness coefficient for the age data, and should return a value of 0.0422. Being very close to zero, this indicates that the age distribution is fairly symmetrical, i.e. neither off-centre to the right nor the left.

9.3.2. Kurtosis

Kurtosis characterizes the relative peakedness or flatness of a distribution compared to the normal distribution (a symmetrical, bell-shaped distribution). Positive kurtosis indicates a relatively peaked distribution. Negative kurtosis indicates a relatively flat distribution.

Excel uses the function:

=KURT(Data range)

to compute the kurtosis statistic.[3]

Thus for the data in Workbook 8.5 kurtosis is computed from:

=KURT(A2:A251) and =KURT(B2:B251)

Enter these functions now to the D6 and E6 cells of the current worksheet (Workbook

---

2 The equation used by Excel for skewness is defined as $n\Sigma(x - \bar{x})^3/(n-1)(n-2)$, i.e. the weighted 3rd moment around the mean.

3 The statistic computed is the weighted 4th moment around the mean.

8.5).

Values of -0.5002 for the occupants data, and -1.069 for the age data should be returned. These values, being both negative, indicate that both data sets are relatively flat, although the occupants data is more peaked that the age data.

Now save this file as Workbook 9.6 (W9_6.XLS).
Exercise 9.3 can be attempted now.

9.4. Descriptive statistics from the Excel Data Analysis routine

In both this and the previous chapter the procedure has been to explain and develop individual Excel functions to calculate the various summary statistics (=AVERAGE, =MEDIAN, etc.). However Excel contains a preprogrammed routine called Data Analysis that will produce all the descriptive statistics automatically. Now that we know what most of these statistics mean we can take advantage of the routine.

Workbook 8.5

First, load Workbook 8.5 (W8_5.XLS).

This contains the by now familiar data on car occupants and their ages.

Now select Tools and then Data Analysis and then Descriptive Statistics.

The dialogue box shown in Fig. 9.1 will appear.

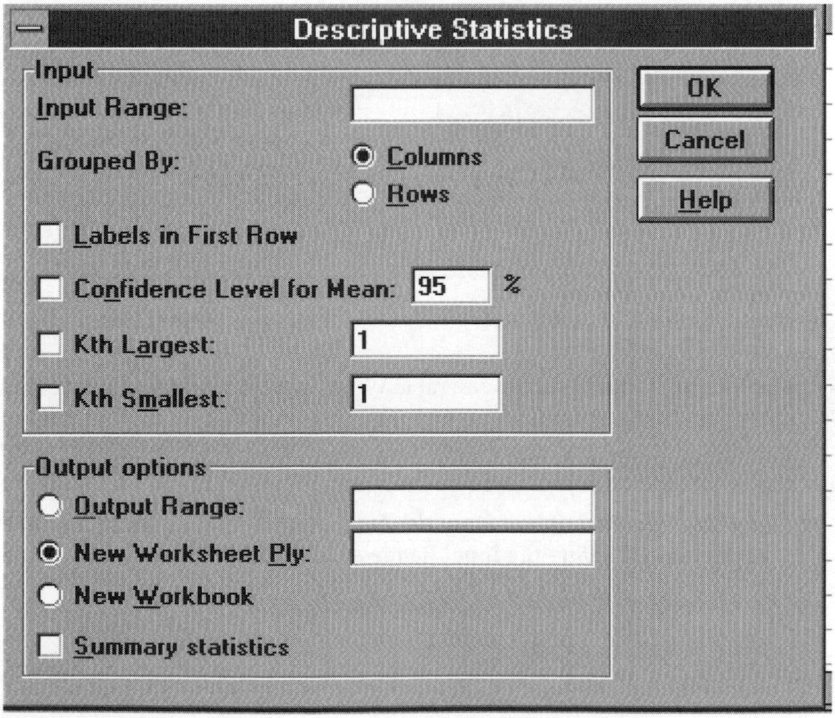

Figure 9.1

First, enter the Input Range for the occupants data (A1:A251) in the top box and en-sure that the data is grouped by Columns. Since we have included the label contained in A1 in the Input Range, now make sure that the Labels in First Row box is checked.

Ignore the 3 boxes below for the moment, and click on the Output Range tab to make it checked.

Then choose a vacant range of the worksheet and enter its coordinates to the Output Range box.

In the illustration we have chosen C1, so the Descriptive Statistics will appear in the range commencing at C1.

Finally, click on the Summary Statistics tab.

The dialogue box should now resemble Fig. 9.2.

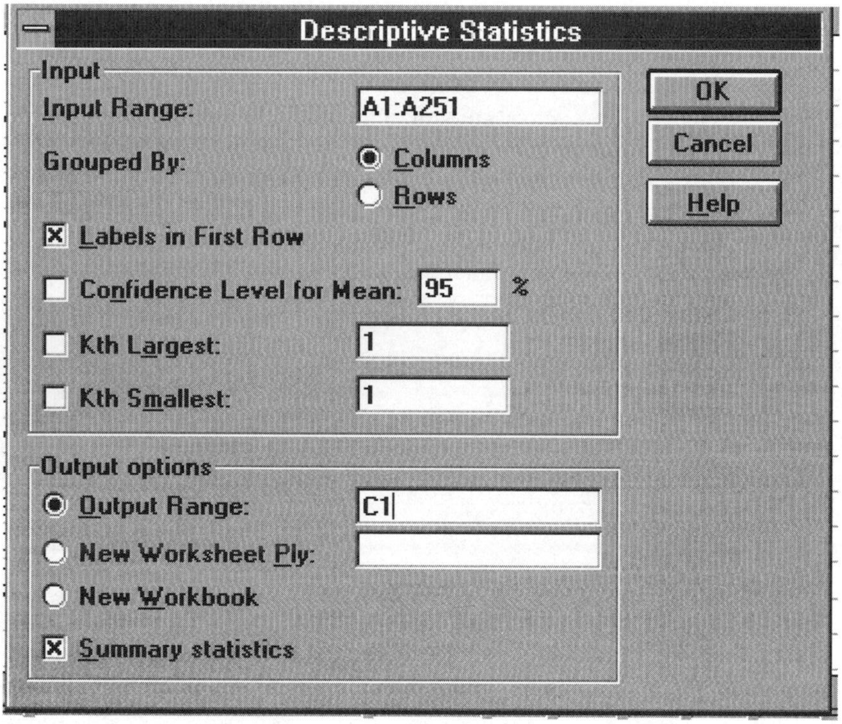

Figure 9.2

If it does, click OK.

Workbook 9.7

The results produced should resemble Workbook 9.7 (after widening column C). Most of the terms should be familiar in the light of previous discussion, but two—Standard Error and Confidence Level—can only be understood once the principles of sampling have been explained. Ignore them at the moment.

To obtain the Descriptive Statistics for the age data set, repeat the procedure outlined above, except define the Input Range as B1:B251 and the Output Range as E1.

The results should resemble Workbook 9.8.

Workbook 9.8

Exercise 9.4 can be attempted now.

	A	B	C	D	E	F	G	H
1	No. of occupants	Age	*No. of occupants*					
2	1	24.07						
3	2	49.42	Mean	2.5				
4		34.78	Standard Error	0.11677				
5	1	62.13	Median	2				
6	3	29.69	Mode	2				
7		49.91	Standard Deviation	1.16775				
8		61.99	Sample Variance	1.36364				
9	2	18.45	Kurtosis	-0.50024				
10		23.21	Skewness	0.48546				
11	1	69.30	Range	4				
12	3	77.46	Minimum	1				
13		22.35	Maximum	5				
14		76.55	Sum	250				
15	4	61.25	Count	100				
16		81.64	Confidence Level(95.000%)	0.22887				
17		17.68						
18		71.85						

Workbook 9.7

9.5. **Z scores**

....

The notion of relative dispersion has already been mentioned in the context of the coefficient of variation. But there is a further measure of relative variation that is frequently used in descriptive statistics. This is known as a **Z score**, and is defined for any individual observation as:

$$Z = (\text{observation value - mean})/\text{standard deviation} = (x_i - \bar{x})/s$$

where s is the standard deviation.

To see this in operation, make up the first 2 columns of Workbook 9.9.

Workbook 9.9

Here, we have the marks obtained by a group of 10 students in a Law examination. The mean and standard deviation mark have been calculated in B13 and B14 respectively and these cells named as M and SD.

Do this now.

To calculate the Z scores for these students add the label:

Z score

Microsoft Excel - W9_8.XLS

File Edit View Insert Format Tools Data Window Help

Courier (W1)   10   B I U

E3   'Mean

	A	B	C	D	E	F
1	No. of occupants	Age	*No. of occupants*		*Age*	
2	1	24.07				
3	2	49.42	Mean	2.5	Mean	40.37552
4		34.78	Standard Error	0.11677	Standard Error	1.4257064
5	1	62.13	Median	2	Median	40.25
6	3	29.69	Mode	2	Mode	0.78
7		49.91	Standard Deviation	1.16775	Standard Deviation	22.542397
8		61.99	Sample Variance	1.36364	Sample Variance	508.15967
9	2	18.45	Kurtosis	-0.50024	Kurtosis	-1.069367
10		23.21	Skewness	0.48546	Skewness	0.0421814
11	1	69.30	Range	4	Range	83.66
12	3	77.46	Minimum	1	Minimum	0.13
13		22.35	Maximum	5	Maximum	83.79
14		76.55	Sum	250	Sum	10093.88
15	4	61.25	Count	100	Count	250
16		81.64	Confidence Level(95.000%)	0.22887	Confidence Level(95.000%)	2.794329
17		17.68				
18		71.85				

Sheet1 / Sheet2 / Sheet3 / Sheet4 / Sheet5 / Sheet

Workbook 9.8

Workbook 9.9

Microsoft Excel - W9_9.XLS

File Edit View Insert Format Tools Data Window Help

SD   =STDEVP(B3:B12)

	A	B	C	D	E	F	G	H	I	J
1	Student	Law	Z							
2	Number	mark %	score							
3	1	67	0.319988							
4	2	89	1.75667							
5	3	56	-0.39835							
6	4	49	-0.85548							
7	5	47	-0.98609							
8	6	58	-0.26775							
9	7	37	-1.63912							
10	8	62	-0.00653							
11	9	76	0.907722							
12	10	80	1.168936							
13	Mean	62.1	0.00							
14	Stand Dev	15.31307	1							
15										

Sheet1 / Sheet2 / Sheet3 / Sheet4 / Sheet5 / Sheet

to the C1 and C2 cells, and then in C3 enter:

=(B3-M)/SD

Then copy this into C4:C12
Finally copy B13:B14 into C13:C14 and format C13:C14 to 2 decimal places.

This will compute the mean and standard deviation of the Z score data.

As you can see, the mean and the standard deviation of the Z scores are 0 and 1 respectively. This is not coincidence, and is a very useful property of this so-called **Z transformation** that will be used in later discussion. In other words, when the Z scores are calculated for a data set, regardless of the data set's own mean and standard deviation, the Z score data will always have zero mean and unit standard deviation.

The computed Z scores measure relative rather than absolute performance, in the sense that each raw score is related both to the mean of the group and to the dispersion of the raw scores within the group. Thus, with a given mean performance by the group, any raw score will translate to a Z score that is lower the greater the group's spread of performance and higher the less the group's overall spread of performance.

As an illustration of the use of Z scores in the computation of relative as opposed to absolute performance, consider Workbook 9.10.

	A	B	C	D
1	Student	Law	IT	Combined
2	Number	mark %	mark %	mark
3	1	67	40	107
4	2	89	71	160
5	3	56	50	106
6	4	49	41	90
7	5	47	45	92
8	6	58	36	94
9	7	37	50	87
10	8	62	50	112
11	9	76	40	116
12	10	80	79	159
13	Mean	62.1	50.2	112.3
14	Stand Dev	15.31307	13.3551	25.3418626

Workbook 9.10

Here, the same group of students' IT marks have been added to column C.

Load W9_9.XLS as a template, insert 3 columns at C and then add the IT marks shown. Then proceed in line with the following discussion.
Calculate the mean and standard deviation of the raw scores for IT in C13 and C14 and then name these cells as MI and SDI.

Now suppose that a prize is to be awarded to the best student in the group. Clearly we need to combine the scores in each subject.

Do this now in column D.

We *could* now sort the data in descending order on combined score to obtain the rankings, but with such a small data set it is clear that student 2 has just 'shaved' the prize by one mark from student 10.

However, whether this will still be the case when we consider relative as opposed to absolute performance remains to be seen, and requires that the Z scores in each subject are calculated.

Consequently, use column E to replicate the students' identification numbers and then in Columns G calculate the Z score for IT by entering the formula:

=(C3-MI)/SDI

to the G3 cell.
Then copy G3 into G4:G12.
Finally, compute the combined Z scores in column H by adding the Law and the IT Z scores and add an appropriate label at the top of column H.

The result should resemble Workbook 9.11. They indicate that student 10 should now win the prize if it is to be awarded in terms of relative rather than absolute performance.[4] This is because, although number 10 scored one mark less overall than number 2, he or she was further ahead of the rest of the class in the subject that he or she was best at.

Workbook 9.11

	A	B	C	D	E	F	G	H	I	J
1	Student	Law	IT	Combined	Student	Law	IT	Combined		
2	Number	mark %	mark %	mark	Number	Z score	Z score	Z score		
3	1	67	40	107	1	0.319988166	-0.76375	-0.44376222		
4	2	89	71	160	2	1.756669725	1.5574518	3.31412148		
5	3	56	50	106	3	-0.39835261	-0.014975	-0.41332811		
6	4	49	41	90	4	-0.85547857	-0.688873	-1.54435146		
7	5	47	45	92	5	-0.98608598	-0.389363	-1.37544892		
8	6	58	36	94	6	-0.2677452	-1.06326	-1.33100553		
9	7	37	50	87	7	-1.63912305	-0.014975	-1.65409855		
10	8	62	50	112	8	-0.00653037	-0.014975	-0.02150587		
11	9	76	40	116	9	0.907721531	-0.76375	0.14397115		
12	10	80	79	159	10	1.16893636	2.1564717	3.32540802		
13	Mean	62.1	50.2	112.3		0.00	0.00			
14	Stand Dev	15.31307	13.3551	25.3418626		1.00	1.00			
15										

Microsoft Excel - W9_11.XLS

File Edit View Insert Format Tools Data Window Help

Courier (W1) 10

H3   =F3+G3

Sheet1 / Sheet2 / Sheet3 / Sheet4 / Sheet5 / Sheet

4 Notice, however, that the original rankings will be unchanged if we take the Z score of the combined mark rather than combining the Z scores of the individual marks.

**Workbook
9.11**

There is no easy answer as to whether performance should be measured in absolute rather than relative terms. However, particularly in cases where performance in a number of examinations is to be aggregated, measuring relative performance is much more likely to take account of differences in the standard of marking and/or the intrinsic difficulty of the examination.

On the other hand, using relative performance only, as a basis for selection can produce disastrous consequences. For example, suppose that it is decided in a particular examination that only those examinees with a positive Z score will be regarded as having passed. Now suppose that in this year the quality of student is excellent—none gets less than 90% in the examination. It will still be the case that, using Z scores, approximately 50% will fail because of their relative rather than their absolute performance.

Then assume that in the next year the quality of student has deteriorated, but that the standard of the examination is unchanged. Application of the positive Z score rule will still ensure that roughly 50% of the candidates pass, yet it should be clear that the passing 50% of this group could well be less able in absolute terms than the failing 50% of the previous year's intake.

Exercise 9.5 can be attempted now.

9.6. **Index numbers**

One of the most frequently encountered methods of presenting data is in terms of index numbers, and is associated with such well-known measures as the Retail Price Index (RPI), the FT-SE index of share prices, or the index of industrial production.

9.6.1. Simple index numbers

An **index number** is simply a statistical method of summarizing data sets in a way that facilitates comparisons both between and within data sets. Usually the data will represent observations on a particular variable in different time periods, and the computed index number provides a simple method of comparing these different time period values.

**Workbook
9.12**

For example, consider Workbook 9.12 which shows the total population of the UK in relation to the EC/EU in selected years.

	A	B	C	D	E	F	G	H	I	J
1	Year	73	78	82	86	89	90	93		
2	UK pop (000s)	56223	56178	56306	56763	57236	57411	57927		
3	EC/EU pop 000s	308770	314869	319377	322335	325785	327907	332894		
4										
5										

Workbook 9.12

Make up this workbook now.

To construct an index number for each of these series, the first thing to do is select a base year, denominate it as 100, and then express each of the data values as a proportion of the value in that base year. Consequently, suppose the base year for the UK is selected as 1986, and for the EC/EU as 1978. The UK index number for 1989 would therefore be computed as $(100)(57236)/(56763) = 100.83$. Similarly, the EC/EU index number for 1982 is $(100)(319377)/(314869) = 101.43$.

In both cases, the fact that the base year has been denominated as 100 allows *subtraction* of 100 from any index to show the percentage increase or decrease in the value of the variable between the chosen period and the base period. Consequently, between 1986 and 1989 the UK population increased by 0.83%, while between 1978 and 1982 the EC/EU population increased by 1.43%

To compute the index numbers for each of the years in both series, proceed as follows. First, in A4 and A5 enter the labels:

UK index no.   EC/EU index no.

Then in B4 enter:

=100*B2/$E2

and in B5 enter:

=100*B3/$C3

Then copy B4:B5 into C4:H5.

Notice that E2 contains the UK population in the chosen base year (1986) and C3 contains the EC/EU population in its chosen base year (1976). The dollar signs attached to each of these cells mean that after copying, each of the population values in both series is related to the chosen base year value.

The effect should resemble Workbook 9.13.

	A	B	C	D	E	F	G	H	I	J
1	Year	73	78	82	86	89	90	93		
2	UK pop (000s)	56223	56178	56306	56763	57236	57411	57927		
3	EC/EU pop 000s	308770	314869	319377	322335	325785	327907	332894		
4	UK index no.	99.04868	98.9694	99.1949	100	100.8333	101.1416	102.0506		
5	EC/EU index no.	98.063	100	101.4317	102.3711	103.4668	104.1408	105.7246		
6										

B4 = =100*B2/$E2

Workbook 9.13

If it does, save the file as W9_13.XLS.

Now notice that although the UK index number series permits comparison over the period in relation to 1986, and the EC/EU series does the same in relation to 1978, the 2 index number series are not directly comparable *with each other*. In other words, although we *can* say that between 1986 and 1993 the UK population increased by 2.05%, the temptation to argue that over the same period the EC/EU population increased by 3.35% (105.72-102.37) must be resisted. This is because the percentage increase or decrease must always be related to the base period, which in the EC/EU case was 1978.

9.6.2. Chain index numbers

Simple index numbers allow the percentage change in any year to be computed in relation to the given base year. However, sometimes it will be desirable to calculate the percentage change in a variable in relation to the previous year's value. If this year on year approach is required, than a **chain index number** should be computed.

A chain index number is simply an ordinary index number in which each period in the series uses the previous period as the base. In other words, the base is continually updating, although the choice of which year to start the chaining establishes that year as *the* base.

Now suppose that we decide to use 1973 as the start of the chain for both the UK and the EC/EU population data. To compute chain index numbers for the current data, load Workbook 9.13 (W9_13.XLS) and read on.

Workbook 9.13

First, in A6 and A7 enter the labels:

UK chain index no.   EC/EU chain index no.

Then in B6 and B7 enter values of 100.
   Next, in C6 enter:

   =100*C2/B2

and in C7 enter:

   =100*C3/B3

Then copy C6:C7 into D6:H7.

Workbook 9.14

The results should resemble Workbook 9.14

	A	B	C	D	E	F	G	H	I
1	Year	73	78	82	86	89	90	93	
2	UK pop (000s)	56223	56178	56306	56763	57236	57411	57927	
3	EC/EU pop 000s	308770	314869	319377	322335	325785	327907	332894	
4	UK index no.	99.04868	98.9694	99.1949	100	100.8333	101.1416	102.0506	
5	EC/EU index no.	98.063	100	101.4317	102.3711	103.4668	104.1408	105.7246	
6	UK chain index no.	100	99.91996	100.2278	100.8116	100.8333	100.3058	100.8988	
7	EC/EU chain index no.	100	101.9753	101.4317	100.9262	101.0703	100.6513	101.5209	
8									

Workbook
9.14

If they do, then save the file as W9_14.XLS.

These chain index numbers indicate whether the rate of change of the population is rising, falling, or constant in relation to the value for the previous year in the series.

9.6.3. Weighted index numbers

So far, the index numbers explained have all related to a single variable in different years (population, for example). However, an index number such as the RPI will contain many different items (representing the typical basket of goods that people buy). So to see how more complex index numbers are constructed, consider the data shown in Workbook 9.15.

	A	B	C	D	E	F	G	H	I
1	Purchases of items of electronic equipment 1980 and 1993 (000s of units)								
2		Quantity	Quantity						
3		1980	1993						
4	televisions	20.2	22.4						
5	video recorders	4.8	12.6						
6	video cameras	0.4	5.3						
7	personal computers	0.8	8.5						

Workbook
9.15

Make up this workbook now.

To obtain an index number that compares the purchase quantities of all items in 1993 with those in 1980, it is simply necessary to sum the quantities for 1993 and express them as a proportion of the sum of the quantities for 1980. When this ratio is multiplied by 100, the **aggregate quantity index number** is obtained.

Conventionally, the more recent year is referred to as the **current** year and given the subscript c, and the more distant year as the **base** year and given the subscript b. Consequently, since the data represent quantities (Q) we can define the aggregate quantity index number as:

$$100(\Sigma Q_c / \Sigma Q_b) = 100(48.8/26.2) = 186.25$$

Confirm this now in your own workbook by using A8 to contain the label:

SUM

and B9 and C9 to contain the formulae:

=SUM(B4:B7)   and   =SUM(C4:C7)

These are the total quantities purchased in each of the years.

Then in A9 enter the label:

Simple quantity index no.

and compute its value in B9 from:

=100*C8/B8

Now save the file as W9_15.XLS.

Clearly, this figure implies that there has been an 86.25% increase in the total volume of purchases of electronic equipment between 1980 and 1993.

Although this is a useful piece of information, the simple index number calculated is deficient in the sense that it does not take account of any price data that could be used to indicate the relative importance of each item from an expenditure point of view. This deficiency is rectified in Workbook 9.16.

	A	B	C	D	E	F	G	H	I
1	Purchases of items of electronic equipment 1980 and 1993 (000s of units)								
2		Quantity	Quantity	Price	Price				
3		1980	1993	1980	1993				
4	televisions	20.2	22.4	260	230				
5	video recorders	4.8	12.6	600	280				
6	video cameras	0.4	5.3	1500	850				
7	personal computers	0.8	8.5	1800	900				

Workbook 9.16

Now use Workbook 9.15 (W9_15.XLS) as a template and add the extra price information indicated.

On the basis of this added information a variety of index numbers can now be computed, with the exact nature of what is being measured being determined by the interplay between the price and quantity variables.

For example, suppose it is required to measure the change in expenditure on all items of electronic equipment between the 2 periods. Clearly expenditure on each item in the current period is given by $P_c Q_c$, and so total expenditure in 1993 is obtained by summing the expenditures on each individual item, i.e. $\Sigma P_c Q_c$. Equivalently, $\Sigma P_b Q_b$ measures total expenditure in the base period and so the expenditure index number (E) is given by:

$$E = 100(\Sigma P_c Q_c / \Sigma P_b Q_b)$$

For the illustrative data this produces:

$$[(22.4)(230) + (12.6)(280) + (5.3)(850) + (8.5)(900)]/[(20.2)(260) + (4.8)(600) + (0.4)(1500) + (0.8)(1800)] = 204.8$$

There has therefore been a 104.8% increase in expenditure on these items of electronic equipment over the period.

Confirm this now in your own workbook by making the following entries.
  In F2 and G2 enter the labels:

$P_b Q_b$ and $P_c Q_c$

Then in F4 and G4 enter the formulae:

$$=B4*D4 \quad \text{and} \quad =C4*E4$$

and copy them into F5:G7.

These values are the expenditures on each of the items in the 2 periods.

Next, in F8 and G8 calculate the total expenditure on all items in each period by copying the SUM formula in E8 along into F8:G8.
Now use A10 to contain the label:

Expenditure index no.

and calculate its value in B10 from:

$$=100*G8/F8$$

The previously calculated value for the index number (204.8) should be confirmed.

Now save this model as W9_16.XLS.

However, the fact that both price and quantity data are available also allows calculation of what are known as **weighted** index numbers, where the weights are used to take account of the relative importance of each item in the data series. Thus if a weighted quantity index number is required, the weights will usually be the prices of the items, while if a weighted price index number is needed, then the weights will usually be the quantities.

But this approach raises the problem of whether the data for the base period or the current period should be used as the weights. The answer is that either base period weights or current period weights can be used provided that consistency is maintained. In other words, both of the weights must refer to the same period in the numerator and the denominator of the index number expression, and these can be either base period or current period values.

For example, if prices are being compared using quantities as weights, then the time subscript for prices must be different on both the numerator and the denominator of the index number expression. Quantity subscripts, however, will refer to the same period. A similar logic applies to quantity index numbers, but in either case that which is being measured by the index number has a different time subscript on the top and bottom of the index number expression. For example, the expression:

$$100(\Sigma P_c Q_c / \Sigma P_c Q_b)$$

defines an aggregate quantity index number that uses *current* period prices as the weights, while

$$100(\Sigma P_b Q_c / \Sigma P_b Q_b)$$

defines an aggregate quantity index number that uses *base* period prices as the weights. For the illustrative data, this means that:

$$100(\Sigma P_c Q_c / \Sigma P_c Q_b) = 295.5$$

and

$$100(\Sigma P_b Q_c / \Sigma P_b Q_b) = 360.1$$

Alternatively, if a price index number is required, then the base weighted index is:

$$100(\Sigma P_c Q_b / \Sigma P_b Q_b)$$

and the current weighted price index number is:

$$100(\Sigma P_c Q_c / P_b Q_c)$$

These evaluate to 69.3 and 56.9 respectively for the illustrated data set, indicating that by either measure there has been a significant reduction in the average price of this basket of electronic goods.

Now confirm these calculations by making the following additions to the current workbook (W9_16.XLS).

In H2:I2 enter the labels:

P_cQ_b and P_bQ_c

Then in H4 and I4 enter the formulae:

=E4*B4   and   =D4*C4

Now copy H4:I4 into H5:I7 and then sum H4:H7 and I4:I7 in H8 and I8.

Rows 4 to 7 of columns F, G, H, and I now contain the following information:

    In F: base period expenditure on each of the items
    In G: current period expenditure on each of the items
    In H: base period quantities valued at current period prices
    In I: current period quantities valued at base period prices

With these figures established, it is now an easy matter to compute each of the 4 weighted index numbers that have been explained.

First add identifying labels to the A11:A14 range. That is:

Q index no. base
Q index no. current P
P index no. base Q
P index no. current Q

Then compute the values of each of these index numbers in B11:B14 from the formulae:

=100*I8/F8
=100*G8/H8
=100*H8/F8
=100*G8/I8

The manual calculations performed earlier should be confirmed by these formulae. If they are, resave the file as W9_16.XLS.

Exercise 9.6 can be attempted now.

9.7. Cross-tabulation

Consider a group of 20 individuals. It would be an easy matter to describe them in a variety of ways. Suppose we choose to use two descriptors—gender and hair colour. Then, each individual could be classified in two ways.

Now suppose we define hair colour to be either Dark (D), Red (R), or Blond (B), and gender to be either Male (M) or Female (F).

Next, consider the following data set, which represents the hypothetical result of such a classification process.

Individual no.	1	2	3	4	5	6	7	8	9	10
Gender	F	F	M	F	F	M	F	F	M	M
Hair colour	D	D	R	R	D	B	D	D	B	B

Individual no.	11	12	13	14	15	16	17	18	19	20
Gender	F	M	M	M	F	F	M	M	F	F
Hair colour	R	D	D	D	B	B	R	D	R	D

The purpose of cross-tabulation is to prepare a table showing the number of individuals in each of the two way classifications. That is, the numbers who are:

M and D   M and R   M and B   F and D   F and R   F and B

Clearly, such a classification procedure is most easily done in terms of a table, and it is called a **contingency table**. The structure of such a table is shown in Table 9.1.

Now, by inspecting the raw data *manually*, complete the table.

Table 9.1

	HAIR COLOUR			
GENDER	B	D	R	TOTAL
F				
M				
Total				

When you have finished, notice that even with a small data set such as this the required classification procedure is extremely tedious (and prone to error). This is where Excel can help.

First open a new workbook and use A1:C1 to contain the labels:

ID number   Gender   Hair colour

Then enter the appropriate raw data in cells A2:C21.
Now select Data from the Menu bar and then Pivot Table.

A Wizard routine will be initiated.

First ensure that the Microsoft Excel List or Data Base box is checked, and then select Next.
At stage 2 of the Wizard tell Excel that the data range to be cross-tabulated is contained in B1:C21, and then click Next.

The stage 3 dialogue box is shown in Fig. 9.3.

Now click and drag the gender button into the ROW area and then click and drag the hair colour button into the COLUMN area.
Next, click and drag the gender button into the DATA area.

The screen should now resemble Fig. 9.4.
However, if the button in the Data area does not indicate Count of Gender, double click on it and then select Count from the list that appears.

Assuming that your screen is the same as Fig. 9.4, select Next to obtain the last Wizard screen.

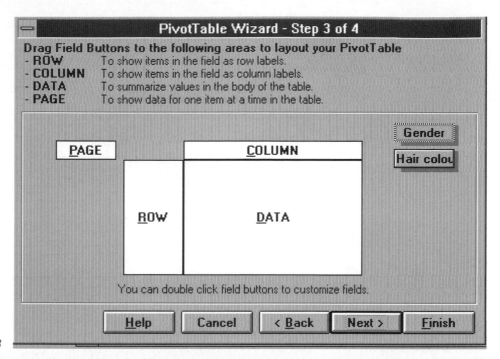

Figure 9.3

Here you must define the location in which Excel is to place the cross-tabulation.

Do this by entering D1 to the top box and then deselect the Save Data with Table Layout model type tab.
Now select Finish.

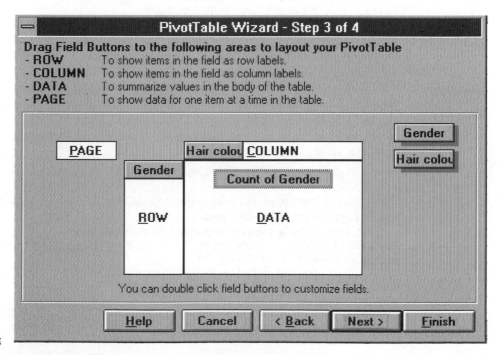

Figure 9.4

The results should look like Workbook 9.17.

	A	B	C	D	E	F	G	H	I
1	ID number	Gender	Hair colour	Count of Gender	Hair colour				
2	1	F	D	Gender	B	D	R	Grand Total	
3	2	F	D	F	2	6	3	11	
4	3	M	R	M	3	4	2	9	
5	4	F	R	Grand Total	5	10	5	20	
6	5	F	D						
7	6	M	B						

Workbook 9.17

If they do, save the model now as W9_17.XLS.

The data have now been cross-tabulated by gender and hair colour and the totals in each of the categories computed.

We should now note that in the previous illustration on cross-tabulation the raw data were already in categorical form (M/F and D/R/B). However, there can be circumstances in which we will have to use Excel to perform this categorization first, before we can use the cross-tabulation routine.

To see an example of this, load Workbook 9.18.

Here, the data from Workbook 8.5 has been reproduced but, in addition, each of the occupants has also been classified by gender (M/F). A section of the workbook is shown in Workbook 9.18.

Workbook 9.18

The task we face is to produce a cross-tabulation of age versus gender, and this immediately raises the problem that the age data have not been categorized. One solution would be to use the Histogram routine to classify the age data into class intervals, and then use these class intervals as the categories for the cross-tabulation. However, this approach requires that the user selects the class intervals or that Excel is allowed to do it for itself. In either case, we have already seen that there are no clear rules for making such a selection.

An alternative but related approach is to categorize the data into its **quartiles** and then use these as the age categories.

To do this, first of all compute the quartiles of the age data in the E2:E5 range of the worksheet from:

=QUARTILE(B2:B251,1)   =QUARTILE(B2:B251,2)

and so on for the next two quartiles.

When formatted to 2 decimal places, values of 21.99, 40.25, 60.12, and 83.79 should be returned.

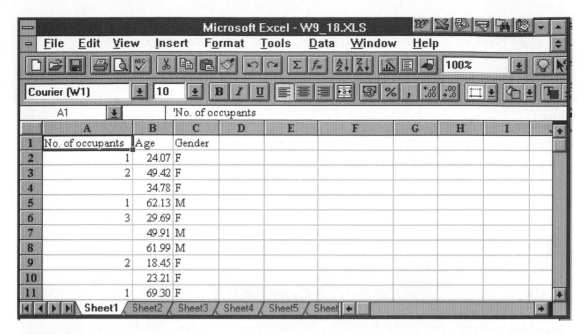

Workbook 9.18

Now we are going to use a VLOOKUP function to classify each age value into its quartile. However, since the VLOOKUP function needs to start at zero we need to add this value to the E1 cell.

So, enter a value of zero to E1.
Now, in F1:F4 enter the labels:

Q1, Q2, Q3, and Q4

The E$1:F$4 range can clearly be regarded as a lookup table and then used to return the quartile associated with each age value. Thus, for example, any age value less than 21.99 will be classified as being in Q1, while any age value of 21.99 or more, but under 40.25, will be placed in Q2.

Now add the label:

Quartile

to the D1 cell, and in D2 enter the formula:

=VLOOKUP(B2,E$1:F$4,2)

Then copy D2 into D3:D251.

The data has now been categorized by both gender and age quartile in columns C and D.

To obtain a cross-tabulation of this data, use the Pivot Table routine as outlined above, except define E7 as the cell in which to start the pivot table (so that the data in E1:F5 is not overwritten).

The results should resemble Workbook 9.19, and indicate that we have a fairly even spread of quartile ages both amongst and between males and females.

Workbook 9.19

If they do, save the file now as W9_19.XLS.

As a final topic in cross-tabulation notice, that the values returned to the body of the table need not necessarily refer to the variables used in the row and column tabulation. For

	A	B	C	D	E	F	G	H	I	J
1	No. of occupants	Age	Gender	Quartile	0	Q1				
2	1	24.07	F	Q2	21.99	Q2				
3	2	49.42	F	Q3	40.25	Q3				
4		34.78	F	Q2	60.12	Q4				
5	1	62.13	M	Q4	83.79					
6	3	29.69	F	Q2						
7		49.91	M	Q3	Count of Quartile	Quartile				
8		61.99	M	Q4	Gender	Q1	Q2	Q3	Q4	Grand Total
9	2	18.45	F	Q1	F	29	32	31	31	123
10		23.21	F	Q2	M	34	30	31	32	127
11	1	69.30	F	Q4	Grand Total	63	62	62	63	250
12	3	77.46	M	Q4						
13		22.35	M	Q2						
14		76.55	M	Q4						

Cell reference E2, formula: =QUARTILE(B2:B251,1)

Workbook 9.19

example, using the data from Workbook 9.18 suppose that we want to perform a cross-tabulation of gender with number of occupants but that we want the average age of the occupants (as opposed to the number of individuals) returned to the body of the table.

Workbook 9.19A

To do this, open Workbook 9.19A (W9_19.XLS).

This is simply Workbook 9.19 modified to provide the full information on the number of occupants in each car (i.e. without any gaps in the data in column A). Thus the data in column A becomes 1, 2, 2, 1, 3, 3, 3, 2, 2, 1 . . . etc. This is necessary so that the eventual cross-tabulation routine does not encounter blank cells.

Now initiate the Pivot Table routine.
At the range prompt, however, define the area containing the data to be A1:C251.

The subsequent prompt will now show 3 variables (number of occupants, age, and gender) as being available for cross-tabulation.

Consequently, click and drag the Gender button to the Row area and the No. of occupants button to the Column area.
Then click and drag the Age button into the central area, double click on it, and select Average.
Finally, supply an output range commencing in E7.

When you have finished, the result should resemble Workbook 9.19B.

Workbook 9.19B

We can now note that:

The oldest average age is observed in cars with only 1 male occupant.
The youngest average age is observed in cars with 4 female occupants.
The average age of those individuals in cars with 2 occupants regardless of gender is 39.94.
The average age of females regardless of the number of occupants in the car is 40.634.
The average age of the entire sample is 40.375.

Exercise 9.7 can be attempted now.

	B	C	D	E	F	G	H	I	J	K
				Microsoft Excel - W9_19B.XLS						
	File	**Edit**	**View**	**Insert**	**Format**	**Tools**	**Data**	**Window**	**Help**	
	J19									
1	Age	Gender	Quartile	0	Q1					
2	24.07	F	Q2	21.99	Q2					
3	49.42	F	Q3	40.25	Q3					
4	34.78	F	Q2	60.12	Q4					
5	62.13	M	Q4	83.79						
6	29.69	F	Q2							
7	49.91	M	Q3	Average of Age	No. of occupants					
8	61.99	M	Q4	Gender	1	2	3	4	5	Grand Total
9	18.45	F	Q1	F	46.12166667	40.4576	40.1	35.9733	44.9	40.63447154
10	23.21	F	Q2	M	48.444	39.3286	43.6	35.9989	35.98	40.12472441
11	69.30	F	Q4	Grand Total	47.17727273	39.9379	41.8	35.9877	39.55	40.37552
12	77.46	M	Q4							
13	22.35	M	Q2							

Sheet1 / Sheet2 / Sheet3 / Sheet4 / Sheet5 / Sheet

Workbook 9.19B

9.8. Exercises

Exercise 9.1

Make up Workbook 9.20.

The data are the daily number of accidents on a motorway network over a period of 365 days. Estimate the mean, variance, and standard deviation number of accidents.

Exercise 9.2

Load Workbook 9.21 (W9_21.XLS) from the accompanying disk. The data are the annual profits (in £000s) of a group of 200 companies.

(i) Calculate the upper and lower quartiles of this data set and hence the range of profits obtained by the middle 50% of companies.

(ii) Within what range do the middle 70% of profit values lie?

Firms with profits that are in the lowest decile are likely to close down in the near future.

(iii) Calculate the level of profits that must be achieved if closure is likely to be avoided.

(iv) Which decile spans the widest range of profit values?

Exercise 9.3

Load Workbook 9.22 (W9_22.XLS). Here, the data from Exercise 9.2 (W9_21.XLS) have been augmented to include the annual profits earned by another group of companies. They are identified as groups A and B.

(i) Is the range of profits earned by the middle 50% of companies in group A higher or lower than for those in group B?

(ii) Compare the degree of skewness between the two groups of companies.

(iii) Compare the degree of kurtosis between the two groups of companies.

When you have finished, save the file as W9_22A.XLS.

Exercise 9.4

Load Workbook 9.22 (W9_22.XLS).

Use the Excel Data Analysis routine to compute the descriptive statistics for both groups of companies. Then answer the following questions.

Workbook 9.20

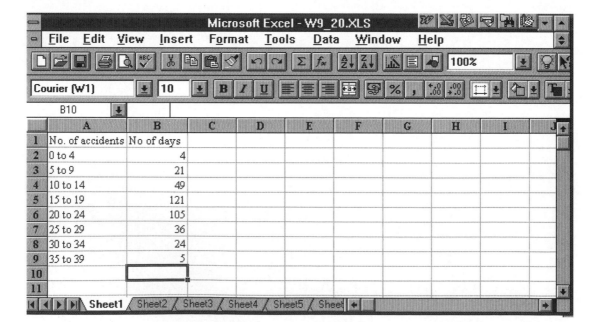

(i) Which group of companies has the highest mean profit?

(ii) In which group of companies are the profit values most dispersed?

(iii) Which group of companies has got the highest relative dispersion of profits?

(iv) Calculate the mean profit earned by the combined group of companies.

(v) Calculate the range of profits earned by the combined group of companies.

When you have finished, save the file as W9_22B.XLS.

Exercise 9.5

Load W9_22.XLS and immediately save the file as W9_22C.XLS.

Use this workbook to show, for the combination of both groups of companies, a high–low ranking of both absolute and relative profit performance.

Hint: identify each company in group A by the labels A1, A2 . . . A200, and those in group B by B1, B2 . . . B200. Then collect the data for the two groups in one long list, compute the Z scores, and then sort the list first of all by raw score and then by Z score.

Exercise 9.6

Load W9_16.XLS and then imagine that 3 more items have been added to the list of electronic goods. The prices and purchase quantities in each of the periods are given as:

	Quantity 1980	Quantity 1993	Price 1980	Price 1993
CD player	0.1	5.9	386.99	145.99
Personal stereo	0.9	12.35	25.99	14.00
Answering machine	1.6	2.1	86.45	35.99

(i) By inserting rows at appropriate location, recompute each of the 5 most important index numbers (expenditure, base and current weighted price, base and current weighted quantity).

(ii) What effect has the introduction of these 3 new products to the basket of goods had upon the original index numbers?

Exercise 9.7

Load W9_23.XLS.

The data are the result of a market experiment in 5 regions of the UK—Southern England (SE), Northern England (NE), Scotland (S), Wales (W), and Northern Ireland (NI). Consumers in each of these areas were asked to test a new product and then say whether they liked it (L), were undecided about it (U), or disliked it (D).

(i) Cross-tabulate these data by region and attitude.

(ii) In which regions of the country might the product be expected to do best and worst?

(iii) By considering the total number of respondents from each region, is there an indication of what type of sampling method was employed?

9.9. Solutions to the exercises

Solution to Exercise 9.1

The solution is shown in Workbook 9.24.

The formulae used are:

In D2: =B2*C2 i.e frequency times mid-point value, copied into D3:D9.

In B10: =SUM(B2:B9) i.e. the sum of the frequencies = the total number of observations.

In D10: =SUM(D2:D9) i.e. the total worth of all the observations.

In B11: =D10/B10 i.e. the mean

In E2: =C2-B$11 i.e. the deviation of the mean from the first midpoint value, copied into E3:E9 to give the rest of the deviations from the mean.

In F2: =B2*(C2-D$11) i.e. frequency times the deviation from the mean, copied into F3:F9 to give the value of the rest of the deviations from the mean.

```
┌─────────────────────────────────────────────────────────────────────────────┐
│  ─                  Microsoft Excel - W9_24.XLS                               │
│  ─   File   Edit   View   Insert   Format   Tools   Data   Window   Help     │
│  [icons]                                             Σ  fx  [icons]  100%     │
│  Courier (W1)    ▼  10  ▼   B  I  U  [icons]  %  ,  [icons]                  │
│       B12        ▼         =G10/B10                                           │
└─────────────────────────────────────────────────────────────────────────────┘
```

	A	B	C	D	E	F	G
1	No. of accidents	No of days (f)	Mid points (Xm)	fXm	Xm - Mean	f(Xm - Mean)	f(Xm - Mean)^2
2	0 to 4	4	2	8	-17.2739726	-69.09589041	1193.560518
3	5 to 9	21	7	147	-12.2739726	-257.7534247	3163.658473
4	10 to 14	49	12	588	-7.2739726	-356.4246575	2592.623194
5	15 to 19	121	17	2057	-2.2739726	-275.1506849	625.6851192
6	20 to 24	105	22	2310	2.726027397	286.2328767	780.2786639
7	25 to 29	36	27	972	7.726027397	278.1369863	2148.893976
8	30 to 34	24	32	768	12.7260274	305.4246575	3886.84256
9	35 to 39	5	37	185	17.7260274	88.63013699	1571.060236
10	Sum	365		7035		0	15962.60
11	Mean =	19.27					
12	Variance =	43.73315819					
13	Stand Dev.	6.613105034					
14							

```
│◄│◄│►│►│ \ Sheet1 / Sheet2 / Sheet3 / Sheet4 / Sheet5 / Sheet │◄│
```

Workbook 9.24

In F10: =SUM(F2:F9) i.e. the sum of all the deviations from the mean, equal to zero as always.

In G2: =B2*(C2-D$11)^2 i.e. frequency times the squared deviation from the mean, copied into G3:G9 to give the value of each of the squared deviations from the mean.

In G10: =SUM(G2:G9) i.e. the sum of squared deviations from the mean.

In B12: =G10/B10 i.e. the variance = sum of squared deviations divided by the sum of the frequencies.

In B13: =B12^0.5 i.e. the standard deviation = the square root of the variance.

Solution to Exercise 9.2

The solution is shown in Workbook 9.25.

(i) With values of 1 and 3 entered to C2 and C3, use D2 and D3 to contain:

=QUARTILE(B3:B202,C2) and
=QUARTILE(B3:B202,C3)

Then compute the inter quartile range in D4 from:

=D3-D2

The middle 50% of companies therefore lie in a profit range of £48.74 thousand.

(ii) With values of 15% and 85% entered to E2 and E3, use F2 and F3 to contain:

=PERCENTILE(B3:B202,E2) and
=PERCENTILE(B3:B202,E3)

Then compute the range between these two percentiles in F4 from:

=F3-F2

The middle 70% of companies therefore lie in a profit range of £66.97 thousand.

(iii) Compute each of the decile values as indicated in the C7:D16 range of Workbook 9.25. The values in C7:C16 are entered directly, and the formula in D7 is:

=PERCENTILE(B$3:B$202,C7)

and this is copied into D8:D16.

The lowest decile spans a range of 0 to £11.0557 thousand, so companies earning less than £11.0557 thousand are likely to close.

(iv) The formula in E7 is:

=D7-0

to obtain the range of the first decile.

Then, in E8 we entered:

=D8-D7

```
X Microsoft Excel - W9_25
File  Edit  View  Insert  Format  Tools  Data  Window  Help
Courier (W1)      10    B  I  U
D7                =PERCENTILE(B$3:B$202,C7)
```

	A	B	C	D	E	F	G	H
1		Annual	quartile	profits	decile	profits		
2	Company	profits (£000s)	1	23.23232	15%	15.05721		
3	1	21.81	3	71.9703	85%	82.0356205		
4	2	77.34	Inter quartile range	48.73797	range of middle 70%	66.9784106		
5	3	36.91						
6	4	87.83	decile		Range	decile no.		
7	5	27.71	10%	11.05774	11.05774057	1		
8	6	84.14	20%	20.86831	9.81057382	2		
9	7	80.36	30%	28.29133	7.423016129	3		
10	8	48.49	40%	36.74261	8.451282668	4		
11	9	22.23	50%	47.87481	11.13219939	5		
12	10	91.25	60%	55.9118	8.036984531	6		
13	11	55.18	70%	66.70928	10.79748599	7		
14	12	81.95	80%	79.3811	12.6718198	8		
15	13	29.26	90%	91.27763	11.89652733	9		
16	14	16.93	100%	99.04884	7.771213655	10		

`Sheet1 / Sheet2 / Sheet3 / Sheet4 / Sheet5 / Sheet6`

Workbook 9.25

and copied this into E9:E16. This gives the profit ranges of each of the other deciles.

Clearly, the widest range is for the 8th decile (£12.6718 thousand).

Solution to Exercise 9.3

The solution is shown in Workbook 9.26

(i) =QUARTILE functions were used in E2:F3 to calculate the upper and lower quartiles of both data sets and the interquartile ranges computed in E4 and F4 from:

=E3-E2 and =F3-F2

Clearly, the middle 50% of companies in group A span a wider range of profits than those in group B (48.7379 > 2034.6305).

(ii) The formulae in E6 and F6 are:

=SKEW(B3:B202) and
=SKEW(C3:C202)

The profits in group A are positively skewed (i.e. the frequency distribution is off-centre to the right) while those for group B are negatively skewed (i.e. the frequency distribution is off-centre to the left).

(iii) The formulae in E7 and F7 are:

=KURT(B3:B202) and
=KURT(C3:C202)

Since kurtosis measures the degree of peakedness in the frequency distributions of the data, it follows that the frequency distribution of profits in both group A and group B are relatively flat (both have negative kurtosis values), with group A being slightly more peaked than group B (-1.122 is closer to 0 than -1.244).

Solution to Exercise 9.4

Use Tools, Data Analysis, and then Descriptive Statistics. The Input Range for group A is B3:B202 and the Output Range is defined as D1. For group B the Input Range is C3:C202 and the Output Range is F1. The Summary Statistics tab was checked in both cases.

The results are shown in Workbook 9.27.

(i) Group A has a higher mean profit than Group B.

(ii) Both the range and the variance are higher for Group A.

	A	B	C	D	E	F	G	H
1		Group A annual	Group B annual	quartile	Group A	Group B		
2	Company r	profits (£000s)	profits (£000s)	1	23.23232	17.94227		
3	1	21.81	3.49	3	71.9703	52.57276		
4	2	77.34	52.16	Interquartile range	48.73797	34.63049		
5	3	36.91	44.99					
6	4	87.83	1.58	skewness	0.128064	-0.15393		
7	5	27.71	42.07	kurtosis	-1.12229	-1.24412		
8	6	84.14	0.51					
9	7	80.36	62.13					
10	8	48.49	36.41					
11	9	22.23	36.51					
12	10	91.25	55.87					
13	11	55.18	40.24					
14	12	81.95	59.55					
15	13	29.26	6.28					
16	14	16.93	48.70					
17	15	46.88	6.94					
18	16	2.94	52.94					
19	17	80.12	64.69					

Cell E2: =QUARTILE(B$3:B$202,D2)

Workbook 9.26

(iii) Calculate the coefficient of variation (CV_A and CV_B) for each group. Thus:

$CV_A = 100(28.67/48.4) = 59.23\%$ and
$CV_B = 100(20.09/35.564) = 56.48\%$.

Relative dispersion is therefore slightly higher in Group A.

(iv) Since there are an equal number of companies in both groups, the combined mean is simply obtained by summing the 2 individual means and then dividing by 2. Thus:

Combined mean = $(48.4 + 35.564)/2 = 41.98$

If however, there had been an unequal number of companies in each group the combined mean would have to be computed in a way that takes account of the unequal numbers. This is called a weighted mean and is calculated as:

weighted mean = $(n_1 \bar{x}_1 + n_2 \bar{x}_2)/(n_1 + n_2)$

(v) The range for the combined group is the largest maximum minus the smallest minimum. Hence:

Combined range = $99.05-0.5149 = 98.5351$

Solution to Exercise 9.5

The combined list of company labels and profits are contained in columns D and E of Workbook 9.22C. These were produced by entering the label: A1 to the D3 cell and then dragging down on the handle until D202. Then the label: B1 was entered to D203 and this was dragged down to D402.

This produces the group and company identifiers—A1, A2, . . . A200, B1, B2, . . . B200. Next, the data in B3:B202 was copied into E3:E202 and then the data in C2:C203 copied into E203:E402.

This produces the combined list of company identifying labels and their profits.

```
┌─────────────────────────────────────────────────────────────────────────────┐
│ —            Microsoft Excel - W9_27.XLS                            ▢ ▢ ▢ ▢ ▢ │
│ — File  Edit  View  Insert  Format  Tools  Data  Window  Help             ▢ │
├─────────────────────────────────────────────────────────────────────────────┤
│ [toolbar icons]                                     100%  ▢  ▢ ▢ │
├─────────────────────────────────────────────────────────────────────────────┤
│ Courier (W1)      ▢  10  ▢   B  I  U   ▤ ▤ ▤ ▥  ▢  %  ,  ▢ ▢  ▢ ▢  ▢ │
├─────────────────────────────────────────────────────────────────────────────┤
│    D25        ▢                                                              │
└─────────────────────────────────────────────────────────────────────────────┘
```

	A	B	C	D	E	F	G
1		Group A annual	Group B annual	*profits (£000s)*		*profits (£000s)*	
2	Company no.	profits (£000s)	profits (£000s)	GROUP A		GROUP B	
3	1	21.81	3.49	Mean	48.4	Mean	35.564
4	2	77.34	52.16	Standard Error	2.028	Standard Error	1.4205
5	3	36.91	44.99	Median	47.87	Median	37.898
6	4	87.83	1.58	Mode	#N/A	Mode	#N/A
7	5	27.71	42.07	Standard Deviation	28.67	Standard Deviation	20.09
8	6	84.14	0.51	Sample Variance	822.2	Sample Variance	403.59
9	7	80.36	62.13	Kurtosis	-1.122	Kurtosis	-1.244
10	8	48.49	36.41	Skewness	0.128	Skewness	-0.154
11	9	22.23	36.51	Range	98.31	Range	67.332
12	10	91.25	55.87	Minimum	0.742	Minimum	0.5149
13	11	55.18	40.24	Maximum	99.05	Maximum	67.847
14	12	81.95	59.55	Sum	9681	Sum	7112.9
15	13	29.26	6.28	Count	200	Count	200
16	14	16.93	48.70	Confidence Level(95.	3.974	Confidence Level(9.	2.7842
17	15	46.88	6.94				

```
│◄│◄│►│►│\ Sheet1 / Sheet2 / Sheet3 / Sheet4 / Sheet5 / Sheet │◄│ ║        │►│
```

Workbook 9.27

Next, the mean and standard deviation of both groups A and B were computed in B203:C203 for the mean, and B204 and C204 for the standard deviation.

To compute the Z scores, the formula in F3 is:

$$=(E3-B\$203)/B\$204$$

and this was copied into F4:F202.

Then in F203 the Z scores for the group B data were calculated from:

$$=(E203-C\$203)/C\$204$$

and this was copied into F204:F402.

Then the D2:F402 area was selected and sorted on raw score to produce the section of the worksheet shown in Workbook 9.28.

With the same area selected, the sort was changed from raw score to Z score and produces the section of the worksheet shown in Workbook 9.29.

Clearly, the rankings have changed as a result of using Z score as opposed to raw score as the basis of the performance measure.

There are many potential reasons for this

ranking reassessment. Although it is clear that companies in Group A are generally more profitable that those in Group B, it could easily be the case that Group A companies are subject to less competition. Consequently, performing well in absolute terms in Group A may well indicate a less efficient company than one in Group B who actually performed less well in terms of absolute profits earned.

Solution to Exercise 9.6

(i) Place the mouse pointer anywhere in row 7 and then click and drag down to row 9 so that these 3 rows are highlighted. Now select Insert from the Menu bar and then Rows. Three rows will be inserted which should now be filled with the data for the 3 new products. Now copy the formulae in F7:I7 into F8:I10.

The index numbers will recompute automatically, and the results should resemble Workbook 9.30.

Clearly, this is a very efficient way of expanding the basket of goods.

Microsoft Excel - W9_28.XLS

File Edit View Insert Format Tools Data Window Help

Courier (W1) 10

G8

	A	B	C	D	E	F	G	H
1		Group A annual	Group B annual		Profit	Profit		
2	Company no.	profits (£000s)	profits (£000s)	Company	Raw score	Z score		
3	1	21.81	3.49	A79	99.05	1.770709		
4	2	77.34	52.16	A50	98.93	1.76639		
5	3	36.91	44.99	A133	98.60	1.755127		
6	4	87.83	1.58	A18	97.70	1.723717		
7	5	27.71	42.07	A136	97.58	1.719487		
8	6	84.14	0.51	A56	97.14	1.704027		
9	7	80.36	62.13	A81	96.56	1.683748		
10	8	48.49	36.41	A112	96.00	1.66419		
11	9	22.23	36.51	A151	95.66	1.652231		
12	10	91.25	55.87	A194	95.36	1.641779		
13	11	55.18	40.24	A187	95.34	1.640877		
14	12	81.95	59.55	A114	94.87	1.624491		
15	13	29.26	6.28	A86	94.32	1.605234		
16	14	16.93	48.70	A106	93.99	1.593918		
17	15	46.88	6.94	A137	93.53	1.577699		
18	16	2.94	52.94	A43	93.29	1.569209		
19	17	80.12	64.69	A90	93.11	1.562902		

Sheet1 / Sheet2 / Sheet3 / Sheet4 / Sheet5 / Sheet

Workbook 9.28

Microsoft Excel - W9_29.XLS

File Edit View Insert Format Tools Data Window Help

Courier (W1) 10

H31

	A	B	C	D	E	F	G	H
1		Group A annual	Group B annual		Profit	Profit		
2	Company no.	profits (£000s)	profits (£000s)	Company	Raw score	Z score		
3	1	21.81	3.49	A79	99.05	1.770709		
4	2	77.34	52.16	A50	98.93	1.76639		
5	3	36.91	44.99	A133	98.60	1.755127		
6	4	87.83	1.58	A18	97.70	1.723717		
7	5	27.71	42.07	A136	97.58	1.719487		
8	6	84.14	0.51	A56	97.14	1.704027		
9	7	80.36	62.13	A81	96.56	1.683748		
10	8	48.49	36.41	A112	96.00	1.66419		
11	9	22.23	36.51	A151	95.66	1.652231		
12	10	91.25	55.87	A194	95.36	1.641779		
13	11	55.18	40.24	A187	95.34	1.640877		
14	12	81.95	59.55	A114	94.87	1.624491		
15	13	29.26	6.28	B91	67.85	1.610956		
16	14	16.93	48.70	B94	67.82	1.609772		
17	15	46.88	6.94	A86	94.32	1.605234		
18	16	2.94	52.94	A106	93.99	1.593918		
19	17	80.12	64.69	B60	67.31	1.584104		

Sheet1 / Sheet2 / Sheet3 / Sheet4 / Sheet5 / Sheet

Workbook 9.29

Workbook 9.30

Microsoft Excel - W9_30.XLS

File Edit View Insert Format Tools Data Window Help

Courier (W1) 10 B I U

B12 =100*C11/B11

	A	B	C	D	E	F	G	H	I	J
1	Purchases of items of electronic equipment 1980 and 1993 (000s of units)									
2		Quantity	Quantity	Price	Price	PbQb	PcQc	PcQb	PbQc	
3		1980	1993	1980	1993	1980	1993			
4	televisions	20.2	22.4	260	230	5252	5152	4646	5824	
5	video recorders	4.8	12.6	600	280	2880	3528	1344	7560	
6	video cameras	0.4	5.3	1500	850	600	4505	340	7950	
7	personal computers	0.8	8.5	1800	900	1440	7650	720	15300	
8	CD players	0.1	5.9	386.99	145.99	38.699	861.34	14.599	2283.2	
9	personal stereos	0.9	12.35	25.99	14	23.391	172.9	12.6	320.98	
10	answering machines	1.6	2.1	86.45	35.99	138.32	75.579	57.584	181.55	
11	SUM	28.8	69.15			10372	21945	7134.78	39420	
12	Simple quantity index no.	240.10417								
13	Expenditure index no.	211.56915								
14	Q index no. base P	380.04439								
15	Q index no. current P	211.56915								
16	P index no. base Q	68.786164								
17	P index no. current Q	55.66959								
18										

Sheet1 / Sheet2 / Sheet3 / Sheet4 / Sheet5 / Sheet

(ii) The introduction of the three new products has had the effect of increasing the expenditure and quantity index numbers, but reducing both price index numbers in comparison with the previous basket of goods.

Workbook 9.31

Solution to Exercise 9.7

(i) Use the Pivot Table routine with a data range of A1:B111 and drag region into the Rows area and attitude into the Columns area. The results should resemble Workbook 9.31.

Microsoft Excel - W9_31.XLS

File Edit View Insert Format Tools Data Window Help

Courier (W1) 10 B I U

H3 =D3/G3

	A	B	C	D	E	F	G	H	I
1	Region	Attitude	Count of Attitude	Attitude					
2	SE	L	Region	D	L	U	Grand Total	D as %	L as %
3	SE	L	NE	7	16	7	30	0.233333	0.533333
4	SE	U	NI	1	3	2	6	0.166667	0.5
5	SE	L	S	3	5	2	10	0.3	0.5
6	SE	D	SE	18	22	16	56	0.321429	0.392857
7	SE	D	W	5	1	2	8	0.625	0.125
8	SE	L	Grand Total	34	47	29	110		
9	SE	L							
10	SE	U							

Sheet1 / Sheet2 / Sheet3 / Sheet4 / Sheet5 / Sheet

(ii) The absolute numbers who liked the product are highest in Southern England, which also possesses the highest number who disliked the product. However, in relative terms, i.e. as a percentage of the number of respondents in each region, the highest proportion of respondents who liked the product was in Northern England. In Southern England, the highest absolute number who disliked the product was also the highest proportion.

These percentage calculations are shown in the H3:I7 range of Workbook 9.31.

(iii) The number of respondents selected from each region are roughly in proportion to the populations of those regions. This is known as quota sampling.

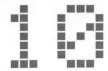

Simple linear regression

Contents

Accompanying data files to be loaded as instructed:

W10_1.XLS   W10_5.XLS   W10_8.XLS   W10_9.XLS   W10_10.XLS   W10_11.XLS
W10_APP2.XLS

10.1. Introduction

Linear regression is the process of fitting a **linear equation** of the form:

$$y = a + bx$$

to a set of data observations on the variables x and y.[1]

The word regression literally means 'moving backwards', but as used in statistics it is probably more helpful to think of it as meaning 'moving towards', or 'fitting'. Viewed in this way, linear regression can be construed as meaning the process of finding the equation of the straight line that has moved towards (i.e. fits) the observed data to the greatest extent.

It is of course possible that the observed data possess x and y coordinates that, of their own accord, (i.e. quite naturally) correspond exactly to the coordinates of a single straight line. But it is much more likely that there will be one or more outlying observations whose coordinates are not consistent with those of a unique straight line. In this case, the regression technique can be thought of as an averaging process whereby the 'best' straight line through the data is fitted.

To understand this more clearly, we will construct an example that will allow us to develop and follow the regression technique to its logical conclusion.

10.2. The linear model

Suppose you have been asked by a client to determine the effect of different application levels of a new brand of fertilizer upon crop yield. Obviously the first step must be to extract whatever relationship exists between crop yield and fertilizer application, and to do this we must first of all define our model and its variables.

As you might expect, the model to be used is a linear one (since at this stage we know of no other). This is a perfectly valid first approach, since linear regression can be performed easily and quickly within Excel.

However, it is as well to bear in mind from the outset that there is no necessary presumption, in business or anywhere else, that relationships must be linear. Indeed, as we will see later, the linear model is often not justified in terms of the data, and may therefore have to be abandoned in favour of some alternative (non-linear) model. At this stage, however, it is the logical first step, and provided we have some mechanism for identifying its limitations, it will get us started.

The presumed model is therefore **linear** and of the form:

$$y = a + bx$$

where *a* is the intercept term and *b* is the gradient term of the presumed line.

But what are the x and y terms of this equation? In this case it is intuitively apparent that it is fertilizer application that influences crop yield rather than vice versa, and as a consequence we can identify crop yield as the **dependent** variable (y) and fertilizer application as the **independent** variable (x). Our presumed model can therefore be stated verbally:

Crop yield is a linear function of fertilizer application

The task of linear regression is to determine the precise nature of this relationship by finding the implied values of the intercept and gradient terms, so that equations such as:

[1] If you are unsure of the meaning of this equation, consult Appendix 10.1 now.

$$y = 5 + 0.9x \text{ or } y = 10 - 1.2x$$

can be obtained.

Once again, it is as well to note at this stage that it will not always be as easy to identify the dependent and independent variables as was done above. In many real-life applications the direction of **causation** (i.e. which variable influences which) will be far from clear, and this can cause untold difficulties. But in our example we can be fairly sure that the relationship is properly defined in terms of causation.

Having defined our model, the next task is to make it more specific by collecting data on the relationship between crop yield and fertilizer application. The standard approach is to perform a controlled experiment, in which different chosen amounts of fertilizer are applied to a set of plants and their yields subsequently recorded after a given time period. Although this is easy enough to describe, there are a number of potential difficulties which have to be considered. The most important of these are:

(i) The values of x (fertilizer application) chosen by the experimenter must include zero. This acts a 'control' in the sense that it provides us with information on what yield is to be expected in the absence of any fertilizer application.

(ii) The non-zero values of x should span a 'reasonable' range, and should not increase in large jumps. This of course begs the question of what is 'reasonable' and what is 'large', and so the experimenter will have to be guided by prior knowledge and a realization that it will usually be impossible to perform the experiment in such a way that completely continuous application levels can be used.

(iii) The application levels must be entirely under the experimenter's control. This may seem to be the case in our example, until it is remembered that measurement error is an unavoidable fact of experimental life. In most cases it will have to be accepted that data are always subject to measurement error even in the controlled laboratory (let alone in the volatile business world) and that the experimental results will inevitably reflect this error. All that can be done is to make the greatest effort to ensure that it is kept to a minimum.

(iv) The conditions under which the experiment is carried out must be fully controlled in terms of all the other factors that influence plant growth (such as water received, soil conditions, and exposure to light). Only if this can be achieved is it possible to identify the single effect of fertilizer application on yield, as opposed to the effect of fertilizer combined with these other factors.

Now, while it may be possible to control those other factors within the confines of the laboratory, it is a different matter in real life, where many business variables are subject to influence by other variables that are entirely beyond the company's control. You only have to think of the effect that an increase in interest rates or a decline in the exchange rate will have upon a firm's profitability to realize that these external factors are uncontrollable from the firm's viewpoint, yet nevertheless exercise a crucial influence.

As if this were not enough, there is a further problem: if you are unaware of which independent variables influence your dependent variable, how can you control for them?

For example, we would all accept that water, light, and soil conditions influence plant growth and would recognize the need to control these, but what if it were to become known that magnetic variation also exercises an effect and that this varies within the laboratory? Previous experiments that did not have a control for this effect would now be partially invalidated by such a discovery, yet were carried out in good faith by controlling for those factors that were known about at the time. The fact that society's knowledge is continually increasing is little comfort to the researcher who is trying to control factors whose effects may have not yet been discovered.

For this reason the relationship to be investigated should always reflect the logical reasons for expecting there to be a relationship to be discovered. It is not acceptable to carry out a 'blanket' approach, whereby every independent variable that you can think of is tried in a regression model until one that 'fits' is discovered, regardless of any apparent reason for expecting there to be a relationship.

Provided these 4 points are fully accommodated in the experimental design, this means that the designated independent variable (x) can truly be regarded as being independent. This is important, since without this knowledge it is much more difficult to identify the exact direction of the causal relationship between x and y. Only if the independent variable is completely under the experimenter's control can it be absolutely clear that it is x that is causing y to change rather than the other way round. Also, such control ensures that x is not related to the other external factors.

Bearing these points in mind we might proceed to establish our application levels as:

grams of fertilizer applied (x): 0, 1, 2, 3, 4, 5, 6, 7, 8, 9, 10

where x is measured in grams of fertilizer application per day.

Once we have decided upon our application levels, the next problem is to decide what to apply them to. Ideally, we should obtain a set of absolutely identical plants and then apply the chosen levels of fertilizer to each of them (i.e. the first plant receives 0 grams, the second plant receives 1 gram, and so on).

However, the problem with this approach is that it is very difficult to be sure that the plants were truly identical even in terms of their physical characteristics, let alone in terms of their genetic make-up. We have to accept that apparently identical plants differ in their inherent vigour, and that this will exercise an effect upon their yield that is not related to the amount of fertilizer received.

To deal with this problem we should apply each application level to 11 (i.e. 0 to 10 inclusive) sets of (say) 30 apparently identical plants and then record the mean yield over the experimental period for each set of plants. This would mean that the first set of 30 plants would each receive 0 grams of fertilizer, the second set of 30 would each receive 1 gram, and so on. The mean weight gain over the period would then be calculated and recorded as the y values corresponding to 0 grams of application, 1 gram, etc.

Suppose now that this is what has been done, with the results shown in Workbook 10.1.

| Workbook 10.1 | **Make up Workbook 10.1 now, or load it from the accompanying disk (W10_1.XLS).** |

Even a cursory examination of the data suggests that fertilizer application has a marked effect upon yield at low application levels, but that this effect diminishes quite quickly (as saturation sets in) and eventually exercises an adverse effect as the plants become overwhelmed (poisoned) by fertilizer. This immediately casts doubt upon our linearity assumption, but we will conveniently overlook this for the moment until we have seen how to perform a linear regression on the data we have obtained. We will, however, return to this problem at a later stage.

10.3. **The scatter diagram**

Our first step should always be to create a **scatter diagram** of the results obtained.

To do this, draw a frame with the Chart Wizard and then define the data range as A3:B14. Then select an XY {Scatter} type of chart and use Option 2. Use the first

column for the Category X axis labels and the first row for the Legend text. Next, supply titles as shown in Fig. 10.1 and select Finish.

Finally, to remove the lines joining up the points, double click on the chart to allow editing and then click on the actual line in the chart. Then double click on any of the data points that are displayed, and from the screen that appears click on the None tab for the line type.

The effect should resemble Fig. 10.1. Notice that this confirms our earlier observation that the relationship does not look particularly linear.

With the scatter of points established we must now try to fit a straight line through these points.

To do this, use A1 and A2 to contain the labels a and b, and then enter values of 0.2 and 0.5 to B1 and B2 respectively.
Then name B1 and B2 as a and b.

These 2 cells contain our guesses for the values of the intercept (a) and the gradient (b), and therefore define a unique straight line that can then be plotted on top of the scatter diagram.

We are therefore guessing that the straight line:

$$y = 0.2 + 0.5x$$

is a reasonable fit to the scatter of points. To see whether it is, we now use column C to compute the values of y that are associated with the equation that we guessed.

To do this, enter the following formula to C4:
=a+b*A4

This gives the value of y predicted by the linear equation that we are using for the first value of x.

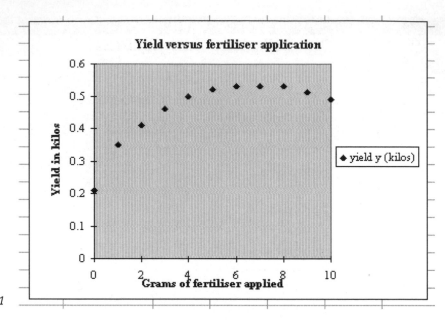

Figure 10.1

Now copy C4 into C5:C14.

This gives the rest of the predicted values for y associated with the remaining values of x.

Finally, in C3 add the label:

predicted y

Note carefully what has been done. Column B contains the actual values of y that were observed in the experiment for each of the chosen values of x. Column C gives the values of y that are predicted for these values of x on the basis of the straight line defined by the values of a and b that we have guessed.

We can now add this predicted line to the scatter points shown in Fig. 10.1.

To do this double click on the chart in the current workbook to allow editing and then click on the Chart Wizard. Now redefine the data range to be charted as A3:C14.

The result should resemble Fig. 10.2.

Now save this model as W10_1A.XLS.

As you can see, the line ($y = 0.2 + 0.5x$) that has been fitted to the data points does not really 'look very good'. It should be clear that we can do better. But this raises the question of how to decide whether we could in fact have done better with some other line.

One answer would be to judge each fitted line by eye, but this raises the objection that not all eyes are the same in terms of what they see. This approach would produce a myriad of different regression equations all from the same data, depending upon who was performing the experiment and how they perceived the data. Obviously this is unsatisfactory if (as should be the case) we require an objective statement of the relationship that produces the same results from a given data set regardless of who is performing the regression. To obtain this we must employ an algebraic approach which is known (for reasons which will become apparent) as 'least squares'.

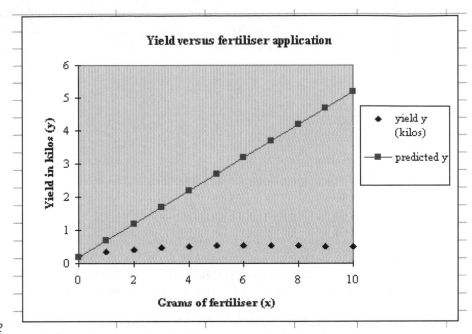

Figure 10.2

10.4. **The 'least squares' regression line**

If we consider carefully what we are attempting to do with our data, it should be apparent that we are trying to fit the 'best' straight line to the data set. This is what would have been hoped for when fitting by eye, since certain lines would be excluded on the basis that 'they don't look right'. But whereas the eye has an intuitive (albeit subjective) grasp of what looks best, how can inanimate algebra select the best line?

The answer is to ask what we really mean by 'best' and then define it in terms that algebra can understand. To do this, it would seem logical to define 'best' as involving the least error, but then we encounter the problem of what is meant by 'error'. To answer this we need to define a few terms.

First, we refer to the observed values as:

x_i, y_i where $i = 1, 2, 3 \ldots 11$

and we refer to the regression line as:

$\hat{y}_i = a + bx_i$

where the 'hat' above the y term indicates that it is a predicted value (i.e. predicted on the basis of the regression equation).

By using this notation we can see that for any observed value of x ($x_2 = 1$ for example), there are two associated values of y:

the observed value ($y_2 = 0.35$)

and the predicted value:

$\hat{y}_2 = a + b(x_2) = 0.2 + 0.5(1) = 0.7$

This being the case, we can define the difference between the observed value of y when $x = x_2$ and the predicted value of y when $x = x_2$ as the second **error** term: e_2. Here, $0.7 - 0.35 = 0.35$.

Furthermore, since there are 11 pairs of x, y observations, it follows that there will be 11 error terms: $e_1, e_2 \ldots e_{11}$, each one associated with the difference between each observed y value and its associated predicted value $(\hat{y}_i)$. We can therefore define any error term as e_i and write:

$$e_i = (y_i - \hat{y}_i)$$

This is a crucial definition.

Now, since there are 11 error terms, it surely makes sense to define the **total error** as the sum of the individual errors i.e.:

$$\text{Total error} = \Sigma e_i = \Sigma\,(y_i - \hat{y}_i)$$

Phrased in these terms we can now see that a reasonable algebraic definition of the 'best' straight line would be:

that line which has the least total error: Σe_i

This would be perfectly valid were it not for the fact that some of the error terms will be positive while others will usually be negative. This means that the positive and negative errors will tend to cancel one another out, with the result that under certain circumstances the total error could be calculated as zero when in fact there is not a single observation actually lying on or close to the line.

Clearly this is unsatisfactory, since an error is an error regardless of whether it is positive or negative, and it is only an algebraic peculiarity that is masking this fact.

To deal with this problem we must employ the same device as was used with the variance—to square each error term and then use the sum of these squared errors as our measure of Total (Squared) Error. When we do this we obtain:

$$\text{Total Squared Error} = \Sigma e_i^2 = \Sigma\,(y_i - \hat{y}_i)^2$$

This statistic is often referred to as the Sum of Squared Errors (SSE), and it is this which is to be made as small as possible. We therefore want to find the values of a and b that define the straight line that:

minimizes the sum of squared errors : Σe_i^2

To see how to do this, we can perform the error calculations in the current workbook.

Make sure the most recent version of Workbook 10.1 (W10_1A.XLS) is on screen. First, in D3 enter the label:

Error

and then in D4 enter the formula:

=B4-C4

Now copy this formula into D5:D14.

These are the error terms, given the observed data and the fitted line. As we said already, some are positive and some are negative, and so a cancelling-out process takes place when they are added up.

Consequently, we should now compute the **squared** errors in column E.

To do this, in E3 enter the label:

Squared error

and then in E4 the formula:

=D4^2

This will square the first error term.

Now copy E4 into E5:E14.

This will produce each of the squared errors for the entire data set.

Finally, in E15 enter:

=SUM(E4:E14)

This computes the Sum of Squared Errors (SSE), and it is this sum that is to be made as small as possible.

The effect should resemble Workbook 10.2. Notice that, given the actual data, each of the individual squared errors, and therefore the Sum of Squared Errors, is entirely determined by the values that have been used for *a* and *b*—that is, by the guess that has been used for the intercept and the gradient of the line to be fitted. Currently, we are using values of a = 0.2 and b = 0.5 and so the SSE is computed as 80.3136. However, if we change these values then both the value of the SSE and the position of the fitted line will change.

	Microsoft Excel - W10_2.XLS						
File	**Edit**	**View**	**Insert**	**Format**	**Tools**	**Data**	**Window** **Help**

Courier (W1) — 10 — | C4 | =a+b*A4

	A	B	C	D	E	F	G
1	a	0.2					
2	b	0.5					
3	fertilizer applied x (grams)	yield y (kilos)	predicted y	Error	Squared error		
4	0	0.21	0.2	0.01	1E-04		
5	1	0.35	0.7	-0.35	0.1225		
6	2	0.41	1.2	-0.79	0.6241		
7	3	0.46	1.7	-1.24	1.5376		
8	4	0.5	2.2	-1.7	2.89		
9	5	0.52	2.7	-2.18	4.7524		
10	6	0.53	3.2	-2.67	7.1289		
11	7	0.53	3.7	-3.17	10.0489		
12	8	0.53	4.2	-3.67	13.4689		
13	9	0.51	4.7	-4.19	17.5561		
14	10	0.49	5.2	-4.71	22.1841		
15					80.3136		

\ Sheet1 / Sheet2 / Sheet3 / Sheet4 / Sheet5 / Sheet

Workbook 10.2 Confirm this now by changing the value of *a* from 0.2 to 0.3 and the value of *b* from 0.5 to 0.05.

The SSE should fall from 80.3136 to 0.2111 and the fitted line should look a lot better. We conclude that this new line ($\hat{y}_i = 0.3 + 0.05x_i$) is a much better 'fit' than the old one, simply because, on balance, all of the actual data points are closer to the fitted line than before.

Now try to reduce the SSE even further by experimenting with different values for *a* and *b*.

If you get close to a value of 0.1 for the SSE then you are doing very well, and if you can manufacture a value of 0.04032 then you can do no better.

When you have finished, save the file as W10_2.XLS.

The trial and error procedure that you have been using indicates what you are trying to do and how you are trying to do it. But it is clearly very inefficient, and offers no indication of when the 'best' line has been achieved. You could keep on changing the values of a and b for a very long time until you felt satisfied that the SSE could be reduced no further, and even then you might be mistaken. There has to be a better way.[2]

This better way is to accept that, after a lot of algebra and a lot of calculus, statisticians have derived two formulae that will calculate the values of a and b that minimize the SSE. These formulae, in turn, have been formulated as dedicated Excel functions. The functions are called =INTERCEPT(Range of y values,Range of x values) and =SLOPE(Range of y values,Range of x values) and are used as follows.[3]

Bring Workbook 10.2 up on screen and read on.
First, use the C1 and C2 cells to contain the labels:

Intercept (a) and Gradient (b)

Next, in D1 enter:

=INTERCEPT(B4:B14,A4:A14)

A value of 0.34136 should be returned.

Then, in D2 enter:

=SLOPE(B4:B14,A4:A14)

A value of 0.02336 should be returned.

These two values are the least squares regression coefficients for the given data, and supply the values of a (0.34136) and b (0.02336) that minimize the SSE. The line defined by these coefficients is therefore:

$$\hat{y}_i = 0.34136 + 0.02336x_i$$

and this is the best line that can be fitted to the data.

Confirm this now by entering the values calculated in D1 and D2 as the values for the guesses of a and b in B1 and B2.

The SSE should now become 0.040319, and this is its minimum value.

Now re-save this file as W10_2.XLS.

Notice, however, that although the SSE is as small as it can be, it is not zero. This should prompt consideration of the difference between 'best' and 'good'. In other words, the values of a and b calculated by the least squares method define the *best* straight line through the data, but whether this best line is good or bad is a separate issue that needs further consideration.

Suppose, for example, that a set of x, y observations corresponded exactly, when plotted, to a circle. Now suppose that you used the =INTERCEPT and =SLOPE functions to fit the best straight line through these data points. The technique would do exactly as it was told, and do its best, but it is patently obvious that its best will not be very good, since a straight line looks nothing like a circle. The phrase 'fitting square pegs into round holes' immediately comes to mind.

---

2 You could use the Solver to minimize the value of the target cell (E15) by changing the values in B1:B2.

3 Note that it must be the range of y values that are used as the 1st argument in the function and the range of x values as the 2nd argument. If you reverse this order then you will regress x on y rather than y on x.

Also notice that the equation obtained from the least squares regression technique is defined for any finite value of x, and not just for those values of x that were observed. This means that we can make predictions about the yield that would result from fertilizer application levels that were not actually applied (1.5 or 11.6 grams, for example).

When these predictions are made on the basis of values of x which lie within the observed experimental range of x values (0 to 10 in this case), this process is known as **interpolation**. On the other hand, when the prediction uses a value of x that is outside the observed range then this is known as **extrapolation**.

As you might imagine, extrapolation is much less accurate than interpolation, for the simple reason, that while a relationship may be perfectly linear within its observed range of x values, there is no mechanism for determining how it behaves outside these x values. It *might* remain linear, but the only way to be sure about this is to extend the range of x values employed.

Exercise 10.1 can be attempted now.

10.5. Measuring the goodness of fit

The previous section has mentioned the distinction between 'best' and 'good' in the context of the relation between the fitted regression line and the actual data. It is now time to develop a statistical measure of the extent to which there is a perfect linear association between the pairs of x, y observations. In other words, a statistic that measures how well the best fitted line corresponds to a perfect straight line.

The simplest measure used is known as the **correlation coefficient** (r) and has a maximum value of 1 and a minimum value of -1. A value of 1 means that there is a perfect direct linear association between the pairs of x, y observations, with direct meaning that as x increases so too does y. For example, consider the following data set:

x	1	2	3	4
y:	3	6	9	12

It should be clear that each value of y is exactly 3 times the corresponding value of x. The fitted regression equation would therefore be:

$$\hat{y} = 3x$$

and the correlation coefficient would be computed as 1.

On the other hand, consider:

x:	1	2	3	4
y:	-3	-6	-9	-12

In this case, the value of y is exactly minus 3 times the value of x, and so the fitted regression equation would be :

$$\hat{y} = -3x$$

However, the relationship, although still perfectly linear, is now indirect in the sense that as x increases y decreases.

For this reason the correlation coefficient would be computed as -1—that is, a perfect **negative** linear association between y and x.

Now consider the following data set

x:	1	2	3	4
y:	-3	6	-9	12

In this case, there is no perfect linear association to be observed. There *is* a pattern—when x is odd $\hat{y} = -3x$, while when x is even $\hat{y} = 3x$—but considering both odd and even values of x leads us to conclude that there is no real linear association between y and x. The computed correlation coefficient would therefore be close to zero.

Excel can compute the correlation coefficient for us with its =CORREL function, the general syntax of which is:

=CORREL(y Range, x Range)

Now load Workbook 10_2.XLS.
   Then, in E1 enter the label:

Corr. Coeff.

and in F1 the formula:

=CORREL(B4:B14,A4:A14)

A value of 0.77348 should be returned to F1, indicating that the strength of the linear association is by no means perfect i.e. it is some way from 1.[4]

Associated with the correlation coefficient is a statistic known as R^2, that is obtained quite simply by squaring the correlation coefficient. Thus, since r always lies between 1 and -1, R^2 will always lie between 0 and 1 and will always be less than or equal to r.

R^2 is known as the **coefficient of determination** and can be understood in the following terms. We already know that the least squares regression line will minimize the Sum of Squared Errors, but how large is this minimum? To answer this, we can note that once we have obtained the fitted regression equation it is an easy matter to calculate these (squared) error terms and sum them to produce the Sum of Squared Errors. This was done in the E15 cell of Workbook 10.2.

Now, since we know this statistic to be the sum of the squared error terms, it would seem logical to regard it as a measure of the unexplained variation in the y variable, (i.e. unexplained by the regression equation). This is exactly what we do. But now we must face the question of whether this Sum of Squared Errors is 'large' or 'small', and this is complicated by the fact that we do not possess a known scale of measurement or a known range of values within which the Sum of Squared Errors is likely to fall. We can partially deal with this problem if we employ the notion of the proportion of the total variation in the y variable that is unexplained, since then we will obtain a statistic which is placed on a scale between 0 and 1.

But how do we calculate the total variation in the y variable? The answer is quite simply to define it as the Sum of Squared Deviations of each observed y value from its mean value, i.e:

$$\Sigma(y_i - \bar{y})^2$$

where, as usual, $\bar{y}$ denotes the mean value of y.

You will notice that this is simply the numerator in the formula for the variance of y which was explained previously and, as we saw there, represents the total variation of each y value around its mean value. It is often referred to as the Total Sum of Squares (TSS).

For ease of calculation in subsequent discussion we can therefore deduce that if:

4　This is what we might have expected given our previous observations about there being a saturation procedure taking place, and that the x, y plot eventually curves downwards.

$$\text{VARP(Data Range)} = (\Sigma (y_i - \bar{y})^2)/n$$

Then

$$\Sigma (y_i - \bar{y})^2 = n*\text{VARP(Data Range)}$$

To summarize, we have:

$$\text{SSE} = \text{UNEXPLAINED VARIATION} = \Sigma e_i{}^2 = \Sigma(y_i - \bar{y}_i)^2$$
$$\text{TSS} = \text{TOTAL SUM OF SQUARES} = \Sigma(y_i - \bar{y})^2$$

From these two definitions it follows that the proportional unexplained variation (PUV) can be written as:

$$\text{PUV} = \text{SSE/TSS}$$

That is:

$$\text{PUV} = \Sigma(e_i{}^2)/\Sigma(y_i - \bar{y})^2$$

Now if this statistic measures the proportional unexplained variation, and if, as it does, it lies between 0 and 1, then it surely follows that the proportional explained variation (PEV) must be given by:

$$\text{PEV} = 1\text{-PUV} = 1 - \Sigma(e_i{}^2)/\Sigma(y_i - \bar{y})^2$$

This is indeed the case, and produces the statistic known as R^2.

It is an extremely important statistic, since it gives us the proportion of the total variation in the y values that is explained by the regression equation of y on x. In this sense it is the regression equation's 'examination' mark, with the 'examination' being the question:

How well does the observed data correspond to a linear function? For the data in our example, Workbook 10.2 has already computed:

$$\text{SSE} = 0.040319$$

Furthermore, you can easily confirm that the TSS in y will be computed to be:[5]

$$\text{TSS} = 0.10036$$

Therefore:

$$\text{PUV} = 0.040319/0.10036 = 0.40174.$$

And:

$$\text{PEV} = R^2 = 1\text{-PUV} = 1\text{-}0.40174 = 0.59826.$$

Now, with Workbook 10.2 on screen use the E2 cell to contain the label:

R Squared

and then in F2 enter:

=F1^2

A result of 0.59826 should be returned, and is precisely the result that we have just computed for the PEV.[6]

Now resave this file as W10_2.XLS.

This means that of the total squared variation that takes place in the y variable, 59.826% is explained by the regression equation that has been fitted, and that 40.173% of the total

---

5 Use any cell to contain: =11*VARP(B4:B14). The indicated result will be returned to that cell.

6 Excel also has a dedicated function to compute the coefficient of determination. It is called RSQ and has the syntax: =RSQ(y Range,x Range). Thus for the current example we would enter: =RSQ(B4:B14,A4:A14).

variation is therefore unexplained. As we saw before, the linear equation is not a very good fit for these data.

The calculations above may seem needlessly complicated in order to obtain a statistic that Excel produces easily, but it must be remembered that any statistic is meaningless unless the principles upon which it is founded are fully appreciated. These have now been explained.

Exercises 10.2, 10.3, and 10.4 can be attempted now.

What the analysis above has done is to allow determination of the extent (if any) of the statistical linear association between y and x. Assuming that this is satisfactorily established, the next question is whether we can conclude from this that we have identified a **causal** relationship between the independent variable and the dependent one.

To answer this you must be absolutely clear about the distinction between **association** and **causation**. To appreciate this, you only have to think of an experiment that records a student's age against the number of examinations that he or she has passed at college or university. Without doubt we would find a high degree of statistical association between these 2 variables (even allowing for mature students and child prodigies), but the direction of causation (if any) is far from clear.

It is certainly not tenable to contend that the number of examinations passed determines a student's age, but could the student's age be determining the number of examinations passed? Obviously there is a sense in which the latter hypothesis is valid, since if examinations are passed then students tend to get older in the process. But although this is a necessary condition it is hardly sufficient, otherwise age alone would be the only requirement in passing examinations.

Clearly there is at least one other variable exercising an influence 'behind the scenes' upon both age and the number of examinations passed, and we might suspect that the student's IQ, or the number of school qualifications obtained, or even the year of study should be investigated.

What these reservations mean is that, although statistical association can perhaps be established, the crucial step involved in turning this association into a causal relationship is fraught with danger. This is particularly so in those areas (common in business) where not only does one variable influence a second variable but the resulting value of this second variable then exercises a secondary influence upon the value of the first variable. For example, it will usually be the case that increased investment will lead to increased profits, but it is also the case that these increased profits provide the funds to finance further investment. Such a situation is known as 'feedback' and is a statistical nightmare for even the most experienced analyst, since it will never be clear which variable is influencing the other. Clearly the direction of causation has been obscured by the feedback.

10.6. Transforming non-linear models into linear ones

As was observed earlier, and as is clear from Fig. 10.1, the data for our fertilizer example do not lend themselves easily to linear interpretation. So the question arises of whether, given our suspicions of non-linearity, we can modify our analysis within the confines of the linear regression model.

The answer is that we can—under certain circumstances. For example, suppose that instead of hypothesizing a linear relationship, we suspected that y and x were related as follows:

$$y = ax^b$$

Clearly (since this equation describes a **polynomial** function), y and x will not be related in a linear fashion unless b = 1 (in which case $y = ax^b$ becomes $y = ax$). In all other cases, the relationship between y and x will be curved (with the curve becoming steeper and steeper if b exceeds 1, but become flatter and flatter if b is less than 1). Clearly this is non-linear behaviour except for the special case of b = 1.

However, if we perform a logarithmic transformation of both sides of the equation then we will obtain:

$$\log y = \log a + b(\log x)$$

At first sight, the effect of this transformation may not be obvious. However, closer inspection of the expression should reveal that this is a linear equation of the standard form, provided we recognize that the variables are now log y and log x, rather than y and x.

In other words, the intercept of the line is log a, the gradient is b (as before), and the variables are log y and log x.

Now all we have to do is to force Excel to perform the regression analysis on the logarithmically transformed variables rather than upon y and x.[7]

To do this, load W10.1 and then make the following additions.
  In C3 and D3 add the labels:

  log x   and   log y

In C4 and D4 enter the formulae:

  =LOG(A4)   and   = LOG(B4)

and then copy these into C5:D14.

Columns C and D now contain our independent (log x) and dependent (log y) variables. Now notice that a problem (#NUM!) has arisen in C4, where we are asking Excel to calculate the value of log 0. Mathematically this is not defined, and for this reason we must regard the regression range as C5:C14 for the independent variable and D5:D14 for the dependent variable. This will exclude the x value of 0 from the regression analysis.[8]

Now calculate the intercept, the gradient, the correlation coefficient, and R^2 for this logarithmically transformed data set by locating the following formulae in F1:F4

  =INTERCEPT(D5:D14,C5:C14)
  =SLOPE(D5:D14,C5:C14)
  =CORREL(D5:D14,C5:C14)
  =RSQ(D5:D14,C5:C14)

After adding identifying labels in E1:E4, the results should resemble Workbook 10.3.

---

7 To see why this works, consult Appendix 10.2.

8 It also, unfortunately, removes the 'control'.

	Microsoft Excel - W10_3.XLS					

File   Edit   View   Insert   Format   Tools   Data   Window   Help

Courier (W1)   10   **B** *I* U   ≡ ≡ ≡   % ,

D4   =LOG(B4)

	A	B	C	D	E	F	G
1					log a	-0.42958	
2					b	0.167842	
3	fertiliser applied x (grams)	yield y (kilos)	log x	log y	r	0.900437	predicted y = ax^b
4	0	0.21	#NUM!	-0.67778	R^2	0.810788	0
5	1	0.35	0	-0.45593			0.371892495
6	2	0.41	0.30103	-0.38722			0.417775384
7	3	0.46	0.477121	-0.33724			0.447196433
8	4	0.5	0.60206	-0.30103			0.469319156
9	5	0.52	0.69897	-0.284			0.487229794
10	6	0.53	0.778151	-0.27572			0.502370078
11	7	0.53	0.845098	-0.27572			0.515537472
12	8	0.53	0.90309	-0.27572			0.52722223
13	9	0.51	0.954243	-0.29243			0.53774855
14	10	0.49	1	-0.3098			0.547342625
15							

Sheet1 / Sheet2 / Sheet3 / Sheet4 / Sheet5 / Sheet

Workbook 10.3

As you can see from Workbook 10.3, the logarithmic regression equation is:

$$\log y = -0.42958 + 0.1678(\log x)$$

This is the linear version of the assumed polynomial expression, but the latter can be identified by noting that since:

$$\log a = -0.42958$$

it follows that:

$$a = 10^{-0.42958} = 0.3718.$$

Furthermore, since b is not in logarithmic form, it is a simple matter to identify the implied polynomial expression as:

$$\hat{y} = 0.3718x^{0.1678}$$

As you can also see, the value of R^2 has increased from its original value of 0.5983 for the assumed linear equation, to 0.81079 for the logarithmic equation (representing the assumed polynomial function). On the basis of this we can conclude that the polynomial function is a better 'fit' to the data than the simple linear function since the R^2 value is closer to 1.

Now although you could graph the regression equation on top of the raw data in its logarithmic form, it will usually be more instructive to graph the implied polynomial form.

Consequently, use column G to compute the predicted values of the polynomial regression equation by entering the following formula to G4:

$$=10\wedge F\$1*A4\wedge F\$2$$

This is equivalent to:

$$y = ax^b$$

when it is remembered that F1 contains the value of log a and F2 contains the value of b.

Then copy G4 into G5:G14, and add the label:

predicted y

to the G3 cell.

Now use the Chart Wizard to draw a frame and define the data range as:

A3:B14,G3:G14

Choose an XY{Scatter} type of chart, Option 2, and use the first column as the Category (X) axis labels and the first row as the legend text. Supply titles and then Finish. Finally, to remove the lines joining up the points in the actual series, double click on the chart to allow editing and then click on the line representing yield in the chart. Then double click on any of the data points that are displayed and from the screen that appears click on the None tab for the line type.

The results should resemble Fig. 10.3.

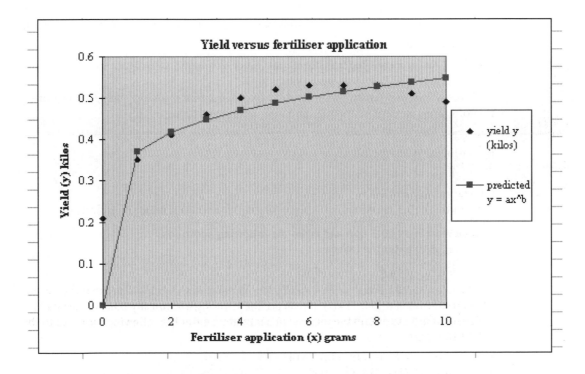

Figure 10.3   **Now save this model as W10_3.XLS.**

The result of this discussion clearly suggests that, as far as this particular data set is concerned, the polynomial equation:

$$\hat{y} = 0.3718x^{0.1678}$$

provides a much better fit to the raw data than the simple linear equation:

$$\hat{y} = 0.34136 + 0.02336x$$

that was obtained earlier. This is clear not only from the charts showing the fitted equations but also from the improved values of r and R^2 obtained by the polynomial 'fit'.

It should be stressed once again, however, that of the alternatives considered the best result still does not confirm the linearity assumption. The relationship is clearly curved, but we have used the linear regression technique to extract the parameters of this curve. This was entirely due to the logarithmic transformation, since it should now be clear that:

$$y = a + bx$$

is linear in x and y. And:

$$y = ax^b$$

is non-linear in x and y. But:

$$\log y = \log a + b \log x$$

is linear in log y and log x.

Finally, you may well be wondering what should be done if neither the linear nor the polynomial functions provide a satisfactory 'fit' to the data. The answer is, that provided we are determined to remain within the confines of the linear regression model, then as another alternative we could hypothesize an **exponential** function of the form:

$$y = ab^x$$

Now, if we perform a logarithmic transformation of both sides of this equation we obtain:

$$\log y = \log a + x \log b$$

This is known as a **semi-log transformation**, since although y is in logarithmic form, x has remained in its original (non-logarithmic) form.

Nevertheless, the transformation is still a linear equation, with log y being a linear function of x. The intercept will be log a and the gradient will be log b. Thus:

$$y = ab^x$$

is non-linear in y and x, but:

$$\log y = \log a + x \log b$$

is linear in log y and x.

Workbook 10.3 can perform the regression for you without major modification.

Load Workbook 10.3 now and make the following additions.
   In E7:E10 enter the labels:

   log a   log b   r   and R^2

Now you must tell Excel that the independent variable is x (A4:A14), and that the dependent variable is log y (D4:D14). This will use the semi-logarithmically transformed data.

Consequently, to obtain the regression parameters enter the following formulae to the F7:F10 range:

   =INTERCEPT(D4:D14,A4:A14)
   =SLOPE(D4:D14,A4:A14)
   =CORREL(D4:D14,A4:A14)
   =RSQ(D4:D14,A4:A14)

(Notice that the problem of taking the logarithm of 0 does not arise in this formulation). The results should resemble Workbook 10.4, where for completeness the results of the simple linear regression have been reproduced in the E13:F16 range.

We have also computed the predicted values resulting from the semi-log transformation in column H.

To do this, enter the following formula to the H4 cell:

   =10^F$7*10^F$8^A4

and copy H4 into H5:H14.

This is the equivalent of $y = ab^x$ when it is remembered that:

$$a = 10^{\log a} = 10\wedge F\$7 = 10^{-0.48736} = 0.3255$$
$$b = 10^{\log b} = 10\wedge F\$8 = 10^{0.02706} = 1.064$$

Therefore, for the semi-log transformation we have:

$$\hat{y} = 0.3255(1.064^x)$$

which is equivalent to:

$$=10\wedge F\$7*10\wedge F\$8\wedge A4$$

when written in terms of cell references.

	A	B	C	D	E	F	G	H
1					log a	-0.42958	DOUBLE LOG	SEMI-LOG
2					b	0.167842	TRANSFORM	TRANSFORM
3	fertiliser x g.	yield y (kilos)	log x	log y	r	0.900437	predicted y = ax^b	predicted y = ab^x
4	0	0.21	#NUM!	-0.6778	R²	0.810788	0	0.325566787
5	1	0.35	0	-0.4559	DOUBLE LOG		0.371892495	0.346498291
6	2	0.41	0.30103	-0.3872			0.417775384	0.368775534
7	3	0.46	0.47712	-0.3372	log a	-0.48736	0.447196433	0.392485037
8	4	0.5	0.60206	-0.301	log b	0.027061	0.469319156	0.417718884
9	5	0.52	0.69897	-0.284	r	0.736759	0.487229794	0.444575077
10	6	0.53	0.77815	-0.2757	R²	0.542814	0.502370078	0.473157923
11	7	0.53	0.8451	-0.2757	SEMI-LOG		0.515537472	0.503578431
12	8	0.53	0.90309	-0.2757			0.52722223	0.53595475
13	9	0.51	0.95424	-0.2924	a	0.341364	0.53774855	0.570412624
14	10	0.49	1	-0.3098	b	0.023364	0.547342625	0.607085881
15					r	0.773479		
16					R²	0.59827		
17					NO LOGS			
18								

Workbook 10.4

When you have made these additions, save the workbook as W10_4.XLS.

The results of this new regression show that R^2 has fallen to 0.5428 and that as a consequence the semi-log transformation has not improved the strength of association in comparison with the double log transformation (or even in comparison with the simple linear model).

Finally, we can use the Chart Wizard to produce a graph showing each of the fitted equations (linear, polynomial, and exponential) on top of the raw data.

Use column I to contain the predictions for the linear equation by the now familiar method. Then define the data range for the chart as:

A3:B14,G3:I14

After adding titles and removing lines as was done previously, the results should resemble Fig. 10.4.

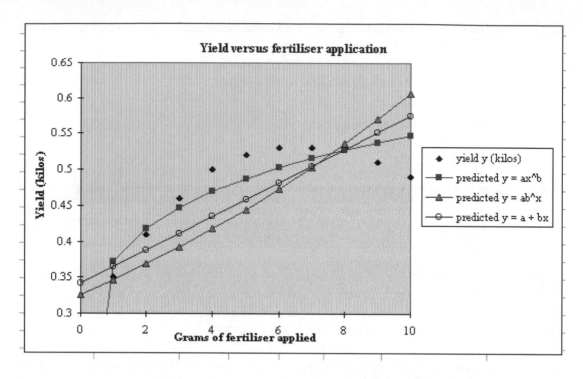

Figure 10.4   As is clear from this diagram (and the three R^2 results) the polynomial equation appears to be the best fit, but even then it still cannot follow the decline in yield that occurs when saturation sets in. Nor does it perform very well for an x value of 0 (the predicted value of y is 0 while the actual value is 0.21). Consequently, we should regard the polynomial function as satisfactory only for a certain range of x values (1 to 7 roughly). Outside this range the actual data is behaving in a way that is not consistent with a single-termed polynomial function.[9]

The preceding analysis has done enough to suggest that there are a number of ways in which the raw data can be transformed so that the linear regression model can still be applied. As a final point in this section, if none of the methods outlined above produces satisfactory values of R^2, then you may just have to accept that the simple linear regression model is incapable of modelling your data set. Other methods are available, but these require further explanation.

Exercise 10.5 can be attempted now.

10.7. **Time series analysis**

An important application of the regression techniques developed in this chapter lies in an area known as **time series analysis**. What this means is that the independent variable is

---

9   We should suspect that the actual data is behaving in a way that might best be described by a quadratic function: $y = ax^2 + bx + c$. Unfortunately, there is no logarithmic transform that can turn a quadratic function into a linear one, and so the simple linear regression technique cannot be used to estimate the quadratic terms. A more powerful technique, known as multiple regression, needs to be used.

taken to be the passage of time, and that the linear regression equation is used to extract the trend that the dependent variable adopts as time passes.

Unfortunately, however, when time is used as the independent variable there are a number of additional complications introduced to the regression technique. These stem from the fact that the dependent variable will often be subject to a number of influences that are highly sensitive to the units in which the passage of time are measured (months, quarters, years, etc.). For example, if only annual data has been observed it will be impossible to identify any seasonal influence (such as more fuel consumed in winter) that acts upon the data. To identify any such effects would require that quarterly data be collected.

However, as long as we recognize these difficulties we can accommodate them in our model and thereby develop a technique for splitting the raw time series data into its various component parts. This is the basic objective of time series analysis.

As a simple starting-point, let us presume that any set of quarterly time series data is composed of three elements: a trend value (t), a seasonal element (s), and a residual component (r). Having defined the components of our model, we now have to decide upon the form that the model should take. In this simple illustration it will be assumed to be additive and adopt the following form:

$$y = t + s + r$$

The first step in the analysis of time series will always be to establish the trend on the basis of the least squares regression equation.

To see how this is done, open a new workbook and enter the following data, or load the file called W10_5.XLS.

In A1:   time (x)

In A2:A21:
1	2	3	4	5	6	7	8	9	10
11	12	13	14	15	16	17	18	19	20

In B1:   y

In B2:B21
20	15	10	18	24	18	13	21	28	22
19	25	32	26	21	29	35	28	22	32

This represents a data set consisting of quarterly observations over a 5-year period with x having been defined in terms of the quarter number (1 to 20).

Now compute the intercept and the gradient of the trend line and use these to calculate the estimated trend in column C. The formulae are:

In I1:   =INTERCEPT(B2:B21,A2:A21)

In I2:   =SLOPE(B2:B21,A2:A21)

In C2   =I$1+I$2*A2   copied into C3:C21

The effect should resemble Workbook 10.5.

Workbook 10.5

If it does, save the file as W10_5.XLS.

Column C provides us with the linear trend values predicted by the regression equation of y on x:

$$y = 14.57895 + 0.79248x$$

The next task is to calculate the de-trended **series.**

In our additive case, the de-trended series will be given by:

de-trended series = y - t

	A	B	C	D	E	F	G	H	I
1	time (x)	y	linear trend					a	14.57895
2	1	20.00	15.37					b	0.792481
3	2	15.00	16.16						
4	3	10.00	16.96						
5	4	18.00	17.75						
6	5	24.00	18.54						
7	6	18.00	19.33						
8	7	13.00	20.13						
9	8	21.00	20.92						
10	9	28.00	21.71						
11	10	22.00	22.50						
12	11	19.00	23.30						
13	12	25.00	24.09						
14	13	32.00	24.88						
15	14	26.00	25.67						
16	15	21.00	26.47						
17	16	29.00	27.26						
18	17	35.00	28.05						
19	18	28.00	28.84						
20	19	22.00	29.64						
21	20	32.00	30.43						
22									

Formula bar: C2 =I$1+I$2*A2

Title bar: Microsoft Excel - W10_5.XLS

Menu: File Edit View Insert Format Tools Data Window Help

Sheet tabs: Sheet1 / Sheet2 / Sheet3 / Sheet4 / Sheet5 / Sheet

Workbook 10.5

This means that the entries in column D should be obtained by subtracting the entries in column C from those in column B.

Do this now by entering the following formula to the D2 cell:

=B2-C2

and copying it into D3:D21.
Then add the label:

de-trended series

to the D1 cell.

The next task is to try and identify the seasonal component (if any) that is contained in the de-trended series. To do this we must collect together all the de-trended values that pertain to the same quarter of the year (i.e quarters 1, 5, 9, 13, 17; 2, 6, 10, 14, 18; etc.).

Consequently, for the first quarter of year 1 the difference between the actual value of y (20.00) and the trend value (15.371429) is 4.63, and for the first quarter of year 2 the difference is 5.46. These 'equivalent quarter' values have been placed in the block of cells commencing in A30, then summed and averaged to produce an average value for the season that they represent. They are displayed in Workbook 10.6.

Workbook 10.6

Make these entries now in the current workbook.

You should be able to see that the 4 entries in the row labelled 'Average' represent an estimate of the seasonal variation of the series, so the next step will be to place them in column

	quarter 1	quarter 2	quarter 3	quarter 4
year 1	4.63	-1.16	-6.96	0.25
year 2	5.46	-1.33	-7.13	0.08
year 3	6.29	-0.50	-4.30	0.91
year 4	7.12	0.33	-5.47	1.74
year 5	6.95	-0.84	-7.64	1.57
Average	6.09	-0.70	-6.30	0.91

Workbook 10.6

E (against their appropriate quarters) and then subtract them from the actual series values to produce what is known as the seasonally adjusted series.

Do this now in columns E and F of your worksheet by making the following entries. First, in E2, E3, E4, and E5 enter:

   =B$35   =C$35   =D$35   =E$35

and then copy E2:E5 into E6:E21.

This will transfer the equivalent quarter seasonal variations to column E.

Next, in F2 enter:

   =B2-E2

and copy this into F3:F21.

These formulae subtract the seasonal variation (s) from the actual series values (y) to give:

   y - s

which is known as the **seasonally adjusted series.**

Finally, the residual elements will be defined by:

   y - s - t

and these should be placed in column G of your worksheet.

Do this now by entering the following formula to G2:

   =B2-E2-C2

and copying it into G3:G21.

When all these calculations have been completed and appropriate labels added, the final worksheet should look something like Workbook 10.7.

Workbook 10.7

If it does, save the file now as W10_7.XLS.

Clearly, the seasonally adjusted series is one of the most important results of this analysis, since it is almost impossible to encounter any set of published statistics without finding that

	Microsoft Excel - W10_7.XLS								
File	Edit	View	Insert	Format	Tools	Data	Window	Help	
F2			=B2-E2						
	A	B	C	D	E	F	G	H	I
1	time (x)	y	linear trend	detrended series	seas var.	seas adjusted	residual	a	14.57895
2	1	20.00	15.37	4.63	6.09	13.91	-1.46	b	0.792481
3	2	15.00	16.16	-1.16	-0.70	15.70	-0.46		
4	3	10.00	16.96	-6.96	-6.30	16.30	-0.66		
5	4	18.00	17.75	0.25	0.91	17.09	-0.66		
6	5	24.00	18.54	5.46	6.09	17.91	-0.63		
7	6	18.00	19.33	-1.33	-0.70	18.70	-0.63		
8	7	13.00	20.13	-7.13	-6.30	19.30	-0.83		
9	8	21.00	20.92	0.08	0.91	20.09	-0.83		
10	9	28.00	21.71	6.29	6.09	21.91	0.20		
11	10	22.00	22.50	-0.50	-0.70	22.70	0.20		
12	11	19.00	23.30	-4.30	-6.30	25.30	2.00		
13	12	25.00	24.09	0.91	0.91	24.09	0.00		
14	13	32.00	24.88	7.12	6.09	25.91	1.03		
15	14	26.00	25.67	0.33	-0.70	26.70	1.03		
16	15	21.00	26.47	-5.47	-6.30	27.30	0.83		
17	16	29.00	27.26	1.74	0.91	28.09	0.83		
18	17	35.00	28.05	6.95	6.09	28.91	0.86		
19	18	28.00	28.84	-0.84	-0.70	28.70	-0.14		
20	19	22.00	29.64	-7.64	-6.30	28.30	-1.34		
21	20	32.00	30.43	1.57	0.91	31.09	0.66		
22									

| Sheet1 | Sheet2 | Sheet3 | Sheet4 | Sheet5 | Sheet |

Workbook 10.7

they have been seasonally adjusted. In its basic form, what the seasonally adjusted series does is to indicate what the behaviour of the dependent variable would have been like had it not been subject to seasonal variation. Now graph the actual series, the trend, and the seasonally adjusted series on the same axes, and you will obtain a more obvious indication of what has been done.

The results should resemble Fig. 10.5. As you can see, the seasonally adjusted data is much closer to the trend than the actual series. This is the entire purpose of seasonal adjustment.

As a final consideration in this section, you should realize that the analysis of time series is an extremely complex undertaking. This stems from the fact that the passage of time is the 'universal variable', i.e. just about everything changes with the advance of time. But whether it is the passage of time *per se* that is causing the dependent variable to change, or the influence of another variable or variables, is difficult to determine. This will often be of minor importance if all we are trying to do is describe and analyse the past behaviour of the dependent variable, but if, as is often the case, we are going to make predictions about the future on the basis of past experience then the influence of other variables cannot be ignored so easily. This forecasting approach is clearly fraught with danger, but as long as we remember that a successful forecast can be thought of as one which performs better than a guess, then we can continue to make predictions and feel at least partially confident that our decision making is more informed than would have been the case if we decided everything by a guess—on the toss of a coin for example.

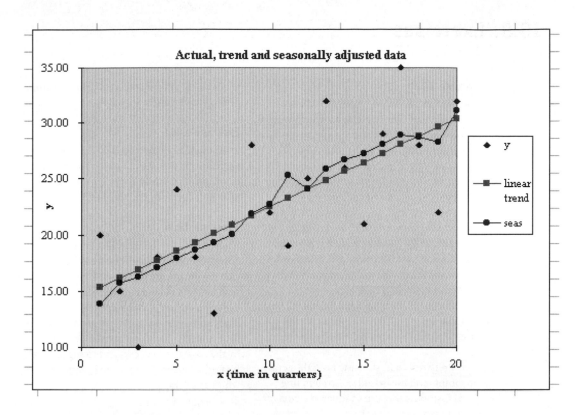

Figure 10.5   **Exercise 10.6 can be attempted now.**

10.8. Exercises

Exercise 10.1

Load the file called W10_8.XLS from the accompanying disk. The data are the results of the following market research experiment by a large company.

The company's total market area was divided into 40 equally populated market areas, and the price to be charged for the product was set to be the same in each area. Then, the weekly amount of advertising expenditure (£x) in each of these market areas was set as indicated in column B. The weekly sales (y units) in each market area was then recorded as shown in column C.

(i) Use linear regression to estimate a linear equation describing how the value of sales (y) varies with the level of advertising expenditure (x).

(ii) Prepare a chart showing both the actual data points and the best fitted straight line.

(iii) Compute the sum of squared errors for the best fitted line.

(iv) If the product sells at a price of £100, and costs £70 per unit to produce, estimate a linear equation for the company's weekly profit in terms of its advertising expenditure (x).

When you have finished the exercise, save the model as W10_12.XLS.

Exercise 10.2

Load the file called W10_9.XLS from the accompanying disk. The data are the relationship between monthly sales of ice cream (x gallons) and monthly sales of peaches (y tonnes) in 20 selected supermarkets.

By calculating the correlation coefficient between y and x, decide whether peaches and ice cream is a popular choice by the customers of this supermarket.

Exercise 10.3

Load the file called W10_12.XLS. Calculate the correlation coefficient and the coefficient of determination for the regression equation of sales on advertising expenditure.

Exercise 10.4

The data shown in Table 10.1 are the correlation coefficients between the examination marks obtained by a group of 100 students in 4 subjects.

Suppose that in their next year of study the students have to specialize in any two of the four subjects. Use the information provided by the correlation coefficient to suggest which two subjects should be taken by students whose marks are:

High in Maths
Low in Maths
High in Stats
Low in Stats
High in Economics
Low in Economics
High in English
Low in English

Exercise 10.5

Load the file called W10_10.XLS from the accompanying disk. The data show the relationship, for a particular product, between the quantity of the product demanded (y units) and the price charged (£x) for 40 different prices. Considering linear, polynomial, and exponential forms of the relationship between y and x, estimate the best-fitting equation to the data. Prepare a

Table 10.1		MATHS	STATS	ECONOMICS	ENGLISH
	Maths	n/a	0.9468	0.3812	-0.8765
	Stats	0.9468	n/a	0.1023	-0.7945
	Economics	0.3812	0.1023	n/a	0.9145
	English	-0.8765	-0.7945	0.9145	n/a

chart showing the best-fitting equation on top of the actual data.

Exercise 10.6

Load the file called W10_11.XLS from the accompanying disk. The data are a supermarket chain's monthly sales of turkeys over a period of 36 months.

(i) Prepare a workbook that will calculate the trend and the seasonally adjusted series for turkey sales.

(ii) Prepare a suitably titled and labelled chart showing the actual series, the trend, and the seasonally adjusted series on the same axes.

(iii) What conclusions can be drawn from the above analysis?

10.9. **Solutions to the exercises**

Solution to Exercise 10.1

The solution is shown in Workbook 10.12 and Fig. 10.6. With the price of the product being £100 and the unit cost being £70 it follows that:

Profit = Sales(Price - Unit cost) - Advertising Expenditure

Workbook 10.12

Which is equivalent to:

Profit = y(100 - 70) - x = 30y - x

Since the regression procedure has established that:

$$y = 3008.462 + 0.217897x$$

it follows that the estimated linear equation for profit is:

Profit = 30(3008.462 + 0.217897x) - x = 90253.86 + 6.5369x - x = 90253.86 + 5.5369x

	Microsoft Excel - W10_12.XLS								
File	Edit	View	Insert	Format	Tools	Data	Window	Help	

Courier (W1) — 10 — B I U

E5 — =(C5-D5)^2

	A	B	C	D	E	F	G	H	I	J
1	Market	Weekly	Weekly	Predicted		a	3008.462	=INTERCEPT(C5:C44,B5:B44)		
2	Area	Advertising	Product	Weekly	Squared	b	0.217897	=SLOPE(C5:C44,B5:B44)		
3		Expenditure	Sales	Sales	Errors					
4		(£x)	(y units)				SUM OF SQUARED ERRORS			
5	1	0	2021	3008.462	975081.6		18649969	=SUM(E5:E44)		
6	2	1000	2376	3226.359	723110.4					
7	3	2000	2689	3444.256	570411.3					
8	4	3000	2987	3662.153	455831.1					
9	5	4000	3146	3880.049	538828.6					
10	6	5000	3325	4097.946	597445.9					
11	7	6000	3891	4315.843	180491.6					
12	8	7000	4071	4533.74	214128.2					
13	9	8000	4456	4751.637	87401.05					
14	10	9000	4879	4969.533	8196.313					
15	11	10000	5213	5187.43	653.8095					
16	12	11000	5489	5405.327	7001.152					

Sheet1 / Sheet2 / Sheet3 / Sheet4 / Sheet5 / Sheet

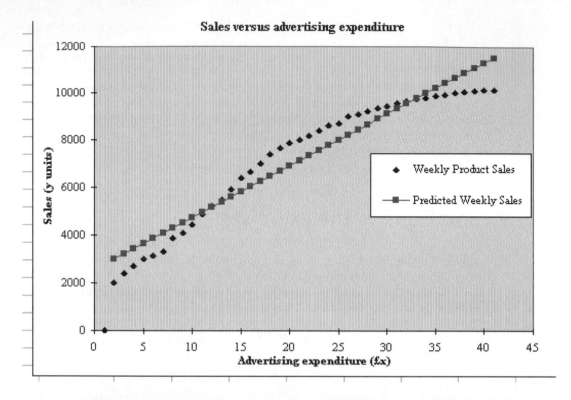

Figure 10.6

Solution to Exercise 10.2

=CORREL(C4:C23,B4:B23) = 0.054573
=RSQ(C4:C23,B4:B23) = 0.002978

Both of these values are very close to zero, indicating that there is neither a strong positive nor a strong negative linear association. If the correlation coefficient had been highly positive then it would suggest that peaches and ice cream are a common joint purchase, and that the products are **complements**. On the other hand, a large negative value for the correlation coefficient would indicate that the products are **substitutes**—when the customer buys more of one she buys less of the other. The calculated value of the correlation coefficient, being so close to zero, suggest that buying patterns of ice cream are not related to (i.e. independent of) buying patterns for peaches.

Solution to Exercise 10.3

=CORREL(C5:C44,B5:B44) = 0.965071
=RSQ(C5:C44,B5:B44) = 0.931362

The fit of the line is clearly not perfect, but both values are sufficiently high to suggest that over the experimental range a good fit has been obtained. However, as with the fertilizer

example, the scatter diagram (Fig. 10.6) indicates that there is a saturation process taking place, and so we should be reluctant to make predictions outside this range.

Solution to Exercise 10.4

The general principle is that if a student is strong in a particular subject then he or she should specialize in that subject *and* in the one with the highest positive correlation coefficient with that subject. On the other hand, if a student is weak in a particular subject then they should specialize in those two subjects which are least positively correlated with the subject in which they are weak.

For example, if the correlation coefficient between Maths and English were -1, then a student who was very weak in Maths should specialize in English. The perfect negative correlation would suggest that they would be very strong in English. Thus:

High marks in:

Maths	Specialize in Maths and Stats (r = 0.9468)
Stats	Specialize in Stats and Maths (r = 0.9468)

Eco-nomics Specialize in Economics and English (r = 0.9145)

English Specialize in English and Economics (r = 0.9145)

Low marks in:

Maths Specialize in English (r = -0.8765) and Economics (r = 0.3812)

Stats Specialize in English (r = -0.7945) and Economics (r = 0.1023)

Eco-nomics Specialize in Stats (r = 0.1023) and Maths (r = 0.3812)

English Specialize in Maths (r = -0.8765) and Stats (r = -0.7945)

Solution to Exercise 10.5

Workbook 10.13

The solution is shown in Workbook 10.13, and Fig. 10.7.

For the simple linear function, the ranges for the =INTERCEPT, =SLOPE, =CORREL, and =RSQ functions were B4:B43,A4:A43.

For the polynomial function a double log transform was used and so the ranges for the =INTERCEPT, =SLOPE, =CORREL, and =RSQ functions were D4:D43,C4:C43. For the exponential function a semi-log transform was used and so the ranges for the =INTERCEPT, =SLOPE, =CORREL, and =RSQ functions were D4:D43,A4:A43.

As you can see, the correlation coefficient and coefficient of determination values are very high for all of the specified models, but the polynomial is the highest. Consequently we conclude that this is the best fit to the data.

The predicted values for each of the equations are computed by entering the following formulae to E4, F4, and G4:

$$=I\$2+I\$3*A4 \qquad =10^{\wedge}I\$8+A4^{\wedge}I\$9$$
(Linear) \qquad (Polynomial)

Microsoft Excel - W10_13

File Edit View Insert Format Tools Data Window Help

F4   =10^I$8*A4^I$9

	A	B	C	D	E	F	G	H	I	J
1		Quantity			Pred-	Pred-	Pred-	LINEAR: y = a + bx		
2	Price	Demanded			-icted	-icted	-icted	a	1627.87	
3	(£x)	(y units)	Log x	Log y	y = a + bx	y = ax^b	y = ab^x	b	-638.931	
4	0.9	1114	-0.046	3.0469	1052.8329	1113.6	1075.3	r	-0.98677	
5	0.92	1089	-0.036	3.037	1040.0543	1089.4	1058.4	R^2	0.973707	
6	0.94	1065	-0.027	3.0273	1027.2757	1066.3	1041.8			
7	0.96	1043	-0.018	3.0183	1014.4971	1044.1	1025.5	POLYNOMIAL: log y = log a + b log x		
8	0.98	1022	-0.009	3.0095	1001.7185	1022.8	1009.4	log a	3.001032	i.e. y = ax^b
9	1	1003	0	3.0013	988.93987	1002.4	993.61	b	-0.99886	i.e. y = 1002x$^{-0.99886}$
10	1.02	982	0.009	2.9921	976.16126	982.75	978.04	r	-0.99995	
11	1.04	963	0.017	2.9836	963.38265	963.87	962.71	R^2	0.999894	
12	1.06	944	0.025	2.975	950.60403	945.7	947.62			
13	1.08	929	0.033	2.968	937.82542	928.21	932.76	EXPONENTIAL: log y = log a + xlog b		
14	1.1	912	0.041	2.96	925.04681	911.35	918.14	log a	3.340292	i.e. y = ab^x
15	1.12	896	0.049	2.9523	912.2682	895.1	903.75	log b	-0.34308	i.e. y = 2186(-0.3427^x)
16	1.14	879	0.057	2.944	899.48959	879.41	889.58	r	-0.99675	
17	1.16	867	0.064	2.938	886.71098	864.27	875.64	R^2	0.993512	

Sheet1 Sheet2 Sheet3 Sheet4 Sheet5 Sheet6

Start Microsoft Excel - W10_13 Paint Shop Pro 15:40

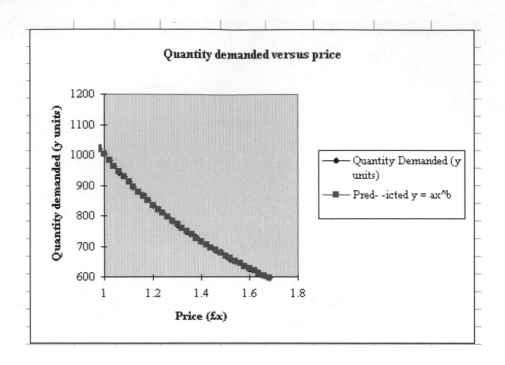

Figure 10.7
=10^I$14*10^(I$15*A4)
(Exponential)

and copying them into E5:G43.

As Fig. 10.7 indicates, when the predicted values for the polynomial equation are plotted on top of the actual data there is very little distinction to be observed.

Solution to Exercise 10.6

A section of the solution is shown in Workbook 10.14.

(i) Cells H1:H4 were used to compute the intercept, slope, correlation coefficient, and R^2 of the x, y data in B5:B40,A5:A40 and then the trend was computed in column C from the formula in C5:

=H$1+H$2*A5

copied into C6:C40.

The de-trended series was calculated in column D by subtracting the trend values from the actual values. Since turkey sales appear to be sensitive to the month rather than the quarter, the seasonal variation was computed on a monthly basis. The calculations for the seasonal variations are shown in Workbook 10.14A.

The average 'equivalent month' seasonal variations were then placed in column E, and in column F these were subtracted from the actual series values to give the seasonally adjusted data.

(ii) The data range for the chart was defined as A4:C40,F4:F40, and produces Fig. 10.8.

(iii) Clearly there are monthly peaks of turkey sales at Christmas and Easter. Nevertheless, the overall trend is of slowly increasing turkey sales (approximately b = 0.03 thousand = 30 per month).

When the seasonally adjusted data is inspected, it would seem to suggest that, although turkey sales are still a seasonal (monthly) event, they are becoming less so. This could be due to the fact that people are increasingly consuming other types of meat on festive occasions, but also because they are consuming relatively more turkey at other times. This is indicated by the fact that the seasonally adjusted figure at Christmas for the 1st year is well above the trend value, whereas for the 2nd and 3rd years the figures are below trend. Christmas sales of turkeys are therefore becoming less substantial in relation to turkey sales in the rest of the year.

	Microsoft Excel - W10_14.XLS							

File **Edit** **View** **Insert** **Format** **Tools** **Data** **Window** **Help**

| | | | | | | | | | | | 100% | | |

Courier (W1) | 10 | B I U | | | | | | % , | | | |

F5 | =B5-E5

	A	B	C	D	E	F	G	H	I
1	Time	Monthly Sales	Trend	de-trended	seasonal	seasonally	a	3.049714	
2	(months)	of Turkeys		series	variation	adjusted	b	0.02934	
3		000's					r	0.208316	
4	x	y	t	y - t	s	y - s	R^2	0.043395	
5	1	3.21	3.0790541	0.130945946	0.00553539	3.204464607			
6	2	2.7	3.1083938	-0.40839382	-0.60047104	3.300471042			
7	3	3	3.1377336	-0.13773359	-0.34647748	3.346477477			
8	4	4.25	3.1670734	1.082926641	1.13084942	3.119150579			
9	5	2.8	3.1964131	-0.39641313	-0.55515701	3.355157014			
10	6	2.5	3.2257529	-0.7257529	-0.77116345	3.271163449			
11	7	2.4	3.2550927	-0.85509266	-0.79716988	3.197169884			
12	8	2.5	3.2844324	-0.78443243	-0.83317632	3.333176319			
13	9	2.8	3.3137722	-0.5137722	-0.47918275	3.279182754			
14	10	2.4	3.343112	-0.94311197	-0.50518919	2.905189189			
15	11	3	3.3724517	-0.37245174	-0.54452896	3.544528958			
16	12	8.9	3.4017915	5.498208494	4.29613127	4.603868726			
17	13	3.4	3.4311313	-0.03113127	0.00553539	3.394464607			
18	14	2.9	3.460471	-0.56047104	-0.60047104	3.500471042			
19	15	3.1	3.4898108	-0.38981081	-0.34647748	3.446477477			

Sheet1 / Sheet2 / Sheet3 / Sheet4 / Sheet5 / Sheet

Workbook 10.14

As regards the Easter peaks of sales, the seasonally adjusted data shows that sales are roughly 'on trend', and so we conclude that the Easter turkey is retaining its traditional role more than the Christmas turkey.

Appendix 10.1. Linear functions

Unless the reader has a clear idea of the algebraic and graphical concept of a straight line, the subsequent discussion will be severely diluted. Consequently, look at the data below.

x	0	1	2	3	4	5	6
y	10	12	14	16	18	20	22

(i) By inspecting the data estimate the equation of the straight line that it represents.

(ii) Prepare a worksheet that will graph x versus y.

(i) We can argue as follows:

when x = 0; y = 10. Therefore the starting value of y is 10.

when x = 1; y = 12. Therefore y has increased by 2 units as a result of a 1 unit increase in x.

when x = 2; y = 14. Therefore y has increased by a further 2 units as a result of another 1 unit increase in x.

We should therefore suspect that that a unit increase in the value of x generally causes the value of y to increase by 2 units. Also, since the

	A	B	C	D	E	F	G	H	I
42		Year 1	Year 2	Year 3	Average				
43	Month 1	0.13095	-0.031131	-0.08320849	0.00553539				
44	Month 2	-0.40839	-0.560471	-0.83254826	-0.60047104				
45	Month 3	-0.13773	-0.389811	-0.51188803	-0.34647748				
46	Month 4	1.08293	1.2808494	1.028772201	1.13084942				
47	Month 5	-0.39641	-0.34849	-0.92056757	-0.55515701				
48	Month 6	-0.72575	-0.44783	-1.13990734	-0.77116345				
49	Month 7	-0.85509	-0.61717	-0.9192471	-0.79716988				
50	Month 8	-0.78443	-0.87651	-0.83858687	-0.83317632				
51	Month 9	-0.51377	-0.165849	-0.75792664	-0.47918275				
52	Month 10	-0.94311	0.0048108	-0.57726641	-0.50518919				
53	Month 11	-0.37245	-0.204529	-1.05660618	-0.54452896				
54	Month 12	5.49821	3.9161313	3.474054054	4.29613127				
55									

Cell reference: E43 = =AVERAGE(B43:D43)

Workbook 10.14A

Figure 10.8

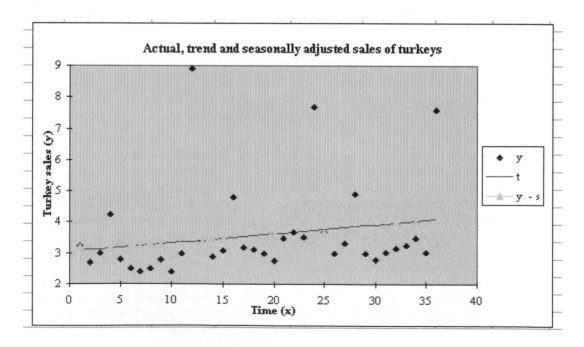

starting value for y was 10 (the value when x = 0), we should think that the general linear expression for y would be given by:

$$y = 10 + 2x$$

(ii) **Enter the values for x in A2:A8 and the values for y in B2:B8. Use A1 and B1 to contain the labels: x, and y.**

Then use the Chart Wizard to draw a frame and define the data range as A1:B8. Select an XY {Scatter} type graph, Option 2 and use the first column for the Category X labels and the first row for the Legend text. Add titles and then choose Finish.

A perfect straight line should be produced.

The discussion above means that:

$$y = a + bx$$

is the general form of the equation of a straight line. To see this, consider the process of cooking a chicken. The cooking instructions will usually say something like:

> Cook for 44 minutes per kilo plus 20 minutes over.

Thus, if x represents the weight of the chicken in kilos, then y (the cooking time) for a 2 kilo bird is given by:

$$y = 20 + 44(2) = 108 \text{ minutes}$$

Hence the cooking time for a chicken weighing x kilos would be:

$$y = 20 + 44x$$

Supply the value of x (i.e. the weight of the chicken) and the cooking time (y) is determined.

Now suppose that the cooking instructions are given as:

> b minutes per kilo plus a minutes over

The cooking time (y) is therefore :

$$y = a + bx$$

This is the general form of the linear relation, but if we use the specific cooking instructions quoted earlier, then clearly a = 20 and b = 44. Thus:

$$y = a + bx \text{ becomes: } y = 20 + 44x$$

In this formulation *a* is known as the intercept and *b* as the gradient. Thus any straight line can be defined by:

$$y = \text{intercept} + \text{gradient}(x) = a + bx$$

In graphical terms, with y on the vertical axis and x on the horizontal axis, the following relationships are true:

(i) When x = 0 the value on the vertical axis (y) is given by the intercept. Thus:

$$y \text{ (when } x = 0) = a.$$

(ii) When x is increased from 0 to 1 the value on the vertical axis (y) increases by b units. Thus:

$$y \text{ (when } x = 1) = a + b$$

(iii) When x is increased from 1 to 2 the value on the vertical axis (y) increases by another b units. Thus:

$$y \text{ (when } x = 2) = y \text{ (when } x = 1) + b = a + b + b = a + 2b$$

(iv) When x is increased from 2 to 3, the value on the vertical axis (y) increases by another b units. Thus:

$$y \text{ (when } x = 3) = y \text{ (when } x = 2) + b = a + 2b + b = a + 3b$$

(v) When x is increased to a value of x:

$$y(\text{when } x = x) = y(\text{when } x = x - 1) + b = a + (x - 1)b + b = a + xb - b + b = a + xb$$
$$= a + bx$$

Appendix 10.2 Logarithmic transformation

Load the file called W10_APP2.XLS.

The data in columns A and B represent a polynomial equation of the form:

$$y = 10x^2$$

for x values between 1 and 10 inclusive.

Fig. A10.1 shows the chart of this relationship to be curved (the data range plotted was A2:B11). Rows 2 to 11 of columns C and D are the logarithms of columns A and

B respectively. That is, C2 and D2 were made to contain:

$$=\text{LOG(A2)} \qquad \text{and} \qquad =\text{LOG(B2)}$$

and both of these formulae were copied into C3:D11.

Fig. A10.2 shows that when log x is plotted against log y (data range C2:D11) the curved relationship between y and x from Fig. A10.1 has become perfectly linear when plotted in logarithmic form. This clearly suggests that the curve:

$$y = 10x^2$$

has been turned into a linear relationship that is given by:

$$\log y = 1 + 2 \log x$$

Notice that nothing has been done to the intrinsic relationship between y and x. It has merely been expressed in a different form that conveniently turns out to be linear (in log y and log x rather than y and x).

As a useful analogy of what has been done here, consider a bicycle wheel. Viewed from the side it clearly looks like a circle. Now suppose that a huge downward force is applied to the wheel. It would eventually become flat and look like a line when viewed from the side.

Taking logarithms of two variables that are related to each other in the form:

$$y = ax^b$$

is exactly equivalent to the application of the downward force on the wheel. All the intrinsic information that the data contain is unchanged, but how it appears is different, and, since we want to use linear regression, becomes much more appropriate for that technique.

Inferential statistics

Contents

Accompanying data files to be loaded as instructed:

W10_2.XLS   W11_3.XLS   W11_4.XLS   W11_7.XLS   W11_8.XLS   W11_9.XLS

W11_12.XL   W11_13.XLS   W11_14.XLS   W11_17.XLS   W11_18.XLS   W11_19.XLS

11.1. Introduction to inference

Previous chapters have explained the concepts involved in *describing* data sets. However, there is a considerable difference between the processes of description and *inference*. In the latter case it is recognized that the data will usually be sample values drawn from some larger data set known as the **population**. This clearly poses the question of whether the sample data that has been gathered can be regarded as truly representative of the population from which it was drawn. Only if this can be established satisfactorily will the sample statistics be of real value in making general statements about the statistical features of the population data. Consequently, establishing or refuting the extent to which sample data are representative of a population is the fundamental task of inference and inferential as opposed to descriptive statistics.

It should also be clear that, since we will usually only possess full knowledge of the sample as opposed to the population data, any inference about population values that we make on the basis of this data will be subject to reservations. In statistical terms these reservations are expressed and measured in terms of probabilities. In other words, on the basis of the sample evidence we might infer something like:

> 'on balance, the sample mean would appear to be representative of the unknown population mean, but there is an x% chance that it is not'

A verbal statement such as this is equivalent to what inferential statistics calls a **hypothesis test**. In other words, the analyst hypothesizes, for example, that the population mean is equal to some constant (k). This is what is called the **null hypothesis**. Then, on the basis of the sample evidence, some simple statistics are calculated to test this hypothesis against the **alternative hypothesis** (usually that the population mean is not equal to k).

On the basis of this test and the probability of the calculated test values occurring, either the null hypothesis is accepted or it is rejected (and by implication, the alternative hypothesis accepted). In either case, however, an inference has been made, and so there will usually be a chance of being wrong (x% in our previous verbal example). Clearly the value of x in a statement such as this will be of considerable importance to the investigator.

More formally, we define the null hypothesis as H_0 and the alternative hypothesis as H_1. We then write

H_0: population statistic = k

and:

H_1: population statistic $\neq$ k

The task of elementary inference is to choose between H_0 and H_1 in a rational way, always being mindful of the fact that such a choice cannot be made without incurring a risk of making the wrong choice. Before we can do this however, a number of concepts require to be explained. The first of these is the notion of probability.

11.2. Principles of probability

As the previous section has suggested, inferential statistics is inevitably concerned with chance, since outcomes and decisions cannot be regarded as definite. Consequently, where chance is involved, a full appreciation of the issues raised by inference will require an understanding of some probability concepts.

The probability of an event is simply its relative frequency of occurrence. Thus if an event can have 5 possible and equally likely outcomes, the probability of any one of them occurring is 1 in 5 = 0.2 = 20%. However, particularly when we are dealing with continuous data, the relationship between the value of the variable (X) and its probability of occurrence is usually expressed in terms of what is known as a **probability density function** (pdf).

To understand this important concept, consider the process of taking observations on the height of individuals. Measuring to 2 decimal places, we could use the Histogram routine explained in Chapter 8 to construct a frequency distribution that would indicate how often particular heights were observed (0.10m, 0.11m, ... 1.9m). However, this frequency curve would change if we decided to measure the heights to 3 decimal places, and then change again if the heights were measured to 4 decimal places. Theoretically, if not practically, there is no obvious limit to the number of decimal places to which height (or age, or time, for that matter) can be measured. This is what is meant by the variable being regarded as continuous.

Consequently, as more and more observations are taken, and as the number of decimal places to which the observations are measured becomes larger and larger, a histogram of the frequencies versus the observed X values tends to become a **smooth curve**. Now if this smooth curve also has the property that the area underneath it is equal to **unity** then it is known as a **probability curve**. The figure of unity is important since it implies that any value of X must lie at or in between the maximum and minimum values for which the pdf is defined. Unity is therefore the probability value of certainty. Furthermore, the height of this probability curve at some value of X is usually denoted by f(x), and this function is called the pdf.

It is crucial to recognize that f(x) does not represent the probability of observing the particular value of X. When the data are continuous, it is only possible to find the probability of observing a value of X in a specified range. Thus the probability that X lies between two specified values (call them a and b) is given by the area under the pdf between X values of a and b. However, on the basis of the pdf it is an easy, if laborious, matter to compute the areas to the right or the left of each of a large number of possible X values.

When this is done the **probability distribution function** is obtained and gives—depending upon how it was constructed—the probability that X is either greater than some specified value, or less than some specified value.[1] This function is also referred to as the **cumulative distribution function**, and is the continuous counterpart of the cumulative frequencies that were explained in Chapter 8.

Fortunately, despite the fact that most commonly used probability density functions involve very complex mathematics, Excel can produce both the f(x) values and the cumulative function values for any of a wide range of commonly encountered density functions. One of these probability density functions that will prove particularly useful is known as the normal distribution.

11.3. **The normal distribution**

One of the most widely used probability distributions is known as the **normal distribution**, and adopts an importance that derives from the historical observation that many random

---

1 When the data are continuous the probability that X is exactly equal to some specified value is effectively regarded as zero. This is because it is impossible to distinguish a value of, say, 1.99999999999999999 from one of 1.99999999999999998.

variables associated with common processes turn out to be normally or approximately normally distributed.

The first point to note is that there is no such thing as *the* normal distribution. Rather, there is a family of distributions in which each member of the family is differentiated from another on the basis of the values of its mean (μ) and its standard deviation (σ). Clearly this implies that there is a different normal distribution for every possible combination of μ and μ, and so there are an infinite number of normal distributions.

When the random variable X is distributed normally with mean μ and standard deviation σ, we symbolize this as:

$$X \sim N(\mu, \sigma)$$

The following are the important characteristics of any normal distribution.

1. It adopts a symmetrical bell shape about its mean so that the curve on either side of μ is a mirror image of the other side.

2. The mean, the median, and the mode are all equal.

3. The curve is asymptotic to the X axis on both sides of the mean. This implies that the value on the Y axis never reaches zero for finite values of X—both positive and negative. In other words, the value on the Y axis will never quite reach zero, regardless of how large or how small X becomes.

4. The total area under the curve is 1. In conjunction with the previous point, this means that the probability of x lying between ∞ and -∞ is 1 (i.e. certain).

5. For any normal distribution:

> approximately 68% of all x values will lie within a range of 1 standard deviation either side of the mean
> approximately 95% of all x values will lie within a range of 2 standard deviations either side of the mean
> approximately 99.7% of all x values will lie within a range of 3 standard deviations either side of the mean

This is true for any normal distribution and allows us to deduce that the probabilities of any X value being more than 1, 2, or 3, standard deviations away from the mean on either side are 0.32, 0.05, and 0.003 respectively. For example, if:

$$X \sim N(5, 2)$$

then approximately 68% of all X values will lie in the range 5-2 = 3 to 5 + 2 = 7, approximately 95% will lie in the range 5-4 = 1 to 5 + 4 = 9, and approximately 99.7% will lie in the range 5-6 = -1 to 5 + 6 = 11.

Equivalently, the probabilities that X will lie outside the ranges 3 to 7, 1 to 9, and -1 to 11 are approximately 32%, 5%, and 0.3% respectively. Furthermore, because of symmetry, the probability that X exceeds 7 is 16% and the probability that X is less than 3 is also 16%. Extending this logic should make it clear that:[2]

> P(X>9) = P(X<1) = 2.5%
> P(X<9) = 100% - P(X>9) = 100% - 2.5% = 97.5%
> P(X>11) = P(X<-1) = 0.15%
> P(X<11) = 100% - P(X>11) = 100% - 0.15% = 99.85%

The equation used to calculate the probabilities associated with any normal distribution is mathematically complex. However, Excel has a dedicated function known as =NORMDIST. The general syntax of this function is:

---

2 P(X>9) symbolizes the probability that X exceeds 9.

=NORMDIST(Required X value, Mean,Standard deviation, FALSE/TRUE)

The last argument (FALSE/TRUE) is a **switch** to tell Excel whether to compute the value of the probability density function (FALSE) or the cumulative probabilities of all the X values up to the required X value (TRUE). In other words, if the switch is set to TRUE then the probability that X will *not* be exceeded is computed.

For example, if:

$$X \sim N(5,2)$$

Then, =NORMDIST(9,5,2,FALSE) will return a value of (0.027), which is the value on the Y axis associated with an X value of 9. This is not the probability of X occurring, however. On the other hand, =NORMDIST(9,5,2,TRUE) will return a value of approximately 97.5% (0.975), which represents the area under the distribution to the left of 9. This *is* a probability, and represents the chances that any value of X is less than 9. We write:

$$P(X<9) \approx 0.975$$

Thus, if we want to prepare a chart of any normal distribution then we should use the FALSE switch to obtain the value of the probability density function at each chosen value of X. However, since the probability associated with any value of X is represented by an area under the curve, we require to set the switch to TRUE in order to obtain the probability of that value of X not being exceeded.

Now we can use the =NORMDIST function to create our own chart of any normal distribution.

To do this, open a new workbook and proceed as follows.
First, in A1 and A2 enter the labels:

Mean   and   Standard deviation

Then in B1 and B2 enter some values for the mean and the standard deviation.

In the illustration we will use 5 and 2 respectively.

Next, in A10 and B10 enter the labels:

X   and   f(x)

We now need to supply a range of X values to be evaluated by the NORMDIST function so that a chart of the pdf can be created. This is not entirely straightforward, since as we have already seen the range of X values over which the normal distribution displays its characteristic bell shape is entirely determined by its mean and its standard deviation.

Thus for example, a normal distribution with mean = 0 and standard deviation = 1 would display almost all of its bell shape over a range of X values between -3 and 3. On the other hand, a normal distribution with $\mu = 0$ and $\sigma = 100$ would only show most of its bell shape over a range of X values spanning the range -300 to 300.

Clearly, if we are to prepare a worksheet that can satisfactorily chart any normal distribution, we need to create a flexible scale that is sensitive to the values of the mean and the standard deviation being used. This is where we can use our previously gained knowledge that in any normal distribution more that 99% of all X values will lie within plus or minus 3 standard deviations of the mean. Thus, if:

$$X \sim N(10,2)$$

we know that a minimum value for X of 10 - 3(2) = 4, and a maximum value for X of 10 + 3(2) = 16 will encompass almost all of the X values.

Equivalently, if:

$$X \sim N(28,4)$$

then the required minimum and maximum values are 28 -3(4) = 16 and 28 + 3(4) = 40. Now suppose that we decide to allocate 100 cells of our worksheet to contain the X values.

Use A11:A111 to contain these values of X.

The first (lowest) value for X will be given by:

$$\mu - 3\sigma$$

and the last (highest) value by:

$$\mu + 3\sigma$$

The range of X values (maximum - minimum) is therefore:

$$(\mu + 3\sigma) - (\mu - 3\sigma) = 6\sigma$$

With 100 cells being used to contain the X values, this means that the X values should increase in steps of $6\sigma/100 = 0.06\sigma$.

Now put these ideas into practice in the current workbook by using A11 to contain:

=B1-3*B2

This is the mean minus 3 times the standard deviation being used i.e. the minimum value of X that we need to plot.

Then in A12 enter:

=A11+0.06*B$2

This is the minimum value of X plus the flexible step value obtained by multiplying the standard deviation by 0.06.

Now copy A12 into A13: A111.

We have now created a truly flexible scale, as can be appreciated if we change either or both of the values for the mean and/or the standard deviation.

For example, make B1 contain 16 (the mean) and make B2 contain 1.5 (the standard deviation).

The values in A11:A111 will now commence at 11.5 and increase in steps of 0.06(1.5) = 0.09 until the maximum value of 20.5 is reached. Using A11:A111 as the scale for the horizontal axis means that the scale for the graph will adjust automatically for each new normal distribution that is to be charted.

Now restore the values in B1 and B2 to 5 and 2 respectively.

With this flexible scale established, it is now an easy matter to compute and display the pdf values associated with each of these X values.

To do this use B11 to contain:

=NORMDIST(A11,B$1,B$2,FALSE)

and then copy B11 into B12:B111.

The normal distribution density function values will be computed, and your workbook should resemble the section shown in Workbook 11.1

		Microsoft Excel - W11_1.XLS				
File **Edit** **View**	**Insert**	**Format** **Tools**	**Data**	**Window**	**Help**	
B11		=NORMDIST(A11,B$1,B$2,FALSE)				

	A	B	C	D	E	F
1	Mean	5				
2	Standard deviation	2				
3						
4						
5						
6						
7						
8						
9						
10	X	f(x)				
11	-1	0.002215924				
12	-0.88	0.002648172				
13	-0.76	0.003153363				
14	-0.64	0.003741436				
15	-0.52	0.004423227				
16	-0.4	0.005210467				
17	-0.28	0.006115763				
18	-0.16	0.007152554				
19	-0.04	0.00833505				
20	0.08	0.009678138				
21	0.2	0.011197265				
22	0.32	0.012908288				

Sheet1 / Sheet2 / Sheet3 / Sheet4 / Sheet6 / Sheet1

Workbook 11.1

Now chart the data in A11:B111 as an XY{Scatter} graph to obtain Fig. 11.1.

All that remains is to make the title 'hot' so that we obtain an indication of which particular normal distribution has been graphed.

To do this, use C1 and C2 to contain the labels:

Normal distribution: mean =   standard deviation =

Then in D1 and D2 enter:

=FIXED(B1,2)   =FIXED(B2,2)

These are the string values of the mean and the standard deviation of the particular normal distribution being charted.

Then in D3 concatenate the text and the string values by entering:

=C1&D1&C2&D2

Now double click on the chart and from the Menu bar select Insert and then Titles. From the list that appears, click on the Chart Title tab and then OK and then on the Formula bar.

Now enter the cell reference of the cell containing the 'hot title' in the form:

=SHEET1!D3

The results should resemble Fig. 11.2. This is a chart of the normal distribution probability

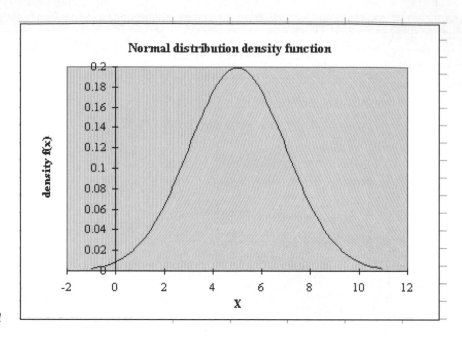

Figure 11.1

density function, and can now display any normal distribution that you choose to define in terms of its mean and standard deviation values. However, the chart itself is not an accurate method of obtaining the specific probabilities associated with one or more designated X values. To do this we need a **normal distribution calculator**.

Accordingly, open a new workbook and proceed as follows.
First, in A1 and A2 enter the labels:

Mean   Standard deviation

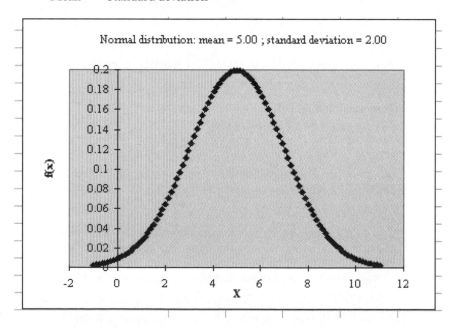

Figure 11.2

Then use B1 and B2 to contain the values of these terms (use 6 for the mean and 2 for the standard deviation).

Now, in A3 enter the label:

Required X value (a)

and enter a value of 10 to B3.

Next, in A5 enter the label:

P(X<a) =

and in B5 the formula:

=NORMDIST(B3,B1,B2,TRUE)

Notice how we are now using the distribution function rather than the density function to obtain the probability represented by the area under the curve. The switch is therefore set to TRUE. A value of 0.97725 will be returned. This is P(X<a) in a distribution where X ~ N(6,2)

Now, in A6 enter the label:

P(X>a) =

and in B6 the formula:

=1-B5

A value of 0.02275 will be returned since the probability that X exceeds *a* must be unity minus the probability that X is less than *a*, when the probability that x = *a* is regarded as being infinitesimally small. Therefore, P(X>a) when X ~ N(6,2) = 0.02275.

We therefore have the ability to calculate the normal distribution probabilities associated with X exceeding *a* and X not exceeding *a* for any specified normal distribution. However, it will often be the case that we require to know the probability of X lying *between* two specified values (or the probability that X lies outside the range specified by two given X values).

To do this, use the current worksheet as a template and change the label in A3 to:

Larger required X value (a)

and then in A4 add the label:

Smaller required X value (b)

Now use B3 and B4 to contain the values 10 and 2.

Next, in A7 enter the label:

P(X<b) =

and in B7 the formula:

=NORMDIST(B4,B1,B2,TRUE)

This will give the probability that X is less than b.

Continuing as before, use A8 to contain the label:

P(X>b) =

and B8 to contain the formula:

=1-B7

To find the probability that X lies between a and b we simply have to note that that since a > b this will be given by:

$$P(X>b) - P(X>a)$$

Therefore use A9 to contain the label:

P(X lies between a and b) =

and then use B9 to contain:

=B8-B6

i.e. P(X>b) - P(X>a) when P(X>b) is in B8 and P(X>a) is in B6.

Finally, to compute the probability that X lies outside the range a to b, we simply have to note that this will be given by:

1 - P(X lies between a and b)

Therefore use A10 to contain the label:

P(X lies outside the range a to b) =

and then, in B10 enter:

=1-B9

The results should resemble Workbook 11.2, and provide a very efficient normal distribution calculator.[3]

	A	B	C	D	E	F	G	H
1	Mean	6						
2	Standard deviation	2						
3	Larger required X value (a)	10						
4	Smaller required X value (b)	2						
5	P(X<a) =	0.97725						
6	P(X>a) =	0.02275						
7	P(X<b) =	0.02275						
8	P(X>b) =	0.97725						
9	P(X lies between a and b)	0.9545						
10	P(X lies outside the range a to b)	0.0455						
11								
12								

B5 = =NORMDIST(B3,B1,B2,TRUE)

Workbook 11.2

Now save this model as W11_2.XLS.

Exercises 11.1 and 11.2 can be attempted now.

_____

3 You should appreciate that in this electronic age Workbook 11.2 is a replacement for printed normal distribution tables that statisticians used to have to consult.

11.4. Comparing two normal distributions

To see the effect upon any normal distribution of changes in the values of the mean and/or the standard deviation, load Workbook 11.3 (W11_3.XLS) from the accompanying disk.

This is a prepared worksheet that will allow such comparisons to be made. The two normal distributions are defined as A and B, and their means and standard deviations can be entered to the B1:B4 range indicated by yellow colouring. This is the only area of the worksheet to which you can enter information—the rest of the sheet is protected.

To start with, let the means and standard deviations of the two distributions be the same—6 for the mean and 2 for the standard deviation.

As the chart indicates, the probability density functions are coincident.

Now increase the mean for distribution B to 9 and observe that the pdf for B has moved to the right.

Its height, spread, and general shape, however, remain the same as for distribution A.

Keep on increasing the mean for B and this effect will continue—the position of the distribution on the X axis moves up but the general shape is unchanged.
Now reset the means of both distributions to 6 and increase the standard deviation for B from 2 to 4.

Once again the chart displays the effect quite clearly—distribution B is now flatter and wider than distribution A, and this will continue as the standard deviation of B is increased.

Now try increasing both the mean and the standard deviation of the B distribution. The chart should indicate that both the position on the X axis and the height and spread for B will have changed.

11.5. Combining normal distributions

Just as any 2 normal distributions can be compared, they can also be combined to create a new composite normal distribution. The 2 commonest combining methods are addition and subtraction. Thus if:

$A \sim N(\mu_a, \sigma_a)$ and $B \sim N(\mu_b, \sigma_b)$ then:
$A + B \sim N[\mu_a + \mu_b, (\sigma_a^2 + \sigma_b^2)^{0.5}]$

For example, if:

$A \sim N(7,3)$ and $B \sim N(1,4)$ then:
$A + B \sim N[7 + 1, (3^2 + 4^2)^{0.5}] = N(8,5)$

On the other hand, if:

$A \sim N(\mu_a, \sigma_a)$ and $B \sim N(\mu_b, \sigma_b)$ then:
$A - B \sim N[\mu_a - \mu_b, (\sigma_a^2 + \sigma_b^2)^{0.5}]$

For example, if:

$A \sim N(7,3)$ and $B \sim N(1,4)$ then:
$A - B \sim N[7 - 1, (3^2 + 4^2)^{0.5}] = N(6,5)$

Notice that the standard deviation of the combined distribution is the same regardless of whether it is the sum or the difference of the individual distributions that is being created, i.e. $(\sigma_a^2 + \sigma_b^2)^{0.5}$ in both cases.

To see the effect of combining any two normal distributions in terms of the probability density functions that are generated, load Workbook 11.4 (W11_4.XLS) now.

This is another prepared workbook that allows you to enter values for the means and the standard deviations of any 2 normal distributions (A and B) in the B1:B4 range and observe the effect upon the probability density functions for the sum and the difference of A and B.

Now use this workbook to confirm the results obtained above by using 7 and 1, and 3 and 4 for the means and standard deviations of the A and B distributions respectively.

As an illustration of the use of combining normal distributions in this way, consider a firm that has issued 2 types of share—ordinary (O) and preference (P). Now suppose that over a long period of time it was observed that the daily closing price (in £s) of these 2 types of share were both normally distributed. To be exact, it was found that:

$$O \sim N(2.5375, 0.9876) \text{ and } P \sim N(1.8765, 0.8125)$$

The problem posed is to calculate the probability that on a randomly selected day a portfolio of one ordinary and one preference share had a combined closing price between £5 and £4.

To answer this question we will need to use two worksheets, so load both W11_2.XLS (the normal distribution calculator) and W11_4.XLS.
With both of these files loaded, use Window from the Menu bar to make W11_4.XLS active.
Now enter the mean and standard deviation closing prices given above for both types of share in the B1:B4 range.

Now note the values that appear in the chart title for the mean and standard deviation of the combined prices (O + P). Values of 4.405 and 1.2789 should have been returned. We therefore know that the combined price of an ordinary and a preference share is distributed normally with mean 4.405 and standard deviation 1.2789.

To obtain the required probability, select Window from the Menu bar and then activate W11_2.XLS.
Now enter the mean and standard deviation values for the combined distribution to the B1 and B2 cells (i.e. 4.405 and 1.2789).

Next we must supply the range of (O + P) values for which the probability is to be calculated (the values of a and b in the design of this worksheet).

Consequently, since a must exceed b for this worksheet to operate correctly, enter a value of 5 to B3 and a value of 4 to B4.

The required probability will be computed in B9 and should equal 0.303378 = 30.3378%.

Exercise 11.3 can be attempted now.

With the properties of any normal distribution established, we can now proceed to use this knowledge in the context of a sampling process.

11.6. **The sampling distribution of the mean**

Consider a production process producing items of output that can each have 0, 1, 2, 3, or 4 identifiable faults. Also suppose that any item of output is equally likely to have 0, 1, 2, 3, or 4 faults.

Consequently, for the production process as a whole, i.e. considering a large number of items, the mean number of faults is given by:

$$(0 + 1 + 2 + 3 + 4)/5 = 2 \text{ faults}$$

This is the population mean number of faults (μ).

It also follows that for this population the variance number of faults (σ^2) is given by:

$$\sigma^2 = [(0 - 2)^2 + (1-2)^2 + (2-2)^2 + (3 -2)^2 + (4 - 2)^2]/5 = (4 + 1 + 0 + 1 + 4)/5 = 10/5 = 2 \text{ faults.}$$

Therefore the population standard deviation number of faults (σ) is:

$$\sigma = 2^{0.5} = \sqrt{2}$$

We therefore have a population in which $\mu = 2$ and $\sigma = \sqrt{2}$.

Now imagine that the firm's quality control department decides to sample some items of output in order to test the presumption that the production process was in fact operating in such a way that the population mean number of faults was 2. Then suppose that the sample size (n) was set at 2, i.e. 2 items were selected at random from a particular output batch.

Because each of the sampled items could have anything between 0 and 4 faults, all possible permutations for the total number of faults in the sample are given by:

	Possible no. of faults	1st item sampled				
		0	1	2	3	4
2nd item sampled	0	0	1	2	3	4
	1	1	2	3	4	5
	2	2	3	4	5	6
	3	3	4	5	6	7
	4	4	5	6	7	8

A similar table can be constructed to show, instead of the total number of faults, the mean number of faults ($\bar{x}$) that could be calculated from any sample that could occur. Thus:

Possible mean no. of faults	1st item sampled				
	0	1	2	3	4
0	0	0.5	1	1.5	2
1	0.5	1	1.5	2	2.5

2nd item sampled

2	1	1.5	2	2.5	3
3	1.5	2	2.5	3	3.5
4	2	2.5	3	3.5	4

Clearly, some sample mean values are more likely to occur that others. For example, a sample mean value of 0 can only be obtained if both items sampled had 0 faults. This only occurs in 1 of the 25 possibilities outlined in the last table.

On the other hand, a sample mean value of 2 can result in a number of ways, viz.

| 1st item sampled | 0 | 1 | 2 | 3 | 4 |
| 2nd item sampled | 4 | 3 | 2 | 1 | 0 |

In any of these cases the sample mean value is 2 faults. This suggests that, from this population, a sample mean value of 2 is 5 times more likely to occur than a sample mean value of 0 (or of 4).

Now, by counting the number of times that a particular value for the sample mean could occur we obtain what is known as the **sampling distribution of the mean**. Thus, for the illustration we have the following distribution of possible sample mean values:

0, 0.5, 0.5, 1, 1, 1, 1.5, 1.5, 1.5, 1.5, 2, 2, 2, 2, 2, 2.5, 2.5, 2.5, 2.5, 3, 3, 3, 3.5, 3.5, 4

Now open a new workbook and use A1 to contain the label:

Possible sample mean values

and then enter the values above to the A2:A26 range.

Since the A2:A26 range contains the distribution of the sample mean values, we can now compute the mean, median, and mode of this distribution of mean values.

Hence use A27:A29 to contain the labels:

Mean of the means   Mode of the means   Median of the means

and in B27:B29 enter the formulae:

=AVERAGE(A2:A26)   =MODE(A2:A26)   =MEDIAN(A2:A26)

The results will all equal 2, and it is no coincidence that this is also the population mean value.

This suggests that the important point to be noted from this discussion is that the mean of the sampling distribution of sample means ($\mu_{\bar{x}}$) is equal to the known population mean μ. Symbolically, we conclude that:

$$\mu_{\bar{x}} = \mu$$

However, although we have only demonstrated this equality for a sample of size $n = 2$, it can be taken on trust that it is also true for samples of any size.

This is the first crucial result in sampling theory. The second crucial result requires that we consider the spread of sample mean values that can occur. The reason for this can be appreciated by observing that although

$$\mu_{\bar{x}} = \mu$$

there are still 20 out of 25 occasions in our illustration when the actual sample mean was not the same as the population mean.

Clearly, the opportunity for sample mean values that deviate from the population mean to be calculated will depend upon the spread that these sample mean values can adopt. We therefore need to calculate the standard deviation of the sampling distribution of means. This statistic is called the **standard error** and is given the symbol:

$$\sigma_{\bar{x}}$$

It is quite simply the standard deviation of the distribution of all possible sample mean values that could be computed from the given sample size.

Consequently, use the current worksheet to calculate this statistic by using A30 to contain the label:

Standard error

and then B30 to contain the formulae:

=STDEVP(A2:A26)

It should be found that a result of 1 is returned. In other words:

$$\sigma_{\bar{x}} = 1$$

Now compare $\sigma_{\bar{x}}$ with σ, i.e. the standard deviation of the sampling distribution with the standard deviation of the population. Clearly, the fact that $\sigma_{\bar{x}}$ is less than σ suggests that there is less variation in the sample mean values than in the population values from which they were drawn. If this were not the case, then there would be little basis for a wide range of sampling procedures.

This relative lack of dispersion in the distribution of the sample mean values when compared to distribution of the population values from which they were drawn is known as the **central limit theorem**, and provides the entire rationale for sampling. Clearly, it also implies that $\sigma_{\bar{x}}$ is a crucial statistic that must be calculated.

However, before we proceed to use the results of this discussion we should recognize that in the illustration a small sample of size 2 was used (so that the arithmetic did not become too tedious). In conjunction with the fact that there were only 5 distinct population values that could occur (0, 1, 2, 3, or 4), this meant that there were only $5^2 = 25$ possible outcomes generating 9 distinct sample mean values. These were easily calculated in a two-way table by inspection and then entered to the workbook so that their standard deviation (the standard error) could be obtained.

However, now suppose that each item could in fact have 10 identifiable faults (0, 1, 2, . . . 9). The number of possible sample outcomes from a sample of n = 2 increases from $5^2 = 25$ to $10^2 = 100$, and there will be 19 distinct sample mean values. Furthermore, if a sample of size n = 3 were taken, then the total number of sample outcomes that could be computed would increase to $5^3 = 125$ if there were 5 possible population values, or $10^3 = 1000$ if there were 10 possible population values.

In general, if there are m distinct values for a population, and if a sample of size n is drawn from that population, then there will be m^n possible sample outcomes and nm – (n – 1) distinct sample mean values. Clearly these numbers can become very large. This would not be a serious problem were it not for the fact that, as we saw in the illustration, the distribution of all possible sample mean values *had* to be specified before its standard error could be calculated. And, as we have already suggested, the standard error is a crucial statistic that must be computed.

For example, with 10 possible population values and a sample size of n = 5, there are a total of $10^5 = 100000$ possible sample mean values (many of which will be the same, of course). Imagine the tedium of having to deduce and then enter each of these values to the worksheet before being able to compute their standard error.

Fortunately there is an easier way. To see this way, reconsider the given and computed statistics from the illustrative example. We have:

$$\mu = 2 \quad \sigma = \sqrt{2} \quad n = 2 \quad \mu_{\bar{x}} = 2 \text{ and } \sigma_{\bar{x}} = 1.$$

The correspondence between μ and $\mu_{\bar{x}}$ is obvious, but is there any identifiable link between σ, n and $\sigma_{\bar{x}}$? The answer is that there is:

$$\sigma_{\bar{x}} = \sigma/\sqrt{n}$$

Hence with $\sigma = \sqrt{2}$ and n = 2 we have:

$$\sigma_{\bar{x}} = \sqrt{2}/\sqrt{2} = 1$$

This is the second crucial result, and means that we have no need to create the sampling distribution of the means in order to calculate the standard error. Hence, for example, with $\sigma = \sqrt{2}$ and n = 4 then $\sigma_{\bar{x}} = \sqrt{2}/\sqrt{4} = 0.702$, while if n increased to 9 then $\sigma_{\bar{x}}$ would fall to $\sqrt{2}/\sqrt{9} = 0.4714$.

Clearly, as the sample size increases the value of $\sigma_{\bar{x}}$ declines, indicating that the variation that can take place in the sample means that *could* be computed also declines.

To see the effect of this discussion, reload Workbook 11.3 (W11_3.XLS) which compares any 2 normal distributions. Now resave the file immediately as W11_5.XLS and make the following additions.
Use C1 to contain the label:

sample size n

and D1 to contain the actual size of the sample—use 2 to start with.

Now since column B contains the pdf values for the normal distribution defined by the mean and standard deviation values in B1 and B2, we can regard this as the (normal) distribution of the population from which the sample was drawn.

In the original worksheet, column C contained the pdf values associated with the mean and standard deviation of the second normal distribution (B). However, since the purpose of this worksheet is to compare the distribution of the population with the sampling distribution we require that the values in B3 and B4 are the mean and the standard deviation of the sampling distribution. In other words, B3 should contain $\mu_{\bar{x}}$ ($=\mu$) and B4 should contain $\sigma_{\bar{x}} = \sigma/\sqrt{n}$).

Therefore in B3 and B4 enter the formulae:

=B1   =B2/D1^0.5

This will compute the standard error on the basis of whatever values have been entered for σ (Standard deviation A), μ (Mean A), and the sample size (n). Furthermore, the value in B4 will be used as the standard error for the pdf to be created in column C (i.e. the sampling distribution of the mean).[4]

As you can see, even with a sample of size n = 2 the spread of the sampling distribution is less that the spread of the population values.

Now keep on increasing n until you are satisfied of the effect, and when you have finished save the file as W11_5.XLS.

This discussion leads us to the 3rd crucial result in sampling theory. We already have:

1. $\mu_{\bar{x}} = \mu$: the mean of the sampling distribution of means is equal to the population mean.

---

4   Note that if n = 1 then $\sigma = \sigma_{\bar{x}}$, and the sampling distribution of the mean and the distribution of the population are coincident.

2. $\sigma_{\bar{x}} = \sigma\sqrt{n}$: the standard error of the sampling distribution of the mean can be computed directly from σ and n without having to create the actual sampling distribution of the mean.

The question now arises of whether we can make any statement about the nature of the distribution of the $\bar{x}$ values around their mean value (the population mean). The answer is that if the sample size is large (more than 30), then the $\bar{x}$ values are perfectly normally distributed, and even if the sample size is less than 30 they are approximately normally distributed. In both cases the normal distribution has mean $= \mu$ and standard deviation $= \sigma\bar{x}$.

Furthermore, this remains true regardless of the distribution of the population values from which the sample was drawn. In other words, if the population values have mean $= \mu$ and standard deviation $= \sigma$, then the distribution of all possible sample mean values, when n exceeds 30, is normal with mean $= \mu$ and standard deviation $=$ the standard error $= \sigma/\sqrt{n}$ $= \sigma_{\bar{x}}$.

This is a truly crucial result, since it allows the following conclusion to be drawn. From the previous discussion on the properties of any normal distribution we know that approximately 95% of all possible values will lie in the range:

mean $\pm$ 2(standard deviations)

Thus, when a sample of size n is taken from a population with mean $= \mu$ and standard deviation $= \sigma$, approximately 95% of all possible sample mean values will lie in the range:

$$\mu \pm 2\sigma/\sqrt{n} = \mu \pm 2\sigma\bar{x}$$

Sample mean values outside this range therefore have only a 5% or less chance of occurring if the population mean is in fact $= \mu$.

For example, suppose that in the production process example there were 10 identifiable numbers of faults:

(0, 1, 2, 3, 4, 5, 6, 7, 8, or 9)

The population mean is therefore 4.5 and $\sigma = 2.87228$.

Now suppose that a sample of size n = 100 is taken from a large batch of output. We can now deduce that:

$$\bar{x} \sim N(4.5, 2.87228/\sqrt{100}) = N(4.5, 2.87228/10) = N(4.5, 0.287228)$$

Therefore, regardless of which one of the 10^{100} possible samples of 100 that could be taken, approximately 95% of the sample means will lie in the range that is given by:

$$\mu \pm 2\sigma_{\bar{x}} = 4.5 \pm 2(0.287228) = 4.5 \pm 0.57446$$

Correspondingly, it therefore follows that approximately 2.5% of all possible sample mean values will lie above 4.5 + 0.57446 = 5.07445, and 2.5% will lie below 4.5 - 0.57446 = 3.9255.

This will always be the case provided the population mean is in fact μ, and should provide a clue as to how we might set about testing the possibility that the population mean has changed from 4.5 (as a result perhaps of some numbers of faults being more likely to occur than others).

Additionally, from our knowledge of the features of any normal distribution we can also argue that approximately 99.7% of all possible sample mean values will lie within a range of 3 standard errors of the mean. Thus:

$$\mu \pm 3\sigma_{\bar{x}} = 4.5 \pm 3(0.287228) = 4.5 \pm 0.86167$$

Once again it follows that approximately 0.15% of all possible sample mean values will exceed 4.5 + 0.86167 = 5.36167 and 0.15% will be less than 4.5 - 0.86167 = 3.6383.

These ranges within which 95% or 99.7% of all possible sample mean values are sure to lie are known as **confidence intervals**, and have **confidence levels** defined by the percentage of values lying within the range. Also, since we know that the sample mean values are normally distributed, we can recall that 2 and 3 are the approximate z values associated with 95% and 99.7% confidence levels respectively.

However, the confidence intervals just created are only approximate because figures of 2 and 3 were used for the standard normal distribution Z values. To obtain the exact Z values associated with any probability in a normal distribution, Excel has a function called =NORMINV. The full general syntax is =NORMINV(Probability x%,Mean,Standard deviation)

Notice that this function returns the value of Z below which x% of all possible Z values lie. Thus =NORMINV(97.5%,0,1) would return a value of approximately 2, since approximately 97.5% of all Z values are below a Z value of 2.

To see how the NORMINV function works, open a new workbook and proceed as follows. First in A1:A4 enter the labels:

> Mean   Standard deviation   Required probability % = P(Z or less)
> Normal value (Z)

Now in B1 and B2 enter values for the mean and the standard deviation.
To create the standard normal distribution N(0,1), use values of 0 and 1 respectively.
Next, in B3 enter the required probability as a percentage.

For example, if we required the Z value associated with 97.5% of all Z values being less than that value we would enter 97.5% for the required probability. This would give the Z value to be used in a 95% confidence interval when the 2.5% of values in the bottom tail of the distribution are also included.

Finally, in B4 enter:
> =NORMINV(B3,B1,B2)

Now save this file as W11_6.XLS.

With the values specified above (97.5%, 0, and 1) it will be found that a Z value of 1.9600 is returned to B4. This is the exact value of the approximate value of 2 that we have previously used.

It is now an easy matter to use this workbook to confirm the Z values associated with the following frequently used confidence levels.

Do this now by sequentially changing the value in B3 to match the values shown in the first row of the illustration below.

P(Z or less)	95%	97.5%	99.5%	99.9%
Z value	1.6449	1.9600	2.5758	3.0902
P(Z or more)	5%	2.5%	0.5%	0.1%
Confidence	90%	95%	99%	99.8%

Now it should be clear that any confidence interval for the sample mean can be generally written as:

$$\bar{x} \pm Z(\text{standard error})$$

and that the Z values for 90%, 95%, 99%, and 99.8% confidence are 1.6449, 1.96, 2.5758, and 3.0902 respectively.

Exercises 11.4 and 11.5 can be attempted now.

11.7. **Testing hypotheses about the population mean**

Now recall that in the previous discussion the population mean and standard deviation were presumed to be known. However, knowledge of the sampling distribution of the mean allows us to make inferences about the population mean in the much more realistic case when the latter is not known. This is the true purpose of sampling, since if we knew the true population mean there would be no need to sample.[5] To make inferences about an unknown population mean, we can put together the three crucial results established earlier in the following way.

Continuing with the current example ($\mu = 4.5$ faults, $\sigma = 2.87228$ faults, $\sigma_{\bar{x}} = 0.287228$ faults, and n = 100), suppose that a sample mean of 5.2 faults was observed. What can we infer? Clearly, since we have already established that 95% of all possible sample mean values will lie in the range given by:

$$\bar{x} \pm 1.96(\text{standard error}) = 5.2 \pm 1.96(0.287223) = 5.2 \pm 0.5629$$

it follows that 95% of all possible sample means will lie between:

5.7629 faults and 4.6370 faults

The hypothesized population mean (4.5) is therefore outside the range of values that are to be expected, and so we must infer either of 2 things.

1. An extremely unlikely event was observed—this particular sample had an exceptionally high number of items with a large number of faults—but the rest of the batch from which the sample was taken was in line with the population mean number of faults (4.5).

2. The production process is not in fact producing output with a population mean number of faults = 4.5.

Which of these 2 possible inferences is to be made depends largely on one thing—the cost of making the wrong inference. These potential costs can be summarized as follows:

	State of nature	
Decision	Process OK (unlikely sample)	Process faulty
Recalibrate machine	Incorrect	Correct
Leave machine alone	Correct	Incorrect

Clearly there are 2 types of *incorrect* inference that can be made in this scenario. Type I is to decide that the specifications of the machine are incorrect and recalibrate the machine when in fact there is nothing wrong with it. This is an **error of commission**, since the presumption of the null hypothesis ($H_0: \mu = 4.5$) has been incorrectly rejected. Type II is to decide to leave the machine alone, accept that the mean number of faulty items is $\mu = 4.5$, and presume that an unlikely sample has been obtained, when in fact the machine needs recalibrating. This is an **error of omission**, since the incorrect null hypothesis has not been rejected. Not surprisingly, these 2 types of error are related, since the more sure we have to be of not incorrectly rejecting a true null hypothesis, the more likely will it be that an untrue null hypothesis will not be correctly rejected.

There is no easy way of resolving this quandary except by reference to the costs involved in making either of the 2 types of error. However, it is the general approach to reject the null

---

5 For the moment we will still assume—albeit somewhat unrealistically—that the population standard deviation is known. However, this assumption will be removed later in the discussion.

hypothesis if the hypothesized population mean lies outside the range of the confidence interval for the calculated sample mean. Thus, with a 90% confidence interval for $\bar{x}$ and with the hypothesized value of μ lying outside this range, we would reject H_0 with 90% confidence and thereby incur a risk of 10% that we reject a true null hypothesis. Similarly with a 95% confidence interval for $\bar{x}$ and with the hypothesized value of μ lying outside this range, we would reject H_0 with 95% confidence and thereby incur a risk of 5% that we reject a true null hypothesis.

Now load Workbook 11.7 (W11_7.XLS).

This is a prepared workbook that can compute the confidence intervals, and then accept or reject the null hypothesis depending upon the sample mean calculated, and the level of confidence required.

Now use this workbook to test the hypothesis that was worked through manually.

That was:

$$H_0: \mu = 4.5 \text{ versus } H_1: \mu \neq 4.5$$

when $\sigma = 2.87228$ faults, sample mean = 5.2 faults, and n = 100.

Enter these 4 values now to the appropriate cells of the highlighted area.
   Now start with a confidence level of 90% and then increase this steadily in steps of 1%.

You should find that H_0 is rejected for all levels of confidence that are less than 98.5%. The upshot of this discussion is that we can only accept the null hypothesis if we require a confidence level of more than 98.5% (and a risk of erroneously rejecting a true null hypothesis of less than 2%). Rejection of H_0 is therefore justified with up to 98.5% confidence (but not with 99% confidence).

Exercise 11.6 can be attempted now.

11.8. Testing hypotheses using a sample test statistic

Creating a confidence interval for the sample mean provides a simple intuitive way of testing certain types of hypotheses about the unknown population mean. The decision rule is simply to accept the null hypothesis ($\mu = k$) if k lies within the range of the confidence interval for the sample mean, otherwise reject it.

However, for reasons that will soon become clear we can also test the null hypothesis versus its alternative by creating what is known as a **test statistic**. Generally, such a statistic is defined as:

$$\frac{\text{sample statistic} - \text{hypothesized population statistic}}{\text{standard error of the sample statistic}}$$

Thus for tests in relation to the sample mean we therefore have:

$$\frac{\text{sample mean} - \text{hypothesized population mean}}{\text{standard error}}$$

Which can be written in symbols as:

$(\bar{x} - \text{hypothesized } \mu)/\sigma_{\bar{x}}$

When H_0: $\mu = k$ this becomes:

$(\bar{x} - k)/(\sigma/\sqrt{n})$

Now, if the population standard deviation is known, and if the sample size exceeds 30, then this test statistic is called Z, since it has a standard normal distribution with mean = 0 and standard deviation = 1. It is therefore a **standard normal variable** ($\mu = 0$ and $\sigma = 1$), and the probabilities associated with given Z values, or the Z values associated with certain probabilities, are easily calculated.

Notice that the test statistic simply calculates the difference between the sample statistic and the hypothesized population value and then standardizes this difference by dividing it by the standard error of the sample statistic. This puts any particular test statistic on the same scale as any other one and means that the behaviour of all variables on this scale is known, since it follows a normal distribution.

For clarity, we will call any Z value calculated from the sample Z_{calc}. Thus:

$Z_{calc} = (\bar{x} - k)/(\sigma/\sqrt{n})$

Now recall that in any standard normal distribution the Z values associated with 95% and 99% confidence intervals are 1.96 and 2.53 respectively. These values are called **critical** Z values, and are denoted by Z_{crit}.

Furthermore, if the null hypothesis is accepted with 95% confidence then there must be a 5% chance of incorrectly rejecting it. This is called the **significance** of the test, and is denoted by α. Thus Z_{crit} for $\alpha = 0.05 = 1.96$ and Z_{crit} for $\alpha = 0.01 = 2.576$. We can symbolize this as:

$Z_{crit,\alpha = 0.05} = 1.96 \qquad Z_{crit,\alpha = 0.01} = 2.576$

Now reconsider the last illustration, where a sample of size n = 100 was taken from a population with a known standard deviation of $\sigma = 2.87228$ faults and where the sample mean was calculated to be $\bar{x} = 5.2$.

The null hypothesis that was to be tested was H_0: $\mu = 4.5$ versus H_1: $\mu \neq 4.5$. Also recall that using the confidence interval approach this null hypothesis was rejected for all confidence levels less than 99%.

The value of the test statistic is easily computed as:

$$Z_{calc} = \frac{5.2 - 4.5}{2.87228/\sqrt{100}}$$

$$Z_{calc} = 0.7/0.287228 = 2.4371$$

Now suppose that we require the risk of incorrectly rejecting H_0 to be no more than 5%. This implies that $\alpha = 0.05$ and that $Z_{crit,\alpha = 0.05} = 1.96$.

Clearly the calculated value of Z exceeds the critical value (2.4371 > 1.96) and so we reject the null hypothesis. This is because the chances of calculating a Z value from the sample that is either greater than 1.96 or less than -1.96 are less than 5%, if the population mean is in fact 4.5. However, now suppose that the costs involved in **incorrectly** rejecting the null hypothesis were enormous. Prudence would require a higher degree of confidence and so α would decline.

So suppose we require 99% confidence. This implies that $\alpha = 0.01$, and we have already seen that $Z_{crit,\alpha = 0.01} = 2.576$. Comparing Z_{calc} with Z_{crit} we now find 2.4371 < 2.576 and so we now have to *accept* H_0.

As well as confirming our previous confidence interval approach, this discussion suggests a simple decision rule, viz.

If $Z_{calc} > Z_{crit,\alpha}$ or $Z_{calc} < -Z_{crit,\alpha}$ then reject H_0

Notice one final advantage of using the test statistic to test hypotheses. In the illustration it is clear that the Z_{calc} lies somewhere between the Z values associated with $\alpha = 0.05$ and $\alpha = 0.01$. But where exactly does it lie? This is the same as asking what is the significance of the calculated Z value. The answer is quite easily obtained from the NORMDIST function.

To see how this is done, open Workbook 11.8 (W11_8.XLS).

This is another prepared workbook that can be used to test any hypothesis both by the confidence interval and the test statistic approaches.

Consequently, add the data for the problem to the highlighted area.

Then observe that the significance of Z is 1.48%. The fact that this value lies in between 1% and 2% explains why in the confidence interval approach we could reject H_0 with 98% confidence (2% significance) but had to accept H_0 if 99% confidence were required (1% significance).

Exercise 11.7 can be attempted now.

11.9. One-tailed and two-tailed hypothesis tests

It should now be pointed out that as long as the nature of the alternative hypothesis is of the form $H_1: \mu \neq k$, then the previous approaches (confidence interval and test statistic) are satisfactory methods of testing hypotheses. However, sometimes the nature of the investigation will be such that an alternative hypothesis of the form $H_1: \mu > k$ or $H_1: \mu < k$ should be used. This would be the case if, for example, we were required to say whether for some process the mean number of faults produced had increased or decreased on the manufacturer's specification.

Alternative hypotheses of the form $H_1: \mu > k$ or $H_1: \mu < k$ have 2 implications for the testing procedures previously explained. First, they are not really testable by the confidence interval approach since, by being symmetrically distributed around the mean, the confidence interval explicitly considers values that are greater than the mean as well as values that are less than the mean.

Second, although the test statistic approach remains valid, the Z_{crit} values associated with any required value of α will have to be adjusted. This is because when the alternative hypothesis is of the form $H_1: \mu \neq k$, the $\alpha\%$ of values that will cause H_0 to be rejected are distributed equally in each tail of the sampling distribution. That is, $\alpha/2\%$ are located in each tail, and values of the test statistic lying in either of these regions will cause H_0 to be rejected. However, when the nature of the alternative hypothesis is $H_1: \mu > k$ or $H_1: \mu < k$, then the $\alpha\%$ of test statistic values that cause rejection of H_0 are concentrated either in one tail of the sampling distribution or in the other.

From this discussion it should be clear that when $H_1: \mu > k$ or $H_1: \mu < k$ we require to perform a **one-tailed test** as opposed to a **two-tailed test** when $H_1: \mu \neq k$. Fortunately, the adjustment to the critical Z values is easily made by noting that 90% of Z values lie between

1.64 and -1.64 (5% in each tail) and 95% of Z values lie between 1.96 and -1.96 (2.5% in each tail). Therefore if we are performing a two-tailed test with $\alpha = 0.05$ the critical Z value is 1.96. However, if it were a one-tailed test (still with $\alpha = 0.05$) then the critical Z value would fall to 1.64.

There is an intuitive meaning to this adjustment. When H_1 is of the form $H_1: \mu \neq k$, this supplies less information to the test than when $H_1: \mu > k$ or $H_1: \mu < k$. In the latter case the possibility that values of μ that are less than k or greater than k have been excluded from the testing process. As long as either of these exclusions is justified theoretically or empirically, then the testing process becomes much more powerful as a result of this extra knowledge. This is reflected in the reduced Z_{crit} values for any chosen α value, and makes it easier to reject the null hypothesis.

The effects upon the critical Z values of one-tailed as opposed to two-tailed tests, for various frequently used levels of significance, are shown below.

α %	10%	5%	2%	1%	0.5%	0.1%
Z_{crit} 2-tailed	1.645	1.96	2.33	2.576	2.807	3.29
Z_{crit} 1-tailed	1.281	1.645	2.05	2.33	2.575	3.09

Now reconsider the last illustration where:

$H_0: \mu = 4.5$ was tested against $H_1: \mu \neq 4.5$

We saw that on the basis of the test statistic ($Z_{calc} = 2.4371$) H_0 was rejected at the both the 5% and the 2% significance levels (2.4371 exceeds both 1.96 and 2.33), but had to be accepted at the 1% significance level (2.4371 does not exceed 2.575). Now suppose that the nature of the alternative hypothesis was changed to:

$H_1: \mu > 4.5$

Clearly the value of the test statistic is unchanged ($Z_{calc} = 2.4371$). However, the critical values for Z are now lower. Thus 2.4371 exceeds 2.33, which is the 1% significance level for a one-tailed test, and so H_0 can now be rejected with 99% confidence. This altered decision is entirely due to the fact that a one-tailed test was employed and that the critical Z values for any given level of significance are all lower.

Either one-tailed or two-tailed tests can be performed in Workbook 11.9.

Workbook 11.9

Load this file now (W11_9.XLS).
Now confirm the analysis that has just been carried out by entering the data for the problem in the highlighted area.

The workbook carries out both the one-tailed and the two-tailed tests and also calculates the significance of the result for both types of test. For example, we saw earlier that the significance of the calculated Z value in the two-tailed test was 1.48%. This is confirmed by the value in B20. However, it should come as no surprise that the significance of the calculated Z value in the one-tailed test has been reduced—exactly halved, in fact—as the value in the B21 cell indicates. The null hypothesis can now be rejected with less risk of error in the one-tailed case than in the two-tailed one.

Exercise 11.8 can be attempted now.

As a practical example of the principles that have been discussed we are now going to carry out a sampling procedure in which you, the reader, can interact.

Open up a new workbook now and proceed as indicated.

First we are going to use an Excel routine known as Random Number Generation to create a random sample.

Consequently, select Tools and then Data Analysis and then Random Number Generation.

The dialogue screen shown in Fig. 11.3 will appear.

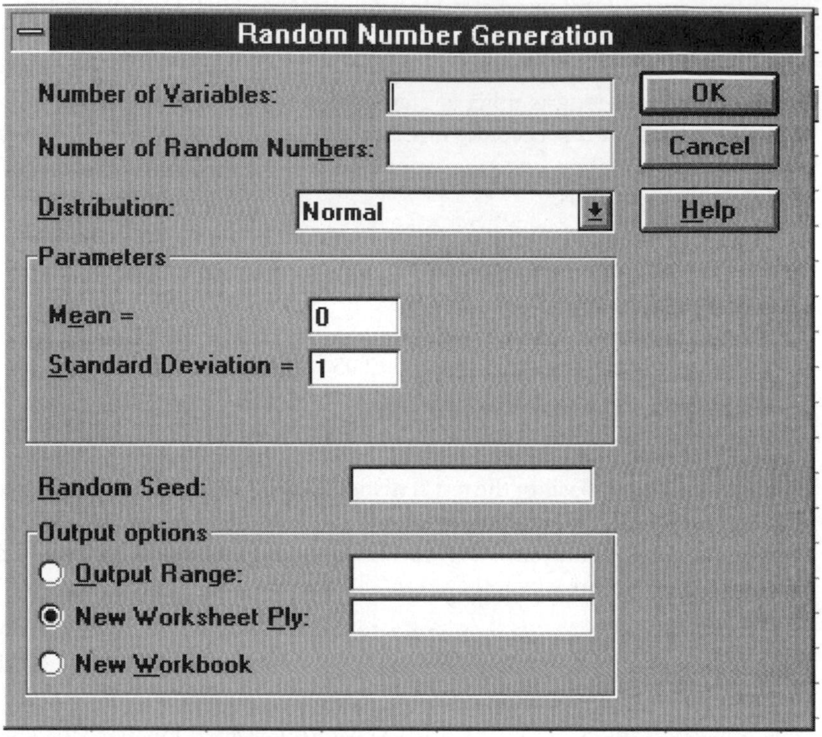

Figure 11.3

We are only going to generate 1 random sample, so in the first box enter a value of 1.
Now, since we want a random sample of 500 values, click on the second box and
enter a value of 500.
Next, in the Distribution box click on the arrow tab to display the options available.

These represent a number of different probability distributions that can be chosen to represent the distribution of the population from which we wish to sample. Many of them will
be unfamiliar, but not the Normal.

So, select this option to continue with the process of generating a random sample of
500 observations from a normally distributed population.

Now you must supply the mean and the standard deviation of the normal distribution from
which you wish to sample. The default values will usually be 0 and 1, i.e. the standard normal distribution.

Consequently, if these values are not already showing enter them now.
Next, click on the Output Range tab and then on the box alongside. Enter the cell reference A1 and press OK.

The 500 sample values will be sent to the A1:A500 range of the worksheet. Assuming that
this has happened, we now need to compute the mean of these values.

So, use B1 to contain the label:

Mean

and in C1 enter the formula:

=AVERAGE(A1:A500)

The author is unable to say what value will be returned to C1, since it will depend entirely upon the random sample that that you have generated. However, it should not be far away from 0.

Now since we know that this was a random sample drawn from a population in which $X \sim N(0,1)$, it follows that the sampling distribution of the mean will be:

$$\bar{x} \sim N(0, 1/\sqrt{500})$$

Consequently, in B2 and B3 enter the labels:

standard error Z_{calc}

and in C2 and C3 the formulae:

=1/500^0.5   and   = (C1-0)/C2

The C3 cell now contains your own individual test statistic on the presumption that the population mean is 0.

Once again, it cannot be said what value has been obtained. However, of all the readers who use this text there will be no more than 5% who obtain a Z_{calc} value in excess of 1.96 or below -1.96. Furthermore there will be no more than 1% of readers who obtain a personal Z_{calc} value in excess of 2.57 or less than -2.57. If you are one of these readers, then you have generated a highly unlikely event.

Now save this file as Workbook 11.10 (W11_10.XLS).

11.10. Hypothesis tests with small samples and/or unknown population standard deviation

All of the previous discussion has been in the context of large samples (n > 30) and situations when the population standard deviation was presumed to be known. However, when σ is unknown and n is less than 30, the distribution of the test statistic is no longer guaranteed to be normal. In such circumstances the test statistic conforms to what is known as a **t distribution**. The t distribution is similar to the standard normal distribution in the sense that it is symmetrically distributed around a mean value of zero. However, its standard deviation is determined by what is known as the number of degrees of freedom.

The latter are computed from the sample size, and represent a measure of the amount of information from the sample data that has been used up. Roughly speaking, each time a statistic is calculated from sample data 1 degree of freedom is used up, so in the case of hypothesis tests about the sample mean the number of degrees of freedom is given by the sample size minus 1 (n - 1)—since the sample mean must have been calculated.

When n is very large the difference between t values and Z values is negligible, however, as n declines the t distribution develops a standard deviation that is increasingly greater than 1. This means that it is more spread out than the standard normal distribution, and so critical values associated with any given α level will be higher. For example, in a two-tailed test we have already seen that 95% of all Z values lie between 1.96 and -1.96. However, in a t distribution with 20 degrees of freedom 95% of all t values will lie between -2.086 and 2.086, while with only 5 degrees of freedom 95% of all t values will lie between -2.571 and 2.571.

Like the normal distribution, the pdf for the t distribution is defined by a complex mathematical equation. However, Excel's TDIST function can compute any required probability for us. The general syntax of this function is:

=TDIST(Required t value, Number of degrees of freedom, Number of tails to be used)

Hence, suppose we required the probability that t exceeded 2.1 in a t distribution with 20 degrees of freedom. We should write:

=TDIST(2.1,20,1)

Take a new workbook and enter this formula now to the A1 cell.

A result of 0.024309 should be returned indicating that:

P(t >2.1) when t has 20 degrees of freedom = 2.4309%

Notice that the fact that the value of the last argument (number of tails to be used) was set to 1 ensured that the returned value was only the area under the pdf to the right of 2.1.

Now suppose that we require the probability that t exceeds 2.1 or is less than -2.1, again with 20 degrees of freedom. To obtain the area in both tails of the distribution, all that needs to be done is to change the value of the last argument in TDIST from 1 to 2.

Do this now in the A2 cell by entering:

=TDIST(2.1,20,2)

A value of 0.048618 should be returned, and indicates the probability that t lies outside the range -2.1 to 2.1.

Excel also has a related function—TINV—that reverses the logic of the TDIST function in the sense that it returns the t value associated with any required level of significance for the given number of degrees of freedom.

The general syntax of TINV is:

=TINV(Required probability,Degrees of freedom)

and returns the value associated with leaving half of the required probability in both tails of the distribution. Consequently, suppose that in a t distribution with 20 degrees of freedom we required the t value associated with 5% of all values being equally distributed in each of the tails. That is:

t* such that $P(t > t^*) + P(t < -t^*) = 0.05$

From our knowledge of the normal distribution we should expect that the t value will not be too far away from 1.96.

Therefore, use the A3 cell of the current worksheet to contain:

=TINV(0.05,20)

A value of 2.085962 will be returned, and indicates that 2.5% of all t values will exceed 2.085962, while another 2.5% of all t values will be less than -2.085962. Clearly these would be the t values to be used in the creation of a 95% confidence interval when the t as opposed to the normal distribution is being used.

As a point of notation, the critical t value obtained from the TINV function is denoted by $t_{\alpha, v}$ where as usual, α is the significance level and v is used to represent the number of degrees of freedom.

It should now be apparent that these larger values for t as opposed to Z mean that a 95% confidence interval using t will be wider than the equivalent one using Z, and so for any given value of α it will be less likely that the null hypothesis is rejected. The upshot of this discussion is that the test statistic will now become:

$$t_{calc} = (\bar{x} - \mu)/\sigma_{\bar{x}}$$

and this calculated t value should be compared with critical t values that will always be greater than the equivalent critical values of Z.

Exercise 11.9 can be attempted now.

Before we put this idea into practice in an example, however, there is a further adjustment that has to be made if the population standard deviation is unknown. In such cases it is clear that we will have to estimate the unknown population standard deviation from the sample. However, it can be shown that applying the formula for the standard deviation that we have been computing up until now[6] underestimates the population standard deviation. When sample data are used to estimate an unknown population standard deviation, the formula to be used is:

$$(SSD/(n-1))^{0.5}$$

In other words, instead of standardizing the sum of squared deviations by dividing by the number of observations, we divide by the number of degrees of freedom (n - 1).

Moving from a Z distribution to a t distribution and adjusting the formula for the sample standard deviation are the only adjustments that are required to allow hypothesis testing in the context of small samples from populations with unknown standard deviations. For example, you may have seen the television programme called *2 Point 4 Children* and wondered what inspired the title. The answer is that at the time of the programme's inception the National Census results revealed that the average family had 2.4 children. Being calculated on the basis of a census this is a **population value**, but since things can change, we could establish the following null hypothesis:

$$H_0: \mu = 2.4$$

and test it against the alternative:

$$H_1: \mu \neq 2.4$$

Now suppose that the census authorities 'lost' the raw data and had failed to take note of the population standard deviation, and that a small sample of families of size n = 16 was taken. Each family was requested to reveal their number of children and then the results recorded. Suppose the following data set was obtained:

X (number of children under 16)   0, 1, 4, 1, 2, 1, 0, 4, 3, 2 ,3, 1, 0, 1, 0, 1

Open a new workbook and enter these data to the A1:A17 range (including the X label). Now use B1 and B2 to contain the labels:

Sample mean   Sample standard deviation

and in C1 and C2 enter the formulae:

=AVERAGE(A2:A17)   and   =STDEV(A2:A17)

The formula in C2 is the sample standard deviation. That is, the STDEVP function calculates the standard deviation on the basis of a divisor of n, whereas the STDEV function uses a divisor of (n - 1). Values of 1.5 and 1.36626 will be returned.

---

6 $(SSD/n)^{0.5}$.

Next use B3 and B4 to contain the labels:

Standard error   Test statistic tcalc

Normally, the standard error is calculated from $\sigma/\sqrt{n}$, but in this case, since σ is unknown we calculate it from $s/\sqrt{n}$, where s is the calculated sample standard deviation.

Consequently, in C3 enter:

=C2/16^0.5

A value of 0.3416 will be returned.

Finally, in C4 calculate the test statistic from:

=(C1-2.4)/C3

A result of -2.635 should be returned.

Finally, use B5 and B6 to contain the labels:

significance %   Critical t

and enter a value of 5% to C5.
Then, in C6 enter:

=TINV(C5,15)

This returns the two-tailed critical t value associated with a t distribution with n - 1 = 15 degrees of freedom. The result should be 2.1314.

Consequently, since the absolute value of the calculated t statistic exceeds the critical t value for $\alpha = 5\%$ (2.635 is absolutely greater than -2.1314), we can reject the null hypothesis with 95% confidence. The result is therefore significant at the 5% level. However, if you change the value in C5 from 5% to 1% then the critical t value will increase to 2.9467 and so H_0: $\mu = 2.4$ can no longer be rejected , meaning that the result is not significant at the 1% level.

In verbal terms this analysis means that the calculated sample mean of 1.5 is *not* consistent with a population mean of 2.4 if we are willing to accept a risk of 5% of incorrectly rejecting H_0. If however, we are only willing to bear a risk of 1% of incorrectly rejecting H_0, then the sample value of 1.5 *is* consistent with a population mean of 2.4.

Now save this file as W11_11.XLS.

These results can be confirmed and the significance of the calculated t value determined from Workbook 11.12.

Workbook 11.12

Load this file now (W11_12.XLS) and confirm that the calculated t value of -2.635 is significant at a level of 1.8747% for the two-tailed alternative hypothesis. Exercise 11.10 can be attempted now.

11.11. **Hypothesis tests using samples from two populations**

The previous discussion has concerned itself with hypothesis tests about a *single* population value—the population mean. However, it is easy to envisage circumstances in which tests require to be performed on the values associated with 2 or more populations.

For example, suppose that an economist argues that the mean weekly pay of all French workers is the same as that for all British workers—both measured in dollars to allow comparison. This is equivalent to the following null hypothesis:

$$H_0: \mu_F = \mu_B$$

or more usefully:

$$H_0: \mu_F - \mu_B = 0$$

where μ_F and μ_B are the respective French and British population mean weekly pay.

Assuming that this null hypothesis is to be tested against the alternative that the population mean pays in the two countries are not equal, this implies:

$$H_1: \mu_F \neq \mu_B \text{ or:}$$
$$H_1: \mu_F - \mu_B \neq 0$$

These two hypotheses must now be tested on the basis of sample evidence, so suppose a random sample of 100 workers was taken from each of the French and British populations, and that the sample means were calculated to be:

$$\bar{x}_F = \$359.84 \text{ and } \bar{x}_B = \$306.48$$

Clearly the sample mean pay is higher for the French than for the British workers, but the question to be answered is whether this is sufficient evidence to allow us to infer that the population mean values are in fact different, or whether the observed difference in the sample means is due to sampling variation.

To answer this question we can employ either of the general approaches to hypothesis testing that have already been explained. That is, we can either construct a confidence interval for the sample mean difference and then see whether the hypothesized population mean difference lies in this range, or we can calculate a test statistic for the difference between the sample mean difference and the hypothesized population mean difference.

Before we can do either of these things, however, we need some information on the standard deviation pay of both populations. So suppose either that these are known or that they have been estimated very accurately from the samples. That is, we have:

$$\sigma_F = \$136.57 \text{ and } \sigma_B = \$125.66$$

Therefore a 95% confidence interval for the difference in the sample means would be given by:

$$(\bar{x}_F - x_B) \pm 1.96(se_{(\bar{x}F - \bar{x}B)})$$

where $se_{(\bar{x}F - \bar{x}B)}$ is the standard error of the sampling distribution of the difference between the sample means.

On the other hand, the test statistic would be calculated from:

$$Z_{calc} = [(\bar{x}_F - \bar{x}_B) - \text{hypothesized value of } (\mu_F - \mu_B)]/se_{(\bar{x}F - \bar{x}B)}$$

Furthermore, since we know that:

$$H_0: \mu_F - \mu_B = 0$$

the test statistic can be reduced to:

$$Z_{calc} = [(\bar{x}_F - \bar{x}_B) - 0]/ se_{(\bar{x}F - \bar{x}B)} = (\bar{x}_F - \bar{x}_B)/se_{(\bar{x}F - \bar{x}B)}$$

Now all that remains is to obtain an expression for $se_{(\bar{x}F - \bar{x}B)}$. This is easily done when it is remembered that when any 2 normal distributions are combined the standard deviation of the sum or the difference is given by the square root of the sum of their individual variances. Thus:

$$se_{(\bar{x}F - \bar{x}B)} = (se_{\bar{x}F}^2 + se_{\bar{x}B}^2)^{0.5}$$

Also:

$$se_{\bar{x}F} = \sigma_F/\sqrt{n_F} \quad \text{and} \quad se_{\bar{x}B} = \sigma_B/\sqrt{n_B}$$

Therefore:

$$se_{\bar{x}F}^2 = \sigma_F^2/n_F \quad \text{and} \quad se_{\bar{x}B}^2 = \sigma_B^2/n_B$$

Consequently:

$$se_{(\bar{x}F - \bar{x}B)} = (\sigma_F^2/n_F + \sigma_B^2/n_B)^{0.5}$$

It is now an easy matter to calculate $se_{(\bar{x}F - \bar{x}B)}$ for the data in our problem from:

$$se_{(\bar{x}F - \bar{x}B)} = (136.57^2/100 + 125.66^2/100)^{0.5} = (186.51 + 157.90)^{0.5} = 344.42^{0.5} = 18.56$$

Now, since we know that:

$$\bar{x}_F - \bar{x}_B = \$359.84 - \$306.48 = \$53.36$$

it follows that the 95% confidence interval for the difference in the sample means will be given by:

$$\bar{x}_F - \bar{x}_B \pm 1.96(se_{(\bar{x}F - \bar{x}B)}) = \$53.36 \pm 1.96(18.56) = \$53.36 \pm \$36.38.$$

Thus 95% of all possible sample mean differences will lie between $89.74 and $16.98.

This range clearly does not include the hypothesized population difference of 0, and so we reject the null hypothesis that mean weekly pays in the 2 countries are equal. This is confirmed if we calculate the test statistic from:

$$Z_{calc} = (\bar{x}_F - \bar{x}_B)/se_{(\bar{x}F - \bar{x}B)} = 53.36/18.56 = 2.875$$

This value is clearly greater than the two-tailed critical Z value for 0.5% significance (2.807), and so we reject the null hypothesis.

We can also determine the significance of this calculated Z value in the context of both a one-tailed and a two-tailed hypothesis test.

To do this, open a new workbook and use A1 to contain:

=NORMDIST(2.875,0,1,TRUE)

A value of 0.99798 will be returned, indicating that 99.798% of all Z values are less than 2.875. Consequently, 0.202% of all Z values will exceed 2.875, and with regards to a one-tailed test this is the significance of the calculated Z value (0.202%).

However, in the context of a two-tailed test we cannot ignore the 0.202% of Z values that lie in the opposite tail of the distribution. Thus for a two-tailed test the significance of a sample mean difference of 2.875 is exactly twice the significance of the one-tailed test—0.404% in this case.

This means that if we were required to perform both a one-tailed and a two-tailed test at the 0.3% level of significance, we would be able to reject H_0 in the one tailed test (0.202% < 0.3%, but would have to accept H_0 in the two-tailed test (0.404% > 0.3%).

Now that we know what is being done, all of these results can be obtained from an Excel Data Analysis routine called Z Test: Two Sample for Means.

Workbook 11.13

To see how it works, load Workbook 11.13 (W11_13.XLS).

Columns A and B of this workbook contain the raw data for French and British weekly pay that were sampled in the last example.

To perform the hypothesis test that that we carried out manually, select Tools, Data Analysis, and then Z Test: Two Sample for Means.

The dialogue box shown in Fig. 11.4 will appear.

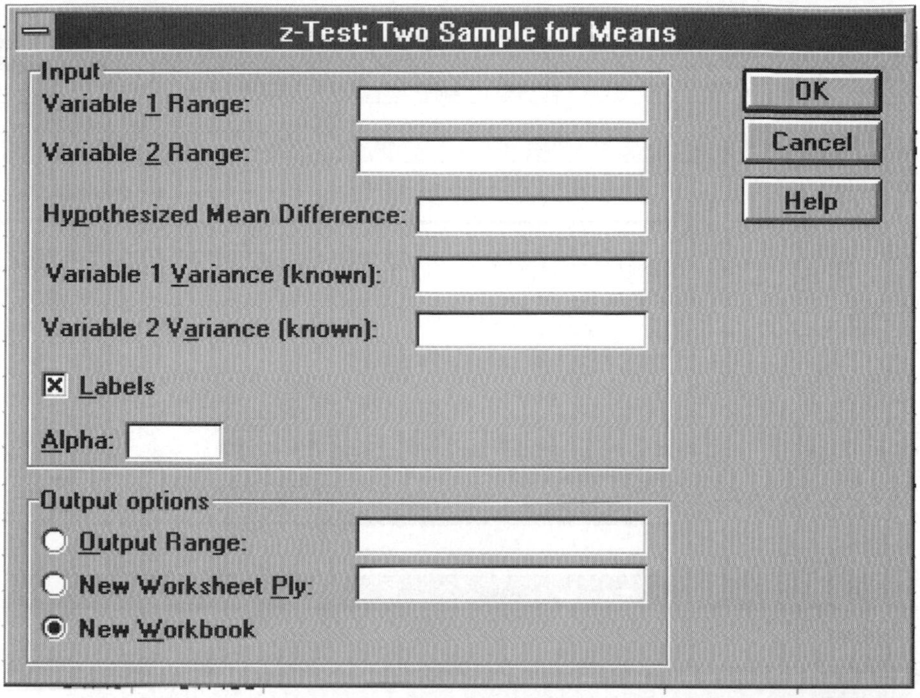

z-Test: Two Sample for Means

Input
Variable 1 Range:
Variable 2 Range:
Hypothesized Mean Difference:
Variable 1 Variance (known):
Variable 2 Variance (known):
[X] Labels
Alpha:

Output options
( ) Output Range:
( ) New Worksheet Ply:
(•) New Workbook

OK
Cancel
Help

Figure 11.4

Now fill in the boxes so that they are the same as Fig. 11.5.

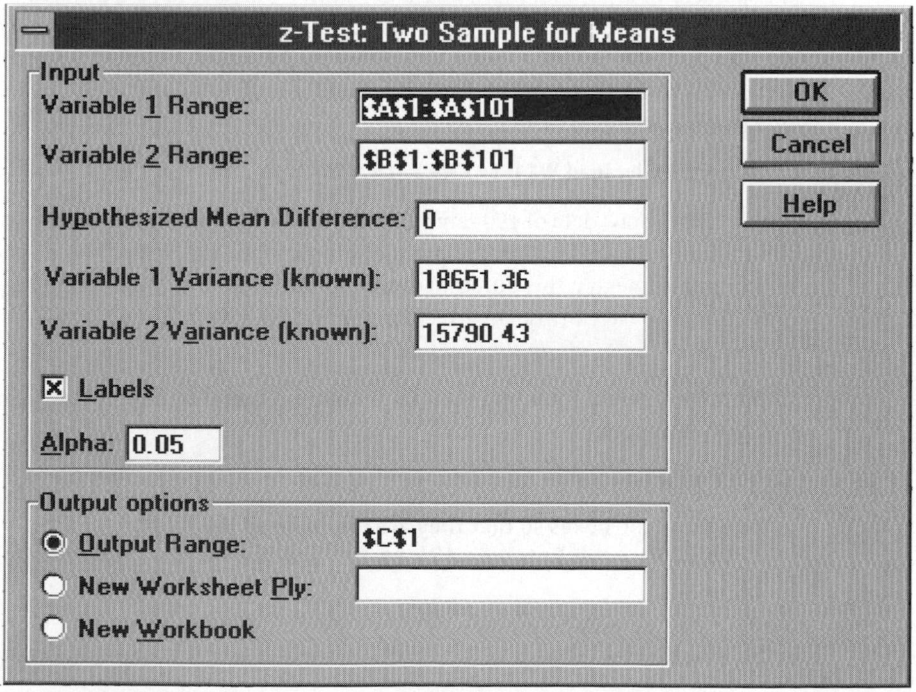

z-Test: Two Sample for Means

Input
Variable 1 Range: $A$1:$A$101
Variable 2 Range: $B$1:$B$101
Hypothesized Mean Difference: 0
Variable 1 Variance (known): 18651.36
Variable 2 Variance (known): 15790.43
[X] Labels
Alpha: 0.05

Output options
(•) Output Range: $C$1
( ) New Worksheet Ply:
( ) New Workbook

OK
Cancel
Help

Figure

When you have finished, click on OK, and the results should resemble Workbook 11.13.

	A	B	C	D	E	F
	File	Edit	View	Insert	Format	Tools	Data	Window	Help
	C18					
	A	B	C	D	E	F
1	France	Britain	z-Test: Two Sample for Means			
2	519.73	333.32				
3	210.44	117.31		*France*	*Britain*	
4	416.13	193.42	Mean	359.8431	306.4813	
5	312.22	229.21	Known Variance	18651.36	15790.43	
6	464.82	223.71	Observations	100	100	
7	302.22	212.76	Hypothesized Mean Difference	0		
8	450	214.54	z	2.875329		
9	144.52	157.78	P(Z<=z) one-tail	0.002018		
10	466.44	330.47	z Critical one-tail	1.644853		
11	591.28	205.6	P(Z<=z) two-tail	0.001009		
12	277.88	356.9	z Critical two-tail	1.959961		
13	432.08	367.01				
14	387.09	324.6				

Sheet1 / Sheet2 / Sheet3 / Sheet4 / Sheet5 / Sheet

Workbook 11.13

As you can see, the results that were obtained manually have been reproduced exactly.[7]

Exercise 11.11 can be attempted now.

Finally, it should be asked how to perform 2 sample hypothesis tests in the much more likely event that the population standard deviations are unknown. In this case the principles are the same, but the population standard deviations will have to be estimated from the sample data by the sample standard deviations, and the distribution of the sampling distribution of the difference between the means is no longer a Z variable, but a t variable instead.

There is no need to go through the calculations manually, however, since Excel has a routine that will perform them for us.

Workbook 11.14

Consequently, load W11.14 (W11_14.XLS).

This is still the raw data of 100 sample observations on French and British weekly pays, but we are now presuming that the population standard deviations are unknown. We will, however, assume that these unknown population standard deviations are equal.

In this case we can use an Excel routine called t Test: Two-Sample Assuming Equal Variances.

Therefore, select Tools and then Data Analysis and then t Test: Two-Sample Assuming Equal Variances.

The dialogue box shown in Fig. 11.6 will appear.

Now fill in the boxes so that they are the same as Fig. 11.7.
When you have finished, click on OK, and the results should resemble Workbook 11.14.

....

7 This is not quite true. There is a bug in the Excel routine that means that the significance of the two-tailed Z value is computed as being exactly half instead of twice the significance of the one-tailed value.

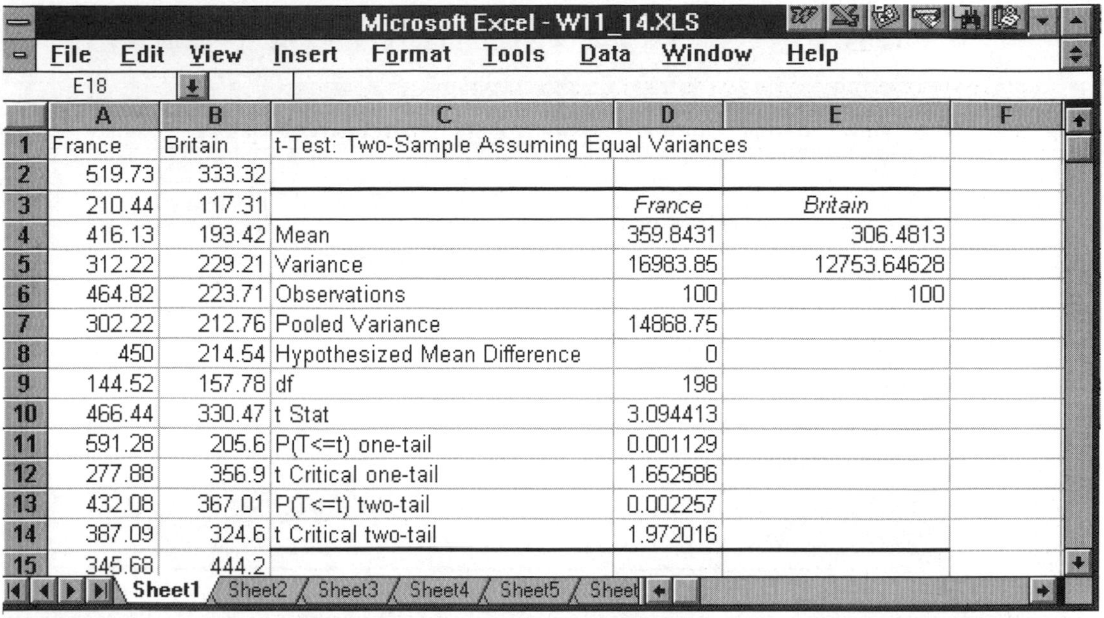

	A	B	C	D	E	F
1	France	Britain	t-Test: Two-Sample Assuming Equal Variances			
2	519.73	333.32				
3	210.44	117.31		*France*	*Britain*	
4	416.13	193.42	Mean	359.8431	306.4813	
5	312.22	229.21	Variance	16983.85	12753.64628	
6	464.82	223.71	Observations	100	100	
7	302.22	212.76	Pooled Variance	14868.75		
8	450	214.54	Hypothesized Mean Difference	0		
9	144.52	157.78	df	198		
10	466.44	330.47	t Stat	3.094413		
11	591.28	205.6	P(T<=t) one-tail	0.001129		
12	277.88	356.9	t Critical one-tail	1.652586		
13	432.08	367.01	P(T<=t) two-tail	0.002257		
14	387.09	324.6	t Critical two-tail	1.972016		
15	345.68	444.2				

Workbook 11.14

There are a few terms that need explaining here. Because the population variances are unknown they are estimated by the sample variances—s_1^2 and s_2^2. Then Excel calculates what is known as the **pooled variance**. This is a weighted average of the sample variances using the degrees of freedom in each sample as the weights. It is calculated as follows:

$$\text{pooled variance} = [(n_1 - 1)s_1^2 + (n_2 - 1)s_2^2]/(n_1 - 1 + n_2 - 1)$$

Hence for the illustration:

$$\text{pooled variance} = [99(16983.84) + 99(12753.64)]/(99 - 1 + 99 - 1) = 14868.75$$

Next, the pooled variance s^2 is used to calculate the standard error of the difference between

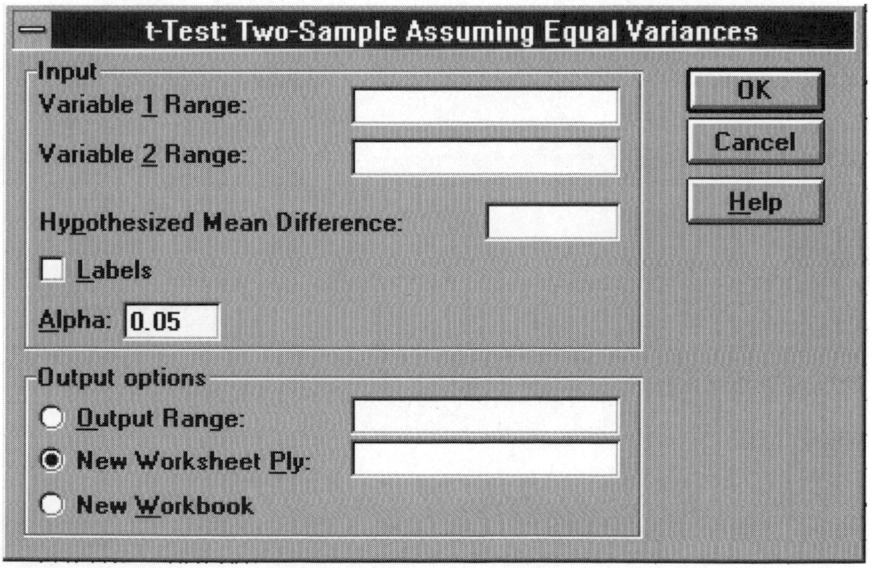

Figure 11.6

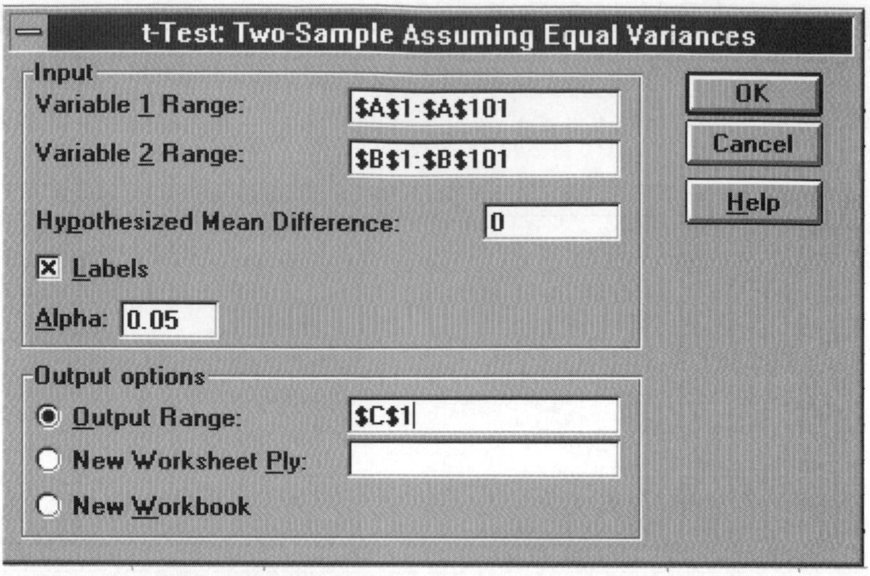

Figure 11.7

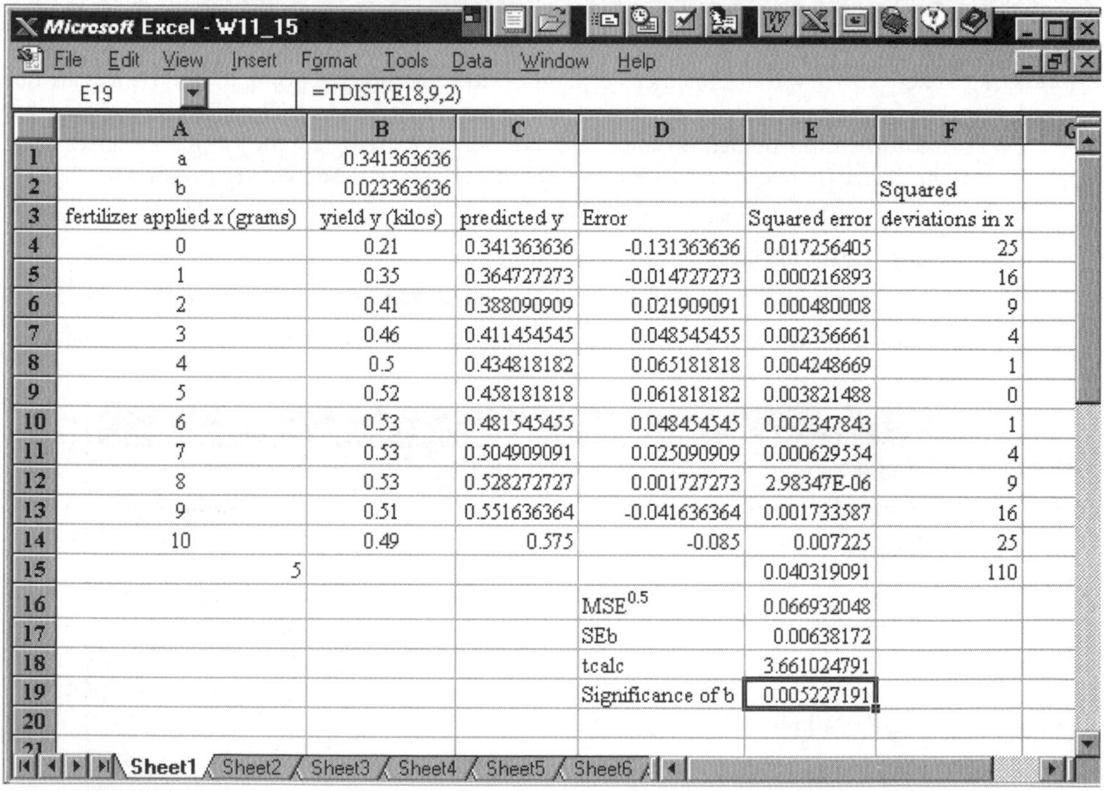

The formula bar shows:

E19 | =TDIST(E18,9,2)

	A	B	C	D	E	F	G
1	a	0.341363636					
2	b	0.023363636				Squared	
3	fertilizer applied x (grams)	yield y (kilos)	predicted y	Error	Squared error	deviations in x	
4	0	0.21	0.341363636	-0.131363636	0.017256405	25	
5	1	0.35	0.364727273	-0.014727273	0.000216893	16	
6	2	0.41	0.388090909	0.021909091	0.000480008	9	
7	3	0.46	0.411454545	0.048545455	0.002356661	4	
8	4	0.5	0.434818182	0.065181818	0.004248669	1	
9	5	0.52	0.458181818	0.061818182	0.003821488	0	
10	6	0.53	0.481545455	0.048454545	0.002347843	1	
11	7	0.53	0.504909091	0.025090909	0.000629554	4	
12	8	0.53	0.528272727	0.001727273	2.98347E-06	9	
13	9	0.51	0.551636364	-0.041636364	0.001733587	16	
14	10	0.49	0.575	-0.085	0.007225	25	
15		5			0.040319091	110	
16				MSE$^{0.5}$	0.066932048		
17				SEb	0.00638172		
18				tcalc	3.661024791		
19				Significance of b	0.005227191		
20							

Sheet1 / Sheet2 / Sheet3 / Sheet4 / Sheet5 / Sheet6

Workbook 11.15

the sample means from:

$$se_{(\bar{x}1 - \bar{x}2)} = (s^2/n_1 + s^2/n_2)^{0.5}$$

Hence for the illustration:

$$se_{(\bar{x}1 - \bar{x}2)} = (14868.75/100 + 14868.75/100)^{0.5} = 17.244$$

This statistic is not produced in the Excel output, but is used to compute the calculated t value.

Finally t_{calc} (what Excel calls t Stat) when a 0 difference is hypothesized is calculated from:

$$t_{calc} = (\bar{x}_1 - \bar{x}_2)/ se_{(\bar{x}1 - \bar{x}2)}$$

This gives:

$$t_{calc} = 53.36/17.244 = 3.0944$$

As you can see, the calculated t value is slightly higher than the z value calculated in the example where the population variances were known. Also, because of the slightly wider range of the t as opposed to the normal distribution, both the one-tailed and the two-tailed critical values are slightly higher. However, because of the assumption that the population variances, although unknown, were equal, both the one-tailed and the two-tailed significance values are lower in the t test than in the z test. This means that for these data we are more likely to reject the null hypothesis with the t test than with the z test.

Exercise 11.12 can be attempted now.

11.12. **Testing the significance of regression parameters**

The previous discussion has explained the principles of sampling theory in the context of the sample mean value that was calculated from a particular population. However, now reconsider the material on linear regression that was provided in Chapter 10. A moment's consideration should suggest that the regression parameters (a and b) must really be regarded as sample values. This is because they are properly regarded as estimates of some unknown population values that would only (perhaps) emerge after a large number of regression experiments.

In formal terms we argue that:

a and b are sample estimates of the (unknown) population parameters α and β

The reasons for any sample value for a or b being different from the true but unknown population parameters have already been suggested, viz.

1. The regression may not have been carried out under controlled conditions.
2. There may have been a high degree of measurement error.
3. Chance may have intervened to produce an unlikely sample result.
4. There may be other variables apart from x that influence y and whose effects have not been taken into account.

For any or all of these reasons, the sample regression equation defined by a and b can be subject to so much sampling variation that a and b are only poor estimates of α and β.

Bearing these points in mind, it should be clear that in the context of linear regression, sampling theory must be used to develop confidence intervals for a and b and to compute sample test statistics so that hypotheses regarding the population parameters can be tested.

Once again the general form of the test statistic:

$$\frac{\text{sample statistic} - \text{hypothesized population statistic}}{\text{standard error of the sample statistic}}$$

will be invaluable as a reminder of what is being done.

Usually we will be more concerned with the gradient term than with the intercept, and so we can start by using the worst case scenario as our null hypothesis about the value of β. This would be:

$H_0: \beta = 0$ versus $H_0: \beta \neq 0$

This implies that there is no real relationship between y and x, since with a gradient of zero the value of y is the same regardless of the value of x. In other words x does not influence y.

The test statistic for this hypothesis is a t variable with (n - 2) degrees of freedom and is defined generally for the null hypothesis that $\beta = 0$ as:

$t_{calc} = b/se_b$

where se_b is the standard error of the slope parameter, i.e. the standard deviation of the sampling distribution of all possible sample slope parameter values that could be calculated.

The formula to calculate se_b is:

$se_b = (SSE/(n - 2))^{0.5}/(SSD_x)^{0.5} = (\Sigma(y - \bar{y})^2/(n - 2))^{0.5}/(\Sigma(x - \bar{x})^2)^{0.5}$

where SSE = the sum of squared errors of the fitted regression equation and SSD_x is the sum of squared deviations in x.

Although not exactly a pleasant expression, there *is* an intuitive meaning to this formula for the standard error of the sample equation's gradient term—se_b. The numerator is simply the mean squared error, and represents the 'average' error involved in the fitted regression equation. Thus, to ignore the denominator for the moment, se_b will clearly be larger the greater are the sum of squared errors, and the smaller are the number of independent observations (degrees of freedom). The expression:

$(SSE/(n - 2))^{0.5}$

is sometimes referred to as the standard error of the estimate, although strictly speaking it is a standard deviation rather than a standard error. Nevertheless, many texts and software packages (including Excel) use this term and denote it by SEE. Thus:

$SEE = (SSE/(n - 2))^{0.5}$

Consequently, with very few observed x, y values and with a poor fit to the raw data provided by the calculated regression equation, the numerator in the expression for se_b will clearly be larger than in cases where a good fit has been obtained on the basis of a large number of observations. From this it also follows that the amount of variation that can take place in the sample values for b is also greater in the former case than in the latter. The larger value for the SEE therefore reflects this increased variation that can take place in the possible values of b that could be calculated, and so means that for any given value of the denominator se_b will be relatively large.

Turning to the denominator, it should be noted that this simply measures the sum of squared deviations of the x values around their mean value (SSD_x). Now recall that in Chapter 10 it was stated that: 'the range of x values employed [in the regression] should span a reasonable range'. Also recall that that this immediately raised the question of what was to be regarded as reasonable.

The value of se_b gives a partial answer to this question. This is because if the range of x values employed is relatively small then so too will be the sum of squared deviations in x. This means that the numerator in the expression for se_b (the SEE) will be divided by a relatively small number with the result that the value for se_b will tend to be relatively large. On the other hand, with a wide range of x values used in the regression, SSD_x will tend to be larger and so the value of se_b, for any given denominator, will tend to decline.

Thus the worst case scenario is one in which there are relatively few observations producing a poor fit to the raw data (creating a large SEE) and in which the (few) observations were concentrated in a narrow range (creating a low SSD_x).

In this case, the value of se_b will be large and indicates to the analyst that there is a high degree of variability in the sample gradient values that could be calculated, and that the particular sample gradient obtained is less likely to be typical of the population gradient than in cases when the variability in the possible sample gradients is low.

Workbook 11.15

To calculate se_b for the example in Workbook 10.2, load W10_2.XLS and immediately resave it as W11_15.XLS.

Some of the required calculations have already been performed for us. Hence, in this workbook the E15 cell contains the sum of squared errors of the fitted regression equation defined by the values for a and b contained in B1 and B2.

Consequently, since we know that the least squares regression parameters for these data are:

$a = 0.341364$ and $b = 0.023364$

enter these values now to B1 and B2.

The SSE in E15 will fall to 0.040319.

Now, since there are 11 pairs of x, y observations in this regression model, it follows that there are $11 - 2 = 9$ degrees of freedom.[8]

Therefore, use D16 to contain the label:

SEE

(i.e. the square root of the mean squared error = the standard error of estimate)

and then in E16 enter the formula:

$=(E15/9)^0.5$

A result of 0.066932 will be returned. This is the mean squared error.

The E16 cell now contains the numerator in the expression for se_b, and all that remains is to compute the denominator (SSD_x).

To do this, first of all compute the mean value of x in A15 from the formula:

$=AVERAGE(A4:A14)$

A value of 5 will be returned.

Now name the A15 cell as XMEAN.
Next, in F2 and F3 enter the label

Squared deviations in x

and then use F4 to contain the formula:

$=(A4-XMEAN)^2$

Then copy F4 into F5:F14.

---

8 One degree of freedom is lost as a result of calculating the intercept from the data, and another one lost from calculating the gradient.

Finally, in F15 compute the sum of squared deviations in x from the formula:

=SUM(F4:F14)

A value of 110 should be returned for SSD_x.[9]

Now add the label:

Se_b

(i.e. standard error of b)

to the D17 cell.

The standard error of b can now be computed by dividing the square root of the mean squared error (E16) by the square root of the sum of squared deviations in x (F15).

Consequently use E17 to contain:

=E16/F15^0.5

A value of 0.00638 should be returned, and this is the standard error of the gradient term i.e. se_b.

With the value of this crucial statistic established, we can now use it to calculate the value of the test statistic for the gradient term. Hence, with the null hypothesis being that $\beta = 0$, the calculated value of t is given by:

$t_{calc} = b/se_b = 0.023364/0.00638 = 3.6611$

You can get the worksheet to calculate this for you if you use D18 to contain the label:

tcalc

and E18 to contain the formula:

=B2/E17

Do this now.

Consequently, since the critical two-tailed value for t with 9 degrees of freedom and $\alpha = 5\%$ is 2.2622 =TINV(5%,9), the fact that 3.661 exceeds 2.262 means that the value of b is significantly different from 0 at the 5% level of significance. Furthermore, since the critical two-tailed value for t with 9 degrees of freedom and $\alpha = 1\%$ is 3.250 =TINV(1%,9), the fact that 3.661 also exceeds 3.250 means that the value of b is significantly different from 0 at the 1% level of significance. It is therefore highly unlikely that a sample regression equation with this calculated value for b could have been obtained from a population in which there was no real linear relation between y an x (i.e. in which $\beta = 0$).

Finally, we can easily compute the significance of the calculated t value that was obtained.

To do this use D19 to contain the label:

significance of b

and then in E19 enter the formula:

=TDIST(E18,9,2)

A value of 0.0052 will be returned and indicates that the calculated value for b is significant at the 0.5% level. There is therefore less than 1 chance in 200 that we will incorrectly reject the null hypothesis that $\beta = 0$ on the basis of this sample of data.

9 A more direct way of calculating the sum of squared deviations in x is to note that the Excel function VARP is defined as: VARP = Sum of squared deviations in x /n. Thus the sum of squared deviations in x = n(VARP). Consequently, use any cell to contain: =VARP(A4:A14)*11. The result will be 110 = SSD_x.

When you have made all these additions to your workbook the results should resemble Workbook 11.15.

Workbook 11.15

If they do, resave the file as W11_15.XLS.

So far, we have only considered the standard error of the gradient term (se_b), but a similar argument applies to the sampling variation that can take place in the intercept term. We denote this variation in the sampling distribution of a by se_a, and could calculate it from another 'messy' formula. However, in the case of the formula for se_a there is no obvious intuitive meaning that can easily be derived from the expression and so we will not reproduce it, nor attempt to calculate it.

This is a perfectly permissible omission, since it should now be pointed out that all of the calculations regarding the standard error of b that have just been performed can be replicated in a dedicated Excel routine called **Regression**. Furthermore, it also performs the required calculations with regard to the intercept term, and so the purpose of the last worksheet was to allow the reader to obtain a 'feel' for the principles involved in the process of obtaining the standard error of *one* regression parameter.

Once this 'feel' has been acquired, we can allow Excel to perform all the necessary calculations for us, since the interpretation of the results obtained remains constant, and as previously explained.

Consequently, load the most recent version of Workbook 11.15 (W11_15.XLS) and read on.

The workbook on screen contains all of the calculations required to compute se_b and to test its significance. Now we are going to replicate them using a dedicated routine.

First, select Tools, Data Analysis, and then Regression.

The dialogue screen shown in Fig. 11.8 will appear.

Now fill in the boxes so that they are the same as Fig. 11.9
When you have finished, click on OK, and the results should resemble Workbook 11.16. If they do, save the file as W11_16.XLS.

Workbook 11.16

Now study this worksheet carefully and observe that all of the calculations performed in Workbook 11.15 have been reproduced exactly, and a few extra ones as well.

Many of these extra ones (especially those under the heading ANOVA) are only relevant in the context of multiple regression, which is the topic of the next chapter and so can be ignored for the moment. However, it should be noted that the Excel output contains confidence intervals for each of the regression parameters in the L17:M18 range. These are the upper and lower values within which 95% of all a and b values are likely to lie. They were calculated from: [10]

$$a \pm t_{\alpha,v}(se_a) = 0.34136 \pm 2.2622(0.03775) = 0.2559 \text{ to } 0.4268$$
$$b \pm t_{\alpha,v}(se_b) = 0.02336 \pm 2.2622(0.00638) = 0.0089 \text{ to } 0.0378$$

However, what has *not* been produced automatically is a **prediction interval** for the predicted value of y for any given value of x, and this is an important omission. To understand why, recall that we have already seen that a and b are both subject to sampling variation, and so cannot be taken as definite values for the population parameters. Now, since any predicted value for y for a given value of x is entirely determined by the values of a and b, it follows that this predicted value of y will also be subject to sampling variation, with the extent

---

[10] For the illustration, $t_{\alpha,v} = t_{0.05,9} = \text{TINV}(5\%,9) = 2.2622$.

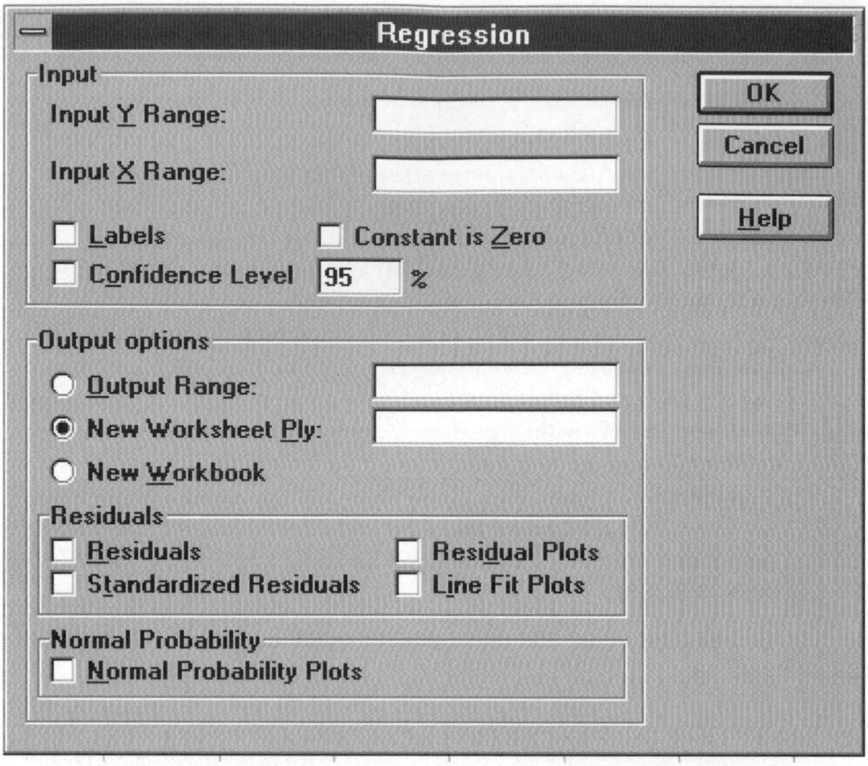

Figure 11.8

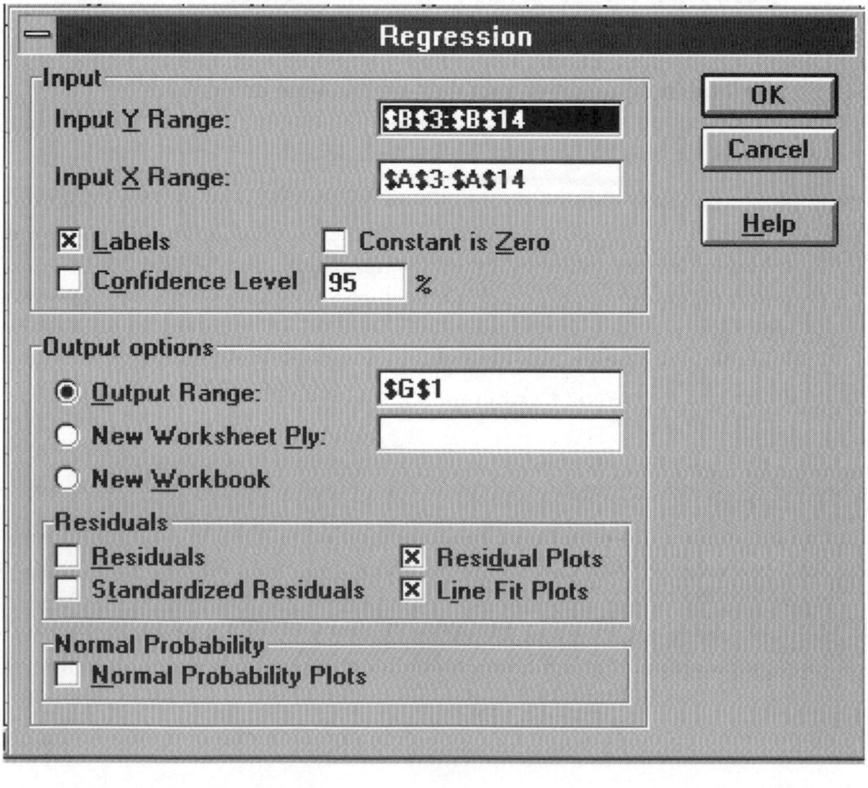

Figure 11.9

	Microsoft Excel - W11_16.XLS						

	File	Edit	View	Insert	Format	Tools	Data	Window	Help	

P15

	G	H	I	J	K	L	M	
1	SUMMARY OUTPUT							
2								
3	*Regression Statistics*							
4	Multiple R	0.773479106						
5	R Square	0.598269928						
6	Adjusted R Squar	0.553633253						
7	Standard Error	0.066932048						
8	Observations	11						
9								
10	ANOVA							
11		*df*	*SS*	*MS*	*F*	*Significance F*		
12	Regression	1	0.060044545	0.060045	13.403103	0.005227191		
13	Residual	9	0.040319091	0.00448				
14	Total	10	0.100363636					
15								
16		*Coefficients*	*Standard Error*	*t Stat*	*P-value*	*Lower 95%*	*Upper 95%*	
17	Intercept	0.341363636	0.037754767	9.041604	8.222E-06	0.255956355	0.42677092	
18	fertilizer applied x	0.023363636	0.00638172	3.661025	0.0052272	0.008927171	0.0378001	
19								

Sheet1 / Sheet2 / Sheet3 / Sheet4 / Sheet5 / Sheet

Workbook 11.16

of this being determined by the degree of sampling variation that can take place in *a* and *b*. We therefore need to create a prediction interval for any value of y that is predicted on the basis of a given value of x and the computed values of a and b.

For example, with a given value of x = 10 the predicted value of y in the illustration is given by:

$$\hat{y} = 0.341364 + 0.023364(10) = 0.575$$

However, to obtain an approximate 95% prediction interval for $\hat{y}$ we must calculate:

$$\hat{y} \pm t_{\alpha,v}(\text{SEE}) = \hat{y} \pm 2.2622(0.0669) = 0.575 \pm 0.1514$$

You can perform these calculations in the current workbook (W11_16.XLS) as follows.

First, use I1: I7 to contain the labels:

value of x   confidence %   predicted y value   2-tailed critical t
prediction interval   upper prediction value   lower prediction value

Now enter the required value of x for which the prediction is to be made to J1 and the required level of confidence for the prediction interval to J2.
    Next, in J3 and J4 enter the formulae:

=H17+H18*J1   and   =TINV(100%-J2,H8-2)

These formulae compute the predicted value of y and the critical t value to be used in the prediction interval given the required degree of confidence.

Now use J5 to contain the formula:

=J4*H7

This computes the width of the prediction interval.

Finally, add and subtract this width from the predicted value in J6 and J7 from the formulae:

=J3+J5   =J3-J5

Results of 0.4236 and 0.7264 for the lower and upper values should be returned, and represent the interval within which approximately 95% of all possible predicted values for the given value of x are certain to lie.

Finally, notice that the Excel output can produce 2 types of chart if required. These will have been produced automatically if both the Line Fit Plots and the Residuals Plots boxes have been checked in the Regression routine. If this is not the case, rerun the routine and check both boxes.

The first of these simply graphs the fitted line on top of the raw data, and should resemble Fig. 11.10. The other chart type is called the **residual plot**, and relates each of the error terms to the associated value of x. For the current illustration it should resemble Fig. 11.11. The residuals plot can often convey much useful information about the properties of the regression model that has been employed. Ideally, these residuals should display no discernible pattern. That is, they should be completely random. When this is not the case then it usually indicates that the model has not been specified properly—perhaps because additional influential independent variables have not been included, or because the model is not really linear.

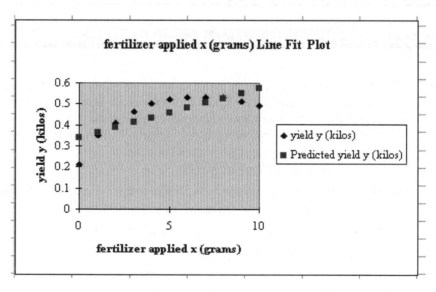

Figure 11.10

For example, if the value of the error in the residuals plot rises steadily as x increases, then this clearly suggests that the amount of error in the fitted regression equation depends upon the magnitude of x. This violates one of the basic assumptions of the regression technique—that the error terms for the population regression equation are randomly distributed with mean zero.

Clearly, in the illustrative example the error terms are negative for low *and* high values of x, and positive for intermediate values, and confirm our previous observation that the raw data are not particularly linear. In other words, there is at least one missing independent variable, and we should suspect that it is a term in x^2 since we have already mentioned in

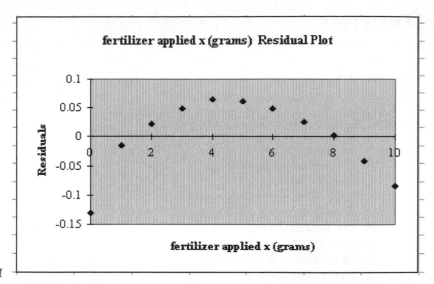

Figure 11.11

Chapter 10 that the relationship between y and x for these data is most probably best estimated by a quadratic function. Consequently, including a term in x^2 and using the more powerful multiple regression technique developed in Chapter 12 would allow a quadratic curve to be fitted to the data.

Exercise 11.13 can be attempted now.

11.13. Exercises

Exercise 11.1

Use Workbook 11.2 to calculate the following probabilities.

(i)   The probability that X exceeds 4 when X ~ N(0.5,1.4)

(ii) The probability that X is less than 4 when X ~ N(0.5,1.4)

(iii) The probability that X lies between -3.6 and 3.8 when X ~ N(0.5,1.4)

(iv) The probability that X exceeds 6 when X ~ N(3,1)

(v)   The probability that X lies between 0 and 6 when X ~ N(3,1)

Exercise 11.2

Over a large number of days the daily closing exchange rate between the £ and the $ was normally distributed with mean = $1.34 and standard deviation = $0.03. Calculate the probability that on a randomly selected day the closing exchange rate will:

(i)   Exceed $1.42.

(ii) Be less than $1.27.

(iii) Lie between $1.29 and $1.38.

Exercise 11.3

A firm produces batches of output in which each item has a unit cost of production that is normally distributed with mean = £6.50 and standard deviation = £0.40.[11] The items of output are sold in a volatile market such that the price received is normally distributed with mean = £7.20 and standard deviation = £0.60.

(i)   Calculate the probability that a randomly selected item from any one of the batches will be sold at a profit in excess of £0.90.

(ii) What proportion of output will be sold at a profit?

(iii) What proportion of output will be sold at a profit of within ± 50% of the mean profit?

(iv) What proportion of output will be sold at a loss of £0.20 or more

Exercise 11.4

Calculate the X values associated with the following normal distribution probabilities:

(i)   P(X > m) = 0.03 when X ~ N(5,4)

(ii) P(X < m) = 0.04 when X ~ N(7,5)

(iii) P(X > m or X < -m) = 0.01 when X ~ N(21,15) i.e. P(X lies outside the range m to -m).

(iv) P(X < m or X > -m) = 0.97 when X ~ N(5,4) i.e. P(X lies between m and -m)

Exercise 11.5

A random sample of size n = 625 was taken from a population with mean = 7 and standard deviation = 2. Using any one of the workbooks from this chapter, calculate the following.

(i)   The probability that a sample mean in excess of 7.1 is obtained

(ii) The probability of obtaining a sample mean that lies outside the range 6.95 to 7.05

(iii) The range within which 96% of all sample mean values will lie

Exercise 11.6

On the basis of the last available census data the mean weekly wage of manual employees in a particular country was 210.67 with a standard deviation of 24.1. To see whether this is still the case, an analyst randomly sampled 900 employees and found that the mean wage was 212.50. Calculate 95% and 99% confidence interval for the sample mean and use these to decide whether there is sufficient evidence from the sample to suggest that the population mean is no longer 210.67.

---

11 The variation in unit cost for different batches is likely to be due to the fact that some batches may have to use more labour paid at overtime rates and use raw materials and energy inputs that vary in the price that the firm has to pay for them.

Exercise 11.7

Using the data from Exercise 11.6, determine the significance of the difference between the calculated sample mean and the hypothesized population mean, and hence determine the greatest degree of confidence with which the null hypothesis can be rejected.

Exercise 11.8

In the context of the data from Exercise 11.6 test:

$$H_0: \mu = 210.67 \quad \text{versus} \quad H_1: \mu > 210.67$$

at both the 2% and 1% levels of significance.

Exercise 11.9

(a) Calculate the following probabilities.

   (i) $P(t > 2)$ when $v = 16$
   (ii) $P(t < -1.8)$ when $v = 12$
   (iii) $P(t > 2.2 \text{ or } < -1.9)$ when $v = 26$
   (iv) $P(t$ lies between -2.3 and 2.3) when $v = 7$

(b) Determine the following critical *2-tailed* t values.

   (i)   t such that 94% of all t values lie between -t and t when $v = 17$
   (ii) t such that 98% of all t values lie between -t and t when $v = 14$
   (iii) t such that 99% of all t values lie between -t and t when $v = 26$
   (iv) t such that 95% of all t values lie between -t and t when $v = 19$

(c) What is the 94% confidence interval t value for a t distribution with 11 degrees of freedom?

Exercise 11.10

Load Workbook 11.17 (W11_17.XLS). The data are the % marks obtained in an economics examination by a random sample of 21 students. The same examination was sat by a population of over 10000 candidates.

   (i)   At the 5% level of significance test the null hypothesis that the population mean mark was 63.5% against the alternative that it was not equal to 63.5%.
   (ii) At the 5% level of significance test the null hypothesis that the population mean mark was 63.5% against the alternative that it was less than 63.5%.

Exercise 11.11

It is frequently claimed by some economists that the fundamental reason for the relative decline in UK manufacturing output and employment is its lack of profitability in relation to service industries.

Consequently, suppose that from past census data the annual net reported profits of all UK manufacturing companies had a standard deviation of 2.89. Also, imagine that for the service sector the standard deviation net reported profits of all firms was 1.96. Now suppose that a random sample of 40 manufacturing and 60 service companies was taken and their annual net reported profits noted.

Load Workbook 11.18 now containing the sample results. Test the hypothesis that there is no difference between manufacturing and service industry net reported profits against the alternative that service industry profits are higher than those in manufacturing.

Use both 5% and 1% levels of significance.

Exercise 11.12

Repeat Exercise 11.11 when the population standard deviation profit in the manufacturing and service sectors are unknown but assumed to be equal.

Exercise 11.13

Load Workbook 11.19 (W11_19.XLS) now. The data are the monthly number of units sold (y) and the monthly selling expenses (£x) of a small firm over a period of 12 months.

Use the Excel Regression routine to perform a linear regression of sales on selling expenses and then answer the following questions.

   (i)   What is the regression equation of y on x?
   (ii) What is the value of the intercept?
   (iii) What is the value of the gradient?
   (iv) If monthly selling expenses were 0, what is the estimated number of units sold.

(v)   If monthly selling expenses were increased by £1000, what is the estimated increase in the number of units sold?

(vi)   If monthly selling expenses were £20000, what is the estimated number of units sold?

(vii)   What proportion of the total variation in the number of units sold is explained by variation in the level of selling expenses?

(viii)   What is the value of the standard error of estimate?

(ix)   Within what range will 95% of all sample values of the intercept lie?

(x)   Within what range will 95% of all sample values of the gradient lie?

(xi)   What is the significance of the intercept term?

(xii)   What is the significance of the gradient term?

(xiii)   Are the intercept and the gradient significantly different from 0 at the 5%, 1%, and 0.5% levels of significance?

(xiv)   If monthly selling expenses were £20000, what range would contain approximately 95% of all sample predictions for the number of units sold.

(xv)   Do the residual terms display a random pattern?

11.14. **Solutions to the exercises**

Solution to Exercise 11.1

Load Workbook 11.2 (W11_2.XLS).

(i) Use B1 and B2 to contain the values 0.5 and 1.4. Then enter a value of 4 to B3.

$P(X > 4) = 0.00621$

(ii) $P(X < 4) = 0.99379$

(iii) Enter 3.8 to B3 and -3.6 to B4.

$P(X$ lies between -3.6 and 3.8$) = 0.989089$

(iv) Change the values in B1 and B2 to 3 and 1 and then enter 6 to B3.

$P(X > 6) = 0.00135$

(v) Enter 6 to B3 and 0 to B4.

$P(X$ lies between 6 and 0$) = 0.9973$

Solution to Exercise 11.2

Load Workbook 11.2 (W11_2.XLS). Enter 1.34 to B1 and 0.03 to B2.

(i) Enter 1.42 to B3.

$P(X > 1.42) = 0.00383$

(ii) Enter 1.27 to B3.

$P(X < 1.27) = 0.009815$

(iii) Enter 1.38 to B3 and 1.29 to B4.

$P(X$ lies between 1.29 and 1.38$) = 0.860998$

Solution to Exercise 11.3

Unit profit (P) is the difference between price and unit cost. So:

$P \sim N(\text{price - unit cost})$
$P \sim N(7.20 - 6.50,(0.60^2 + 0.40^2)^{0.5})$
$P \sim N(0.70,0.72)$

Now load Workbook 11.2 (W11_2.XLS) and enter values of 0.7 and 0.72 to B1 and B2.

(i) Enter a value of 0.90 to B3.

$P(P > 0.90) = 0.390592$

(ii) Enter a value of 0 to B3.

$P(P > 0) = 0.83453$

Therefore 83.453% of output will be sold at a profit.

(iii) The mean profit on any item is £0.70, and so we require the proportion of output that is sold at a profit of between:

£0.70 + 0.5(£0.7) and £0.7-0.5(£0.7) i.e. between £1.05 and £0.35

So, enter values of 1.05 and 0.35 to B3 and B4.

$P(P$ lies between 1.35 and 0.35$) = 0.373112$.

Therefore 37.3112% of output will be sold at within ± 50% of the mean profit.

(iv) Enter a value of -0.20 to B3.

$P(P < -0.20) = 0.10565$

Therefore 10.565% of output will be sold at a loss of £0.20 or worse.

Solution to Exercise 11.4

Open a new workbook and use A1 to contain the following formulae:

(i) =NORMINV(97%,5,4) = 12.52316

97% of all X values are less than 12.52316

(ii) =NORMINV(4%,7,5) = -1.75343

4% of all X values are less than -1.75343

(iii) =NORMINV(99.5%,21,15) = 59.637

99.5% of all X values are less than 59.637

So, 0.5% of all X values are greater than 59.637. Therefore, the other 0.5% of X values are in the other tail, i.e. to the left of:

21-(59.637-21) = -17.637

Consequently, 1% of all X values lie outside the interval:

-17.637 to 59.637

(iv) =NORMINV(98.5%,5,4) = 13.68

98.5% of all X values are less than 13.38

So, 1.5% of all X values are greater than 13.68 Therefore, the other 1.5% of X values are in the other tail, i.e. to the left of:

5 - (13.68-5) = -3.68

Consequently, 3% of all X values lie outside the interval:

-3.68 to 13.68

and 97% of all X values lie inside this interval.

All of these results can be confirmed in Workbook 11.2 (W11_2.XLS). Load this workbook now.

For example, to confirm part (iv) above, enter values of 5 and 4 to B1 and B2, and then enter values of 13.68 and -3.68 to B3 and B4. Then, it should be found that:

P(X lies between a and b) = 0.97.

Solution to Exercise 11.5

We have:

$\mu = 7, \sigma = 2$, and $n = 625$

Therefore:

$\bar{x} \sim N(7, 2/\sqrt{625}) = N(7,2/25) = N(7,0.08)$

Now load Workbook 11.2 (W11_2.XLS).

(i) Enter values of 7 and 0.08 to B1 and B2 and then enter 7.1 to B3

Therefore $P(\bar{x} > 7.1) = 0.10565$

(ii) Enter a value of 7.05 to B3 and 6.95 to B4.

Then, $P(\bar{x}$ lies outside the range 6.95 to 7.05) = 0.531971

(iii) Use any cell of the current workbook to contain:

=NORMINV(98%,7,0.08)

A value of 7.1643 will be returned.

Thus 2% of all sample mean values will exceed 7.1643 and 2% of all sample mean values will be less than 7 - 0.1643 = 6.8357. Therefore 96% of all sample mean values will lie between these values. Confirm this now by entering values of 7.1643 and 6.8357 to B3 and B4. It will then be found that:

P(X lies between a and b) = 0.96.

Solution to Exercise 11.6

Load Workbook 11.7 (W11_7.XLS). Enter the population standard deviation value of 24.1 to B2 and the hypothesized population mean value of 210.67 to B3. The sample size of 900 should be entered to B4 and the calculated sample mean value of 212.50 to B5.

To obtain a 95% confidence interval, enter 95% to B6. The B11 cell indicates that 95% of all sample means will lie within ± 1.5745 of 212.50, that is, between 210.92 and 214.07.

The hypothesized population mean of 210.67 does not lie in this interval and so we reject H_0. This is not the case, however, if a 99% confidence interval is used. You can see this if you enter 99% to B6, whereupon the confidence interval will widen to ± 2.069. The hypothesized mean is now within 212.50 ± this interval, and so H_0 can no longer be rejected.

Solution to Exercise 11.7

Load Workbook 11.8 (W11_8.XLS). Enter the population standard deviation value of 24.1 to B2 and the hypothesized population mean value of 210.67 to B3. The sample size of 900 should be entered to B4 and the calculated sample mean value of 212.50 to B5.

The significance of the difference between the sample mean and the hypothesized population mean is shown in B18 to be 2.2726%. This is less than 5% but greater than 1%, and so the result is significant at the 5% level but not at the 1% level. Therefore the greatest degree of confidence with which H_0

can be rejected is 100% - 2.2726% = 97.7274%.

Solution to Exercise 11.8

Load Workbook 11.9 (W11_9.XLS) and make the equivalent entries as in Exercises 11.6 and 11.7. In other words, enter the population standard deviation value of 24.1 to B3, and the hypothesized population mean value of 210.67 to B4. The sample size of 900 should be entered to B5 and the calculated sample mean value of 212.50 to B6.

Since this is a one-tailed test the significance is returned to B21 and should equal 1.1363%. This is less than 2% but greater than 1%, and so the result is significant at the 2% level but not at the 1% level.

Notice that in the previous two-tailed test, the significance was 2.2726% and therefore would not have been significant at the 2% level. This change has resulted entirely from using the one-tailed as opposed to the two-tailed approach.

Solution to Exercise 11.9

(a) Open a new workbook and use A1 to contain the following formulae:

(i) =TDIST(2,16,1) = 0.031386 = P(t > 2)

(ii) The Excel TDIST function cannot accept negative values for the required value, even although the probabilities associated with such negative values do exist. Consequently, either use symmetry or take the absolute value of the negative amount. That is:

P(t < -1.8) = P(t > 1.8) by symmetry.

Therefore:

=TDIST(1.8,12,1) = P(t > 1.8) = P(t < -1.8) = 0.048516

Alternatively:

=TDIST(ABS(-1.8),12,1) = 0.048516

(iii) P(t > 2.2) = TDIST(2.2,26,1) = 0.0184

and:

P(t < - 1.9) = P(t > 1.9) = TDIST(1.9,26,1) = 0.0343

Therefore:

P(t lies outside the range -1.9 to 2.2) = 0.0184 + 0.0343 = 0.0527

(iv) Because -2.3 and 2.3 are exact mirror values of each other in a t distribution we can change the last argument of the TDIST function from 1 to 2 and obtain the combined probabilities in both tails of the distribution. Hence:

=TDIST(2.3,7,2) = 0.0550

Therefore 5.5% of all t values lie outside the range -2.3 to 2.3, and so 94.5% of all values will lie inside this range.

(b) Open a new workbook and, remembering that the Excel TINV function is two-tailed by definition, use A1 to contain the following formulae:

(i)   =TINV(6%,17) = 2.0150
(ii) =TINV(2%,14) = 2.6245
(iii) =TINV(1%,26) = 2.7787
(iv) = TINV(5%,19) = 2.0930

(c) =TINV(6%,11) = ±2.09614

Solution to Exercise 11.10

First, calculate the sample mean and the sample standard deviation in any vacant cells. Values of 58.714 and 11.803 should be returned.[12] Now load Workbook 11.12 (W11_12.XLS) and make the following entries.

Enter the estimated standard deviation value of 11.803 to B3 and the hypothesized population mean value of 63.5 to B4. The sample size of 21 should be entered to B5 and the calculated sample mean value of 58.714 to B6. The two-tailed and one-tailed test statistic significance values are returned to the B21 and B22 cells.

(i) Since in the two-tailed test 7.7925% exceeds 5%, the null hypothesis has to be accepted at the 5% level of significance.

(ii) Since in the one-tailed test 3.8963% is less than 5%, the null hypothesis can be rejected at the 5% level of significance.

Solution to Exercise 11.11

(i) With Workbook 11.18 (W11_18.XLS) loaded, run the Z Test: Two Sample for Means from the Data Analysis option. Define the variable 1 range as A1:A31 and the variable 2

---

12 If a value of 11.51869 instead of 11.803 is returned for the standard deviation you have used the =STDEVP function rather than the =STDEV function which employs a denominator of (n - 1) rather than n.

	C	D	E	F	G
1	z-Test: Two Sample for Means				
2					
3		*Manufacturing profits £m*	*Service profits £m*		
4	Mean	0.91	1.5975		
5	Known Variance	2.89	1.96		
6	Observations	30	40		
7	Hypothesized Mean Difference	0			
8	z	-1.803391778			
9	P(Z<=z) one-tail	0.0356633			
10	z Critical one-tail	1.644853			
11	P(Z<=z) two-tail	0.01783165			
12	z Critical two-tail	1.959961082			
13					

Workbook 11.18A

range as B1:B41, and then check the Labels box. Set the Hypothesized Mean Difference to 0, then enter the Known Variances for variables 1 and 2 as 2.89 and 1.96.

Now select Alpha to be 0.05 and then check the output tab and enter C1 as the Output Range. The results should resemble Workbook 11_18A. If they do, save the file as W11_18A.XLS.

The calculated Z value is -1.80339, and since we are required to perform a one-tailed test this must be compared with a critical Z value of 1.6448. Since the absolute value of -1.80339 exceeds 1.6448 we can reject the null hypothesis at the 5% one-tailed level. The significance of the calculated Z value for the one-tailed test is shown as 0.03566 (although once again the bug in the routine means that the significance for the two-tailed test should be 0.071327 rather than 0.01783).

(ii) Since the significance of the calculated Z value for the difference between the sample means is 0.03566, it follows that H_0 must be accepted at the 1% significance level. This could be confirmed by running the Z test routine again and changing the Alpha value from 5% to 1%. The calculated Z value will remain unchanged (-1.80339), but the critical Z value for the one-tailed test will increase to 2.3263 and so H_0 can no longer be rejected.

Solution to Exercise 11.12

Load Workbook 11.18 (W11_18.XLS). Then use the t Test: Two—Sample Assuming Equal Variances routine with data ranges of A1:A31 and B1:B41, a Hypothesized Mean Difference of 0, Labels checked, Alpha = 0.05, and an Output Range of C1. The results should resemble Workbook 11_18B.

As you can see, the calculated test statistic (now t instead of Z in the previous Exercise) has declined to -1.6704 and the one-tailed significance of t is 4.971%. This still allows rejection of H_0 at the 5% level, but it is a much closer decision than in Exercise 11.11, when the population variances were known.

Once again, it will not be possible to reject H_0 at the 1% level.

Solution to Exercise 11.13

Run the Regression routine from Data Analysis with the settings indicated in Fig. 11.12. This will produce the output shown in Workbook 11.19A.

(i) The regression equation of y on x is $\hat{y} = -1292.3 + 0.09289x$.

(ii) The value of the intercept is -1292.3.

(iii) The value of the gradient is 0.09289.

(iv) If monthly selling expenses were 0, then the estimated number of units sold would be

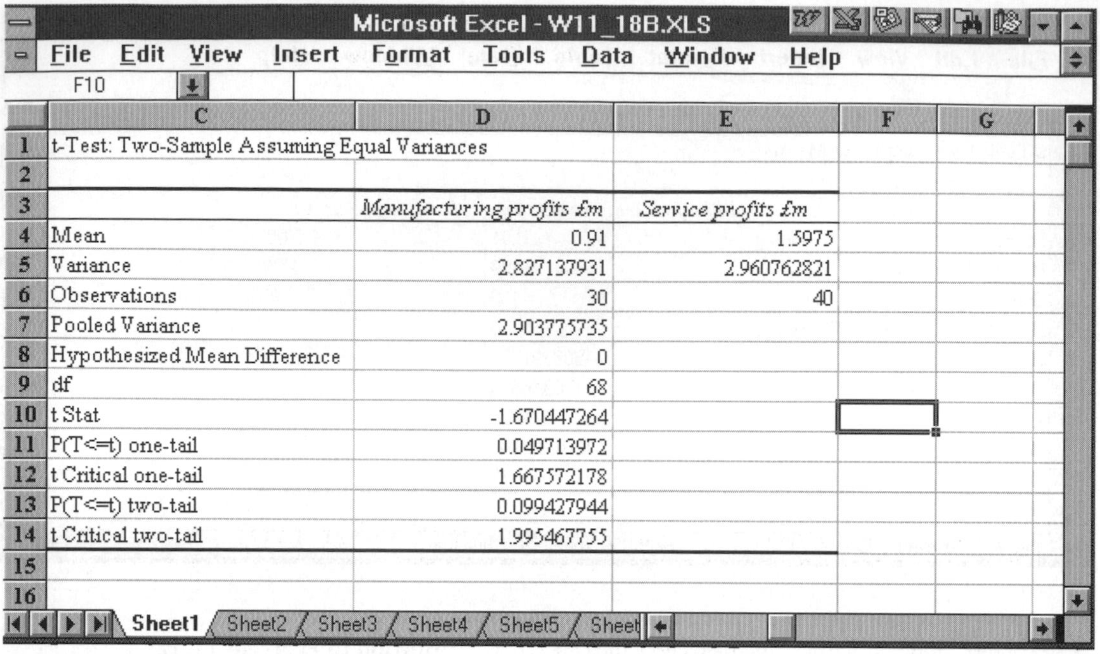

Microsoft Excel - W11_18B.XLS

File   Edit   View   Insert   Format   Tools   Data   Window   Help

F10

	C	D	E	F	G
1	t-Test: Two-Sample Assuming Equal Variances				
2					
3		*Manufacturing profits £m*	*Service profits £m*		
4	Mean	0.91	1.5975		
5	Variance	2.827137931	2.960762821		
6	Observations	30	40		
7	Pooled Variance	2.903775735			
8	Hypothesized Mean Difference	0			
9	df	68			
10	t Stat	-1.670447264			
11	P(T<=t) one-tail	0.049713972			
12	t Critical one-tail	1.667572178			
13	P(T<=t) two-tail	0.099427944			
14	t Critical two-tail	1.995467755			
15					
16					

Sheet1 / Sheet2 / Sheet3 / Sheet4 / Sheet5 / Sheet

**Workbook
11.18B**

Regression

Input

Input Y Range: $B$1:$B$13

Input X Range: $C$1:$C$13

[X] Labels   [ ] Constant is Zero
[ ] Confidence Level 95 %

OK
Cancel
Help

Output options

(●) Output Range: $D$1
( ) New Worksheet Ply:
( ) New Workbook

Residuals
[ ] Residuals   [X] Residual Plots
[ ] Standardized Residuals [X] Line Fit Plots

Normal Probability
[ ] Normal Probability Plots

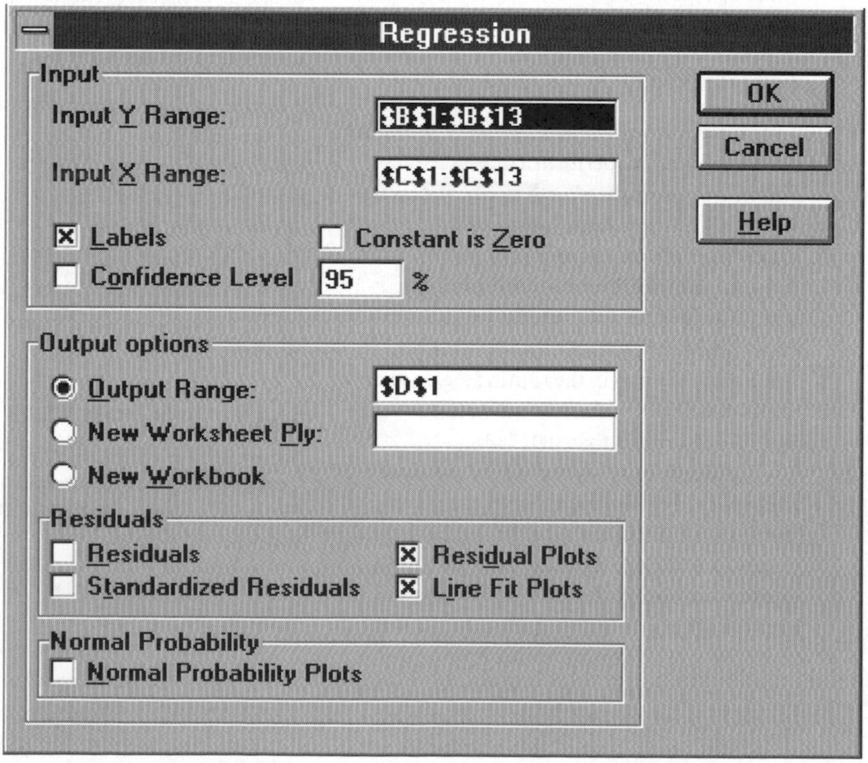

Figure 11.12

	Microsoft Excel - W11_19A.XLS

File　Edit　View　Insert　Format　Tools　Data　Window　Help

K10

	D	E	F	G	H	I	J
1	SUMMARY OUTPUT						
2							
3	*Regression Statistics*						
4	Multiple R	0.93682566					
5	R Square	0.87764231					
6	Adjusted R Square	0.86540654					
7	Standard Error	222.809522					
8	Observations	12					
9							
10	ANOVA						
11		*df*	*SS*	*MS*	*F*	*Significance F*	
12	Regression	1	3560850.835	3560851	71.727598	7.1231E-06	
13	Residual	10	496440.832	49644.08			
14	Total	11	4057291.667				
15							
16		*Coefficients*	*Standard Error*	*t Stat*	*P-value*	*Lower 95%*	*Upper 95%*
17	Intercept	-1292.3061	396.4503079	-3.25969	0.0085786	-2175.652626	-408.9596522
18	Selling Expenses (£x)	0.09289176	0.010968167	8.469215	7.123E-06	0.068453158	0.117330364
19							

Sheet1 / Sheet2 / Sheet3 / Sheet4 / Sheet5 / Sheet

Workbook 11.19A

-1292.3. This makes little sense, and so we might want to suppress the constant. You can do this in the Regression dialogue box by checking the tab that says Constant equal to 0?

(v) If monthly selling expenses were increased by £1000, the estimated increase in the number of units sold would be:

£1000(0.09289) = 92.89 units

(vi) If monthly selling expenses were £20000, the estimated number of units sold would be:

-1292.3 + 20000(0.09289) = 565.5 units.

(vii) The proportion of the total variation in the number of units sold explained by variation in the level of selling expenses is given by R Square = 0.8776 = 87.66%.

(viii) The standard error of estimate is 222.81.

(ix) 95% of all sample values of the intercept will lie between the lower and the upper confidence values for a. That is, between -2175.65 and -408.96.

(x) 95% of all sample values of the gradient will lie between the lower and the upper confidence values for b. That is, between 0.068 and 0.117.

(xi) The significance of the intercept term is given by the P value for a = 0.008.

(xii) The significance of the gradient term is given by the P value for b = 0.0000007

(xiii) As can also be seen from the t values (-3.259 and 8.469) both the intercept and the gradient are significantly different from 0 at the 1% level at least.

(xiv) If monthly selling expenses were £20000, then approximately 95% of all sample predictions for the number of units sold would lie within:[13]

$$\hat{y} \pm t_{0.05,10}(SEE) = 565.5 \pm 2.228(222.8)$$
i.e. between 1061.89 and -69.10.

Since we cannot have negative sales, we should be very sceptical about the validity of this prediction interval.

....

13 A strange coincidence is to be noted in the line below—the standard error of estimate is exactly 100 times the critical t value for the confidence interval.

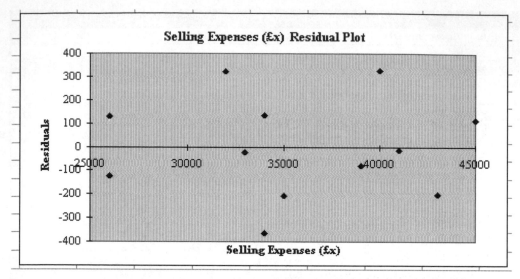

Figure 11.13   (xv) A plot of the residual terms is shown in Fig. 11.13.[14] As can be seen, there is no obvious pattern to the residuals and so we conclude that they would appear to be randomly distributed.

14 This is not the *exact* plot produced by Excel. In this routine Excel usually starts the scale for the horizontal axis at 0—even if there are no observations until a much higher value of x is reached. Consequently, in this example we have used the graph scale option to make the minimum value of x to be plotted equal to 25000. To do this, simply double click on the chart and then double click on any of the scale values on the horizontal axis. Then select Scale and make the minimum value equal 25000.

12

Multiple regression

Contents

Accompanying data files to be loaded as instructed:

W10_1.XLS   W12_1.XLS   W12_5.XLS   W12_7.XLS   W12_8.XLS   W12_9.XLS   W12_10.XLS   W12_10B.XLS

12.1. **Introduction**

Chapters 10 and 11 have explained the processes of performing simple linear regression with one dependent variable and one independent, or explanatory variable, and then testing the significance of the intercept and gradient terms that are estimated.

Throughout this previous discussion, however, it was frequently suggested that this simple linear regression model may be incapable of modelling the data adequately. If this inadequacy is simply a result of non-linearities in the data, then the double or single log transformation techniques explained in Chapter 10 may be able to provide an effective remedy. However, it was also suggested that another potential source of inadequacy in the simple model is the possibility that the dependent variable does not depend simply upon one independent variable, but rather upon a number of independent variables.

In such circumstances, instead of presuming a simple model of the form:

$$y = f(x)$$

we need to define a more extensive model of the general type:

$$y = f(x_1, x_2, \ldots x_n)$$

where $x_1, x_2, \ldots x_n$ represent n distinct independent variables.

In this case we are presuming what is known as a **multiple regression** model, that can be specified generally as:

$$\hat{y} = b_0 + b_1x_1 + b_2x_2 + b_3x_3 + \ldots b_nx_n$$

where the coefficients of the multiple regression model ($b_0, b_1, b_2 \ldots b_n$) are sample estimates of the unknown population parameters ($\beta_0, \beta_1, \beta_2, \ldots \beta_n$) and can be interpreted as follows.

The b_0 term is equivalent to the intercept term in the simple model, and therefore gives the estimated value of the dependent variable when all of the independent variables adopt values of zero. Once again, as explained with regard to the simple model, there may be no clear economic interpretation of this value in certain circumstances.

The b_1 to b_n coefficients are regarded as partial slope coefficients in the sense that if independent variables 2 to n are all held constant, the value of b_1 gives the change in the value of the dependent variable resulting from a unit change in the value of independent variable number 1. For example, if:

$$\hat{y} = 65.2 + 0.45x_1 + 0.8x_2 - 0.1x_3$$

then if x_2 and x_3 are held constant, a one unit increase in the value of x_1 will cause $\hat{y}$ to increase by 0.45 units. Equivalently, if x_1 and x_2 are held constant, a one unit increase in the value of x_3 will cause $\hat{y}$ to decrease by 0.1 units (since b_3 is negative).

The task of multiple regression is, therefore, to obtain least squares regression estimates of $\beta_0, \beta_1, \beta_2 \ldots \beta_n$ (the unknown population regression parameters of the regression model), with these estimates being provided by $b_0, b_1, b_2, \ldots b_n$ (the sample regression parameters). Furthermore, as with the simple case, we will need to test the significance of each of the b_0 to b_n coefficients in the context of a series of null hypotheses that each population coefficient is zero. In this sense, multiple regression is no more than a logical extension of the principles employed in creating and testing a simple linear regression model.

However, moving from one independent variable to more than one does create a number of potential difficulties that were not encountered in the simple model. The most important of these concerns the relationships between the independent variables. In particular, the integrity of the multiple regression technique usually requires that each of the independent variables is largely independent of the others.

To appreciate this point, reconsider the illustration from Chapter 10 on yield and fertilizer application, and recall that the fit obtained was not particularly good ($R^2 = 0.59827$). Consequently, suppose the investigator decided to add a second independent variable in an attempt to improve the fit of the relationship. However, also suppose that this new independent variable was merely the first independent variable (grams of fertilizer applied) measured in kilos. Clearly, x_1 and x_2 are bound to be perfect linear multiples of each other ($x_2 = x_1/1000$), and so the addition of x_2 to the model has added no new information. We would therefore expect no increase in the explanatory power of the model as a result of adding x_2 to the analysis. However, a multiple regression of y on x_1 and x_2 could still be performed and would (sometimes) produce values for b_0, b_1, and b_2.

Yet it should be clear that as a method of distinguishing between the relative effects of each of the two independent variables it is highly unsatisfactory. Coefficients for b_0, b_1, and b_2 might be obtained from the multiple regression technique, but the values of b_1 and b_2 are essentially arbitrary, in the sense that there is no good reason for preferring one particular combination of values to any other.[1]

The problem created for the multiple regression technique by highly correlated independent variables is known as multicollinearity, and can often be difficult to eliminate without considerable respecification of the general regression model—that is, careful choice of different independent variables, and possibly of the nature of the mathematical form of the postulated relationship.

At this stage it is also worth pointing out that mere statistical associations between sets of dependent and independent variables can often be very difficult to interpret in a logical manner. This is because a number of difficulties can be encountered in regression analysis. Not the least of these is the problem that statistical association by itself does not necessarily imply a causal relationship between the dependent and independent variables. In other words, the fact that a dependent variable and an independent variable are strongly correlated cannot always be extended to a logical conclusion that it is the value of the independent variable that is causing the value of the dependent variable to be whatever it is.

For example, there is a famous 'chestnut' in statistics that tells how a Swedish statistician managed to obtain a perfect correlation between the annual Swedish birth rate and the annual number of storks which migrated to Sweden. So, do storks migrating to Sweden also bring Swedish babies with them? The reason for this famous, but obviously spurious, association is (probably) chance, but in other, more serious applications it can be much more difficult to dismiss a high degree of observed correlation on the grounds of patent nonsense and chance.

For instance, 2 variables between which there is a logical reason for expecting a high degree of correlation, may well be tracking some third variable that the analyst has failed to include in the model. Thus we would almost certainly find a high degree of correlation between the number of clients visiting travel agents and the amount of expenditure on holidays. But which of these is causing which? Do we visit a travel agent because we intend to spend money on a holiday, or do we decide to spend money on a holiday because we have visited a travel agent? Either is a plausible hypothesis, but we might also suspect that both visits to travel agents and holiday expenditures could be tied in to some other variable such as average family disposable income. This could well be the real causal variable, with each

---

1 As an analogy of what is happening here ask yourself the following question: is it the upper or the lower blade of a pair of scissors that does the cutting?

of the others being tied together by the fact that if we go on holiday we tend to go to a travel agent, and if we go to a travel agent we (usually) intend going on holiday.

Furthermore, even if a high degree of observed correlation truly reflects a causal relationship, the direction of causality may be far from clear. For example, does advertising expenditure cause sales to be higher, or do high volumes of sales cause high levels of advertising expenditure by providing the funds that are required for the campaigns? Or does causality run in both directions? There is no easy answer to these difficulties, apart from the general advice that regression models should always reflect some logical a priori reason for expecting there to be a relationship between the specified variables.

Finally, there are a number of additional problems that assume greater significance in the multiple as opposed to the simple regression context. Before these can be considered however, it will be necessary to examine some multiple regression output, and clarify some terms.

12.2. A multiple regression routine

Workbook 12.1

Load Workbook 12.1 (W12_1.XLS).

Here, we have the data from Exercise 11.13 on unit sales and selling expenses. In addition however, we have included data for a second independent variable representing price. We therefore suppose a simple demand estimation model of the form:

Unit sales $= b_0 + b_1$ selling expenses $+ b_2$ price

Now recall that for the simple model involving only unit sales and selling expenses, the solution to Exercise 11.13 determined that:

Unit sales $= -1292 + 0.0929$ selling expenses

with t_{calc} for the intercept $= -3.26$ and t_{calc} for the gradient $= 8.47$.

Also, the standard error of estimate was 222.8 and the (simple) $R^2 = 87.8\%$.

Now access Regression from Data Analysis and make the dialogue box resemble Fig. 12.1.

After you have clicked on OK, the regression output should resemble Workbook 12.1. As you can see, the structure of this output is very similar to that obtained in the solution to Exercise 11.13, except that an additional line of output has been added in row 33 to accommodate the 2nd independent variable (price).

However, there were a number of terms in the output that were ignored in Chapter 11 (since they pertained to multiple, as opposed to simple, regression), and which must now be explained. Starting at the top of the output, we should note that in multiple regression models where more than one independent variable is considered, the squared value of the coefficient of multiple correlation is used in a similar manner to the simple R^2 value. The square of the coefficient of multiple correlation, called the **coefficient of determination**, or R^2, shows how well a multiple regression model explains changes in the value of the dependent variable—that is, the percentage of the total variation in the dependent variable that is explained by the collective effect of the independent variables.

Thus for this model, $R^2 = 0.9445$ and so Multiple R (the multiple correlation coeffi-

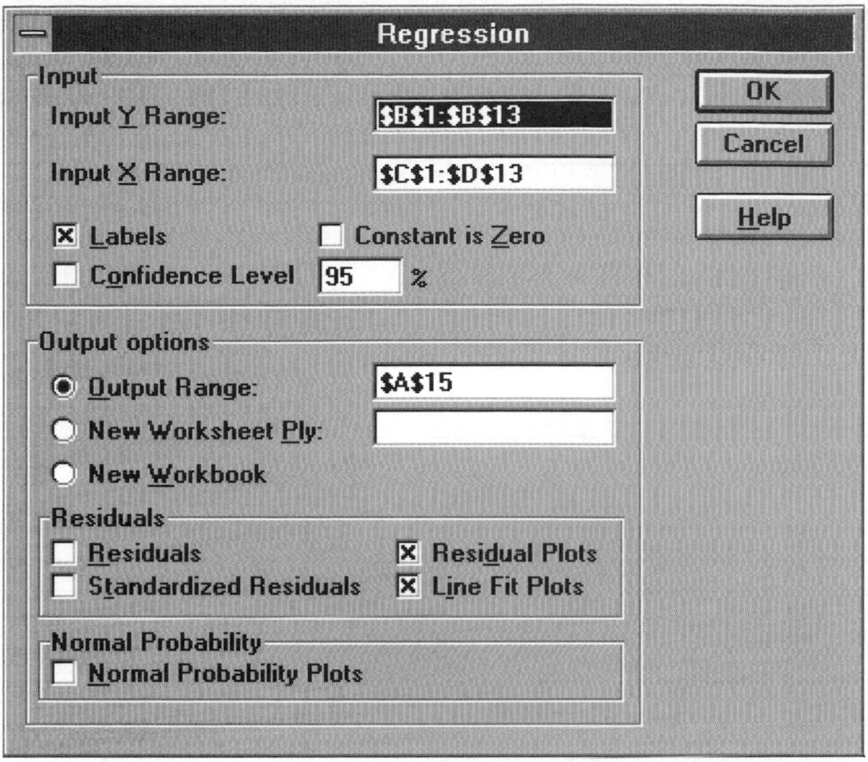

Figure 12.1

cient) = 0.97187 i.e. the square root of R^2. These are the values that have been returned in B19 and B18 for R Square and Multiple R. In the next line we have the Adjusted R Square = 0.9322. This requires further elaboration.

We have already seen in Chapter 10 that an R^2 of 100% results when each data point lies exactly on the regression line. Although this might suggest that any regression model with an R^2 of 100% would prove highly reliable as a predictive device, this is not always the case. This is because it can be shown that the coefficient of determination for any regression equation is artificially high when too small a sample is used to estimate the model's coefficients. In fact, R^2 will always equal 100% when the number of coefficients estimated from the model equals or exceeds the number of observations. This is quite simply because it is then possible to place each data point exactly on the regression plane.

Consequently, to conduct meaningful regression analysis, the sample used to estimate the regression equation must be sufficiently large to give an accurate reflection of the important characteristics of the overall population. This typically means that, in practice, 30 or more data observations are needed to fit a regression model adequately. More precisely, what is usually required is 30 or more degrees of freedom.

For example, to calculate an intercept term, at least 1 observation is needed; to calculate an intercept term plus one slope coefficient, at least 2 observations are required; and so on. Since for any regression model R^2 approaches 100% as the number of degrees of freedom approaches zero, a method has been developed for correcting or adjusting R^2 to take account of the number of degrees of freedom available in the model. This produces the **corrected coefficient of determination**, denoted in Excel by Adjusted R Square and calculated using the expression:

Adjusted R Square = $R^2 - (k - 1)(1 - R^2)/(n - k)$

	Microsoft Excel - W12_1.XLS					
File	Edit	View	Insert	Format	Tools	Data	Window	Help

	A	B	C	D	E	F	G
15	SUMMARY OUTPUT						
16							
17	*Regression Statistics*						
18	Multiple R	0.971877067					
19	R Square	0.944545033					
20	Adjusted R Square	0.932221707					
21	Standard Error	158.11282					
22	Observations	12					
23							
24	ANOVA						
25		*df*	*SS*	*MS*	*F*	*Significance F*	
26	Regression	2	3832294.692	1916147.3	76.6469	2.22706E-06	
27	Residual	9	224996.9747	24999.664			
28	Total	11	4057291.667				
29							
30		*Coefficients*	*Standard Error*	*t Stat*	*P-value*	*Lower 95%*	*Upper 95%*
31	Intercept	-270.0315922	418.8033277	-0.644769	0.53516	-1217.431262	677.36808
32	Selling Expenses (£x)	0.099520446	0.008039126	12.379511	5.9E-07	0.081334666	0.1177062
33	Price (£)	-0.396440205	0.120310842	-3.295133	0.0093	-0.668602446	-0.124278
34							

Sheet1 / Sheet2 / Sheet3 / Sheet4 / Sheet5 / Sheet6

Workbook 12.1

where n is the number of independent variable observations and k is the number of estimated coefficients (intercept plus the number of partial slope coefficients). From this expression it is clear that the downward adjustment to R^2 is large when n, the sample size, is small relative to k, the number of coefficients being estimated.

Consequently, for the current model we have n = 12 and k = 3, with the result that:

$$\text{Adjusted R Square} = 0.9445 - (3 - 1)(1 - 0.9445)/(12 - 3) = 0.9322$$

This is exactly the value that has been returned to the B20 cell, and indicates that the addition of the price data has increased R^2 from a value of 0.878 for the simple model to a value of 0.9445 for the multiple regression model. The value of the Adjusted R Squared has also increased from 0.865 to 0.9322.

In the next line of output we have the standard error of estimate. This is calculated in exactly the same way as in the simple regression case, viz:

> The square root of (the sum of squared errors divided by the number of degrees of freedom)

Compared to the simple model, the standard error of estimate has declined from 222.8 to 158.11 and adds further support to the contention that the addition of the price variable has increased the explanatory power of the model.

Moving down to the next section of the output, we encounter the heading called ANOVA. This is an acronym for Analysis of Variance, and is a statistical method that is not covered in this text. However, it is an easy matter to explain the nature of this output without having to delve into a full discussion of the ANOVA technique.

The first thing to recall is that both simple and multiple regression techniques use calculated t statistics to determine the significance of individual regression parameters. Thus, for example, it may be the case that the intercept term and 2 out of 4 partial slope coefficients are significantly different from zero at the required level of significance. This immediately raises the question of whether the regression model as a whole can be regarded as significant when two of its individual parameters are not.

The ANOVA technique produces a statistic called F that provides evidence on whether a statistically significant proportion of total variation in the dependent variable has been explained. Like the Adjusted R Squared value, the F statistic is adjusted for degrees of freedom and can be defined in terms of R^2 as:

$$F = R^2(n - k)/(1 - R^2)(k - 1)$$

Thus, for the current illustration with $R^2 = 0.9445$, n =12, and k = 3, we have:

$$F = 0.9445(12 - 3)/(1 - 0.9445)(3 - 1) = 76.59$$

which is almost exactly the value contained in the E26 cell of the output.[2]

The F statistic is used to indicate whether a significant share of the variation in the dependent variable has been explained by the regression model. The hypothesis that is actually tested is that the dependent variable is statistically unrelated to all of the independent variables included in the model. If this hypothesis cannot be rejected, then the total explained variation of the model is quite small. At the extreme, if $R^2 = 0$ then so too will be the F statistic, and the regression equation provides absolutely no explanation of the variation in the dependent variable.

As the F statistic increases from zero, the hypothesis that the dependent variable is not statistically related to one or more of the regression's independent variables becomes easier to reject. At some point the F statistic becomes sufficiently large to reject the independence hypothesis and warrants the conclusion that at least some of the model's independent variables are significant factors in explaining variation in the dependent variable. Consequently, the calculated F statistic for the model (76.65 in this case) must be compared to the distribution of F values that can occur before it can be decided whether the calculated value is large or small, in relation to the range of F values that could be computed.

Fortunately, to save consultation of F tables, the value in F26 gives the probability of a value as high as the calculated F value being equalled or exceeded. Thus, in the context of the illustration there is less than a 0.000002227 chance of obtaining such a large value of F when in fact the collective effect of the independent variables of the regression model explains none of the variation in the dependent variable.

Finally, moving down to the output commencing in A30, we see that the introduction of the second independent variable has altered the coefficients that were previously computed for the simple regression model in Exercise 11.13. In particular, the intercept has been substantially increased, from -1292.3 to -270.03.

As regards the significance of the coefficients, the calculated t statistic for the intercept has risen from -3.26 to -0.6447 and its significance has consequently been reduced. This is what would have been hoped for, since a large highly significant intercept term is effectively suggesting that a large part of the explanation of the variation in the dependent variable is to be found in terms of a coefficient that is not related to the values of the independent variables.

The calculated t statistic for the coefficient of the selling expenses variable has increased from 8.47 to 12.38, and as a result has become more significant than previously. Finally, the calculated t statistic for the coefficient of the price variable is -3.295 and is significantly

---

2 The slight discrepancy is simply due to the number of decimal places to which the calculations were taken.

different from zero at the 0.93% level. Also notice that because the residuals chart box was checked in the regression routine, Excel has produced a number of residual charts.

However, before looking at these it must be appreciated that this regression model no longer represents a line, as in the simple case, but rather a plane. Consequently, without resorting to three-dimensional geometry, displaying the fitted relationship between $\hat{y}$ and the 2 independent variables can only be done in a partial manner. In other words, in 2 dimensions we can only display charts of $\hat{y}$ versus selling expenses for a given value, or a series of given values, of price, and we can only display $\hat{y}$ versus price for a given value, or a series of given values, of selling expenses.

This is equally true for the residuals, and so the Excel residual chart output produces the (overall) residuals plotted against each of the independent variables. These are shown in Figs. 12.2 and 12.3.

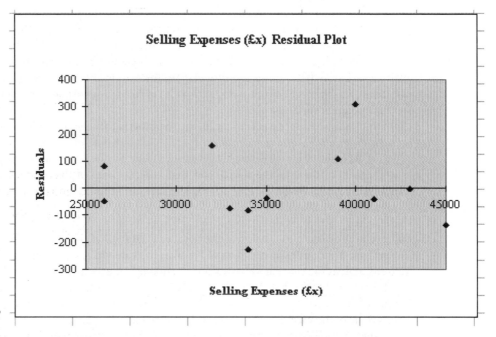

Figure 12.2

The information contained in the residual plots will be considered in more detail in section 12.5. At the moment it is sufficient to note that there is no obvious pattern contained in either of the charts, although this could well be due to the relatively small number of observations being used in the model.

It should now be clear that the net result of this discussion is to suggest that the introduction of price as an additional independent variable has improved the overall explanatory power of the presumed regression model. Once again, however, as in the simple regression routine, Excel has not produced prediction intervals for $\hat{y}$ given any chosen values for each of the independent variables.

To do this, use C17:C23 to contain the following labels:

Selling Expenses	Price	Predicted unit sales	Significance %
Critical t value	Lower predicted sales	Upper predicted sales	

Then, in D17 and D18 enter the chosen values for Selling Expenses and Price—use 25000 and 2000 respectively.

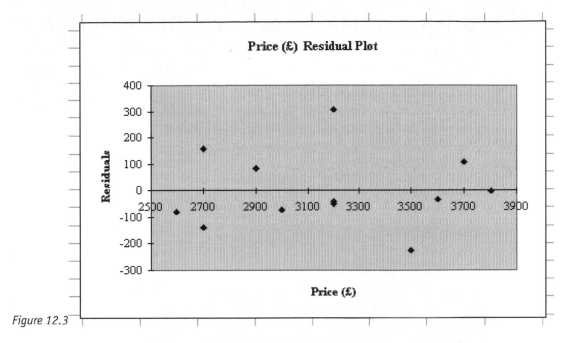

Figure 12.3

Next, compute the predicted level of sales in D19 from the formula:

=B31+B32*D17+B33*D18

This is the unit sales predicted by the regression model for the given values of selling expenses and price that were entered to D17 and D18, and should return a value of 1425.09.

Next, in D20 enter the required level of significance as a percentage (use 5%) and then in D21 calculate the critical t value to be used in the prediction interval from:

=TINV(D20,B27)

This will return the two-tailed t value and should give a result of 2.262

Then, in D22 compute the lower prediction interval from:

=D19-D21*B21

i.e. the predicted sales level minus the critical t value times the standard error of estimate.

Finally, the upper predicted value is then calculated in D23 in a similar manner from:

=D19+D21*B21

These prediction intervals should range from1067.42 to 1782.77 and indicate that if selling expenses and price were set at 25000 and 2000 respectively, the predicted level of sales would be 95% certain to lie between approximately 1067 and 1782.

When you have finished save this file as W12_1A.XLS.
Exercise 12.1 can be attempted now.

12.3. Using multiple regression to fit non-linear models

The previous section has indicated how the multiple regression technique can be used to improve the explanatory power of simple regression models by adding independent variables. However, if the underlying nature of the relationship is fundamentally non-linear then adding independent variables in a linear form may produce little or no effect.

Nevertheless, as with the simple model, if the true relationship can be represented by a simple polynomial or exponential function of 2 or more independent variables then double logarithmic or semi-logarithmic transformations can be performed to eliminate the non-linearities. Hence, if we presumed a model of the form:

$$\hat{y} = b_0 x_1^{b1} x_2^{b2}$$

then:

$$\log \hat{y} = \log b_0 + b_1 \log x_1 + b_2 \log x_2$$

becomes a multiple regression model that is linear in $\log y$, $\log x_1$, and $\log x_2$. Consequently, the procedure would be to turn y, x_1, and x_2 into their logarithmic forms and then regress $\log y$ on $\log x_1$ and $\log x_2$.

Alternatively, if the presumed model is of the form:

$$\hat{y} = b_0 b_1^{x1} b_2^{x2}$$

then

$$\log \hat{y} = \log b_0 + x_1 \log b_1 + x_2 \log b_2$$

becomes a multiple regression model that is linear in $\log y$, x_1, and x_2. In this case, therefore, the procedure would be to turn the dependent variable into its logarithmic form and then regress it on x_1 and x_2 (in their natural form).

Notice that, although both of the transformations involve taking logarithms of the dependent, or all of the variables, the fundamental form of the model is significantly different in each case. This is because the single log transformation ($\log y$ with $x_1, x_2, \ldots x_n$) implies an exponential function that has the property that when all of the independent variables are zero valued, the value of the dependent variable is b_0. That is:

$$\hat{y} = b_0 \, b_1{}^0 b_2{}^0 b_3{}^0 \ldots b_n{}^0 = b_0 \text{ (since all } b^0 = 1)$$

On the other hand, the double log transformation implies a polynomial function that has the property that when all of the independent variables are zero valued, the value of the independent variable is also zero. That is:

$$\hat{y} = b^0 \, 0^{b1} \, 0^{b2} \, 0^{b3} \ldots 0^{bn} = 0$$

This fundamental difference in the underlying properties of the 2 types of transformed models clearly has an important implication for business modelling.

For example, if it were felt by the analyst that any estimated cost function must include a term to represent fixed costs, then fitting a double log transformation model to the data is clearly not appropriate even if it were to produce a better fit than the single log transform model or the simple additive form. This is because:

$$y = b_0 x^{b1} = 0 \text{ when } x = 0 \text{ implying that fixed costs are zero}$$

whereas:

$$y = b_0 b_1{}^x = b_0 \text{ when } x = 0 \text{ implying that fixed costs are } b_0$$

Now however, suppose that the presumed form was:

$$y = b_0 + b_1x + b_2x^2$$

This is a quadratic function, that double or semi-logarithmic transformations of any or all of the variables can no longer turn into a linear form. We must therefore adopt a different approach. This is where the multiple regression technique is essential since, although there is only 1 independent variable (x) in the model, the procedure will be to regard the terms in x and x^2 as distinct variables (x_1 and x_2) and then apply the knowledge that $x_2 = x_1^2$. That is, we presume a model of the form:

$$y = b_0 + b_1x_1 + b_2x_2$$

and then regress y on x_1 and x_2 but with the value of x_2 being given by $x_2 = x_1^2$.

Workbook 10.1

To see this procedure in operation, load Workbook 10.1 (W10_1.XLS).

This is the simple yield–fertilizer application model from Chapter 10 that we have already suggested contains quadratic properties.

Now insert a column at B and in B3 add the label:

x squared

Next, in B4 compute the square of x from the formula:

=A4^2

and copy this into B5:B14.

Columns A and B now contain the values of x and x^2, with column C containing the (unaltered) values of y.

Now access Regression from Data Analysis and make the dialogue box look like Fig. 12.4. Select OK, and the result should resemble Workbook 12.2.

Workbook 12.2

If it does, save the file as W12_2.XLS.

Clearly the effect has been to generate a regression equation of the form:

$$\hat{y} = 0.2419 + 0.08968x_1 - 0.0066x_2$$

which, when it is remembered that $x_2 = x_1^2$, is readily written in its quadratic form as:

$$\hat{y} = 0.2419 + 0.08968x_1 - 0.0066x_1^2$$

Now recall that in the simple model R^2 was calculated to be 0.59827.

The effect of introducing the variable in x^2 has clearly been to increase the value of R^2 dramatically, so that even after adjustment we find that 96.78% of the total variation in yield is explained by variation in the values of x and x^2. Furthermore, each of the regression parameters is significantly different from zero at significance levels well below 0.001%. The net result is therefore to suggest that a robust regression model has been created that can satisfactorily deal with the non-linear nature of the relationship between yield and fertilizer application in a way that was beyond the capabilities of the simple model (even when logarithmically transformed).[3]

Exercises 12.2 and 12.3 can be attempted now.

---

3 Remember that logarithmic transformation can only turn rising or falling curves into rising or falling lines. They cannot model adequately a curve that rises and then falls, or falls and then rises.

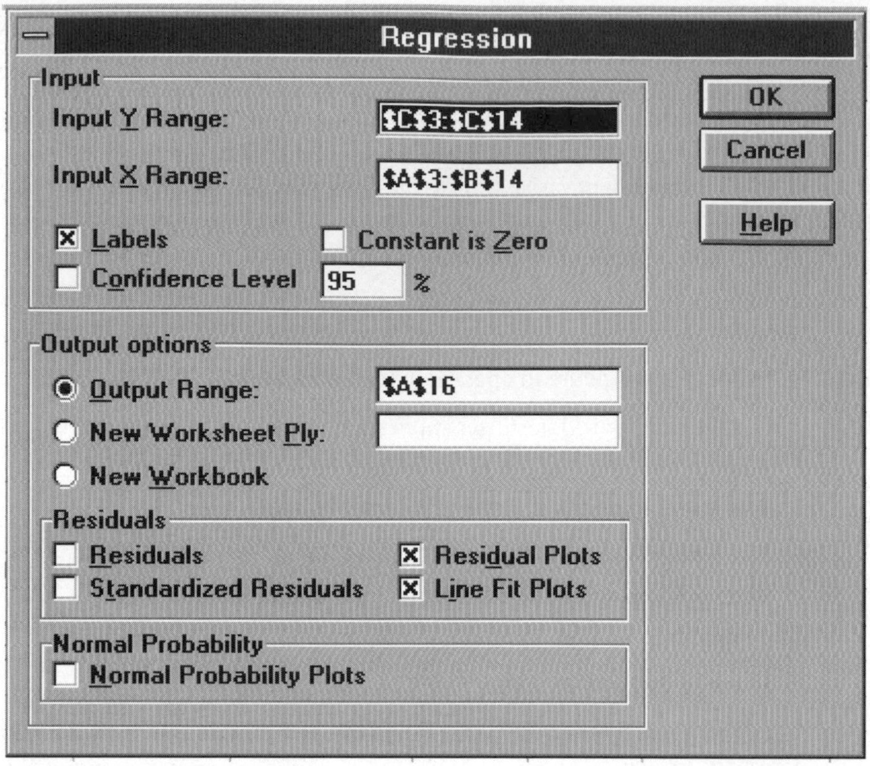

Figure 12.4

12.4. **The problem of multicollinearity**

In the introductory section of this chapter it was pointed out that a high degree of linear association between any 2 or more of the independent variables makes it difficult for the multiple regression technique to distinguish between the relative effects of each of these highly correlated independent variables upon the value of $\hat{y}$. It was also pointed out that the phenomenon of highly or perfectly correlated independent variables is known as multicollinearity.

As a classic example of the problems that can be created by multicollinearity, reconsider the example from Chapter 10 on yield versus fertilizer application. In this simple example it was assumed that only 1 type of fertilizer was applied to the plants. Yet clearly different types of plant respond differently to different types of fertilizer (nitrogen-based, phosphorus-based, potassium-based, or some mixture of these).

Consequently, suppose that it is decided to give each plant simultaneous equal controlled doses (x_1 and x_2) of both of two types of fertilizer (call them A and B) and then record the yield. This clearly means that the independent variables are identical in numerical terms, but not necessarily identical in terms of their effect upon the yield of the plant. This raises the problem of how the regression procedure is to be able to distinguish between the relative effects of, say, 3g of A and 3g of B, when they are both applied at the same time and in the same amounts?

To obtain a dramatic illustration of the problem that multicollinearity causes, reload Workbook 12.2 and make the following changes.

	A	B	C	D	E	F	G
	Microsoft Excel - W12_2.XLS						
	File _Edit_ _View_ _Insert_ _Format_ _Tools_ _Data_ _Window_ _Help_						
	Courier (W1)	10					100%
16	SUMMARY OUTPUT						
17							
18	_Regression Statistics_						
19	Multiple R	0.987039291					
20	R Square	0.974246563					
21	Adjusted R Square	0.967808203					
22	Standard Error	0.017974665					
23	Observations	11					
24							
25	ANOVA						
26		_df_	_SS_	_MS_	_F_	_Significance F_	
27	Regression	2	0.097778928	0.048889	151.3191	4.39887E-07	
28	Residual	8	0.002584709	0.000323			
29	Total	10	0.100363636				
30							
31		_Coefficients_	_Standard Error_	_t Stat_	_P-value_	_Lower 95%_	_Upper 95%_
32	Intercept	0.241888112	0.013694048	17.66374	1.08E-07	0.210309561	0.27346666
33	fertiliser applied x (grams)	0.089680653	0.006371278	14.07577	6.3E-07	0.07498845	0.10437286
34	x squared	-0.006631702	0.000613645	-10.8071	4.74E-06	-0.00804677	-0.0052166
35							

Sheet1 / Sheet2 / Sheet3 / Sheet4 / Sheet5 / Sheet

Workbook 12.2

Alter the labels in A3 and B3 to:

grams of A   and   grams of B

Next, copy the values in A4:A14 into B4:B14.

This creates a situation in which the amount of each fertilizer applied is the same.

Now run the Regression routine with the same settings as before.

Eventually an error message will appear saying that the LINEST() function encountered an error.

In short, the Excel Regression routine is smart enough to know that the 2 independent variables are identical, and therefore perfectly correlated, and that there is no point in having both of them included in the model. One or other will suffice.

Save this file now as W12_3.XLS.

However, the routine is not quite so smart when, instead of making the values in columns A and B identical, they are made to be a constant multiple of each other.

To see this, use Workbook 12.3 (W12_3.XLS) as a template, and then change the labels in A3 and B3 to:

A grams   and   A kilos

Now recall our earlier discussion about one source of multicollinearity being the possibility that the *same* variable was being measured in *different* units. This can be done in the current worksheet by making the following changes.

In B4 enter the formula:

=A4/1000

and copy this into B5:B14.

Column B now contains the application levels of fertilizer A measured in kilograms, while column A contains the same information expressed in grams.

Now run the Regression routine again with the same settings as before, and you will find that the previous error message no longer appears.

However, the output should indicate that the coefficient of the A kilos variable is zero, and that the significance values for the coefficients of both variables have become #NUM or very large indeed.

This is the essence of the problem created by multicollinearity. The multiple regression technique can still estimate (some) regression parameters but is incapable of distinguishing the relative effects of one perfectly correlated independent variable from its partner(s).

Now save the file as W12_4.XLS.

Returning to the problem of separating the effects of the 2 different types of fertilizer, one approach is to respecify the model in such a way that we obtain a range of application levels for each of the fertilizers. Consequently, we should apply 0, 1, 2, 3 . . . 10 grams of A with 0 grams of B, record the yields, then apply 0, 1, 2, 3, . . . 10 grams of A with 1 gram of B, and then record the yields that accrue from this set of application levels. This process continues until we have applied 0 to 10 grams of A with 10 grams of B and recorded each of the intermediate yields obtained. This will give us 11 times 11 = 121 observation values, with each one being a unique combination of 0 to 10 grams of A with 0, 1, 2, . . . 10 grams of B.

Now suppose that this procedure has been carried out and the results were as recorded in Workbook 12.5.

Load this Workbook now (W12_5.XLS).

Now run the Regression routine using the C1:C122 range for the dependent variable (yield) and the A1:B122 range for the independent variables (grams of A and B). Then send the output to the range commencing in D1.

Workbook 12.5

The resulting output should resemble Workbook 12.5. As you can see, the coefficients of both independent variables have been determined and are significantly different from zero. We also have a much higher R^2 than with the simple model that applied only one type of fertilizer (0.8709 > 0.59827). This is partially due to the simple fact of adding another independent variable (regardless of its true importance in terms of explanatory power), but there is more to it than this.

Recall that in the simple model, the obvious non-linear nature of the relationship between yield and application levels of type A fertilizer was attributed to eventual overdosing. Now observe that from the model that we have just constructed this overdosing effect would appear to have been eliminated, or at least moderated, if the high R^2 value is anything to go by. Why should this be the case?

One answer is to be found in terms of the phenomenon of **synergy**. This concept suggests that on its own, each type of fertilizer would eventually poison the plants if applied in sufficient quantities, but applied in tandem they each have a moderating effect upon the over-

	D	E	F	G	H	I	J
	| Microsoft Excel - W12_5.XLS						
	<u>F</u>ile <u>E</u>dit <u>V</u>iew <u>I</u>nsert F<u>o</u>rmat <u>T</u>ools <u>D</u>ata <u>W</u>indow <u>H</u>elp						
1	SUMMARY OUTPUT						
2							
3	*Regression Statistics*						
4	Multiple R	0.93325977					
5	R Square	0.87097379					
6	Adjusted R Square	0.86878691					
7	Standard Error	0.05383366					
8	Observations	121					
9							
10	ANOVA						
11		*df*	*SS*	*MS*	*F*	*Significance F*	
12	Regression	2	2.308431541	1.154216	398.2714	3.3884E-53	
13	Residual	118	0.341971451	0.002898			
14	Total	120	2.650402992				
15							
16		*Coefficients*	*Standard Error*	*t Stat*	*P-value*	*Lower 95%*	*Upper 95%*
17	Intercept	0.26348347	0.011987727	21.97943	1.57E-43	0.23974453	0.28722241
18	grams of A	0.04256033	0.001547609	27.5007	3.8E-53	0.03949565	0.04562501
19	grams of B	0.00981901	0.001547609	6.344631	4.28E-09	0.00675432	0.01288369
20							

Sheet1 / Sheet2 / Sheet3 / Sheet4 / Sheet5 / Sheet

Workbook 12.5

dosing capabilities of the other. It is almost certain that if sufficient amounts of both were applied then the poisoning effect would eventually re-emerge, but over the application levels that we are currently considering, the effect of combining the two is to make yields higher at all high application levels than would have otherwise been the case if only one or the other had been applied at that high application level.

It is, of course, a separate issue as to whether applying both types of fertilizer as opposed to only one or the other makes economic sense. Each of the fertilisers will have a cost to the grower, and depending upon these costs it may be much more expensive to have to apply high levels of both in order to avoid overdosing rather than simply applying low levels of one or the other. Synergistic effects crop[4] up in a number of areas in business and economics. For example, on their own, investment in highly technical equipment and investment in employee training will eventually encounter the phenomenon of diminishing returns (the employees are not sufficiently trained to operate the equipment, or there is insufficient equipment to make the best use of a highly trained workforce). Yet taken together, the effects upon productivity of high levels of both types of investment are often synergistic, in the sense that the 'sum of the parts is less than the whole'.

As a final point of consideration, remember that because of the controlled nature of the yield–fertilizer application model, we were able to devise a method of including both variables while avoiding the multicollinearity problem. In real business life, however, the ability to exercise such control is rarely present. Data on inflation rates, household expenditure, exchange rates, or house prices 'are what they are' and have to be taken as given by the analyst.

---

4 No pun intended.

This raises the practical problem of how to avoid multicollinearity in regression models where many of the independent variables are bound to be highly correlated by the very nature of the variable that they are measuring. For example, the fact that all expenditure-type data require that prices have been used to evaluate the amount spent on the quantities purchased means that these data will be highly correlated with one or other of the various measures of inflation. Consequently, if the Retail Price Index or an index of nominal household expenditure are both included as independent variables in a regression model, it is almost certain that multicollinearity will be present.

One practical approach for dealing with multicollinearity is to deflate or otherwise transform the independent variables. For example, to discover the separate effects of rising price levels from rising income levels on the level of demand for a particular product, it may be necessary to convert nominal data into real terms that are adjusted for the rate of inflation. To do this, simply divide the nominal data by the chosen inflation index (Index of Retail Prices, Consumer Price Index, etc.). Alternatively, if both age and experience are believed to contribute to employee productivity, it may be possible to combine the 2 variables by multiplying them together and creating an employee 'age and experience' variable.

As another approach, it is sometimes suggested to remove all but one of the correlated independent variables from the regression model. Even then, however, the resulting coefficient estimate assigned to the remaining variable will inevitably reflect not only its direct influence but also that via the other excluded variables. The regression model has still not identified the separate effects of the mutually correlated variables.

In our illustration the correlation between the independent variables was perfectly obvious. However, this will not always be the case, and so we should always test for multicollinearity in any model that we are using by computing the correlation coefficients between each of the independent variables. For example, if the dependent variable is contained in A2:A22, and 4 independent variables in B2:E22, then we should take an unused area of our worksheet and enter:

$$=CORREL(B2:B22,C2:C22) \quad \text{i.e. } x_1 \text{ with } x_2$$
$$=CORREL(B2:B22,D2:D22) \quad \text{i.e. } x_1 \text{ with } x_3$$
$$=CORREL(B2:B22,E2:E22) \quad \text{i.e. } x_1 \text{ with } x_4$$
$$=CORREL(C2:C22,D2:D22) \quad \text{i.e. } x_2 \text{ with } x_3$$
$$=CORREL(C2:C22,E2:E22) \quad \text{i.e. } x_2 \text{ with } x_4$$
$$=CORREL(D2:D22,E2:E22) \quad \text{i.e. } x_3 \text{ with } x_4$$

This will give a clear indication of which (if any) of the independent variables are correlated with any other, and is called a **correlation matrix**.

Exercise 12.4 can be attempted now.

12.5. **Residuals analysis**

The least squares regression technique makes 3 assumptions about the nature of the distribution of the error term. To be exact, the residuals are assumed to be **independently normally distributed** with a **zero mean** and a **constant variance**. A violation of any one of these assumptions can often impair the validity of the regression technique.

As we have seen, Excel can be instructed to provide plots of residuals versus each of the independent variables, and each of these should be examined in turn, to see whether the residuals appear to be normally distributed and have a mean equal to zero. In most cases such charts will not form a perfect normal curve, but any serious deviation in terms of outlying values will often be indicated.

A plot of the residuals in their order of occurrence provides another useful means for detecting violations of basic assumptions. If the relationship between the dependent variable and the independent variables is fundamentally linear, then a random pattern should appear in the residual plot. The residuals should display a horizontal band centred about the assumed mean value of zero (i.e. the horizontal axis), and within that band there should also be no clear systematic pattern. On the other hand, if curvature or some other systematic pattern is observed then the model should be respecified to take account of the non-linear relationship that the form of the residuals are suggesting. Any of the logarithmic transformations that have been suggested previously can be used to do this.

Any systematic, repetitive sequence in the residuals plot indicates that these residuals are not truly independent but are **serially correlated** or **autocorrelated**. This problem occurs quite frequently and, because of the multi-dimensional nature of multiple regression models, is not always easily detected using simple two-dimensional graphical plots of the residuals. For this reason the **Durbin–Watson statistic**, defined as the sum of squared first differences of the residuals divided by the sum of squared residuals, should always be calculated and used to measure the extent of serial correlation. This statistic, D, is calculated by the equation:

$$D = \Sigma(e_t - e_{(t-1)})^2 / \Sigma e_t^2$$

where as usual, each error term (e_t) is defined as:

$$e_t = (y_t - \hat{y}_t)$$

However, after some algebra, the last equation for D can also be rewritten as

$$D = 2(1 - \rho)$$

where ρ is the correlation coefficient between **successive residuals**, i.e. $e_2, e_3, \ldots e_t$ correlated with $e_1, e_2, \ldots e_{(t-1)}$. This version of D is a lot easier to use in Excel than the first, and it also has an intuitive connotation.

This is because, if $D = 2(1 - \rho)$, it follows that if there is a zero correlation between the successive error terms then D will equal 2, indicating that the residuals are serially independent. However, as ρ approaches plus or minus one, D will approach 0 or 4. In the former case the perfect positive correlation between the error terms indicates positive serial correlation and D will approach 0. In the latter case, the perfect negative correlation in the error terms indicates negative serial correlation, and will cause D to rise towards its upper limit of 4. Consequently a value of approximately 2 for D indicates the absence of serial correlation; while values close to 0 or 4 indicate that the residuals are not randomly distributed.

Excel can perform these calculations for us if we write some of the formulae ourselves.

| **Workbook 12.1** | **To see how to do this, load Workbook 12.1 (W12_1.XLS).** |

Now run the Regression routine with the Residuals box checked, and make the output commence in A15.

The residuals will be contained in C40:C51.

Now we want to correlate each residual with the previous one.

Consequently, select the C41:C51 area with the mouse and copy this area to D40.

This means that in columns C and D we have e_1 paired with e_2, e_3 paired with e_4, and so on.[5]

---

[5] Notice that this process has cost 1 degree of freedom, since with a total of 12 residuals we can only create 11 successive pairs.

Now, use E41 and E42 to contain the labels:

ρ and   D

Next, F41 and F42 enter the formulae:

=CORREL(D40:D50,C40:C50)   and   =2*(1-F41)

The first of these formulae calculates the correlation coefficient (ρ) between the successive residual terms (-0.3914 should be returned) and the second computes the Durbin–Watson statistic from $2(1 - \rho)$. A value of 2.6338 should be returned, and is sufficiently close to the ideal value of 2 to suggest that serial correlation is not a particularly serious problem in this model.[6]

Now, save this file as W12_6.XLS
Exercise 12.5 can be attempted now.

12.6. Some final considerations

In business and economic data analysis concerned with cost or demand or any other type of relationship, the general form of the presumed regression equation should always be based upon principles derived from economic theory.

However, the particular as opposed to the general form of the regression model is often a subject worthy of some experimentation. This is because there are a large number of specific mathematical functions that are all consistent with the general functional requirement—for example, that as the price increases the quantity demanded falls, or that as output increases so too does the total cost of production.

This means that after the data on relevant dependent and independent variables have been collected, there may be little prior reason to suspect whether the linear, polynomial, or exponential form of the regression equation model is most appropriate. Trying each form and then relying on the form that consistently provides the best fit is a perfectly reasonable approach.

Excel can help here with its **Trendline** routine.

Workbook 10.1

To see how it works, load Workbook 10.1 (W10_1.XLS).

This is the simple yield–fertilizer application model to which we fitted a quadratic function of the form:

$$\hat{y} = 0.2419 + 0.08968x - 0.0066x^2$$

in Workbook 12.2.

Now, use the Chart Wizard to draw a frame, and then create the XY {Scatter} graph of y on x as was done in Chapter 10.
Next, activate the chart by double clicking and then click on any part of data series in the chart. The data points will become visible.
Now, select Insert from the Menu bar and choose Trendline.

---

6 Strictly speaking this may not be true. The Durbin–Watson statistic is dependent upon the values of the residual terms, which in turn depend upon the values of the independent variables used in the model. Unfortunately, there is no way of correcting D to make the distribution of its values independent of the independent variable values employed. This means that there is a 'grey area' of D values for which we simply do not know whether the correlation between the successive error terms is significant or not.

The Trendline type dialogue box will appear as shown in Fig. 12.5. Not all of the possible trend lines will always be deemed by Excel to be appropriate, but in this case Linear, Exponential, Polynomial, and Moving Average are available.

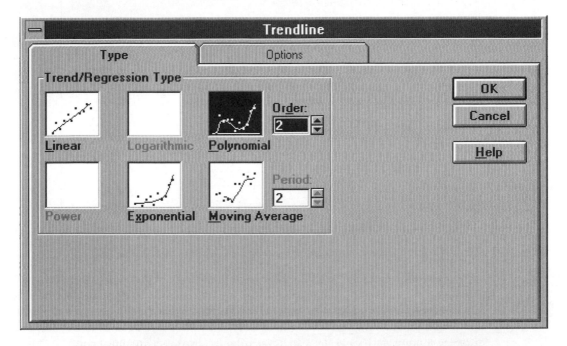

Figure 12.5   **Now, since earlier discussion has suggested that a quadratic form seems to fit this data set best, click on the Polynomial type and leave the order at 2 (i.e. the maximum power of the polynomial function to be fitted is 2).**

Then click on the Options tab and check the boxes for Display Equation on Chart and Display R-squared value on Chart. Make sure that the Set Intercept box is not checked.

Finally, click OK and the results should resemble Fig. 12.6.

If they do, save the file as W12_2A.XLS.

If the displayed equation and R² are obscured by the data plot, click on the equation to obtain a hatched box, and then position the mouse pointer on the perimeter of this box, depress the left-hand mouse button, and drag it to an empty area of the chart.

These are exactly the results that were obtained for the fitted quadratic equation in section 12.3. Clearly this is a very useful procedure for getting a 'feel' for the data without having to write formulae to compute any of the various transformations that have been explained in earlier discussion.

Finally, although Excel does not formally support it, there is a regression method called **stepwise multiple regression**, that relies upon the underlying correlation between the dependent and independent variables to indicate which particular independent variables should be included in the model. In this method, independent variables are selected by the statistical package being used, in line with their individual ability to reduce the overall level of unexplained variation. Clearly, stepwise regression is a highly experimental approach, since it would be possible to include every possible independent variable that could be imagined and then let the technique decide which of these independent variables are worthwhile and which are not. However, although this seems like the answer to an analyst's prayer, there is rarely a silver lining without a cloud.

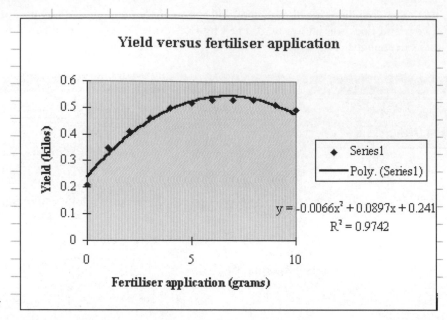

Figure 12.6

The benefit of such an experimental approach lies in its potential to improve the regression model fit and thereby improve the overall level of explanatory power concerning the economic relationships that are of interest. On the other hand, the danger of experimentation is that the resulting regression model might bear little resemblance to a robust and durable economic relation, i.e. one that is sensible in terms of economic theory.

This is because, as was explained earlier in the degrees of freedom discussion, R^2 can always be increased by the addition of further independent variables, even if no true relation exists between the dependent variable and the independent variables that were added. This means that an approach where every imaginable variable is tried can lead to models which are only picking up idiosyncratic aspects of unique samples of data but which prove incapable of providing a high degree of real explanatory power when removed from the context of that sample data.

12.7. **Exercises**

Exercise 12.1

Load Workbook 12.7 (W12_7.XLS). The data are the unit sales of a particular product in each of 35 market areas, along with the price charged, the amount of advertising expenditure, and an index of family income in those market areas.

(i) Prepare a multiple regression model of unit sales in terms of price, advertising expenditure, and family income.

(ii) Provide a brief interpretation of the results obtained.

Exercise 12.2

Elementary production theory suggests that there will usually be a relationship between the physical output obtained from a production process and the physical amount of various inputs that are used in the process. This relationship between inputs and output is known as the **production function.**

Now load Workbook 12.8 (W12_8.XLS). The data are the output obtained from various application levels of 2 inputs (A and B).

Derive a multiple regression equation that can satisfactorily model the relationship between output and inputs.

Exercise 12.3

Load Workbook 12.9 (W12_9.XLS). The data are the relationship between total production costs and output for a small firm.

Determine the equation of the multiple regression model that provides the best fit to the data for the relationship between total costs and output.

Exercise 12.4

Load Workbook 12.10 (W12_10.XLS). Here, the data from Exercise 12.1 have been augmented to include a 4th independent variable representing the mean price charged for the product by this firm's competitors in each market area.

(i) Test for multicollinearity between the independent price variables.

(ii) If this test suggests that multicollinearity is a problem try to devise a method of overcoming the difficulty while still retaining as many independent variables as possible in the model.

When you have finished, save the file as W12_10A.XLS.

Exercise 12.5

Load Workbook 12.10B (W12_10B.XLS). This is the reduced version of the model developed in the solution to Exercise 12.4.

By computing the residuals of the fitted model, determine whether serial correlation in the error terms is liable to be a problem.

12.8. **Solutions to the exercises**

Solution to Exercise 12.1

(i) The regression output is shown in Workbook 12.11.

(ii) As you can see, the adjusted R^2 is 0.7044, but only the coefficient of the advertising expenditure variable is significantly different

from zero at the 1% level of significance. However, the F statistic is significantly different from zero, and so the independent variables, collectively, are explaining more than none of the variation in the dependent variable.

Microsoft Excel - W12_11.XLS

File   Edit   View   Insert   Format   Tools   Data   Window   Help

	F	G	H	I	J	K	L
1	SUMMARY OUTPUT						
2							
3	*Regression Statistics*						
4	Multiple R	0.85468572					
5	R Square	0.73048768					
6	Adjusted R Square	0.70440584					
7	Standard Error	48.0047346					
8	Observations	35					
9							
10	ANOVA						
11		*df*	*SS*	*MS*	*F*	*Significance F*	
12	Regression	3	193626.1948	64542	28.0075	5.86762E-09	
13	Residual	31	71438.09093	2304.5			
14	Total	34	265064.2857				
15							
16		*Coefficients*	*Standard Error*	*t Stat*	*P-value*	*Lower 95%*	*Upper 95%*
17	Intercept	624.322839	489.4550991	1.2755	0.21159	-373.9279735	1622.5737
18	Price	-40.7263867	50.06974262	-0.813	0.4222	-142.844357	61.391584
19	Advertising expenditure	7.10177082	2.357945208	3.0118	0.00513	2.292707177	11.910834
20	Family income	0.50421653	2.976461635	0.1694	0.86658	-5.566320379	6.5747534
21							

Sheet1 / Sheet2 / Sheet3 / Sheet4 / Sheet5 / Sheet

Workbook 12.11

Solution to Exercise 12.2

Simple inspection of the data reveals that if either or both of the inputs are used in zero quantities, then the resulting output is also zero. Consequently, a simple additive linear model would appear inappropriate, since this would produce a term in b_0 that was not necessarily equal to 0, implying that there was some output to be obtained from zero application levels of either or both inputs.

One potential remedy to this problem is to check the Constant is Zero box in the Regression routine dialogue screen. This will suppress the constant. Even then, however, we should also try both semi-logarithmic and double logarithmic transformations of the variables in order to investigate the possibility that the underlying relationship is exponential or polynomial. However, this immediately raises the problem that the logarithm of zero is not defined, yet the data contain zero values for both the dependent variable and the independent variables. This means that Excel will return an error message whenever you instruct it to calculate the logarithm of zero,

and so the only solution is to discard those data points that contain zero values for y in the semi-log transformation and those data points that contain zero values for any of the variables in the double log transformation.

Provided the adjustments described above have been made, the regression outputs for each of the three main possibilities are as shown in Workbooks 12.12, 12.13, and 12.14

Workbook 12.12 $\hat{y} = b_1 x_1 + b_2 x_2$ (Constant is Zero)

The simple additive linear model with the constant suppressed performs quite well. The fitted equation is given by:

$$\hat{y} = 0.1527 \text{ input A} + 0.7503 \text{ input B}$$

The adjusted R^2 value is 0.7074 and both coefficients are significantly different from zero at the 1% significance level. The intercept term, being suppressed is shown to be not relevant.

Workbook 12.13 $\log \hat{y} = \log b_0 + x_1 \log b_1 + x_2 \log b_2$ $(\hat{y} = b_0 b_1{}^{x_1} b_2{}^{x_2})$

Compared to the simple linear additive model, this exponential form has improved the fit simply because the significance of each of the regression coefficients has increased, as has the value of the F statistic and the adjusted R^2 value.

The fitted equation is therefore:

$$\log \hat{y} = -0.1921 + 0.0407 \text{ input A} + 0.1797 \text{ input B}$$

This can be expressed in terms of $\hat{y}$ as:

$$\hat{y} = 10^{(-0.1921 + 0.0407 \text{ input A} + 0.1797 \text{ input B})}$$

or:

$$\hat{y} = (10^{-0.1921})(10^{0.0407 \text{ input A}})(10^{0.1797})^{\text{input B}}$$

This means that:

$$b_0 = 10^{-0.1921} = 0.6425; b_1 = 10^{0.0407} = 1.0982; b_2 = 10^{0.1797} = 1.2014$$

and that

$$\hat{y} = b_0 b_1{}^{x1} b_2{}^{x2}$$

is equivalent to:

$$\hat{y} = 0.6425(1.0982^{\text{input A}})(1.2014^{\text{input B}})$$

Workbook 12.12 Workbook 12.14 $\log \hat{y} = \log b_0 + b_1 \log x_1 + b_2 \log x_2$ $(\hat{y} = b_0 x_1{}^{b1} x_2{}^{b2})$

As you can see, the double log transformation in Workbook 12.14 provides the greatest degree of explanatory power and also has the most significant regression coefficients for the independent variables. We therefore conclude that:

$$\log \hat{y} = -0.0321 + 0.3158 \log \text{ input A} + 0.7520 \log \text{ input}$$

or:

$$\hat{y} = (10^{-0.0321})(\text{input A}^{0.3158})(\text{input B}^{0.7520}) = 0.9287(\text{input A}^{0.3158})(\text{input B}^{0.7520})$$

is the best model that can be fitted.[7]

Solution to Exercise 12.3

The first thing to do is obtain a scatter plot of the data with total costs on the vertical axis and output on the horizontal axis. This produces Fig. 12.7.

As is clear from this figure, and as is also

Microsoft Excel - W12_12.XLS

File Edit View Insert Format Tools Data Window Help

	D	E	F	G	H	I	J
1	SUMMARY OUTPUT						
2							
3	*Regression Statistics*						
4	Multiple R	0.86550076					
5	R Square	0.74909156					
6	Adjusted R Square	0.70739461					
7	Standard Error	0.67762876					
8	Observations	32					
9							
10	ANOVA						
11		*df*	*SS*	*MS*	*F*	*Significance F*	
12	Regression	2	41.12676542	20.5634	44.7828	1.35636E-09	
13	Residual	30	13.77542208	0.45918			
14	Total	32	54.9021875				
15							
16		*Coefficients*	*Standard Error*	*t Stat*	*P-value*	*Lower 95%*	*Upper 95%*
17	Intercept	0	#N/A	#N/A	#N/A	#N/A	#N/A
18	Input A	0.15275974	0.038611482	3.95633	0.00043	0.073904655	0.23161483
19	Input B	0.75032468	0.086337899	8.69056	1.1E-09	0.573999345	0.92665001
20							
21							

Sheet1 / Sheet2 / Sheet3 / Sheet4 / Sheet5 / Sheet

---

7 The fitted model is known as a Cobb–Douglas production function and may be more familiar to you in the form: Q = $AK^\alpha L^\beta$, where Q is output, K and L are units of capital and labour employed, and A, α, and β are constants.

	Microsoft Excel - W12_13.XLS					
	File **Edit** **View** **Insert** **Format** **Tools** **Data** **Window** **Help**					
	E	F	G	H	I	J	K
1	SUMMARY OUTPUT						
2							
3	*Regression Statistics*						
4	Multiple R	0.96654611					
5	R Square	0.93421139					
6	Adjusted R Square	0.92690154					
7	Standard Error	0.04808759					
8	Observations	21					
9							
10	ANOVA						
11		*df*	*SS*	*MS*	*F*	*Significance F*	
12	Regression	2	0.591061843	0.29553	127.802	2.30864E-11	
13	Residual	18	0.041623489	0.00231			
14	Total	20	0.632685332				
15							
16		*Coefficients*	*Standard Error*	*t Stat*	*P-value*	*Lower 95%*	*Upper 95%*
17	Intercept	-0.19208694	0.034803241	-5.5192	3.1E-05	-0.265205896	-0.118968
18	Input A	0.04069353	0.005246786	7.7559	3.8E-07	0.029670432	0.05171663
19	Input B	0.17967449	0.012851948	13.9803	4.2E-11	0.15267353	0.20667546
20							

Sheet1 / Sheet2 / Sheet3 / Sheet4 / Sheet5 / Sheet

Workbook 12.13 suggested by elementary cost analysis, the curved nature of the relationship suggests that some form of polynomial function would provide the best fit. This is indeed the case, but rather than using a quadratic function as in the previous illustration, a cubic function will be fitted. That is, we presume a model of the form:

$$\hat{y} = b_0 + b_1x + b_2x^2 + b_3x^3$$

As with the quadratic function explained in the main body of the text, this cubic

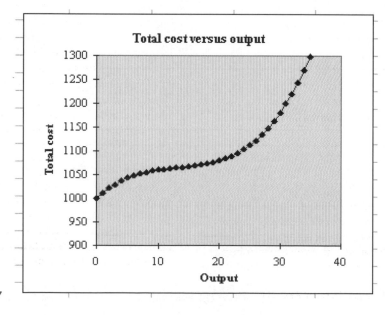

Figure 12.7

```
─                      Microsoft Excel - W12_14.XLS        [icons]  ▼ ▲
□   File   Edit   View   Insert   Format   Tools   Data   Window   Help        ◆
    N17        ↓
        G              H            I          J          K          L          M       ▲
1   SUMMARY OUTPUT
2
3       Regression Statistics
4   Multiple R          0.98972321
5   R Square            0.97955203
6   Adjusted R Square   0.97728003
7   Standard Error      0.02680913
8   Observations        21
9
10  ANOVA
11                      df           SS         MS          F        Significance F
12  Regression          2            0.6197482  0.3098741   431.14143  6.2496E-16
13  Residual            18           0.01293713 0.00071873
14  Total               20           0.63268533
15
16                  Coefficients Standard Erro.  t Stat    P-value    Lower 95%   Upper 95%
17  Intercept       -0.03207608  0.01482719   -2.16332892  0.04421542 -0.063226872 -0.000925
18  log input A     0.31581046   0.02124651   14.8641119   1.5009E-11  0.271173167  0.360447
19  log input B     0.75206793   0.029697     25.324712    1.5818E-15  0.689676805  0.814459
20
  ◄ ◄ ► ►│\ Sheet1 / Sheet2 / Sheet3 / Sheet4 / Sheet5 / Sheet ◄
```

Workbook 12.14

specification requires that we fit a multiple regression in 3 independent variables, x_1, x_2, and x_3, where:

$$x_2 = x_1^2 \text{ and } x_3 = x_1^3$$

Consequently, insert 2 columns at B and then write formulae to compute the square of output in column B and the cube of output in column C. Then use D1:D37 as the dependent variable range and A1:C37 as the independent variables range (making sure that the labels box is checked in the regression dialogue screen). Output the results to E1 and the effect shown in Workbook 12.15 should be obtained.

Clearly the cubic equation that best fits the data is given by:

$$\hat{y} = 1000 + 12x - 0.8x^2 + 0.02x^3$$

Furthermore, the adjusted R^2 is 1 and all of the coefficients are significantly different from zero, as is the computed F statistic. In fact there is such a good fit that you might suspect a bit of 'cheating' in the creation of the data set.[8]

Solution to Exercise 12.4

The introduction of the variable for competitors' mean price in the market area could clearly create multicollinearity problems if, for example, this firm was a price leader and if the competitors followed these prices closely. In such circumstances the correlation between the price that the firm charges (own price) and the mean price charged by competitors would be very high. This can be confirmed or denied for the data by computing the correlation coefficients between each of the independent variables. The results of doing this are shown in Workbook 12.16.

As was suspected, own price and competitors' price are highly correlated and so there is a multicollinearity problem here. However, this is compounded by the fact that, as the correlation matrix shows, all of the independent variables are highly correlated with each other. Hence, multicollinearity is a

---

8 And you would be absolutely right in your suspicions.

Microsoft Excel - W12_15.XLS

File **Edit** **View** **Insert** **Format** **Tools** **Data** **Window** **Help**

	E	F	G	H	I	J	K
1	SUMMARY OUTPUT						
2							
3	*Regression Statistics*						
4	Multiple R	1					
5	R Square	1					
6	Adjusted R Square	1					
7	Standard Error	3.7954E-12					
8	Observations	36					
9							
10	ANOVA						
11		*df*	*SS*	*MS*	*F*	*Significance F*	
12	Regression	3	184037.852	61346	4.259E+27	0	
13	Residual	32	4.60959E-22	1.4E-23			
14	Total	35	184037.852				
15							
16		*Coefficients*	*Standard Error*	*t Stat*	*P-value*	*Lower 95%*	*Upper 95%*
17	Intercept	1000	2.288E-12	4.4E+14	0	1000	1000
18	Output	12	5.74195E-13	2.1E+13	0	12	12
19	Output squared	-0.8	3.84335E-14	-2E+13	0	-0.8	-0.8
20	Output cubed	0.02	7.21321E-16	2.8E+13	0	0.02	0.02
21							

Sheet1 / Sheet2 / Sheet3 / Sheet4 / Sheet5 / Sheet

Workbook 12.15

problem not only between the own price and the competitors' price variables but also among each of the others. This could well be due to a deliberate pricing strategy on behalf of this firm, since the high positive correlation between its own price and family income suggests that the firm is deliberately positioning itself in each market area by matching the price that it charges to the level of income in that area.

Workbook 12.16

Thus, if the firm charges relatively high prices in areas with high incomes (and vice versa), and if competitors follow these prices closely, then we are bound to find a close 3-way link between own price, family incomes, and competitors' price. Furthermore, the high negative correlation between own price and advertising expenditure suggests that there may be an additional strategy of applying high levels of advertising expenditure where prices

Microsoft Excel - W12_16.XLS

File **Edit** **View** **Insert** **Format** **Tools** **Data** **Window** **Help**

F40   =CORREL(C2:C36,F2:F36)

	B	C	D	E	F	G
37						
38			CORRELATION MATRIX			
39		Own price	Advertising expenditure	Family income	Competitors' price	
40	Own price	1	-0.907201819	0.90469026	0.970320587	
41	Advertising expenditure		1	-0.835866833	-0.855690051	
42	Family income			1	0.867559462	
43	Competitors' price				1	
44						

Sheet1 / Sheet2 / Sheet3 / Sheet4 / Sheet5 / Sheet

Microsoft Excel - W12_17.XLS							

File Edit View Insert Format Tools Data Window Help

P1 =CORREL(G2:G36,H2:H36)

	I	J	K	L	M	N	O	P
1	SUMMARY OUTPUT		CORRELATION COEFFICIENT BETWEEN OP/CP AND A/I =					0.637749
2								
3	*Regression Statistics*							
4	Multiple R	0.844032358						
5	R Square	0.712390621						
6	Adjusted R Square	0.694415035						
7	Standard Error	48.80925074						
8	Observations	35						
9								
10	ANOVA							
11		*df*	*SS*	*MS*	*F*	*Significance F*		
12	Regression	2	188829.3111	94415	39.631	2.19204E-09		
13	Residual	32	76234.97466	2382.3				
14	Total	34	265064.2857					
15								
16		*Coefficients*	*Standard Error*	*t Stat*	*P-value*	*Lower 95%*	*Upper 95%*	
17	Intercept	104.4108465	409.5313758	0.255	0.80039	-729.7765618	938.598255	
18	OP/CP	141.0028886	432.0377482	0.3264	0.74627	-739.0284613	1021.03424	
19	A/I	694.2685284	104.4849148	6.6447	1.7E-07	481.4399017	907.097155	
20								

\ Sheet1 / Sheet2 / Sheet3 / Sheet4 / Sheet5 / Sheet6

Workbook 12.17

are low (because incomes are low). This creates a further link in the chain between the independent variables that apply to this firm; and, of course, if competitors follow this pricing strategy then widespread high correlations between all of the independent variables become inevitable.

One possible way of dealing with this widespread multicollinearity problem is to define 2 new variables that represent the ratio between own price and competitors' average price, and the ratio between advertising expenditure and family income. This means that our model could become:

unit sales = $b_0 + b_1$(OP/CP) + b_2 (A/I)

where OP is own price, CP is competitors' price, A is advertising expenditure, and I is family income.

When these data are computed in a workbook and the Regression routine invoked, the results shown in Workbook 12.17 are obtained. The extent of correlation between each of the new independent variables has been reduced ($\rho = 0.6377$) and as a result, from the point of view of multicollinearity some of the integrity of the model has been restored without having to discard important variables from the model. At the same time, however, the OP/CP variable is not significant, although the F statistic is. This is a worrying development, since we really should expect a demand model to have *some* version of a price variable with a significant coefficient. Consequently, the next stage of investigation should be to consider some form of non-linear model.[9]

A final point to note is that the use of these 2-ratio variables inevitably means that the resulting model is less precise. This is because, although it will still be possible to predict unit sales on the basis of given ratio values for OP/CP and A/I, any one ratio value is consistent with a large number of absolute values for each of the terms in the ratio. For

9 If you try both semi-log and double log transformation of the data, unfortunately neither of these presumed models can make the coefficient of CP/OP variable significantly different from zero.

example, a value for OP/CP of 1.1 could be produced by any of the following combinations of OP and CP:

1.1, 1; 11, 10; 110, 100; and so on

Clearly, since the same argument applies to the A/I ratio this implies that the absolute value of any of the variables is being regarded as unimportant in determining the unit sales. It is only the absolute values of the ratios of the 2 sets of variables that is important.

Whether or not this is a reasonable conclusion is difficult to say. On the one hand, we can be fairly sure that the higher the OP/CP ratio, the lower will be the demand for this firm's product relative to the demand for competitors' output. Yet, whether there will be a significant absolute level of demand for the product at all will largely be determined by the absolute price that is charged in relation to the level of family incomes (since high absolute incomes are required to afford high absolute prices).

This means that the use of relative as opposed to absolute prices in a regression

model can only be fully justified to the extent that there is some general link between absolute prices and absolute incomes (via general inflation, for example).

Solution to Exercise 12.5

The Durbin–Watson statistic is calculated as shown in Workbook 12.18. The residuals were calculated in F25:F60 by checking the Residuals box in the Regression dialogue box and sending the entire regression output to D1. Then F26:F59 was copied into G25:G59 to produce the residuals lagged by 1 period (e_1, e_2; e_2, e_3; etc.). Finally F26:F59 was correlated with G26:G29 in I25 to give the correlation coefficient between the successive residuals and then the Durbin–Watson statistic calculated in I26 as $2(1 - \rho)$.

Since the Durbin–Watson statistic is very close to its ideal value of 2, the implication from these calculations is that serial correlation is not present to any great degree in this model.

Workbook 12.18

	Microsoft Excel - W12_18.XLS					
File	Edit	View	Insert	Format	Tools	Data Window Help

I25 =CORREL(F26:F59,G26:G59)

	D	E	F	G	H	I
23	RESIDUAL OUTPUT					
24						
25	*Observation*	*Predicted unit sales*	*Residuals*	Lagged residuals	r =	-0.037577554
26	1	539.7855895	-9.78558948	-20.91979706	D =	2.075155108
27	2	510.9197971	-20.91979706	-19.18074361		
28	3	499.1807436	-19.18074361	-7.21606246		
29	4	437.2160625	-7.21606246	48.5847866		
30	5	621.4152134	48.5847866	-19.37467231		
31	6	519.3746723	-19.37467231	58.25425396		
32	7	501.745746	58.25425396	-34.17135798		
33	8	464.171358	-34.17135798	-17.33840979		
34	9	427.3384098	-17.33840979	44.21519548		
35	10	705.7848045	44.21519548	6.052499617		
36	11	493.9475004	6.052499617	-3.665774342		
37	12	463.6657743	-3.665774342	58.32720812		
38	13	501.6727919	58.32720812	-124.7622383		
39	14	544.7622383	-124.7622383	-53.78463542		
40	15	533.7846354	-53.78463542	135.6838643		
41	16	564.3161357	135.6838643	89.54895359		
42	17	520.4510464	89.54895359	3.279268165		

Sheet1 / Sheet2 / Sheet3 / Sheet4 / Sheet5 / Sheet

Index

······